BENEFIT–COST ANALYSIS

In Theory and Practice

Richard O. Zerbe, Jr.
Dwight D. Dively
University of Washington

HarperCollins*CollegePublishers*

This book is dedicated to the generations of benefit–cost students who have taken our class, and to Arnold Harberger and George Tolley who inspired us.

Sponsoring Editor: Bruce Kaplan
Project Editor: Steven Pisano
Design Supervisor and Cover Design: Mary Archondes
Cover Photo: Bonneville Dam, Columbia River Gorge, Oregon.
  Photograph © Wolfgang Kaehler.
Production Administrator: Jeffrey Taub
Compositor: Publication Services, Inc.
Printer and Binder: R. R. Donnelly & Sons Company
Cover Printer: The Lehigh Press, Inc.

Benefit–Cost Analysis: In Theory and Practice

Copyright © 1994 by HarperCollins College Publishers

Library of Congress Cataloging-in-Publication Data

Zerbe, Richard O.
    Benefit–cost analysis in theory and practice / Richard O. Zerbe,
Jr., Dwight D. Dively.
        p.   cm.
    Includes bibliographical references and index.
    ISBN 0-673-18066-2
    1. Cost effectiveness.   2. Cost effectiveness—Case studies.
    I. Dively, Dwight.   II. Title.
    HD47.4.Z47   1994
    658.15′22—dc20
                                                          93-4495
                                                          CIP

94 95 96   9 8 7 6 5 4 3 2

Contents

Preface

B enefit–cost analysis has a bad reputation in some circles, particularly in the environmental area. It has been called a dogmatic approach that "knows the price of everything and the value of nothing." We wrote this book to show what a wonderfully broad and textured approach to policy problems this type of analysis can bring.

Benefit–Cost Analysis: In Theory and Practice is anchored in an earlier tradition in which analysis was embedded broadly in the social and moral sciences, when it was called *benefit–cost analysis* because of the fruitfulness of its methodology rather than the more mechanistic *cost–benefit analysis* it sometimes has now become. It combines economic theory, economic practice, policy analysis, and philosophy and ethics. We have tried to make considerations of distribution and of the theory of value an integral part of the book. We have also tried to provide sufficient grounding in the theory by providing numerous examples and applications, as well as separate chapters that provide case studies. Furthermore, we have tried to show the richness of the benefit–cost methodology for the public sector by employing financial concepts used extensively in the private sector. In this way, we intend this textbook to be a useful reference tool to government workers, private practitioners, and teachers from a variety of disciplines: economists, engineers, education specialists, and policy scientists. Therefore, this text can be used in public policy programs and public affairs programs as well as economics courses, and students need only the rudiments of economics learned in an introductory economics course.

Many people have contributed to this book. For numerous suggestions for improvements in content, presentation, and style, we would like to thank our reviewers: James Davies, University of Western Ontario; Andrew Postlewaite, University of Pennsylvania; Michael Salinger, Columbia University; W. G. Waters, University of British Columbia; and Allan Zelenitz, Carnegie-Mellon University. Their help has been invaluable. We also want to thank the many students too numerous to mention here who have helped improve the book, in particular Jonathan Lesser, Betsy Cody, Karen Reed, Mariam Roskin, and Agnes McGoven.

Richard O. Zerbe, Jr.
Dwight D. Dively

1

Introduction to Benefit–Cost Analysis

1.1. INTRODUCTION

Benefit–cost analysis is an art consisting of a series of techniques useful for decision making. Because we believe that benefit–cost analysis is an art we use the term *benefit–cost* rather than the term *cost–benefit*. The term *benefit–cost* is more closely identified with the earlier development of this approach that recognized the relationship of benefit–cost analysis to important questions of ethics and values and to interesting questions of economic theory. The term *cost–benefit analysis* is perhaps more identified with the use of this technique by engineers in a more mechanistic fashion. (See Swartzman et al., 1982, Chap. 5.)

As with any art, benefit–cost analysis can be done well or poorly and there are issues of science in using the art. Benefit–cost analysis is an art that to be done well requires an appreciation of a substantial amount of economics as well as sensitivity to ethical and philosophical issues. For this reason, benefit–cost analysis should be treated as an aid to decision making and not as the decision itself. Although we consider many narrow and technical issues of benefit–cost analysis, we think it is most useful to treat it as a tool for organizing thinking about decisions. Not only have we found this a useful approach, but it is one that also obviates many criticisms.

Not only is benefit–cost analysis useful in itself, but the use of benefit–cost analysis shapes the framework for decisions. Such analysis requires a formal report and assessment and the application of a series of evaluation techniques. This has an extremely positive result. The techniques and data are exposed to possible criticism, discussion, revision, and improvement. Prominent examples are seen in the evolution of analyses performed by the Corps of Engineers and by the Bureau of Reclamation over the years. Criticisms and suggestion have worked to improve the quality of these agencies' analyses.

1.1.1.   What Is Benefit–Cost Analyst?

Benefit–cost analysis is a set of procedures for defining and comparing benefits and costs. In this sense it is a way of organizing and analyzing data as an aid to thinking. This concept of benefit analysis leads to what we regard as a fundamental rule of benefit–cost analysis:

> Decisions are made by decision makers, and benefit–cost analysis is properly regarded as an aid to decision making and not the decision itself.

The well-informed benefit–cost analyst is aware that benefit–cost analysis cannot perfectly capture the thinking of the decision maker. The informed decision maker and analyst are aware that data are always imperfect, that the very process of qualification imposes limitations on the conceptual framework, and that philosophical and normative assumptions always remain embedded in the analysis. In fact, benefit–cost analysis is intrinsically dependent on the political process for the specification of rights on which to calculate benefits and costs. (See Chapters 6 and 12 for a discussion of this issue.)

1.2.   THE JUSTIFICATION FOR BENEFIT–COST ANALYSIS

On the most basic practical level the justification for benefit–cost analysis is simply that knowledge about benefits and costs is useful in making decisions. This is true for a world of private as well as public decision making, and benefit–cost analysis can be regarded as a sort of profit and loss accounting such as used by the private sector but with a different perspective.

1.3.   WHEN SHOULD BENEFIT–COST ANALYSIS BE USED?

Viewing benefit–cost analysis broadly, rational decision makers can be said to always use benefit–cost analysis in the sense that your decisions arise from a weighing of benefits and costs. Benefit–cost analysis is similar to profit and loss accounting used in private business. Traditionally, benefit–cost analysis is associated with government intervention and with the evaluation of government action and government projects.

1.4.   THE STEPS OF ANALYSIS

At a general level, benefit–cost analysis is indistinguishable from policy analysis. The procedures for analysis are then those for any policy analysis. The following framework may be a useful starting point:

1. *Who is the client?* This question should be asked regardless of whether or not the analyst is being paid, or has been explicitly hired. An analysis requires a perspective, and the purpose of this question is to make the perspective clear to the analyst. Only when this is done can the next questions be asked.
2. *What are the goals of the analysis?* This question is one of defining the problem.

3. *What is the objective?* The answer to this lays out how the problem is to be treated as a practical matter. Here you specify the objective that gives operational definition to the goal.

4. *What are the alternatives?* This step is crucial to a successful analysis. (See Chapter 26, the case of the Tellico dam, for an example in which this was not done.) The analyst should use his or her imagination and lay out as many alternatives as feasibly possible. Some of these alternatives can often be dismissed easily but a review reduces the chances of ignoring a superior alternative.

5. *What are the consequences of each of the alternatives?* Answering this question involves a choice of techniques for predicting physical consequences.

6. *How are the physical consequences to be valued?* A technique must be chosen for valuing outcomes. This, of course, is part of the heart of benefit–cost analysis.

7. *How certain are the predicted consequences?* Outcomes are always uncertain and this issue should, therefore, always be explicitly addressed.

8. *What is the choice?* This step draws together the results of the benefit–cost analysis and the predictions that underlie it, along with other, perhaps political, considerations, relevant to the choice. This step is for the analyst who recommends a choice to the decision maker.

9. *What is the decision?* This step is for the decision maker who may be someone different from the analyst. But this step precedes the next step which ideally should be performed by the analyst.

10. *How do the outcomes compare with the predictions?* The analyst should monitor the outcomes, compare the actual results with those predicted, and consider why the results are different. This is a step whose importance is seldom recognized.

1.5.   PRACTICE

Stokey and Zeckhauser (1978) end their discussion of thinking about policy choices with the advice to practice. Practice on all kinds of situations. Practice thinking in terms of your day-to-day tasks and in terms of your own decisions. Practice especially presenting your conclusions systematically. "Make up your mind that at least once every day you will deliberately apply the outline set forth above to a problem you face. You'll be amazed at what it will do for your reputation for perceptiveness and good judgment." (Stokey and Zeckhauser, 1968, p. 7.) This is good advice for those interested in applying benefit–cost analysis.

1.6.   AN EXAMPLE: THE MID-STATE PROJECT

It is useful to consider an example of one of these criticisms to give a flavor of benefit–cost analysis and of the sort of issues that reoccur. Hanke and Walker (1974) examine the Mid-State project, a proposed project of the Bureau of Reclamation. This example is taken from their work.

The Mid-State project would serve an area of highly productive agricultural land lying along the north side of the Platte River valley in south central Nebraska. It was conceived in 1943 by local farmers who believed that the project could be financed locally. Even with a federal loan the project had become infeasible on a local basis. Therefore, the district sought the aid of the Bureau of Reclamation.

Hanke and Walker note that the Bureau of Reclamation has traditionally been accused of using the tools of economic analysis to justify decisions that have been determined politically. Economists often conclude that the bureau tends to overstate benefits and understate costs and that this policy enables projects to be built that would not be feasible if "proper" evaluation techniques were employed. The bureau's procedures for benefit–cost analysis are held to be deficient because they (1) omit opportunity costs of the water diverted for project purposes, (2) improperly include secondary benefits, (3) employ low discount rates, and (4) exaggerate primary benefits through the farm budget procedures by valuing farm output on the basis of support prices, by not accounting for the effects of variability in the supply of project water, and by not properly evaluating the opportunity costs of farm investment and owner–operator labor. In addition, questions have been raised about the valuation of recreational benefits. Finally, the bureau has a record of underestimating costs, as verified by the bureau's own studies made in 1951, 1955, and 1960.

The 1967 statement of the Mid-State project indicates that annual costs were expected to be $4,543,000, and annual benefits were estimated to be $5,661,000. Since the alleged benefits exceed the costs (a benefit–cost ratio of 1.24), the project has been designated as "justified." On the basis of existing data and a less favorable choice of criteria and parameter values, Hanke and Walker find that the results can be changed substantially. If liberal assumptions regarding economic parameters are made, the benefit–cost ratio of the project is 0.87. Under more severe, although not unrealistic, assumptions the benefit–cost ratio falls to 0.23.

The benefit and cost figures as prepared by the bureau for the project are summarized in Table 1.1.

1.6.1. Reevaluation

Hanke and Walker note that the Bureau of Reclamation's analysis of the benefits and costs from the Mid-State project can be altered substantially through a reappraisal of certain economic assumptions and procedures. They base such a reevaluation upon what they believe to be the dominant opinion of the economics profession and a critical view of certain logical procedures of the bureau's analysis. Hanke and Walker note that on the basis of the following three factors one would conclude that the Mid-State project is an unsound investment: (1) The discount rate used in the analysis is inappropriately low, (2) multipurpose benefits from flood control and fish and wildlife enhancement have been overstated, and (3) "new lands" do not yield significant or national benefits.

Discount Rate. The discount rate to be used in calculating the present values of benefits and costs of federal water resource projects has long been of great

TABLE 1.1   1967 Bureau of Reclamation Benefits and Costs for the Mid-State Nebraska Project

Description	Value ($)
Benefits	
44,000 acres, dry farming to irrigation, direct benefits, $59.86/acre	2,471,000*
44,000 acres, dry farming to irrigation, secondary benefits, $12.11/acre	204,000†
96,000 acres, pumping to project waters, $12.17/acre	1,096,000*
163,000 acres, balance of irrigated lands, benefiting from groundwater stabilization, $5.05/acre	772,000*
Recreation	
General use for 300,000 days	156,000
Boating for 27,000 days	15,000
Camping for 9,000 days	4,500
Total	175,500
Fish and wildlife	
Fishing	306,000
Hunting	24,000
Trapping	12,000
Annual equivalent investment ($2,540,000) in lands for wildlife refuge	83,000
Total	425,000
Flood control	518,000
Total annual benefits	5,661,500
Costs	
Annual equivalent investment costs ($112,234,000 at 3⅛%)	3,680,000
Annual operation, maintenance, and replacement costs	863,000
Total annual costs	4,543,000
Benefit–cost ratio	1.24

SOURCE: Hanke and Walker (1974).

*Irrigation benefits are discounted by 0.938 to take account of 5-year development lag before full benefits are realized; 5 years is probably an optimistic figure.

†Actual figure for secondary benefits is $500,000, but the bureau has chosen to subtract disbenefits (primary and secondary) from lands lost to project right-of-ways, reservoirs, etc., rather than show them as a separate figure.

concern to federal agencies and their clientele groups because projects are often quite sensitive to changes in the rate.

The Mid-State project was last evaluated in 1967 at a discount rate of 3.125 percent. At that time, discount rates for project analysis by all federal water agencies were derived from the average rate of interest payable by the Treasury on outstanding long-term government bonds. This policy was thought to reflect the cost of capital for federal investments. The agencies were able to avoid using a rate that reflected the cost of capital by using the coupon rates on bonds of long maturity rather than using current yields. For example, the discount rate used in 1967 was 3.125 percent, but the current yield that same year was 4.85 percent. At this latter rate of interest the benefit–cost ratio of Mid-State would have been only 0.89.

If the Mid-State project were being evaluated by using the rate at the time of the reevaluation by Hanke and Walker of 5.37 percent, it would fail the test of economic viability for both 50 and 100 years, with a benefit–cost ratio of 0.87 for 50 years. At the higher rates of 7 percent (Water Resources Council recommendation) and 10 percent (Office of Management and Budget

TABLE 1.2

Source	Discount Rate	Benefit–Cost Ratio
1. Bureau of Reclamation	3.125% (coupon yield)	1.24
2. Hanke and Walker	4.85% (current yield)	0.89
3. Hanke and Walker	5.375 (WRC-old)	0.87
4. Hanke and Walker	7.0 (WRC*-new)	0.63
5. Hanke and Walker	10.0 (OMB†)	0.46

SOURCE: Compiled from Hanke-Walker (1974).
*Water Resources Council.
†Office of Management and Budget.

requirement) the project fails by a larger margin, with benefit–cost ratios of 0.63 and 0.46, respectively (Table 1.2). Note how powerful the effect of the discount rate is on the benefit–cost ratio.

Multipurpose Benefits: Flood Control, Recreation, and Fish and Wildlife

1. The reduction in the number of dams from 23 to 2 clearly reduces the capacity of the project to check flooding. The total flood control benefits for the new Mid-State project plan will be $341,400 rather than $518,000.
2. Recreation benefits are also diminished by the reduction in amount of surface and shoreline area that will result from fewer reservoirs. Moreover, the increased severity of water level fluctuations in the storage reservoirs may worsen the quality of recreation. However, since we cannot reconstruct the original analysis, we cannot make an appropriate adjustment for the probable reductions in recreation benefits.
3. Fish and wildlife benefits claimed for the Mid-State project have been overstated. One of the most important objections to the project is its damaging effect on the Platte River wildlife environment. A study by the Bureau of Sport Fisheries and Wildlife shows that if the Mid-State diversions had been attempted over the period of record (1931–1960), the Platte River would have been dried up 184 out of 360 months. In 7 of the 30 years there would be no flow in the river for the entire 12 months. Hence, if Mid-State were allowed to divert the proposed amount of water for irrigation, waterfowl habitats would be eliminated from the diversion dam to the confluence of the Loup River, 150 miles downstream. The instream fishery would be destroyed, the central flyway would be disrupted, and several rare or endangered species, including the whooping crane, the sandhill crane, and the bald eagle, would be jeopardized further.

The water of the Platte River has many demands for its use and should not be treated as if it were a free good with no opportunity costs. In many areas, for instance, water diverted by the bureau to agriculture has alternative uses at a much higher value in municipal and industrial sectors. Water also has both aesthetic and economically significant uses if it is left instream for fish, wildlife, and recreation. It may even be reused downstream for further irrigation. There is no economic validity in the common misconception that the water of the Platte River is "now being wasted in the Gulf of Mexico" (U.S. Congress, 1964). The bureau's benefit–cost analysis takes no account of opportunity costs of water. Hanke and Walker clearly make a cogent and powerful criticism of the bureau's failure to assign an opportunity cost to water.

> Opportunity cost is the value of opportunities lost by a decision. Opportunity cost is the basic definition of cost in economics.

New Lands Benefits.   The bureau proposes to convert 44,000 acres of dry farming land to irrigation in the Mid-State project area. For the economic justification of the project the benefits from these "new lands" are essential, amounting to $2,471,000, or 43 percent, of the total benefits.

The bureau estimates cropping patterns, yields, sales value, and costs of inputs, and these data are used to calculate net farm income with and without project water. The difference in aggregate farm net income with and without the project represents net primary benefits for "new lands."

Criticisms can be leveled at the bureau's treatment of three important variables in the farm budgets: the value (price) of farm products, the interest rate for farm borrowing, and the opportunity cost of owner–operator labor.

Under a regime of government price and output controls in the agricultural sector, prevailing commodity prices are not an acceptable measure of market value for purposes of benefit–cost analysis because they include a significant proportion of transfer payments to farmers. Recognizing this situation, the WRC issued a new set of price guidelines in 1966, known as "adjusted normalized" prices, which were considerably lower than previous price schedules used by the agencies in project evaluation.

Two changes of lesser impact have also been made in arriving at the final figures. First, the cost of farm borrowing has been raised from 5 percent to 7.5 percent. A 5 percent interest rate can only be obtained on subsidized loans from federal agencies such as the Federal Home Administration. The market rate, on the other hand, is approximately 7.5 percent. Second, the opportunity cost of owner–operator labor has been raised from $0.51 per hour to $1.25 per hour. The cost of this added time is the alternative labor opportunities foregone outside the farm (for example, as hired help at $1.25), not the average return to family labor on the farm itself (approximately $0.50). In this case the opportunity cost of owner–operator labor is not significant ($81,600), but in projects that bring uncultivated land into production this economic cost can be significant.

The impact on new lands benefits from correcting the three most tractable variables in the farm budgets, prices, interest, and labor cost, is substantial. The original benefit estimate of the bureau, $2,470,700, falls to $1,136,400. Had the Mid-State project been reevaluated in 1967 by using adjusted normalized prices, which had been issued a year earlier, the resulting benefit–cost ratio would have been only 0.95 (all other things held constant), and the project would not have been approved by Congress.

1.6.2. Secondary Benefits

In arriving at final benefit–cost figures, secondary benefits associated with new lands benefits have been eliminated because there is no a priori reason to believe that secondary benefits actually result from the Mid-State project and no empirical evidence to the contrary has been put forward by the bureau in any of the documents concerning the project. Secondary benefits are defined by the bureau as the added net profits of agricultural supply and processing industries brought about by the increased productivity of the project area. The actual method of computation is a simplified system of multiplication factors for each crop applied uniformly to every project, regardless of actual conditions among secondary industries, for example, 83 percent of the increase in direct cotton benefits equals secondary benefits from cotton.

In order for secondary benefits to exist, secondary industries must either be suffering from secular stagnation and underemployment or be able to take advantage of economies of scale due to the expansion of farm output. Otherwise, increased profits in one industry or in one region will be no more than transfers of economic activity from some other industry or region. Since there is no evidence that the conditions put forward by Margolis (1957) exist in the prosperous Mid-State area, secondary benefits have been eliminated from the analysis because they represent pecuniary transfers and not real effects.

By using adjusted normalized prices for direct new lands benefits, eliminating secondary benefits, and taking account of fish and wildlife losses, the benefit–cost ratio for the Mid-State project is lowered to a high of 0.63 at the original 3.125 percent interest rate and a low of 0.23 at a 10 percent interest rate. Table 1.3 contains a summary of results. From these figures it appears that the Mid-State project is a poor investment for the nation.

1.7. ADDITIONAL PROBLEMS OF NEW LANDS BENEFITS AND BUREAU POLICY

The preceding revisions of the farm budgets for the Mid-State project do not by any means resolve satisfactorily all the problems attending a logically complete benefit–cost analysis of increased farm output from a reclamation project. Government programs such as acreage retirement, price maintenance, and community purchases not only create income transfers to farmers (their main objective) but entail real resource costs in the form of storage, insurance, depreciation, and interest.

Also, there is a policy consideration that makes the inclusion of new lands questionable. If it is claimed that there is a serious groundwater depletion problem in the Mid-State area, it seems that the problem will only be aggravated by expanding the demand for water through the addition of irrigation acreage (new lands). Other alternatives for dealing with the alleged problem of groundwater depletion are never considered.

TABLE 1.3 Summary of Benefit–Cost Reevaluation of the Mid-State Project

Description	Value ($)	Total Annual Benefits ($)	Benefit–Cost Ratios			
			$I = 3.125\%$ C = 4,543,000* (C = 5,283,200)	$I = 5.375\%$ C = 6,487,000	$I = 7\%$ C = 9,002,800	$I = 10\%$ C = 12,193,000
Total benefits (unchanged from 1967 bureau estimates)						
New lands	2,471,000					
Secondary	499,000					
Land acquisition/withdrawal	−295,000					
Supplemental water	1,096,000					
Groundwater stabilization	772,000					
Flood control	518,000					
Recreation	175,500					
Fish and wildlife	425,000	5,661,500	1.24(1.07)*	0.87	0.63	0.46
Total benefits after reducing multipurpose benefits						
Fish and wildlife (adjusted)	−347,000					
Flood control (adjusted)	341,500					
All other benefits (unadjusted)	4,718,500	4,713,000	1.03(0.89)	0.72	0.52	0.38
Total benefits after reducing new lands benefits and multipurpose benefits						
New lands (adjusted)	1,136,500					
Secondary (adjusted)	0					
Fish and wildlife (adjusted)	−347,000					
Flood control (adjusted)	341,000					
All other benefits (unadjusted)	1,748,500	2,879,000	0.63(0.54)	0.44	0.31	0.23

SOURCE: Hanke and Walker (1974), Table 14.9. Costs equal annual equivalent costs of $112,000,000 at given interest rates plus annual operating costs of $863,000.
*This cost is for a 100-year period of analysis. All others are for a 50-year period of analysis.

CONCLUSION

The preceding analysis takes a critical view of the Mid-State project and the Bureau of Reclamation's practices in using benefit–cost analysis. The results differ significantly from those presented by the bureau. It would seem that the bureau's justification of reclamation is indeed on arid ground.

The issues raised by Hanke and Walker include the following:

1. The choice of discount rate. (See Chapters 3, 13, and 14.)
2. The valuation of nonmarketed goods. (See Chapter 18 and other chapters.)
3. The treatment of secondary benefits. (See Chapter 18.)
4. The treatment of government subsidies. (See Chapter 7.)
5. The determination of opportunity costs. (See Chapter 22 and elsewhere.)
6. The failure to fully consider alternatives. (See Chapter 22.)
7. The issue of who are the winners and losers, the size of their income changes, and how this should or could effect the decision is not considered by Hanke and Walker. (See Chapter 11.)
8. Similarly, the question of how risk and uncertainty are to be incorporated can be important, though it is not considered by either the bureau or by Hanke and Walker. (These issues are considered in Chapters 15, 16, and 17.)

All these issues and others are apt to arise in modern benefit–cost analysis. Some issues such as choice of a discount rate remain unsettled even, to a degree, among professional economists, though this may soon no longer be the case. Other issues such as the treatment of secondary benefits appear fairly well settled.

QUESTIONS AND PROBLEMS

1. The Boston school district plans to build a new high school. It owns a 10-acre site at a suitable location, Beaverbrook (site A), which it has held for the past 10 years and for which it originally paid $500,000. In the past 10 years, land prices generally have increased by about 100 percent, whereas the prices of most goods measured by the CPI have increased only 65 percent. The current market value of the Beaverbrook site, however, is $1,500,000, the value of the land there having increased more than land in many other locations. A building on site A must be sound-proofed, because the street noise level is quite high, and, as a consequence of the sound-proofing, the building must also be air-conditititioned. The capital cost of building the high school on site A would be $2,000,000, which would include sound-proofing and air-conditioning.

   An alternative, site B, consists of 20 acres and could be bought as a 10-acre site for $1,250,000, or the full 20 acres could be purchased for $2,000,000. The advantage of purchasing the full 20 acres is that a grade school could also be built on the site. Although the grade school is not yet needed, the school district has decided that if it purchases site B, it will purchase the full 20 acres. The capital cost of building the high school on site B is $1,000,000. Site B is not as conveniently located as site A although there is no problem with noise pollution at site B. Because of the less convenient location, site B would incur additional busing costs of $100,000 a year for 10 years. You are asked to assume no additional busing costs after 10 years.

Because we have not yet considered discount rates, you are asked to assume for now that future values equal present values, or, that the discount rate is zero.

a. The school district asks your advice. They assure you that they would be equally satisfied with site A or site B and that the decision should be made on financial grounds.

b. Suppose that your advice is sought instead by parents who are opposed to site B because of the additional busing. What additions or changes to the financial analysis might you make?

REFERENCES

Hanke, Steve H., and Richard A. Walker, "Benefit–Cost Analysis Reconsidered: An Evaluation of the Mid-State Project," *Water Resources Journal* 10(5), 898–909, (1974), reprinted in Haveman and Margolis, pp. 324–349.

Hunter, Arthur, Jr., George Tolley, and Robert G. Fabian, "Benefit–Cost Analysis and the Common Sense of Environment Policy," in: Daniel Swartzman, Richard A. Liroff, and Kevin Croke (eds.), *Cost–Benefit Analysis and Environmental Regulations: Politics, Ethics, and Methods,* Chap. 5, Washington, DC: The Conservation Foundation (1982).

Margolis, J., "Secondary Benefits, External Economies, and the Justification of Public Investment," *Review of Economic Statistics* 39, 284–291, 1957.

Stokey, Edith, and Richard Zeckhauser, *A Primer for Policy Analysis*, New York: W. W. Norton (1978).

2

Rationale for
Benefit–Cost Analysis

2.1. INTRODUCTION

Chapter 1 indicated that benefit–cost analysis is a sort of profit and loss accounting, but with a government perspective. But, why is a government perspective
needed? That is, why is government intervention needed, and what situations
might call for the use of benefit–cost analysis? The very use of benefit–cost
analysis implies that some at least believe the existing situation can be improved. Economists have derived a series of conditions which, when violated,
imply the possibility that the situation can be improved at least according to
certain economic criteria. We assume that you are already familiar with these
criteria. Nevertheless, it is useful to summarize them.

Economic efficiency requires that, at the margin, the ratio in which goods
are valued must be the same for all individuals, and the ratio in which inputs
are productive must be the same for different goods produced. This latter ratio
also must reflect the relative scarcity of the inputs so that the ratio of marginal
products of labor to capital are equal to the ratio of the wage rate to the return
to capital. For overall efficiency, production efficiency must also accord with
consumption efficiency so that what people want is what is produced. This
is expressed by the condition that the rate at which one commodity can be
transformed into another through production at the margin equals the relative
marginal values of the two commodities. These efficiency conditions taken
together produce a type of efficiency called *Pareto efficiency*. This is attained
when no further changes can be made without harming someone. A change
from one position to another position in which the welfare of one person
is improved and no one is harmed is called a *Pareto superior move*. This is
a movement toward Pareto efficiency. Most suggested policy changes, however,

do not involve Pareto superior moves. Most changes make some people better off and others less well off.

Pareto efficiency does not indicate how wealth or utility is to be distributed. Distributional issues as well as efficiency ones must be examined. If utility were capable of measurement, efficiency could be defined in terms of the maximization of overall utility for society and a "bliss" point attained. Nevertheless, for any given distribution of utility, welfare could be made greater (a Pareto improvement is possible) whenever the efficiency conditions are not met.

Benefit–cost analysis is concerned with the question of when we can reasonably say that a policy change is a good one. Given a choice among investment decisions for which there are both gains and losses, on the basis of what principles should a choice be made? The problems of efficiency and distribution are precisely those with which benefit–cost analysis attempts to grapple. These questions are the subject of this book. In this chapter we discuss situations that might prevent the attainment of efficiency, and thus describe situations in which benefit–cost analysis might be useful. We will consider the anatomy of "market failure."[1] These categories of "market failure" include in general the divergence of private and social costs, external effects, collective and public goods, monopoly power, and costly information. Although there is a certain artificiality about these categories, they are useful. We consider them below.

2.2. THE RATIONALE FOR BENEFIT–COST ANALYSIS

Discussion of Pareto efficiency often proceeds as if the cost of carrying out transactions were zero. In fact, the world is not one of costless markets. Markets are costly to establish and they are costly to operate once established. Markets are a type of good in scarce supply, and the optimality conditions must be qualified to consider the costs of markets. Markets themselves do not operate in a vacuum. They exist in a legal and institutional context that defines ownership, enforces contracts, governs fraud, and sets up a myriad of rules that affect the efficiency with which the market operates. In many cases a political or bureaucratic "market" is substituted for an economic one. So, potentially, government action, and therefore, potentially, benefit–cost analysis are required.

One way to proceed is to imagine that the world is one of markets that can be costlessly operated. Transaction costs are zero, and so are costs of acquiring market information. In such a world, there would be no deviation from the efficiency conditions except that we would still need to specify a social welfare function in order to decide what the appropriate distribution of utility would be. There would be a market for clean air and clean water, and all congestion would be optional because it would be priced. All land use decisions would reflect a full consideration of benefits and costs. There would

---

[1]The term is in quotes because Coase (1960) has shown us the artificiality of the term. As Coase notes, the issues concern the efficiency of alternative arrangements. We believe that considering the sources of divergence between private and public costs and benefits is useful in discussing alternative arrangements. See Zerbe (1980).

even be a market for income redistribution that reflected people's willingness to pay for the welfare of others.

Clearly this is not the case. Economists have, therefore, developed a short-hand vocabulary to describe aspects of the costs of markets and of transactions, and it is this vocabulary that helps point the way toward areas where benefit–cost analysis might be of help and of interest.

2.3. THE DIVERGENCE OF PRIVATE AND SOCIAL COSTS OR BENEFITS

All the situations described by this vocabulary can be placed into the general category of situations in which there is a divergence between marginal private and marginal social costs or between marginal private and marginal social benefits. This divergence is a necessary condition, but not a sufficient condition for action to improve the situation. If there is no divergence, government action cannot improve the situation. To say that there is a government action that would improve the situation is to say that there are benefits or costs that will not be considered by private decision makers. So, the divergence is necessary for action to be contemplated. But, whether or not government action will improve the situation can only be determined by further analysis—such as benefit–cost analysis, for there are also costs to government intervention. *The only general rule then is to compare the total effects (benefits and costs) of alternative arrangements* (Coase, 1960).

2.4. EXTERNAL EFFECTS (EXTERNALITIES)

External effects are costs or benefits not reflected fully in decision making or in prices. Since all "market failures" are a result of a divergence of private and social costs or benefits, all "market failures" may be viewed in some sense as externalities. Note that, by the definition of externality, government action will itself usually produce external effects. In practice, most external effects reflect the high cost of running a market because those who would benefit from some action do not pay for the benefit either because (1) for technological reasons it is too difficult to collect from potential payers, or (2) the absence of ownership or other legal barrier does not allow collection of payments for provision of the good. Consider briefly the situation when ownership is not clear.

The Buffalo.   Great buffalo herds once roamed the Western United States. These herds were not owned. Their hides had value and could be sold in the Eastern United States. In considering whether or not to kill an additional buffalo a hunter would consider the cost of powder and shot, the opportunity costs of his time, the cost of shipping the buffalo to the East, and so forth. The hunter would not fully consider the value of the buffalo as a reproductive animal because the hunter, not owning the buffalo, would not gain its value in reproduction. Nor would the hunter fully consider the value of buffalo for possible future harvest because a buffalo passed up today might be harvested by someone else tomorrow. Thus the costs to the hunter from killing an additional buffalo would be less than the marginal social costs. These lower private marginal costs would then lead, as shown in Figure 2.1, to a kill rate determined by the intersection of marginal private costs and demand. Because marginal private costs were less than marginal social costs, this kill rate would be greater than the kill rate determined by the intersection of marginal social cost and demand. Since the privately determined kill rate was greater than the reproduction rate, the buffalo was headed toward extinction. An externality existed in the sense that the decision to kill an additional buffalo imposed certain costs on consumers of the buffalo that were not considered by the hunter. That is, certain benefits from not killing an additional buffalo were ignored. Possibly the rights to harvest from any one buffalo herd could have been sold or assigned to some private owner. If this owner could have effectively enforced his property rights against other hunters, the creation of private ownership of the buffalo would have eliminated the externality and eliminated the divergence between private and social costs.

Examples such as this one, in which ownership is not well defined, have broad application, leading to common pool problems in, for example, fisheries, use of the radio spectrum, use of water, and so on.

The Common Pool Problem.   The story of the buffalo represents something more than just an external effect. Incomplete property rights are often reflected in a common pool problem, in a tragedy of the commons. The fact that the buffalo herd is not owned, means that additional hunters will seek to exploit the herd as long as it is profitable. No one hunter, or hunting party, will take account of their kills on reducing the availability of buffalo for the other hunters. Each hunter leaves fewer buffalo making each buffalo harder to find for subsequent hunters. No one has an incentive to ensure that the buffalo will reproduce in

FIGURE 2.1   The divergence of MSC and MPC with lack of ownership.

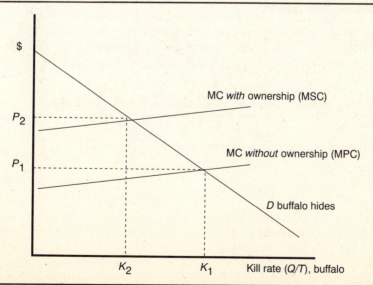

sufficient numbers to maintain the viability of the herd. Buffalo will be killed while not mature and female buffalo bearing calves will be killed because little value is given by the non-owner to the future value of the live calf.

The Dissipation of Rents.   Suppose that a particular herd is called the Rolling Thunder Herd, or RTH for short. Consider how each hunter that pursues the RTH herd affects the number of buffalo available from the herd. Each hunter that enters the business of pursuing the RTH reduces the number of buffalo available for others. This relationship is shown in Table 2.1. If the hunter does not hunt, he might farm or spend the day in the local tavern. Let us say that the value of this alternative activity is equivalent to 60 buffalo per day. As long as the number of buffalo the hunter can kill in a day exceeds 60, the hunter will kill buffalo. The buffalo killed per day falls as each hunter hunts until the number of buffalo killed per hunter reaches 60 with eight hunters for a total of 480 buffalo killed per day. With eight hunters, there is no net gain from pursuing buffalo.

Figure 2.2 shows the relationship between the number of hunters and the buffalo killed per day per hunter. The number of hunters times buffalo killed per day per hunter gives total buffalo kills per day. Any number greater than 60 per day per hunter is a producer surplus. (Note the curve in Figure 2.2 is not a demand curve. Why?) With no restrictions on the entry of new hunters all rents are dissipated at the equilibrium of eight hunters and 480 buffalo harvested per day.

Ownership.   The government, racked by guilt over the treatment of Native Americans or, more likely, impressed by new armaments that the Native Americans gained from abroad, decides to give ownership of the RTH herd to the Crow tribe represented by Chief Big Thunder.

The Chief decides to sell rights to kill buffalo from the herd because the opportunity cost of killing buffalo exceeds the equivalent of 60 buffalo per day now that there is ownership. Ownership internalizes costs which were previously external social costs, in this case the future resources available from a sustained herd of buffalo. Given the hunters' demand curve (derived from a consumers' demand curve for buffalo), the maximum entry price that can be set to attract only one hunter is just less than the value of 140 buffalo (200-60). Table 2.1 shows the number of hunters and the buffalo killed

TABLE 2.1   Number of Hunters and Buffalo Kill Rate per Hunter

Number of Hunters	Buffalo per Hunter	Total Buffalo Kill/Day	Marginal Buffalo Kill/Day
1	200	200	200
2	180	360	160
3	160	480	120
4	140	560	80
5	120	600	40
6	100	600	0
7	80	560	−40
8	60	480	−80
9	40	360	−120
10	20	200	−160

at various entry prices. Each day of hunting has an opportunity cost to the hunter.

As Figure 2.2 shows, Chief Big Thunder finds that at an entry price of just less than 80 buffalo per day there are four hunters and the Crow are able to gain a total of 320 buffalo per day as shown in Figure 2.2. The hunters still gain no rent; they are not significantly better off than before. Social welfare of the Crow is higher by almost 320 buffalo than when there was no ownership. Moreover, the hunters are no worse off than before so that this change to ownership is a Pareto move. In addition, the Crow now have an incentive to prevent the herd from diminishing in size. Only if the demand for buffalo were extremely high now, relative to what it would be in the future, would it pay to exterminate the herd. Note that this example assumes that the Crow may exclude

FIGURE 2.2

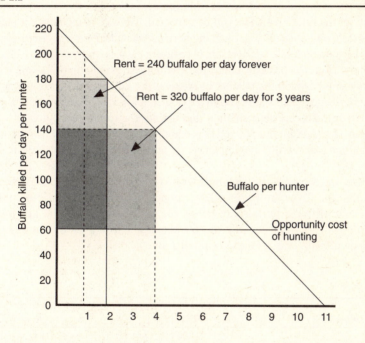

TABLE 2.2   Profits to Chief at Various Entry Prices

Entry Fee to Kill Buffalo	Number of Hunters	Gain to Crow/Day
140	1	140
120	2	240
100	3	300
80	4	320
60	5	300
40	6	240
20	7	140
0	8	0
−40	9	−360

outside (nonpaying) hunters without cost. This, of course, may not be the case. If these exclusion costs are high enough no market may exist.

Ownership and Time.   The analysis so far shows the kill rate as higher with ownership than without (560 vs. 480). We arrived at this somewhat counter-intuitive result by neglecting to add time to the Chief's planning horizon. In fact, because the Chief can claim ownership to both present *and* future benefits of buffalo stock, he will want to choose a daily rate lower than 560 so as to prevent early extinction.

With a kill rate of 600 buffalo per day we might assume that the herd would be eliminated within three years. With a kill rate of 360 or less the herd would last forever, and so on. Table 2.3 shows the period of time a herd will last for different kill rates.

Thus, in making a decision about what entry fee to charge, the Native Americans will consider the future rents that can be collected. We will assume that for planning purposes the Crow use a 30-year planning horizon when the herd will last forever, and that they have no preference for present over future gains so that rents received in different time periods can be easily compared.[2] With these assumptions, Table 2.4 shows the relationship between the number of hunters, the kill rate, the entry fee, and the total rents collected. Rents are maximized now at a kill rate of 360 per day with two hunting parties. The previous solution that ignores the future years gives a value of rents of only 1.17 million (for 560 total) as compared with the wealth-maximizing rent of 2.63 million. At a wealth-maximizing entry fee of 120 buffalo per day, the herd will last forever.

When we compare the situation with ownership to that of no ownership, we find that the Crow are better off by about 2.63 million buffalo, the hunters are no worse off, the buffalo are better off in the sense that the kill rate has fallen from 480 buffalo per day to 360 buffalo per day. Clearly, in this instance, the grant of ownership was a Pareto optimal move.

TABLE 2.3

Number of Buffalo Hunters	Total Buffalo Kill/Day	Number of Years Herd Will Last
1	200	30 years (forever)
2	360	30 years (forever)
3	480	15 years
4	560	10 years
5	600	3 years
6	600	3 years

[2]Rents received in the future are counted equally with rents received in the past. We will see later, in Chapter 4, that this is not a correct procedure. The use of correct procedures will not, however, invalidate the above point.

TABLE 2.4

Number of Buffalo Hunters	Total Kill/Day	Life of Herd (in Years)	Rent per Day per Hunter	Total Entry Fee (Rent/Day)	Total Rent/Year	Total Value of Rent for Life of Herd (30 years) (millions)
1	200	30 (forever)	140	140	51,100	1.53
2	360	30 (forever)	120	240	87,600	2.63
3	480	15	100	300	109,500	1.64
4	560	10	80	320	116,800	1.17
5	600	3	60	300	109,500	0.33
6	600	3	40	240	87,600	0.26
7	560	15	20	210	76,650	1.15
8	480	10	0	0	0	0
9	360	30 (forever)	−20	−180	−65,700	Neg.
10	200	30 (forever)	−40	−400	−146,000	Neg.

The analysis of the effects of different ownership arrangements has many applications in fisheries, water allocation and a host of natural resource areas, and in the production of many goods. When OPEC was formed, the production of oil fell and prices rose. This was widely attributed to the exercise of monopoly power by OPEC. The analysis here suggests the possibility of another explanation. Saudi Arabia and other countries gained ownership of oil production in their respective countries at the same time as they cut production. Previously existing oil companies, fearful of a takeover, may have been pumping oil at a furious rate and supplying more than optimally efficient in the long term. That is, oil companies may have supplied more than they would have if they were certain of maintaining ownership. A more secure ownership could properly take into account the value of future oil so that the opportunity costs to OPEC of pumping was higher and production fell.

Application to Benefit–Cost Analysis.   These sorts of common pool problems arise frequently. A benefit–cost analysis can provide information about the benefits and costs of providing alternative solutions. Perhaps ownership of buffalo herds could in fact have been assigned to various parties. The assignment of such ownership would, however, have a cost, and ownership would itself involve enforcement costs to be effective. The government could have simply sold the herds at auction. As long as the proceeds from the auction exceeded the auction costs, the government would make money, and the bids would be the best estimation of the net benefits of privatizing the herds.

There is a proposal by some land use planners, most notably by a husband–wife team, the Poppers, to turn parts of the Western plains into a buffalo commons. The evaluation of this idea would be an interesting challenge for a benefit–cost analyst.

The Highway.   Excess highway congestion is an example of an externality that may exist because technological conditions may make it too costly to collect fees from those that use the highway. When deciding whether or not to make a trip during rush hour or at an off-peak hour, you examine the private costs and benefits. You do not consider that traveling at a time of congestion may impose costs on your fellow drivers. Since there are costs not considered by you in your private decision, we can say that an externality exists.

Suppose there are two roads between two points, A and B.[3] One is narrow but has a good surface and the other is infinitely broad so that it can never be congested, but has a lower-quality surface. On the broad road, speed tends to be at 45 miles per hour because it is uncomfortable to drive any faster on the surface. (Also, perhaps this is the speed limit and the highway is well patrolled.) During rush hour the speeds on the two roads will be the same (assuming speed is the only cost involved in the choice between the two roads) because the narrow highway will be congested until the speed is the same as the broad highway. Suppose now that you remove some of the traffic from the narrow highway and put the traffic on the broad highway. There will be no loss to those moved to the broad highway because their speed is the same as before. However, average speed on the narrow highway will increase because there is now less congestion. The divergence between private and social costs creates a situation where there is a potential for an efficiency improvement.

Application to Benefit–Cost Analysis.   Professor William Vickery of New York University has been a prominent economic analyst of schemes to price highway use. Calculations show that congestion costs are often quite large. Benefit–cost analysis can be useful in determining the benefits from reducing congestion and the costs of alternative measures to effect a reduction in congestion.

2.5. MARKET POWER

A firm may have significant ability to raise its price above its marginal or average costs without losing its market. Monopolies are generally regarded as bad because they restrict output. Buyers are still willing to pay the full social cost of additional output. A producer will produce an additional unit only as long as the *marginal revenue* from that unit is greater than the marginal cost of producing the unit. For the purchaser, the value of the good will be at least equal to the sales price, otherwise he would not buy the good. The value of the last unit bought will just equal the sales price. For a firm without market power the marginal revenue will equal the sales price and thus the seller's marginal revenue will equal the price or value placed on the good by the buyer. The marginal revenue of an additional unit to a monopolist, however, is less than the sales price. A (nondiscriminating) monopolist can sell more only by decreasing the sales price. Although he sells the new unit at the new sales price, his marginal revenue is less than the sales price because the expansion in sales lowers the price for all units.

---

[3]This example is roughly based on an example used by Frank Knight (1924).

FIGURE 2.3

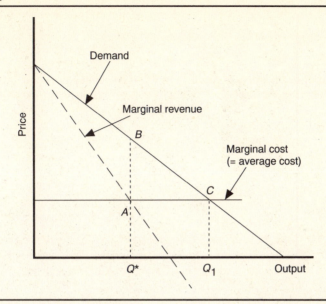

Figure 2.3 shows the demand and marginal revenue curves facing a firm with market power. The value of the resources used to produce one more unit of the good is shown by the marginal cost curve. The willingness to pay for one more unit of the good is shown by the demand curve. The monopolist will operate at Q^* where marginal revenue equals marginal cost. At Q, the willingness to pay for one more unit exceeds the value of what is given up (the marginal cost) so there is a welfare loss to society.

Monopoly may arise because of technological conditions. Average costs may fall over the range of output demanded by the market so that the price set equal to marginal costs may be less than average costs. This is shown by Figure 2.4.

A monopolist will operate at output Q^*, again where marginal revenue equals marginal cost. Output should, however, be no less than output Q_1, and perhaps as much as Q_2. The astute student may note that buyers are willing to pay more than the marginal costs of production for the output between Q_1 and Q_2. The student may also note that in order to produce at Q_2, the deficit represented by the difference between average cost and price, where price is equal to marginal cost, will have to be financed by imposing costs somewhere else. The question that has to be answered to determine where the optimal output lies is what are the costs of financing this deficit and are these costs less than the benefits?

Applications to Benefit–Cost Analysis.   Benefit–cost analysis is now perhaps the primary tool used by both lawyers and economists in antitrust cases. The legality of business behavior and structure is in large part determined by benefit–cost considerations.

FIGURE 2.4

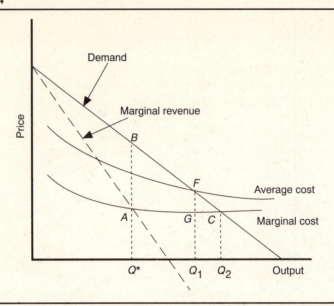

2.6.   GOODS WITH HIGH EXCLUSION COSTS

2.6.1.   Public Goods

One class of goods for which exclusion costs may be high are called public goods. We define public goods as those meeting two conditions: (1) joint consumption and (2) high exclusion costs.[4] Listening to a lecture, enjoying a public park, using the highway, riding on an airplane, watching a movie, or using a lighthouse all have the quality that one person may consume the good at the same time as someone else. This feature of a public good is sometimes called nonrivalry, and public goods are said to be nonrivalrous. The second quality of public goods is that the costs of excluding those who do not pay from using the good are high. Goods with high exclusion costs are often called collective goods so that public goods are also collective goods. It is the quality of collectiveness, rather than the nonrivalry, that suggests the possibility for market intervention.

In fact, many public goods cease being public goods as their rate of use increases. Beaches, parks, and highways become crowded so that people interfere with each other, and use of the good is no longer nonrivalrous. These are called *congestible public goods*. Congestion represents an external effect because one person, in making a decision to use the facility, will not consider the congestion cost his decision imposes on others. In any event, the key market problem is not the absence of rivalry in consumption, but the high cost of excluding nonpayers.

---

[4]Public goods are sometimes defined as having only the quality of nonrivalry.

Air Pollution.   Clean air is a classic example of a public good. Clean air can be enjoyed by many people at the same time so that it is nonrivalrous, and the cost of excluding someone consuming the clean air is high. The negative effects of air pollution are not fully considered because the market for clean air is very imperfect. In considering whether or not to expand the production of a good that produces pollution, the private decision maker will ordinarily give insufficient weight to the damage caused by pollution because most of this damage is caused elsewhere and because there is no market for clean air such that the producer can be paid, or conversely could pay, a price equal to the marginal cost of pollution reduction. You may be willing to pay the factory to reduce its pollution but your neighbor who doesn't pay will also benefit from reduced pollution. Each of you has an incentive to have the other pay and to "free ride" on the other. In the case of air pollution there are poorly defined ownership rights to clean air but, more importantly, and presumably the reason for the lack of clearly defined rights, nonpayers who benefit from reduced pollution cannot be excluded from the benefits because it is too costly. This leads to too much pollution, in the benefit–cost sense, in that there is a willingness to pay for cleaner air that exceeds the cost of attaining it and that private benefits to pollution reduction are less than the public benefits.

The Greenhouse Effect.   One example of air pollution of considerable concern is the effect of CO_2 emissions on global warming. Scientific literature holds that the accumulation of CO_2 (and other) emissions is expected to produce significant climate change over the next century. These predictions have led to a clamorous alarm over the consequences of the greenhouse effect. William Nordhaus of Yale University has suggested that a benefit–cost approach might be useful in making policy decisions with respect to this problem notwithstanding the level of uncertainty that exists.

Nordhaus (1991) points out that an appropriate strategy for coping with greenhouse warming should weigh the benefits and costs of different policies. What will be the damage to the economy if greenhouse gases are allowed to accumulate? What would be the costs of reducing the accumulation of gases? Even though considerable uncertainty exists it may be possible to give some guidance and some bounds to the answers to these questions.

A possible answer to these questions in graphical terms is shown by Figure 2.5. Here the horizontal axis measures the degree of control of greenhouse gases. As the degree of control increases the marginal costs of abatement also increase. The first units of gases reduced are also the most damaging. The marginal damage function then falls as an increasing number of units of gases are abated. The economically optimum level of control of gases is given by the intersection of the marginal control cost function and the marginal damage function. Since the areas under the marginal curves represent the total for costs or benefits, we can compare the costs and benefits of the optimum level of control. If the level of reduction of gases is at the optimum level at point E, the total cost of the abatement is given by the area A. The total saving in the reduction of damages to the economy is given by areas B plus A. The net benefit would then be area B. The net benefit would be positive. (The reader

FIGURE 2.5

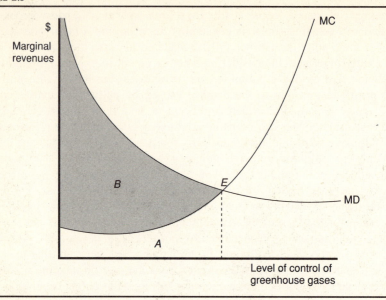

should describe the new equilibrium when the marginal control costs are higher or lower and when the marginal damage function is higher or lower. Having depicted these new equilibria, the reader should now compare geometrically the net benefit with that of Figure 2.5.)

Nordhaus attempts to describe approximately the shape and position of these marginal curves. For the damage function Nordhaus concludes that the best estimate, though highly tentative, is that a doubling of CO_2 emissions from the current level would result in damages of about $\frac{1}{4}$ percent of GNP. Nordhaus further "estimates" that this could be 1 percent of global output, and that at the outside this might be as high as 2 percent of global output. Nordhaus estimates that about 14 percent of greenhouse gases can be reduced at extremely low cost, and that above that level costs rise rapidly. In particular he estimates that the first 14 percent could be reduced for a cost of about $2/ton for the marginal unit of gases eliminated. The marginal costs of reducing these gases by, say, 30 percent approach $50/ton. The marginal costs of a 50 percent reduction would be about $120/ton. The total costs of a 14 percent reduction are about $3 billion. The total costs of a 50 percent reduction are about $201 billion.

The combination of marginal damage function for the best estimate of damage and marginal costs function leads to an estimate of the optimum level of reduction of about 10 percent at a total cost of less than $3 billion (Figure 2.6).

If the medium damage function is used (a doubling leads to a damage of about 1 percent of global output), the optimal reduction is about 17 percent of the greenhouse gases. For the outside estimate of damages from a doubling of gases of about 25 percent of global output, the optimal reduction is about 50 percent.

FIGURE 2.6 Efficient GHG reduction, alternate damage estimates.

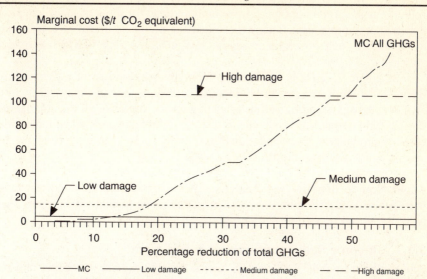

Even though a study such as this is highly tentative, it is useful in a number of respects. It suggests that (1) for policy purposes a reduction of 10 percent in greenhouse gases might well be undertaken without delay, and (2) the conclusion is highly sensitive to a number of the parameters and assumptions and points to areas in which further work may help to give clearer estimates; thus it helps to strip the problem of choice to those fundamentals that must underlie any rational decision.

The Lighthouse. Consider another example. Suppose there is a promontory of land, surrounded by rocks, that juts out into the ocean. There are 10 shipping companies that use the shipping lanes that pass by the promontory; each shipping company has 10 ships. On the average two ships per year are wrecked on the point with loss of lives and cargo. These losses could be prevented by building a lighthouse. To build and operate the lighthouse would cost the equivalent of one ship per year. Since this would save two ships per year it seems that a benefit–cost analysis would suggest that the lighthouse be built. Will this be done privately? This is unclear. Each shipping company individually loses only $\frac{2}{10}$ of a ship per year so alone they have no incentive to build the lighthouse unless they can charge others for it. But, how can you exclude nonpaying companies from using the lighthouse?

The technical difficulties of such exclusion may prevent the lighthouse from being built by any single company. The companies together might build the lighthouse, but again any one company has an incentive to stay out of the agreement, let the other companies build it, and reap the benefits. There is a free-rider problem and there is a divergence between private and public benefits. There remains a number of possible private solutions to this problem. (Can you come up with some?) One possibility is that the government could provide incentives for a private agreement. Another possibility is that the government could arrange for the lighthouse to be built and pay for it out of taxes levied on the shipping companies. Benefit–cost analysis might be useful in considering the value of such government action, and in comparing it with alternative policies.

In Figure 2.7, D_i is the demand for lighthouse service of one company. Because the ships can use the lighthouse services simultaneously, the market demand curve is found by vertically adding up the curves of all the companies. The efficient output is given by the intersection of market demand with marginal costs of production. Each individual user pays P_i and the total payment per unit of lighthouse operation is P_t.

Application to Benefit–Cost Analysis.   Public goods are an important class in which private operation may be impossible or inefficient. Such goods then represent a rich opportunity for benefit–cost analysis.

2.6.2.   Income Redistribution as a Public Good

One important public good that is also a collective good is income redistribution. In, say, the town of Nitro, West Virginia, each of 1000 richer people would be willing to contribute $100 to their 100 poorer fellow citizens as long as the contribution was made by all. Suppose that each member of the richer group gains a benefit of $0.10 for each $1 transferred, up to a total of $100 per person, because he or she values an increase in well-being of the poorer group. No one person would be willing to contribute by himself since he gains $0.10 but loses $1 for each dollar he gives. The total gain to the richer group from the transfer of a dollar to the poorer group would, however, be $100 ($1 × $0.10 × 1000 people), minus the $1.00 in cost for a net gain of $99.00.

FIGURE 2.7   Efficient equilibrium for *public good.* (If the good is also collective good, no market may exist without government action.)

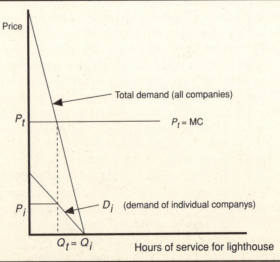

Price

P_t — Total demand (all companies)

$P_t = MC$

D_i (demand of individual companys)

P_i

$Q_t = Q_i$ Hours of service for lighthouse

For a transfer of $100 from each of the 1000 richer people, the total net gain to the rich would be $100,000 transferred with a gain of $99 per dollar transferred or a total of $9,900,000 [$99/dollar transferred times $100,000 transferred or ($100,000 × 0.1 × 1000) − $1 × 100, 000]. For the individual who alone transfers $100, however, there would be a loss of $100 minus the gain of $10 in satisfaction for a net loss of $90. Again, there is a divergence in private and social benefits.

Figure 2.8 shows the private demand for redistribution and the total demand. The representation in the figure differs from that discussed above because the figure gives the more realistic representation that the marginal value to the rich of a dollar transferred falls as more dollars are transferred. The point illustrated is, however, the same. The purely private decision to transfer money to the poorer group does not take into account the value of the transfer to others and thus results in a smaller transfer than is socially optimal.

To this point the discussion of redistribution has taken place as if the only value from redistribution arises from the desires of the rich. The redistribution also has value to the poor. Suppose that each dollar transferred to the poor has a value to them of $1.00. The $1 in cost to the rich from the transfer of $1 is offset by the benefit to the poor of the dollar received. Assuming that transfers can be made costlessly to the poor, it would seem that the social benefits of transfer would exceed social costs (which here are zero), as long as the rich place any positive value at all on the transfer of a marginal dollar to the poor. In Figure 2.8, then, the redistribution would extend to the point at which the total demand curve crosses the zero marginal cost curve, the x axis,

FIGURE 2.8   An individual would redistribute zero because he loses a dollar while gaining 10¢ in satisfaction. Collectively, however, the 1000 individuals would vote to redistribute $100,000 or $100 a piece. If the costs of $1.00 are offset by a gain of $1.00 to the poor, for each dollar transferred, and there are no other costs of transfer, $150,000 would be the optimum to transfer, subject to rights of the rich.

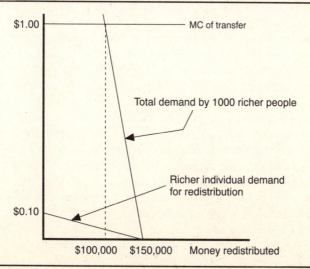

at point Q_2. Notice, however, that this would involve taking money from the rich that they would not agree, even collectively, to give. Would a benefit–cost analysis require that the redistribution proceed beyond the point that the givers are collectively willing to give? This raises the questions of the measure of efficiency that is used to decide policy and of the assignment of rights and finally of the relationship of benefit–cost analysis to such questions. These issues are discussed in Chapters 6 and 12.

Application to Benefit–Cost Analysis.   Benefit–cost analysis can be used to analyze projects whose main purpose is income redistribution. But, any project involves some income redistributions and this attribute of the project can be analyzed using benefit–cost analysis. Techniques for doing this are discussed in Chapter 11.

2.6.3.   The Market for Information

Information can be a pure public good. The costs of excluding others from the information can be large, yet information is often a good that can be used by many people at once (e.g., information that a hurricane is coming). Thus information often has the quality of a public good. Information about the weather may be usable by many without diminishing the ability of others to use it, and it may be difficult to exclude those who have not paid for the information from receiving it. Thus, the government provides considerable information about the weather. Similarly, the Coast Guard provides information to ships about weather and other conditions.

A number of government services are directly motivated by concerns about imperfect information. In 1968, the government passed a Truth in Lending bill requiring lenders to indicate, according to standard formulas, the interest rate being charged. The Federal Trade Commission has adopted rules that attempt to eliminate clearly false advertising that may hurt consumers. The Food and Drug Administration has adopted a number of regulations concerning labeling of foods and medicines and requires that drugs pass safety and efficacy tests before they are marketed.

Standards in quality or in size are set by both government and by industry organizations, some of which facilitate the workings of the market. The U.S. Department of Agriculture, for example, defines choice beef and other grades. Standards for electrical equipment are set by Underwriter Laboratories, and so on.

Information may also be indirectly provided by government action. You wish to place your child in a day care facility while you attend a university. Different centers make different and extravagant claims about their competence and care, but you find these difficult to evaluate, and you are aware that problems have surfaced at some facilities. Perhaps licensing of day care facilities by the government would be a least-cost method of providing information that such facilities meet at least minimal standards. Of course such information can be provided in different ways; an independent rating service may provide ratings for day care facilities or large chain organizations may provide a reliable brand name. Both alternatives have advantages and disadvantages. Yet, special government provision of licensing may have sufficient advantages to pass a benefit–cost test.

A major argument for licensing of physicians is that it is costly for consumers to gather information about their quality, and that licensing tends to guarantee a minimum quality. Perhaps a government provision that requires physicians to prominently post information about themselves would be even more cost beneficial than licensing.

Application to Benefit–Cost Analysis.   The examples here as elsewhere illustrate situations in which benefit–cost analysis may be usefully applied to determine whether or not any policy change might be desirable and to show which of the alternative policies might be the better policy.

2.6.4.   Collective Goods

Collective goods are also goods for whom the cost of excluding those who benefit from them but do not pay for them are high. Thus, collective goods include not only public goods but also goods that are rivalrous in consumption, but which have high exclusion costs. Some goods may be insufficiently provided because high exclusion costs limit the extent to which a market can operate or prevent the operation of a market altogether. Highway congestion indicates that the use of the highway is not a pure public good, but this is still a good that may be best provided by the government. This is because first, exclusion costs are high so that the private market may underprovide highways relative to the desired quantity indicated by a benefit–cost test. Second, the private market may also impose high costs of collection in charging drivers who may have to stop frequently to pay tolls, a cost that could be avoided by government provision.

The argument that the private market may underprovide a good relative to some ideal and may also incur revenue-collection costs is not a sufficient argument for government provision of the good. There is no guarantee that the government will provide the "correct" level of the good, and, of course, the government must also fund provision of the good so that there are costs imposed involving the collection of the necessary revenues, whether provision is by the government or by the private sector. Government provision of a good may be inferior to even quite imperfect private provision of the good. The costs associated with both the funding and the output level may be different under a government regime from that under a private regime and benefit–cost analysis may be useful in determining the better policy.

Clearly, the line between collective goods and public goods on the one hand, and goods best provided by the market on the other hand is not firm. How high should exclusion costs be before the good may be best provided by the government? How high should exclusion costs be or what should be the extent of nonrivalry in consumption, before a good is called a public good?

Table 2.5 shows the degree of nonrivalry on the horizontal axis, and the costs of exclusion on the vertical axis. Pure public goods are found then in the southeast corner. Clean air and national defense may be examples. Pure private goods will then be found in the northwest corner. Sweaters, coffee, pencils, books, and records are examples. In the northeast are goods that are nonrivalrous in consumption, but which have low exclusion costs. These goods normally will be privately provided. Examples are movies or certain private

TABLE 2.5   Market Failure and Public Expenditure—Public Goods and Publicly Provided Private Goods

		Degree of Rivalry	
		Rivalrous	*Nonrivalrous*
Costs of Exclusion	*Excludable*	Private good	Public or private provision
	Nonexcludable	Common property resources (fish) Collective goods	Public good (National defense)

parks or lectures, which are nonrivalrous at least up to the capacity of the facility. The line drawn vertically in Table 2.5 separates collective goods from others and nonrivalrous from rivalrous goods. The argument for government intervention is strongest for those goods that are public or collective goods.

Application to Benefit–Cost Analysis.   Markets associated with goods that have high exclusion costs include both public and collective goods, representing perhaps the largest class in which private operation is sometimes not as efficient as government operation. It is these markets in which benefit–cost analysis has one of its most important roles. (Why are fire fighting and postal services in large measure provided by government?)

SUMMARY

As an approach to analyzing government decision making, the theoretical basis for the use of benefit–cost analysis rests on a divergence between private and social costs. This divergence in turn lies in the existence of external effects that reflect inefficiencies in the definition or delineation of property rights, the existence of collective goods, monopoly, or of costly information.

While a divergence between private and social costs is a necessary condition for government intervention, it is not a sufficient condition. That is, the existence of external effects, etc., does not indicate that any intervention should occur, rather these concepts relating to the divergence of private and social cost suggest places to look for changes in policies or programs. Benefit–cost analysis, by providing an approach to organizing and evaluating data, is an aid to considering whether action, and what sort of action, is warranted.

QUESTIONS AND PROBLEMS

1. Explain why monopoly may cause harm in terms of economic welfare (consumer and producer surplus). Use a diagram.
2. The Wantebe Indians live by catching fish. No one owns the right to fish. They face the following schedule of available fish:

Number of Indian Fishermen	Number of Fish Available per Day per Indian
1	10
2	9
3	8
4	7
5	6
6	5
7	4
8	3
9	2
10	1

The opportunity cost of catching fish is two fish per day.

a. How many Indians per day will fish?

b. What is the producer or consumer surplus (rents) to the Wantebes who fish?

A giant takes over the fishing area, that is, he "owns" it.

c. What entry fee will he charge for fishing?

d. What total rents per day can he collect?

e. How many Indians will fish per day now?

It turns out that the above numbers give a rent for fish catching that fails to replenish the fish stock. The giant wishes to maximize his rents over a period of years, not just today.

   f. Will the giant weight future rents equal to current rents if his interest rate is positive? Explain.

   g. Explain in detail why a consideration of the future may result in the giant raising his entry fee as compared with the answer in part c without an example.

3. Give three examples in which the lack of property right definition increases the cost or lowers the efficiency of market operation. Suggest a change in property rights definition that would effect an improvement.

4. A factory produces wodgets but also dumps 1 lb of smoke into the air per wodget. The smoke tends to create health problems for *everyone* living within 10 miles of the factory.

   a. Is it likely that the factory will produce the "right" amount of wodgets? Explain.

   b. Suppose the people living within 10 miles of the factory attempt to get together and attempt to bribe the factory to cut back its output. Is this type of action likely to be successful given the public good nature of the problem? Explain.

   c. What will happen to the "right" amount of wodgets as the population around the factory increases over time? Explain.

5. Do you agree with the following statement? "When externalities and public goods result in inefficient resource allocation, government intervention is justified." Explain why you agree or disagree.

6. Give three examples in which high exclusion costs make the operation of the market less efficient. Explain what would happen if a change in technology occurred that reduced exclusion costs.

7. There are 50 ships using a rocky harbor. Each ship has the same demand for using the lighthouse. This demand is

$$L = 20 - 1/2P$$

where L is days of lighthouse operation per year.

a. What is the aggregate demand for use of the lighthouse?
b. If the long- and short-run marginal cost of having a lighthouse is a constant $100 per unit of service, what is the efficient level of service?
c. Suppose the 50 ships are owned by 10 shipping companies each with 5 ships. If eight of the companies build the lighthouse what will be their total demand?
d. What will be the level of output for these eight companies assuming that the other two companies are excluded from using the lighthouse?
e. What is the free rider problem?

REFERENCES

Browning, Edgar, and Jacquelene Browning, *Public Finance and the Price System*. New York: Macmillan, 1987.

Coase, Ronald, "The Problem of Social Cost," *Journal of Law and Economics*, 1960.

Hyman, David, *Public Finance,* 2nd ed., New York: The Dryden Press, 1987.

Knight, Frank H., "Some Fallacies in the Interpretation of Social Cost," *Quarterly Journal of Economics,* 38, 582–606, August 1924.

Nordhaus, William D., "To Slow or Not to Slow," *The Economic Journal,* 101(407), 920–937, July 1991.

Stokey, Edith, and Richard Zeckhauser, *A Primer for Policy Analysis*. New York: W. W. Norton, 1978.

Zerbe, Richard O., Jr., "The Problem of Social Cost in Retrospect," *Research in Law and Economics,* 2, 83–102, 1980.

3

Aggregation of Benefits and Cost over Time

3.1. INTRODUCTION

Benefits and costs accrue at different points in time. A benefit of $100 ten years from now is not equivalent to a benefit of $100 now, but how are these to be compared? We will first consider economic principles that apply to the situation of a single individual who faces no uncertainty and who consumes one commodity in two time periods. These principles will then be generalized to cover the more realistic situation in which there are many individuals, commodities, and time periods. We will consider here the interest rate in a first-best world, a world in which the economic efficiency conditions are met. (In a later chapter we will consider the interest rate in a second-best world, a world in which efficiency conditions are not met.)

Even in a first-best world, there remains the problem that the interest rate used, because it determines relative allocations over time, will affect the distribution of goods and utility among different generations of people. Since future generations are not part of either the decision-making or the trading process, ethical questions may be raised about how efficiency is defined. That is, questions may be raised about whose welfare is being maximized. We shall consider approaches for dealing with this problem.

3.2. THE INTEREST RATE IN A FIRST-BEST WORLD

The individual in year 0 has a certain stock of storable commodity X. He will decide how much of X to consume this year and how much next year. Figure 3.1 shows the indifference curve of individual i as between consumption this year and next year. This curve should have the usual convexity

FIGURE 3.1   Intertemporal consumption choice.

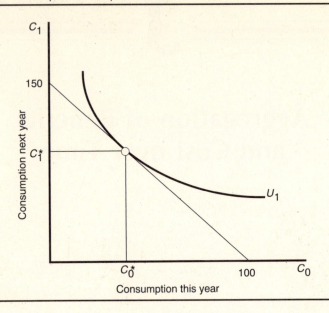

properties. That is, consumption next year becomes relatively more important in comparison with consumption this year as i consumes a greater portion of his stock of the commodity now. The marginal rate of substitution (MRS_{0i}) is shown by the slope of i's indifference curve and shows for individual i the amount of consumption next year equivalent to 1 unit of consumption this year. For example, if Ed Freedman is just willing to sacrifice 1 unit of consumption today for $1\frac{1}{2}$ units tomorrow his MRS_{0i} would be 1.5. We shall say that the marginal rate of time preference of an individual i, the $MRTP_i$ is equal to the MRS_{0i} minus 1. That is if Ed Freedman's MRS_{0i} is equal to 1.5, his $MRTP_i$ is equal to 50 percent. Efficiency requires that the MRS_{0i} be also equal to the price of 1 unit of the commodity this year relative to the price of 1 unit of the commodity next year. This familiar condition is for consumer equilibrium given a budget constraint whose slope reflects the relative prices of the two commodities. Thus we have the following condition for efficiency:

$$MRS_{0i} = \frac{P_0}{P_1} = MRTP + 1 \qquad (3.1)$$

Let us suppose that if commodity X is not consumed, it can be invested productively. (The commodity might be a tree that could be used now or could be allowed to grow until next year.) The opportunity cost of consuming today will then be the loss of available consumption the next year. The cost will depend on the rate at which a unit of the commodity this year, X_0, can be transferred into a unit of next year's commodity, X_1. This is shown by the marginal rate of transformation, which is the amount of consumption next year that can be gained by sacrificing one unit of consumption this year. This is

FIGURE 3.2 Efficiency in intertemporal choice.

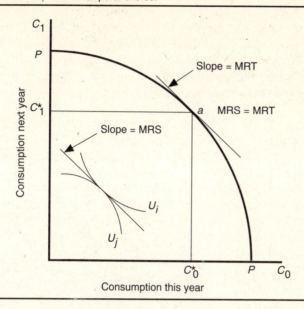

given by the production possibility curve, PP, in Figure 3.2. The MRT is equal to the marginal opportunity cost rate of capital, MOCR[1] plus 1. Thus, if Ed Freedman is able to save 1 unit of commodity X today and obtain 1.8 units next year, his MRT is 1.8 and his MOCR is equal to 80 percent. Efficiency requires that the marginal rate of substitution equal the marginal rate of transformation. If these are not equal there exist Pareto optimal trades through which gains can be realized. Figure 3.2 shows an Edgeworth box that contains the indifference curves for i and for j. The MRS is shown equal to the MRT. Efficiency then requires that

$$MRS_{01} - 1 = MRT_{01} - 1 = MRTP_{01} = MOCR \qquad (3.2)$$

That is, dynamic efficiency requires that the marginal rate of time preference is equal to the marginal opportunity cost of capital. Thus, if for Ed Freedman the MOCR is 80 percent and his MRTP is 50 percent, he should forego additional consumption now for 80 percent more next year. This sort of trading by Ed will continue until his MRTP = MOCR.

These results can be easily generalized to many individuals, time periods, and commodities. We know that the MRS_{0i} of each individual must be equal for an efficient equilibrium. Figure 3.2 shows the MRS for individual i equal to the MRS for individual j. Thus the same conditions hold for many individuals as for the one. Present and future consumption can be regarded as two goods such as apples and oranges. The consumer equilibrium will occur along the contract curve formed by the tangency of consumers' indifference curves with

---

[1]The MOCR is also known as the investment rate of return.

respect to present and future consumption. Since the slopes of the indifference curve represent 1 plus the interest rate, in equilibrium each consumer's MRTP will equal every other consumer's MRTP. If consumers have different MRTPs they will profitably trade present and future incomes until their rates are equal. Consumers who value the future will borrow from those who value the present and both would gain. This would continue until the differences in the MRTPs disappear. The rate of time preference associated with many individuals is called the *social rate of time preference* (SRTP).

Commodity X can be regarded as the composite commodity, that is, money, so that the example using one commodity can be generalized to all commodities. The production possibility curve is then the transformation curve expressing the rate at which real income today can be transformed into real income next year. The general opportunity cost rate of return shown by the transformation curve, minus 1, is the *social opportunity cost rate* (SOCR). The years 0 and 1 can be interpreted as any two adjacent years so that the efficiency conditions can be generalized to hold for multiple time periods. Thus the generalized condition for efficiency is that

$$SRTP = SOCR \hspace{3cm} (3.3)$$

for all time periods.

To further understand this condition, suppose the condition were not true and that the MRTP were 10 percent while the MOCR was 20 percent. Consumers would increase their investments since their return is greater than their MRTP. As consumers decrease their present consumption (i.e., increase savings) and increase investment, their MRTPs rise as present consumption becomes relatively more valuable, and the marginal rate of investment return falls as the better investment possibilities are exhausted. This process continues until the SRTP of consumers equals the SOCR. Thus we have the following rule for a first-best world:

> In an economy with perfect competition, no transactions costs, no uncertainty or risk and no taxes, the rate of interest would be the market rate and this rate would be equal to both the SRTP and the SOCR.

In benefit–cost analysis we consider making an investment today that will yield benefits tomorrow. In a first-best world, the criterion would be whether or not the yield to the investment is as great as the market rate of interest. The way in which this is usually determined is to use the interest rate to discount future earnings. Thus the interest rate that is relevant for benefit–cost analysis is called the *discount rate. In this first-best economy the correct discount rate for benefit–cost analysis is just the market rate.*

This analysis has important implications for comparing income at one time with income for a different time period in a first-best world. The interest rate used for borrowing and lending by every individual will be the same and this interest rate will be the marginal return on investment in the economy, which is equal to the SRTP. *In this economy the correct discount rate for benefit–cost analysis is just the market rate.*

3.3.   THE PRESENT VALUE CRITERION

The amount of consumption C_1 that one would require next year to be willing to give up C_0 in consumption this year is equal to the MRS. That is,

$$\frac{C_1}{C_0} = \text{MRS}_{01} \tag{3.4}$$

The MRS_{01} is equal to 1 plus the SRTP. Thus, we have $C_1/C_0 = \text{MRS}_{01} = 1 + \text{SRTP}$, or

$$C_0 = \frac{C_1}{1 + \text{SRTP}} \tag{3.5}$$

The division process of Equation (3.5) is called *discounting*. Thus, when we know C_1 we can find its equivalent as C_0 at time 0 by discounting.

Suppose consumption is delayed two periods. The value at the end of the first period can be found from Equation (3.5) as $C_2/(1 + \text{SRTP}) = C_1$. We can also use Equation (3.5) to find the value of C_1 at time period 0. This will be $C_0 = C_2/(1 + \text{SRTP})^2$. Extending this to many periods, consumption at time t can be given in terms of equivalent consumption at time 0 as $C_0 = C_t/(1 + \text{SRTP})^t$. Consider now a sacrifice of consumption today that yields a gain of consumption next year. Clearly if the gain tomorrow divided by $1 + \text{SRTP}$ is greater than the sacrifice of consumption today, the project will be worthwhile.

The present equivalent of future amounts is called the *present value*. For simplicity call the SRTP, r. Then we can say that each consumption gain or loss as of time t is expressed in terms of an equivalent gain or loss at the present time (present value) by dividing the gain or loss by $(1 + r)^t$. That is,

$$\text{PV} = \sum_{t=0}^{T} \frac{C_t}{(1 + r)^t} \tag{3.6}$$

Not all the benefits and costs of a project will go to, or come from, consumption. Some will go to, or come from, investment. However, in a first-best world, a dollar will have the same social value in every use so that a dollar of investment is equivalent to a dollar of consumption. Thus, calling benefits B and costs C we have the net present value rule for a first-best world, which calls for investment in a project if the net present value is greater than zero. The rule for project acceptance is

$$\text{NPV} = \sum_{t=1}^{T} \frac{B - C}{(1 + r)^t} > 0 \tag{3.7}$$

where NPV is net present value. *This is then the fundamental equation for evaluating projects in a first-best world.* The NPV of benefits minus costs must be positive. Adjustments to costs and benefits must be made for a second-best world and these adjustments are discussed in Chapter 13.

3.4. THE ETHICAL BASIS FOR THE INTEREST (DISCOUNT) RATE

Investments are made that involve returns that accrue beyond the lifetime of a single individual. How are investments decisions to be made, and what discount rate should be chosen? Consider a market economy in which generations of people overlap. Suppose that there is an investment of $1000 that will pay off only after 100 years. The expected payoff is, however, at an attractive rate of, say, 20 percent per year. We can imagine a buyer for this investment in year 100 because the investment is ready to pay off at that time. John Jones, the owner who wishes to sell at that time, will have bought it earlier from, say, John Smith, realizing that he could sell it later. Smith in turn had bought the asset from John Doe, and so on back through the generations.

Now, of course, we won't know the actual demands of future generations. But, we don't know the actual demands of our future selves. Present generations must make guesses about those future demands.

3.4.1. Initial Position

One way to usefully think about representing future generations is to imagine that you are a chooser in an initial position that needs to make a choice of a discount rate in a world that lasts for two generations. *An initial position is one in which the chooser must choose a discount rate before she knows to what generation she will belong.* The chooser once having chosen the discount rate has an equal chance of belonging to any generation.

We can imagine that the chooser will value equally her utility in any generation. An economy that is not growing would present the chooser with a straight-line 45° production possibility curve. The equilibrium MRS would be 1 and the discount rate would be 0 as shown by Figure 3.3.

Her choice of a positive discount rate depends on her placing more value on a dollar in the present generation than in a future generation. She seems likely to do this only if her wealth is growing so that the value of an additional dollar is falling. (In economist's jargon, there is a declining marginal utility of income.) The chooser will in fact equate her MRS between present and future consumption with the MRT just as we found for a single individual considering a choice between today and tomorrow. For the chooser, as for the individual discussed earlier, as long as the MRT is greater than the MRS she will gain from sacrificing $1 in this generation (or today) and gaining more than $1 in the future generation (or tomorrow).

3.4.2. Future Generations

Some commentators argue that the utility of future generations should not be discounted. On this basis some argue that the correct discount rate is 0.[2] We find this view unacceptable for three reasons. First, a society with a discount rate

---

[2]This would be true only for an economy that was not growing. Suppose that utility were treated equally in each generation and wealth were growing. The marginal utility of income would be falling with increased wealth and future wealth would generate less utility per dollar, resulting in the use of positive time preference for income and a positive interest rate.

FIGURE 3.3   The chooser in a no-growth economy (initial position).

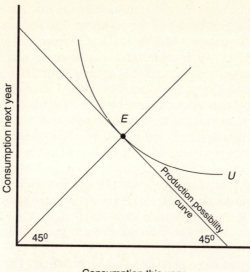

of zero would be a society with a very high   savings rate, and, *ceteris paribus,* a high rate of economic growth. Each generation would be richer than the previous. A discount rate of zero can, in fact, be considered a device by which the relatively poor, the present generation, could subsidize the relatively rich, a future generation. Second, we think the treatment of future generations can be regarded as similar to the problem an individual faces when making future decisions for a self that will be at least somewhat different in the future. Third, the issue of considering future generations is best addressed not through the discount rate but through a consideration of whether or not future generations should be given property rights in present property. The rate of extraction of a natural finite resource or the preservation of forest and the like will depend not only on the discount rate but also on whether or not present property rights are attributed to future generations. The chooser in an initial position would clearly opt to allocate some property rights to a future generation because, as can be shown, this would increase the sum of utilities.

If the discount rate were 0, all projects would be undertaken that had any positive wealth-maximizing rate, that is, that produced any positive wealth at all. Note that the use of an interest rate of 0 would only be appropriate when the yield to private capital were also 0. This is merely the efficiency condition stated above in which the MRTP = MOCR. Otherwise one would make poor investment choices. This can be understood by considering choosing between two projects when the interest rate is 0 but the yield to capital is not. Suppose both projects cost $100 now. Project A yields $150 next year. The second project, project B, yields $150.10 a hundred years from now. With a 0 interest rate project B is the better project. Clearly, however, as long as there is almost any positive return to investment, the proceeds from project A can be invested to produce more than $150.10 at the end of a hundred years.

3.5. A GROWTH RATE APPROACH

Note that the problem of the determination of the discount rate is related to the question of the growth rate of the economy. The discount rate directly affects the level of investment and the level of investment helps determine the economic growth rate. We might imagine that the chooser in the initial position would choose a rule which maximized consumption in each generation and in which each generation saved the same proportion of their national product. The relative sacrifice of consumption would then be the same in each generation. The proportion of national product saved implies a growth rate, which in turn implies an interest rate. Thus, one way to pose the question of a correct social rate of discount is to ask, what proportion of national product should be saved?

One answer is to choose that savings rate that yields the largest possible per capita consumption for every generation consistent with a constant growth rate and a fixed proportion of national product saved. What savings rate would that be? What would be the discount rate associated with this savings rate?

It turns out that these questions can be answered. The growth path that maximizes consumption requires that *the marginal return to capital must equal the growth rate of the economy due to technological change*. If society is undersaving and the capital labor ratio is too low, the return to capital will be higher than the growth rate. Projects should be discounted at the lower growth rate rather than by the higher rate of the return to capital. A greater number of investments would then be undertaken than if the higher rate of return to capital were used. If society is oversaving so that the capital labor ratio is too high, the rate of return to capital will be too low and lower than the growth rate. Projects should then be discounted by the higher discount rate suggested by the growth rate.

For the United States the growth rate has averaged about 3.5 percent per year for most of this century. This is then the discount rate that comes out of this analysis. It is a rate that seems to give a reasonably sensible number, and a number that is independent of inappropriate fiscal and monetary policies.

Estimates of the after-tax return to investment are higher than this at about 4 percent to 5 percent, suggesting that the United States is undersaving. (After-tax returns refer to the rate calculated on returns after taxes are paid.)

3.6. TAKING INTO ACCOUNT THE MARGINAL UTILITY OF MONEY

Earlier we suggested that an appealing procedure to choose an interest rate is that of a chooser in an initial position. We also suggested that such a chooser would treat all utility equally, including the utility of future generations, and would therefore discount the future in an economy in which income was growing. This consideration can be incorporated into the growth framework discussed here. That is, the chooser maximizes the sustainable level of consumption subject to consideration of the reduction in the marginal utility of money due to greater income. Thus, where welfare depends on consumption per person, the discount rate will be given by[3]

$$r = n_2 e + n_1 \tag{3.8}$$

where e is the absolute value of the elasticity of marginal utility of consumption with respect to consumption, n_1 is economic growth from increases in the numbers of workers, and n_2 is growth that arises from technological change. [For a derivation of this see R. Layard (1972, p. 42).] This results in a higher discount rate than the unadjusted growth rate considered above because the higher incomes of the future are worth less due to the declining marginal utility of income. If there is no per capita increase in consumption then n_2 is 0 and the discount rate is n_1, the rate of population growth increase. If population growth is zero the discount rate will be some multiple of the rate of growth of output per person.

Some suggestions put e in the range between 1 and 2.5. Population growth in the United States has run around 1 percent, and output growth per capita has been about 2.5 percent. Using the range for e of between 1 and 2.5, this gives a range of real discount rates between 3.5 percent and 7.25 percent.[4] These rates are considerably lower than the rates currently used by the federal government to evaluate projects. The government rates are at or around real rates of 10 percent.[5] In Chapter 13 we will discuss briefly government rates.

QUESTIONS AND PROBLEMS

1. Suppose that we are in a first–best world. The SRTP is 4 percent. A project is considered in which the costs are $100 in time 0. The benefits in each of the first three periods are $40, and zero thereafter.
   a. By what criterion would you decide whether or not the project is worthwhile?
   b. By this criterion is the project worthwhile?
   c. Suppose that in this first–best world you use the market interest rate to evaluate the project. Would your answer to part b above change? Why or why not?
2. Imagine that you are a chooser in an initial position. Your only choice is constrained to be the level of the discount rate.
   a. If the economy was expected to be richer in the second generation than in the first, would you choose a higher or lower discount rate than if the wealth level was expected to be the same in both generations? Explain.
   b. Suppose that the lower the choice of discount rate, the greater will be the wealth of the second generation relative to the first generation. How would this affect your choice of discount rate?
   c. If your lifetime income was expected to be double your current income, would the value of an additional dollar to you decrease? If your answer is yes does this suggest your discount rate should be positive in a growing economy? Why?

---

[3]The term $n_2 e$ gives the growth in terms of dollars adjusted upward to take into account the change in the marginal utility of income.
[4]If e is around 1.5, this gives a discount rate of $r = 2.5\%(1.5) + 1\% = 4.75\%$.
[5]Rates for some agencies such as the Bureau of Reclamation are based on long-term bond rates and are used as real rates even though the bond rates themselves are nominal and are not adjusted for inflation.

3. In Chapter 1 we considered the problem of the Boston school district. Reevaluate the two sites, given that the discount rate used by the school district is 6 percent, and the time horizon of the district is 10 years.

REFERENCES

Halvorsen, Robert, and Michael Ruby, *Benefit–Cost Analysis of Air Pollution Control,* Lexington Books, 1981, chap. 4.

Layard, Richard, "Introduction," in *Cost–Benefit Analysis: Selected Readings,* edited by R. Layard, Harmondsworth: Penguin, 1972, pp. 9–70.

4

Introduction to Financial Calculations

The introductory chapters of this book have discussed the concept of the *time value of money,* which suggests that a benefit received today is worth more than one received in the future. Several tools for financial analysis have been developed in order to translate this concept into measurable comparisons. In essence, these tools are designed to compare costs and benefits that are received at different times in a way that reflects the true value of these payments to the recipient.

In the simplest case, an individual payment made at a particular time can be evaluated. Tools to accomplish this are usually called *interest calculations* or *single payment formulas* and are discussed in the first major section of this chapter. In more complex cases, multiple payments are made at several times. Tools to assist with financial analysis in these cases are called *series calculations* or *multiple payment formulas,* and are discussed in the second major section of this chapter. Each section is crucial to an understanding of the techniques for financial decision making, which are described in Chapter 9.

The techniques of financial analysis used in benefit–cost calculations are the same ones used for many other purposes, such as determining mortgage payments or calculating the value of an insurance policy. Thus, many of the equations in this chapter may be familiar. Students with some previous finance experience may wish to skip some of the simpler sections and focus on the more complex calculations. Students without previous finance experience should review the entire chapter, since more complex calculations are developed from the simpler concepts introduced at the outset.

It is important to recognize that financial analysis is only a *part* of most benefit–cost analyses. There are some concerns, such as aesthetic beauty or income distribution, which are not ordinarily a part of financial analysis. These issues will be discussed in later chapters. For now, it is important to remember that the techniques of financial analysis are merely tools and do not produce definitive judgments. Decisions lie ultimately in the hands of the policy maker, who must balance financial data with other considerations. Complete and accurate financial information is an important part of such decisions, but it is not the decision itself.

4.1. PRESENT AND FUTURE VALUE

Most of the financial analysis discussed in this chapter focuses on the concepts of *present value* and *future value*. The present value of an asset is how much it is worth to you today; the future value of an asset is how much it will be worth to you at some specified time in the future.

Consider an example. Let us assume that you are owed $10 next week. Its present value is how much it is worth to you today; if you accept $9 we can conclude the debt has a present value of $9 (or less; you might secretly have been willing to settle for $8). If you reject a $9 offer, it means you place a present value of more than $9 on the debt.

To understand future value, let us change the example. The individual who owes you $10 calls and says she doesn't want to pay you back next week, but will give you $12 the week after that. Would you accept this new deal? If you do, we can conclude that the future value of the $10 debt is $12 one week later (again, it may be less than that; you might have settled for $11). If you don't accept the deal, we can conclude that your future value of the $10 debt is more than $12 one week later, that is, you would want more than $12 to extend the debt.

Thus, the present value of an amount to be received in the future must be less than the amount itself; a payment of $10 next week may be worth only $9 to you today. In the jargon of finance, we say the $10 next week is *discounted* to $9 today. Similarly, the future value of an amount you get today must be greater than the amount itself; instead of $10 today you might demand $12 next week.[1]

The concepts of present value, future value, and discounting lie at the heart of financial analysis. Before we consider how to calculate them, we need to develop an understanding of interest rates.

4.2. INTEREST CALCULATIONS AND SINGLE PAYMENT FORMULAS

Most of us are familiar with the concept of interest. In essence, interest is an amount paid for the use of someone else's money. When you borrow money, you are said to pay interest to the individual who provides the funds; when you loan money (or put it in a savings account, after which the bank loans it out

---

[1] This discussion assumes that the actual value of a dollar remains unchanged. For now, we will assume that the value of a dollar is constant and will postpone discussion of inflation and deflation to a subsequent chapter.

for you), you receive interest from the borrower. Interest is usually expressed as a percentage of the amount involved. The amount involved is referred to as the *principal* and the percentage is called the *interest rate*.

There is a vast economics literature that describes theoretical approaches to the analysis of interest. This literature is important in defining what an interest rate represents and in providing guidance about what interest rate to use in a particular type of calculation. We will delve into these subjects in later chapters. For now, we will focus on how to use the interest rate once it is determined.

While the basic concepts of interest are widely understood, it is less frequently noted that there are several types of interest. The important types will be described here.

4.2.1. Simple and Compound Interest

Simple interest is calculated using the principal and a fixed interest rate. Let P be the principal and r be the effective interest rate for a given period (the period usually is, but does not have to be, one year). The amount of interest paid per period is I:

$$I = rP \qquad (4.1)$$

This same amount, I, is paid in every period. Thus, the total value of the investment after t periods (F_t) is simply the original principal plus the accumulated interest payments:

$$F_t = P + trP \qquad (4.2)$$

which can be reduced to the fundamental equation for simple interest:

$$F_t = P(1 + rt) \qquad (4.3)$$

The major disadvantage of simple interest from an investor's standpoint is that interest is not paid on interest already received. Interest is paid only on the original principal, and thus the amount of interest paid per period is constant. Because of this problem, simple interest is rarely encountered in modern finance.

Almost all interest charges today use *compound interest* in one form or another. Savings accounts, contracts, and credit cards all use compound interest. As the name implies, interest is compounded under this system; in other words, interest is paid on the interest payments made previously.

Using the nomenclature used above, the amount of interest paid in the first period is still rP; this represents the amount earned before compounding begins. Thus, the value after one period (F_1) again is

$$F_1 = P + rP \qquad (4.4)$$

In the second period, interest is paid on F_1, not just on P. The amount of interest paid in the second period therefore is

$$rF_1 = r(P + rP) = rP + r^2P \qquad (4.5)$$

EXAMPLE 4.1

Compound Interest

$1000 is invested for five years at 8 percent compound annual interest. How much is it worth at the end of that time?

$$F_t = P(1 + r)^t$$

$$P = \$1000 \qquad r = 0.08 \qquad t = 5$$

$$F_5 = \$1000(1 + 0.08)^5$$

$$= \$1469.33$$

Note that compound interest has produced a result larger than simple interest. This should not be surprising; interest is now being paid not just on the principal but also on the accumulated interest.

This means the value after two periods (F_2) is

$$F_2 = F_1 + rF_1 = P + 2rP + r^2P = P(1 + r)^2 \tag{4.6}$$

This result can be generalized to multiple periods. For t periods:

$$F_t = P(1 + r)^t \tag{4.7}$$

where F_t is the value after t periods. Equation (4.7) is the fundamental formula for compound interest and is one of the most important equations of finance.

4.2.2.   Nominal and Effective Rates

Compound interest is often compounded several times per year: semiannually (twice a year), quarterly (four times a year), monthly, weekly, or even daily. One often sees advertisements such as "interest of 6 percent compounded quarterly." This interest rate, in this case 6 percent, is referred to as the *nominal interest rate*. The actual interest rate being paid, once allowance is made for compounding, is called the *effective interest rate*. The effective rate is simply equal to the compounded nominal rate.

Before considering the relationship between nominal and effective interest rates, let us examine the meaning of interest rates for periods of less than one year. If i is the nominal annual rate and h is the number of compoundings per year, then the rate for the shorter period is simply i/h. For example, a monthly rate would be $i/12$, since there are 12 months in a year. Similarly, a quarterly rate would be $i/4$. By convention, a daily rate is usually expressed as $i/360$, since this is easier to compute than a rate that allows for different numbers of days per month.

This calculation of periodic rates provides the foundation for understanding the relationship between nominal and effective rates. To demonstrate this relationship, consider the following example. Let i be the nominal interest rate and h be the number of compoundings per period. In this example, let us consider a rate of 6 percent per year compounded monthly. The monthly

EXAMPLE 4.2

Nominal and Effective Interest Rates

A bank is offering a savings account paying 8 percent interest, compounded monthly. What is the effective annual interest rate?

$$r = \left(1 + \frac{i}{h}\right)^h - 1$$

$$i = 0.08 \qquad h = 12$$

$$r = \left(1 + \frac{0.08}{12}\right)^{12} - 1$$

$$= 0.083 = 8.3\%$$

compoundings mean $h = 12$. The 6 percent rate is expressed in annual terms, but we clearly need a monthly rate to do the compounding. The monthly rate is simply i/h, the periodic rate divided by the number of compoundings per period. In this case, $i/h = 6\%/12 = 0.5\%$ per month. One dollar invested for a year at this monthly rate would grow to

$$F_{12} = \$1(1 + 0.005)^{12} = \$1.0617$$

The dollar has grown by 6.17 percent, which is therefore the effective annual interest rate, r. In general, the effective rate can be found directly from

$$r = \left(1 + \frac{i}{h}\right)^h - 1 \qquad (4.8)$$

Applying this equation to our example gives

$$r = \left(1 + \frac{0.06}{12}\right)^{12} - 1 = 0.0617 = 6.2\%$$

which is the same result we found previously.

The important result of Equation (4.8) is that the effective interest rate, r, is 6.17 percent, while the nominal rate, i, was only 6 percent. The effect of compounding is to increase the actual return on an investment by raising the interest rate. Thus, a rate of 6 percent compounded monthly will produce a higher return than a rate of 6 percent compounded annually. The effective rate will always be greater than or equal to the nominal rate, as long as h is greater than or equal to one.

4.2.3. Multiple Compoundings per Period

The value of an investment that is subject to periodic compounding can be found by combining results we have obtained previously. By substituting Equation (4.8) for the effective interest rate into Equation (4.7) for the value of an investment, we obtain

EXAMPLE 4.3
Multiple Compoundings per Period

Repeat Example 4.1, but use a nominal rate of 8 percent compounded (a) semiannually, (b) quarterly, (c) monthly, and (d) weekly.

$$F_t = P\left(1 + \frac{i}{h}\right)^{ht}$$

(a) $h = 2$ $P = \$1000$ $i = 0.08$ $t = 5$

$$F_5 = \$1000\left(1 + \frac{0.08}{2}\right)^{2(5)}$$

$$= \$1480.24$$

Similarly,

(b) $h = 4$, $F_5 = \$1485.95$

(c) $h = 12$, $F_5 = \$1489.85$

(d) $h = 52$, $F_5 = \$1491.37$

Note how the value increases as the number of compoundings per period increases.

$$F_t = P\left[1 + \left(1 + \frac{i}{h}\right)^{h} - 1\right]^{t} \tag{4.9}$$

which reduces to

$$F_t = P\left(1 + \frac{i}{h}\right)^{ht} \tag{4.10}$$

Equation (4.10) gives the value of an investment after t periods when interest is compounded h times per period.

An investment problem involving multiple compoundings can be approached in two equivalent ways. One method is to convert the nominal rate into an effective rate using Equation (4.8), then use this effective rate in Equation (4.7) to find the value of the investment. The second method is to use Equation (4.10) directly. The second method is faster, but the first may be easier to understand. Use whichever method is best for you.

4.2.4. Interest Rates with Different Periods

In certain circumstances, it may be necessary to convert interest rates based on a certain period to rates having a different period. For example, we may desire to convert a quarterly rate to a semiannual rate. This type of conversion is often used in calculations involving bonds.

We have already seen an example of this when we converted nominal rates to effective annual rates using Equation (4.8). A similar approach works here.

EXAMPLE 4.4

Different Interest Periods

Bank A offers savings accounts paying 8 percent interest compounded quarterly. Bank B offers accounts with interest compounded semiannually. What nominal rate of interest does bank B need to offer to make its accounts as attractive as bank A's?

$$\left(1 + \frac{i_1}{h_1}\right)^{h_1} = \left(1 + \frac{i_2}{h_2}\right)^{h_2}$$

$$i_1 = 0.08 \qquad h_1 = 4 \qquad h_2 = 2$$

$$\left(1 + \frac{0.08}{4}\right)^4 = \left(1 + \frac{i_2}{2}\right)^2$$

$$1.0824 = \left(1 + \frac{i_2}{2}\right)^2$$

$$i_2 = 0.0808 = 8.08\%$$

Note that since bank B compounds less often, it must offer a slightly higher interest rate.

Let i_1 be the nominal rate paid for period h_1, and let i_2 be a different rate paid for period h_2. Both rates can be converted to effective rates using Equation (4.8):

$$r = \left(1 + \frac{i_1}{h_1}\right)^{h_1} - 1 \qquad (4.11)$$

$$r = \left(1 + \frac{i_2}{h_2}\right)^{h_2} - 1 \qquad (4.12)$$

If the two nominal rates are equivalent, they must yield the same effective annual rate, r. If they do, Equations (4.11) and (4.12) can be set equal to one another:

$$\left(1 + \frac{i_1}{h_1}\right)^{h_1} = \left(1 + \frac{i_2}{h_2}\right)^{h_2} \qquad (4.13)$$

Note that the -1 terms drop out. Equation (4.13) allows a nominal rate that has one period to be converted to an equivalent rate with a different period.

4.2.5. Average Return

One subject that frequently arises concerning interest rates is how to average rates over time. Rates have tended to change frequently in recent years, so it has become important to be able to calculate an accurate average return.

If interest is being compounded and the interest rate is different for different periods, one cannot simply calculate an arithmetic average to get the true

EXAMPLE 4.5

Different Interest Periods

An investor is offered a bond paying 12.5 percent interest compounded semiannually. She wants to compare this return to another investment that provides interest on a weekly basis. What nominal rate must this investment offer to be as attractive as the bond?

$$\left(1 + \frac{i_1}{h_1}\right)^{h_1} = \left(1 + \frac{i_2}{h_2}\right)^{h_2}$$

$$i_1 = 0.125 \qquad h_1 = 2 \qquad h_2 = 52$$

$$\left(1 + \frac{0.125}{2}\right)^{2} = \left(1 + \frac{i_2}{52}\right)^{52}$$

$$i_2 = 0.1214 = 12.14\%$$

Since the alternative investment is compounded more often, it can have a somewhat lower nominal rate and still be attractive.

EXAMPLE 4.6

Average Interest Rates

An investment of $500 earns 5 percent the first year, 20 percent the second year, and 8 percent the third year. What is the average interest rate?

$$F_3 = P(1 + r_1)(1 + r_2)(1 + r_3)$$

$$P = \$500 \qquad r_1 = 0.05 \qquad r_2 = 0.20 \qquad r_3 = 0.08$$

$$F_3 = \$500(1 + 0.05)(1 + 0.20)(1 + 0.08)$$

$$= \$680.40$$

$$1 + \bar{r} = \left(\frac{F_t}{P}\right)^{1/t}$$

$$= \left(\frac{\$680.40}{\$500.00}\right)^{1/3}$$

$$\bar{r} = 0.1081 = 10.81\%$$

Note that this is less than the arithmetic average of 11 percent.

average return. Consider $1000 invested at 6 percent interest the first year and 20 percent the second year. At the end of one year, this is worth $1000(1 + 0.06) = \$1060$. After the second year, the value is $\$1060(1 + 0.20) = \$1272$. From the compound interest equation, we can calculate:

$$\$1272 = \$1000(1 + \bar{r})^2$$

where $\bar{r}$ is the average interest rate. In this case, $\bar{r} = 0.1278$.

Consider the result of an arithmetic average of interest rates: $(0.06 + 0.20)/2 = 0.13$. This is not the same as the correct average return. A simple arithmetic average does not work; $\bar{r}$ is found instead from the geometric average:

$$1 + \bar{r} = \left(\frac{F_t}{P}\right)^{1/t} \tag{4.14}$$

The true average interest rate, $\bar{r}$, will always be less than or equal to the arithmetic average interest rate.

4.2.6. Discounting

One important application of interest calculations is called *discounting*. This procedure is used to find the value at a given time of a single payment that will be made at a different time.

In the simplest case, we would like to find the current value of an amount to be received in the future. This process is often referred to as "discounting to the present." From Equation (4.7) we know that

$$F_t = P(1 + r)^t \tag{4.7}$$

Hence, the present value of an amount to be received in the future is simply

$$P = \frac{F_t}{(1 + r)^t} \tag{4.15}$$

In more complex cases, we might wish to find the value, F_2, at some time in the future, t_2, of an amount, F_1, to be received at a different time, t_1. The first time can be either before or after the second time. Let us begin by finding the present value of the amount received at t_1 by using Equation (4.15):

$$P = \frac{F_1}{(1 + r)^{t_1}} \tag{4.16}$$

The present value can be converted to a value at time t_2 by applying Equation (4.7):

$$F_2 = P(1 + r)^{t_2} \tag{4.17}$$

Substituting Equation (4.16) into Equation (4.17) gives

$$F_2 = \frac{F_1(1 + r)^{t_2}}{(1 + r)^{t_1}} \tag{4.18}$$

which reduces to

$$F_2 = F_1(1 + r)^{t_2 - t_1} \tag{4.19}$$

Equation (4.19) allows values at one time to be converted to values at a different time. In this equation, r is called the *discount rate* and is an estimate of how rapidly the value of money changes during the time period in question. Deciding upon values for r is often a difficult task and will be addressed in a later chapter. When using Equation (4.19), it is essential that t_1 and t_2 be expressed in periods equivalent to those used for r. If r is an effective annual rate, then t_1 and t_2 must be expressed in years.

EXAMPLE 4.7

Discounting

A company expects to receive a payment of $2500 from a customer in three years.

(a) If the prevailing interest rate is 11 percent, how much is that payment worth today?
(b) If payment is postponed by a year, how much should the company demand?

(a)
$$P = \frac{F_t}{(1 + r)^t}$$

$$F_3 = \$2500 \qquad r = 0.11 \qquad t = 3$$

$$P = \frac{\$2500}{(1 + 0.11)^3}$$

$$= \$1827.98$$

The payment is worth $1827.98 today.

(b)
$$F_2 = F_1(1 + r)^{t_2 - t_1}$$

$$F_3 = \$2500 \qquad r = 0.11 \qquad t_1 = 3 \qquad t_2 = 4$$

$$F_4 = \$2500(1 + 0.11)^{4-3}$$

$$= \$2775.00$$

The company should demand $2775.00 if payment is delayed by a year. The answer in (b) could also be found by converting the answer in (a):

$$F_t = P(1 + r)^t$$

$$P = \$1827.98 \qquad r = 0.11 \qquad t = 4$$

$$F_4 = \$1827.98(1 + 0.11)^4$$

$$= \$2775.00$$

4.3.   SERIES

Many financial situations involve a series of payments made at different times. For example, an auto or home loan is usually repaid with constant monthly payments. Similarly, an investment may yield annual benefits, such as dividends. Calculations involving these types of cash flows are often simplified by using financial series formulas.

4.3.1.   Annuities or Uniform Series

An *annuity* is a stream of constant payments made at fixed intervals for a given length of time, and is also called a *uniform series*. The auto loan repayment mentioned above is an example of this. An annuity has four basic characteristics:

1. The payment amount, A, is constant.[2]
2. The interest rate, r, is constant.
3. The payments are made at specific intervals. It is conventional to base calculations on the assumption that payments are made at the end of the periods, and we shall employ that convention here. Most annuities actually do pay benefits at the end of the periods, and in other types of analysis the periods can often be chosen so that this assumption holds true. This assumption is by no means necessary, however, and alternative derivations could be made for payments at the start of the periods, the middle of the periods, and so on. Appendix 4A presents information about payments made at different times during the periods.
4. The payments are made for a fixed number of periods, n. The periods are often years, but, of course, any other period could be used.

Two calculations involving series are of great importance. First, how much is the stream of payments worth today; that is, what is its present value? Second, how much is the stream worth at some later date; in other words, what is its future value? The derivation of equations to answer these questions is not particularly complex and is worth understanding.

4.3.2. Future Value of an Annuity

Let us begin by analyzing the future value, which we will call F. This is analogous to the F_t used for single payment formulas. The t is usually omitted in the series calculations since only one future value is generally of interest— the one at the end of n periods. We know the annuity consists of a series of payments of amount A made at constant intervals of time for n periods. Each payment receives interest from the date it is made until the end of the nth period, at which time we are calculating the future value. Thus, the last payment receives no interest, the payment before it receives interest for one period, and so on:

$$F = A(1 + r)^{n-1} + A(1 + r)^{n-2} + \cdots + A(1 + r) + A \qquad (4.20)$$

Note that the first payment receives interest for $n - 1$ periods, not n periods. This is because of our assumption that payments are made at the end of the periods, so that the first payment begins to earn interest in the second period.

Equation (4.20) could be evaluated directly to find the future value, but the calculations become rather tedious. We will try to reduce this equation to a simpler form. We begin by noting that the equation is a geometric progression; that is, each term differs from its predecessor by a constant multiplicative factor of $(1 + r)$. As a first step, multiply Equation (4.20) by $(1 + r)$, which yields

$$F(1 + r) = A(1 + r)^n + A(1 + r)^{n-1} + \cdots + A(1 + r)^2 + A(1 + r) \qquad (4.21)$$

---

[2]A thoughtful reader might ask whether these payments are constant in real or in nominal terms, that is, do they remove the effects of inflation or leave them in? Either is possible as long as the interest rate is treated consistently. A nominal payment requires the use of a nominal interest rate; a real payment requires a real interest rate. A full treatment of inflation will be found in Chapter 9.

EXAMPLE 4.8

Future Value of an Annuity

$1000 is deposited at the end of each year in a bank account earning 8.5 percent interest, compounded annually. At the end of 7 years, how much is the account worth?

$$F = A\left[\frac{(1+r)^n - 1}{r}\right]$$

$$A = \$1000 \qquad r = 0.085 \qquad n = 7$$

$$F = \$1000\left[\frac{(1 + 0.085)^7 - 1}{0.085}\right]$$

$$= \$9060.50$$

Now, subtract Equation (4.20) from Equation (4.21). Note that every term except the first term in Equation (4.21) and the last term in Equation (4.20) drops out:

$$F(1 + r) - F = A(1 + r)^n - A \tag{4.22}$$

Factoring and rearranging this equation yields

$$F = A\left[\frac{(1 + r)^n - 1}{r}\right] \tag{4.23}$$

This is the future value of an annuity. Equation (4.23) is another of the most important equations of finance.

The term $[(1 + r)^n - 1]/r$ in Equation (4.23) is called the *uniform series compound amount factor,* and is denoted by $(F/A, r\%, n)$.[3] Before electronic calculators were available, large tables of compound amount factors were prepared to simplify computation.[4] These are now largely superfluous.

Equation (4.23) can also be used in reverse to find the annual amount A that is needed to accumulate a total amount F after n periods. It is obvious that

$$A = F\left[\frac{r}{(1 + r)^n - 1}\right] \tag{4.24}$$

This equation is useful in applications involving government bonds. Some cities issue bonds in the amount F that are repayable at a given date in the future. (Of course, investors would not pay the full amount F for the bonds, or they would not make any money. Alternatively, they might pay F for the bonds but also receive periodic interest payments.) To accumulate the cash needed to

---

[3] Some finance texts use the symbol $s_{\overline{n}|r}$ for the uniform series compound amount factor.
[4] Such tables can be found in Donald Newnan, *Engineering Economic Analysis,* San Jose, Calif.: Engineering Press, 1980, and many other books.

EXAMPLE 4.9
Future Value of an Annuity

Repeat Example 4.8 using 8.5 percent interest compounded quarterly. First, find the effective annual interest rate using Equation (4.8):

$$r = \left(1 + \frac{i}{h}\right)^h - 1$$

$$i = 0.085 \qquad h = 4$$

$$r = \left(1 + \frac{0.085}{4}\right)^4 - 1$$

$$= 0.08775$$

Then solve the annuity as before:

$$F = A\left[\frac{(1 + r)^n - 1}{r}\right]$$

$$A = \$1000 \qquad r = 0.08775 \qquad n = 7$$

$$F = \$9137.18$$

Note how the future value is increased by the quarterly compounding.

EXAMPLE 4.10
Sinking Funds

The city of Bedrock has issued $10,000,000 of bonds to finance a new municipal aggregate plant. If the bonds are redeemable at the end of 20 years, and the city can earn 7 percent effective annual interest on its sinking fund, how much should Bedrock put into the fund every year in order to accumulate enough money to retire the bonds?

$$A = F\left[\frac{r}{(1 + r)^n - 1}\right]$$

$$F = \$10,000,000 \qquad r = 0.07 \qquad n = 20$$

$$A = \$10,000,000\left[\frac{0.07}{(1 + 0.07)^{20} - 1}\right]$$

$$= \$243,929.26$$

This represents the amount Bedrock must put into its sinking fund each year in order to accumulate $10,000,000 in 20 years so it can pay off the bonds.

redeem the bonds, annual payments of the amount A are made into a *sinking fund* that then receives interest. Hence the term in brackets in Equation (4.24) is called the *uniform series sinking fund factor,* and is denoted by $(A/F, r\%, n)$.

4.3.3. Present Value of an Annuity

The present value of the stream of payments to be received in the future is simply the sum of the discounted payments. For example, a payment received at the end of one period is worth $A(1 + r)^{-1}$ today. For a series of equal payments,

$$P = A(1 + r)^{-1} + A(1 + r)^{-2} + \cdots + A(1 + r)^{-(n-1)} + A(1 + r)^{-n} \quad (4.25)$$

where P is the present value.

To derive a simpler expression, we will use a technique similar to the one used for future value. The future value could be converted directly to the present value by using Equation (4.15), but the slightly longer derivation given here will help to illustrate once again the basic technique used in the previous section. Multiply Equation (4.25) by $(1 + r)$, to produce

$$P(1 + r) = A + A(1 + r)^{-1} + \cdots + A(1 + r)^{-(n-2)} + A(1 + r)^{-(n-1)} \quad (4.26)$$

Now subtract Equation (4.25) from Equation (4.26), and notice how most of the terms cancel out:

$$P(1 + r) - P = A - A(1 + r)^{-n} \quad (4.27)$$

This reduces to

$$P = A\left[\frac{1 - (1 + r)^{-n}}{r}\right] \quad (4.28)$$

Equation (4.28) gives the present value of an annuity and is analogous to Equation (4.23) for the future value. The quantity in brackets is called the *uniform series present worth factor,* and is denoted by $(P/A, r\%, n)$.[5]

As we noted earlier, an equation of this type can be used in reverse to find the amount of the payment needed to produce a given present value:

$$A = P\left[\frac{r}{1 - (1 + r)^{-n}}\right] \quad (4.29)$$

The quantity in brackets is called the *uniform series capital recovery factor,* which is denoted by $(A/P, r\%, n)$.

Equation (4.29) is often used to determine the annual expenditure A needed to pay for an immediate outlay P. Since these annual expenditures will be equal, this approach is often called the *levelized costs calculation.* Utility companies, for example, use Equation (4.29) to determine how much their rates must increase to pay for a new facility. If the facility costs P to build and must be paid for in n years, A is the extra amount needed each year to pay off the plant.

---

[5] Finance texts use the symbol $a_{\overline{n}|r}$.

EXAMPLE 4.11

Present Value of an Annuity

Find the present value of the payment stream outlined in Example 4.8.

$$P = A\left[\frac{1 - (1 + r)^{-n}}{r}\right]$$

$$A = \$1000 \qquad r = 0.085 \qquad n = 7$$

$$P = \$1000\left[\frac{1 - (1 + 0.085)^{-7}}{0.085}\right]$$

$$= \$5118.51$$

4.3.4. Annuities with Different Interest Periods

As we discussed in an earlier section of this chapter, it is often necessary to convert interest rates based on one period (such as years) into rates having a different period (such as months). The same situation sometimes arises in calculating the present or future value of an annuity. In these cases, the annuity's payment period is not the same as the time period used to express the interest rate. Bonds are good examples of this problem since many bonds offer semiannual payments and interest rates are rarely expressed in these terms.

There are two approaches to analyzing the value of annuities when the interest period and payment period differ. The first approach involves the use of effective annual rates and can be described in three steps:

1. Convert the given interest rate i to an effective annual interest rate r using Equation (4.8):

$$r = \left(1 + \frac{i}{h}\right)^{h} - 1 \tag{4.8}$$

2. Convert the effective annual interest rate r to the rate for the period of the annuity by using Equation (4.8) in reverse and solving for i/h.
3. Find the value of the annuity using i/h, which is the effective rate for the period in question.

A somewhat faster but perhaps less obvious method converts the interest rate directly and omits the intermediate step of employing an effective annual interest rate. This approach involves a two-step process:

1. Convert the given rate i_1 to the effective interest rate for the period of the annuity (i_2/h_2) using Equation (4.13):

$$\left(1 + \frac{i_1}{h_1}\right)^{h_1} = \left(1 + \frac{i_2}{h_2}\right)^{h_2} \tag{4.13}$$

2. Find the value of the annuity using i_2/h_2.

Either of these approaches is valid, and both will yield the same result. Use whichever approach is most understandable for you.

EXAMPLE 4.12

Annuities with Different Interest Periods

A 10-year bond with a face value (also referred to as its principal or par value) of $1000 pays interest at a rate of 10 percent compounded semi-annually. If the appropriate market-clearing interest rate is 8 percent compounded quarterly, what is the present value of the bond?

A bond of this type can be thought of as a combination of a single payment and an annuity. The single payment is the $1000 that will be provided at the end of 10 years. The annuity consists of the semiannual interest payments that are made every 6 months for the lifetime of the bond. The amount of these semiannual payments is the semiannual interest rate (in this case 10%/2 = 5%) times the face value of the bond ($1000), which yields $50.

Let us first consider this problem using the three-step approach outlined above.

1. Find the effective annual interest rate.

$$r = \left(1 + \frac{i}{h}\right)^h - 1$$

$$i = 8\% \qquad h = 4$$

$$r = \left(1 + \frac{0.08}{4}\right)^4 - 1$$

$$= 0.0824 \text{ or } 8.24\%$$

2. Convert the effective annual rate to the rate for the period of the annuity.

$$r = 0.0824 \qquad h = 2$$

$$0.0824 = \left(1 + \frac{i}{h}\right)^2 - 1$$

$$\frac{i}{h} = 0.0404 \text{ or } 4.04\%$$

3. Find the value of the annuity.

There are two parts of the annuity to evaluate. The present value of the face value can be found from Equation (4.15):

$$P = \frac{F_t}{(1 + r)^t}$$

4.3.5. Combining Annuities and Discounting

Many cash flows can be analyzed by using a combination of single payment discounting and annuities. Such situations often arise in cases where annual payments are constant, except in one or two years. The exceptions may arise due to extraordinary circumstances, such as a lump sum payoff at the end of an investment or a 1-year maintenance cost during the lifespan of a project.

In this case, the appropriate effective interest rate to use is the value of i/h found in step 2. Since interest is compounded semiannually, there are two periods each year for 10 years, meaning that there are 20 compoundings to consider. Thus,

$$P = \frac{\$1000}{(1 + 0.0404)^{20}}$$

$$= \$452.89$$

The value of the semiannual interest payments can be found by using Equation (4.28):

$$P = A\left[\frac{1 - (1 + r)^{-n}}{r}\right]$$

Again, 0.0404 should be used for the interest rate and 20 for the number of periods:

$$P = \$50\left[\frac{1 - (1.0404)^{-20}}{0.0404}\right]$$

$$= \$677.12$$

Therefore the total present value of this bond is

$$P = \$452.89 + \$677.12$$

$$= \$1130.01$$

The problem could also be solved using the second approach discussed above:

1. Convert the interest rate to the effective rate for the period of the annuity.

$$\left(1 + \frac{i_1}{h_1}\right)^{h_1} = \left(1 + \frac{i_2}{h_2}\right)^{h_2}$$

$$i_1 = 8\% \qquad h_1 = 4 \qquad h_2 = 2$$

$$\left(1 + \frac{0.08}{4}\right)^4 = \left(1 + \frac{i_2}{h_2}\right)^2$$

$$\frac{i_2}{h_2} = 0.0404$$

Note that this is the same effective rate as was calculated using the other approach.

2. Find the value of the annuity. This calculation is exactly the same as in step 3 of the first approach.

To analyze these situations, the cash flow should be split into two parts: (1) a constant annual stream of payments, and (2) one or more single payments. The sum of these two parts should equal the actual cash flow. Once the two parts are identified, the present values of the streams can be calculated separately. The total present value is simply the sum of the two present values.

EXAMPLE 4.13

Combining Annuities and Discounting

An investment provides an annual payment of $500 for 4 years. At the same time as the last annual payment is received, a separate bonus payment of $250 is provided. What is the present value of this investment if the investor uses a discount rate of 10 percent?

This investment can be analyzed in two parts: (1) a 4-year annuity at $500 per year, and (2) a single payment of $250 received at the end of the fourth year. For the annuity:

$$P = A\left[\frac{1 - (1 + r)^{-n}}{r}\right]$$

$$A = \$500 \qquad r = 0.10 \qquad n = 4$$

$$P = \$500\left[\frac{1 - (1 + 0.10)^{-4}}{0.10}\right]$$

$$= \$1584.93$$

For the single payment:

$$P = \frac{F_t}{(1 + r)^t}$$

$$F_4 = \$250 \qquad r = 0.10 \qquad t = 4$$

$$P = \frac{\$250}{(1 + 0.10)^4}$$

$$= \$170.75$$

Thus, the total value of the investment is $1584.93 plus $170.75, which equals $1755.68.

4.3.6. Perpetuities

A perpetuity is a special type of annuity in which the initial amount invested is sufficiently large to produce periodic payments of a fixed amount forever. We would like to know the present value of such an investment.

Recall Equation (4.28), which gave us the present value of an annuity:

$$P = A\left[\frac{1 - (1 + r)^{-n}}{r}\right] \tag{4.28}$$

Now, if we receive payments forever, n approaches infinity. Since $(1 + r)^{-1}$ is less than 1, as n approaches infinity this quantity approaches 0. Therefore, for a perpetuity:

$$P = \frac{A}{r} \tag{4.30}$$

The present value is simply the periodic payment divided by the interest rate.

EXAMPLE 4.14

Perpetuities

An investor wants to buy a perpetuity that will provide $500 per year forever, and can get an effective annual interest rate of 12 percent. How much should he invest?

$$P = \frac{A}{r}$$

$$A = \$500 \qquad r = 0.12$$

$$P = \frac{\$500}{0.12}$$

$$= \$4166.67$$

4.3.7.   Uniform Gradients

Another common type of series is the *uniform gradient* or *arithmetic series*. The amount of the periodic payment is not constant; instead, each payment is larger than its predecessor by a fixed amount. A uniform gradient has these characteristics:

1. Successive payments differ by the amount G. We will assume that the first payment is 0, so the second is G, the third is $2G$, and so on. This assumption greatly simplifies the calculations. We will see how to handle series in which the initial payment is not 0 in a subsequent section.
2. The interest rate r is constant.
3. Payments are made at the end of fixed periods.
4. A total of n payments are made. Since the first is 0, the last payment is $(n - 1)G$.

Thus, the gradient consists of these payments:

$$0 + G + 2G + 3G + \cdots + (n - 2)G + (n - 1)G \qquad (4.31)$$

As before, we are interested in the present and future values of this payment stream. The equations for these values are derived in a fashion similar to those for an annuity. These derivations can be found in many finance textbooks.

The future value of a uniform gradient can be found from

$$F = \frac{G}{r}\left[\frac{(1 + r)^n - 1}{r} - n\right] \qquad (4.32)$$

It, of course, can be used in reverse to find the amount G if the future value is known.

The present value of a uniform gradient is given by

$$P = \frac{G}{r}\left[\frac{1 - (1 + r)^{-n}}{r} - \frac{n}{(1 + r)^n}\right] \qquad (4.33)$$

As always, this equation can also be used to find G if P is known.

EXAMPLE 4.15

Present Value of a Uniform Gradient

An investment yields a series of gradient payments starting with $750 at the end of the second year and increasing by $750 each year thereafter. The lifespan of the investment is 15 years and the prevailing effective annual interest rate is 10 percent. What is the present value of this investment?

$$P = \frac{G}{r}\left[\frac{1-(1+r)^{-n}}{r} - \frac{n}{(1+r)^n}\right]$$

$$G = \$750 \qquad r = 0.10 \qquad n = 15$$

$$P = \frac{\$750}{0.10}\left[\frac{1-(1.10)^{-15}}{0.10} - \frac{15}{(1.10)^{15}}\right]$$

$$= \$30,113.99$$

4.3.8. Combining Uniform Series with Uniform Gradients

Earlier, we assumed that a uniform gradient started with a zero payment at the end of the first period. We need to be able to handle a situation in which the gradient starts with the first period; for example, a payment of $100 is made at the end of the first year, $200 at the end of the second year, $300 at the end of the third year, and so on. This is actually a special case of a more general problem in which the gradient begins from some base. For example, the first payment could be $1000, the second $1100, the third $1200, and so on. Here the base is $1000 and the gradient amount is $100.

Problems of this type are easy to handle: simply treat the base and the gradient separately. The base is a uniform series, in this case $1000. The gradient is a uniform gradient of $100. Calculate the desired values for each separate series and then sum them to get the overall result.

4.3.9. Uniform Growth Series

A type of series that grows by a uniform percentage each year is called a *uniform growth series* or a *geometric series*. The four basic characteristics of such a series are the following:

1. Successive payments differ by the factor $(1+g)$, where g is the growth rate. The basic amount of the series is X, so the first payment is $X(1+g)$, the second is $X(1+g)^2$, and so on.
2. The interest rate r is constant.
3. Payments are made at the end of fixed periods.
4. A total of n payments are made. The final payment is thus $X(1+g)^n$.

The uniform growth series therefore consists of these payments:

$$X(1+g) + X(1+g)^2 + \cdots + X(1+g)^{n-1} + X(1+g)^n \qquad (4.34)$$

As always, we want to find the present and future values.

EXAMPLE 4.16

Present Value of a Uniform Growth Series

An investment produces a stream of payments that grow by 15 percent each year from a base amount of $1000. If the effective annual interest rate is 10 percent and the payments continue for 10 years, what is the present value of the investment?

$$P = X\left[\frac{1 - (1 + k)^{-n}}{k}\right]$$

$$1 + k = \frac{1 + r}{1 + g}$$

$$X = \$1000 \qquad g = 0.15 \qquad r = 0.10 \qquad n = 10$$

$$1 + k = \frac{1.10}{1.15}$$

$$k = -0.04348$$

$$P = \$1000\left[\frac{1 - (1 - 0.04348)^{-10}}{-0.04348}\right]$$

$$= \$12,873.97$$

Let us first consider present value. If we discount each payment, we see that the present value P is

$$P = \frac{X(1 + g)}{1 + r} + \frac{X(1 + g)^2}{(1 + r)^2} + \cdots + \frac{X(1 + g)^{n-1}}{(1 + r)^{n-1}} + \frac{X(1 + g)^n}{(1 + r)^n} \qquad (4.35)$$

We could proceed as before and try to eliminate terms, but there is a simpler approach. Let us define an effective growth rate k, such that:

$$1 + k = \frac{1 + r}{1 + g} \qquad (4.36)$$

k is thus a combination of the effects of growth and discounting. Substituting Equation (4.36) into Equation (4.35):

$$P = \frac{X}{1 + k} + \frac{X}{(1 + k)^2} + \cdots + \frac{X}{(1 + k)^{n-1}} + \frac{X}{(1 + k)^n} \qquad (4.37)$$

Compare this to Equation (4.25) for an annuity. The forms are identical. We can therefore use Equation (4.28) to give us the present value:

$$P = X\left[\frac{1 - (1 + k)^{-n}}{k}\right] \qquad (4.38)$$

It is difficult, and not really necessary, to derive a unique expression for the future value of a uniform growth series. The simplest way to get the future

EXAMPLE 4.17

Combining Analytical Techniques

An investor has purchased an interest in Megabucks Oil Company. The firm expects to pay the investor the following amounts over the next 7 years:

Year	1	2	3	4	5	6	7
Amount	$1000	$1200	$1400	$1600	$1800	$2000	$5000

The investor's interest in Megabucks terminates at the end of 7 years. A salesperson of Megabucks' stock has claimed that this investment has a future value after 7 years of over $20,000. If the appropriate effective annual interest rate is 10 percent, and if all payments are made at the end of the year, is the salesperson correct?

To solve this problem you could simply treat each payment separately and find its future value. However, it is probably quicker to observe that the payment stream consists of a $1000 annuity, a uniform gradient of $200 per year, and a single payment of $2800 in year 7:

Year	1	2	3	4	5	6	7
Annuity	$1000	$1000	$1000	$1000	$1000	$1000	$1000
Gradient		200	400	600	800	1000	1200
Single payment							2800
Total	$1000	$1200	$1400	$1600	$1800	$2000	$5000

value is to find the present value first and convert it to the future value. This can be done using Equation (4.7):

$$F = P(1 + r)^n \qquad (4.7)$$

Substituting Equation (4.38) into Equation (4.7) yields

$$F = X \left[\frac{1 - (1 + k)^{-n}}{k} \right] (1 + r)^n \qquad (4.39)$$

which is the future value of a uniform growth series.

4.4. COMBINING ANALYTICAL TECHNIQUES

An understanding of the concepts of interest and the use of equations for single payments and series greatly simplifies financial analysis. Without the formulas presented in this chapter, financial analysis would be an extremely tedious and time-consuming process. By carefully combining these formulas, a wide

Thus, find the future value of each cash stream and sum the results. For the annuity:

$$F = A\left[\frac{(1 + r)^n - 1}{r}\right]$$

$$= \$1000\left[\frac{(1 + 0.10)^7 - 1}{0.10}\right]$$

$$= \$9487.17$$

For the gradient:

$$F = \frac{G}{r}\left[\frac{(1 + r)^n - 1}{r} - n\right]$$

$$= \frac{\$200}{0.10}\left[\frac{(1 + 0.10)^7 - 1}{0.10} - 7\right]$$

$$= \$4974.34$$

The single payment earns no interest since it is received at the end of year 7. Hence it is just worth $2800. The future value is

$$F = \$9487.17 + \$4974.34 + \$2800.00$$

$$= \$17,261.51$$

Despite the salesperson's promise, this investment is not worth $20,000 after 7 years.

variety of seemingly complex problems can be converted to straightforward tasks. Example 4.17 shows how this can be done.

QUESTIONS AND PROBLEMS

1. An investor places $500 in a savings account paying 5.75 percent interest. What is the value of the investment at the end of 3 years if the interest is compounded
   a. Annually?
   b. Monthly?
   c. Weekly?
2. What is the effective annual interest rate of an investment offering 10 percent interest compounded
   a. Semiannually?
   b. Monthly?
   c. Weekly?
   d. Daily?

3. A city in the Midwest issued a series of bonds in 1869 that offered to pay 3 percent annual interest as long as the bond was held. The face value of the bonds was $100. In 1980, an individual discovered one of the bonds in an old trunk and attempted to cash it in. Considerable controversy arose as to whether the bond was to pay simple interest or compound interest. Calculate the amount of interest the bondholder would receive in both cases and explain why these results might have been controversial.

4. Bank A offers savings accounts with interest compounded monthly, while bank B offers savings accounts with interest compounded quarterly. If bank A is offering 6 percent nominal interest, how much does bank B need to offer in order to effectively compete?

5. An investor buys a security that offers a 5 percent return the first year, a 2 percent return the second year, a 13 percent return the third year, and a 20 percent return the final year. He assumes this means his average return is 10 percent. Is this correct? If not, what is the correct average return?

6. Your great aunt wants to establish a trust fund for you that will pay you $100,000 at the end of 10 years. You thank her for her generosity, but suggest that immediate cash would be nicer. However, your great aunt has read this book and knows about the time value of money. If she believes that the appropriate discount rate is 9 percent, how much should she give you today to be equivalent to the $100,000 trust fund?

7. A firm is owed $10,000 six months in the future. The debtor requests a three-month extension. If the firm uses an effective monthly interest rate of 1 percent, how much should they ask for if payment is delayed?

8. A life insurance agent offers to sell you an annuity that will pay you $1000 per year for 15 years. Each payment will be made at the end of the year. You expect interest rates to average 13 percent over that time period. The agent wants to charge you $7000 for the annuity, noting that you will get $15,000 back and therefore more than double your money. Is he right? Is the annuity a good investment?

9. How much should a city place into its sinking fund each year to cover $17,000,000 worth of bonds? Assume the sinking fund earns 8 percent effective annual interest and the bonds are redeemable after 14 years.

10. Find the value of a $10,000 corporate bond with a 20-year maturity, payments every six months, and paying 7 percent nominal annual interest if the appropriate market-clearing interest rate is
    a. 10 percent compounded semiannually.
    b. 12 percent compounded annually.
    c. 8 percent compounded monthly.

11. What is the present value of a uniform gradient lasting for 10 years and with a payment increment of $500? Use an effective annual interest rate of 7 percent.

12. What is the present value of the gradient described in Problem 11 if it begins from a base of $1000? The $1000 is paid at the end of the first year.

13. What is the future value after 10 years of a uniform growth series that starts at $500 and grows by 5 percent per year? Use an effective annual interest rate of 6.5 percent.

14. An individual invests $1000 per year for 45 years in a retirement account earning interest at an effective annual rate of 9 percent. When she retires, she expects to live for another 20 years. If the 9 percent interest rate continues to hold, how much can she draw out each month and use up all of her money in exactly 20 years?

15. Almost all American workers are required to pay Social Security taxes. Besides the taxes deducted from each worker's paycheck, a slightly higher tax rate is charged to their employers, whose payments are also funneled into the Social Security trust

funds. The current combined tax rate is about 15 percent. If an individual works for 35 years, earns $20,000 per year, and the combined Social Security tax rate is 15 percent, how much will his payments be worth at retirement if the trust funds earn 6 percent effective annual interest? For simplicity, assume payments are made once per year.

a. If the individual then receives $2000 per month after retirement, how long must he live to recover the money he and his employer paid in? Assume the fund continues to earn 6 percent interest after retirement.

b. If the monthly payment is only $1000, how long must he live to recover the money? Explain this result.

APPENDIX 4A

Other Types of Annuities

The equations given in the text for the present and future value of an annuity assume that payments are made at the end of the periods. This need not be true. For example, if payments are made at the beginning of the periods, different equations for present and future value are required. For the future value, each payment would receive interest for one period more than is shown in the text since each is received a full period early. After all, receiving a payment at the start of a period is just the same as receiving it at the end of the previous period. Hence, the earlier result for future value:

$$F = A\left[\frac{(1 + r)^n - 1}{r}\right] \qquad (4.23)$$

becomes

$$F = A\left[\frac{(1 + r)^n - 1}{r}\right](1 + r) \qquad (4.A.1)$$

for payments at the start of periods.

We can use this result to find the present value of an annuity for which the payments are made at the start of the periods. From Equation (4.15) we know that

$$P = \frac{F}{(1 + r)^n} \qquad (4.15)$$

Substituting Equation (4.A.1) into Equation (4.15) gives

$$P = \frac{A\{[(1 + r)^n - 1]/r\}(1 + r)}{(1 + r)^n} \qquad (4.A.2)$$

which reduces to

$$P = A\left[\frac{1 - (1 + r)^{-n}}{r}\right](1 + r) \qquad (4.A.3)$$

68

Equation (4.A.3) gives the present value of an annuity that has payments at the beginning of the periods.

Similar equations can be developed for payments made at other times by applying the appropriate amount of additional interest to the equations given in the text. For example, if payments are made in the middle of the periods, the factor $(1 + r)^{1/2}$ should be used.

5

Measures of Welfare Loss for an Individual

5.1. INTRODUCTION

This chapter asks what is a benefit or a cost? This far from trivial question is in fact one of the fundamental questions to be asked in benefit–cost analysis. Appreciating the conceptual nature of benefits and costs is useful in performing any sort of a policy analysis, even one where the data are insufficient to carry out a full benefit–cost analysis. Thus, understanding the nature of a benefit or a cost is useful, and perhaps even essential, in performing any sort of a policy analysis.

We begin to address the question of defining benefits and costs in this chapter and continue this task in the two succeeding chapters. This chapter is concerned with the problem of measuring welfare change for a single individual, individual i. This chapter uses some descriptive calculus but knowledge of calculus is not necessary to understand this chapter.

5.2. A WELFARE FUNCTION FOR INDIVIDUAL i

We start with a definition that utility is what individual i attempts to maximize when she makes choices. That is, by definition we shall say that an individual attempts to maximize utility in making decisions. Utility does not necessarily represent pleasure in some hedonistic sense. Rather, it is simply a device to help explain what people choose. The attainment of justice and the appreciation of art, as well as a new automobile, are all activities or goods that give rise to utility because they are things that are chosen. Utility itself is a function of goods and services broadly conceived, and of the utility of others. For now we shall ignore the dependence of utility on the utility of others to simplify the exposition. These goods, services, and activities that yield utility are designated by X_j's. The utility of individual i can then be expressed as

$$U_i = U(X_1, X_2, \ldots, X_N) \tag{5.1}$$

where each X represents a good or service. A change in utility for the ith person from a change in the quantity of the jth good will be given by

$$dU_i = \sum_{j_i} \frac{\partial U_i}{\partial X_{ij}} dX_{ij} \tag{5.2}$$

This says that a change in utility from an action that changes the quantities of goods or services is the change in quantity of the good or service going to person i, dX_{ij}, times the marginal utility of the good or service for person i, summed over all the X_j affected goods.

For individual i the additional utility created by a new unit of good X_j is equal to the (explicit or implicit) price times i's marginal utility of income. That is, the value to you of a new book costing \$3.00 is three times the number of utils each dollar is worth to you. If each dollar were worth 5 utils, the book would be worth 15 utils to you. In symbols this is

$$\frac{\partial U_i}{\partial X_{ij}} = \frac{\partial U_i}{\partial Y_i} P_j$$

where Y represents income and P_j represents the price of good X_j. The term $\partial U_i / \partial Y_i$ is i's marginal utility of income, that is, the utility of an additional dollar. If the above expression for $\partial U_i \partial X_{ij}$ is substituted into Equation (5.2), this gives

$$dU_i = \sum_{j_i} \frac{\partial U_i}{\partial Y_i} P_j \, dX_{ij} \tag{5.3}$$

The term $P_j \, dX_{ij}$ may be thought of as an income change—the change in the amount of the jth good dX_{ij} times the price of the good P_j. The income change for i is weighted by the value of her marginal utility of income, $\partial U_i / \partial Y_i$, to give the utility change associated with the income change. (Technical Note 5A derives similar equations allowing for interdependent utility.)

5.3.   THE WILLINGNESS TO PAY AND TO ACCEPT

The remainder of this chapter is concerned with measuring $\sum (\partial U_i / \partial Y_i) P_j \, dX_{ij}$. To do this we introduce the concepts of *willingness to pay* (WTP) for a good or to avoid a cost and the *willingness to accept payment* (WTA) to forego a good or to bear a cost. To see the way the WTP and the WTA work, suppose that you have an income of \$40,000 per year and are just willing to pay \$10,000 for a new Mazda. The \$10,000 would be your WTP. It is constrained by your income. We can regard this as the WTP for a price decrease of the one Mazda to zero. Now suppose instead that your rich uncle gives you this same Mazda. You would be willing, say, to sell it for \$12,000. This would be your WTA. We could regard this as your WTA to forego the Mazda (or to forego the

TECHNICAL NOTE 5A
Interdependent Utility Functions

Here we recognize that i cares not only for the goods and services that she receives, but for the goods and services that others receive. That is, in Equation (5.1) i's utility should be set out as a function of the utility of others as well as of the goods and services she receives. This is because she may care for other persons in society so that her utility is higher when some of these people receive an increased income, or she may care negatively about increases in goods going to others because she is envious of them, or dislikes some of them and so forth.

We shall measure the weight that i gives to increases in k's income by the amount i is willing to pay for the increase in k's income. (We could also measure this by the amount i is willing to accept to require k to forego an increase in income.) Suppose that we designate the weight, measured by i's willingness to pay, that i gives to changes in person k's income as W_{ki}. Thus, when person k's income increases by Y we shall say that person i's income changes by $W_{ki}(Y)$. There has been no change in i's money income but there has been a change in her income in the sense that her welfare has changed as a result of changes in k's welfare. If we were to express i's initial reaction to any income that k receives it would be

$$du_i = \sum_j \sum_k \frac{\partial U_i}{\partial Y_i} W_{ki} P_j \, dX_{kj} \tag{5.4}$$

In Equation (5.4) the income of k is valued by i. This is summed over all of the k persons 1 through n in society so that one of these persons in the summation is i herself. The weight i gives to her own income is set equal to 1. Equation (5.4), however, does not yet capture the full interdependence of i and k. It is not sufficient to just measure i's willingness to pay for the initial increase in k's income.

Consider for a moment that you are person i and that person k is someone that you care about, and also that person k in turn cares about you. In this situation, when person k's income increases there is also an increase in your satisfaction, and you are, in fact, willing to pay something for this increase in person k's income. This amount you are willing to pay is our measure of the value to you of the increase in k's income. The increase in your satisfaction resulting from person k's larger income in turn increases the satisfaction of person k, and this in turn increases your satisfaction, and so on. It is not sufficient, therefore, to introduce just the term W_{ki} that only measures your willingness to pay for k's initial increase in income. We must also take into account the secondary increases in your willingness to pay arising from increases in your satisfaction that arise from increases in k's satisfaction and so on. Fortunately, this interdependence effect reduces to a simple term in almost

ability to buy the Mazda at zero price). The WTP and the WTA may differ because your income situation is different in the two cases. The WTP is constrained by your income and also by the fact that your income is lower than for the WTA. In the case of the WTA you already have the Mazda and the value of the Mazda must be included as part of your real income. The fact

all cases.[1] As long as the weight that person i gives to changes in person k's income, W_{ki}, times the weight that person k gives to changes in i's income, W_{ik} is less than one, then the effect of the interdependence reduces to a simple "interdependence multiplier" that is equal to[2]

$$M_{ki} = \frac{1}{(1 - W_{ki}W_{ik})}$$

For example, if $W_{ki} = .5$ and $W_{ik} = .3$ then the interdependence multiplier is 1.18. That is, the effect of the interdependence is to increase i's total welfare change by 1.18 over the initial effect of a change in k's income on i. If we imagine that typical interdependence weights are small, say 0.1, then the multiplier is close to 1, or 1.01 in this case.

Suppose that k's income changes by \$100 and that i values this change at \$0.10 on the dollar, that is, $W_{ki} = 0.1$. In turn k values changes in i's income at 0.2. The initial effect of k's change in income on i is then \$100 times 0.1 or \$10, and the multiplier is 1.02, giving a total change on i's income of \$10.20.

Using the interdependence multiplier in conjunction with Equation (5.3) gives the change in i's utility resulting from a policy that can then be expressed as

$$du_i = \sum_k \sum_j \frac{\partial U_i}{\partial Y_i}(M_{ki})(W_{ki})(P_j \, dX_{kj}) \qquad (5.5)$$

This says that a change in i's utility that results from a policy action is the change in the quantity of the jth good going to person k, times the price of the jth good, times the weight that i gives to changes in the income of person k, times the interdependence multiplier, times the marginal utility of income for person i.

---

[1] For example, if your value increases in k's income at 1.5 times the increase in your own income, k must value increases in your income at 0.67 or more before the product of the two weights is greater than one.

[2] Person k's initial change in income is $P_j \delta X_{kj}$. Each dollar that person k receives is worth W_{ki} to person i in terms of i's willingness to pay for a change in person k's income change. Thus, person i's valuation of k's initial change in income will be $(W_{ki})P_j\delta X_{ij}$. In addition to this effect, there will be a string of second- and third-, etc., round effects that takes into account the fact that any increase in i's real income will lead in turn to a change in k's real income because k cares about i, which in turn leads to a further increase in i's income, etc. This leads to the following series of the terms:

$$(W_{ki})P_j\Delta X_{kj} + (W_{ki})P_j\Delta X_{kj}(W_{ik})(W_{ki})$$

$$+ (W_{ki})P_j\Delta X_{ij}[(W_{ik})(W_{ki})]^2 + \cdots + W_{ki}P_j\Delta X_{ij}[(W_{ik})(W_{ki})]^{n-1}$$

Via the formula for the summation of a multiplicative series this reduces to $(W_{ki}P_j\Delta X_{kj})$ (M_{ki}).

---

that you are richer in the case of the WTA question means that the value of additional money may be less. More money is required to represent the utility of the car.

The willingness to pay and the willingness to accept are measured by the *compensating variation* (CV) and *equivalent variation* (EV), respectively.

For a single individual the compensating and equivalent variations give an exact ordinal ranking of choices and are known as *exact utility indicators*. These measures may be approximated by *consumer* or *producer surplus*, which are the traditional measures of welfare change in benefit–cost analysis.

In benefit–cost analysis, the concepts of willingness to pay or accept, and the concepts of consumer and producer surplus, are the building blocks for determining the benefits and costs of alternative policies. It is empirical estimates of these concepts that are, in fact, added together to give total benefits and costs.

When prices do not change, the expression $\sum_j P_j \, dX_{ij}$ is just equal to the change in real income. The welfare measure of a straight change in income is, of course, just the change in income. With prices given, the minimum sum you would accept to forego $100 is just $100. The maximum sum you would pay to receive $100 is also $100.

When prices do change, the meaning of a change in income is less clear because the change in income will depend on which prices are used to measure income. A fall in the price of books changes your real income. But, by how much? Is the value of the change in books to be determined by using old or new prices or by some combination of old and new? We now turn to this problem.

5.3.1. The Problem

The central problem of benefit–cost analysis is that of choosing among alternatives on the basis of utility maximization. In this chapter we consider the choice problem for a single individual. The problem can be illustrated by Figure 5.1. Here we have indifference curves, U_1, U_2, and U_3, for individual 1. We wish to compare three bundles, X_1, X_2, and X_3, lying on these curves. The bundle X_2 is the initial point. There are alternative actions which can move individuals to either point X_1 on U_1 or X_3 on U_3. In benefit–cost analysis the question is, how do we value moves to these alternative positions? The answer is easy and unambiguous in the abstract. The value is given by the change in utility in moving from U_2 to U_3, or from U_2 to U_1. Can we measure these changes?

5.3.2. Cardinal Utility

Measurable utility is called *cardinal utility*. It does not exist except as an abstract concept since there is no agreed upon standard or method of measurement. Full cardinal utility requires that you be able to answer questions such as how much happier are you at the beach than in economics class, or even how much happier are you eating chocolate ice cream than is Sally at the beach. A cardinal measure of utility implies the ability to measure happiness across different activities and across different people. We have no measure to do this; certainly we have no agreed upon measure.

Consequently, in Figure 5.1 we have no way of measuring the magnitude of the utility change from position X_2 to X_3, or more generally, of measuring the utility change from one utility position to any other. Had we such a measure, economics would be quite a different science.

FIGURE 5.1   Three choices for $X - Y$ combinations.

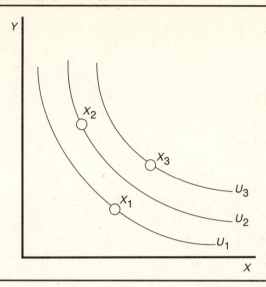

5.3.3.   Ordinal Utility

An ordinal measure of utility is one in which we can *rank* the utilities of different positions. An ordinal measure would allow us to say, with reference to Figure 5.1, that position 3 > position 2 > position 1 (where > reads "is preferred to"). The question is, can we in principle devise a measure that gives the correct ranking of the relative positions?

5.3.4.   The Equivalent Variation

Consider a single consumer h with a budget line BB that is just tangent to U_2 at point 2. Such a line is drawn in Figure 5.2. The consumer wishes to compare the utility on U_2 with the utility on U_1 and U_3. Now consider budget lines CC and AA parallel to BB and just tangent to U_3 and U_1, respectively. The order in which the budget lines cross the axis necessarily gives an ordinal measure that correctly ranks the three alternative positions. *This is because each budget line is parallel and is just tangent to an alternative indifference curve, so that one budget line will lie above another only if the utility curve to which it is tangent lies above the utility curve to which the lower budget line is tangent.* Thus, the relative position of budget lines parallel to the original budget line and tangent to respective indifference curves gives a ranking of alternative positions. The vertical difference between parallel budget lines can be measured by, for example, the income differences as measured along the y axis. Thus, budget line BB is higher than AA by the income difference BA. The budget line BB is lower than CC by the distance CB. If relative prices are the same at positions 1, 2, and 3 on U_1, U_2, and U_3 so that all lie also on the parallel budget lines, the vertical distance between these budget lines represents the income differences, the $P_j \, dX_{ij}$ of Equation (5.3), when prices do not change. That is, for positions 1, 2, and 3 the distances

FIGURE 5.2   The equivalent variation.

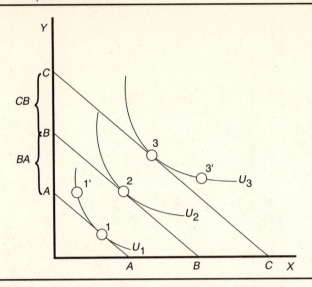

BA and *CB* represent just the income changes, the measure of the welfare change.

Suppose, however, one is attempting to compare positions as 1′, 2, and 3′ on U_1, U_2, and U_3 for which relative prices are different. Positions 1′ and 3′ indicate the same utility levels as positions 1 and 3. Thus the difference in the parallel budget lines *AA*, *BB*, and *CC* will also rank the utility level of the positions 1′, 2, and 3′.

The differences between indifference curves measured by parallel budget lines reflecting original prices are called *equivalent variations* (EVs), and they belong to a class known as *exact utility indicators* because they give an exact ranking of alternative positions for a single individual.

The EV is the money which, in the absence of the suggested change, will give the individual the same level of welfare as would the suggested change. We might speak of the decrease in new car prices that would follow from a tariff decrease. In the absence of a change in the tariff and the price decrease, you can imagine a sum of money that could be given that would leave your utility level the same as if the price decrease occurred. This sum of money is the EV.

Similarly, we might consider the increase in the price of new cars that would follow a tariff increase. In the absence of the tariff and price increase, there is a sum of money you could give up that would leave you just as well or as poorly off as if the price increase had occurred. Again this sum is the EV.

Another way to interpret the EV is to note that it is the income one would accept to forego the benefits of a price decrease. Similarly, it is the income one would pay to avoid a price increase. The EV assumes one has the right to the price decrease but has no right to avoid the price increase. In Figure 5.3, suppose there is a price decrease for good X for individual *h*. The price decrease

FIGURE 5.3   Equivalent variation for a price decrease.

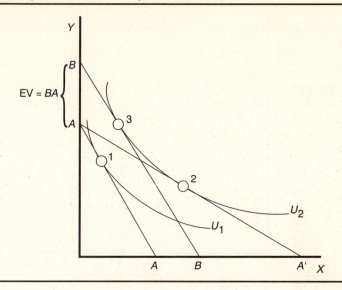

rotates AA to AA' and moves the consumer from point 1 on indifference curve U_1 to point 2 on indifference curve U_2. The EV is determined by drawing a new budget line, BB, parallel to the original one, AA, and tangent to U_2. The difference in the incomes represented by AA and BB is measured by BA, which is the EV. This is the income individual h would accept in lieu of the price decrease. With this income, he would be just as well off as with the price decrease to budget line AA'. (The student should work out the EV geometry for a price increase.)

5.3.5.   The Compensating Variation

The equivalent variation is not the only measure of the difference in indifference curves. The vertical difference between indifference curves generally varies at different points along the curves. Thus, a measure of the ranking of indifference curves will depend on the prices used to make the measure. There is, then, an infinite number of measured differences in indifference curves because there is an infinite number of budget lines that could be used to compare the two indifference curves. The EV is a natural measure because it uses original prices and has an intuitive interpretation.

Another natural measure is the *compensating variation*. When final prices are used to measure the distance between indifference curves, the measure of the distance between indifference curves is called the *compensating variation* (CV). Although other measures could be devised, the EV and CV are the most useful in practical terms because they have a natural interpretation in terms of willingness to pay or accept welfare changes.

Consider Figure 5.4, in which a price decrease rotates budget line AA to AA' and moves the consumer from point 1 on U_1 to point 2 on U_2. The CV

FIGURE 5.4   The compensating variaton.

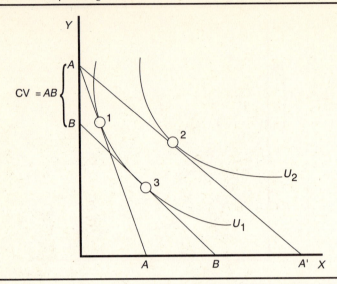

measures the distance between the indifference curves measured in *final* prices. Thus we draw *BB* parallel to *AA'*. The difference between *AA'* and *BB* is *AB*, which is the CV. *The CV is the money transfer which, following some economic change, would leave you as well off as before the change. The CV is the sum of money the consumer would pay to have a price decrease.* That is, the CV is the sum of money that could be taken from *h* after the price change and leave *h* as well off as before the change. *In the case of a price increase, the CV is similarly the sum of money the consumer would accept to tolerate the price increase.* That is, the CV is the sum of money that could be given to *h* that would leave *h* just as well off as if the price had not increased. The CV will also give a correct ordinal ranking of utility changes as long as alternatives are compared *pairwise*. No such restriction is necessary for the EV. (See Technical Note 5B.) The CV is measured using final prices.

5.3.6.   The EV and CV for Interdependent Utilities

Earlier we indicated that the welfare of individual *i* is a function of both the goods and services she receives and of the utility of others. We have shown the EV and the CV of *i* for goods and services. The EV or CV of *i* can also be shown for income received by others. Suppose that *i* cares positively about *k*. In Figure 5.5 the horizontal axis shows *k*'s income, the indifference curves reflect points of indifference for *i* between his own and *k*'s income, and position *E* shows the initial equilibrium between the budget line *MN* and *i*'s indifference curve reflecting the amount *i* gives to *k*. Suppose now that the cost of giving to *k* decreases so that the budget line rotates to *MN'* with a new equilibrium at *E'*. The distance *MA* shows *i*'s CV, and the distance *MB* shows *i*'s EV.

FIGURE 5.5   CV and EV for interdependent utilities.

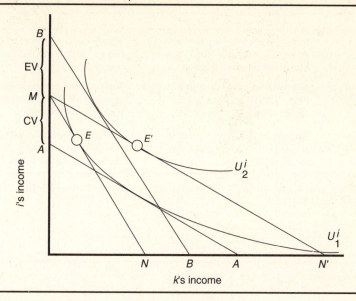

5.3.7.   The Relationship of the CV and EV

Table 5.1 summarizes the EV and CV measures. The CV for a price decrease from A to B is equal in magnitude, but of opposite sign, to the EV for a price increase from B to A. In Figure 5.6, we show again on the same graph the equivalent and compensating variations. The consumer is initially at equilibrium at point 1 with budget line AA. The price of X decreases and a new equilibrium is reached along U_2 at 2. The EV for a move from 1 to 2 is found by increasing the consumer income at the *original* price until the new income is sufficient to attain the utility level associated with the lower price. The new budget line parallel to the original budget line and tangent to U_2 is BB. This gives an EV of BA.

The CV for a price increase moving the consumer from 2 to 1 is measured at *final* prices and will be AB. This is equal in magnitude but opposite in sign (BA is positive, AB is negative) to the EV for the move from 1 to 2.

For a price decrease, then, the CV is the amount the consumer would *pay* (the willingness to pay) to have the change. The EV is the amount the consumer would accept to forego the change. For a price increase, the CV is the amount the consumer would *accept* to put up with the price increase. The EV is the amount the consumer would pay to avoid it.

For a price fall, the size of the CV is bounded by the initial income; it is the amount the consumer could pay. There is no such limitation for the EV for a price fall. The most the CV could be for a price fall starting with a budget of M_1 is M_1. For a normal good, then, the EV will exceed the CV for a price fall because the EV measure starts from a higher base utility in which the marginal utility of income is lower than for the CV. This is reversed for a price increase and the absolute value of the CV will be greater than the absolute value of the EV.

TABLE 5.1

	Compensating Variation	*Equivalent Variation*
	Money which can be taken or given to leave one as well off as before the economic change	Money taken or given that leaves one as well off as after the economic change
Welfare gain (benefit)	Amount he would be willing to pay (WTP) for the change (finite—limited by his income)	Amount he would be willing to accept (WTA) to forego the change (could be infinite)
Welfare loss (cost)	Amount he would be willing to accept (WTA) as compensation for the change (could be infinite)	Amount he would be willing to pay (WTP) to avert the change (finite—limited by income)

SOURCE: Adapted from R. Layard and A. A. Walters, *Microeconomic Theory,* McGraw Hill: New York, 1978, pp. 150–152.

FIGURE 5.6   Relation of the CV and EV to each other.

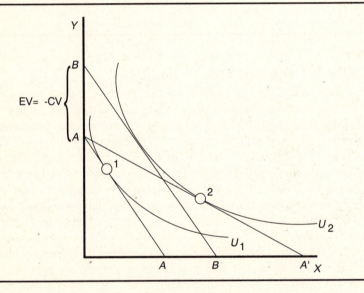

For a price fall, the CV assumes the consumer has no "right" to the price decrease and must purchase it. The EV assumes the consumer has a right to the decrease and must be bribed to give up the right. Where the right is very valuable so that initial utility levels are quite different, the difference in the EV and CV can be great. Respecting your right to life, the honest murderer asks, how much must I pay you (i.e., what would you *accept*) to be allowed to shoot you? The robber-murderer, however, asks, what sum will you pay for me not to shoot you? The unconstrained sum is larger than the constrained sum. The income effect is quite large because where there is the right to life the utility level is much higher than where there is no such right.

5.4.   THE COMPENSATED DEMAND CURVE

It is useful to relate the EV and CV to demand curves. For this purpose we introduce the Hicksian demand curve. *The ordinary (or Marshallian) demand curve gives quantities demanded at various prices holding income constant with utility varied.* In contrast, the Hicksian demand curve gives quantities demanded at various prices by holding *utility* constant and by letting income vary. In Figure 5.7, D_0 is the ordinary (Marshallian) demand curve. The curves H_1 and H_2 are the compensated Hicksian demand curves corresponding to the EV and CV.[3] The compensated demand curve H_1 is derived by beginning with an initial utility and an initial level of money income that is the same as for the ordinary demand curve at point 1. As price falls along the Hicksian curve, income is taken away to maintain the level of utility. The amount taken away is the CV. Fewer goods will be purchased along a Hicksian than a Marshallian demand curve for a given price drop, assuming the product is a normal good, because income is removed to hold utility constant in deriving the compensated demand curve, while it is not taken away along the ordinary demand curve.

The Hicksian curve H_2 corresponds to the EV for a price fall. Along the curve the consumer is given money income to forego the price decrease. The additional money income means the consumer will purchase more goods than along an ordinary demand curve.

FIGURE 5.7   Compensated and Marshallian demand curve.

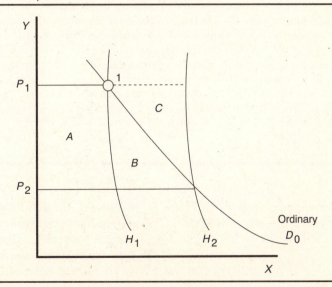

[3]A geometric proof that the areas inside the compensated demand curves are the EV and CV is furnished by Richard Just, et al., (1982). For an expression of the relationship, see Technical Note 5B.

TECHNICAL NOTE 5B
EV, CV, and Consumer Surplus

In Figure 5.8, the consumer is initially in equilibrium at price P_1. This established a point, point a, on both the Hicksian and Marshallian curves shown. Let the price decrease to P_2. The consumer equilibrium moves to b and this establishes another point, point b, on the *ordinary* demand curve D_0 at P_2X_2. The Hicksian demand curve H_1 corresponding to the CV for a price decrease going through point a is generated by determining the quantity purchased at each price, by adjusting income so that the consumer remains on the same indifference curve. For the price reduction to P_2 a compensating variation of $Y_0 - Y_1$ must be subtracted to keep the consumer on U_1. As long as X is a normal good, this reduction in income means the consumer will purchase less than if the price is reduced without subtracting income as is done with the ordinary demand curve. For a normal good then the fact that income must be subtracted as price falls to keep the consumer on the same indifference curve U_1 means that H_1 will be within D_0. The equilibrium of the income-adjusted budget line with the assigned indifference curve U_1 at c results in purchase of X_3, which is less than purchases of X_2 for which income is now adjusted. (The move from a to c represents a price substitution response to the relative price change.) The area behind H_1 is labeled A and is the CV. The area behind the ordinary demand curve is labeled $A + B$.

The analysis is similar for the EV. The compensated demand curve corresponding to the EV is H_2 and holds utility constant at U_2. Point b represents the consumer's original position in terms of the EV calculation. The budget line Y_0Y_0 for the EV reflecting price P_1 lies above the budget line for the CV Y_1Y_1 also reflecting price P_1. The budget line for the EV reflects the additional income required to achieve utility level U_2 rather than utility level U_1. This income is $Y_3 - Y_0$, which is the EV. Because the compensated demand curve H_2 reflects the higher income corresponding to the utility level U_2, the curve H_2 lies above the curve H_1 for a normal good. Also, H_2 will lie above the ordinary demand curve for a normal good until price P_2 is reached, because at P_2 the ordinary demand curve also reflects utility level U_2. In Figure 5.8b the EV is shown by $A + B + C$. Figure 5.9 shows the EV, CV, and CS in separate panels.

For a price drop from P_1 to P_2 the CV is area A. The EV for the price drop is indicated by area $A + B + C$. The relationship between the CV and the EV is shown again in Figure 5.8 (see Technical Note 5B). For a normal good, then, the Hicksian compensated variation for a price reduction must be entirely inside the ordinary demand curve. (A normal good is one with a positive income effect.) Again this is because the Hicksian demand curve associated with U_1 removes income from the consumer as price is reduced.

For a price reduction from P_1 to P_2 there is a Hicksian compensated demand curve associated with the EV, which corresponds to holding utility constant at original prices at the final utility level U_2 rather than the initial level U_1. In Figure 5.8 this is the curve H_2 (U_2). The consumer facing price P_1 must

FIGURE 5.8   CV, EV, and compensated demand curves.

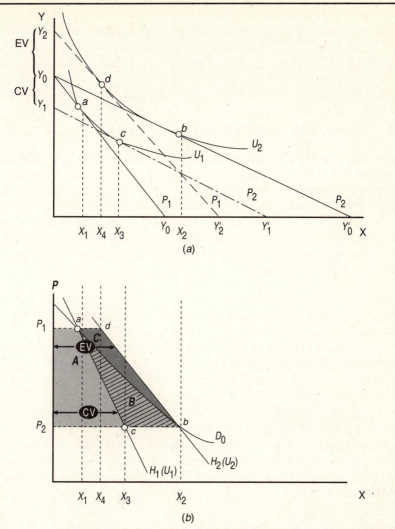

(a)

(b)

be given an amount $Y_2 - Y_0$ to forego the price decrease to P_2. This is the EV. There is a positive income effect (for a normal good), and the consumer will purchase more than without the income adjustment. The Hicksian compensated demand curve corresponding to the EV for a price reduction will then lie entirely outside the ordinary demand curve for a normal good.

What is the compensated demand curve corresponding to the CV for a price *increase* from P_2 to P_1? Initially, the consumer is at point b, which lies on both the ordinary demand curve and on the compensated demand curve H_2. When the price increases to P_1, $Y_2 - Y_0$ is the amount of income or compensating variation that must be given to keep the consumer at the initial utility U_2. The consumer given $Y_2 - Y_0$ will purchase X_4 units and again point d represents a point on the compensated demand curve H_2. Here $H_2(U_2)$ corresponds to the

CV. Again, for a normal good the income effect is positive and the consumer's purchases will be greater than that shown by the ordinary demand curve when he does not receive compensation for the price increase. You will recall that the CV for a price increase is equal to the negative of the EV for a similar price decrease. Thus, the H_2 curve corresponds to the EV for a price decrease or the CV for a price increase. Similarly the H_1 curve corresponds to the CV for a price decrease and to the EV for a price increase. (See Technical Note 5C.)

5.5. CONSUMER AND PRODUCER SURPLUS

The willingness to pay or accept as measured by the compensating and equivalent variations is the correct theoretical measure for welfare changes. However, in practice, the measures are difficult to obtain since deriving compensated demand curves requires holding utility levels constant. Ordinary demand curves in which income is held constant are more likely to be available and are, therefore, more likely to be used. Welfare measures associated with ordinary demand curves that approximate the compensating and equivalent variations are called *consumer and producer surpluses*.

5.5.1. Consumer Surplus

Consumer surplus is approximately the amount one would pay for the good, over what one does pay, rather than do without the good.

Consumer surplus (CS) is the usual measure of welfare change in benefit–cost analysis. It approximates the exact utility indicators, the CV and EV. The CS is represented by the area beneath the ordinary demand curve, but above the price. In Figure 5.9, D_0 is an ordinary demand curve for individual h, and P_0 is the price. Area A is the consumer surplus. The consumer actually pays P_0 per unit of the good for a total payment of P_0Q_0 represented by area B. If confronted by a choice of paying $A + B$ for Q_0 units or doing without Q_0 altogether, individual h would pay $A + B$ but no more. Since individual h in fact must pay only B for Q_0, area A remains as consumer surplus. (See Technical Note 5D.)

FIGURE 5.9 Consumer surplus.

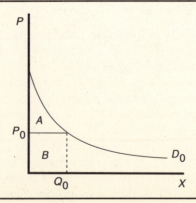

TECHNICAL NOTE 5C
Expenditure Functions

Much of modern welfare theory is expressed in terms of an expenditure function. The cost of securing a level of utility U^0 where other prices P_2^0 are constant and the price of good 1 is P_1^0 is expressed by $C(P_1^0, P_2^0, U^0)$. This is known as an *expenditure function*. The CV is the income needed to obtain the intended utility level at the original price minus the income needed to achieve the intended utility level after the price change. This measure is given by

$$CV = C[P_1^0, P_2^0, U^0)] - C[(P_1^1, P_2^0, U^0)]$$

for a price decrease $P_1^0 > P_1^1$ so that CV > 0.

Another expression for the CV equation where there is a single price change from P_1^0 to P_1^1 is

$$CV = \int_{P_1^1}^{P_1^0} \frac{\partial C}{\partial P_1}(P_1^0, P_2^0, U^0)\, dP_1$$

That is, the CV is the sum of the quantities along the compensated demand curve as the price varies between P_1^0 and P_1^1.

The EV is the income needed to achieve the final level of utility U^1 with prices at their original level, minus the income needed to achieve the final utility level after the price changes. The EV for the price change for P_1^0 to P_1^1 is

$$EV = C[P_1^0, P_2^0, U^1] - C[P_1^1, P_2^0, U^1]$$

and expressed as an integral is

$$EV = \int_{P_1^1}^{P_1^0} \frac{\partial C}{\partial P_1}(P_1^0, P_2^0, U^1)\, dP_1$$

Again, the above indicates the EV is the area behind the corresponding compensated demand curve.

The above equations make it clear that the only difference between the CV and the EV is the level of utility at which the cost difference is evaluated. The CV is concerned with the original utility level, the EV with the final utility level.

In a move from position 1 to position 2 the initial utility level is designated U^1 and the final level U^2, but in a move from position 2 to 1 the initial utility level is U^2. Since the CV is evaluated at the initial utility level and the EV at the final utility level, the CV for a move from position 1 to 2 must equal the absolute value of the EV for a move from position 2 to 1. (The student should write out these expressions so that this is clear.)

TECHNICAL NOTE 5D
Consumer Surplus

In the diagram a consumer has income of Y_0 and purchases X_1 units of good X achieving indifference curve U_1. There will also be an indifference curve U_0 going through Y_0 and representing the consumer's initial level of utility before purchasing X. The consumer actually spends $Y_0 - Y_1$ to achieve U_1 and buy X_1. If the consumer spent $Y_0 - Y_2$ for X_1 units he would remain on the original indifference curve U_0. The amount $Y_0 - Y_2$ is, then, the amount the consumer would pay rather than give up X_1 altogether. The amount $Y_0 - Y_1$ is the amount the consumer must pay to buy X_1. The difference is $[(Y_0 - Y_2) - (Y_0 - Y_1)] = Y_1 - Y_2$, and is consumer surplus. The expression for producer surplus is similar but for workers can be more complex. (See Just et al., 1982.)

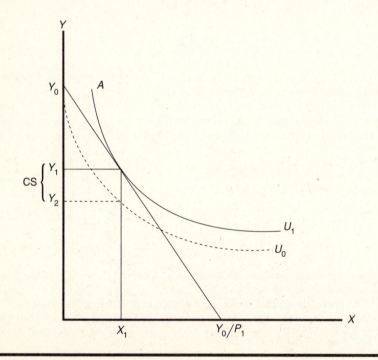

The relations between CS and the EV and CV for a price decrease are shown in Figures 5.8 and 5.10.

The curves H_1 (U_1) and H_2 (U_2) are compensated demand curves. H_1 (U_1) corresponds to utility level U_1, the level before the price decrease. H_2 (U_2) corresponds to the utility level after the price decrease. The CV is given by area A in Figure 5.8(b) and the EV will be area $A + B + C$. The line D_0 is the ordinary demand curve. It goes through points a and b or H_1 and H_2. The CS is area $A + B$, the area between the prices along the ordinary demand curve. For a derivation of CS, see Technical Note 5D and the accompanying diagram.

FIGURE 5.10   Relation between EV, CV, and CS.

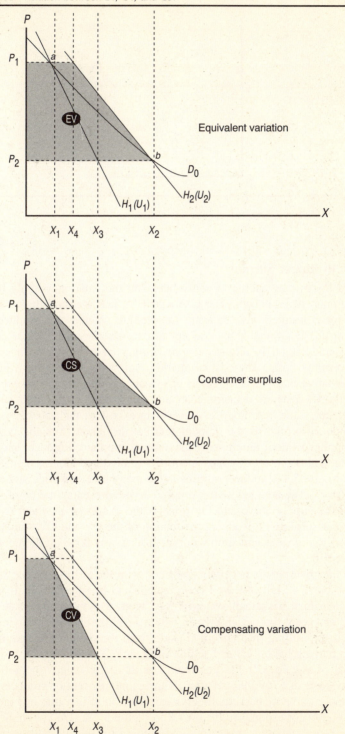

FIGURE 5.11   Producer surplus.

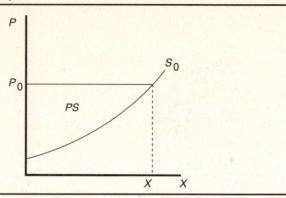

5.5.2. Producer Surplus

Gains or losses may accrue to consumers, but they also may apply to suppliers of inputs, to producers. The CVs and EVs that measure the welfare gain or loss for consumers also measure the welfare changes for producers. *Producer surplus* is an analogous concept to consumer surplus. Producer surplus is easily understood in relation to *opportunity cost*. All costs in economics are opportunity costs. The cost of attending class Tuesday is the value of the best alternative that you have given up. Costs are thus always associated with decisions. All costs are decision costs and opportunity costs. Producer surplus is a payment value that producers receive in excess of their costs.

Producer surplus is the amount that can be taken from the producer or input supplier without diminishing the amount supplied. Producer surplus (PS) is measured along a supply curve just as CS is measured along a demand curve. Thus in Figure 5.11 producer surplus is the area *below* the price and above the supply curve. The area below the supply curve represents total costs. The area between the supply curve and the price is the excess of payment over costs, or producer surplus. PS is an approximation of the EV and CV which can also be related to compensated supply curves just as was done on the demand side in Figure 5.8.

Producer surplus is normally identified with the term *economic rent*. Suppose you are $7'4''$ tall, are well coordinated, and like basketball. If you don't play professional basketball you will, say, work as an insurance salesman for $30,000 per year. You can, however, obtain $800,000 per year playing basketball. You like selling insurance and aside from the money you are indifferent between playing basketball and selling insurance. You would play professional basketball if it paid $30,001 per year. The $800,000 minus the $30,001 opportunity cost, or $769,999 per year, is the economic rent or producer surplus. Your supply curve of basketball services would look like that in Figure 5.12. The $769,999 corresponds to the area R in Figure 5.12. (Do you think attempts by owners of competing teams to avoid bidding for players will be influenced by the size of the economic rent?)

FIGURE 5.12   Economic rent.

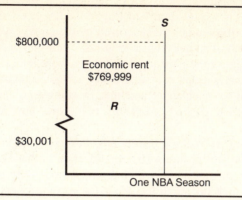

One NBA Season

5.5.3   Profit and Producer Surplus

Changes in profits of supplying firms are often equal to changes in production surplus or are good proxies for such changes. The firm's profit is $\pi = $ TR $-$ TVC $-$ TFC, where TR is total revenues, TVC is total variable cost, and TFC is total fixed cost. Producer surplus is TR$-$TVC. Thus producer surplus exceeds profit by total fixed costs. Except for plant closings or expansion TFC does not change, thus changes in profits are equal to changes in producer surplus. Changes in profit, and thus producer surplus, are equal to changes in total revenue minus changes in variable cost. Thus changes in producer surplus are normally equal to changes in revenues minus changes in variable costs.

5.6.   HOW ACCURATE IS CS AS AN APPROXIMATION OF THE EVs AND CVs?

Since the work of J. R. Hicks in the 1940s, it has been known that the EV or CV was the proper measure of welfare changes. However, information was generally available to determine only ordinary demand curves and the associated consumer surpluses. This information was thought insufficient to determine compensated demand curves. The question became, what did consumer surpluses measure?

The concept of consumer surplus originated in 1884 with Jules Dupuis was publicized by Alfred Marshall, and has been controversial ever since. Paul Samuelson concluded that "consumer surplus is a worse than useless concept...," and I. M. D. Little later referred to consumer surplus as "little more than a theoretical toy."

It is well known that the amount of consumer surplus is "path dependent." That is, the magnitude of consumer surplus will depend on *which* price is varied first, and in a case where money income is varied as well, whether price or income is first varied. Even for a single price change there are income effects and a path-dependency problem. The CV and EV, however, are not path dependent.

In spite of criticisms, benefit–cost analysts and some theorists persisted in their use of consumer surplus. This perspective was justified. In 1976,

Robert Willig, in a path-breaking effort, showed that under ordinary conditions, consumer surplus is a good approximation of the EV or CV and that the error of approximation will often be overshadowed by the errors involved in estimating the demand curves. The question is then how well do consumer and producer surpluses approximate the EV and CV? Willig's work indicates that for ordinary cases the consumer surplus is a sufficiently accurate approximation regardless of the path used to calculate it and that in any event, the EV and CV can be well estimated if desired. Appendix 6A shows how Willig's results can be used.

As important as Willig's results are, however, they are applicable only with a significant qualification. This qualification is that Willig's results, even when he allows for multiple price changes, are not fully general equilibrium results because they do not fully allow for income effects. (This important qualification is not always recognized.) We discuss a full general equilibrium approach in Chapter 21.

SUMMARY

Within this chapter we analyzed the conceptual nature of benefits and costs, a useful step in performing any sort of policy analysis. We discussed the problems of measuring welfare changes for a *single* individual and developed a welfare function for such an individual using Equation (5.3). This equation measures changes in an individual's utility based on the individual's marginal utility of income and income effects resulting from changes in prices of all goods and services.

We then acknowledged that an individual cares for the utility of others as well as the goods and services she receives. In the technical notes, we developed an "interdependence multiplier" to account for such interdependent utility measures. We went on to introduce the concepts of *willingness to pay* and *willingness to accept* which may be measured by the compensating and equivalent variation (CV and EV). In explaining these concepts we introduced *compensated demand curves*. Because utility is impossible to measure, we used the CV and EV to establish an exact, ordinal ranking of utility.

To simplify utility measurement further, we noted that the CV and EV may be approximated by estimates of consumer and producer surplus. These are the traditional measures of welfare changes in benefit–cost analysis. In the following chapter we will discuss techniques to assess changes in welfare for *many* individuals and to develop a broader, social welfare function.

QUESTIONS AND PROBLEMS

1. Mr. James used to shop at Tradewell and at Safeway for groceries. Now he only shops at Tradewell. The store management convinced Mr. James that he was better off shopping at Tradewell through a demonstration project that showed to Mr. James' satisfaction that Tradewell is cheaper than Safeway. In this project Mr. James was just leaving Tradewell with a bag of groceries. Tradewell management examined the bag and offered Mr. James $1,000 if the *same* market basket of goods was cheaper at Safeway. It turned out that the basket of goods was not cheaper at Safeway so that Tradewell was able to keep its $1000 and Mr. James and many others were convinced that Tradewell was the cheaper store.

You are hired by Safeway to show that Mr. James would have been better off (*hint:* more consumer surplus) shopping at Safeway. You determine that all nonprice services and attributes are the same at the two stores.

a. Explain how it might be that Safeway is right?
b. For simplicity assume only three goods are involved at the two stores, meat, fruit, and canned goods, and that Mr. James's demand curve for all three goods is as follows:

Price	Quantity
$10	1
9	2
8	3

Prices at the two stores are as follows:

	Meat	Fruit	Canned Goods
Tradewell	10	8	10
Safeway	8	10	8

c. Calculate the consumer surplus for Mr. James for shopping at the two stores. At which store does Mr. James have a higher consumer surplus?

2. Can you think of empirical evidence consistent with the independence multiplier not being infinite?

3. Consider a policy that increases records for Don and increases books for Dick. That is, Don will obtain 2 records and Dick will gain 5 books. Records are $4 apiece while books are $8 each. Suppose, however, that Don cares negatively about Dick's income. Don's marginal utility of income is 2 and Dick's is 4. Suppose also that Don gives income going to Dick a weight of minus 1 (-0.2) while Dick gives no weight to changes in Don's income.

a. What will be the effect of the policy change on Don's utility?
b. Suppose that Dick gains 5 books and Don gains 2 records, but that Don weights Dick's utility by a negative 0.5, what would be the effect of the policy on Don's utility?
c. What if Don's negative weight for Dick's utility were greater than 1. How would this effect Don's utility from policies giving Dick and Don the same income?
d. Suppose that Don negatively weights increases in Dick's income but that Dick positively weights increases in Don's income. (1) Would the interdependence multiplier be greater or less than 1? (2) Is it possible that an increase in Don's income would make Don worse off while making Dick better off? If so, make up an example that illustrates this.

REFERENCES

Hicks, John R., "The Four Consumer Surpluses," *Review of Economic Studies* 11(1), 31–41, Winter, 1943.

Just, Richard, et al., *Applied Welfare Economics and Public Policy,* Englewood Cliffs, N.J.: Prentice-Hall, 1982.

Mishan, E. J., et al., *Cost-Benefit Analysis: An Informal Introduction* (third edition), London: George Allen & Unwin, 1984.

Willig, Robert D., "Consumer's Surplus Without Apology," *American Economic Review* 66(4), 589–597, September 1976.

6

The Measurement of Aggregate Welfare Changes

6.1. INTRODUCTION

The previous chapter introduced the concepts of equivalent and compensating variations (EV and CV) and their proxy, consumer surplus (CS). These concepts were applied to determine the welfare ranking of a single individual. The economic approach is very powerful in considering the welfare position of a single individual. The EV and the CV give an exact ordinal ranking of choices on a utility basis. Utility itself and goods and services are defined broadly to cover all choices so the economic approach gives a sort of *deus ex machina* decision criterion. In addition, the EV and the CV can be derived from ordinary demand curve data, or the EV and CV can be reasonably approximated by CS. However, policy questions do not generally concern only a single individual.

6.2. THE AGGREGATION PROBLEM

A central problem of any social welfare or social value theory, including benefit–cost analysis, is the problem of aggregation over individuals. Once we have calculated Robert's and Alice's CVs and EVs we need to decide how each is to be weighted.

Economic efficiency is consistent with many different utility and income distributions. In a policy sense, the Pareto requirements for efficiency are consistent with different assignments of rights among individuals or groups. So, the problem of locating the optimal point on the utility frontier is a problem of social choice and individual and social justice.

The sad fact is that the aggregations of CVs or EVs over several individuals, unlike the CVs or EVs for one person, have no meaning as indicators of ordinal utility, unless we are willing to make additional and restrictive assumptions. That is, suppose project A shows a CV for Robert's Plotnick of +5 and for Alice's Rivlin of −2, for a total of +3. Suppose project B shows a CV for Alice of +4 and a CV for Robert of −2 for a net total of +2. It is not possible to say whether project A or B is superior without a scheme to compare Robert's and Alice's CVs. That is, the net total of +3 for project A and the net total of +2 for project B are net totals of what? They are income measures that when broken apart into the CV for Alice and the CV for Bob serve to rank Alice's and Bob's choices, but when the CVs of Bob and Alice are combined they do not rank their choices. Robert's and Alice's CVs are not measured in units of utility. Rather, they only indicate ordinal ranking for the individuals. Alice's CV of +4 in project B may yield her much more satisfaction than Robert's CV of +5 in project A. Any solution or approach to comparing the welfare of different individuals must clearly and directly involve ethical choices.

6.3. THE SOCIAL WELFARE FUNCTION

Economists approach the social choice problem by postulating a *social welfare* function. A very general function is one called a Samuelson-Bergson welfare function. The social welfare function is a decision rule for making choices in which the welfare of more than one person or household is affected. To begin at a general level, consider social welfare as a function of the utilities of the individuals in society, where we suppose temporarily that these utilities are measurable:

$$W = W(U_1, U_2, \ldots, U_N) \tag{6.1}$$

Equation (6.1) shows social welfare W as a function of the utilities of N different individuals. Mathematically, a change in welfare is found by totally differentiating Equation (6.1) to give a change in welfare:

$$dW = \sum_{i=1}^{N} \frac{\partial W}{\partial U_i} dU_i \tag{6.2}$$

This says that a change in social welfare (dW) is given by the change in the ith person's utility (dU_i) multiplied by the weight given the ith person's utility ($\partial W/\partial U_i$), and that this is summed over all N persons. The weight given the ith person's utility in the social welfare function is called the *marginal social utility* of i or the MSU_i. It was unnecessary to consider this term when we were interested in only one person's welfare since by definition that $MSU_i = 1$.

We already have an expression for a change in one person's utility, person i, from Chapter 5. It is necessary now only to let person i be any person in the society and to incorporate the expression for a change in i's welfare from Chapter 5, as expressed in Equation (5.3), into Equation (6.1). This gives

$$dW = \sum_j \sum_i \frac{\partial W}{\partial U_i} \frac{\partial U}{\partial Y_i} P_j \, dX_{ij} \tag{6.3}$$

WELFARE WITH INTERDEPENDENT UTILITY

To take into account interdependent utility effects as shown in Technical Note 5A, the equivalent to Equation (6.3) is

$$dW = \sum_j \sum_k \sum_i \frac{\partial W}{\partial U_i} \frac{\partial U}{\partial Y_i} (M_{ki})(W_{ki}) P_j \, dX_{kj} \qquad (6.3a)$$

The last term, $P_j dX_{kj}$, represents the income going to person k. Second, there is i's increase in satisfaction (measured by WTP or WTA) from increases in income going to person k. The terms $(M_{ki})(W_{ki})$ (see Technical Note 5A for definitions) in conjunction with $P_j \, dX_{kj}$ capture this. When person k is in fact person i, the term $P_j \, dX_{kj}$ represents the income going directly to person i, and the terms $(M_{ki})(W_{ki})$ are 1 since this is the weight i gives to herself.

In Equation (6.3), the summation sign that applies to person i requires every person in the society to be person i in turn, unlike Equation (5.3) in Chapter 5. That is, the income change for each person (person i) is measured by the CV or EV value, and this is converted into utility units by multiplying by i's marginal utility of income, and then these utility units are weighted by the marginal social utility of person i $\partial W/\partial U_i$. These values are summed over all of the affected X_j goods and over all of the i and k persons. (We could imagine that interdependence of utility effects might also be captured through the MSU_1 term, rather than as shown in the boxed materials.)

Reading the right-hand side, the last term in Equation (6.3) represents the change in income as measured by the CV or the EV. The income change for person i consists first of the income going directly to person i which is shown by $P_j \, dX_{ij}$. The income value of the change to individual i is now weighted by i's marginal utility of money, $\partial U_i/\partial Y_i$. Finally, the change in i's utility is weighted by the marginal social utility of i. These effects are summed over all persons i and over all k persons and also over all j goods.

To see how Equation (6.3) works, suppose that a policy increases goods going to Don and Dick so that Don's CV value of the goods going to him is $100 and Dick's valuation of the goods that he receives directly is $50. Suppose further that both Don and Dick have a marginal utility of income of 1 and a marginal social utility weight of 1. The increase in Don's utility will be the $50 CV that he receives initially times Don's marginal utilty of income (MUY) to give 50 in utils. These 50 utils are then multiplied by Don's MSU to contribute 50 social welfare units. The $100 that Dick receives is multiplied by his marginal utility of income of 1 and by his MSU which is also to contribute 100 units to social welfare. The total addition to social welfare would then be 150 units.

AN INTERDEPENDENT UTILITY EXAMPLE

The above example in an interdependent utility context requires that we specify the interdependent weights. Suppose that Don weighs a change in Dick's income by 0.1 and Dick weighs an increase in Don's income by 0.2 so that the interdependence multiplier would be just 1.02.

The increase in Don's income will be first the $50 CV that he receives initially. But Don will also be affected by the fact that Dick values Don's change in income. This effect can be combined with the first direct increase in Don's income by multiplying by the interdependence multiplier to give $51 as an income measure of Don's welfare change. This is multiplied by Don's MUY to give 51 in utils, and by the social utility of Don which is also 1 to contribute 51 in social welfare units.

The $100 that Dick receives is valued by Don as $100 × 0.1 or $10 in income. When multiplied by the interdependence multiplier and converted to utility units the $10 income measure of welfare change is worth 10.2 utils to Don. So Don's welfare change is 51 plus 10.2 or 61.2 utils. When multiplied by Don's MSU of 1 the contribution will be 61.2 in units of social welfare.

Similarly, the $100 that Dick receives is worth $102 or 102 utils to himself when the effect on Don is considered, and the $50 that Don receives is worth 10.2 utils to Dick (10 units directly and 0.2 unit through the interdependence multiplier). Dick's gain is then 112.2 utils. This is multiplied by 1 to give a contribution to society of 61.2 plus 112.2 for a total gain of 173.4 in social welfare units. Notice that the social gain when interdependent utilities are taken into account is about 16 percent higher than when they are not taken into account. (Is this reasonable?)

For convenience we will give symbols for the following terms:

$$\text{Marginal utility of } i\text{'s income} = \pi_i$$
$$\text{Marginal social utility of } i \text{ (MSU}_i) = \theta_i$$

This allows us to rewrite Equation (6.3) as

$$dW = \sum_i \sum_j \theta_i \pi_i P_j \, dX_{ij} \tag{6.4}$$

Equation (6.4) can in turn be rewritten as Equation (6.5):

$$dW = \sum \sum P_j \, dX_{ij} + \sum \sum (\theta_i \pi_i - 1) P_j \, dX_{ij} \tag{6.5}$$

By adding together the two terms of Equation (6.5), the student will see that it is the same as Equation (6.4), which is in turn the same as Equation (6.3). Equation (6.5) expresses the change in welfare as the sum of an efficiency effect ($P_j \, dX_{ij}$) and a distribution effect [$(\theta_i \pi_i - 1) P_j \, dX_{ij}$]. Equation (6.5) says that a change in welfare is given by the changes in the incomes (the efficiency effect), plus the distribution effect in which changes in income are weighted by the individual's marginal utility of income (π_i), and finally by the social weight given the individual (θ_i).

It is possible to simplify Equation (6.5) by substituting the marginal social utility of income (α_i) for these two effects, the MUY and the MSU.[1] The marginal social utility of income (MSUY) is the social weight given to an additional dollar that goes to i. This gives

$$dW = \sum_j \sum_i P_j \, dX_{ij} + \sum_j \sum_i (\alpha_i - 1) P_j \, dX_{ij} \qquad (6.6)$$

THE FUNDAMENTAL INTERDEPENDENT UTILITY WELFARE EQUATION

The equivalent equation in an interdependent utility context is

$$dW = \sum_j \sum_k \sum_i (M_{ki})(W_{ki}) P_j \, dX_{ij} + \sum_j \sum_k \sum_i (\alpha_i - 1)(M_{ki})(W_{ki}) P_j \, dX_{kj}$$

$$(6.6a)$$

In practice it may be difficult to measure the amount that others would pay to see an increase in k's income. That is, the practical EV or CV measures may not include $(M_{ki})(W_{ki})$. In this case it is useful to think of the interdependence effect as being embodied in the MSUY. More social weight is given to changes in income for persons others care more about.

Here and in the following chapters we explore the efficiency and distribution effects of Equation (6.6). Again, the first term on the right-hand side is the efficiency effect. The second term is the distributional effect, which depends on the marginal social utility of income and the social weight given the individual. *Equation (6.6) is a fundamental welfare equation for the economic analysis of normative issues.*

The efficiency effects are found by aggregating the CVs or EVs, and the distributional effects determine the weight to be given to the income changes for different classes of affected individuals. The consideration of distributional effects is discussed in Chapter 11. Another method is to ignore the distributional effects. The approach that ignores the distributional effects is the subject of the remainder of this chapter.

6.4. KALDOR–HICKS AND POTENTIAL PARETO CRITERION

The best-known attempts to formulate a principle for aggregating preferences are known as *compensation tests*. A very common approach, and one by tradition associated with benefit–cost analysis, is to decide that changes in Robert's

---

[1]The reader may believe we do not need to include the θ_i, the MSU of person i, since we already have the interdependence effect. In fact, a powerful argument can be made for dropping this term. This argument is sometimes called utilitarianism.

and Alice's incomes receive an equal weight, that the MSUY = 1. The decision criterion that makes this assumption is called the Kaldor, the Hicks, or the Scitovsky potential Pareto criterion. The Kaldor criterion (named for Nicholas Kaldor, 1939) can be expressed as follows:

Kaldor: The winners from a project *could* in principle compensate the losers from the project.

More formally, the Kaldor criterion says that state A is preferable to state B if it is possible in principle to undertake costless lump-sum transfers *in state A* so that it would be superior to state B.

State of the world A might be one in which a dam exists that did not exist in state B, and in which as a consequence of building the dam, the income distribution and the pattern of production is different in state A than in B. Suppose that the gain to the winners in moving from state B to A is $100. The loss to the losers is $90. Suppose that if the losers in the move from state B to state A were given $90 as compensation, the losers could buy the same set of goods or a set of equivalently valuable goods to those they had in state B. Suppose also that the winners, having given up $90 in state A, still have access to a set of goods that is better than the set they had available to them in state B. Then, the gains to the winners could be redistributed to the losers to cover their loss of $90, leaving $10 as net gains to the winners. In this situation the move from B to A is said to satisfy the Kaldor compensation test. The compensation test, however, is a hypothetical test.[2] The compensation is not in fact to be carried out. We can assume that this results in a net increase in the utility of society if we assume that the marginal utility of income is the same for the gainers and losers and is invariant to the move from B to A. If the compensation is actually carried out, the move from B to A would satisfy the Pareto test, and no such assumption about the marginal utility of money is required.

Hicks (1939) suggested a slightly different criterion:

Hicks: The losers could not bribe the potential winners not to undertake the project.

More formally, state A is preferable to state B if, *in state B,* it is not hypothetically possible to carry out lump-sum redistributions so that everyone could be made as well off as in state A.

If the potential losers in state B would lose $90, and the potential winners would gain $100, state A is preferred to state B because the losers could not hypothetically bribe the winners to not undertake the project.

It may seem that the Kaldor and Hicks criteria are the same. This is not, however, the case because the Kaldor test envisions redistributions as carried

---

[2]There are two versions of the compensation test. The strong version limits the hypothetical redistribution to the goods produced in state A. The weak version allows the aggregate production to change hypothetically as the redistribution is carried out. The weak test envisions compensation being carried out in terms of purchasing power.

out in state A, while the Hicks test envisions such redistributions as being carried out in state B. The available production sets may not, for example, be the same in the two states.

A *necessary* condition for the Kaldor test to be passed is that the sum of the CVs is positive. Unfortunately, a positive sum of CVs does not guarantee that this test will be passed. (That is, in technical terms a positive sum of CVs is a necessary but not a sufficient condition for the Kaldor test.) A *sufficient* condition for the Hicks test is that the sum of the EVs is positive. But unfortunately, the Hicks test may be passed even though the sum of EVs is not positive. That is, a positive sum of EVs is a sufficient but not a necessary condition to pass the Hicks test. (For further treatment of this issue see Boadway and Bruce, 1984.)

It is possible that the use of the Kaldor or the Hicks test alone will result in a reversal paradox. From state B a move to state A may look good. But, having arrived at state A, from state A a move to state B may now look good. As a consequence Scitovsky (1941) proposed the following criterion:

Scitovsky: Both the Kaldor and Hicks criteria are met.

The Kaldor–Hicks criterion is also called the *potential Pareto criterion* since a project is held to be worthwhile if a Pareto superior redistribution *could* occur. Suppose we are in state B and are considering a move to state A. If the sum of the CVs and EVs are both positive, there will be no reversal paradox. And, we can also say that the Hicks compensation test *is* passed and that the Kaldor test *may* be passed. Were the sum of the EVs and CVs negative, we could say that the Kaldor test is not passed and that the Hicks test may not be passed.

The Kaldor–Hicks decision criterion "solves" the social welfare problem by assuming each person has the same marginal social utility of income (MSUY). A dollar is counted the same regardless of who receives it. (For least restrictive assumptions, under which CVs and EVs can be aggregated, see Technical Note 6A on the Gorman form.) The expression for a welfare change is similar to that for a single individual and is

$$dW = \sum_j \sum_i P_j \, dX_{ij} \tag{6.7}$$

This differs from the measure of change for a single individual only in the summation sign, $\sum$, indicating the changes in the EVs or the CVs summed across individuals. The Kaldor–Hicks approach ignores the distributional aspects of benefit–cost decisions. The approach does, however, take into account interdependent utilities, although this is not always recognized. Kaldor–Hicks has the severe limitation that it ignores distributional effects. Chapter 12 points out that using Kaldor–Hicks is nevertheless justified where the cost of determining a policy's distributional effects or the costs of responding to them are larger than the expected benefits from taking the distributional effects into account.

TECHNICAL NOTE 6A
The Gorman Demand and Utility Equations

We present here the most general utility and demand equations for which CVs and EVs can be aggregated across individuals so as to say that social welfare is increased. This equation is called the Gorman form. The Gorman form for the situation in which all individuals face the same prices is

$$X_i = A_i(P) + B(P)(Y_i) \qquad (6.8)$$

This says the quantity of X_i consumed by i is a function of price P_i and this can vary by individuals as indicated by the subscript i. To the effect of price on X_i is added a term $B(P)Y_i$ which indicates X_i is also a function of income. The effect of income is, however, multiplied by a coefficient B which can vary with price but which does not vary with income with individuals. The Gorman form implies linear Engel curves, and a constant marginal utility of income across individuals and incomes. The Engel curve shows the relationship between income and quantity demanded as in Figure 6.1. The curve E is of the Gorman form and is derived from indifference curves in Figure 6.1(a) which correspond with the Engel curve.

The Gorman demand form more generally associated with Equation (6.8) implies an associated aggregate utility function that is similar to the demand form and is

$$U_i = A_i(P) + B(P)Y_i \qquad (6.9)$$

which says that aggregate utility is a function of prices and of income. This is known as the unrestricted Gorman form. (The indifference curves arising from the unrestricted Gorman form are said to be quasihomothetic.) Marginal utility will vary with prices, but not by incomes. The marginal utility with respect to income associated with the above equation is just $\partial U / \partial Y = B$, a constant. That is, the Gorman form assumes a constant marginal utility of income for all individuals. There is some empirical evidence that aggregate demand curves fit the general Gorman form. On balance, the evidence is mixed. We do not, however, find plausible an approach that assumes marginal utilities of income are the same across individuals and incomes.

If we impose a restriction on the general Gorman form such that demand is zero when income is zero, the term $A_i(P)$ disappears. This results in utility functions that are homothetic and identical for individuals. A homothetic utility function requires indifference curves that satisfy a requirement that any ray drawn from the origin will cut indifference curves at points of equal slope. This implies that a change in income, relative prices remaining the same, will not change the *relative* proportions of goods consumed. (That is, income elasticity is 1 for everyone. Engel curves are linear and homogeneous; they go through the origin.) Empirically, demand curves do not fit the restricted Gorman form, the form that demand is zero when income is zero. That is, income elasticities are not always one.

Figure 6.1 Gorman form Engle curves.

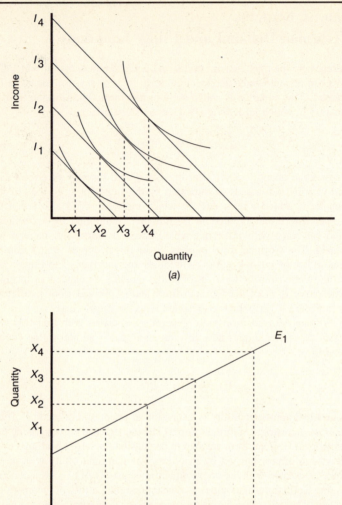

6.5. THE AGGREGATION OF EVs AND CVs

Assuming that Kaldor–Hicks is the appropriate criterion (that is, assuming the Gorman form), the individual measures of welfare, the EV and CV, can be aggregated to give a measure of social welfare.

Figure 6.2 shows compensated demand curves for Robert Plotnick and Alice Rivlin. The areas below these curves are the EVs. Bob's EV is *A* and

Figure 6.2   Aggregate compensated demand curves.

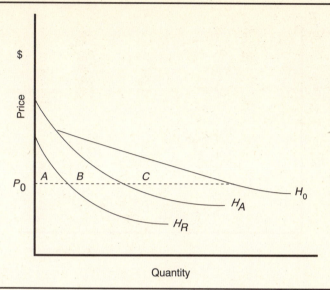

Alice's is $A + B$. The aggregate EV is found by summing Bob and Alice's compensated demand curves to give H_0. The aggregate EV is then area $A + (A + B)$, or, $A + B + C$ where area A is equal to area C.

6.6.   AGGREGATION OF CONSUMER AND PRODUCER SURPLUSES

To this point, our discussion has proceeded in terms of the EVs and CVs. We must now address the issue of using consumer and producer surpluses to approximate the EV and CV. First, we consider aggregating the surpluses, then we consider how accurate they are at approximating the EV and CV. Aggregate consumer and producer surplus measures may be produced in the same manner as the aggregate CVs and EVs. In Figure 6.3(a) D_R and D_A are Robert's and Alice's ordinary demand curves for books. The aggregate demand curve is D_0, which is found by summing D_R and D_A horizontally. At price P_0 Robert's consumer surplus is represented by area A and Alice's consumer surplus is represented by area $A + B$. The total consumer surplus is measured by the aggregate demand curve D_0, and is $A + B + A'$ where area A' equals area A.

Similarly, in Figure 6.3(b) S_R and S_A represent Robert's and Alice's labor supply curves. The aggregate labor supply curve is given by S_0 and is found by horizontally summing Robert's and Alice's labor supply curves. At a wage rate of W_0, Robert's producer surplus is represented by A and Alice's producer surplus is represented by area $A + B$. The aggregate producer surplus is then given by $A + B + A'$, as shown along the aggregate labor supply curve.

Figure 6.3 Aggregate demand and supply curves.

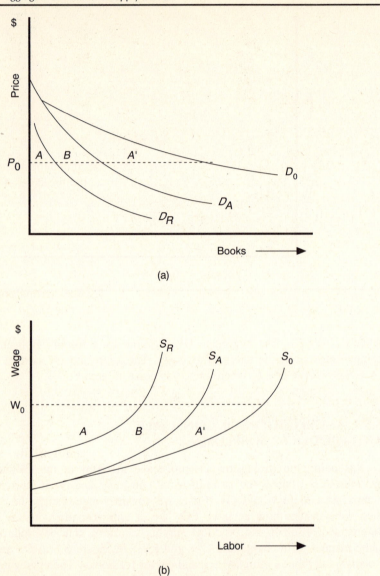

(a)

(b)

6.7.   AGGREGATION EXAMPLES

Let us consider how the EV and/or the CV or CS might be used in judging some contemplated action. The EV or CV can be expressed in terms of whether it is the sum one would *accept* or would *pay* for a particular result. We will label these amounts as *accept* or *pay*.

We label the existing situation I. The contemplated change is to situation II. Situation I is, say, without an airport and without the noise pollution which

TABLE 6.1

	Residents	Airlines	Net Social Value
Value of moving from I to II CV (I → II)	−$5000 accept	+$2000 pay	−$3000
Value of *not* moving from I to II EV(I ↛ II)	+$3500 pay	−$3000 accept	+$500
Value of moving from I to II EV (I → II)	−$3500 pay	+$3000 accept	−$500

an airport would produce. Situation II is with the airport and the noise pollution. We assume for simplicity that the only effects from the presence of the airport are that area residents would suffer harm and that the airlines would gain from the airport. The least amount that residents would *accept* to allow the airport is $5000. The most the residents would *pay* to avoid the airport is $3500. The airlines would pay $2000 to have the airport, but would accept $3000 to forego it.

The CV for a move from I to II would be the $2000 the airlines are willing to *pay* minus the $5000 *accept* from the residents, for a negative $3000. This measures the value of a move from I to II when I is the starting point.

The EV for not moving from I to II would be the $3500 the residents are willing to pay minus the $3000 the airlines are willing to accept to give up the airport, for a positive $500 which is the value of *not* moving from I to II when I is the starting point. The EV is customarily expressed in positive language, that is, as the value of making the move rather than of *not* making the move. Thus the value of moving from I to II is just a negative $500. Its value is typically expressed as the sign reversal of the final result when orginially WTP is positive and WTA is negative; it may also be calculated in one step by reversing the signs on WTP and WTA, and this aspect of its meaning and calculation is something for the student to be very careful about.

These results are summarized in Table 6.1 where the one-step calculation for the positive language conception of the EV is included, as it is in the following table. Clearly, situation I is preferable from a social standpoint when situation I is the starting point. In this circumstance, the CV tells us that the value of moving to situation I is a negative $3000. The EV tells us that the value of moving to situation II is a negative $500 (because the value of *not* moving to situation II would be a positive $500).

6.7.1. The Symmetry of the EV and the CV

It is instructive now to look at the CV and EV for a move from situation II to I, when the airport exists and the proposed change is to eliminate it. The CV will be the amount the residents would pay to make the move and eliminate the airport minus the amount the airlines would accept to make the move and relinquish the airport. The EV is the amount the airlines would pay not to have the change and keep the airport minus the amount the residents would accept not to have the change and tolerate the airport; remembering, however, that the EV is expressed as the value of making the move rather than of *not* making the move, the one-step calculation is included by reversing the signs on the WTP and WTA figures. Table 6.2 summarizes the results so far.

TABLE 6.2

	Residents	Airlines	Net Social Value
Value of II CV (I → II)	−$5000 accept	+$2000 pay	−$3000
Value of *not* II EV (I ↛ II)	+$3500 pay	−$3000 accept	+$500
Value of II EV (I → II)	−$3500 pay	+$3000 accept	−$500
Value of I CV (II → I)	+$3500 pay	−$3000 accept	+$500
Value of *not* I EV (II ↛ I)	−$5000 accept	+$2000 pay	−$3000
Value of I EV (II → I)	+$5000 accept	−$2000 pay	+$3000

It is clear from Table 6.2 that the CV from I to II equals the EV (expressed in its *not*-move version) from II to I. This is mechanically true since the CV is a measure of the difference between indifference curves using final prices. The EV is measured using original prices. But the final prices in a move from I to II are the original prices in a move from II to I. Thus in comparing two situations, the CV (I→II) and the CV (II→I) give all necessary information. Since this is so, we shall use only the CVs in our further examples; the reader will understand that the EVs could be used as well.

6.7.2 Aggregate Ambiguities

In Table 6.2, the value of situation I was greater than II, as measured by CV (II → I), and the value of II was less than I, as measured by CV (I → II). Clearly there is no ambiguity. Situation I is preferred to II. Could the aggregate results, however, be ambiguous?

There are two possibilities:

(1) CV (I → II) > 0 and CV (II → I) > 0
(2) CV (I → II) < 0 and CV (II → I) < 0

In case (1) the criterion says first that situation II is preferred to I and then that I is preferred to II. This case is, however, a logical impossibility. To see why, let us re-create the airport example with new numbers. Suppose the airlines learn the airport will be more valuable than they first thought. The new willingness to pay and accept figures are shown in Table 6.3.

The CV (I → II) is positive, indicating that solution II is preferred. In order for CV (II → I) to also be positive, the absolute value of the *accept* figure for the airlines must be less than *pay* figures of $6000. But for a normal good, it cannot be true that the (absolute value of) *accept* figure will be less than the *pay* figure. As we discussed earlier, the accept figure assumes the person(s) must be bribed away from a preferred position. The accept figure thus starts from a higher real income base than the pay figure and if the income effect

TABLE 6.3

	Residents	Airlines	Net Social Value
Value of II CV (I → II)	−$5000 accept	+$6000 pay	+$1000
Value of I CV (II → I)	+$3500 pay	−$? accept	+$?

TABLE 6.4

	Residents	Airlines	Net Social Value
Value of II CV (I → II)	−$5000 accept	+$3000 pay	−$2000
Value of I CV (II → I)	+$3500 pay	−$4000 accept	−$500

is positive, the accept figure must be greater. (The student can work out the reasoning where the good is not normal. What about the situation where the good is normal for one group, but not for another?)

The truly ambiguous case is (2). That is,

$$(2)\ \ CV(I \rightarrow II) < 0 \text{ and } CV(II \rightarrow I) < 0$$

This says that the relative value of II is negative and that the relative value of I is also negative. This case could occur with the *pay, accept* figures in Table 6.4.

This illustrates a perfectly possible case. The (absolute value of the) accept figures are larger than the pay figures and there is no violation of the principle of consumer choice. *In this example, the result, whether I or II, will be determined by the starting point.* A move away from the starting point (for example, a move from I to II when I is the starting point) cannot be justified by the CV or by a dual EV-CV criterion.

6.8.   BENEFIT–COST ANALYSIS AND THE ASSIGNMENT OF RIGHTS

The starting point is itself determined by the assignment of property rights. If the residents have the right to quiet, this right must be purchased from them by the airlines. Then, the CV(I → II) is the relevant one, and in the example at hand, the airlines are unable to purchase this right from the residents and the airport is not built.

On the other hand, if the residents are deemed to have no right to quiet, but the airport has the right to exist, the residents must then bribe the airport to exist elsewhere (or nowhere). Again, in the example at hand, the residents are unable to do this. The airport is built, or, if already built, it remains.

Thus the results of a benefit–cost analysis might depend on the assignment of property rights. The assignment of rights is important only in the ambiguous case in which CV (I → II) indicates position II is not preferred and CV (II → I) indicates position I is not preferred. In our airport example we must make a decision as to whether the residents have the right to quiet or the airport has the right to make noise. Otherwise, we may encounter ambiguous results. If the analyst cannot assign rights she should acknowledge the inability to give a definitive answer.

The assignment of property rights can be important in benefit–cost cases where there is a substantial difference between the accept and pay figures (the income effect is large). Such differences often arise in benefit–cost decisions concerning environmental amenities as well as in other situations. For example,

Figure 6.4   EV and CV and the indeterminacy of marginal rights.

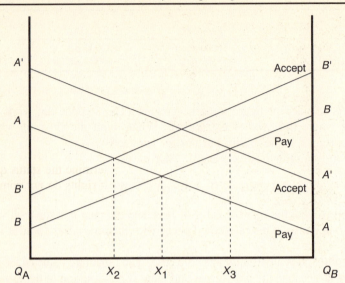

an analysis of a proposal to classify an area as wilderness or not, or a proposal to raise a dam in order to lower electricity prices while flooding forest land, could depend crucially on the assignment of rights. The analyst must face the issue squarely. Where the assignment of rights is unclear and the results depend on the assignment, the analyst must point this out.

We can further analyze this problem with the help of Figure 6.4. Here the amount of good X that is allocated to group A is shown by the horizontal distance from Q_A and the amount of the good that is allocated to group B is shown by the horizontal distance from Q_B. The curve AA shows the maximum sum of money A would *pay* for successive units. The curve $A'A'$ shows the minimum amounts A would *accept* for giving up successive units of X to B. Similarly, BB shows the maximum amount B would *pay* for successive units and $B'B'$ the minimum amounts B would accept to give up units of X. If A has a right to the entire quantity the final allocation will be $Q_A X_3$ to A and $Q_B X_3$ to B. B must buy X from A and this split at X_3 is given by the intersection of A's accept curve $A'A'$ with B's pay curve BB. Similarly, if B owns the good, A will buy $Q_A X_2$ and B will retain $Q_B X_2$.

How should the right to previously unallocated goods be allocated? A should have at least $Q_A X_2$ units and B should have at least $Q_B X_3$ units as measured by a benefit–cost test. This is because even if B owned $Q_A X_2$ units he would sell them to A since A's willingness to pay for $Q_A X_2$ units exceeds what B would accept. Similarly, A would sell $Q_B X_3$ units to B.

The question reduces then to the one of how to allocate the units between X_2 and X_3. There is no simple economic answer to this question and we leave it to you to contemplate the solution. We note, however, that any reasonable allocation might be Kaldor–Hicks superior to leaving the right unassigned and that an allocation with some compensation to the loser might be Pareto superior if the alternative is an anarchy in which valuations of the units X_2X_3 by A and B would be very low.[3]

6.9. HUMAN PERCEPTION OF GAINS AND LOSSES

Is the value of a dollar gained about the same as the value of a dollar lost but with sign reversed? Most economic literature would suggest yes. Even the indifference curves drawn in intermediate texts require that the answer is yes. The answer, however, is no. The status quo has particular meaning in decision making. People do not merely compare end points among possible outcomes, but rather compare changes from some reference point—a point that represents the status quo point. Obviously, legal rights help determine the status quo and therefore the evaluation of gains and losses, but such rights do not completely determine the status quo.

Because of the difference between the EV and the CV, that is, because of the difference between the WTP and the WTA, we expect some difference in evaluation between buying and selling positions due to income (and substitution) effects. Preference for the status quo, however, creates a difference between buying and selling positions and between losses and gains beyond the expected differences, that is, differences due to income or substitution effects. This effect now called variously the *endowment effect* or *status quo bias* is now well established. Experimental results (see Knetsch, 1989, 1990, 1991; Kahneman, Ketsch, and Thaler, 1990, 1991) show, for example, that the value one puts on even common and inexpensive items such as pens and coffee mugs depends on whether or not one starts from a position of ownership.

Frey and Pommerehne (1987) call attention to the asymmetry in the international trade of art objects. Fund-raising activities to prevent the loss of national art are much more successful than those undertaken to buy new art. This suggests that the appropriate valuation of preservation activities is not the WTP but rather the WTA and that the differences between these two measures will be greater than previously thought.

The value of restoring harmed individuals seems to differ from an equivalent monetary compensation. Compensation for a loss appears to be viewed as a gain from a new reference point incorporating the harm, and as such is valued less than the initial loss from the initial reference point. A mitigation measure, however, appears to be viewed as reducing the loss and thus carries more weight. Slightly more than one-half the students in a survey preferred, for example, to have an accidentally destroyed "old textbook used in an earlier course" replaced rather than to receive cash sufficient to buy a new book (Knetsch, 1990). Between 80 and 90 percent of survey respondents expressed a preference for spending money to reduce nuisances associated with a new waste disposal facility rather than paying compensation to people affected even when the compensation was greater than the amount spent on mitigation or greater than any loss in property values.

These differences in valuation have profound implications for benefit–cost evaluation. For example, recognition of the greater weight given to losses

---

[3]For more on rights and benefit–cost analysis see Zerbe (1991) and Heyne (1988).

than to gains will provide greater justification for preserving environmentally sensitive areas and cultural and physical resources. They suggest the particular value of environmental restoration as compared to monetary compensation after damage. The outcry about loss of environmental amenities associated with our national image, such as old-growth forests, is then not surprising; real harm is being done. The results suggest not only that legal rights are losses from positions to which people feel an entitlement by reason of experience or expectation but also are particularly powerful.

QUESTIONS AND PROBLEMS

1. Government subsidies to the arts will result in increases in the number of books and records that go to Don and Dick who are the only persons affected by the policy. Suppose that you are given the following information about the effects of the policy: Dick will gain directly a CV of $100 and Don a CV of $50.
   a. Is this a worthwhile policy using Kaldor–Hicks and ignoring interdependent utilities?
   b. Suppose the Kaldor–Hicks measure of welfare is used. What is the value of the policy, considering distributional effects?
   The above CVs do not take into account, however, Dick's negative investment in Don's income. Dick values increases in Don's income negatively to the extent of $0.10 on the dollar that he would be willing to pay to prevent any increase in Don's income. Dick would require or accept $0.20 on the dollar, however, to allow any increase in Don's income. Don is indifferent to changes in Dick's income. The marginal social weight given to Dick's income is 0.8 and the marginal social weight given to Don's income is 1.0. Dick's marginal utility of income is 2.0 and Don's is 1.0.
   c. Calculate the effect of the arts policy on social welfare, taking into account the distributional effects, the social weight given to each person's income, and the marginal utility of income.
   d. Ethically speaking, should Dick's negative evaluation of Don's income be counted?
2. How should criminal gains be counted in benefit–cost analysis?
3. The city of Pineville is considering building a garbage dump. There are three alternatives. The first is to put the dump in a north-end site; the second is to put the dump in a south-end site; the third possibility is to pay the county to take the trash to the county dump. Some north-end citizens feel they would gain from having the north-end site. It would be quicker to make trips to the dump to get rid of refuse. We will call this group N_1. Others prefer the south-end site for a similar reason. We shall call this group S_1. Yet another group in the north end opposes the dump location because they feel it makes their neighborhood a less attractive place to live. We shall call this group N_2. Similarly, another group in the south end prefers the dump to be located elsewhere, and we will call this group S_2. The garbage must be disposed of, otherwise the social costs will be very great.
   You conduct an investigation to determine the benefits and costs of the different alternatives. First you are able to estimate the following willingness to pay and accept figures:

   N_1:   willing to pay to have the site in the north end, $100
   N_1:   willing to accept having the site elsewhere than in the north end, $150

N_1: willing to pay to have the garbage disposed of rather than accumulate at home, $1000

N_2: willing to pay not to have the site in the north end, $100

N_2: willing to accept having the site in the north end, $300

N_2: willing to pay rather than to have the garbage accumulate at home, $1000

S_1: willing to pay to have the site in the south end, $50

S_1: willing to accept having the site elsewhere than in the south end, $80

S_1: willing to pay to have the garbage not accumulate at home, $700

S_2: willing to pay to have the site elsewhere but in the south end, $75

S_2: willing to accept having the site in the south end, $95

S_2: willing to pay to not have the garbage accumulate at home, $850

In addition to these costs and benefits, there are construction costs associated with building and operating the site either in the north or the south end. The present value of these costs are $1650 for the north end site and $850 for the south end. Finally, the county will charge $3000 to dispose of the garbage.

a. Suppose that there is no right to have the dump in any particular location so that by the CV criteria a Kaldor–Hicks test will be met only if the winners could compensate the losers. On the basis of the CV, calculate the benefits and costs of the three alternatives.

b. Will the answer be different in terms of the choice of alternatives if the city is determined to choose one of the three alternatives and if you don't know the WTP of disposal? Why or why not?

c. Will the answer be different if the EV is calculated instead of the CV? Explain the relationship between the EV for building a site and the CV for not building a site.

REFERENCES

Boadway, Robin W., and Neil Bruce, *Welfare Economics,* Oxford: Basil Blackwell, 1984.

Frey, B. S., and W. W. Pommerehne, "International Trade in Art: Attitudes and Behavior," *Riv. Int. Sci. Econom. Comm.* 34, 465–486, 1987.

Gorman, W. M., "Community Preference Fields," *Econometrica,* January 1953.

Hausman, Jerry A., "Exact Consumer Surplus and Deadweight Loss," *American Economic Review* 71(4), 1981, 662–676.

Heyne, Paul, "The Foundations of Law and Economics," *Research in Law and Economics* 11, 53–71, 1988.

Hicks, John R., "The Foundations of Welfare Economics," *Economic Journal* 49, 696–712, 1939.

Just, Richard E., et al., *Applied Welfare Economics and Public Policy,* Englewood Cliffs, NJ: Prentice-Hall, 1982.

Kahneman, Daniel, Jack L. Knetsch, and Richard Thaler, "Experimental Tests of the Endowment Effect and the Coase Theorem," *Journal of Political Economy* 98(6), 1325–1348, December 1990.

Kahneman, Daniel, Jack L. Knetsch, and Richard H. Thaler, "The Endowment Effect, Loss Aversion, and Status Quo Bias," *Journal of Economic Perspectives* 5(1) 193–206, Winter 1991.

Kaldor, Nicholas, "Welfare Propositions in Economics and Interpersonal Comparisons of Utility," *Economic Journal* 49, 549–552, 1939.

Knetsch, Jack L., "The Endowment Effect and Evidence of Nonreversible Indifference Curves," *American Economic Review* 79(5), 1277–1284, 1989.

Knetsch, Jack L. "Environmental Policy Implications of Disparities Between Willingness to Pay and Compensation Demanded Measures of Values," *Journal of Environmental Economics and Management* 18, 227–237, 1990.

Knetsch, Jack L. "Preferences and Nonreversibility of Indifference Curves," *Journal of Economic Behavior and Organization* 17, 131–139, 1992.

Scitovsky, T., "A Note on Welfare Propositions in Economics," *Review of Economic Studies* 9(1), 77–88, November 1941.

Willig, R., "Consumer's Surplus Without Apology," *American Economic Review* 66, 589–597, 1976.

Zerbe, R. O., Jr., Comment: "Does Benefit Cost Analysis Stand Alone? Rights and Standing," *Journal of Policy Analysis and Management,* 96–105, 1991.

APPENDIX 6A

The Willig Estimates of the Accuracy of Consumer Surplus

For many years there has been a controversy over whether or not benefit–cost analysis had any theoretical basis. It was known that the CV and EV measures were what were needed and that consumer surplus (CS) measures were generally all that were available. And, it was known that consumer surplus *did not* equal either the CV or EV. This led well-known economists such as Paul Samuelson and I. M. P. Little to dismiss consumer surplus as "little more than a theoretical toy" and, of course by implication, benefit–cost analysis was also dismissed. This concern over how good a measure is the CS is surprising in view of the much more fundamental and serious problem posed by welfare assumptions required to aggregate the EVs and CVs across individuals. In any event, in 1976 Robert Willig showed that CS is in fact a good estimate of either the EV or CV.

Willig derives upper and lower levels on the percentage errors from approximating the compensating and equivalent variations by using consumer surplus.[1] Willig shows that the maximum and minimum values for the CV and EV are:

$$\overline{CV} = \Delta CS - e_1^c \, | \, \Delta CS \, | \tag{6.A.1}$$
$$\underline{CV} = \Delta CS - e_2^c \, | \, \Delta CS \, | \tag{6.A.2}$$
$$\overline{EV} = \Delta CS + e_2^e \, | \, \Delta CS \, | \tag{6.A.3}$$
$$\underline{EV} = \Delta CS + e_1^e \, | \, \Delta CS \, | \tag{6.A.4}$$

The $\overline{CV}$ and $\overline{EV}$ are the upward bounds on the EV and CV. The $\underline{EV}$ and $\underline{CV}$ are the lower bounds. In these equations e_1 and e_2 represent the lower and upper bounds of an error term that can be calculated with varying degrees of precision. These equations become handy rules of thumb where "e" is approximated by e_a, where

---

[1] See Just et al. (1982), Appendix B, for a thorough treatement of these issues.

$$e_a = 3\frac{(E_y S)}{2} \quad \text{and} \quad S = \frac{CS}{M_0}$$

M_0 is initial income and E_y is income elasticity. There will be a maximum and minimum e_a according to whether e is calculated by using the *minimum* or *maximum* income elasticity for any market affected over the range of the actual price change. Thus if e_a is used one can approximate the range of EV and CV by using the upper and lower bounds on E_y.

Greater accuracy can be obtained by using more accurate calculations of e_{min} or e_{max}. These more elaborate and accurate expressions for e are identified as e_c and e_e and are shown in Table 6.A.1, along with values of e_a for various combinations of E_Y and S. As shown in Table 6.A.1 there is an e_a, e_c, and an e_e for each income elasticity and for each value of S.[2] The second and third entries are e_c and e_e. The absolute value of these entries shows the relative error in using consumer surplus to estimate the CV or EV.

An estimate of the CV or the EV can be made using the average income elasticity. This is, of course, the answer obtained with an average of the minimum and maximum CV or EV. That is, for most cases accurate estimates of the CV and EV are

$$CV = CS_i - e_B CS \qquad (6.A.5)$$
$$EV = CS_i + e_B CS \qquad (6.A.6)$$

where e_B is the average of either the e_a's or e_c's or e_e's. Again, greater accuracy can be obtained by using the e_c's and e_e's indicated by the second and third entries in Table 6.A.1.

Using the rule of thumb and an average e_B results in small errors of approximation for most cases. *No more than about 2 percent error is incurred if e_B is less than or equal to 8 percent and if income elasticity varies by less than 50 percent among commodities and over the path of the price changes.* If income elasticity is constant the error will be less than 1 percent as long as e_B is less than or equal to 10 percent. These are conditions likely to be widely met. When these conditions are not satisfied or more accuracy is desired, the second and third entries of Table 6.A.1 can be used.

EXAMPLES FOR ONE PRICE CHANGE

Example 1
Consider the following example. A family of three members earning about $20,000 per year before taxes will typically spend about $1000 per year on clothing or about 5 percent of their income (adjusted from 1972 BLS consumer expenditures survey). A project will lower the price of all clothing by 10

---

[2]Just et al., provide an algorithm for computing even tighter and more accurate error bounds using information about income elasticities in *each* affected market (Just et al., 1982, app. B, pp. 381–382).

TABLE 6.A1[a]

η	s							
	-0.10	-0.05	0.00	0.05	0.10	0.15	0.20	0.25
	-0.05050	-0.02525	0.00000	-0.02525	-0.05050	-0.07575	-0.10100	-0.12625
-1.01	-0.04597	-0.02405	0.00000	-0.02660	-0.05632	-0.08993	-0.12852	-0.17374
	-0.05632	-0.02660	0.00000	-0.02405	-0.04597	-0.06609	-0.08467	-0.10190
	-0.04000	-0.02000	0.00000	-0.02000	-0.04000	-0.06000	-0.08000	-0.10000
-0.8	-0.03687	-0.01917	0.00000	-0.02091	-0.04390	-0.06938	-0.09795	-0.13042
	-0.04390	-0.02091	0.00000	-0.01917	-0.03687	-0.05328	-0.06858	-0.08290
	-0.03000	-0.01500	0.00000	-0.01500	-0.03000	-0.04500	-0.06000	-0.07500
-0.6	-0.02798	-0.01447	0.00000	-0.01557	-0.03243	-0.05079	-0.07094	-0.09327
	-0.03243	-0.01557	0.00000	-0.01447	-0.02798	-0.04065	-0.05257	-0.06383
	-0.02000	-0.01000	0.00000	-0.01000	-0.02000	-0.03000	-0.04000	-0.05000
-0.4	-0.01888	-0.00971	0.00000	-0.01031	-0.02130	-0.03307	-0.04574	-0.05946
	-0.02130	-0.01031	0.00000	-0.00971	-0.01888	-0.02758	-0.03585	-0.04372
	-0.01000	-0.00500	0.00000	-0.00500	-0.01000	-0.01500	-0.02000	-0.02500
-0.2	-0.00956	-0.00488	0.00000	-0.00512	-0.01049	-0.01616	-0.02215	-0.02850
	-0.01049	-0.00512	0.00000	-0.00488	-0.00956	-0.01404	-0.01834	-0.02248
	0.00000	0.00000	0.00000	0.00000	0.00000	0.00000	0.00000	0.00000
0.0	0.00000	0.00000	0.00000	0.00000	0.00000	0.00000	0.00000	0.00000
	0.00000	0.00000	0.00000	0.00000	0.00000	0.00000	0.00000	0.00000
	0.01000	0.00500	0.00000	0.00500	0.01000	0.01500	0.02000	0.02500
0.2	0.00980	0.00494	0.00000	0.00504	0.01020	0.01547	0.02086	0.02637
	0.01020	0.00504	0.00000	0.00494	0.00980	0.01457	0.01925	0.02384
	0.02000	0.01000	0.00000	0.01000	0.02000	0.03000	0.04000	0.05000
0.4	0.01986	0.00996	0.00000	0.01003	0.02013	0.03030	0.04055	0.05087
	0.02013	0.01003	0.00000	0.00996	0.01986	0.02970	0.03948	0.04920
	0.03000	0.01500	0.00000	0.01500	0.03000	0.04500	0.06000	0.07500
0.6	0.03019	0.01504	0.00000	0.01494	0.02979	0.04454	0.05919	0.07373
	0.02979	0.01494	0.00000	0.01504	0.03019	0.04544	0.06079	0.07623
	0.04000	0.02000	0.00000	0.02000	0.04000	0.06000	0.08000	0.10000
0.8	0.04080	0.02019	0.00000	0.01979	0.03920	0.05822	0.07686	0.09512
	0.03920	0.01979	0.00000	0.02019	0.04080	0.06182	0.08326	0.10512
	0.05050	0.02525	0.00000	0.02525	0.05050	0.07575	0.10100	0.12625
1.01	0.05231	0.02586	0.00000	0.02489	0.04889	0.07209	0.09452	0.11623
	0.04889	0.02489	0.00000	0.02586	0.05231	0.07977	0.10829	0.13774
	0.06000	0.03000	0.00000	0.03000	0.06000	0.09000	0.12000	0.15000
1.2	0.06291	0.03071	0.00000	0.02933	0.05731	0.08406	0.10964	0.13410
	0.05731	0.02933	0.00000	0.03071	0.06291	0.09669	0.13216	0.16942
	0.07000	0.03500	0.00000	0.03500	0.07000	0.10500	0.14000	0.17500
1.4	0.07444	0.03608	0.00000	0.03397	0.06602	0.09627	0.12487	0.15194
	0.06602	0.03397	0.00000	0.03608	0.07444	0.11529	0.15886	0.20539
	0.08000	0.04000	0.00000	0.04000	0.08000	0.12000	0.16000	0.20000
1.6	0.08630	0.04152	0.00000	0.03858	0.07451	0.10805	0.13942	0.16881
	0.07451	0.03858	0.00000	0.04152	0.08630	0.13474	0.18726	0.24439
	0.09000	0.04500	0.00000	0.04500	0.09000	0.13500	0.18000	0.22500
1.8	0.09852	0.04703	0.00000	0.04313	0.08281	0.11943	0.15334	0.18480
	0.08281	0.04313	0.00000	0.04703	0.09852	0.15510	0.21757	0.28685
	0.10000	0.05000	0.00000	0.05000	0.10000	0.15000	0.20000	0.25000
2.0	0.11111	0.05263	0.00000	0.04761	0.09090	0.13043	0.16666	0.20000
	0.09090	0.04761	0.00000	0.05263	0.11111	0.17647	0.25000	0.33333

[a] Each group of three numbers includes

$$\hat{\epsilon} = \frac{\eta|s|}{2}, \quad \epsilon^c = -\frac{[1 + (\eta - 1)s]^{1/(1-\eta)} - 1 + s}{|s|} \quad \text{and} \quad \epsilon^e = -\frac{[1 - (\eta - 1)s]^{1/(1-\eta)} - 1 - s}{|s|}$$

respectively. From *Applied Welfare Economics and Public Policy,* by Richard Just et al., Englewood Cliffs, NJ: Prentice-Hall, 1982.

percent. Suppose the demand elasticity for clothing is about -1. The change in CS will be about \$105. This change in CS is calculated as follows. For a straight-line demand curve the change in CS will be

$$\Delta CS = \Delta P Q_0 + \frac{1}{2}\Delta P \Delta Q$$

We are given that $P_0 Q_0 = 1000$ so that $Q_0 = 1000/P_0$. We also are given $\Delta P/P_0 = 10\%$ so that $\Delta P = 0.1 P_0$. Thus, $\Delta P Q_0 = (0.1 P_0)(1000/P_0) = \$100.00$. From the expression for price elasticity we have

$$\Delta Q = \frac{E_d \Delta P Q_0}{P_0}$$

where E_d is the demand elasticity. Where E_d is 1, we have

$$\frac{1}{2}\Delta P \Delta Q = \frac{1}{2}[(0.1 P_0)(\Delta Q)] = \$5.00$$

Thus the change in CS is \$100 + \$5 = \$105.00. Then e_a will equal $(E_y/2)$ (\$105/\$20,000) or $0.0026 E_y$.

Often income elasticities are close to 1. An income elasticity of 1 means that the percentage change in the quantity purchased is equal to the percentage in income. An income elasticity of 2 or 3 indicates the percentage change in purchases of the good are two to three times the percentage change in income. These are large income elasticities. If the average income elasticity for clothing were 3, e_a would still be only 0.008 on our example. The use of consumer surplus would involve less than a 1 percent error in terms of measuring the EV.

An estimate of the CV or the EV, which we label CBV and EBV, can be made using the average income elasticity. This is, of course, the answer when an average of the minimum and maximum CV or EV is used. An error larger than 5 percent is likely only for budget items that represent a large fraction of income.

Example 2

Suppose your family spends 25 percent of its income on housing. Suppose the project in question lowers housing prices by 50 percent and suppose again the demand elasticity is about 1. Consumer surplus will be about +\$3125. (The student should draw a demand curve and calculate this.) The e_a would then be $E_y 3125/40,000 = .078 E_y$. And, if the average income elasticity were 1.8, e_a would be 14.04 percent. This is, of course, a much more substantial error than in the previous example, but it is a pretty spectacular case.

If more precise estimates of the EV and CV are desired, Equations (6.A.5) and (6.A.6) can be used to estimate them by applying more accurate estimates of e_c and e_e. More precise estimates of the e_c and e_e are given as the second and third entries of Table 6.A.1 where the income elasticity is constant. Table 6.A.1 gives an exact measure of the CV or EV. To use the table we need E_y and S where E_y in our example is 1.8 and $S = 3125/20,000 = 0.156$.

Using the table for $S = 0.15$ and $E_Y = 1.8$ we have $e_c = 0.1551$ and an $e_e = 0.1194$. The CS overestimates the CV by 15.51 percent and underestimates the EV by 11.94 percent. Exact measures of the CV and EV are

$$CV = 3125 - 0.1551(3125) = 2640$$
$$EV = 3125 + 0.1194(3125) = 3498$$

Suppose income elasticity were not constant but instead $E_{y\ min} = 1.6$ and $E_{y\ max} = 2.0$. Then e_c would be between 13.47 percent and 17.65 percent and e_e between 10.8 percent and 13.04 percent. This would indicate that the change in consumer surplus overstated the CV by between 13.47 percent and 17.65 percent and understated the EV by between 10.8 percent and 13.04 percent. Minimum and maximum CV and EV could be

$$\overline{CV} = 2704\ \overline{EV} = 3532$$
$$\underline{CV} = 2573\ \underline{EV} = 3462$$

Although CS is not a particularly accurate measure in this spectacular case, the difference in the maximum and minimum estimates is only about 5 percent for the CV and about 3 percent for the EV. There is, however, a 37 percent difference between the maximum value of the EV and the minimum value of the CV. This is not primarily an inaccuracy of approximation, but simply a difference in the EV and CV. Where the difference between the CV and EV is this substantial one should point out that the legal interpretation of where rights lie becomes important in the benefit–cost analysis.

Example 3

Suppose the consumer demand for shoes is given by

$$Q = 6 - 0.1P + 0.0001M$$

where Q = quantity of shoes purchased in 1 year, P = the price of shoes, and M = income. Suppose the initial price is \$40, P_0 = \$40, and consumer income, M_0, is \$20,000. Now consider the welfare effects of a tax on shoes of \$20 per pair that raises the price of shoes to \$60 per pair. The situation is shown in Figure 6.A.1. The change in CS will be $-\$60$. How accurate is this consumer surplus as a measure of the CV or EV? Using e_a as an approximation of e we have

$$e_a = \frac{E_y S}{2} \qquad E_y = \left(\frac{M_0}{Q_0}\right)\frac{\Delta Q}{\Delta M} \qquad \text{and} \qquad S = \frac{\Delta CS}{M_0}$$

From Equation (6.A.5), $\Delta Q/\Delta M = 0.0001$ and $M_0/Q_0 = 20,000/Q$. Thus $E_y = 2/Q$. As price rises from \$40 to \$60, quantity varies from 4 to 2. Thus E_y rises from 0.5 to 1. Thus e_a varies from 0.00075 to 0.0015. The CV will thus be between CS(1.00075) and CS(1.0015) or between 60.01 and -60.09. Clearly, CS is a very accurate approximation of the CV. The accuracy of the

Figure 6.A.1   Single price change.

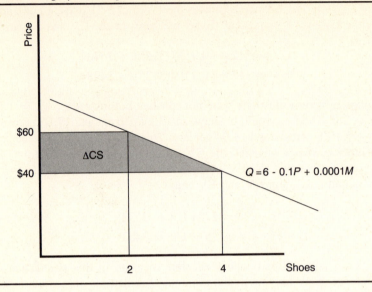

CS can be improved by using an average E_y. Since E_y varies from a low of 0.5 to a high of 1, the average is 0.75 and

$$e_a = \frac{0.75(\$60.00)}{40,000} = 0.001$$

$$CV^b = -\$60 - 0.001(\$60) = -\$60.06$$

The more accurate expression obtained by using the average is clearly unnecessary in this case.

Example 4

Suppose, however, the consumer is crazy about the shoes and the demand equation is

$$Q = 6 - 0.1p + .01M$$

Again let a tax be placed raising the price from \$40 to \$60. The change in CS is now $-\$4020$.

$$E_Y = \left(\frac{20,000}{Q}\right)(0.01) = \frac{200}{Q}$$

Q will go from 202 to 204, and E_y will then vary from 1 to 0.99. The e_a varies from $(1)(4020)/40,000$ to $(0.99)(4020)/40,000$ or from 0.10 to 0.099.

And the CV lies between $[-4020 - 0.099(4020)]$ and $[-4020 - 0.10(4020)]$ or from -4418 to -4422. The average of the above estimates for the CV can be used or obtained by using the average income elasticity which would give

$$CV = 4419.99$$

Even greater accuracy can be obtained by using Table 6.A.1 and using values of e_c and e_e.

AN EXAMPLE WITH MULTIPLE PRICE CHANGES

Suppose we have the following demand curves for one individual and two substitute commodities:

$$Q_1 = 20 - 5P_1 + 2P_2 + 0.01M$$
$$Q_2 = 15 - 5P_2 + 3P_1 + 0.005M$$

The problem is to evaluate the welfare effects of a change in P_1 from 1 to 2 accompanied by a change in P_2 from 1 to 2. Assume initial income is $1000. Let $P_1^0 = 1$ and $P_2^0 = 1$.

The path-dependency problem of CS is clearly evident here. The CS will vary depending on which price is changed first. In Figure 6.A.2 D_1^1 and D_2^1 are the original demand curves for goods 1 and 2.

If P_1^1 changes first to P_1^2 we have a loss of consumer surplus of area A for good 1. The demand for good 2 increases to D_2^2. If now the price of good 2 increases from P_2^1 to P_2^2 the loss of consumer surplus is area $B + B'$. Thus the change in CS is area $A + B + B'$. Instead, suppose the price of good 2 changes first. The loss of CS in this market would be area B. The demand curve for 1 would shift to D_1^2 and the change in consumer surplus in the market will be $A + A'$. The changes in CS would be $A + A' + B$. In general, this will not equal area $A + B + B'$. The point of Willig's analysis is, however, that usually this makes little difference.

In the problem at hand, let us calculate CS along the path generated by first varying the price of good 1 and then by varying the price of good 2. This gives the results of Figure 6.A.2. For good 1 initial quantity will be 27 at price $P_1^1 = 1$ and the final quantity will be 22 at $P_1^2 = 2$. Assuming the price of good 2 remains constant at price $P_2^1 = 1$, the change in consumer surplus for market 1 will then be $\Delta CS_1 = -24.5$. In market 2 the change in consumer surplus as price changes from P_2^1 to P_2^2 while the price of good 1 remains at the higher price will be $CS = 21.00$. The total change in consumer surplus then will be $CS_1 + CS_2 = -45.5$.

How accurately does this measure the welfare change? How might we estimate the actual CV or EV? We use the rule of thumb estimates by using e_a to put bounds on the CV or EV.

E_y will vary from 0.37 to 0.45. As Q_2 varies from 26 to 16, E_y varies from 0.19 to 0.31 for the second equation. Thus the minimum and maximum

Figure 6.A.2 Multiple price changes.

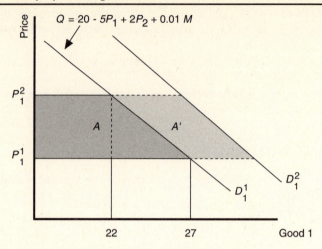

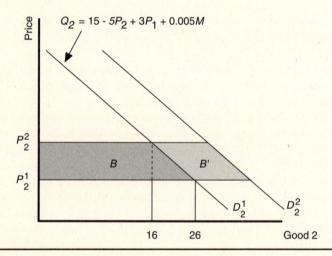

income elasticities along the price path are 0.45 and 0.19. Their average is 0.32. Then,

$$\min e_a = 0.19 \left[\frac{-45.5}{2(1000)} \right] = -0.004$$

$$\max e_a = 0.45 \left[\frac{-45.5}{2(1000)} \right] = -0.01$$

$$e_B = \frac{0.004 + 0.01}{2} = 0.007$$

$$\overline{CV} = -45.5 - (0.004)(45.5) = -45.68$$

$$CV = -45.5 - (0.01)(45.5) = -45.96$$

$$EV = -45.5 + (0.01)(45.5) = -45.04$$

$$EV = -45.5 + (0.004)(45.5) = -45.32$$
$$CV_B = -45.5 - (0.007)(45.5) = -45.82$$
$$EV_B = -45.5 + (0.007)(45.5) = -45.18$$

These indicate the following: The CS overestimates the CV (absolute value) by about 0.6 percent. The CS underestimates the EV by about 0.6 percent. The best estimate of the CV lies within 0.3 percent of the CV's bounds and the best estimate of the EV lies within 0.3 percent of the EV's bounds.

Greater accuracy for the error bounds can be obtained from Table 6.A.1. The first entry in Table 6.A.1 gives the value of e_a a different value from E_y. The accuracy of the error bounds can be improved by using the second entry for error-bound calculations of the CV and the third entry for error-bound calculations of the EV. A comparison of the first entry with the second or third entry indicates the inaccuracy from using the rule of thumb. We use the minimum E_y of 0.19 and the maximum of 0.45 and $S = -45.5/1000 = 0.046 = 0.05E_y$ in conjunction with Table 6.A.1. The table entry at $S = -0.05$ for E_y between 0.2 and 0.6 indicates that almost no inaccuracy is introduced by using this rule of thumb.

A CHANGE IN INCOME AND PRICES

The welfare value of a change in income is just the change in income. *Thus, when prices and income both change, the CV and EV are found by calculating the price effects as measured along the compensated demand curves plus the change in income.* When prices and income both change, however, the income change causes a shift in both the ordinary and compensated curves. The question is which curve, the initial or final curve, is to be used for calculating the welfare price effects?

The problem and its solution can be understood by examining Figure 6.A.3. In this figure $D(M_0)$ is the initial ordinary demand curve and $H(U_0)$ and

Figure 6.A.3   A change in income and prices.

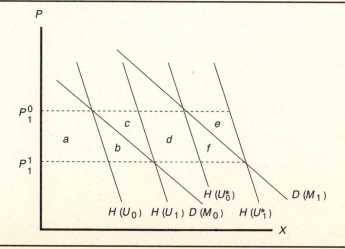

$H(U_1)$ are the compensated demand curves associated with the price change from P^0 to P^1. $D(M_1)$ is the final ordinary demand curve after the income change and $H(U_0^*)$ and $H(U_1^*)$ are the associated compensated demand curves. The CV is conditioned at the initial utility level so $H(U_0)$ is the appropriate compensated demand curve. The CV will then be

$$CV = M_1 - M_0 + \text{ area } a$$

where $M_1 - M_0$ represents the income change. Area a can be estimated by calculating area $a + b$ using the initial ordinary demand curve $D(M_0)$ and correcting by Willig's formula by subtracting area b. If instead we use the final demand curve with Willig's corrections we would have the CV as $M_1 - M_0 + a + b + c + d$ which would be an overestimate by areas $b + c + d$. *To estimate the CV in the case of price and income changes we evaluate changes at the initial income level first and add to these the change in income.*

The EV is evaluated by the final utility level so the EV associated with the price and income change in Figure 6.A.3 is given by

$$EV = M_1 - M_0 + a + b + c + d + e + f$$

This may be estimated by using the final ordinary demand curve $D(M_1)$ to obtain areas $a + b + c + d + f$. Then one uses Willig's corrections to add in area e. *Thus the EV is estimated by the final income level* and the effect of the price change is added to the income change.

7

Calculation of Costs and Benefits in Partial Equilibrium

7.1. INTRODUCTION

Chapters 5 and 6 introduced the concepts of consumer and producer surplus, and in this chapter we will see how these concepts can be applied in a practical context. As in Chapter 6, we are concerned with Kaldor–Hicks efficiency. That is, we will continue to assume that the marginal social utility of money is the same for all individuals.

We will focus on conceptual calculations of costs and benefits. One of the early steps in benefit–cost analysis should be to trace through the effects of the contemplated action on different markets and determine conceptually the nature of the costs and benefits that are created. The conceptual determination of benefits and costs should precede any empirical estimates. But often this is not done. This chapter emphasizes that a failure to systematically consider costs and benefits in the context of the appropriate supply and demand analysis can lead to error.

7.2. PARTIAL AND GENERAL EQUILIBRIUM ANALYSIS

For simplicity, we will assume first that only one market is affected by the policy and examine the effects in this market only. This approach of ignoring other markets is called *partial equilibrium analysis*. For example, an analysis of whether or not a bridge ought to be upgraded can reasonably be handled by examining the value of time saved for those trips that are already being taken, plus the net value of the additional trips induced by the better bridge. It is reasonable to examine only the market for use of the bridge, that is, to use partial equilibrium analysis, to examine the benefits and costs of upgrading the bridge. However, if the better bridge materially affected home location and the price of bus or taxi service then, perhaps, a more general analysis would be required. Of course, effects in other markets are often important and need to be taken into account. In these cases, partial equilibrium analysis is insufficient. The consideration of the various interrelated markets is called *general equilibrium analysis*. We consider effects in several markets toward the end of this chapter. Full general equilibrium analysis is taken up in Chapter 21.

7.3. CONSUMER AND PRODUCER SURPLUSES REVISITED

The demand curve shows approximately the willingness to pay for one unit, two units of the good, etc. Thus the area under the demand curve for one unit of a widget in Figure 7.1, area A, shows the gross value or willingness to pay for that unit. Area B shows the willingness to pay for a second unit, and so on. Thus the total area under the demand curve shows the total willingness to pay, that is, the total value, for Q^* units of the good. In Figure 7.2, the price of the good is P^*, and the area above this price shows the excess of the willingness to pay over what is actually paid, the consumer surplus, area A. Similarly, the supply curve shows the opportunity cost of providing various levels of output or service. Payments that exceed this opportunity cost are called producer surplus. In Figure 7.2, area B shows the producer surplus.

External effects give rise to producer and consumer surpluses. Traffic congestion increases the price of taking trips, consumers are willing to pay to reduce air pollution, and so forth. The value of an external effect can be expressed as the willingness to pay to gain the value of a positive external effect or to avoid the harm of a negative external effect. These are changes in producer and consumer surpluses but we will refer to them as changes in the value of the external effect as a convenience in the benefit–cost accounting.

Figure 7.1

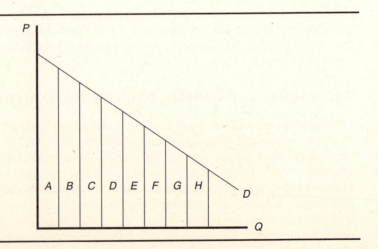

Figure 7.2

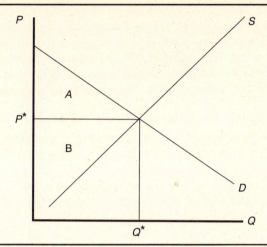

7.3.1. Transfers

Payments from one party to another are neither benefits nor costs (as long as different people are regarded as having the same marginal utility of income), but are transfers. Thus, if widgets are a constant-cost industry and are taxed so that consumers pay the full amount of the tax, the tax results in a loss of consumer surplus by widget consumers most of which is offset by tax revenues received by others.

7.3.2. An Expression for a Change in Welfare

Armed with these concepts and definitions, we are now in a position to give a general expression for the welfare change from a policy:

> The change in welfare in partial equilibrium analysis is the sum of the changes in producer and consumer surplus, plus changes in government revenue, plus changes in the value of external effects.

The fundamental equation we apply in this chapter is

$$\Delta W = \Delta CS + \Delta PS + \Delta GR + \Delta EE \qquad (7.1)$$

where W = welfare
    CS = consumer surplus
    PS = producer surplus
    GR = government revenues
    EE = external effects

In a deeper sense, the last four of these terms are changes in consumer and producer surplus, but it is convenient to maintain the above divisions for heuristic purposes. External effects convey benefits or losses to individuals that are also reflected in a willingness to pay or to accept. Why are increases in government revenue regarded as an increase in welfare? Tax revenue because it can be used to purchase government goods or to reduce other taxes will offset the loss of consumer surplus due to higher taxes. The change in government revenue to the extent that it is offset by a decrease in consumer surplus will be a welfare transfer and not a net contributor to government revenue. We will see, however, that government revenues can increase more than the concomitant loss in consumer surplus. We will now explore Equation (7.1) in a variety of contexts.

7.3.3.   Changes in Consumer and Producer Surplus

Figure 7.3 shows the welfare effects of creating a monopoly in an industry subject to constant long-run costs (flat long-run supply curve).

When the industry is organized competitively, price is equal to marginal costs and is P_0, output is Q_0, and consumer surplus consists of areas A, B, and C. This consumer surplus (CS_0) in the initial state is equal to

$$CS_0 = A + B + C$$

Producer surplus is zero because there is no area below the price (P_0) and above the supply curve. Thus

$$PS_0 = 0$$

There are no taxes or distortions, so there is no change in government revenues or in external effects (government revenues = 0 and external effects = 0).

When the industry is organized as a monopoly the producer can charge more than the marginal cost. In Figure 7.3, the monopoly price is shown as P_1, leading to an output of Q_1. Therefore,

$$CS_1 = A \qquad PS_1 = B$$

We can compare these two states before and after the monopoly by determining the producer and consumer surplus in the initial state, then determining the

Figure 7.3   A butter monopolist with constant costs.

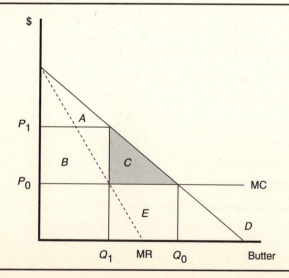

EXAMPLE 7.1

The following example shows the importance of going through the diagrammatic exercise. Railroad regulation in the 1890s increased rates for long-haul traffic and decreased rates for short-haul traffic (for more details, see Chapter 8). In Figure 7.4, the original unregulated rate for short-haul traffic is P_M. The rate after regulation is P_R. Producer and consumer surpluses before and after regulation are as follows:

$$CS_0 = Z \qquad PS_0 = A + B$$

$$CS_1 = Z + A + C \qquad PS_1 = B + D$$

The changes in PS and CS are

$$\Delta CS = (Z + A + C) - Z = A + C$$

$$\Delta PS = (B + D) - (A + B) = D - A$$

$$\Delta W = (A + C) + (D - A) = C + D$$

In the long-haul market shown in Figure 7.4b the price is raised from P_0 to P_R'. The change in welfare in the long-haul market results in a loss of areas C' and D', whose size differs from the size of C and D, the gains in the short-haul market. The overall effect of the change in welfare then is

$$W = +(C + D) - (C' + D')$$

One published analysis of the welfare effect of railroad regulation neglected to draw a diagram such as Figure 7.4.[1] The resulting analysis ignored areas D and D'. This omission substantially biased the welfare change calculations. On the basis of the erroneous analysis the authors concluded that the welfare effect of early railroad regulation was negative. A correct calculation indicates the effect is positive.[2] *The important lesson here is that clear diagrams help to correctly identify all welfare changes and avoid errors.*

[1] See Spann and Erickson (1971).
[2] For correct calculations see Zerbe (1980).

producer and consumer surplus in the final state, and then subtracting the values in the initial state from those in the final state.

In this case we subtract consumer and producer surpluses in the competitive state from the values in the monopoly state.

This gives us:

$$\Delta CS = A - (A + B + C) = -(B + C)$$

$$\Delta PS = B - 0 = B$$

Combining the change in producer and consumer surplus gives us the change in welfare:

$$\Delta W = -C$$

Figure 7.4   The railroad market in 1890.

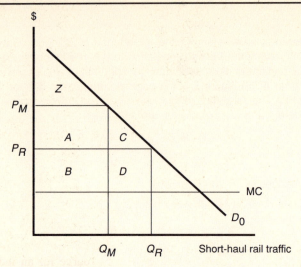

Price moves from P_M to P_R. The change in welfare is $\Delta W_{SH} = +(C+D)$

(a)

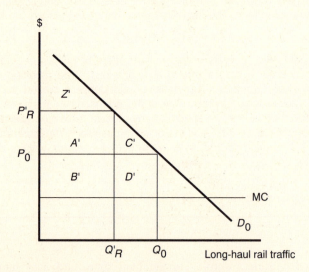

Price moves from P_0 to P'_R. The change in welfare is $\Delta W_{LH} = -(C'+D')$

(b)

This indicates a negative change in welfare and is equal to area C. Welfare is, *ceteris paribus,* less under monopoly than under competition. Area C is often called the *deadweight loss triangle* because in moving from marginal cost pricing at P_0 to monopoly pricing at P_1 area C is lost; no one gets it.

Area C can be understood intuitively as a loss by considering the effects of output changes. Consider the vertical areas which are benefits or costs created by output changes. The area under the demand curve represents gross willingness to pay. It also approximates the value of production. The area under the supply curve represents total variable costs. Thus a change in the area under the supply curve represents a change in costs and a change in the area under the demand curve measures a change in benefits. In moving from production at Q_0 to production at Q_1, we sacrifice production that has a gross value of area $C + E$. However, we free resources of value E for use elsewhere.

The loss in the value of good X (area $C + E$) over the gain from other goods arising from the resources freed (area E) is then area $(C + E) - E$, or area C.

7.4.   CHANGES IN TAX REVENUES—
A FLAT SUPPLY CURVE

A similar analysis can be used to show the welfare effects of a tax under partial equilibrium. Again we use the long-run supply curve for an industry subject to constant costs with a price equal to long-run marginal costs. This is shown in Figure 7.5. Originally the industry is at P_0Q_0. The tax T is charged to the producer and is added to marginal costs. Price to the consumer increases to P_1. Output is now Q_1. In the initial situation we have

$$CS_0 = A + B + C \qquad PS_0 = 0$$

and after tax we have

$$CS_1 = A \qquad PS_1 = 0$$

Note that this differs from our previous analysis in that the producer surplus after the tax is 0, not B. This is because the tax raises the producer's marginal

Figure 7.5   A per unit tax with constant costs.

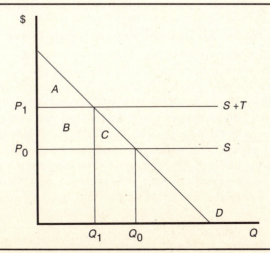

costs to $S + T$. That is, the net price to the producer is still P_0. The change in combined producer and consumer surplus is

$$\Delta(\text{PS} + \text{CS}) = A - (A + B + C) = -(B + C)$$

We have not called this the change in welfare because area B is not lost. Area B is tax revenues, the tax T times the output Q_1.

How should taxes be counted? The convention in partial equilibrium is to regard each dollar of tax revenue as a gain of a dollar. That is, tax revenues are regarded as a transfer from tax payers to tax recipients. A dollar lost by tax payers is regarded as a dollar gain to recipients. Tax revenues are a measure of the excess of willingness to pay by consumers over the costs of production. They are then a form of welfare change just as consumer and producer surpluses. Thus there is no welfare loss of area B, since the tax revenues are a gain to those on whom the tax dollars are spent though a loss to consumers who pay the taxes. (In general equilibrium we would need to take into account the effects of the government spending the tax revenue in various markets.) The loss of tax dollars is shown as a loss of consumer surplus and the gain is shown as a gain in tax revenues. Thus, the equation for the welfare change under partial equilibrium, with taxes but without external effects, is

$$\Delta W = \Delta \text{CS} + \Delta \text{PS} + \Delta \text{GR} \qquad (7.2)$$

where CS = consumer surplus, PS = producer surplus, and GR = government revenues. Hence the change in welfare for the tax example is

$$\Delta W = -(B + C) + B = -C$$

When tax policy is considered, area C is called the *excess burden of taxation*. It is, of course, a welfare loss area. This area is the appropriate measure of the welfare loss. Again we can understand area C as a net welfare loss by thinking in terms of quantity changes. The area under the demand curve is an approximation of the gross willingness to pay or the gross benefits. The area under the supply curve represents total costs. The net loss is area C.

7.4.1. Taxes Again: An Upward Sloping Supply Curve

The analysis differs slightly when the supply curve is upward sloping. In Figure 7.6, the original position is P_0 and Q_0. With taxes levied equal to T per unit, the final position is $P_1 Q_1$. Figure 7.6 indicates the relevant welfare areas. Note that area D in Figure 7.6 is not really a triangle because the demand curve is not linear. We assume, however, that along the relevant part of the demand curve an assumption of a linear demand schedule yields reasonable approximations.

In order to calculate CS and PS we recall that CS is measured by the area *above* the price but under the demand curve. The producer surplus is measured by the area *below* the price but above the supply curve. As shown in Figure 7.6, originally we have

$$\text{CS}_0 = A + B + C + D$$
$$\text{PS}_0 = G + E + F$$

Figure 7.6 The welfare loss from tax: upward sloping slowly.

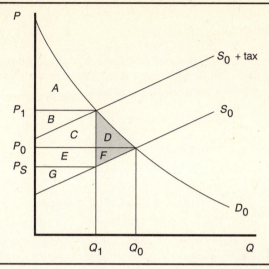

After the tax we have

$$CS_1 = A$$
$$PS_1 = G$$
$$GR = B + C + E$$

(Notice that we calculate producer surplus on the original supply curve because this shows the price the producer receives; it is the net tax price to the producer.) Now the change in welfare will be

$$\Delta CS = A - (A + B + C + D) = -(B + C + D)$$
$$\Delta PS = G - (G + E + F) = -(E + F)$$
$$\Delta GR = (B + C + E)$$
$$\Delta W = -(B + C + D) - (E + F) + (B + C + E)$$

or

$$\Delta W = -(D + F)$$

Again, the change in welfare is the dead weight welfare loss triangle, the excess burden of taxation.

7.4.2. The Size of Loss Triangles

To a linear approximation the size of the *excess burden* or dead weight loss triangle can be measured as

$$\Delta W = -\frac{1}{2} T \Delta Q \tag{7.3}$$

where T is the size of the tax. This is true because area $D + F$ is almost half of a box whose sides are T and ΔQ.

EXAMPLE 7.2

Suppose 100 million pounds of butter are sold per year for $1.50 per pound. The demand elasticity for butter is 1.5 and is produced under conditions of constant costs (the supply curve is flat). What is the deadweight loss that will result from a tax of $0.25 per pound?

$$\Delta W = -\frac{1}{2}P_0Q_0t^2E_d$$

$$P_0 = \$1.50$$
$$Q_0 = 100 \text{ million}$$
$$E_d = 1.5$$
$$T = 0.25 \ (t = 0.25/1.5 = 0.167)$$
$$\Delta W = -3.125 \text{ million}$$

Equations (7.4) and (7.5) can apply to either the initial or final equilibrium as long as consistent values are used; that is, initial values must be used together or final values used together in calculating the distortion. Thus instead of P_0Q_0 we could use final prices and quantities as long as we used elasticity figures associated with final prices.

For small taxes, the welfare loss can be expressed in terms of the absolute values of the elasticities of demand and supply (E_d and E_s) as below [see, e.g., Bishop (1968) for a derivation].[3] We will define t as the percentage tax. Notice that $T = tP_s$ where P_s is the equilibrium price minus the tax, or, the final price to supplier. Then the welfare loss is approximately given by

$$\Delta W = \frac{-\frac{1}{2}P_0Q_0t^2}{1/E_d + 1/E_s} \tag{7.4}$$

where Q_0 and P_0 are the original price and quantity.

For a flat supply curve $1/E_s$ becomes zero as E_s approaches infinity, and the formula may be simplified as

$$\Delta W = -\frac{1}{2}P_0Q_0t^2E_d \tag{7.5}$$

Equations (7.4) and (7.5) apply to percentage or ad valorem taxes. These equations may also be expressed in terms of the absolute size of the tax, T, by remembering that $t = T/P_d$.

The question asked at the end of Example 7.3 is answered in Equation (7.5'). In formula (7.4), t is the tax distortion as a percent of the initial price. Sometimes, however, it is convenient to calculate the welfare loss in terms of

---

[3]For large taxes, exact expressions can be derived if one has sufficient information about the demand and supply curves. For example, it is easy to derive exact expressions for welfare changes when one knows that the demand and supply curves are linear.

EXAMPLE 7.3

In the previous example, suppose the values remain the same except the supply elasticity is 1.2. What will be the deadweight loss? Now we need to apply equation (7.4).

$$\Delta W = \frac{-\frac{1}{2}P_0 Q_0 (t)^2}{1/E_d + 1/E_s}$$

$$\Delta W = -\$1.28 \text{ million}$$

Note that this is less than when the supply curve was flat. Can you explain (use a diagram) why the result is less for this case? If the taxes were such that the final equilibrium price was the same in both cases, would the loss be greater with an upward-sloping or flat supply curve?

EXAMPLE 7.4

In Example 7.2, suppose that t^* is 0.167, and the other values remain the same except the supply elasticity is 1.2. What will be the deadweight loss? Notice that a t^* of this size will yield the same final equilibrium price as Example 7.2.

$$\Delta W = -\frac{1}{2}P_0 Q_0 E_d (t^*)^2 [1 + E_d / E_s]$$

$$= -\frac{1}{2}(1.50)(100)(1.5)(0.167)^2 [1 + 1.5/1.2]$$

$$= -\$7.03125 \text{ million}$$

Note that this is greater than when the supply curve was flat because the size of the tax is larger than in Example 7.2 (45 cents versus 25 cents).

the change in price as above. In this case we will refer to t^* as the percentage price distortion between the final and the initial price. The welfare loss will be:

$$\Delta W = -\frac{1}{2}P_0 Q_0 E_d (t^*)^2 [1 + E_d / E_s] \tag{7.5'}$$

The logic of this formula is clear. Notice that, adjusting for the definition of distortion, the first part is equivalent to Equation (7.5). The terms to the left of the brackets capture the size of the deadweight loss that is consumer surplus, and thus are multiplied by 1 within the brackets. The size of the deadweight loss that is producer surplus will be in inverse relationship to the elasticities: this portion of the loss is found by multiplying the terms to the left of the brackets by the ratio of demand to supply elasticity. Notice that in the case where the supply elasticity is infinite, Equation (7.5') reduces to Equation (7.5) because

t^* then equals t and E_s disappears. Equation (7.5) can apply to either the initial or final equilibrium as long as consistent values are used; that is, initial values must be used together or final values used together in calculating the distortion. Thus instead of $P_0 Q_0$ we could use final prices and quantities as long as we used elasticity figures associated with final prices.

7.5. SHIFTS IN SUPPLY CURVES

A straightforward but common problem is calculating the welfare change from, say, an invention that shifts the supply curve for butter production to the right. Such a shift is shown in Figure 7.7(a). The original position is at P_0 and Q_0. The final position is at P_1 and Q_1. We have

$$
\begin{aligned}
CS_0 &= A & PS_0 &= B + D \\
GR_0 &= 0 & EE_0 &= 0 \\
CS_1 &= A + B + C & PS_1 &= D + E \\
GR_1 &= 0 & EE_1 &= 0 \\
\Delta CS &= (A + B + C) - A = B + C & \Delta GR &= 0 \\
\Delta PS &= (D + E) - (B + D) = E - B & \Delta EE &= 0
\end{aligned}
$$

$$
\begin{aligned}
\Delta W &= \Delta CS + \Delta PS + \Delta TR + \Delta EE \\
&= (B + C) + (E - B) = C + E
\end{aligned}
$$

The change in welfare is the area between the two supply curves bounded by the demand curve.

The student can satisfy himself that this answer makes sense intuitively. Figure 7.7(b) shows the same area divided up somewhat differently. Areas H and J make up the same area as E and C in Figure 7.7(a). Area H is clearly the resource (cost) saving from producing the original quantity Q_0 at the new lower costs. Areas J and L represent the gross value of the additional production as valued by demanders. The area under the supply curve (area L) represents the additional cost. The difference between the gross value J and L and the additional cost L is, of course, just area J. Thus the net benefit is area $H + J$, which is the same as we found in Figure 7.7(a).

Although this problem is straightforward, analysts examining this type of problem occasionally count areas $L + J$ as the net benefit, or more simply measure welfare changes by the change in output times the price. This may or may not be close to areas $H + J$. In any event, this type of error will not be made by students of this book.

7.6. WELFARE CHANGES WITH EXTERNAL EFFECTS

The student will recall that the rationale for using benefit–cost analysis arises when there is a divergence between private and social costs and benefits. Such divergence does not mean action should be taken. The existence of such a divergence, however, suggests the possibility of improvement. Taxes create one divergence because private decision makers may not fully consider the effects generated by their decision. Monopoly represents another divergence because

Figure 7.7

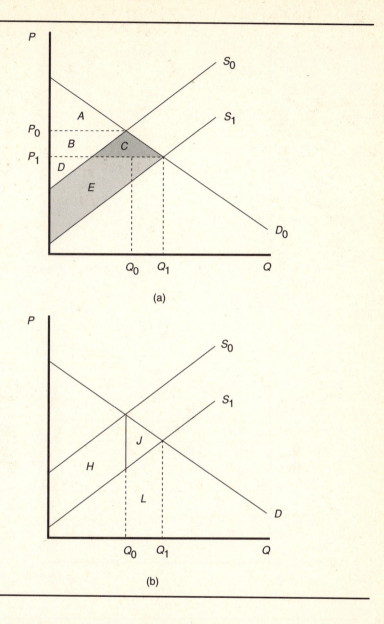

(a)

(b)

the marginal social gain from expanding production is greater than the private gain the monopolist considers. Pollution and other factors that cause benefits or costs that are not fully reflected directly in the price system are another source of divergence between private and social cost. This sort of divergence results in the decision maker failing to consider relevant effects of the decision and is known as a technological externality. Changes in pollution damage or in other external effects are, of course, welfare changes that should be counted in the benefit–cost analysis. In Figure 7.8a we depict the electric power industry.

Figure 7.8 Welfare loss with external effects (D = damage/KWH).

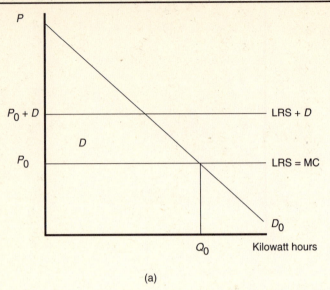

(a)

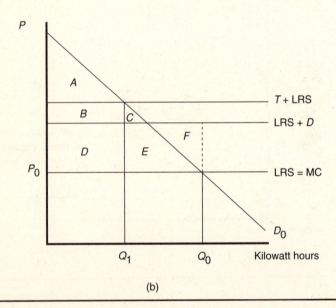

(b)

We assume the long-run marginal and average cost curve is flat (the industry produces under conditions of constant costs), and we label this curve the long-run supply curve (LRS) in Figures 7.8(a) and (b). The industry also pollutes. Each kilowatt hour of output is associated with D pollution damage. We wish to evaluate the welfare effects of a tax on kilowatt hours.

Figure 7.8(b) depicts the industry after the per-unit tax is levied. We apply Equation (7.1). Initially we have prices at P_0 and quantity demanded at Q_0.

Consumers pay no taxes and are not billed for pollution damage. There-fore,

$$CS_0 = A + B + C + D + E$$
$$PS_0 = 0 \qquad GR_0 = 0$$
$$EE_0 = -(D + E + F)$$

when EE is the external pollution effect on welfare. EE is negative because it is damage. It includes an area F which is above the demand curve. After the tax we have

$$CS_1 = A \qquad PS_1 = 0 \qquad GR_1 = B + D \qquad EE_1 = -D$$

Subtracting the initial welfare state from the final state we have

$$\Delta CS = A - (A + B + C + D + E) = -(B + C + D + E)$$
$$\Delta PS = 0 \qquad \Delta GR = B + D$$
$$\Delta EE = -D + (D + E + F) = +(E + F)$$

The change in welfare is

$$\Delta W = \Delta CS + \Delta PS + \Delta TR + \Delta EE$$
$$= -(B + C + D + E) + (B + D) + (E + F)$$
$$= -C + F$$

The change in welfare will be positive if area F exceeds area C. This is a remarkable result. It indicates that tax revenues may be generated even while increasing welfare, if the taxes are raised from a tax on the output of a pol-luting industry. The result is not surprising. The tax itself creates the usual excess burden areas C and E. But, pollution damage is reduced by an amount represented by areas $F + E$. Areas $F + E$ are a gain, areas $C + E$ are a loss, and the net result, areas $F - C$, could be positive or negative.

7.7. MORE COMPLICATED EXAMPLES

7.7.1. A Wheat Program

A. Where There Are No Taxes.   The government proposes a program to buy wheat from farmers in order to raise the price of wheat. We do not know the benefits of the program; that is, we do not know where the wheat will go, etc. We are, however, asked to find the *costs* of the program. Again our first step is to discover the relevant conceptual areas, using supply and demand analysis.

Figure 7.9 shows the initial demand and supply for wheat, D_0 and S_0. The line $D_0 + G$ shows the demand after the government begins buying. It consists of the original demand D_0 plus the government demand. The initial equilibrium is at P_0, the final equilibrium is at P_1. At the price P_1, total consumption other than government consumption falls to Q_C; some original consumption has been priced out of the market.

Figure 7.9

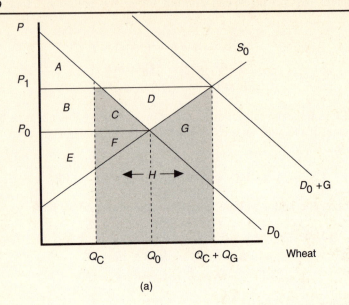

(a)

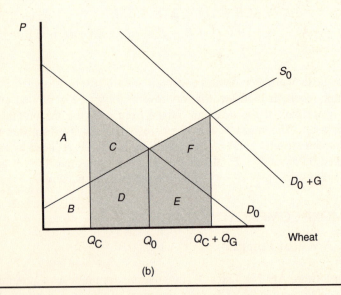

(b)

The general formula requires that we calculate the sum of changes in consumer and producer surplus, government revenues, and external effects. Originally the price is at P_0 and we have

$$CS_0 = A + B + C$$
$$PS_0 = E + F$$
$$GR = 0$$
$$EE = 0$$

After the move to P_1 we have

$$CS_1 = A$$
$$PS_1 = B + C + D + E + F$$
$$GR_1 = -(C + D + F + G + H)$$
$$EE = 0$$

Government revenues are negative because money is spent for the wheat. The loss of consumer surplus occurs because the government program has raised the price. Note that consumers will buy only Q_C after the price change, meaning the government must pay for all of area $C + D + F + G + H$. The overall changes are

$$\Delta CS = A - (A + B + C) = -(B + C)$$
$$\Delta PS = B + C + D + E + F - (E + F) = B + C + D$$
$$\Delta GR = -(C + D + F + G + H)$$
$$\Delta W = \Delta CS + \Delta PS + \Delta GR$$
$$= -(B + C) + (B + C + D) - (C + D + F + G + H)$$
$$= -(C + F + G + H)$$

Area $C + F + G + H$ represents the welfare cost of the program. Notice that this area is somewhat less than the money costs to the government. The money cost is the quantity the government buys times the price or $(Q_0 + Q_G - Q_C)P_1$. This equals area $(C + F + G + H) + D$. The money cost exceeds the opportunity cost by area D. This is because the project does indeed create a gain (producer surplus) for farmers. Nevertheless the program causes a net welfare loss unless the government's use of the wheat has a value equal to the program's net welfare cost of $C + F + G + H$.

Again we can look at the problem in terms of quantity changes. We indicated that the area under the demand curve gives an approximation of the gross benefits or the gross value. The area under the supply curve indicates resource or opportunity costs. Figure 7.9(b) shows the solution when approached in this manner.

Initial area under demand curve $= A + B + C + D$
Initial area under supply curve $= B + D$
Initial net surplus $= A + B + C + D - (B + D) = A + C$
Area under demand curve $= A + B$
Area under supply curve $= B + D + E + F$
Net surplus $= (A + B) - (B + D + E + F) = A - (D + E + F)$
Change in net surplus $= A - (D + E + F) - (A + C) = -(C + D + E + F)$

Notice that this area is just the area found to represent the cost in the previous example using the method of consumer and producer surpluses.

B. A Wheat Program with a Tax. This example is the same as the previous one except that the government taxes the wheat before and after the government support program. In Figure 7.10, the initial equilibrium is at P_0 and Q_0. After the government enters as a buyer, consumers purchase Q_1. Total purchases are

Figure 7.10   The cost of a government price support program for wheat when wheat is taxed.

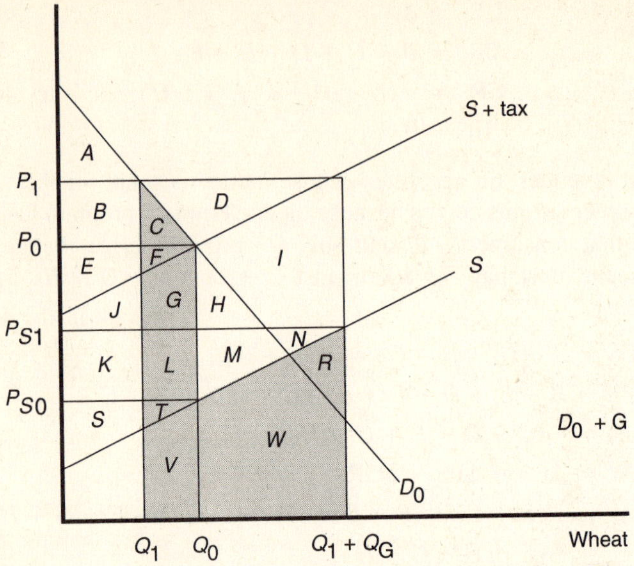

$Q_1 + Q_G$. The final price is P_1. P_{S0} is the initial price to suppliers and P_{S1} the final supply price. With the tax only we have

$$CS_0 = A + B + C$$
$$PS_0 = S + T$$
$$GR_0 = E + F + J + G + K + L$$

With the tax and government purchase we now have

$$CS_1 = A$$
$$PS_1 = K + L + M + N + S + T$$

The new tax revenues consist of taxes collected minus government spending:

$$GR_1 = B + C + D + E + F + I + J + G + H$$
$$- (C + D + F + G + H + I + L + M + N + T + R + V + W)$$
$$= (B + E + J) - (L + M + N + T + R + V + W)$$

The welfare loss can be calculated as

$$\Delta CS = -(B + C)$$
$$\Delta PS = K + L + M + N$$
$$\Delta GR = B - (F + G + K + L) - (L + M + N + T + R + V + W)$$
$$\Delta W = -(C + F + G + L + T + R + V + W)$$

This is the shaded area in Figure 7.10, and it has a logical interpretation. The area $R + V + W$ is the change in costs required to achieve the greater production.

The area $T + L + G + F + C$ is the net loss of the benefit to consumers plus the loss of tax revenues that occurs because of the price supports.

7.7.2. The Problem of Highway Congestion

There are many goods that are not priced or are underpriced in terms of social costs. Public parks, beaches, libraries, and highways are examples. When the price is too low customers will tend to consume a greater quantity than if prices could be costlessly and correctly set. Prices that are too low will result in congestion. During the 1973 oil crisis price controls on gasoline resulted in long lines at gas stations. For congestible public goods, too low or nonexistent prices result in a level of congestion that is larger than would exist if prices could be levied easily. National parks become overcrowded in the summer as do beaches. Roads are often overcrowded especially during rush hours.

Roads, highways, and arterials are not priced in accord with marginal costs. This leads to a socially inefficient level of congestion on the highways and arterials. The absence of prices for highway use leads to (*a*) overcrowding, (*b*) distortion in the allocation of traffic volume among roads, (*c*) distortion in the allocation of automobiles on one road at different points in time (that is, a too high traffic volume during peak periods and a too low volume during off peak periods), and (*d*) inefficient sizes and numbers of roads. In the following example, we ignore the problem of inefficient size and number of highways.

Overcrowding.   In Figure 7.11 traffic volume is the good provided. With price at P_1, below the optimum price P_0, traffic volume is Q_1, which is greater than the optimum of Q_0. Area C is the deadweight loss. Why is P_1, the actual price, not usually equal to the optimum price?

We can explore this question and this example in greater depth by examining how the marginal social cost curve can be derived. Traffic engineers

Figure 7.11   Congestion costs from overuse.

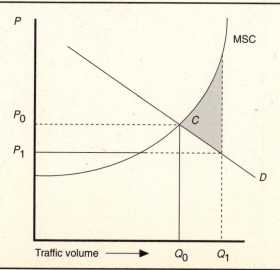

calculate the speed-volume relationship for highways. These relationships may be used in calculating congestion costs. Figure 7.12 shows a typical relationship. As average volume per lane increases, speed falls until capacity is reached at around 2000 cars per lane per hour. Travel time increases as speed falls. Engineers refer to this point as the point of (maximum) highway capacity. This point is typically reached when speeds are below 35 mph, depending on the road. Beyond this point hypercongestion occurs, since both speed and traffic flow fall.

From the speed curve we may calculate the trip times for various levels of traffic flow. By estimating the value of time and the costs of operating an automobile at various speeds, we may convert the speed-volume curve into a cost-volume curve, as in Figure 7.13. When the volume and density of automobiles are low, such as at Q_c, there are no congestion costs. Each driver correctly perceives the average trip time, and the marginal driver's decision to make the trip does not impose costs on anyone else. However, as traffic volume exceeds Q_c, this is no longer the case. The marginal driver contributes to congestion and slows down other drivers. There is then a divergence between marginal social costs and marginal private costs. Marginal social costs increase without limit as the traffic volume asymptotically approaches 2000 to 2500 cars per lane per hour. In Figure 7.13, the demand curve for drivers is shown as D. Since drivers recognize only their marginal private costs, MPC, they will consume Q_0 of highway use. However, the actual marginal social costs, MSC, would yield only Q_1 of highway use. This traffic volume could be achieved by a tax on highway use equal to the divergence between marginal private and marginal social cost. This tax or price for using the highways would vary by the level of traffic congestion. This idea of pricing the highways is perhaps not as far fetched as it may seem. Technology currently exists, and is used by the

Figure 7.12

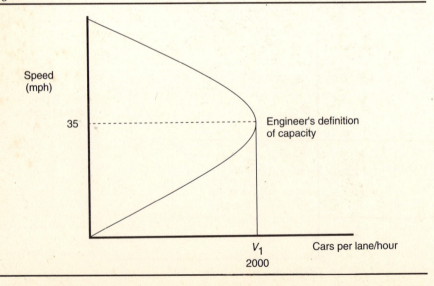

Figure 7.13

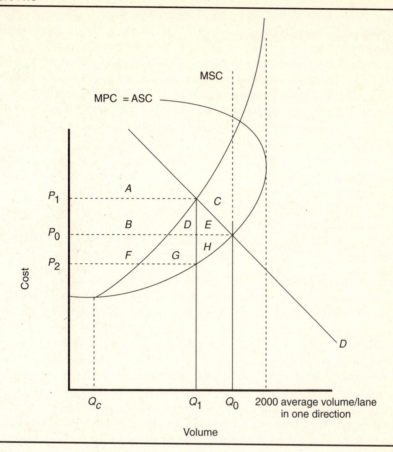

railroads, to monitor each car each time of day as the car passes fixed points. This is done by a number attached to the car which is read electronically. The correct traffic volume could also possibly be achieved by other traffic control means.

The social loss is shown by the difference in benefits and costs between the efficient and actual traffic volumes. This is shown by area C in Figure 7.13. Area C is the excess of congestion costs over the benefits from additional traffic volume between Q_1 and Q_0.

There is another way to look at this cost saving. Initially drivers are bearing an average cost of P_0. Consumer surplus is $A + B + D + E$. When traffic volume falls to Q_1, average costs are P_2. Consumer surplus is now $A + B + D + F + G$. The net gain in CS is $F + G - E$. Area $F + G$ is the cost saving for drivers, $Q_0 - Q_1$, still driving. Drivers now not driving were bearing average cost of P_0 and the cost to these drivers was area H. The gross benefits are the areas under the demand curve, areas $H + E$. The difference is area E. Area E is lost because of the reduction in traffic volume. The net effect of moving to the reduced volume is thus $F + G - E$, which is identically, though not obviously, equal to area C. Area $F + G$ is interesting because it is readily observable. It is the drop in trip time multiplied by the volume of traffic times the cost of time. Since area E is likely to be small, area $F + G$ is a reasonable approximation for the congestion saving.

The method of examining the savings can be derived from the surpluses (area behind the curves) approach. There are no producers in this example, only government-supplied highways. There is therefore no producer surplus but there can be changes in government revenues. Imagine that the move from Q_0 to Q_1 is accomplished by imposing an optimal tax equal to $P_1 - P_2$. We have then

$$
\begin{aligned}
CS_0 &= A + B + D + E & PS_0 &= 0 \\
GR_0 &= 0 & CS_1 &= A \\
PS_1 &= 0 & GR_1 &= B + D + F + G \\
\Delta CS &= -(B + D + E) & \Delta PS &= 0 \\
\Delta GR &= B + D + F + G \\
\Delta W &= \Delta CS + \Delta GR + \Delta PS = F + G - E
\end{aligned}
$$

Distortion Among Roads. Similar losses occur because traffic is not optimally distributed among roads. Frank Knight (1924) illustrates this with his famous two-road example. Let there be two roads connecting the same destinations. One road is infinitely broad but poorly surfaced so that cars have a maximum safe speed of 45 mph. The other road is narrow and well surfaced and cars could go 70 mph with similar safety. During periods of heavy traffic (which might be at all times) the speed on these roads becomes the same, 45 mph. As long as the narrow road is faster drivers will use this road, increasing congestion and reducing speed. When the traffic volumes on the roads are in equilibrium, speeds on each road will be equal at 45 mph. Now suppose we force some traffic from the narrow road to the broad road. This is a Pareto improvement because those moved to the broad road go the same speed as before and those left on the narrow road can go faster. There is a social welfare gain. The purpose of this example is to show intuitively that overcrowding can occur and that better pricing in use of highways can yield a welfare gain.

Allocation Over Time. An example similar to the two-road example gives some intuition of the loss because of misallocation over time. Consider a driver who is indifferent between travel during the peak traffic period when trip time is longer but time of day is more convenient, and travel during the off peak period when the trip time is shorter but at a less convenient time. If this driver is forced to travel during off peak time he is indifferent but other peak drivers gain because peak speed increases.[4]

---

[4]The reader may be interested in knowing what the efficient pricing rules are for highway use. These rules are designed to achieve efficient allocation among highways, efficient allocation of traffic at different points in time, and an efficient size and number of highways. These rules can avoid the type of welfare losses from inefficient pricing discussed in the text. The rules for efficient use of resources characterized by peak demand (i.e., congestion) for highways are essentially the same as for commodities subject to short-run demand fluctuations. These rules are

7.7.3. The Size of a Congestion Tax

Keefer (1958) calculated the top half of a speed-volume relationship for Chicago highways. Keefer's equations are of the form

$$S = a - bX \tag{7.6}$$

where S = the average speed in miles per hour; X = volume of traffic per 10-ft moving lane per hour; and a, b are coefficients determined by Keefer from observation.

   This equation is an approximation of the bottom half of Figure 7.12. We can convert this into an expression relating time to traffic volume and then assign a cost to time. From this we can derive the MSC curve and find the optimal congestion tax as MSC $-C$ where C represents average costs. If we set distance equal to one, then time $T = 1/S$, and we have

$$T = \frac{1}{a - bX} \tag{7.7}$$

where T is in hours per mile.

   If c is average costs/hour, total costs per mile are

$$TC = \frac{c}{a - bX} \tag{7.8}$$

where TC is total costs per mile. Marginal social costs are then

$$MSC = \frac{bc}{(a - bX)^2} \tag{7.9}$$

Average costs per mile will be TC/X and the optimum congestion tax will be

$$\text{Tax} = \text{MSC} - \text{average costs per mile} \tag{7.10}$$

   Using this relationship, actual estimates of the values for parameters a and b, and figures for the value of time equal to 75 percent of the wage rate, we calculate the optimum tax for Chicago expressways in 1974. These are as shown in Table 7.1.

   Krauss et al. (1976) found that optimum tolls range from about 0.1 cents per person mile for a rural road at off peak time to 7.7 cents per person mile for an urban expressway near a central business district (figures are in 1974 dollars). Krauss et al. suggest that total welfare losses on the order of

---

1. Price equals short-run marginal cost.
2. The efficient size of highway (efficient size of plant) is determined by equality of quasi rents from a unit of highway (producer surplus) *at the margin* with the cost of the unit.
3. Simultaneously satisfying rules 1 and 2 will yield total revenues just sufficient to cover total costs if the production process is one of constant returns to scale. (Constant returns to scale means that a doubling of inputs will double outputs.) Since the size of a proposed highway can be increased without increasing the costs proportionately, returns to scale are increasing rather than constant. In this case a subsidy is required in addition to the prices indicated by rule 1 to cover total costs.

TABLE 7.1   Unaccounted-for Social Congestion Costs for Chicago Highways and Arterials (1974)

Vehicles per Lane per Hour	Traffic Flow Expressways (cents/car mile)	Arterials (cents/car mile)
200	0.07	0.70
400	1.37	1.71
600	2.23	2.73
800	4.16	5.89
1000	4.44	10.44
1200	5.92	18.99
1400	9.55	37.09
1600	11.20	

0.09 to 1.35 percent of GNP are associated with inefficient pricing of urban expressways. In 1976 this was about $90 to $1350 million per year.[5]

7.8.   PARTIAL EQUILIBRIUM IN SEVERAL MARKETS

When the policy changes do not involve large income changes and only a few regional or local markets are affected, a simple extension of the partial equilibrium analysis can be used. In this section we illustrate the following partial equilibrium propositions. We must caution, however, that the partial equilibrium results may differ from the correct general equilibrium results. These rules apply directly to general equilibrium if welfare results are calculated allowing for substitution and income effects. These propositions are

1. Markets indirectly affected by a policy may be ignored if in these markets price is not affected and there are no distortions.
2. When distortions exist in indirectly affected markets but price doesn't change, the welfare effect will be given by multiplying the size of the distortions per unit by the change in the number of units. The sign of the distortion should be clear from the context. An increase in pollution or other negative externality is an additional cost; an increase in a positive externality or in tax revenues is a benefit.
3. When price is changed in several markets the welfare effects can be approximately pictured by analyzing the changes in each market sequentially; though the order of the sequence usually makes little difference, it can sometimes affect the results of the analysis.

---

[5]We assume conservatively that vehicle operating costs are constant per mile for Chicago expressways at different speeds. For arterials, lower speeds are common and it is necessary to take into account the fact that greater highway density imposes greater direct costs as well as greater time costs. Johnson (8) derives the following linear equations based on data from a Chicago Transportation Study report:

$$C = 0.829 + 0.312t$$

where C = unit operating cost in cents per mile and t = unit time in minutes per mile. The range of t is 1.71 to 5.45, or, in terms of speed, between 11 and 35 mph. If this is modified for inflation and changes in the price of gasoline, we obtain, in 1974 dollars, $C = 5.97 + 1.02t$.

4. When price is changed in indirectly affected markets and there are no distortions in these markets, the net change in welfare is zero. The change in consumer surplus is approximately offset by the change in producer surplus.

5. When price is changed in indirectly affected distorted markets there is a net welfare change. This welfare change is approximated by the average value of the price distortion times the change in quantity.

7.8.1. An Example: Flat Supply Curves

Consider a local market for butter and margarine in which the demands are interrelated. Figure 7.14 shows the two markets in initial equilibrium.

D_B^1 is the existing demand curve for butter and D_M^1 is the existing demand curve for margarine. The demand curve D_B^2 is the demand curve for butter that *would be observed* if the margarine market *did not* exist. Now consider a policy change that increases the marginal cost and price of butter from P_B^1 to P_B^2. The new equilibrium is shown in Figure 7.14. The increase in the price of butter increases the demand for margarine to D_M^2.

The loss of consumer surplus from the policy is given by looking only at the butter market, and it is area A. This can be seen by comparing the areas of consumer surplus before and after the price increase. It does not include area C or D. This point is difficult to understand. The key to understanding it is to appreciate the following rule: There can be no loss of consumer surplus when the price has not changed. Margarine consumers cannot be better or worse off than before the policy change. Former butter consumers who have been priced out of the butter market will gain because they can switch to margarine but this mitigation of loss has already been counted in the butter market. In a sense these areas (C and D) are already accounted for in limiting the loss of CS in the butter market to area A rather than to area $A + B$, which would be the correct measure of loss if the margarine market did not exist. That is, area D is not an offset to the loss of CS represented by A in the butter market because the existence of the margarine market has already offset the loss of CS in the butter market, limiting it to area A rather than area $A + B$. Areas C and D do not count as a CS gain in analyzing the higher price of butter and area B does not count as an additional CS loss unless the margarine market does not exist. As long as the price of margarine does not change there is no change in CS in the margarine market and the effect of the margarine market has already been taken into account in the demand for butter. The rule is that there are no changes in CS or PS in a market unless price changes in the market.

Suppose now having implemented a policy that increases the cost and price of butter, another policy is implemented that increases the cost and price of margarine. What is the welfare effect of the price increase? Figure 7.15 is the same as Figure 7.14 but with the upward shift in the cost curve for margarine to MC_M^2. Areas D and E reflect the increased importance of the margarine market due to the higher price of butter. That is, they represent the potential consumer surplus that can be gained or lost by price decreases or increases. The relevant demand curve for the change in consumer surplus in the margarine market is $\mathbf{D}_M^2$. The loss of consumer surplus due to the increase in margarine cost and price is then measured along the new demand curve D_M^2.

Figure 7.14

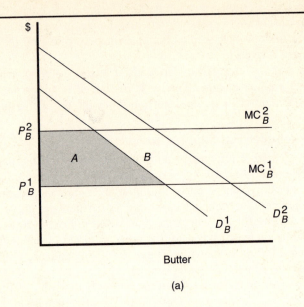

Butter

(a)

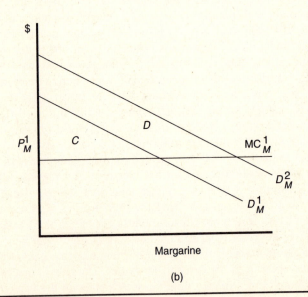

Margarine

(b)

The loss in the margarine market would be $C + D$; this is in addition to the original loss of A in the market for butter.

7.8.2. The Three-Park Problem

An application of these principles is shown by the following three-park problem. Consider the interrelated demand for three parks that are imperfect substitutes for each other. These parks are A, B, and C. They are unpriced and share consumer surplus areas A, B, and C. A policy is considered that will eliminate all three parks. It might appear that an analyst should count the value of the

Figure 7.15

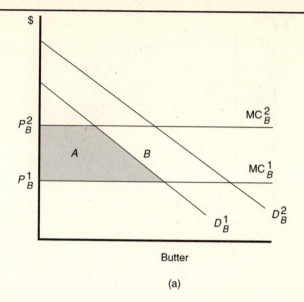

Butter

(a)

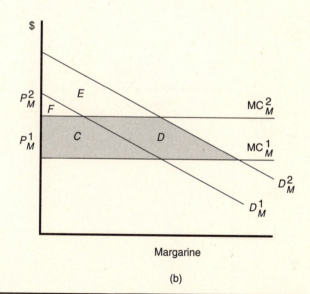

Margarine

(b)

loss of these parks as areas $A + B + C$. This analysis will, however, understate the value of the parks because it does not recognize that the welfare loss from the elimination of any one park is contingent on the other parks remaining in existence.

The correct loss may be determined by considering the parks as being eliminated in sequence in any order. Suppose A is eliminated first. The CS loss is area A. The demand curves for B and C will shift to the right as shown in Figure 7.16. When park B is eliminated the additional loss is $B + B'$. Now the

Figure 7.16

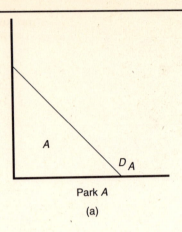

Park *A*

(a)

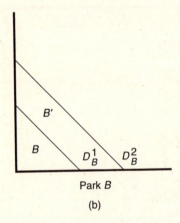

Park *B*

(b)

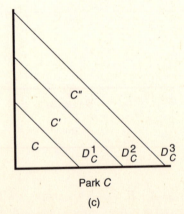

Park *C*

(c)

demand curve for C will again shift to the right. When park C is eliminated the additional loss will be $C + C' + C''$. Thus the loss from eliminating the three parks is $A + B + B' + C + C' + C''$. This differs from the loss initially calculated by $B' + C' + C''$ and this can be very large.

Mistakes of this type occur frequently in practice. Analysts sometimes calculate the benefits of additional lakes such as those arising from a dam using a formula that ignores the number of lakes already in the area. But the value of an additional lake will usually be less if substitute lakes already exist. An overestimation or underestimation of the value of additional lakes may occur depending on whether or not there are many or few lakes already there.

7.8.3. The Problem of the Second Best:
Distortions in One Market

In the butter and margarine example we saw that the partial equilibrium welfare effect of policies can be determined by examining only the primary market when there are no distortions or price changes in the indirectly affected markets. Now consider the case where there is a distortion in the secondary market.

The second-best theory says that when there is a distortion in one market so that the first-best welfare conditions are not met, and given that this distortion may not be removed, the welfare maximum requires an optimal distortion in other markets rather than the first-best conditions in these markets. The approximate welfare effect in the secondary market is found by multiplying the size of the distortion by the change in quantity. Here our purpose is to show that the distortion in indirectly affected markets can increase or decrease the magnitude of the welfare effects and to indicate how this can be calculated.

Consider a proposal to tax margarine, given an existing tax on butter. The situation before and after the tax on margarine is depicted in Figure 7.17. The initial price for margarine is P_M^1 and the final price is P_M^2. The taxed price for butter remains at P_B^2 but the demand increases from D_B^1 to D_B^2 after the tax on margarine. As a result the quantity of butter purchased increases from Q_B^1 to Q_B^2. In the margarine market we have the following:

$$\Delta CS = -(B + C) \qquad \Delta PS = 0 \qquad \Delta GR = B \qquad \Delta W = -C$$

In the butter market we have

$$\Delta CS = 0 \qquad \Delta PS = 0 \qquad \Delta GR = +(D + E) \qquad \Delta W = D + E$$

Thus the overall change in welfare is

$$\Delta W = -C + (D + E)$$

This amount could be positive or negative. How is it that the welfare effect of the margarine tax could be positive, or in any case smaller than the simple deadweight loss area C? The box $D + E$ is just the size of the distortion (the tax), times the change in quantity which gives the change in tax revenue. The change in tax revenue in the butter market arises even though there is no change in PS or CS in this market. Clearly then, the increase in tax revenues in the butter market is an increase in net welfare for this market. The original tax on butter distorts the choice between margarine and butter. The tax on margarine reduces this distortion and there is a gain from reducing this distortion.

Figure 7.17

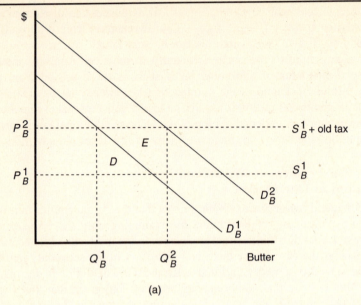

(a)

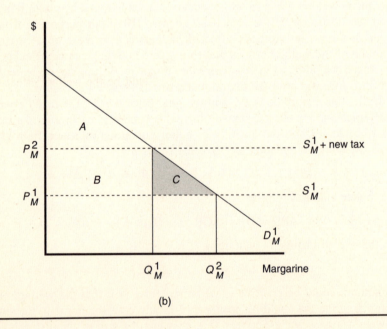

(b)

The tax on margarine reduces welfare because it raises the price to consumers, but it also increases welfare because it reduces the distortion in the choice between butter and margarine. This is seen more clearly in considering inputs to a production process. Suppose screws and nails are substitutes, either of which could be used in making a structure. In some instances screws are better and in others nails are better. Assume that screws normally would be used for job A. Suppose screws are taxed and nails are not. Given the higher price for screws produced by the tax, nails are the better buy. The tax on screws results in the use of nails as a substitute, even though without the tax screws should be used. But if nails were also appropriately taxed, screws would be chosen where they were the better choice without the tax and vice versa.

The tax on nails tends to reduce welfare insofar as it raises the price to consumers. But the tax tends to increase welfare insofar as it reduces the distortion in the choice between nails and screws. Thus it happens that the net welfare effect could be positive or negative. The logic applies to the butter and margarine example as well. One may wish to think of butter and margarine as contributing to the production of utility. (Of course, the nails and screws can be thought of in this way also.) The tax on butter will cause margarine to be chosen when butter would produce more utility per dollar, were it not taxed. Thus the existence of a tax on butter similar to that on margarine reduces the welfare loss.

The following questions are left to the student to answer:

a. How would the results differ if margarine and butter were complements?
b. Suppose butter was subsidized. What would be the welfare effects of a tax on margarine?

7.8.4. Price Changes in Several Markets

Figure 7.18 shows the initial equilibrium in the butter and margarine markets when there are no distortions. A tax is placed on butter that increases the price from P_B^1 to P_B^2. This increase in the price for butter, however, shifts the demand for margarine to the right, increasing the price in the margarine market from P_M^1 to P_M^2. The gain of producer surplus in the margarine market is clearly area $A + B$. From the previous discussion, we know that area C does not represent a welfare change.

The loss of consumer surplus in the margarine market would be area A if measured along demand curve D_M^1. The loss would however be $A + B + D$ if measured along demand curve D_M^2. It is reasonable to think of the demand curve D_M^1 moving up to D_M^2 and tracing out a path along the supply curve. That is, the loss of consumer surplus is approximated by using a sort of average of D_M^1 and D_M^2. The loss of consumer surplus is then calculated as area $A + B$. But this is just equal to the gain in producer surplus. Thus there is no net welfare change in the margarine market. The approximate partial equilibrium welfare loss from the tax on butter is just the traditional deadweight loss in the butter market, area E.

Figure 7.18

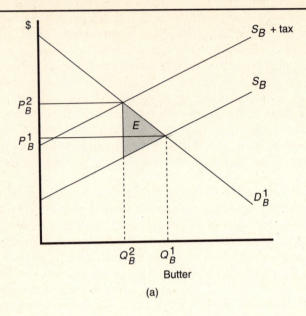

(a)

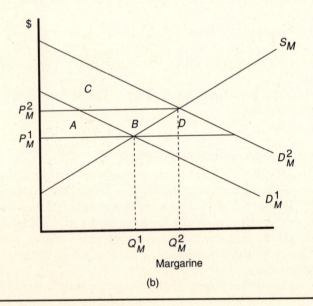

(b)

SUMMARY

The partial equilibrium values of welfare change may be found by the following rules:

1. The welfare change is the sum of the changes in (*a*) consumer surplus, (*b*) producer surplus, (*c*) tax revenues, and (*d*) externality changes.
2. Markets indirectly affected by a policy may be ignored in terms of efficiency effects, if in these markets price is not affected and there are no distortions.
3. When distortions exist in indirectly affected markets but price doesn't change, the welfare effect will be given by multiplying the size of the distortions per unit by the change in the number of units. The sign of the distortion should be clear from the context. An increase in pollution or another negative externality is an additional cost; an increase in a positive externality or in tax revenues is a benefit.
4. When price is changed in several markets the welfare effects can be approximately pictured by analyzing the changes in each market sequentially though the order of the sequence usually makes little difference.
5. When price is changed in indirectly affected markets and there are no distortions in these markets, the net change in welfare is zero. The change in consumer surplus is approximately offset by the change in producer surplus.
6. When price is changed in indirectly affected distorted markets there is a net welfare change. This welfare change is approximated by the average value of the price distortion times the change in quantity.

This chapter has given an intuitive explanation of an extension of partial equilibrium analysis to several markets. The more theoretically sound approach, however, is through general equilibrium analysis, which is considered in Chapter 21.

QUESTIONS AND PROBLEMS

1. Consider the following projects and explain whether or not partial equilibrium analysis would probably be sufficient or whether general equilibrium analysis should be required. Explain what information you would like to have to make your decision about which type of analysis should be used.
   a. A new bridge is being considered in light of the traffic congestion on the existing bridge.
   b. A new federal dam is suggested for the Columbia River.
   c. A federal gasoline tax is suggested.
   d. A national cigarette tax is also suggested.
   e. A cigarette tax is being considered by the city of New Haven, Connecticut.
2. Given a demand elasticity of 0.5 and a supply elasticity of 1.0 for ball point pens, and total sales in 1991 of $150 million, consider the welfare and transfer of the following taxes in partial equilibrium:
   a. The tax will be 10 cents per unit and the initial price is $1.00. What is the excess burden and the size of tax revenues?

    b. The tax will be 20 percent of the selling price. What will be the final selling price, the excess burden, and tax revenues?

    c. Instead of a tax, there will be a subsidy of 12 percent of the selling price. What will be the selling price, the welfare loss, and the total amount of the subsidy?

3. The government is considering purchasing military hardware from a firm whose production is now taxed on a constant per unit basis, but whose production also produces X pollution damage per unit produced. Show geometrically the welfare cost of the government purchase.

4. Suppose that hypercongestion exists during some rush hour periods each day on the Dan Ryan expressway. That is, the traffic volume on the Dan Ryan expressway during peak periods is below maximum capacity but speeds are low. The demand curve intersects the marginal private cost curve on its upper portion. Show in a diagram the welfare gain of moving to an optimum congestion level.

5. A leading textbook on traffic engineering (*Traffic Flow Fundamentals* by Adolf D. May, Prentice-Hall, 1990, pp. 292–293) reports speed-density and speed-volume relationships for the Eisenhower Expressway in Chicago. May notes that the maximum vehicle flow occurs at a speed of about 40 mph. He then says, "the optimum speed appears to be on the order of 40 mph." Should a benefit–cost analyst agree or disagree with this concept of optimum? Why or why not? Would the economically optimal speed be higher or lower?

6. Consider the market for home heating. Suppose there are three sources of home heating, gas, oil, and electricity.

    a. Show in a diagram the welfare effects of a tax on gas if all these sources have flat long-run supply curves, and there are no external effects nor distortions in any related markets.

    b. Given the above tax on gas, what (show in a diagram) will now be the welfare effect of a tax on oil?

    c. What would be the welfare effects (show in a diagram) of the tax on gas as in part a above if supply curves for gas, oil, and electricity are upward sloping?

    d. What will be the effects of the tax on oil given the tax on gas when supply curves on the gas, oil, and electricity are upward sloping?

    e. Show the effect of the above oil tax on welfare when not only are the supply curves upward sloping, but electricity produces pollution.

7. Total costs for using I-5 between Seattle and Tacoma, Washington, during rush hour are given by TSC = $100 + 0.0025X^2$, where X = traffic volume in cars per hour. (Assume one person per car.) The marginal cost, including social congestion costs, of traffic volume will then be $0.005X$. If traffic volume is 1800 cars per hour,

    a. What will be the total social costs?

    b. What will be the marginal social costs at the same volume of traffic?

    c. At a traffic volume of 1200 cars per lane per hour, what will be the marginal private cost of travel? (Marginal private cost equals average social costs.)

    d. If the optimum traffic volume is 1200 cars per lane per day, what will be the size of the Pigovian tax (optimal externality tax) at this level of traffic volume? Explain the calculation.

    e. If 1200 cars per lane per hour is the optimum traffic volume, what would be the marginal willingness to pay at this level?

REFERENCES

Bishop, Robert L., "The Effects of Specific and Ad Valorem Taxes," *Quarterly Journal of Economics* 82(2), 192–218, May 1968.

Johnson, M. Bruce, "On the Economics of Road Congestion," *Econometrica* XXXII (1–2), 137–150, January–April 1964.

Keefer, L. E., "The Relation Between Speed and Volume on Urban Streets," Highway Research Board Report, 37th Annual Meeting, 1958.

Knight, Frank H., "Some Fallacies in the Interpretation of Social Cost," *Quarterly Journal of Economics* 38, 582–606, August 1924.

Krauss, Marvin, et al., "The Welfare Costs of Nonoptimum Pricing and Investment Policies for Freeway Transportation," *American Economic Review* 66(7), September 1976.

Ruby, Michael G., "Benefit Cost Analysis with Uncertain Information: An Application in Air Pollution Control," Ph.D. thesis, University of Washington, 1981.

Spann, R. M., and E. W. Erickson, "The Economics of Railroading: The Beginning of Capitalization and Regulation," *The Journal of Economics* 12(2), 2–21, Spring 1971.

Zerbe, Jr., R. O., "The Costs and Benefits of Early Regulations of the Railroads," *The Bell Journal of Economics* 11(2), 343–350, Spring 1980.

Zerbe, Jr., R. O., and Kevin Croke, Jr., *Urban Transportation for the Environment*, Cambridge, MA: Ballinger, 1974.

8

Applications of Benefit–Cost Analysis (Partial Equilibrium) to Regulatory Issues

Benefit–cost analysis is widely used in the evaluation of government regulation of business. Three cases presented here are examples of benefit–cost application in a regulatory context. The first case involves regulation of the railroads, the second the regulation of product liability insurance markets, the third considers interaction of domestic regulation and international markets. Together these cases illustrate methodology for applying benefit–cost analysis as well as illuminate a number of important regulation issues.

8.1. FIRST CASE: EARLY REGULATION OF THE RAILROADS

8.1.1. Introduction

The Interstate Commerce Commission (ICC) is a classic regulatory agency, and its origins and operation have been analyzed extensively. Railroad regulation is often seen as representing either "capture" of the ICC by the railroads or as an example of self-interest legislation in which those regulated "purchase" regulatory legislation [Stigler (1971)]. However, an analysis of the early legislation and problems posed by no regulation shows that the prevailing view of early railroad regulation is not entirely correct.

   This short discussion treats only a small part of railroad regulation. For evaluations of more recent railroad regulation the reader is referred to Moore (1974) and to Friedlaender (1969, 1971) and to Hilton (1966). Our discussion concerns only early regulation of the railroads and is based on work by Zerbe (1980).

   This early regulation is generally seen as representing either captive or special interest regulation. Posner (1974), for example, states "[A] major purpose . . . of the original Interstate Commerce Act was to shore up the railroads' cartels" (p. 342). Others have argued that the original ICC regulation was not in the public interest and that the ICC regulation services are a classic example of regulation for the benefit of the regulated.

A different view is presented here. In the late 1800s the demand for railroad regulation was both widespread and persistent. Railroad regulation, some of which was bitterly fought by the railroads, existed in about 25 states before 1887 when the Interstate Commerce Act was established [see references in Zerbe (1980)].

The railroads' interest in interstate regulation before 1887 was primarily defensive. They were interested in federal regulation mainly because they correctly saw it as inevitable and as a refuge from state regulation. The 1887 Act embodied the substantive provisions of the shipper-written Regan Bill with the administrative machinery of the railroads' Cullen Bill. In the short run everyone probably got something from the 1887 Act. Politically, it seemed an ideal compromise and if, as some of the calculations here indicate, both consumers and producers gained in the short run, perhaps it was.

The primary purpose of the 1887 regulation was not to maintain railroad cartels, but rather to reduce rate instability [Hilton (1966)] and to increase rate "fairness" [Friedlaender (1971), Friedlaender and deNeufville (1979), Hilton (1966)]. The unfairness problem developed because rates for long hauls where there were competing railroads were less than rates on short hauls where the individual railroad had a monopoly. The rate level was a secondary consideration. The ICC, to a remarkable degree, did what it was supposed to do. The probability seems high, given the calculations here, that there were net social benefits from early ICC regulation.

8.1.2. The Problem

Rates were regulated separately in the short-haul and long-haul markets. An important part of the regulation was to prohibit short-haul rates that were greater than long-haul rates. The result of this regulation was that rates rose in the long-haul market and fell in the short-haul market.

Consider Figure 8.1. D is the demand for short-haul services; MC is marginal cost per ton mile, which is horizontal; P_m is a monopolist's price for these services in the absence of ICC regulation; and Q_m is the associated output. P_r and Q_r are the ICC-regulated price and the associated output, respectively. Consumer surplus before the regulated decrease in rates is simply area Z.

After the decrease in rates from P_m to P_r, consumer surplus is $Z + A + B$. The change in consumer surplus is

$$\Delta CS = A + B \tag{8.1}$$

Producer surplus before the decrease in rates is $A + C$. After the decrease it is $C + D$. The change in producer surplus is therefore

$$\Delta PS = D - A \tag{8.2}$$

We define the net welfare effect (ΔW) as the sum of producer and consumer surplus or

$$\Delta W = A + B - A + D = B + D \tag{8.3}$$

Figure 8.1   Effects in the short-haul market.

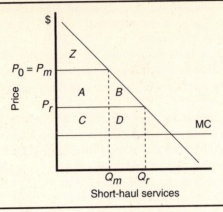

Short-haul services

Figure 8.2   Effects in the long-haul market.

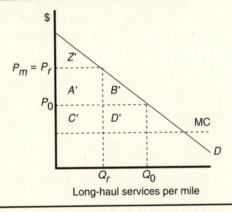

Long-haul services per mile

In the long-haul market, price before regulation is positioned as P_0 in Figure 8.2. Regulation increases price to P_r; for convenience P_r in Figure 8.2 is positioned the same as P_m in Figure 8.1. Thus, the relationships in Equations (8.1) through (8.3) hold also for the long-haul market, except that the right-hand side of the equations is reversed in sign. Thus the welfare change for the long-haul market is

$$\Delta W = -(B + D) \tag{8.4}$$

where it is understood that the demand and cost curves for the long- and short-haul markets are different so the size of areas B and D are also different.

This straightforward application of partial equilibrium analysis shows the value of explicitly drawing the supply and demand curves and calculating the relevant triangles and boxes. It is too easy otherwise to leave out something like area D in Figure 8.1 as did one published analysis.

8.1.3. Calculating the Welfare Effect

The welfare effect of the ICC regulations can be calculated for the following available data.

	Short-Haul Market	Long-Haul Market
P_0	2.5¢/ton mile	$0.3/ton mile
P_m	3.33¢/ton mile	$0.5/ton mile
Q_0	6.4 billion ton miles	23.0 billion ton miles
MC	$1.14/ton mile	$0.2/ton mile

The (absolute value) of the elasticity of demand (E_m) over the regulated quantity can be calculated from the following:

$$E_m = \frac{P_m}{P_m - \text{MC}} \tag{8.5}$$

$$Q_m = \frac{P_m Q_0}{P_m + \Delta P \ (E_m)} \tag{8.6}$$

$$\Delta Q = (\%\Delta P)Q_m E_m \tag{8.7}$$

Equation (8.5) is derived from the following relationship:

$$\text{MR} = \text{MC } P_m \left(1 + \frac{1}{E_m}\right)$$

Equations (8.6) and (8.7) are derived directly from the formula for demand elasticity. These give us the additional information.

	Short-Haul Market	Long-Haul Market
E_m	1.52	1.67
Q_m	4.63 billion ton miles	14.15 billion ton miles
ΔQ	1.77 billion ton miles	9.45 billion ton miles

Assuming a linear demand curve approximates the true demand curve, we then obtain:

Short-haul market:

$$\Delta CS = A + B = (P_m - P_0) Q_m + \frac{1}{2}(P_m - P_0) \Delta Q = +45.8 \text{ million}$$

$$\Delta PS = D - A = (P_0 - \text{MC}) \Delta Q - (P_m - P_0)Q_m = -14.54$$

$$\Delta W = \Delta CS + \Delta PS = +31.26$$

Long-haul market:

$$\Delta CS = -(B + C) = -37.75$$

$$\Delta PS = -(E - B) = +18.85$$

$$\Delta W = \Delta CS + \Delta PS = -18.90$$

The results are summarized in Table 8.1.

TABLE 8.1 Estimated Gains and Losses from Early Railroad Regulation

	Short-Haul Market	*Long-Haul Market*	*Total*
Consumer surplus	+$45.80	−$37.75	+$8.05
Producer surplus	−14.54	+18.85	+4.31
Total	$31.26	−$18.90	+$12.36

To see how robust these figures are we have calculated the welfare figures for alternative assumptions about marginal costs and for alternative constant elasticity demand curves rather than direct linear curves. For 30 reasonable alternative cases, the welfare gain is positive in 21 cases. These calculations do not allow for the fact that actual railroad freight rates on long-haul traffic were often below the regulated rates due to railroads cheating on the rates to gain additional business. The calculations also do not account for any gain in rate stability or in the feeling of fairness arising from railroad regulation which were among the stated goals of the regulation.

The benefit–cost analysis provided here indicates that the early regulation of the railroads probably produced welfare gains, contrary to the assertions of many critics. Yet, as the calculations of Moore (1974) and Friedlaender (1971) indicate, from the present-day perspective, the welfare effect of the ICC has been negative. This is because other technologies arose to compete with the railroads while regulation limited competitive responses by the railroad and maintained uncompetitive prices. This raises the question of how the 1887 problems could have been solved without incurring the long-run regulatory costs. Short-run problems often appear to give rise to a regulatory solution which imposes long-run costs. A policy question that remains, then, is how could the losses from later unneeded railroad regulation have been avoided while capturing these early gains?

8.2. SECOND CASE: CASE STUDY OF PROPERTY LIABILITY INSURANCE REGULATION

8.2.1. Introduction

This case study, which is based on work by Frech and Samprone (1980), examines the welfare loss from price regulation in the product liability insurance industry. This study provides an interesting exercise because it illustrates a useful technique for measuring the welfare loss where quality changes are potentially significant. Many analyses of welfare loss due to regulation overvalue the loss because no allowance is made for the positive welfare effects of competition on those margins not being regulated. This is especially true of older analyses.

Consider the simple example represented by Figure 8.3. Let P_r be the regulated price and P_0 the unregulated price. For simplicity, assume a flat marginal cost equal to the unregulated price. The industry may have persuaded the regulators to set a price above marginal and average costs such as P_r. The traditional method of analyzing welfare loss calculates the loss of consumer surplus from price regulations as area $A + B$. In the traditional analysis of a monopoly, or of an industry which has secured government price regulation,

Figure 8.3   Regulation of product liability insurance.

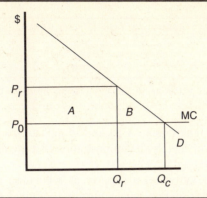

area A would be regarded as a producers' gain that offsets the loss of consumer surplus also represented by area A. In this case the deadweight loss, that is, the net welfare loss, would be represented by just area B.

Firms may, however, compete to gain monopoly profits represented by area A and in the extreme case resources may be spent which completely exhaust area A so that area A also represents social waste, that is, welfare loss.

Even where firms compete away all or part of area A, areas A and B together will be an overestimate of loss where the regulated firms compete on margins other than price to the benefit of consumers in those markets. For example, firms can compete in quality. A firm considering whether to lower its prices or raise its quality would make the usual sort of marginal benefit–marginal cost comparison. Decreasing the price and raising the quality are to some extent competitive substitutes. Thus if prices cannot be used as a competitive weapon because they are regulated, quality changes become more important. Area $A + B$ may thus be an overestimate of welfare loss because regulation may lead to an increase in quality that generates additional consumer surplus not measured by the preregulation demand. Thus the traditional analysis may misrepresent the effect of regulation on welfare because first, no account is taken of quality changes, thus tending to overestimate loss, and second, because no account is taken of market competition for available producer surplus, thus tending to underestimate the loss. The following analysis develops these points in a particular context, the context of the market for product liability insurance.

8.2.2.   The Setting for the Property Liability Insurance Industry

Rate regulation in the property liability insurance industry occurs at the state level. An individual company or a rating bureau representing the company submits rates to the state's insurance department for approval. A rate bureau classifies risks and sets insurance rates on the basis of statistical evidence submitted to it. The rates become effective when approved by the department or when a specified period of time has passed without departmental action (usually 30 days). Once a company's rates are approved the company cannot change them unless a request for a rate deviation is filed and approved with

TABLE 8.2   Concentration in the Property-Liability Insurance Industry for 1972–1974

Year	Top Four Firms or Groups	Top Eight Firms or Groups	Top Twenty Firms or Groups
1972	20.0	30.1	53.9
1973	19.9	32.2	54.3
1974	20.6	33.9	55.5

Source: Best's Aggregates and Averages: Property Liability Insurance Edition (1973, 1974, 1975).

the state insurance department. A request to deviate from previously approved rates must be accompanied by a demonstration that the deviation is justified by lower losses or increased expenses.

The traditional rationale in support of regulation asserts that regulation protects the customer in two ways. First it is argued that independent pricing may lead to price competition that results in rates inadequate to maintain the solvency of the insurance company and that therefore state regulations are needed to allow cooperative pricing to ensure the solvency of the insurance industry. Second, it is argued that, given the rate regulation, additional regulation is required to protect consumers from abusive practices that could arise from cooperative pricing.

Aside from state regulation the structure of the industry is competitive. As Table 8.2 shows, the percentage of the market held by the top 4, the top 8, and the top 20 firms is not especially high. These are the type of concentration ratios that are traditionally associated with the absence of monopoly power. In addition, there are no serious entry or exit restrictions that limit competition. Thus, the main distinction between the property liability insurance industry and many other competitive industries is that in many states insurance rates are regulated.

8.2.3.   Direct Evidence of Nonprice Competition

Two alternative sales methods are employed by the property liability insurance industry: the independent agency system and direct writing. The independent agency method provides more consumer services but is also more costly. Independent agents solicit insurance business for themselves and place this business with an affiliated company on a commission basis. Independent agents retain the property rights to policies they place with affiliate companies so that companies that obtain policies from independent agents are legally prohibited from renewing expired policies by directly contacting the policyholder. The company must instead renew the policy through the original agent. In contrast, other agents (direct writers) deal exclusively with a single company. In the second case the rights of policy renewals belong to the company. This results in an expense saving for the companies that operate through direct writers since a centralized processing system can be used for billing and renewals. Direct writing agents are paid either a commission or a salary, or both. When a commission is paid, the initial and renewal commission rates are lower than that of the independent agent.

Independent agents provide the consumer with more services than do direct writing agents. Probably the most important service of the independent

TABLE 8.3   Independent Agents' Mean Market Share (%), 1973

Private Passenger	Regulated Sector Mean	Competitive Sector Mean	t-Statistic for Difference Between Means
Automobile liability	51.39	45.10	1.81[b]
	(0.12)[a]	(0.11)	
Automobile physical damage	49.71	43.98	1.75[b]
	(0.11)	(0.10)	

[a] Value in parentheses is the standard deviation.
[b] Significant at a 5% level, based on a one-tail test.
SOURCE: Best's Executive Data System (1974).

agent is finding the company best suited to the consumer's needs. To some individuals, this search service and the fact that independent agents represent the policyholder rather than the company are sufficient to justify the higher price of their policies. In states where prices are set by regulation, and as a result are higher, nonprice competition is stimulated; the more service–intensive and more costly independent agent system becomes more attractive. Table 8.3 shows that the use of independent agents is more common in regulated states. The direct evidence on sales methods and indirect evidence on entry indicates that the higher-regulated insurance prices stimulate additional nonprice competition rather than higher profits. Thus, to refer again to Figure 8.3 it appears that box A is competed away and is not producer surplus.

8.2.4.   The Concept of the Welfare Loss

The welfare loss due to rate regulation is measured by the difference between consumer surplus with and without rate regulation. Producer surplus may be ignored because we assume both constant production costs and nonprice competition that together imply producer surplus is always zero. The difference in consumer surplus with and without regulation is measured as follows:

$$W = \int_0^{Q_c} \Delta(P, S) \, dQ - P_c Q_c - \int_0^{Q_r} \Delta(P, \bar{S}) \, dQ - P_c Q_c \qquad (8.8)$$

where P = the price of the insurance produce,
S = the quantity of complementary services provided per unit of risk reduction under competitive conditions
$\bar{S}$ = the quantity of complementary services provided per unit of risk reduction under regulated conditions
P_c, Q_c = the equilibrium price and quantity demanded under competitive conditions
P_r, Q_r = the price and quantity demanded under regulated conditions

The first expression on the right-hand side of the equation gives the area under the demand curve from zero quantity to the competitive quantity, Q_c. From this is subtracted the competitive price times the competitive quantity. This remaining consumer surplus is shown by area A in Figure 8.4(a). From this is subtracted the consumer surplus under regulation. This is shown in

Figure 8.4   Consumer surplus and product liability insurance.

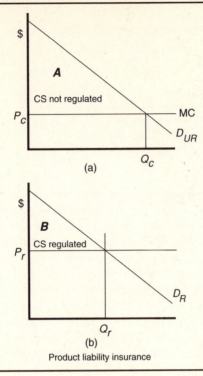

(a)

(b)

Product liability insurance

Figure 8.4(b).[1] Competition for quality moves the demand curve for product liability insurance to the right, thus the demand curve in Figure 8.4(b) lies to the right of the demand curve in Figure 8.4(a). Because the quality of the regulated product is higher, consumers are willing to pay more for each additional quantity of service. The consumer surplus under regulation is the area under the new demand curve between zero quantity and the regulated quantity, minus the regulated price times the regulated quantity. This is area B in Figure 8.4(b). In order to better understand the effect on consumer surplus, Figures 8.4(a) and (b) are collapsed into a single diagram, Figure 8.5. In Figure 8.5 consumer surplus without regulation is given by area $A + C + D$. Consumer surplus with regulation is given by area $A + B + B'$. Thus the net consumer loss due to regulation is given by area $(C + D) - (B + B')$.

There will be clear upper and lower bounds on the magnitude of this loss. The upper bound will occur if customers are satiated with services at the initial equilibrium. In this case the customer's valuation of the insurance product is not influenced by additional services and the regulatory price increase simply causes a movement up along the original demand curve. This means that the welfare loss attributed to rate regulation is at a maximum and is equal to area

---

[1]In Frech and Samprone's original article the last plus sign in their equation, No. 1, should be a minus sign. See Frech and Samprone (1980, p. 433).

Figure 8.5   Welfare loss due to nonprice competitiion.

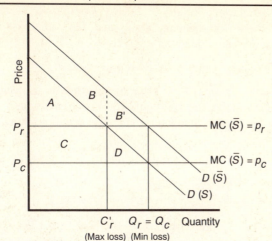

$C + D$ alone. Using the terminology of Equation (8.8) the maximum welfare loss area is equal to[2]

$$(P_r - P_c)Q_r + \int_{Q_r^*}^{Q_c} \Delta(P, S)\, dQ - (Q_c - Q_r)\, P_c \qquad (8.9)$$

Alternatively, Equation (8.9) shows the welfare loss due to pure rent-seeking behavior which confers no offsetting benefits.

The minimum welfare loss caused by regulation is zero. This occurs if consumers are indifferent between the lower price and lower quality without regulation and the higher price and higher quality with regulation. That is, the additional services supplied by the producers engaging in nonprice competition cause the demand curve to shift out such that area $C + D$ is just equal to area $B + B'$ in Figure 8.5. The welfare loss cannot be negative, that is, a welfare gain, since this would imply consumers were better off because of the additional services, but if this were the case consumers would have purchased the services in the absence of regulation. Therefore the actual welfare loss attributable to rate regulation must fall somewhere between zero and the maximum set by Equation (8.9).

8.2.5. Calculation of the Welfare Loss

The price of automobile insurance is defined as the ratio of premiums paid to losses paid out for that type of insurance. The quantity (Q_i) of the ith type of automobile insurance is defined as the losses incurred for that type (the ith type) of insurance for the year divided by the number of residents in the state. That is the quantity as defined as the loss per resident. Income will also affect

---

[2]Frech and Samprone (1980) represent the maximum welfare loss as their equation 2 on p. 434. This equation is incorrect. Their diagram of the welfare loss on p. 435 is, however, correct.

the quantity of insurance purchased. Thus income is another variable used to explain quantity purchased. Finally a dummy variable R_i is introduced that takes the value of one for regulated states and zero otherwise. The general form, then, of the demand equations is given by

$$Q_i = a_{i0} + a_{i1}P_i + a_{i2}Y + a_{i3}R_i \tag{8.10}$$

where Y is per capita income, P_i is price of the ith type of insurance, and R_i represents whether or not a state is regulated. These equations were estimated in linear form for the various states for 1973. The equations actually calculated are as follows:

$$Q_L = 50.34 - 24.03P_L + 0.0033Y_1 - 2.25R_L$$
$$ (6.34) \quad (-6.59) \quad\;\; (3.75) \quad\;\; (-1.72) \tag{8.11}$$
$$N = 51 \quad\;\; R_2 = 0.163 \quad\;\; F = 27.2$$

$$Q_D = 33.38 - 14.52P_D + 0.0014Y + 0.17R_D$$
$$ (7.44) \quad (-5.34) \quad\;\; (2.09) \quad\;\; (0.18) \tag{8.12}$$
$$N = 51 \quad\;\; R_2 = 0.39 \quad\;\; F = 8.1$$

where the L subscript indicates automobile liability insurance, the D subscript indicates automobile physical damage insurance, and t-statistics are in parentheses.[3] (Apparently the income variables standardize the size of the risk faced by consumers. Income accounts for the value of the insured automobile and the size of the personal liability judgments which tend to be higher in wealthier states.)

For our purposes the striking finding of Equations (8.11) and (8.12) is the small and statistically insignificant effect of the nonprice competition variable. In Equation (8.12) this variable even has the incorrect sign. Thus the hypothesis that consumers place no value on additional services cannot be rejected.

8.2.6. Two Hypotheses

The welfare loss is at the theoretical maximum when regulation has no effect on the quantity. That is, if regulation has a positive effect on service quality because independent agents are better at finding a company best suited for the customer's needs, then regulation should increase the insured against losses incurred per resident, holding income constant. Regulations should increase Q_L and Q_D of Equations (8.11) and (8.12). The fact that the R variables are not significant in these equations, or have the wrong sign, means that the hypothesis of maximum welfare loss due to regulation cannot be rejected at usual significant levels. In the common language of statistics, the null hypothesis that extra nonprice competition has no effect on demand cannot be rejected at the usual levels of significance.

---

[3]The equations provide a good deal of explanatory power for a cross-sectional study and excellent precision in estimating most of the coefficients. To standardize for risk, additional explanatory variables were tried including urbanization and the proportion of drivers under 25 but they failed to account for any additional variation and failed to noticeably alter the above coefficients. It seems that income alone is adequate.

We could, however, define the null hypothesis as one that says that the welfare loss due to rate regulation is zero. This would be the minimum welfare loss shown by the previous analysis. This hypothesis requires that

$$\frac{\Delta Q}{\Delta R} = \frac{\Delta P}{\Delta R} \times \frac{\Delta Q}{\Delta P} \tag{8.13}$$

The $\Delta Q/\Delta R$ term is given by the coefficient on the R variable in Equations (8.11) and (8.12). The $\Delta P/\Delta R$ term is given by the regulatory price increase and the $\Delta Q/\Delta P$ variable is given by the coefficient of the price variable in Equations (8.11) and (8.12). The regulatory price increase for the liability insurance (0.082) and the price increase for the null hypothesis and no loss requires that $\Delta Q/\Delta R = 1.97$ for Equation (8.11) and that $\Delta P/\Delta R = 0.89$ for Equation (8.12). These values are sufficiently different from the actual values that the null hypothesis can be reasonably rejected. That is, we can say with some degree of assurance that welfare is reduced by automobile insurance regulation especially for liability, and that the loss might be the maximum loss.

Conclusion.   The above analysis indicates that there is a welfare loss from regulation; however, point estimates of the loss cannot be very precise. Nonetheless, the best estimates are presented as a suggestive measure in Table 8.4.

For the automobile liability industry, the estimate of a negative effect of regulation on the demand curve can be ruled out on theoretical grounds. The evidence shows, however, that there is no positive effect on demand. Therefore, the best point estimate for that sector is no effect on demand and, hence, a maximum welfare loss.

For automobile physical damage insurance, the point estimate indicates that consumers value each additional dollar's worth of nonprice competition at about fourteen cents. The measure of the welfare loss must net out this increase in welfare due to the extra services. Thus, the information contained in Equations (8.11) and (8.12) gives the results in Table 8.4.

Summary.   First, it is clear that the demand for automobile insurance is relatively price-sensitive and can be quite well explained with the aid of a simple economic model.

TABLE 8.4   Impact of Automobile Insurance Rate Regulation, 1973

Welfare Loss	Per Capita	Total (millions)
Liability[a]	$3.68	$429.50
Physical damage[b]	1.44	168.10
Total	$5.12	$597.60
Mean per capita demand[c]	Competitive	Regulated
Auto liability	$28.09	$23.29
Auto physical damage	17.07	15.82

[a] From Equation (8.11).
[b] From Equation (8.12).
[c] From Best's Review.

Second, although the estimates of the impact of extra nonprice competition on demand are not as precise as one might like, one can be fairly certain that the extra services provided as a result of price regulation are not worth their costs to consumers, especially for liability insurance.

Third, the exact welfare loss estimates are somewhat tentative because of the lack of precise point estimates. Nonetheless, the resulting figure of $597.60 million suggests that the current deregulation movement can lead to a surprisingly large gain in economic efficiency.

8.3.   THIRD CASE: THE SOCIAL COST OF THE U.S. TOBACCO PROGRAM

We present this brief case to show again how easy it is to incorrectly count the relevant boxes and triangles in partial equilibrium analysis. The analyst takes a risk if he assumes he has a conceptual understanding of the boxes and triangles without systematically working through the geometrical analysis.

The first tobacco price support program in the United States was authorized under the Agricultural Adjustment Act of 1933. Several changes in its operation have been made, but all programs between 1933 and about 1975 followed the same basic principles. We first examine the social costs of the program as it existed before 1975.

Prior to the program's implementation, tobacco production varied between years, causing prices to fluctuate widely. Agricultural prices in general were perceived to be low in relation to other prices. The program's goal was to achieve economic parity and to ensure a certain income stability for tobacco growers. This was achieved by a restriction of output that resulted in higher prices. The program, initiated by dissatisfied growers and their Congressmen, made rental, deficiency, and adjustment payments to farmers who stayed within their allotted acreages.

The Agricultural Adjustment Act gives the Secretary of Agriculture the power to set production quotas and to assign allotted acreages to farmers. The tobacco program controls production essentially in two ways. First, it restricts the number of acres per farm that can be planted with tobacco. In the past, tobacco acreage allotments have been reduced continuously as technical development increased production per acre. Second, it restricts the movement of tobacco allotments from one farm to another. This is an effort to slow down yield increases due to movement of allotments from low- to high-yielding farms.

8.3.1.   The Effect of Acreage Control

The restrictions on using land for tobacco means that land is combined in less than optimal proportions with other inputs, such as labor, fertilizer and machinery. Thus the marginal cost curve will be shifted up by the acreage control, and as a result the price will be higher and the quantity produced less.

The calculation of the change in producer and consumer surplus is complicated by the fact that the United States has monopoly power in selling tobacco

Figure 8.6 Tobacco program.

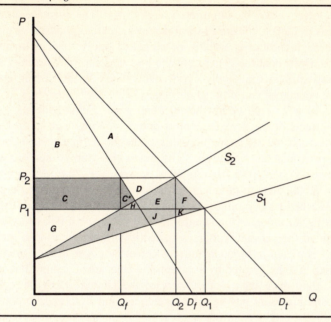

abroad. Thus, the higher price generates monopoly profits, which are a welfare gain (producer surplus) from the point of view of U.S. citizens.[4]

Figure 8.6 shows the original supply, without the acreage controls, as S_1. The supply curve S_2 shows the new higher marginal cost curve. P_1 is the original price and P_2 the price after controls. D_f represents the demand for tobacco by foreigners. D_t represents the total demand, so that domestic demand is represented by the difference between D_t and D_f. Following the usual convention we count changes in foreigners' consumer or producer surpluses as zero. Then
Domestic consumer surplus

$$CS_1 = A + D + E + F \text{ (Note } B + C + C' + H \text{ do not count in this analysis}$$
$$\text{as they are CS for foreigners.)}$$
$$CS_2 = A$$
$$\Delta CS = -(D + E + F)$$

Producer surplus

$$PS_1 = G + I + J + K \qquad PS_2 = G + C + C' + D$$
$$\Delta PS = PS_2 - PS_1 = [C + (C' + D)] - (I + J + K)$$
$$\Delta W = \Delta CS + \Delta PS = (C + C') - (E + F + I + J + K)$$

The change in welfare is then $(C + C') - (E + F + I + J + K)$.

---

[4]This assumes the production technology does not require fixed proportions among imports.

8.3.2. Interpretation

The welfare effects can be interpreted as follows. The increase in tobacco prices reduces domestic consumer surplus and increases producer surplus. Part of the increase in producer surplus is from monopoly rents extracted from foreigners, and part is at the expense of the loss in domestic consumer surplus. The rightward shift in the supply curve also causes an increase in costs that reduces both consumer and product surplus.

It is very easy to miscount the relevant areas. Some analysts evaluated the welfare effects of the acreage control policy as above but ignored area C' (see Figure 8.6). It is easy to see how this came about. The analysts explained the areas approximately as follows: "The net social gain is area C, which is the net monopoly gain from foreign sales, less area F, the loss in consumer surplus, less K, the loss in producer surplus from the reduction in output, less $I + J + E + M$, the loss in producer surplus from the increase in production costs from restricting an input." One should not, however, be quick to assume that one has counted the geometrical areas correctly without working it through.

Area C' is a gain in producer surplus offset by a loss in foreign consumer surplus, which is to be ignored by assumption. Thus area C' should be included as a welfare gain from the point of view of the United States. It is true that area C' doesn't represent payment by foreigners, but by domestic consumers. Shouldn't then the producer surplus represented by area C' be offset by an equal loss of consumer surplus? The answer is *yes, but the loss of consumer surplus has already been offset as part of area E.* To count E as a loss and then to also exclude area C' is to *double count* some losses of consumer surplus.

The student should calculate the change in producer and consumer surplus by working through a version of the diagram in which domestic demand is given first and foreign demand is given by the difference between total and domestic demand. Since even sophisticated analysts can make mistakes, our advice, if you are supervising or carrying out a benefit–cost analysis, is to require that the gains and losses be systematically derived as in Chapter 7.

8.3.3. Counting Foreigners' Gains and Losses

We will now evaluate the effect of the policy-counting gains and losses to foreigners. With reference to Figure 8.6 we have

$$CS_1 = (A + D + E + F) + (B + C + C' + H)$$
$$CS_2 = A + B$$
$$\Delta CS = -(D + E + F + C + C' + H)$$
$$\Delta PS = PS_2 - PS_1 = (C + C' + D) - (I + J + K)$$
$$\text{and } \Delta W = \Delta CS + \Delta PS = -(E + F + H + I + J + K)$$

This is just the increase in costs $(I + H + J + E)$ plus the loss due to the fall in production $(F + K)$. Taking into account the effect of foreign losses eliminates gains $C + C'$ which were positive in the previous analysis in Figure 8.6. From an international perspective the welfare effects of the program must be negative.

Determining the Magnitude of Gains and Losses.   Johnson made estimates of the welfare losses from the tobacco program both in 1965 and in 1980. Our estimates of the welfare cost of the program assume that the curves bounding the relevant areas of Figure 8.6 can be estimated using the techniques of Chapter 7. The size of the monopoly rents can be calculated as the increase in price times foreign sales. The size of the efficiency loss due to the leftward shift in supply is calculated by Johnson, and the size of area C' and of area $F + K$ can be calculated as below.

Estimates of elasticities are made by Johnson (1965, 1980, and by others).[5] We will use a demand elasticity calculated as a weighted average of domestic and foreign demand elasticities of 0.2. The supply elasticity is estimated as 0.3. The percentage price distortion is thought to be about 0.30. We will use estimates of price and quantity after the tobacco program of 60.4 cents per pound and 1267 million pounds. (Note that if we use the price and quantity figures after the tobacco program we must use elasticity figures that apply after the program.)

It makes a crucial difference whether we regard the percentage price distortion as the distortion from what would otherwise be the equilibrium price or as a distortion similar to an ad valorem tax, that is, as a percentage of the final price. The student may recall that this difference was discussed briefly in Chapter 7. We will assume that the distortion refers to a percentage distortion from the original price. This means that we should use Formula (7.5') to calculate area C:

$$\Delta W(F + K) = -\frac{1}{2}P_0 Q_0 E_d (t^2)\left(1 + \frac{E_d}{E_s}\right)$$

where $P_0 Q_0$ represent original price and quantities, E_d is total demand elasticity, E_s is supply elasticity, and t is the percentage price distortion, as compared to the original price.

Applying this formula gives a welfare triangle loss of about $29,000,000,[6] as follows.

$$E + K = \frac{1}{2}\,(765,000,000)\,(0.5)(0.3)^2\left(1 + \frac{.2}{.3}\right) = 29,000,000 \text{ per year}$$

The area of monopoly rent gained from foreigners, area C, is the price increase times the quantity exported. The price increase estimated above is $(t \times 60.4)$ or 18 cents and the quantity exported is about 474,000,000 pounds. Thus the monopoly rent collected is $85.3 million per year. Johnson estimates the efficiency loss of areas $I + J + E$ as about $80 million per year.

---

[5]Johnson gives a range of estimates.
[6]If we determine the distortion is a percentage distortion from final price as with an ad valorem tax, we would use Equation (7.4) and have an estimate of loss of $8,262,000. (The student may wish to draw a diagram that makes clear where the difference in the two figures arises. Notice that where the percentage distortion is interpreted as a percentage of what would be the equilibrium price, the difference between the demand and supply prices is much larger than when the percentage distortion is based on the final price.)

The size of area C' can be estimated from the foreign demand elasticity. This is estimated to be about 1.5. (We assume this is the elasticity estimate at the final not the initial price.) The size of area C' will be approximately $\frac{1}{2}(\Delta Q \cdot \Delta P)$ if we assume that area H is small so that area C is approximately a triangle. The change in price is 18 cents. The change in foreign quantity can be estimated, by $E_f = (\Delta Q/Q)/(P/\Delta P)$ and solving for ΔQ, as about 212,000,000 pounds. The size of area C' is then about $19 million per year. This gives the estimates of losses and gains shown in Table 8.5.

Clearly the gain represented by area C' of $19 million is a nontrivial gain that should not be ignored.[7] These estimates are sensitive to the elasticities assumed, however. For example, Johnson suggests that the loss supply efficiency might have been $80 million instead of only $25 million.

What does seem likely is that domestic welfare losses were mitigated by the collection of foreign rents and may have been positive in 1965, but, as Johnson (1980) shows, were certainly positive in 1980.

Discussion.   This case study gives the student more practice in calculating the lost producer and consumer surplus and shows how simple calculations of welfare areas may be made. This section also introduces the common practice of ignoring the welfare of foreigners in these calculations. The student should evaluate this practice in light of equity and distributional issues raised in Chapters 11 and 12. Also, in considering a general equilibrium model in which effects on foreign income are felt domestically through changes in export demand, the gains from collecting rents from foreigners may be much less. It is not surprising that there is a decline in welfare losses as markets adjust to reduce these losses.

There are several other policy issues that can be discussed in a benefit–cost framework, which are of interest with respect to the tobacco program. First, one of the objectives of the tobacco program was to increase price stability for tobacco. Johnson (1980, at 52f) finds that the program has achieved this to a remarkable degree, and has also stabilized output. Such stability has a value if it reduces risk. What is the value of this stability? Decreases in tobacco use have occurred as information about its health effects have become better known. The tobacco program raises the price of tobacco, reduces the amount demanded, and decreases consumer surplus. Is part of this loss in consumer surplus a false loss? An argument could be made that less tobacco would be consumed if information about its health effects were costless.

TABLE 8.5

	Long-Run Estimate (millions per year)
Welfare triangle $(F + K)$	−29.0
Export monopoly (C)	+85.0
Supply distortion $(E + H + I + J)$	−25.0
Area C' (uncounted producer surplus)	+19.0
Total welfare change	+50.0

---

[7] Johnson's estimates for areas other than area C are slightly different.

Figure 8.7 Tobacco health effects considered.

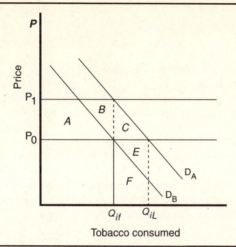

Figure 8.7 shows a full information demand curve compared with the actual demand curve. Area $B + C$ would be a recorded loss of consumer surplus that may not in fact be a loss of consumer surplus. One way to think about this is to imagine a temporary demand for a good that once it is tried is found to be worthless. Ex ante there is loss of consumer surplus along D_{1L} of $A + B + C$ if government action raises the price of this good. Ex post those that didn't buy the good because of the higher price find they are better off because they did not buy the good. They have saved a net value equal to the amount they would have spent on the good, or $E + F$. In the tobacco case, ex post those that did not buy because of the higher price may feel they have saved a good deal more than just the cost of the good purchased.

Another policy issue raised by this exercise is whether or not the domestic gains from the program are at a maximum. Given the positive domestic welfare effects of the program, one can ask if the price were higher would the gains be even greater? Johnson suggests that this is in fact the case.

If a major goal of the program is to extract monopoly rents from foreign demanders, could this be done more efficiently through an export tax? Is such a tax constitutional?

QUESTIONS AND PROBLEMS

First Case

1. The analysis here is limited in a number of ways. For example, suppose after rates are raised in the long-haul market that railroads compete on quality of service so that the quality of service was better after than before regulation. How would that affect the above calculations? (See the next case.)
2. Was the present value of initial railroad regulation positive? To answer the question one would have to develop a counterfactual scenario assuming that railroads were left unregulated in 1887. Attempt to develop a framework and to conceptualize how you might answer this question.

3. Suppose railroads were able to cheat on the cartel level of rates so that actual rates in one or both markets were less than the regulated rates. How would this affect the calculation of the regulation welfare cost?

Second Case

1. A fundamental question raised by the price regulations here is who gains. That is, if the potential producer surplus, area *D*, is competed away as waste should the industry be in favor of these regulations? The analysis also indicates that consumers lose so, again we ask, who gains? What theory of regulation, if any, can explain these results?
2. Does the absence of producer surplus created by the regulations imply that there would be no opposition to deregulating the industry? Why or why not?
3. Consider minimum quality regulations of MDs, insurance brokers, barbers, widgets, or other goods or services. Under what conditions could the benefits from regulation exceed the costs, unlike the case of the product liability insurance industry? Diagram the benefit–cost areas for this case and explain the logic.

Third Case

1. Should benefit–cost analysis count everyone's gains and losses the same (foreigners, criminals, etc.)?

REFERENCES

First Case

Friedlaender, A. F., *The Dilemma of Freight Transportation Regulation,* Washington, D.C.: The Brookings Institution, 1969.

Friedlaender, A. F., "The Social Costs of Regulating the Railroads," *American Economic Review* 61, 226–234, May 1971.

Friedlaender, A. F., and R. DeNeufville, "The Political Rationality of Federal Transportation Policy," *Research in Law and Economics* 1, 97–114, April 1979.

Hilton, G., "The Consistency of the Interstate Commerce Act," *Journal of Law and Economics* 8, 87–113, October 1966.

Kolko, G., *Railroads and Regulation, 1877–1916,* Princeton, N.J.: Princeton University Press, 1965.

Moore, T. G., "Deregulatory Surface Freight Transportation," in *Promoting Competition in Regulated Markets,* A. Phillips, ed., Washington, D.C.: The Brookings Institution, 1974.

Posner, R. A., "Theories of Regulation," *Bell Journal of Economics* 5(2), 335–358, Autumn 1974.

Spann, R. M., and E. W. Erickson, "The Economics of Railroading: The Beginning of Cartelization and Regulation," *Bell Journal of Economics and Management Science* 1(2), 227–244, Autumn 1970.

Stigler, G., "The Theory of Economic Regulations," *Bell Journal of Economics* 2(1), 2–21, Spring 1971.

Zerbe, R. O., "The Costs and Benefits of Early Regulation of the Railroads," *Bell Journal of Economics* 11(1), Spring 1980.

Second Case

Frech III, H. E., and Joseph C. Samprone, Jr., "The Welfare Loss of Excess Nonprice Competition: The Case of Property–Liability Insurance Regulation," *Journal of Law and Economics* 23(2), 429–440, October 1980.

Third Case

Johnson, P., "The Social Cost of the Tobacco Program," *Journal of Farm Economics* 47(2), 242–255, 1965.

Johnson, P., *The Economics of the Tobacco Industry,* New York: Praeger, 1984.

Johnson, P., and D. Norton, "Social Cost of the Tobacco Program Redux," *American Journal of Agricultural Economics* 65(1), 117–119, 1982.

Lancaster, F., "Effects of Allotment Reconstitution on Tobacco Fields," *Journal of Farm Economics* 46(6), 1415–1420, 1965.

9

Making Financial Decisions

In Chapter 4 we outlined the basic concepts and mathematics of financial analysis, and Chapters 5 through 8 provided a theoretical background for measuring benefits and costs. In this chapter we will see how this information can be used in practice to make financial decisions. For the moment we will restrict our scope to those problems that involve financial information alone. There are, of course, other issues that often are in benefit–cost analysis, such as externalities or considerations of income distribution. We will deal with these in later chapters.

We will describe three basic categories of problems that can be approached using financial analysis. The first category involves assessing the desirability of a single project or investment. We want to know whether the undertaking will increase or decrease our *real wealth*. This does not mean that the undertaking simply yields more money than we put in; for example, an investment of $100 today that returns $101 in 10 years would hardly be desirable. Rather, we want to ensure that the undertaking makes us better off than alternative decisions, including the decision to do nothing.

The second category of problem involves the comparison of different projects. Obviously, we want to check that each increases our real wealth. Beyond that, we want to see which one provides the largest increase. The techniques of financial analysis can be used to help identify the preferred project.

The third category covers activities that we need to undertake, even though they do not increase real wealth in the same way. Once again, we wish to compare different alternatives to accomplish the objective involved. For example, a homeowner may need a new roof and wants to identify which material would be best. Or, a state highway department decides to rebuild a highway and needs to know which design to choose. In this category, financial analysis helps to select the alternative that accomplishes the goal with the smallest decrease in real wealth, or in other words, at the lowest possible cost.[1]

Several different methods are used to make financial decisions, including net present value, benefit–cost ratios, internal rate of return, and the payback period. Net present value is preferred by most experts because it always provides the correct answer and is relatively easy to calculate. This method will be described in the first section of this chapter. The other approaches will be discussed and compared in the second section. The final section will provide a brief introduction to the types of information needed to calculate cash flows.

9.1. NET PRESENT VALUE

The most widely used technique of financial analysis involves calculating *net present value* (NPV). The theoretical rationale for the NPV was discussed in Chapter 3. In financial terms, the NPV of a project is simply the sum of its discounted cash flows. If the NPV is greater than zero, the project increases real wealth. If the NPV is less than zero, the project decreases real wealth. This technique is sometimes called *present worth analysis*.

Net present value has two major advantages over other approaches. First, when used properly, it gives the correct financial decision in all cases. This differentiates the NPV from some of the other approaches that will be discussed later in this chapter. Second, NPV is relatively simple to calculate, while other techniques are sometimes complex.

9.1.1. Calculating the Net Present Value

In general, we need to make five assumptions in order to use the NPV approach:

1. The discount rate(s) is (are) given. The rate can vary over time, but we must assume a value for the discount rate during each period. For convenience, we will assume the rate does not include any risk premium since the risk of the project (its chance of failure) can be included in other ways.

2. Capital is readily available. We will borrow money if necessary in order to undertake projects with positive NPVs. In a developed country, this assumption is usually realistic; in Third World nations it may be less so.

3. The interest rate for borrowing is the same as the interest rate for lending. This is not strictly true, since financial institutions require differential interest rates in order to cover overhead expenses and make a profit. However, capital markets in most Western countries closely approximate the perfect markets described by economic theory, so this assumption is usually acceptable.

---

[1] Of course, activities in this category do produce benefits. For example, the homeowner stays dry and drivers get a new road. These benefits are not expressed in financial terms, however, so the projects seem to decrease real wealth. It is crucial to note that the alternatives being considered must each achieve the goal in question, otherwise the financial comparison is irrelevant.

4. Cash flow projections include all relevant costs and benefits, including such items as maintenance and taxes. This requires a careful assessment of all the project's impacts before we make our analysis. Unless otherwise noted, all cash flows occur at the end of the periods.
5. If we are comparing projects, we need to use a complete list of options. This means all projects are mutually exclusive; we could not choose part of one project and combine it with part of another. If such a combination is possible, it should be considered as a separate option.

If these five assumptions hold, we can calculate the NPV from estimates of benefits and costs over time. As was discussed in Chapter 4, cash flows incurred in the distant future must be discounted more heavily than those occurring earlier to account for the time value of money. Thus, we estimate benefits and costs, discount them to the present, and then sum the discounted benefits and discounted costs:

$$\text{NPV} = \sum_{t=0}^{n} \frac{B_t}{(1 + r_t)^t} - \sum_{t=0}^{n} \frac{C_t}{(1 + r_t)^t} \tag{9.1}$$

B_t represents the benefits we derive from the project in period t; since we are considering only financial flows, this would be the income or the revenue produced by the project. C_t is the cost in period t, n is the lifespan of the project, and r_t is the effective interest rate for period t. The NPV is simply the difference between the discounted benefits and discounted costs. If the NPV is greater than zero, the project increases real wealth.

Note that there can be B_0 and C_0 terms in the equation. These represent immediate effects; for convenience, we describe them as taking place at $t = 0$. B_0 is usually zero, but many projects have immediate costs, C_0, such as the purchase price of a new machine. As we would expect, the cash flows at $t = 0$ are not discounted since the denominator of the equation is equal to 1.

Two observations should be made about Equation (9.1). First, it applies in all cases, even if we are considering nonfinancial impacts such as environmental degradation. The net present value of a project is always the difference between the discounted benefits and the discounted costs. *Equation (9.1) is thus the fundamental financial equation of benefit–cost analysis.*

Second, the period chosen need not be in years, although this is often used. Time can be expressed in months, days, decades, or whatever units may be convenient. However, one must be sure to express costs and benefits using the same period, and r_t must be the effective interest rate for that period.

9.1.2. Net Present Value for Single Projects

Equation (9.1) is easy to use if we follow a simple series of steps. When evaluating a single project, there are four things to do:

1. Choose an appropriate period, usually years. Write down the cash flows for these periods.
2. Find the correct effective discount rate or rates.
3. Calculate the NPV using Equation (9.1).
4. Compare the NPV with 0. If the NPV exceeds 0, the project increases real wealth and should be accepted.

EXAMPLE 9.1

Net Present Value

The Husky Dogsled Company is considering buying a new piece of equipment to help in its manufacturing process. It would cost $40,000 immediately but would save $7500 each year for the next 10 years. However, at the end of the fifth year a one-time maintenance expense of $5000 would be incurred. If the relevant effective annual discount rate is 8 percent, should Husky Dogsled buy the machine?

1. Choose the period and write down the cash flows. The logical period is years. Then,

$$B_0 = 0 \qquad B_1 = \cdots = B_{10} = \$7500$$

$$C_0 = \$40,000 \qquad C_5 = \$5000$$

2. Find the correct discount rate.

$$r_1 = \cdots = r_{10} = 0.08$$

3. Calculate the NPV.

$$NPV = \sum_{t=0}^{n} \frac{B_t}{(1 + r_t)^t} - \sum_{t=0}^{n} \frac{C_t}{(1 + r_t)^t}$$

$$= \left[\sum_{t=1}^{10} \frac{\$7500}{(1 + 0.08)^t} \right] - \left[\$40,000 + \frac{\$5000}{(1 + 0.08)^5} \right]$$

The term in the first set of brackets is the benefit stream, and the two costs are enclosed in the second set of brackets. Note that the $5000 maintenance expense is discounted from the fifth year.

The benefits represent the present value of an annuity of $7500 received for 10 years and discounted at 8 percent. We can use Equation (4.28) from Chapter 4 to find the present value of an annuity.

$$P = A \left[\frac{1 - (1 + r)^{-n}}{r} \right]$$

Therefore,

$$NPV = \$7500 \left[\frac{1 - (1.08)^{-10}}{0.08} \right] - \$40,000 - \left[\frac{\$5000}{(1.08)^5} \right]$$

$$= \$50,325.61 - \$40,000 - \$3402.92$$

$$= \$6922.69$$

4. Compare the NPV with 0. Since the NPV is greater than 0, the machine is a good investment. It produces a discounted savings of $6922.69.

Following these steps will make NPV computations clear and simple. Once we gain experience with the technique, we will be able to combine several of the initial steps and proceed directly to the NPV calculation. However, the first two examples in this chapter trace through all the steps to show how the technique works.

EXAMPLE 9.2

Net Present Value

The law firm of Bear, Bear, Bear, and Goldilocks is planning to purchase a new computer. It costs $1700 and would save $150 per month in secretarial costs. It would be worn out after one year. The firm must pay an effective annual interest rate of 12 percent. Is the computer a good investment?

1. Choose the period and write down the cash flows. In this case, the logical period is months.

$$B_0 = 0 \qquad B_1 = \cdots = B_{12} = \$150 \qquad C_0 = \$1700$$

2. Find the correct discount rate. The effective annual rate is 12 percent. Since the period being used is months, we must use Equation (4.8) from Chapter 4 and solve for i/h to find the effective monthly rate:

$$r = \left(1 + \frac{i}{h}\right)^h - 1$$

$$r = 0.12 \qquad h = 12$$

$$0.12 = \left(1 + \frac{i}{12}\right)^{12} - 1$$

$$\frac{i}{12} = 0.009489$$

Thus, the monthly interest rate is 0.9489 percent.

3. Calculate the NPV.

$$NPV = \sum_{t=0}^{n} \frac{B_t}{(1 + r_t)^t} - \sum_{t=0}^{n} \frac{C_t}{(1 + r_t)^t}$$

$$= \sum_{t=1}^{12} \frac{\$150}{(1.009489)^t} - \$1700$$

$$= \$150 \left[\frac{1 - (1.009489)^{-12}}{0.009489} \right] - \$1700$$

$$= \$1693.73 - \$1700.00$$

$$= -\$6.27$$

4. Compare the NPV with 0. Since the NPV is less than 0, the computer is not a good investment. However, you may not be making this decision for financial reasons alone. The computer may make the secretary happier and be well worth the $6.27!

9.1.3. Net Present Value for Comparing Projects

When projects are being compared, there are five basic steps in using Equation (9.1):

1. Identify all possible alternatives. Recall that they must be mutually exclusive.

EXAMPLE 9.3

Net Present Value for Comparing Projects

The Bedrock city government plans to build a new road to the municipal aggregate plant. One contractor proposes to build the road for $100,000, after which it would need only $10,000 worth of maintenance in the seventh year. Another proposes a cheaper project costing $75,000, but this road would require $5000 of maintenance each year. The two roads are otherwise equivalent and each would last for 10 years. Bedrock can borrow money at an effective annual rate of 7 percent. Which contractor should it choose?

In this case, Bedrock should choose the less expensive project. There are no financial benefits here: The benefits of the road go to the users and are the same for both proposals since the highways are equivalent.

1. Identify all possible alternatives. There are only two proposals, and they are mutually exclusive, as required.
2. Choose the period and write down the cash flows for each project. The logical period is years.
   For project 1:

   $$B_t = 0 \qquad C_0 = \$100{,}000 \qquad C_7 = \$10{,}000$$

   For project 2:

   $$B_t = 0 \qquad C_0 = \$75{,}000 \qquad C_1 = \cdots = C_{10} = \$5000$$

3. Find the correct discount rate. For both projects,

   $$r_1 = \cdots = r_{10} = 0.07$$

4. Calculate the NPV of each project.

$$NPV = \sum_{t=0}^{n} \frac{B_t}{(1 + r_t)^t} - \sum_{t=0}^{n} \frac{C_t}{(1 + r_t)^t}$$

   For project 1:

$$NPV_1 = -\$100{,}000 - \frac{\$10{,}000}{(1.07)^7}$$

$$= -\$100{,}000 - \$6227.50$$

$$= -\$106{.}227.50$$

   For project 2:

$$NPV_2 = -\$75{,}000 - \$5000 \left[\frac{1 - (1.07)^{-10}}{0.07} \right]$$

$$= -\$75{,}000 - \$35{,}117.91$$

$$= -\$110{,}117.91$$

   Note that the annuity equation was used for project 2's maintenance costs.

5. Compare the NPVs. Project 1 has the lower cost; that is, its NPV is closest to zero. Since the roads yield identical benefits, Bedrock should choose the cheaper project, that of contractor 1.

2. Choose an appropriate period and list the cash flows for each project.
3. Find the effective discount rate or rates.
4. Calculate the NPV of each project using Equation (9.1).
5. Compare the NPVs. The project with the highest NPV is the one that does the most to increase real wealth. In the case of projects that cost money but do not yield financial benefits, the option with the NPV closest to 0 is the best choice, since it produces the desired outcome with the smallest decline in wealth.

Examples 9.1 through 9.3 illustrate the basic calculations for net present value. You should use this stepwise procedure until you are comfortable with the technique. Later examples in this chapter will use a somewhat abbreviated form in order to save space. However, any of them can be solved using the approaches described above.

9.1.4.   Effect of Different Discount Rates

The choice of the discount rate is often the most difficult part of financial analysis. In some cases, a small change in r can lead to significant changes in NPV. It is important for a financial analyst to recognize this influence and make allowances for it.

The appropriate discount rate is sometimes known with considerable certainty, particularly if the project covers only a short time span. When the rate is not guaranteed or can vary over time, it is often desirable to calculate the NPV using a range of discount rates. This information allows the decision maker to see the possible results of the project under a variety of assumptions. Uncertainty will be handled in more detail in a subsequent chapter.

Example 9.4 shows how a given project may be extremely desirable (case a) or undesirable (case d) depending upon the discount rate. In this case, most of the change resulted from the $100 payment in year 5; a discount rate of 5 percent makes this worth $78.35 today, while a 20 percent rate reduces its value to only $40.19. Interest rates have been quite variable for the last decade, and it may be difficult to predict whether a 5 percent or a 20 percent rate is appropriate for five years in the future. Considering a range of possibilities thus becomes essential to complete financial analysis.

9.1.5.   Different Project Lifespans

One of the most common uses of NPV calculations is to compare alternative projects. In many cases the proposals have equal lifespans, such as two designs for a bridge that will last for 50 years, or two financial investments that have 10-year maturities. Similarly, projects are often undertaken to fulfill a certain purpose, and the lifespans of the projects are irrelevant as long as the purpose is achieved before their termination. In all these cases the projects can be compared directly and the one with the largest NPV selected.

Sometimes, though, projects have different lifespans and cannot be compared directly. For example, a firm might have to choose between two machines to produce a certain item, with one machine lasting for four years and the other for five. The firm will want to buy new machines of the same types once the first purchases wear out. The NPVs cannot be compared directly because the

EXAMPLE 9.4

Effect of Discount Rates

Consider a project with the following cash flows:

Year	0	1	2	3	4	5
Costs	$100					
Benefits		$20	$20	$20	$20	$100

What is its NPV at an effective annual discount rate of (a) 5 percent, (b) 10 percent, (c) 15 percent, and (d) 20 percent?

$$NPV = \sum_{t=0}^{n} \frac{B_t}{(1 + r_t)^t} - \sum_{t=0}^{n} \frac{C_t}{(1 + r_t)^t}$$

In all cases, the benefits consist of a four-year annuity of $20 per year plus $100 in year 5. The only cost is $C_0 = \$100$.

(a) $r_1 = \cdots = r_5 = 0.05$

$$NPV = \$20 \left[\frac{1 - (1.05)^{-4}}{0.05} \right] + \frac{\$100}{(1.05)^5} - \$100$$

$$= \$49.27$$

Similarly,

(b) NPV = $25.49
(c) NPV = $6.82
(d) NPV = −$8.04

projects are not equivalent. A direct comparison often tends to underestimate the benefits of the longer-lived asset since such an asset does not need to be replaced as frequently. It is thus essential to use some method to compensate for different lifespans when comparing projects so that the most realistic set of cash flows is utilized.

There are four common approaches to the problem of different lifespans: replication, equivalent annuities, assigning a terminal value, and using the best available alternative rate. Each of these methods is discussed separately below.

Replication.   *Replication* is the most obvious solution but can be extremely tedious. This process involves repeating the projects until they both terminate at the same time. In our earlier comparison of machines, this would involve buying four successive 5-year machines and five 4-year machines, and then comparing the NPVs for the entire 20-year cycle. This frequently involves considerable calculation. Also, in some cases the projects cannot be replicated; perhaps the 4-year machine is a discontinued model and cannot be purchased again. This problem and the lengthy calculations involved lead us to recommend against the replication method except in very simple cases.

EXAMPLE 9.5

Equivalent Annuities

Machine A costs $5000 and lasts for four years. Machine B costs $2000 but lasts only two years. Machine A requires no maintenance, but B requires $1000 worth of maintenance one year after purchase. The effective annual discount rate is 9 percent. If the two machines produce equal outputs, which is the better buy?

Machine A has an NPV of −$5000 (it has an initial cost of $5000 and no other costs or benefits). The equation for the present value of an annuity is

$$P = A\left[\frac{1 - (1 + r)^{-n}}{r}\right]$$

$$-\$5000 = A\left[\frac{1 - (1.09)^{-4}}{0.09}\right]$$

$$A = -\$1543.34$$

This result means the firm must pay $1543.34 per year in order to cover the entire cost of $5000.

One cycle of machine B would generate a cash flow of −$2000 immediately and −$1000 after one year. The NPV would be

$$NPV = -\$2000 - \frac{\$1000}{1.09}$$

$$= -\$2917.43$$

The equivalent annuity is

$$-\$2917.43 = A\left[\frac{1 - (1.09)^{-2}}{0.09}\right]$$

$$A = -\$1658.47$$

The firm must pay $1658.47 per year for machine B.

Thus, machine A is cheaper on an annual basis and is thus the better investment.

Equivalent Annuities. The method of *equivalent annuities* will handle the same types of problems as replication without the tedious calculations. This method also assumes that projects can be repeated. The cash flows of each project are converted into annuities for which the required investment is the same every period. In this way, the differences in project lifespans and cash flows can be smoothed out, and the two projects can be compared directly. This method works because the annuities are the value per period of each project if they continue forever.

To use equivalent annuities, find the NPV of one cycle of each investment. Then, find the equivalent annuity that would produce this same NPV. This can be done using Equation (4.28) from Chapter 4:

$$P = A\left[\frac{1 - (1 + r)^{-n}}{r}\right] \tag{4.28}$$

Substitute the NPV for P, use appropriate values for r and n, and calculate A, the annuity amount. Repeat the calculation for each option. The project with the largest periodic benefit, A, is the preferred one.

Assigning a Terminal Value.   If the project cannot be replicated, the method of *assigning a terminal value* will work. This method can also be used in situations where projects can be repeated, but the first two methods are somewhat better in this case.

As the name implies, the method of assigning a terminal value requires a cash value to be placed on a project whose lifespan has not been exhausted. For example, if one project lasts for ten years and another lasts for seven, we can

---

EXAMPLE 9.6

Assigning a Terminal Value

High-Tech, Inc., can buy one of two computers to help monitor its production process. Computer A costs $97,000 and saves $25,000 per year in production costs. It has an expected life of five years and can be resold for $50,000 after three years. Computer B has a lifespan of only three years, costs $45,000, and saves $20,000 per year. Since computer technology changes rapidly, neither computer can be repurchased in the future. High-Tech's effective annual discount rate is 9 percent. Which computer is a better investment?

$$\text{NPV} = \sum_{t=0}^{n} \frac{B_t}{(1 + r_t)^t} - \sum_{t=0}^{n} \frac{C_t}{(1 + r_t)^t}$$

Since the projects cannot be replicated, a terminal value must be assigned to computer A after three years.
  For computer A:

$$B_1 = \cdots = B_5 = \$25{,}000 \qquad C_0 = \$97{,}000 \qquad F_3 = \$50{,}000$$

F_3 is the value after three years.

$$\text{NPV}_A = \$25{,}000 \left[\frac{1 - (1.09)^{-3}}{0.09} \right] + \frac{\$50{,}000}{(1.09)^3} - \$97{,}000$$

$$= \$63{,}282.37 + \$38{,}609.17 - \$97{,}000$$

$$\text{NPV}_A = \$4{,}891.54$$

  For computer B:

$$B_1 = B_2 = B_3 = \$20{,}000 \qquad C_0 = \$45{,}000$$

$$\text{NPV}_B = \$20{,}000 \left[\frac{1 - (1.09)^{-3}}{0.09} \right] - \$45{,}000$$

$$= \$50{,}625.89 - \$45{,}000$$

$$= \$5625.89$$

Computer B is the better investment.

EXAMPLE 9.7

Best Available Alternative Rate

A skier is considering the one-time purchase of a portion of a condominium. For $10,000 she can buy two weeks of usage each year for the next 20 years of a condo at Downhill Villas. She expects this will save her $1500 per year. For $7500, she can buy similar usage rights for 15 years at Slalom Acres. This will save her $1375 per season. Her effective annual discount rate is 10 percent. However, after 15 years she will be planning for retirement and will invest only in low-risk government bonds that are expected to yield 7 percent. Which condominium is the better investment?

$$NPV = \sum_{t=0}^{n} \frac{B_t}{(1 + r_t)^t} - \sum_{t=0}^{n} \frac{C_t}{(1 + r_t)^t}$$

At Downhill Villas:

$$NPV_1 = \$1500 \left[\frac{1 - (1.10)^{-20}}{0.10} \right] - \$10,000$$

$$= \$12,770.35 - \$10,000$$

$$= \$2770.35$$

At Slalom Acres:

$$NPV_2 = \$1375 \left[\frac{1 - (1.10)^{-15}}{0.10} \right] - \$7500$$

$$= \$10,458.36 - \$7500$$

$$= \$2958.36$$

choose a period of comparison equal to the lifespan of the shorter-lived asset, in this case seven years. The NPV of the seven-year asset is found as usual. For the ten-year project, we must assign it a cash value at the end of seven years. While this may seem somewhat arbitrary, it is often quite easy to determine the market value of a used asset, particularly a machine or a building. The NPV is then computed for the first seven years of cash flows, including the terminal value. In almost all cases, the NPV for the seven years of cash flows will be different from the NPV for the entire ten years due to costs and imperfections in the resale market. If the projects cannot be replicated and the NPV of the ten-year project is the same after either seven or ten years, the two projects can be compared directly without allowing for different lifespans.

This method also works for situations in which the time period we are concerned about is not equal to the lifespan of either asset. In the preceding example in this section, we might be interested in the value of the assets over five years. In this case, we would need to assign terminal values to both projects at the end of five years and compute their NPVs.

Best Available Alternative Rate.   The *best available alternative rate* (BAAR) is a concept that is frequently useful in financial analysis. The BAAR is the highest return that can be earned by a given investor and will, of course, depend

It appears that Slalom Acres is the better investment. However, the lifespans are not equal, so we need to reinvest the savings from the Slalom Acres condo for five more years. The skier demands safe investments so can earn only 7 percent.

In year 15, the $10,458.36 of benefits are worth

$$\$10,458.36(1.10)^{15} = \$43,687.17$$

This is simply the future value of the project at the end of 15 years. Note how the 10 percent discount rate was used, since this is what applied during this period. The $43,687.17 is now invested for five years at 7 percent yielding

$$\$43,687.17(1.07)^5 = \$61,273.52$$

This is the total benefit from the Slalom Acres investment. Discounting this back to the present using the 10 percent discount rate gives

$$\frac{\$61,273.52}{(1.10)^{20}} = \$9107.92$$

This is the total discounted benefit from the condo at Slalom Acres. Therefore its true NPV is

$$NPV_2 = \$9107.92 - \$7500$$
$$= \$1607.92$$

So, when the lifespans are equalized, Downhill Villas is the better investment.

---

upon circumstances. An investor with a large sum of money can often earn higher interest than one with a few hundred dollars. Furthermore, the possible returns will vary over time. In many cases, the BAAR will be the same as the discount rate: Since an investor can earn interest at the BAAR, he should discount future returns from a project by that amount.

One application of the BAAR is as a fourth method for finding the NPVs of projects with different lifespans. If the projects will not be replicated, the proceeds from the shorter-lived one can be reinvested at the BAAR until the lifespans are equal. Then the total returns can be computed and the project with the highest NPV chosen. If the BAAR is the same as the discount rate, the projects can be compared directly without allowing for differences in lifespans. In this case, reinvesting at the BAAR will be exactly balanced by discounting, meaning that the NPV of the shorter project will not change following its termination. If the BAAR is not the same as the discount rate, then the proceeds from the shorter project should be invested at the BAAR until the lifespans of the projects are equal.

It is often necessary to compare projects having different lifespans. If the projects do not need to be repeated after their termination, and if the best available alternative investment rate is the same as the discount rate, the NPVs of the projects can be compared directly without allowing for their different lifespans. If, however, replication is desired or if the alternative reinvestment rate is not the same as the discount rate, one of the techniques described above must be used.

We can summarize the methods for comparing projects with different lifespans as follows:

1. Replication is useful only for simple projects with easily matched lifespans. Otherwise, the calculations are too lengthy.
2. Equivalent annuities works well whenever projects can be replicated.
3. Assigning a terminal value is useful for projects that cannot be replicated or when the period of analysis does not correspond to either lifespan. This method suffers from the somewhat arbitrary nature of the terminal value.
4. The BAAR is ideal for projects that will not be replicated and when the alternative investment rate differs from the discount rate. (If the BAAR equals the discount rate, the NPVs can be compared directly without compensating for the difference in lifespans. Use a BAAR of 10 percent in Example 9.7 and prove this for yourself.)

9.1.6.   Net Terminal Value

Before moving on to a discussion of alternatives to net present value, we will take a quick look at the method of *net terminal value* (NTV). This method is occasionally used in lieu of NPV and produces directly comparable results. That is, any project that is accepted by the NPV criterion will be accepted by the NTV standard.

To find NTV, simply calculate the value of the project at its termination. Instead of discounting the cash flows, credit them with interest until the termination of the project:

$$\text{NTV} = \sum_{t=0}^{n} B_t (1 + r_t)^{n-t} - \sum_{t=o}^{n} C_t (1 + r_t)^{n-t} \tag{9.2}$$

Thus, a cash flow produced in the final year (year n) receives no interest, while an initial cash flow (year 0) receives interest for n years.

Equation (4.15) of Chapter 4 showed how present and future values are related. It should not be surprising that the NTV and NPV methods produce comparable results. Most analysts use NPV, and we suggest that you follow this convention.

9.2.   ALTERNATIVES TO NET PRESENT VALUE

In the first section of this chapter, we discussed net present value (NPV) as a method of making financial decisions. NPV can be used to identify projects that increase real wealth and hence are attractive investments, and it can also be used to set priorities among different projects. There are several other techniques that can be used for these purposes, including some that are commonly employed in business and government. These techniques will be described in this section.

Many alternative methods of financial analysis have been developed over the years, but most fall into one of five classes: benefit–cost ratios, payback period, return on book value, internal rate of return, or wealth-maximizing rate. Particular attention will be paid to benefit–cost ratios, the internal rate of return, and the wealth-maximizing rate since these methods have considerable conceptual appeal and are commonly used by private firms and government agencies.

Each of the techniques described in this chapter has particular strengths and weaknesses. Some of the techniques, including some forms of the payback period and return on book value, can produce erroneous results. In general, many analysts prefer to use NPV or benefit–cost ratios in making benefit–cost calculations, although some of the other methods have value in particular circumstances.

It is important to learn about these alternative approaches for at least three reasons:

1. Some of the techniques can provide information to supplement the results of the NPV analysis. This may allow a financial decision to be better understood and explained.
2. Many organizations use a method of financial analysis other than the NPV, so a familiarity with these techniques and their advantages and disadvantages is valuable.
3. Knowledge of alternative techniques for financial analysis is essential to being a good critic of presentations or publications that use these methods.

9.2.1. Benefit–Cost Ratios

Like NPV, *benefit–cost ratios* (BCR) provide direct relationships between the benefits and costs of a project and use these relationships to decide whether a particular project is a good investment. There are three forms of the BCR that are commonly encountered: the undiscounted BCR, the discounted BCR, and the net BCR.

In its simplest form, known as the *undiscounted BCR* ((BCR_u), the ratio is simply the total benefits from a project divided by the total costs:

$$BCR_u = \sum_{t=0}^{n} \frac{B_t}{C_t} \tag{9.3}$$

where B_t represents the benefits in period t, C_t represents the costs in period t, and n is the project lifespan. Any project whose BCR_u exceeds 1 has benefits that exceed costs, and hence is a good investment according to this criterion.

No discounting occurs in this form of the BCR, so payments in the distant future are treated as equivalent to payments made immediately. This is clearly incorrect, since the time value of money is completely ignored. Despite this obvious flaw, this method is occasionally encountered in practice because of its extreme simplicity, and is sometimes used to "justify" projects with large initial outlays whose benefits occur in the distant future. This method should not be used.

More sophisticated forms of the BCR discount cash flows in order to recognize the time value of money. The formula for the *discounted BCR* (BCR_d) is

$$BCR_d = \frac{\sum\limits_{t=0}^{n} \frac{B_t}{(1 + r_t)^t}}{\sum\limits_{t=0}^{n} \frac{C_t}{(1 + r_t)^t}} \tag{9.4}$$

where r_t is the appropriate discount rate for period t. Again, if the BCR exceeds 1, the project increases real wealth.

This version of the BCR produces correct decisions about projects since it allows for the time value of money. It is very similar to the calculation of NPV, which is

$$NPV = \sum_{t=0}^{n} \frac{B_t}{(1 + r_t)^t} - \sum_{t=0}^{n} \frac{C_t}{(1 + r_t)^t} \tag{9.1}$$

The only difference is the operation used to compare costs and benefits: NPV uses subtraction, BCR_d uses division. An NPV greater than 0 is equivalent to a BCR_d greater than 1 and an NPV less than 0 is equivalent to a BCR_d less than 1. NPV and the discounted BCR will always produce identical decisions about projects.

The value of the discounted BCR is sensitive to how cash flows are defined. In some cases, a cash flow can be interpreted as either a positive cost (an increase in total costs) or a negative benefit (a decrease in total benefits).

The value of the BCR_d changes depending upon which of these choices is made. Consider a situation in which a project's discounted benefits are $100 and its discounted costs are $50. Now, a new expense of $25 at the outset is added. If treated as a negative benefit, the BCR_d would be $(100 - 25)/50 = 1.5$. If treated as a positive cost, the BCR_d would be $100/(50 + 25) = 1.33$.

For single projects, the choice does not affect the decision about a project's desirability since the two values for the BCR_d will both be less than 1 or greater than 1. However, the results of a comparison of projects will not necessarily be correct unless cash flows are treated consistently. It should be noted that this problem does not affect the NPV since it uses subtraction rather than division to compare projects.

Furthermore, the BCR_d can be subject to problems of scale if used to compare projects. A project with total costs of $100,000 may generate a greater increase in real wealth than one with total costs of $100, but the ratio of benefits to costs may not be as high. Thus, projects must have an equal outlay basis if they are to be compared. This issue is discussed in more detail in a subsequent section.

Another version of the BCR that is sometimes encountered is the *net BCR* (BCR_n). The net BCR is defined as the ratio of the discounted net benefits (benefits minus costs) to the discounted costs, and is usually expressed as a percentage:

$$BCR_n = \frac{\sum\limits_{t=0}^{n} \frac{B_t}{(1 + r_t)^t} - \sum\limits_{t=0}^{n} \frac{C_t}{(1 + r_t)^t}}{\sum\limits_{t=0}^{n} \frac{C_t}{(1 + r_t)^t}} \times 100\% \tag{9.5}$$

EXAMPLE 9.8

Discounted Benefit–Cost Ratio

A project is expected to yield the following cash flows:

Year	0	1	2	3
C_t	$100	$100		
B_t				$250

Find the discounted BCR of this project. Also, find the project's NPV. Use a discount rate of 10 percent. Do either of these methods suggest that the project is desirable?

For BCR:

$$BCR_d = \frac{\sum\limits_{t=0}^{n} \dfrac{B_t}{(1+r_t)^t}}{\sum\limits_{t=0}^{n} \dfrac{C_t}{(1+r_t)^t}}$$

$$= \frac{\dfrac{\$250}{(1.10)^3}}{\left[\dfrac{\$100}{(1.10)^0} + \dfrac{\$100}{1.10}\right]}$$

$$= \frac{\$187.83}{\$100.00 + \$90.91}$$

$$= 0.98$$

For NPV:

$$NPV = \sum_{t=0}^{n} \frac{B_t}{(1+r_t)^t} - \sum_{t=0}^{n} \frac{C_t}{(1+r_t)^t}$$

$$= \$187.83 - (\$100.00 + \$90.91)$$

$$= -\$3.08$$

Both methods suggest that the project should be rejected. When a 10 percent discount rate is used, the value of the $250 obtained after three years is reduced enough to make it less valuable than the original outlays. At a lower discount rate this project would be attractive. Try a discount rate of 9 percent or less and see for yourself.

The numerator is simply the NPV, so Equation (9.5) is equivalent to

$$BCR_n = \left[\frac{NPV}{\sum\limits_{t=0}^{n} \dfrac{C_t}{(1+r_t)^t}}\right] \times 100\% \tag{9.6}$$

The net BCR is closely related to the discounted BCR. Equation (9.5) can be rewritten as

$$BCR_n = \frac{\displaystyle\sum_{t=0}^{n} \frac{B_t}{(1+r_t)^t} - \sum_{t=0}^{n} \frac{C_t}{(1+r_t)^t}}{\displaystyle\sum_{t=0}^{n} \frac{C_t}{(1+r_t)^t}} \times 100\% \qquad (9.7)$$

which is equivalent to

$$BCR_n = \left[\frac{\displaystyle\sum_{t=0}^{n} \frac{B_t}{(1+r_t)^t}}{\displaystyle\sum_{t=0}^{n} \frac{C_t}{(1+r_t)^t}} - 1 \right] \times 100\% \qquad (9.8)$$

The first term on the right-hand side of the equation is the discounted BCR. Hence,

$$BCR_n = (BCR_d - 1) \times 100\% \qquad (9.9)$$

The net BCR shows the percentage increase in real wealth generated by a project. Any project with a net BCR greater than 0 should be accepted. Once again, this method produces results exactly comparable to NPV since it allows for the time value of money.

As with the discounted BCR, the net BCR must be used carefully in cases where a cash flow can be treated as either a cost or a benefit. If a particular cash flow were treated as a positive cost, it would appear in both the numerator and the denominator of the net BCR calculation. If, instead, the cash flow were treated as a negative benefit, it would appear only in the numerator. These two options would lead to different values for the net BCR. Thus, if the net BCR is used to compare projects, cash flows must be defined consistently. The net BCR is also subject to the same problems of scale that were described for the discounted BCR.

The BCR can be used to compare projects, just as the NPV was. Either the discounted BCR or the net BCR will give an accurate comparison between projects, with the project having the highest BCR being the most desirable.

As noted previously, care must be taken when identifying the alternatives for comparison. Since we are computing a ratio, the result is sensitive to the absolute sizes of the costs and benefits. For example, consider two exclusive nonrepeatable investments. The first requires an outlay of $1000, yields $1025 immediately, and, therefore, has an NPV of $25 and a BCR_d of 1.025. The second investment requires $100, yields $110 immediately, and produces an NPV of only $10 but a BCR_d of 1.10. The first investment increases wealth by a larger amount ($25 instead of $10) and thus is preferable, but the BCR of the second is larger. Does this mean that the BCR is an invalid technique?

No, it simply means that alternative investments must be specified carefully. *The investments must have an equivalent outlay* if they are to be compared. In our example above, one investment required $1000, the other only $100. If the second investment were replicable, we could have purchased it ten

EXAMPLE 9.9

Net Benefit–Cost Ratio

Repeat Example 9.8 using the net BCR. Use a discount rate of 10 percent. Is this an attractive investment?

$$
BCR_n = \frac{\sum\limits_{t=0}^{n} \dfrac{B_t}{(1 + r_t)^t} - \sum\limits_{t=0}^{n} \dfrac{C_t}{(1 + r_t)^t}}{\sum\limits_{t=0}^{n} \dfrac{C_t}{(1 + r_t)^t}} \times 100\%
$$

$$
= \frac{\dfrac{\$250}{(1.10)^3} - \dfrac{\$100}{1} - \dfrac{\$100}{1.10}}{\dfrac{\$100}{1} + \dfrac{\$100}{1.10}} \times 100\%
$$

$$
= \frac{-\$3.08}{\$190.91} \times 100\%
$$

$$
= -1.61\%
$$

Since the net BCR is less than 0, this project is not desirable. It represents a net loss of 1.61 percent of real wealth.

---

times so its total cost would also be $1000. However, we were told that the second investment could not be repeated. Thus, we still have $900 left when compared to the first investment. So, the second investment should be treated as a cost of $1000($100 + $900), with a yield of $1010($110 + $900). Then, its BCR_d is 1.01, and the BCR produces the same ranking as the NPV.

In general, projects must have an equal outlay basis if the BCR is to be used for comparison. If projects can be replicated, this should be done until outlays are equal. If projects cannot be replicated, then the remaining funds should be invested at the best available alternative rate (BAAR). The BAAR is usually equal to the discount rate. When projects are compared on an equal outlay basis, the BCR methods identify the project that does the most to increase real wealth.

In addition, cash flows must be defined consistently if projects are to be compared. For example, consider a project with discounted benefits of $130 and discounted costs of $100. An additional expense of $20 is required in the first year. If this expense is treated as a cost, the BCR_d is $130/$120, or 1.083. If this expense is treated as a reduction in benefits, the BCR_d is $110/$100, or 1.100. In either case, the project is desirable. However, if this project is being compared to an alternative with a BCR_d of 1.090, which choice should we make?

This example indicates the importance of defining cash flows consistently when using the BCR to compare projects. All cash flows of a particular type should be defined as either positive costs or negative benefits.

EXAMPLE 9.10

Comparing Projects Using the BCR

An investor has $500 to invest. Her stockbroker identifies two possible investments, whose cash flows occur as follows:

Year	0	1	2	3	4
Investment A					
Benefits		$180	$180	$180	$180
Costs	$500				
Investment B					
Benefits					500
Costs	300				

Neither investment is replicable. Any leftover funds can be invested at the discount rate, which is 7 percent. Using the discounted BCR approach, identify the best investment.

$$BCR_d = \frac{\sum\limits_{t=0}^{n} \dfrac{B_t}{(1 + r_t)^t}}{\sum\limits_{t=0}^{n} \dfrac{C_t}{(1 + r_t)^t}}$$

For investment A:

$$BCR_d = \frac{\sum\limits_{t=0}^{n} \dfrac{\$180}{(1.07)^t}}{\dfrac{\$500}{(1.07)^0}}$$

The BCR_d and BCR_n can be used to compare projects if two rules are observed:

1. Cash flows must be defined consistently for all projects.
2. Projects must have equal outlays, or be adjusted through replication or additional investment until outlays are equal.

The project with the largest BCR is preferred.

9.2.2. Payback Period

The second alternative method of financial decision making is based on the concept of a *payback period*. The payback period is defined as the time required for a project's total benefits to exceed its total costs. At that time, the project can be said to have "paid back" its initial cost, hence the name payback period. For some applications, there is considerable intuitive appeal to this concept since it allows projects to be judged by how rapidly they pay off, but the payback period sometimes can lead to poor financial decisions, as discussed below.

Payback is often used in work related to utilities. One of its most common applications is in the analysis of energy conservation programs. In such cases,

The benefits represent a four-year uniform series or annuity. We can use Equation (4.28) to find the discounted value of such a stream of payments:

$$BCR_d = \frac{\$180\left(\left[1 - (1.07)^{-4}\right]/0.07\right)}{\$500}$$

$$= 1.22$$

For investment B:

$$BCR_d = \frac{\$500/(1.07)^4}{\$300}$$

$$= 1.27$$

Thus, investment B appears to be the better choice. However, it costs only $300 and we must compare projects on an equal outlay basis. To do so, we can invest the remaining $200 at the BAAR, in this case 7 percent. At the end of four years, this yields $200(1.07)^4 = \$262.16$. So, the initial cost for investment B is $500, and the total benefit at the end of four years is $762.16. Therefore,

$$BCR_d = \frac{\$762.16/(1.07)^4}{\$500}$$

$$= 1.16$$

When the two investments are compared on an equal outlay basis, we see that investment A is the best choice.

---

the returns from an investment in conservation are analyzed to see how long it will take for the savings to pay back the initial cost. For example, a homeowner may want to know how long it will take for an investment in insulation to pay off through reduced heating bills. Payback analysis is also being applied to other public projects, such as water conservation efforts and solid waste reduction programs.

Payback is also commonly encountered in industries whose products have short lifespans in the marketplace. For example, a company manufacturing a new computer chip knows that the chip is likely to be superseded by a superior design within two to three years. Thus, the company may believe that the simplest way to evaluate the product's success is to see if it pays back its costs within that two- to three-year period.

The payback period is most easily understood if all cash flows are treated simultaneously, instead of considering costs and benefits separately. Let X_t be any cash flows in period t; X_t is negative if it is a cost and positive if it is a benefit. Let p be the payback period. Then, in its simplest form, the payback period is found when

$$\sum_{t=0}^{p} X_t \geq 0 \tag{9.10}$$

The cash flows from a project are simply added chronologically until the sum is positive; the payback period p is the time needed to reach this positive sum.

This simple undiscounted version has the obvious flaw of disregarding the time value of money and therefore should be avoided. If discounting is included, the equation for the payback period becomes

$$\sum_{t=0}^{p} \frac{X_t}{(1 + r_t)^t} \geq 0 \tag{9.11}$$

In this case, the discounted cash flows are summed until a positive result is obtained.[2]

The payback method suffers from two major problems that make it a poor substitute for the NPV technique. First, any decision rule about which projects to accept and reject must be arbitrary. Obviously, a project that never pays back its costs is hardly desirable, but beyond that no definitive judgments can be made. Is a payback period of 100 years acceptable? Why not 10 years? Or even 1 year? Most organizations using the payback technique have chosen some acceptable period, such as 3 or 4 years, and reject all projects that have paybacks longer than that period. This often results in the rejection of projects with positive NPVs, which is hardly defensible as an analytical technique.

The second problem with the payback method is that it ignores cash flows that occur beyond the payback period. A project with a large expense in a later year, such as a maintenance charge for a machine, might be unacceptable from the NPV approach but would be approved by payback analysis since this charge might never be considered when the cash flows are summed chronologically.[3] Similarly, a project with long-term returns often looks less desirable than one with short-term returns when the payback technique is used, even though the first project may do more to increase real wealth. In general, the payback method favors short-term projects over long-term ones, even if the financial benefits of a long-term project are far greater. Given these problems, it should be apparent that the payback approach is arbitrary and can lead to poor financial decisions.

If the payback technique is so bad, why bother with it at all? There are at least three reasons to be familiar with this method:

1. Payback has considerable conceptual appeal for many decision makers, since it provides information about how long it takes for a project to pay

---

[2]This is equivalent to saying that the payback period occurs when discounted benefits exceed discounted costs:

$$\frac{B_t}{(1 + r_t)^t} \geq \frac{C_t}{(1 + r_t)^t}$$

[3]One could imagine a payback methodology that considers later costs, such as one that requires total discounted benefits at time p to exceed the grand total of discounted costs for the lifespan of the project. Yet this too is arbitrary, for it counts costs but not benefits in certain periods and can still lead to incorrect financial decisions. A modified method of this type is, however, clearly better than the simple method used by most organizations.

EXAMPLE 9.11

Payback

Metropolitan Bus Lines is considering the installation of new transmission components in its fleet that will decrease fuel consumption. For an initial cost of $500 each, these components will save $150 in fuel per year for six years, after which they must be replaced. Metropolitan faces a discount rate of 8 percent. As a rule, the agency has decided to accept projects with a payback period of three years or less. Would they buy the transmission components? Is their decision the correct one from a rigorous financial standpoint?

$$\sum_{t=0}^{p} \frac{X_t}{(1 + r_t)^t} \geq 0$$

For this project,

$$X_0 = -\$500 \qquad X_1 = \cdots = X_6 = \$150$$

If $p = 1$, then,

$$\sum_{t=0}^{1} \frac{X_t}{(1 + r_t)^t} = -\$500 + \left(\frac{\$150}{1.08}\right)$$

$$= -\$361.11$$

Similarly,

for $p = 2$,	$= -\$232.51$
$p = 3$,	$= -\$113.44$
$p = 4$,	$= -\$3.19$
$p = 5$,	$= \$98.90$

The payback period is five years. Since Metropolitan uses a three-year limit, they would not purchase the transmission components. However, the NPV of the project is

$$NPV = -\$500 + \$150 \left[\frac{1 - (1.08)^{-6}}{0.08} \right]$$

$$= \$193.43$$

Since the NPV is positive, the project increases real wealth and should be accepted. The arbitrary nature of the payback period leads to the rejection of a desirable project.

off. Many organizations use payback analysis because of this seemingly logical appeal.

2. The payback period may provide valuable information if used in conjunction with other techniques. By calculating the payback period, an organization can determine how long it will take to recover its initial investment, which may be an important consideration if cash flow is a problem.

3. Payback can be a fairly accurate representation of true results in situations where benefits are constant or increase over a long period of time. This helps to justify the use of payback methodologies in energy conservation analyses.

Payback analysis should *not* be used to make financial decisions, but can be used to provide supplemental information.

9.2.3.   Return on Book Value

The third alternative method of financial analysis is known as the *return on book value* or the *accounting rate of return*. This method employs financial analysis based on *accounting* cash flows rather than the *actual* cash flows used by other methods of financial analysis. These accounting values are often called *book values* and are the figures commonly cited in newspaper articles and corporate reports.

Calculating the return on book value (RBV) is quite simple. The average book income and the average book value of the project are determined based upon the expected lifespan of the project. The book income is the actual cash income plus adjustments for depreciation and other effects. The book value of the project is how much the original investment is supposedly worth at a given time once allowances are made for maintenance, depreciation, and so on. The RBV is then defined as

$$\text{RBV} = \frac{\text{average book income}}{\text{average book value}} \tag{9.12}$$

Organizations using this approach employ a variety of arbitrary rules to decide what is an acceptable RBV. The most common standard seems to be the organization's average RBV; any project that exceeds this average is accepted.

Although this method is commonly used, it has little to recommend it. It does not explicitly discount cash flows, although depreciation allowances do provide a form of discounting. It does not have a consistent, logical decision rule that determines which projects should be accepted. Finally, while book values and incomes are useful in some contexts, proper financial analysis requires the use of real cash flows. Using book values creates a substantial risk of making incorrect financial decisions.

The use of book values is a major issue of contention between accountants and economists. Accountants rely on book values because they have been developed as a product of standard accounting rules and are often especially useful for tax purposes. Information on this basis is commonly available in government and corporate reports and financial summaries, and thus is easy to obtain. Economists criticize the use of book values because such values are not true indicators of real wealth. Unfortunately, the types of information sought by economists are often harder to obtain. Thus, despite the obvious flaws in the return on book value approach, it is likely to continue to be used.

9.2.4.   Internal Rate of Return

The most popular alternative to net present value is the *internal rate of return* (IRR). The IRR is the discount rate for which a project's benefits exactly balance its costs and can be thought of as the "break-even" rate. At the IRR, the NPV of a project is exactly equal to 0, as shown in Figure 9.1.

This method has many proponents who find it more concrete and less esoteric than the NPV technique. These advocates criticize NPV since it requires that a discount rate be assumed, and prefer instead to perform one IRR computation rather than calculate the NPV for a variety of discount rates.

Unfortunately, the IRR can be difficult to calculate and can give misleading results in some situations, and thus cannot be generally recommended. Before discussing these issues, we will see how to calculate and use the IRR.

As noted earlier, the IRR is the discount rate that sets a project's discounted benefits equal to its discounted costs:

$$\sum_{t=0}^{n} \frac{B_t}{(1 + \text{IRR})^t} = \sum_{t=0}^{n} \frac{C_t}{(1 + \text{IRR})^t} \qquad (9.13)$$

Using the terminology developed earlier in this chapter, this is equivalent to

$$\sum_{t=0}^{n} \frac{X_t}{(1 + \text{IRR})^t} = 0 \qquad (9.14)$$

where X_t represents any cash flow. X_t is positive for benefits and negative for costs.

The IRR is usually found by iteration, which is a process that repeats the same series of calculations until an acceptable result is obtained. There are a few very simple cases in which the IRR can be found directly, but these are

Figure 9.1.

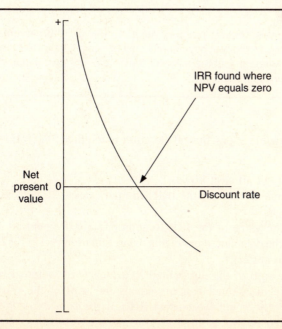

EXAMPLE 9.12

Internal Rate of Return

A project has the following costs and benefits:

Year	0	1	2	3
Costs	$1500		$200	
Benefits		$750	750	$750
Net cash flow	−1500	750	550	750

Find the internal rate of return. If the opportunity cost of capital is 11 percent, is this project desirable?

$$\sum_{t=0}^{n} \frac{X_t}{(1 + IRR)^t} = 0$$

As a first estimate, let IRR = 10%.

$$\sum_{t=0}^{n} \frac{X_t}{(1 + IRR)^t} = -\$1500 + \frac{\$750}{1.10} + \frac{\$550}{(1.10)^2} + \frac{\$750}{(1.10)^3}$$

$$= \$199.85$$

Since the sum is positive, guess a higher IRR. Let IRR = 12%. Calculating as before,

$$\sum_{t=0}^{n} \frac{X_t}{(1 + IRR)^t} = \$141.93$$

Repeating this iterative process yields an IRR of 17.5 percent. Since this exceeds the 11 percent opportunity cost of capital, the project will generate more than enough income to cover the cost of borrowing. It is therefore an attractive investment.

---

rarely encountered in practice. If iteration is required, the following procedure can be used:

1. Write out all cash flows.
2. Assume a value for the IRR. In many cases, 10 percent makes a good first guess.
3. Use the value of the IRR to appropriately discount all payments, then sum the discounted payments using Equation (9.14) [or Equation (9.13) if you prefer].
4. If the sum of the discounted X_t equals 0 (or, alternatively, if the sum of the discounted benefits equals the sum of the discounted costs), you have found the correct IRR. If the sum exceeds 0 (benefits exceed costs), guess a higher IRR and return to step 3. If the sum is less

than 0 (costs exceed benefits), choose a lower IRR and again return to step 3.

This approach will gradually converge until an IRR is found for which the sum of the discounted cash flows is approximately equal to 0. It is rarely necessary to be extremely precise; an IRR calculated to the nearest one-tenth of 1 percent (0.1 percent) is almost always adequate. Many computers and calculators are programmed to calculate the IRR.

Once the IRR is found, it is easy to decide if a project is worthwhile. If the actual interest rate on borrowed capital (to be precise, the opportunity cost of capital) is less than the IRR, the project is desirable since it earns returns at a higher rate than the borrowing rate. On the other hand, if the borrowing rate is greater than the IRR, the project cannot earn enough to pay for the borrowed funds and thus is not desirable. This conceptual appeal of simply comparing rates of return is one of the main benefits of the IRR approach.

The preceding example shows how the IRR can be used for a series of relatively simple cash flows. The calculations are straightforward and produce a single result. This occurs whenever an initial investment is followed by a stream of benefits. In other words, the IRR technique works for single projects when initial negative cash flows are followed by a series of nonnegative cash flows.[4]

In these relatively simple cases, the IRR produces results equivalent to the NPV. An IRR greater than the opportunity cost of capital corresponds exactly to an NPV greater than 0. The IRR approach is perfectly acceptable in these situations, although it often takes longer to calculate than the NPV.

As the cash flows from a project become more complicated, the IRR approach begins to lose its utility. There are two major problems that occur. First, the calculations become more complex and time-consuming. Finding the IRR of a project with varying cash flows over a ten-year period is an elaborate task, especially if several iterations are required. This problem can be partially overcome if computers or programmable calculators are available. In contrast, the NPV requires only one repetition of the calculation.

The second and more fundamental problem arises if negative cash flows occur after positive cash flows. In the simple case outlined above, negative cash flows occurred only at the start of the project; if negative cash flows also take place later in the project, the IRR approach may produce multiple solutions.

This occurs because the polynomial used to calculate the IRR now has more than one sign change. The simple case had a period of negative cash flows followed by a period of positive cash flows. The sign of the cash flows changed once, from negative to positive. If a negative cash flow occurs later in the project, additional sign changes are introduced. Each sign change has the potential for creating an additional positive root of the polynomial, and hence an additional value for the IRR.[5]

---

[4]Cash flows of zero are permitted.

[5]This result is embodied in a concept known as Descartes rule. The rule states that for any real polynomial with p sign changes, the number of positive roots is equal to $p - 2q$, where q is any nonnegative integer. Thus, for three sign changes, there can be either three positive roots ($q = 0$) or one positive root ($q = 1$). Likewise, for four sign changes, there can be four positive roots ($q = 0$), two positive roots ($q = 1$), or zero positive roots ($q = 2$).

EXAMPLE 9.13

Multiple Roots for the IRR

A project has the following cash flows:

Year	0	1	2
Net cash flow	−$1000	$10,000	−$9500

Find the IRR. Note that with two sign changes there can be as many as two positive roots to the IRR polynomial.

$$\sum_{t=0}^{n} \frac{X_t}{(1 + IRR)^t} = 0$$

As a first estimate, let IRR = 10%.

$$\sum_{t=0}^{n} \frac{X_t}{(1 + IRR)^t} = -\$1000 + \frac{\$10,000}{1.10} - \frac{\$9500}{(1.10)^2}$$

$$= \$239.67$$

Iteration yields two values for the IRR:

$$IRR_1 = 6.3\% \qquad IRR_2 = 793\%$$

Figure 9.2.

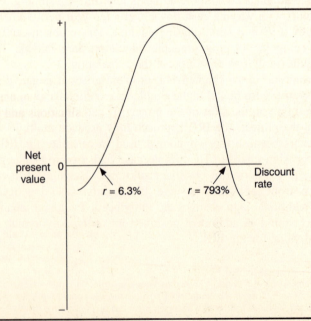

EXAMPLE 9.14

IRR for Complex Cash Flows

For the project described in Example 9.13, find the NPV at a discount rate of 5 percent. Compare the results with an analysis based on the 6.3 percent internal rate of return calculated in Example 9.13.

$$\text{NPV} = \sum_{t=0}^{n} \frac{B_t}{(1 + r_t)^t} - \sum_{t=0}^{n} \frac{C_t}{(1 + r_t)^t}$$

$$= \frac{\$10,000}{1.05} - \left[\$1000 + \frac{\$9500}{(1.05)^2} \right]$$

$$= -\$92.97$$

Using the NPV rule, the project would be rejected. However, the IRR technique would accept the project, since the IRR of 6.3 percent exceeds the 5 percent opportunity cost of capital. In this case, the IRR approach produces the wrong investment decision.

Example 9.13 shows how these multiple roots can occur. The smaller root results from very slight discounting of later payments, while the larger root discounts the outlay in the second year to almost nothing. Either root allows the sum of the discounted cash flows to equal 0.[6]

If the NPV is calculated for Example 9.13 using a variety of discount rates, the result shown in Figure 9.2 can be obtained. This shows that for discount rates between 6.3 percent and 793 percent, the NPV is positive. For other values of the discount rate, the NPV is negative. Thus, the IRR finds the points at which the NPV is zero, but cannot determine which is the "correct" rate for using the IRR decision rule.

Furthermore, the IRR can lead to erroneous investment decisions in complex cases. An analyst relying upon the IRR of 6.3 percent calculated in Example 9.13 would be sadly mistaken, as shown in the next example. The IRR does not represent the real return of a project in such situations and should not be used to make financial decisions.

The IRR can be used to compare projects. The IRR for each project is calculated and the one with the highest return is chosen. As described above, this technique is only valid for projects with cash flows having only one sign change.

---

[6]Although the mathematics are correct, it is hard to believe that this project could return either 6.3 percent or 793 percent. In fact, it does not. These widely divergent roots result from a hidden assumption in the IRR approach: It assumes that the project can both borrow and lend at the internal rate of return. In other words, excess funds generated by the project can be invested externally at the IRR, and then tapped later to offset negative cash flows. There is no reason to assume that such external investment is possible. In fact, external investment at more than the market rate is essentially impossible; certainly returns of 793 percent are hard to find. Thus, the assumption upon which the IRR rests in these cases is untenable.

Projects should be compared on an equal outlay basis. As was discussed for benefit–cost ratios, a project may have a higher IRR but do less to increase real wealth simply because its outlay is smaller. This necessitates the use of equal outlays when comparing projects. An equal outlay basis can be obtained by replication or the use of the best available alternative rate.

For example, consider a situation where a toll bridge authority has decided to purchase automatic toll collecting machines to supplement human toll collectors. The authority is considering machines produced by the Acme Company and the Fair Change Company. Both machines cost $1000 and last for three years. The Acme model requires a shorter break-in period and thus produces savings more quickly than the Fair Change model. The Fair Change model requires less maintenance, however, so it produces greater savings in later years. The net cash flows for the two machines are:

Year	0	1	2	3
Acme	−$1000	$250	$500	$600
Fair Change	−1000	0	600	800

The toll bridge authority uses the IRR to compare projects. The IRR for Acme is 14.5 percent, while the IRR for Fair Change is 14.1 percent. The Acme model is therefore selected.

This conclusion is shown graphically in Figure 9.3. This chart shows the NPV of the two models for various interest rates. At low rates, the Fair Change model has a higher NPV, but as the interest rate rises the Acme model's NPV passes that of the Fair Change model. This occurs because the Acme model's benefits are realized earlier than those of the Fair Change model and thus are not discounted so heavily at high interest rates.

Figure 9.3 also shows the approximate values of the IRR for the two projects. The IRR is found at the point where the project's discounted benefits equal its discounted costs, which is where the NPV = 0. This point in the figure occurs at about 14.5 percent for the Acme model and at slightly over 14 percent for the Fair Change model. These correspond to the results given above.

This figure illustrates another potential flaw of the IRR technique when comparing projects. As noted earlier, the NPV of the Fair Change model exceeds that of the Acme model at low discount rates. If the actual discount rate is low, the Fair Change model is the better investment. However, the IRR calculation does not reveal this, since it does not compare the projects at actual discount rates. Hence, the IRR can produce misleading results when comparing projects.

In general, the IRR has little to recommend it over the NPV technique. It can sometimes provide useful information, but the calculation difficulties and the possibilities for error make it an unreliable guide.

9.2.5. Wealth-Maximizing Rate

The *wealth-maximizing rate* (WMR) can be used to provide an accurate estimate of the return from projects. It avoids the flaws of the IRR by producing a single,

Figure 9.3.

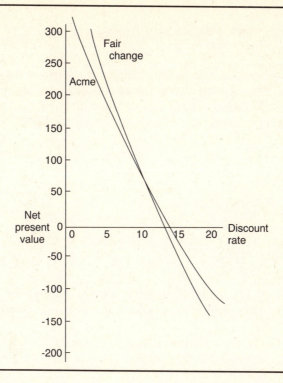

accurate result. The WMR can be used to evaluate single projects or to compare multiple projects.[7]

The WMR is a measure of the percentage increase in real wealth generated by a project. The WMR is defined as the compounded rate of return obtained on the original investment, C_0. If n is the lifespan of the project and F is the future value at the end of that lifespan, then

$$F = C_0(1 + \text{WMR})^n \qquad (9.15)$$

The WMR is simply a measure of the growth of the original investment during the lifespan of the project.

The future value F is the result of a stream of benefits B_t. However, the benefits obtained in early periods do not sit idly waiting for the final summation; instead, they can earn interest until the termination of the project. This interest is accumulated at the best available alternative rate (BAAR), which was discussed in Section 9.1.5. The BAAR is the best rate of return available outside of the project and may vary depending upon the amount of money involved. Thus, the future value of the project is the sum of the benefits and the appropriate

---

[7]Richard Zerbe, "Consistency Among Cost-Benefit Criteria," *Policy and Information* 7(1), 125–132, 1983.

amount of interest each benefit stream earns:

$$F = \sum_{t=0}^{n} B_t(1 + \text{BAAR})^{n-t} \qquad (9.16)$$

Equation (9.16) assumes that benefits are paid at the end of the periods; if this is not the case, the equation can be adjusted as described in Appendix 4.A.

Since both Equations (9.15) and (9.16) yield the future value, they can be set equal to one another to find an equation for the WMR:

$$C_0(1 + \text{WMR})^n = \sum_{t=0}^{n} B_t(1 + \text{BAAR})^{n-t} \qquad (9.17)$$

This in turn can be rearranged to

$$\text{WMR} = \sqrt[n]{\frac{\sum_{t=0}^{n} B_t(1 + \text{BAAR})^{n-t}}{C_0}} - 1 \qquad (9.18)$$

Equations (9.17) and (9.18) provide ways to calculate the WMR for any project with an initial negative cash flow followed by a series of positive cash flows.

The WMR differs from the IRR in one important respect. The IRR, as we have seen, assumed that the benefits from a project could be reinvested at the IRR rather than at market rates.[8] The fallacy of this assumption renders the IRR inaccurate in many situations. The WMR, in contrast, allows external reinvestment only at the BAAR, a rate that can be obtained in the market. This change makes the WMR accurate in cases where the IRR fails.

The WMR can be used to evaluate whether a project increases or decreases real wealth. The WMR is calculated using either Equation (9.17) or (9.18). A decision about the desirability of a project is then made using one of the following rules:

1. If the BAAR is the same as the loan rate (the rate at which borrowed funds are available), a project is attractive if the WMR exceeds the BAAR.
2. If the BAAR is greater than the loan rate, the project is attractive if the WMR exceeds the BAAR. A WMR greater than the loan rate but less than the BAAR is not sufficient, since this indicates that funds should be invested at the BAAR rather than in the project.

---

[8]The expression for the IRR that would correspond to this equation is

$$C_0(1 + \text{IRR})^n = B_t(1 + \text{IRR})^{n-t}$$

This expression shows explicitly how the IRR approach assumes that benefits can be reinvested at the IRR, which of course is not realistic. The WMR is thus a combination of the real "internal rate of return," which is producing the benefits, and the BAAR, which is allowing them to be reinvested.

EXAMPLE 9.15

WMR for Single Projects

An investor is offered a share in a gold mine that is expected to yield $1000 per year for four years, at an initial cost of $3000. The best alternative investment she can make is a mutual fund earning 11 percent per year. If she can borrow money at this 11 percent figure, should she invest in this gold mine? Use the WMR approach to find an answer.

$$C_0(1 + WMR)^n = \sum_{t=0}^{n} B_t(1 + BAAR)^{n-t}$$

$$C_0 = \$3000 \qquad B_1 = \cdots = B_4 = \$1000 \qquad n = 4 \qquad BAAR = 11\%$$

$$\$3000(1 + WMR)^4 = \sum_{t=0}^{n} \$1000(1.11)^{n-t}$$

Applying Equation (4.23) for the future value of an annuity to the right-hand side of this equation gives

$$\$3000(1 + WMR)^4 = \$1000\left[\frac{(1.11)^4 - 1}{0.11}\right]$$

$$\$3000(1 + WMR)^4 = \$4709.73$$

$$WMR = 0.119 = 11.9\%$$

Since the WMR exceeds the BAAR, the investor should purchase a share of the gold mine.

---

3. If the BAAR is less than the loan rate, the project is attractive if the WMR exceeds the BAAR and if funds are already available. If funds must be borrowed to undertake the project, the WMR must exceed the loan rate in order for the project to be attractive; it makes no sense to borrow money if the project will not repay the borrowing costs.

Given the simple economic models normally used, the first situation (where the BAAR and the loan rate are identical) will be the most common. The second situation is virtually impossible, and the third will arise only in unusual circumstances. Thus, a project will usually be acceptable if the WMR exceeds the BAAR.

The WMR can also be used to compare different projects to find the one that does the most to increase real wealth. The projects must meet two conditions:

1. The projects must be given equal lifespans. If the projects do not initially have equal lifespans, the short-lived projects should be replicated until the same lifespan is achieved. If replication is not possible, the proceeds of the short-lived projects should be reinvested at the BAAR until the period of comparison is equal.

EXAMPLE 9.16

WMR for Comparing Projects

The trustee of an estate has $10,000 to invest for a period of four years. He is offered the following four investments. Investment A costs $5000, lasts for four years, and yields $2800 every second year. It is replicable in increments of $5000 at any time. Investment B costs $8000 and produces $2400 per year for four years. Investment C costs $2500 and yields $1000 per year for three years. It is replicable in increments of $2500. Investment D costs $10,000 and produces $15,000 after four years. The best available alternative rate and the loan rate are both 9 percent. Which investment should the trustee choose, if any?

The first step is to make the investments equal in lifespan and initial outlay. For investment A, this means buying two shares initially to use up the $10,000. For investment B, the remaining $2000 should be invested for four years at the BAAR, yielding $2000(1.09)^4 = \$2823.16$. For investment C, four shares should be purchased at the outset. To ensure comparability with the other three projects, this investment must be treated as if it had a lifespan of four years. Investment D meets the requirements without modification. The cash flows for these investments are shown below:

Year	A	B	C	D
0	−$10,000	−$8000 + −$2000	−$10,000	−$10,000
1		$2400	4000	
2	5600	2400	4000	
3		2400	4000	
4	5600	$2400 + $2823.16		15,000

$$C_0(1 + WMR)^n = \sum_{t=0}^{n} B_t(1 + BAAR)^{n-t}$$

In all cases, $C_0 = \$10,000$, $n = 4$, and BAAR = 9%.
    For investment A:

$$\$10,000(1 + WMR)^4 = \$5600(1.09)^2 + \$5600$$

$$WMR_A = 5.21\%$$

Similarly:

$$WMR_B = 8.38\%$$

$$WMR_C = 9.34\%$$

$$WMR_D = 10.67\%$$

Investment D is the best choice. Since its WMR exceeds the BAAR, it is an attractive investment and should be purchased.

2. The projects must be given the same initial cost basis; that is, the C_0 for each project must be identical. Again, projects should be replicated if necessary to achieve this condition; otherwise, excess funds should be invested at the BAAR.

These two conditions are necessitated by the nature of the WMR. It calculates the return based upon a period of n years; if the lifespans of the projects are not equal, they cannot be successfully compared. Likewise, the WMR is based upon a ratio of benefits to initial costs; if the initial costs are not identical for the projects, the largest ratio may not represent the largest increase in real wealth.

Once all projects are expressed with equivalent lifespans and outlays, the WMR of each can be found using either Equation (9.17) or (9.18). The project with the highest WMR is the most desirable. The WMR of the best project should then be evaluated using the rules given for single projects to make sure that the best project leads to an increase in real wealth.

9.2.6. Reconciliation of Different Approaches

If used properly, the NPV, BCR_d, BCR_n, and WMR will provide consistent evaluations of individual projects and consistent rankings among multiple projects. Although the calculations are different, each of these methods uses real values for costs and benefits, discounts cash flows to reflect the time value of money, and employs a logical decision rule.

For individual projects, each of the four methods yields a single result that can be compared to the appropriate decision rule. A project that is acceptable using one method will also be acceptable using all the other methods. Projects chosen using any of the four methods will increase real wealth.

These four methods can also be used to compare projects. If the following three rules are observed, the NPV, BCR_d, BCR_n, and WMR will produce consistent ranking of projects:

1. The projects must have or be given identical lifespans.
2. The projects must have or be given identical initial outlays.
3. If projects have different lifespans or initial outlays, replication should be used to produce identical lifespans and outlays. If replication is not possible, funds should be invested at the best available alternative rate in order to ensure identical lifespans and outlays.

These three conditions are illustrated in Example 9.17.

9.3. CASH FLOWS

To this point, we have simply assumed the amounts of the cash flows generated by a project. There are many factors that can influence these cash flows, and it will be worthwhile to develop a basic understanding of these factors. Four of particular importance are salvage value, taxes, depreciation, and inflation. We will discuss these factors in this section.

The discussions that follow present a simplified version of cash flow analysis. Accounting practices and tax laws are often extremely complex, and these

EXAMPLE 9.17

Comparability of Methods

An investor has $100 to invest in one of three projects. The expected cash flows from these projects are as follows:

Year	0	1	2	3	4
Project A	−$100	$ 50	$50	$50	$50
Project B	−20		40		
Project C	−100	160			

Compare these projects using the NPV, BCR_d, BCR_n, and WMR. None of the projects can be replicated. Use a discount rate and a BAAR of 10 percent.

If the projects are compared directly, the NPVs, BCR_ds, BCR_ns, and WMRs can be calculated using the equations provided in this chapter. However, the immediate use of these formulas does not ensure consistency among the projects.

To compare the projects properly, project B must have the same outlay as projects A and C. Since the projects cannot be replicated, the additional $80 for B should be invested at the BAAR. After four years, this $80 will have grown to

$$\$80(1.10)^4 = \$117.13$$

This makes the total cash flows appear as follows:

Year	0	1	2	3	4
Project A	−$100	$ 50	$50	$50	$ 50
Project B	−100		40		117
Project C	−100	160			

The NPV, BCR_d, and WMR can be calculated for each project using the usual equations. The following results are obtained:

Project	NPV	BCR_d	BCR_n	WMR
A	$58.49	1.58	58.49%	23.4%
B	13.06	1.13	13.06	13.4
C	45.45	1.45	45.45	20.8

Each of these calculations shows that project A is best, followed by project C, and then project B.

complexities are beyond the scope of this book or the needs of most benefit–cost analysts. While the details are not of particular importance, it is crucial to have a basic understanding of the general principles involved.

9.3.1. Salvage Value

Some investments involve tangible assets, such as equipment or machinery. These investments wear out over time and must be replaced. The asset may not be entirely worthless at the end of its life, however, so it may be possible to sell the item. The resulting gain is called the *salvage value* and needs to be included as a positive cash flow.

9.3.2. Taxes

The income of a firm is subject to taxation. The earnings from a project therefore do not necessarily all accrue to the firm—some may go for taxes. Likewise, individuals must pay taxes on investment earnings. Taxes are thus another cost of most investments. State, regional, and local governments and nonprofit agencies may or may not pay taxes on projects depending on specific circumstances.

However, in most cases the actual cash income from a project is more than the taxable income. Most governments allow certain deductions to be made from the actual cash income when computing the taxable income. One example of this was the 10 percent tax credit for certain new investments that was available in the 1970s and early 1980s. This meant that a firm buying a piece of equipment for $1000 received a $100 credit against its taxes for that year. Another major deduction is for depreciation.

9.3.3. Depreciation

Depreciation is an allowance made for the use of a tangible asset. An asset such as a building or machine gradually wears out, and its value therefore decreases, or depreciates. In computing taxable income from an investment, most governments allow a firm or individual to deduct an appropriate amount of depreciation from its cash income.

There are several methods of computing the amount of depreciation allowable in a given year. Until recently, the three most commonly used ones in the United States were *straight-line*, *double-declining-balance*, and *sum-of-the-year's-digits*. Beginning in the late 1970s, economists and policy analysts began to explore ways in which depreciation could be used to influence economic incentives and purchasing decisions. This led to revisions to the tax laws in the United States that affect how depreciation is calculated. In 1981, the *Accelerated Cost Recovery System* (ACRS) was adopted, which essentially supplanted the other methods. This approach was intended to allow depreciation to occur more rapidly, thereby providing a tax reduction for organizations that purchased capital goods. In 1987, ACRS was replaced by the *Modified Accelerated Cost Recovery System* (MACRS) as part of the overall tax reform. All five techniques are described briefly for the reader's reference.

Straight-line depreciation is the most logical method and is the simplest to use. The salvage value S is deducted from the cost of the asset, K, with the

EXAMPLE 9.18

Straight-Line Depreciation

A firm purchases a new set of conveyors for its assembly line. The conveyors cost $18,000 and will be worth $2000 as scrap at the end of their useful life. Government regulations specify that the useful life of such an asset is five years. How much depreciation can the firm take each year if it uses the straight-line method?

$$d(t) = \frac{K - S}{N}$$

$$K = \$18,000 \qquad S = \$2000 \qquad N = 5$$

$$d(t) = \frac{\$18,000 - \$2000}{5}$$

$$= \$3200$$

The firm can charge $3200 worth of depreciation each year.

---

result being the total amount that can be depreciated. This total is divided by the lifespan of the asset, N, to yield the amount of depreciation per year, $d(t)$:

$$d(t) = \frac{K - S}{N} \qquad (9.19)$$

In straight-line depreciation, $d(t)$ is constant for each year of the asset's life.

The useful life of the asset is generally specified by the U.S. Treasury Department and similar agencies in other countries in order to ensure consistent depreciation practices by firms. Until recently, there have been long lists of the expected lifespans of different types of assets. As described below, recent changes in tax laws have led to considerable simplification of these lists.

The other methods allow for faster depreciation of assets than does the straight-line approach; that is, more depreciation is taken in earlier years than in later ones. From a financial point of view this is desirable because it reduces taxes initially, at the price of higher taxes later. Accelerated depreciation is usually justified on the grounds that it compensates for inflation (which is decreasing the real value of the depreciation charges) and that it encourages capital investment. The additional capital investment, it is claimed, will stimulate the economy and provide jobs. There has been considerable debate among economists and policy makers about the virtues of accelerated depreciation.

The first of the accelerated depreciation methods is called the *double-declining-balance* method. It is based on the *book value* of the asset, a term that stems from a firm's financial records, which are known to accountants as *books*. The initial book value, $B(1)$, is simply the purchase price, K. The value in any subsequent year, $B(t + 1)$, is the previous year's value, $B(t)$, minus that year's depreciation, $d(t)$:

$$B(t + 1) = B(t) - d(t) \qquad (9.20)$$

In the double-declining-balance method, $d(t)$ is found from

$$d(t) = \frac{2B(t)}{N}$$ (9.21)

This method usually ignores salvage values.

The double-declining-balance method allows different amounts of depreciation in each year. This method does not fully depreciate the asset; that is, the total of the depreciation allowances does not equal the purchase price. This somewhat disconcerting result is simply a vestige of the method of calculation and is more than offset by the accelerated depreciation allowed. In practice, most firms shift from double-declining-balance to straight-line depreciation at some time during the life of the asset. To do this, the book value at the time of the changeover is used as the depreciable amount, K. This amount is then fully depreciated over the remaining life of the asset.

Sum-of-the-year's-digits depreciation is a bit more complicated than the two previous methods. The amount of depreciation in year t, $d(t)$, is given by

$$d(t) = \left[\frac{N - (t - 1)}{N(N + 1)/2}\right] K$$ (9.22)

where again N is the lifespan of the asset and K is the initial cost. Salvage value is generally ignored.

Like the double-declining-balance method, sum-of-the-year's-digits produces more depreciation in early years than in later ones. Sum-of-the-year's-digits does, however, lead to full depreciation of the asset.

The Economic Recovery Tax Act of 1981 and the Tax Reform Act of 1986 made major changes in the methods used to calculate depreciation in the United States. The two most important changes were in how the lifespans of assets are determined and in the amounts of depreciation allowable in each year. These two changes are discussed below.

For many years, the U.S. government has specified the expected lifespans of assets to ensure the consistent use of depreciation calculations. By 1981, a total of 30 different categories of assets existed, each with its own depreciable lifespan. Many assets were assigned lifespans of 25 years or more, which made accelerated depreciation extremely beneficial to firms.

Under the provisions of the Economic Recovery Tax Act of 1981, depreciation schedules were vastly simplified. Four general categories of assets were identified, each with its own depreciable life. These new categories allowed simpler and more equitable evaluations of the lifespans of assets.

The second major change made by the Economic Recovery Tax Act was to eliminate the two existing methods of accelerated depreciation in most cases and substitute the Accelerated Cost Recovery System (ACRS). The ACRS method was simply a table showing the percentage of an asset's purchase price that could be depreciated in a given year. Different percentages were used for the four lifespans described above. The percentages were derived by Congress using a combination of the double-declining-balance method in the first year followed by the sum-of-the-year's-digits method in subsequent years.

In 1986, the United States again changed the allowable methods of depreciation as part of an overall revision of the tax code. Although these reforms were euphemistically known as "tax simplification," the changes greatly complicated depreciation calculations. Property placed into service starting in 1987 now falls into one of eight classifications:

1. Three-year property, which includes only a few specialized items
2. Five-year property, which includes automobiles, trucks, computers, and research equipment
3. Seven-year property, which includes office furniture
4. Ten-year property, which includes ships
5. Fifteen-year property, which includes telecommunications equipment and wastewater treatments plants
6. Twenty-year property, which includes sewers
7. Residential rental property, which is assigned a depreciable life of 27.5 years
8. Nonresidential real property, which is assigned a depreciable life of 31.5 years

In addition to these classification changes, the Tax Reform Act of 1986 eliminated the use of ACRS for property placed into service after 1986. Instead, a Modified ACRS was developed (which is referred to as MACRS) that uses the following depreciation approaches:

1. Property in the 3-, 5-, 7-, and 10-year classes is depreciated at first by using the double-declining-balance method, followed by switching to the straight-line method in the first year that straight-line would result in a higher depreciation allowance.
2. Property in the 15- and 20-year classes is depreciated at first by using the 150 percent declining-balance method, followed by switching to the straight-line method in the first year that straight-line would result in a higher depreciation allowance. The 150 percent declining-balance is identical to double-declining-balance, except that 1.5 is substituted for 2 in Equation (9.21).
3. Residential rental property and nonresidential real property are depreciated by using the straight-line method.

In addition to these approaches, a taxpayer can elect to use straight-line depreciation for any property placed into service after 1986. There are also some types of property that must be depreciated by using the straight-line approach, including property that is tax-exempt or was financed with tax-exempt bonds. This provision often affects property of state and local governments or private property that was paid for with debt issues by state or local governments.

There are a variety of other complications and restrictions in MACRS that are not discussed here. However, this description provides an overall understanding of the depreciation concepts that are currently in place.

Tax Credits.   In addition to depreciation, tax credits are sometimes given for certain types of investments. Tax credits are usually intended as rewards for expenses favored by the government, such as research or job creation. Tax credits may be structured as reductions from income or as direct credits against taxes that are due. Tax credits often have a significant effect on the value of an investment and thus must be carefully considered in financial analyses.

Taxable Income.   Once depreciation is calculated, the taxable income can be found. If Y is the project's cash income, $d(t)$ the allowable depreciation for the year, and YT is the taxable income:

$$YT = Y - d(t) \tag{9.23}$$

For simplicity, this expression does not reflect any tax credits, which would further reduce taxable income. If τ is the tax rate, the after-tax income (YA) of the project is

$$YA = Y - \tau YT = Y - \tau[Y - d(t)] \tag{9.24}$$

This expression also does not reflect tax credits. It can be rearranged to

$$YA = Y(1 - \tau) + \tau\, d(t) \tag{9.25}$$

The term $\tau\, d(t)$ is a positive cash flow resulting from depreciation and is called the *tax shield*. In some sense this is not a "real" cash flow since depreciation is not generating any income. It does act to reduce taxes, though, so the effect is the same as if it were a real revenue producer.

The after-tax income is what should be used in financial analysis. Costs and benefits are combined into a single income figure for the year, the after-tax income is determined, and these are used to find the NPV:

$$NPV = \sum_{t=0}^{n} \frac{YA(t)}{[1 + r(t)]^t} \tag{9.26}$$

where $YA(t)$ represents the after-tax income for year t. Note again that there can be an initial income in year 0; this usually represents the purchase price and is thus negative.

In some cases, the benefits of tax credits and depreciation cannot be fully utilized in a single year since an organization may not have sufficient before-tax income. In such cases, unused depreciation and tax credits can be preserved for use in future years, a process known as "carrying forward." There are often limits on the number of years for which tax credits can be carried forward. Sometimes such credits can be retroactively applied to taxes paid in previous years, too.

9.3.4. Inflation

Net present value calculations provide a valuable theoretical approach for handling financial analyses, but many practical questions have been left unanswered. One such question involves the treatment of *inflation* in benefit–cost analyses. Inflation refers to a general increase in prices throughout the economy. A general decrease in prices throughout the economy is referred to as *deflation*. There are many causes of inflation, and economists disagree about which ones are the most important.

Many benefit–cost calculations require accurate estimates of cash flows and discount rates. However, these estimates are likely to be strongly affected by inflation. For example, the maintenance costs for a highway with a 20-year lifespan are almost certain to increase over time as the costs of materials and labor rise. Similarly, the employment benefits of a program that creates jobs will increase if wages rise over time.

EXAMPLE 9.19

Cash Flows with Straight-Line Depreciation

A firm buys a machine for $1000 that will save $500 per year for four years. At the end of that time it will be worn out but will be worth $200 as scrap. In addition, a maintenance expense of $100 will be incurred at the end of year 3. The firm uses straight-line depreciation and faces a tax rate of 46 percent. There are no tax credits and this project can be considered separately from the firm's other activities. If the effective annual discount rate is 13 percent, what is the NPV of the machine?

Consider the cash flows:

Year	0	1	2	3	4
Costs	$1000			$100	
Benefits		$500	$500	500	$500 + $200 scrap
Net income	−1000	500	500	400	700

For straight-line depreciation:

$$d(t) = \frac{K - S}{N}$$

$$K = \$1000 \qquad S = \$200 \qquad N = 4$$

$$d(t) = \frac{\$1000 - \$200}{4}$$

$$= \$200$$

After-tax incomes are found from

$$YA = Y(1 - \tau) + \tau d(t)$$

For year 1:

$$YA_1 = \$500(1 - 0.46) + 0.46(\$200)$$

$$= \$362$$

Similarly,

$$YA_2 = \$362 \qquad YA_3 = \$308 \qquad YA_4 = \$470$$

The NPV is

$$NPV = \sum_{t=0}^{n} \frac{YA(t)}{[1 + r(t)]^t}$$

$$= -\$1000 + \frac{\$362}{1.13} + \frac{\$362}{(1.13)^2} + \frac{\$308}{(1.13)^3} + \frac{\$470}{(1.13)^4}$$

$$= \$105.57$$

EXAMPLE 9.20

Nominal Cash Flows

An investment of $100 yields a nominal benefit of $250 after three years. If the nominal discount rate is 10 percent, what is the NPV?

$$NPV = \sum_{t=0}^{n} \frac{B(t)}{[1 + r(t)]^t} - \sum_{t=0}^{n} \frac{C(t)}{[1 + r(t)]^t}$$

$$C_0 = \$100 \qquad B_3 = \$250 \qquad r = 0.10 \qquad n = 3$$

$$NPV = \frac{\$250}{(1.10)^3} - \$100$$

$$= \$87.83$$

To account for inflation, cash flows and discount rates can be expressed in one of two ways. A *nominal amount* includes the effects of inflation and thus is not directly comparable from year to year. That is, a dollar today is not the same in nominal terms as a dollar a year from now, since the dollar next year is inflated and has less actual purchasing power. For example, the dollar might buy 50 grapes this year but only 45 grapes next year. Similarly, a *nominal interest rate* includes both the time value of money and the effects of inflation. Thus, an 8 percent nominal rate may consist of 3 percent for the time value of money plus 5 percent to compensate for the general increase in prices throughout the economy.

A cash flow can also be expressed as a *real amount*, which has the effects of inflation removed. A dollar has the same purchasing power, regardless of when it is earned. Similarly, a *real interest rate* reflects only the time value of money, not changes in the general price level. Thus, in periods of inflation, nominal interest rates will be higher than real ones, since nominal rates also include the effects of a higher level of prices throughout the economy.

Either nominal or real values can be used in benefit–cost analysis, *as long as they are used consistently*. That is, nominal cash flows require nominal discount rates, and real cash flows require real discount rates. Both methods of accounting for inflation are acceptable as long as one is used throughout the entire analysis. Thus, cash flows should be given consistently in either real or nominal terms, and the final benefit–cost results (such as net present value) should be calculated in the same terms.

It is sometimes necessary to convert nominal rates into real ones, or vice versa. If r is the nominal interest rate, R is the real interest rate, and i is the inflation rate, then

$$1 + R = \frac{1 + r}{1 + i} \tag{9.27}$$

The real interest rate is simply the nominal rate with the effect of inflation removed. The real interest rate R is often approximated by $r - i$, although Equation (9.27) gives a more precise result.

EXAMPLE 9.21

Real Cash Flows

For the investment described in Example 9.20, the real value of the cash benefit after three years is $204.07. If the inflation rate is 7 percent per year, what is the NPV in real terms?

First, find the real discount rate:

$$1 + R = \frac{1 + r}{1 + i}$$

$$r = 0.10 \qquad i = 0.07$$

$$1 + R = \frac{1.10}{1.07}$$

$$R = 0.028$$

Second, find the NPV:

$$NPV = \sum_{t=0}^{n} \frac{B(t)}{[1 + r(t)]^t} - \sum_{t=0}^{n} \frac{C(t)}{[1 + r(t)]^t}$$

$$= \frac{\$204.07}{(1.028)^3} - \$100$$

$$= \$87.85$$

The result is the same as Example 9.20, except for a round-off error. The correct value for the NPV is obtained as long as either real or nominal values are used consistently.

Inflation can also have an indirect effect on cash flows if taxes are involved. Tax rates historically have been imposed on nominal income; in other words, the tax system usually does not remove the effects of inflation when calculating tax payments. If inflation exists, nominal income can rise while real income stays constant or even declines. Furthermore, many taxes are progressive; that is, the tax rates increase as income increases. Thus, the percentage of income paid as taxes can rise, even though real income has not changed. In this case, a stream of constant real payments over time will lose a progressively larger portion to taxes each year if there is a positive inflation rate. This phenomenon is known as "bracket creep" since the taxpayer is moving into higher tax brackets.

In the United States, some taxes are now indexed to allow for the effects of inflation. For example, federal personal income taxes were indexed for inflation beginning in 1984. However, many taxes are still imposed on nominal income, so the effect of inflation on taxes should still be considered when conducting financial analyses for individuals or taxable entities.

Inflation can be measured in several different ways. In the United States, three of the most important measures of inflation are the gross domestic product deflators, the consumer price indexes, and the producer price indexes. These three measures are described below.

The gross domestic product (GDP) is a measure of the current market value of all final goods and services produced in the domestic economy. It represents the overall size of the U.S. economy, including purchases by individuals and governments, and gross private domestic investment. GDP figures are commonly used by government agencies and private firms to assess the status and growth of the economy.

The GDP can also be used to provide measures of inflation called *implicit price deflators*. In principle, these measures are found by calculating the nominal GDP at current prices, and then calculating the real GDP at the prices that prevailed in some earlier base year. The ratio of the nominal GDP to the real GDP provides an index of the price change from the base year to the present year.

In practice, it is very difficult to evaluate all individual purchases at both current and base year prices. Instead, the Bureau of Economic Analysis of the Department of Commerce calculates the current GDP by aggregating purchases of goods and services in broad categories, such as housing and clothing. The current market value of each of these categories is then deflated to the base year using an appropriate price index, and the deflated amounts are summed to represent the value of the GDP in base year prices. The price indexes used are obtained from other government agencies. The implicit price deflator is then calculated by dividing the current GDP by the value of the same quantities of goods and services in the base year. The base year is currently 1982.

Several different implicit price deflators are prepared from GDP data. The most commonly used is the *GDP deflator*, which includes changes for all goods and services in the economy. A second inflation measure derived from GDP calculations is the *personal consumption expenditures (PCE) index*, which measures the change in prices of goods and services purchased by individuals. Other measures are calculated to provide inflation estimates for government purchases.

The second major group of inflation measures are the *consumer price indexes* (CPI). These indexes measure the price of a fixed market basket of goods and services purchased by consumers, including food, housing, energy, clothing, medical care, and a variety of other items. The ratio of the prices of this market basket in different years provides a measure of inflation.

Since the CPI is based on a fixed market basket, it measures only changes in prices and not changes in the mix of products purchased. The current base year for the CPI is the average of 1982–1984, a period with very low inflation. All CPI figures are reported in terms that reflect growth from a value of 100 assigned to this base.

Several types of CPIs exist. The most commonly used is the CPI for all urban consumers, known as CPI-U. The CPI-U covers about 80 percent of the civilian population. Another type of CPI is the CPI for urban wage earners and clerical workers, known as CPI-W. This measure includes only about half the people covered by the CPI-U since it excludes professionals, short-term and self-employed workers, the unemployed, and people outside of the labor force. Until 1978, only the CPI-W was available; now both measures are calculated monthly by the Department of Labor's Bureau of Labor Statistics.

In addition to the aggregate CPI, values for the individual components of the CPI are also reported. This information is often useful for analyzing policies that affect certain sectors of the economy or in preparing inflation analyses for projects that will involve only a limited range of goods or services. CPIs for different metropolitan areas are published. These are especially useful for state and local policy analysts.

A third set of inflation measures are the *producer price indexes* (PPI). These indexes provide measures of price changes for private industries, and are analogous to the consumer price indexes for individuals. Three types of PPIs are available: (1) measures by state of processing, which reflect price trends at different production levels; (2) measures by industry, which reflect price changes for different industrial sectors; and (3) measures by commodity, which reflect price changes for different materials.

The PPIs are calculated by the Bureau of Labor Statistics based on industry surveys. Like the CPI, the PPI uses a fixed mix of outputs for each industry, and thus reflects only price changes. The PPI uses a base year of 1982 and reports price trends in comparison with a value of 100 for 1982. The methods for calculating the PPIs were extensively revised in the early 1980s to accommodate recent economic changes.

Figure 9.4 compares the GDP deflator, CPI, and PPI since 1950. The values are remarkably similar, with the GDP deflator and the CPI being especially close in most years. The PPI tends to oscillate more than the other measures since it reflects a narrower segment of the overall economy and industrial prices tend to change more rapidly than consumer prices.

With so many different measures of inflation available, the choice of which one to use for policy analysis is often controversial. For example, in the early 1980s there were lengthy debates about whether the CPI or the GDP deflator should be chosen as the cost-of-living index for increasing federal transfer payments. The CPI had historically been used for this purpose, but some analysts argued that it overstated inflation because it did not allow for changes in the mix of goods purchased and suffered from other structural flaws. A switch to the GDP deflator was proposed as a way to save money, since the GDP deflator

Figure 9.4. Comparison of inflation measures: 1950–1990.

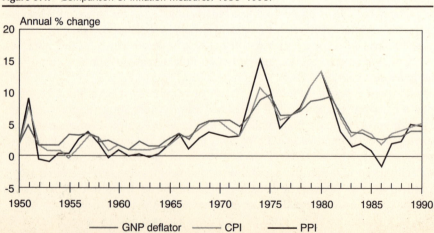

had been several points lower than the CPI in the late 1970s and early 1980s. However, the debate ignored the historical comparison of the two measures shown in Figure 9.4, which indicates that the CPI and GDP deflator are usually very similar. In fact, in 1982 and 1983 the GDP deflator actually exceeded the CPI.

Like policy makers, economists have been unable to agree on the best single measure of inflation for policy analysis. Some favor measures that are closely targeted to the project being examined. For example, the costs of a construction project should be analyzed using measures developed for construction. Other experts suggest that broad consumer inflation measures, such as the CPI, should be used for all public projects. They argue that government is an agent for the public, and therefore the costs and benefits of public projects should be analyzed using inflation measures that reflect prices facing the public.

While the second approach has merit, we believe that it masks important distinctions between different types of public projects. Consider a situation in which a policy maker must choose between an expanded food service program for the elderly and a new highway project. In order to make a choice, the policy maker needs accurate information about the future costs of each project. If we know that food costs are expected to increase by 5 percent per year and highway construction costs are expected to increase by 10 percent per year, shouldn't such information be included in the analysis?

Thus, we recommend that inflation measures be selected using the following principles:

1. The measure selected should reflect the relative price facing the project. A project that has a specialized purpose, such as the production of energy, should be evaluated using a specialized measure of inflation.
2. The measure selected should be appropriate for the region in which the benefits and costs are to be incurred. A project in New England should be evaluated using inflation measures that apply there, rather than national measures or measures for some other geographical area.
3. The measure selected should correspond to the types of economic activity involved. A project that directly affects consumers should be evaluated using a version of the CPI, while a project that affects many sectors of the economy should be evaluated using the GDP deflator.

These principles apply to large projects for which careful assessments of inflation are needed. In many cases, such as small projects, short duration projects, and preliminary estimates, complex inflation analysis is unnecessary. In these situations, a general inflation measure can be used, with the GDP deflator probably being the best choice.

All these general inflation measures suffer from one potential problem: They do not explicitly show changes in relative prices. In other words, these measures do not reflect the change in the price of one product in comparison with another. Such changes in relative prices are often critical in benefit–cost analysis. For example, assume you are a financial analyst for an organization that uses a great deal of energy, such as an aluminum refinery or a transit system. You need to choose an inflation rate for a benefit–cost analysis and decide that the PPI is the best option. However, energy prices have tended to change in ways very different than the overall PPI. Thus, if you used the overall

PPI for the analysis, the results would probably not reflect the conditions facing your energy-intensive enterprise.

This example illustrates the dangers of using broad general inflation measures when relative measures are more relevant. In a situation such as this, you should identify an inflation measure that best represents the project being considered. You may wish to use one of the specialized indexes available, such as the PPI Fuel and Power Index, or you may want to construct your own index using data from other sources.

Several sources of information about future inflation are available. The federal government and many state governments prepare estimates of future inflation as part of their budgeting processes. In addition, several private economic consultants have developed econometric models that are used to predict future inflation. These predictions are sometimes discussed in national publications, but usually must be purchased from the private firm.

It should be noted that few, if any, organizations have correctly predicted inflation rates in recent years. The volatility of energy prices, dramatic changes in national and world economies, and changes in federal monetary and fiscal policies have all had significant and unpredicted effects on inflation rates. Thus, if a careful assessment of the impact of inflation on a project is needed, it is best not to rely on one inflation projection. Instead, the benefit–cost analysis should be conducted using a variety of inflation rates.

SUMMARY

This chapter has described the use of net present value (NPV) in making financial decisions. The NPV represents the sum of a project's discounted cash flows and signifies whether a project increases or decreases real wealth. NPV can be calculated using Equation (9.1). NPV can be used to evaluate the desirability of a single project or the relative value of a series of alternatives.

Each of the alternatives to net present value is used by some firms and agencies, and hence familiarity with these techniques may be useful. However, some of the approaches can lead to erroneous conclusions. The payback and return on book value methods should be avoided for this reason.

Despite its many proponents, the internal rate of return offers few advantages over the NPV and has several pitfalls. It can be used by those who find it more understandable than the NPV, but great care must be exercised in using the IRR for complex problems. The wealth-maximizing rate is better than the IRR since it provides accurate evaluations of projects with an initial investment followed by a stream of benefits and is simpler to calculate.

The discounted and net benefit–cost ratios are similar to the NPV and can be used in all situations. The BCRs are essentially rearrangements of the NPV and sometimes produce information in a more interesting or compelling form. Thus, we recommend the NPV approach, supplemented by the BCR and the WMR where appropriate.

One problem that often arises when comparing projects is that they may have different lifespans. There are four common methods to deal with such a situation: replication, equivalent annuities, assigning a terminal value, and the best available alternative rate. The choice among these options depends on the nature of the alternatives.

The figures used for the NPV calculation often stem from an analysis of cash flows. Cash flows are affected by salvage values, taxes, and depreciation. Most depreciation calculations are now based on the Modified Accelerated Cost Recover System, known as MACRS.

Many benefit–cost analyses can be profoundly affected by inflation, which is a general increase in prices throughout the economy. In these situations, all figures should be presented either in nominal terms, which include the effects of inflation, or in real terms, which have the effects of inflation removed. Several measures of inflation are commonly available, including the gross domestic product deflator, the consumer price index, and the producer price index. The choice of inflation measures depends on the type of project being studied.

QUESTIONS AND PROBLEMS

1. A municipal subway system is contemplating the purchase of an electronic fare system to replace traditional tokens. Each installation is expected to cost $50,000 and save $8000 per year in labor costs over the ten-year lifespan of the equipment. An annual maintenance expense of $500 will be required. The subway system uses a 7 percent discount rate. Should the system buy the electronic equipment?
2. Find the NPV of a project with the following cash flows:

Year	0	1	2	3	4	5
Costs	$10,000			$5000		$ 2000
Benefits		$2000	$4000	6000	$8000	10,000

Use a discount rate of 9.5 percent. Is the project desirable?
3. A farmer has been offered a new device to dispense insecticide at a cost of $5000. The device has an expected lifetime of six months. The device will save $1500 worth of crops each month for six months, and the insecticide will cost $200 per month. Since the insecticide will pollute the runoff from the farmer's fields, the local pollution control authority will charge the farmer $300 per month for six months beginning in the third month of use (it takes some time for the insecticide to pollute the runoff). If the farmer uses a 10 percent effective annual discount rate, is this device a good investment?
4. A city is planning a new convention center and has received bids from two contractors. One contractor's proposal would cost $15,000,000 to build plus upkeep of $175,000 per year for its expected 30-year lifespan. Annual revenues are expected to be $1,000,000. The second contractor proposes a larger facility capable of earning $2,000,000 each year for 30 years at an initial cost of $25,000,000. Its larger size requires maintenance expenses of $400,000 per year. It would also need $5,000,000 in renovations in years 11 and 21. If the city uses a discount rate of 7 percent and uses net present value as its evaluation criterion, should it build either facility? If so, which one?
5. A military procurement officer must purchase fuel filters for a new tank. One model is expected to last two months and costs $200. Another model costs $550 and lasts six months. This model requires a $25 cleaning after four months. The military uses an 8.3 percent annual discount rate for such equipment. Which filter is the best choice according to the:
   (a) Replication method?
   (b) Equivalent annuities method?

6. Ten-Four Trucking needs to buy another truck for its fleet. It can purchase a new vehicle for $67,000, which will generate $15,000 in revenue for seven years to pay off the investment cost. (That is, $15,000 per year is available to recoup the initial investment after all operating costs have been covered.) Alternatively, it can buy a used truck for $38,000, which will generate $13,000 per year for four years. Neither investment is directly replicable, although Ten-Four will need to replace the vehicle once it wears out. Assume both vehicles have a $5000 salvage value at the end of their lives, and that the new truck is worth $23,000 after four years. If Ten-Four has a 12 percent discount rate, which truck is the better investment?

7. A project has the following cash flows:

Year	0	1	2	3	4
Costs	$10,000		$1000		
Benefits		$3000	3000	$3000	$3000

Find the discounted and net benefit–cost ratios for this project using a discount rate of 5 percent. Is the project a good investment? Would the BCR_d and BCR_n increase or decrease if the discount rate were 10 percent?

8. A county government has received a federal grant of $10,000,000 to provide new health care services. The grant can be used in one of three ways:

   (1) A new health care facility can be built. Construction would cost $6,000,000 in year 0 and $4,000,000 in year 1. The facility would yield benefits of $1,000,000 per year for 20 years starting in year 2.

   (2) An old facility can be remodeled at a cost of $8,000,000 in year 0. The improved facility would have additional benefits of $1,500,000 per year for ten years, starting in year 1.

   (3) Equipment can be purchased for existing health care facilities. Four sets of equipment would be purchased at $2,500,000 each. One set of equipment would be purchased each year, starting in year 0. Each year's equipment will last for five years after its purchase. Each year's equipment will produce annual benefits of $750,000 per year during each year of its lifespan.

The county can earn 4 percent annual interest on funds until they are needed. The federal government will allow the county to keep half of any funds it does not need for the project, but the other half must be returned after two years. Any funds kept by the county should be regarded as benefits in the year they are obtained. The county uses a discount rate of 7 percent. Using either the BCR_d or the BCR_n, determine which project is the best. Differences in project lifespans can be ignored.

9. A large industrial firm makes project decisions using a payback period of four years. An inventor has a new device that will last for seven years and save the company $100,000 in electricity costs annually. The inventor wants $325,000 for the device. Will the firm purchase the invention? If the company's discount rate is 10 percent, should the company purchase the invention if it used net present value analysis rather than the payback approach? Would either of these answers be different if the inventor wanted to be paid in five annual payments of $90,000 due at the end of each year, plus an initial payment of $50,000?

10. A project has the following cash flows:

Year	0	1	2	3	4
Costs	$10,000	$1000	$1000		
Benefits		3000	3500	$4000	$4500

Find the internal rate of return. If the opportunity cost of capital is 7 percent, is this project a good investment?

11. A project has the following cash flows:

Year	0	1	2	3
Costs	$10,000			
Benefits		$4000	$4000	$4000

The opportunity cost of capital and the discount rate are 8 percent. Find the NPV, BCR_d, BCR_n, and IRR. Using each of these measures, determine if the project is a good investment.

12. A project has the following cash flows:

Year	0	1	2	3
Costs	$10,000	$5000		
Benefits		4000	$6000	$8000

The opportunity cost of capital and the discount rate are 8 percent. Find the NPV, BCR_d, BCR_n, and IRR. Using each of these measures, determine if the project is a good investment.

13. A project has the following cash flows:

Year	0	1	2	3
Costs	$10,000		$10,000	
Benefits		$8000	8000	$8000

The opportunity cost of capital and the discount rate are 8 percent. Find the NPV, BCR_d, BCR_n, and IRR. Using each of these measures, determine if the project is a good investment.

14. For $10,000, the Little Red School District can join a purchasing consortium that will save the district about $3000 per year for five years. If the district does not join the consortium, the money will be placed in a reserve account earning 7 percent per year. The current borrowing rate is also 7 percent. Using the WMR approach, determine if the school district should join the consortium.

15. The manager of a city's pension fund has $1,000,000 to invest. She has three investment alternatives:

   (1) Alternative A requires an initial investment of $250,000, lasts for two years, and earns interest at a rate of 7 percent compounded annually. It is replicable at any time in increments of $250,000.

   (2) Alternative B requires an initial investment of $850,000 and yields $1,250,000 after four years.

   (3) Alternative C requires an initial investment of $1,000,000 and returns $375,000 per year for three years. It cannot be replicated.

   The best available alternative rate and the loan rate are both 8 percent. Using the WMR approach, determine which of these investments are attractive. If more than one is attractive, determine which is the best investment.

16. A firm is considering investing $78,000 in new production equipment. It would receive a 10 percent tax credit for the equipment and would use ACRS depreciation

for the five-year lifespan of the equipment. Unused tax credits can be carried forward into future years until they are exhausted. The equipment would generate $20,000 in revenue annually after operating costs have been deducted. The firm has a tax rate of 46 percent and uses an 8 percent discount rate. If this investment can be considered separately from the firm's other activities, is it worth purchasing?

17. Find the annual depreciation allowances for the five-year depreciable life of a $19,000 investment using:
    (a) Straight-line depreciation
    (b) Double-declining-balance depreciation
    (c) Double-declining-balance depreciation, switching to straight-line in the fourth year
    (d) Sum-of-the-year's-digits depreciation
    (e) The Accelerated Cost Recovery System

REFERENCES

Brealey, Richard, and Myers, Stewart, *Principles of Corporate Finance*, New York: McGraw-Hill, 1981, Chapters 5–6.

Hoel, Arline, Clarkson, Kenneth, and Miller, Roger, *Economics Sourcebook of Government Statistics*, Lexington, KY: Lexington Books, 1983, Chapter 1.

Newnan, Donald, *Engineering Economic Analysis*, 2nd Edition, San Jose: Engineering Press, 1983, Chapters 9–10.

Riggs, James, *Essentials of Engineering Economics*, New York: McGraw-Hill, 1982, Chapters 2–4.

Zerbe, Jr., Richard O. "Consistency Among Cost–Benefit Criteria," *Policy and Information* 7(1) (1963).

10

Case Study of Options for Sludge Disposal

The following case study highlights some of the uses of financial information in conducting a benefit–cost analysis. It illustrates the importance of the discount rate and shows how disagreements about assumptions can affect the outcome of the financial analysis. The case study also shows how nonfinancial factors can play a major role in reaching benefit–cost decisions. These nonfinancial factors will be discussed in more detail in subsequent chapters, but are introduced here to make the case study correspond more closely to real decisions.

10.1. THE PROBLEM

The Regional Sewage Treatment District is responsible for treating sewage from several cities in a metropolitan area. The district is planning on upgrading its facilities in order to more effectively remove pollutants. As part of the upgrade, the district must choose a method to dispose of the sludge that remains after processing. This sludge is a bulky semisolid material that has a low level of toxicity. Current environmental regulations allow the sludge to be disposed of in landfills, used as a fertilizer, or applied to forests.

The district's treatment plant is located along the shoreline of a major bay. The plant location adjoins a large park that is maintained in a near-natural state. Access to the plant is by a road through the park; the road also passes through a large, high-income residential neighborhood.

Sludge disposal is currently handled by trucking the material from the plant, through the park and neighborhood, to a forested area about 30 miles away. The sludge is then sprayed on the ground in the forest as a soil amendment. The current systems at the plant produce about three truckloads of sludge per day. This disposal system has been in place for about 20 years and has proven to be very reliable and cost-effective. In recent years, however, a few complaints about the truck traffic have been received from residents in the nearby area, and a few other complaints have been made by people living near the rural forest.

The district's plan for upgrading the treatment plant will increase the quantities of sludge. Initially, the district planned to simply continue using its current disposal method, but on a larger scale. However, a private firm has now proposed an alternative processing and disposal method that is supposed to have several important advantages over the current disposal technology. The governing board of the district, which is made up of representatives from the participating cities, is now trying to choose which disposal method to implement.

10.2.   THE OPTIONS

Regardless of which option is chosen, the amount of sludge that must be handled will increase. However, the two options differ dramatically in their financing, costs, and social impacts:

1. *Current disposal method*. The district's staff has recommended continuing the present disposal method after the plant upgrades are completed. Their preference is based largely on the reliability and technical simplicity of the existing process. This approach would necessitate purchase of additional land for disposal, but district staff believe that the timber sales from this land would ultimately offset these costs. Continuing the present disposal method would also require a slight expansion of the treatment plant, which would result in the loss of 2 acres of park land. The number of loaded sludge truck trips would increase to 11 per day.

2. *Vendor's method*. The vendor's proposed approach would rely on an entirely different treatment method that converts the sludge into a dry pelletized fertilizer that would be sold for agricultural uses. This approach would eliminate the need to purchase additional rural land, would save 2 acres at the treatment plant, and would require less obtrusive facilities. It would also increase sludge trucks trips over current levels, but only by seven trips per day. However, the district staff has pointed out that the vendor's approach has never been tried on a commercial scale, so its effectiveness and reliability are uncertain. Furthermore, there are no guaranteed markets for the fertilizer that is produced. To overcome these objections, the vendor proposes to operate the new process on a test basis for five years at no cost to the district. During this period, the district would continue to use its existing sludge treatment process for about two-thirds of the sludge, while the remainder would be handled through the vendor's process. If the test succeeded, the district would be obligated to switch all sludge handling to the new process after five years.

In addition to the issues discussed above, two other factors may influence the choice among the options:

1. Environmental Regulations.   There is considerable uncertainty about future regulatory practices for sewage sludge. State and federal agencies are currently reviewing standards for allowable toxics and are studying alternative procedures for sludge disposal. District staff believe that regulatory changes might adversely affect the vendor's proposal to use sludge as fertilizer since this plan is experimental and could introduce toxics into the food chain. In contrast, the vendor believes that changes in environmental regulations would hurt the current disposal practice since it produces sludge with slightly higher levels of toxicity than does the new process.

2. Costs.   The district staff have presented data that show the current process to be less expensive to build and operate on a life cycle cost basis. District staff analyzed the costs of the two options using a 5.5 percent inflation rate and a 2.0 percent real discount rate. The resulting cost estimates for the alternatives are shown in Table 10.1. The vendor has reviewed these calculations and has criticized them for two reasons.

First, the vendor believes a real discount rate of 5.0 percent should be used. District staff have indicated that they always use a 2.0 percent real discount rate since it is an appropriate rate for a public agency that builds systems required for environmental protection. The vendor argues for 5.0 percent since it more accurately reflects the cost of capital in the private sector and that funds diverted from private to public uses should also be discounted at this rate. For comparison purposes, the city in which the plant is located currently uses a discount rate of 3.0 percent for most public works projects. The actual borrowing to finance the expansion of the treatment plant is expected to be issued at a nominal rate of 8.0 percent.

Second, the vendor believes the district has overvalued the timber that would be harvested from the rural forest. The vendor thinks this overvaluation has occurred because an overly optimistic current timber value has been used and because timber prices were assumed to rise faster than inflation in the district's analysis. The district assumed a starting price of $230 per million board-feet, compared with $180 recommended by the vendor. The district used timber price trends from 1929 to 1986, which showed an average real price growth rate of 1.25 percent, while the vendor relied on trends from 1975 to 1985, which showed timber prices to be declining. A chart showing these price trends is shown in Figure 10.1. The vendor also pointed out that the district's timber prices are for different areas than are being used for sludge disposal. If the changes proposed by the vendor are made, the vendor's proposal is less expensive on a life cycle basis, as shown in Table 10.1.

TABLE 10.1   Results of Life Cycle Cost Analyses

Analyst	District Proposal (million)	Vendor Proposal (million)
District	$54.2	$59.1
Vendor	52.4	40.7

Figure 10.1

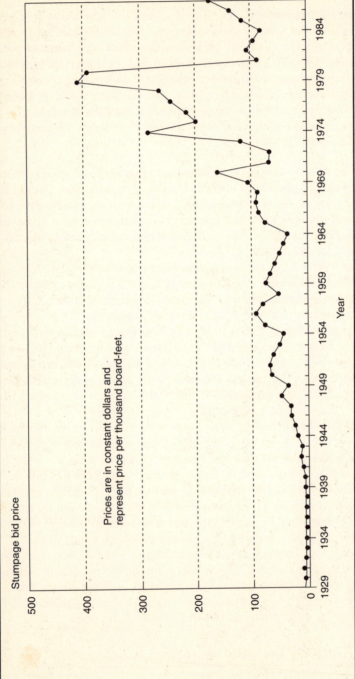

Stumpage bid price

Prices are in constant dollars and represent price per thousand board-feet.

Year

10.3. THE QUESTION

You are a staff person for a councilmember of one of the cities that is a member of the Regional Sewage Treatment District. Your city includes the site of the treatment plant, along with the park and residential neighborhood that adjoin it. Your councilmember wants to know how to vote at the district's meeting next week. The councilmember is very concerned about costs and is sensitive to environmental and neighborhood concerns. The councilmember has a record of supporting the recommendations of the district staff, especially since the staff is highly regarded and has received numerous national honors.

However, the councilmember is also being extensively lobbied by the vendor and by elected officials who support the vendor's plan. The vendor continues to claim that the new treatment process would be less expensive and points out that it is supported by many neighborhood groups. Several other elected officials have met privately with your councilmember and have indicated that support of the vendor's proposal would win the gratitude and votes of people in the neighborhood.

Your councilmember has posed several specific questions for your staff team, including

1. Which cost analysis is correct?
2. Which of the proposed discount rates is more reasonable?
3. Which analysis of timber prices is more reasonable?
4. How can the risk of the vendor's proposal be considered? Does the offer of a test for five years provide a sufficient guarantee?
5. What other factors should affect a decision? How can these be balanced against the cost and risk factors?

There is not sufficient time for a complete independent analysis of the project. You have time to discuss the project with the district, the vendor, and other city agencies. You also have time to talk with a few neighborhood and special interest groups.

What recommendation would you make to your councilmember? How would you arrive at this recommendation? To assist your analysis, Table 10.2 shows the annual costs of the two options.

When this situation actually occurred, the councilmember's staff developed a five-step process for preparing a recommendation:

1. Collect and review existing documents on the alternatives and their costs, benefits, and risks.
2. Discuss the options with staff from the district and the vendor to isolate areas of disagreement and concern.
3. Check the financial analyses of the two parties to ensure that the calculations were properly done.
4. Prepare an independent financial analysis based on the staff's best judgment about the issues in dispute.
5. Identify other factors that should be weighed by the councilmember in reaching a decision.

TABLE 10.2   Annual Costs of Options (in nominal thousands of dollars, not discounted)

Year	District Proposal (with District Timber Prices)	District Proposal (with Vendor Timber Prices)	Vendor Proposal
1989	$ 1,077	$ 1,077	$ 0
1990	1,866	1,866	0
1991	2,533	2,533	0
1992	14,627	14,627	0
1993	10,193	10,287	3,961
1994	10,956	11,013	4,083
1995	2,738	2,834	4,211
1996	5,737	5,756	7,105
1997	4,591	4,999	7,319
1998	4,693	5,175	7,565
1999	7,141	7,198	7,824
2000	4,752	5,388	8,120
2001	6,144	6,513	8,386
2002	7,946	8,447	8,691
2003	7,176	7,507	9,012
2004	7,317	7,758	9,377
2005	6,961	7,665	9,709
2006	10,500	10,500	10,086
2007	10,238	10,238	10,484
2008	8,219	9,122	10,934
2009	8,705	9,680	11,347
2010	6,921	8,826	11,815
2011	10,785	11,512	12,308
2012	(76,221)	(35,185)	12,863

Information gathered during the first two steps has been presented above. When this situation actually occurred, the staff's check of the financial calculations done by the district and the vendor showed that these calculations were accurate under the assumptions used by the two groups. Thus, the substantive part of the staff's analysis focused on the last two steps in the process.

10.4.   THE ANSWER

After reviewing the two financial analyses, staff concluded that these differed only because of assumptions about the discount rate and timber prices. The district and the vendor agreed on all the other parameters, including annual cash flows and inflation rates. Thus, the staff began the financial analysis by comparing the two sets of differing assumptions:

1. *Discount rate.* The district used a real discount rate of 2.0 percent and the vendor used a rate of 5.0 percent. The councilmember's staff sought alternative discount rate information in two ways. First, they identified the real discount rate used by their city for public works projects, which turned out to be 3.0 percent. Second, they investigated the cost of the actual borrowing that would be needed to finance the expansion

of the treatment plant. Under conditions at the time, this borrowing would be expected to have an interest rate of about 8.0 percent, which represents a premium of about 2.5 percent above inflation. Thus, the staff concluded that a real discount rate of about 3.0 percent was more appropriate than either of the assumptions used by the two parties.

2. *Timber prices.* Timber prices are an important aspect of the district's proposal since timber sales offset much of the cost of buying forest land for sludge disposal. Staff reviewed the timber price assumptions made by the district and the vendor. The district used a starting price of $230 per million board-feet and the vendor used a price of $180. This difference had only a modest effect on the outcome of the financial analysis. The principal difference between the analyses was related to assumptions about future timber prices. The district analyzed price trends from 1929 to 1986 and calculated that prices grew by an average of 1.25 percent more than inflation during that period. This assumption was used in the district's analysis of future timber price growth. The vendor examined the same data but claimed that only recent information should be used. By examining the period from 1975 to 1985, the vendor determined that real timber prices have actually declined. Thus, the vendor's financial analysis assumes that timber prices will grow only at the inflation rate, and the vendor claims that this is a conservative assumption.

The councilmember's staff found flaws in both timber price analyses. The district analysis failed to note that almost all the growth in prices had occurred during the early and mid-1970s, and prices had actually declined since then. Thus, the concept of an average growth rate may be very misleading. The vendor analysis covered a period from a high price peak to a low price trough, which is an inappropriate period for developing a long-term price trend. Prices have actually risen significantly since the final year chosen by the vendor for the timber price analysis. In addition, the staff noted that timber prices are highly variable depending upon location, species, accessibility, and growth rate. The information that was used for the financial analyses was based on statewide averages, not prices for timber from locations comparable to the rural forest used for sludge disposal. This problem made the timber price analyses even more suspect.

The councilmember's staff did not have time to prepare an independent timber price calculation. Thus, they decided that neither analysis was especially reliable but that no other information could be obtained. They decided to analyze each option using its own timber price assumptions, but to point out the flaws in each set of assumptions.

The final financial analysis prepared by the staff consisted of a recalculation of the estimates provided by the district and the vendor using a real discount rate of 3.0 percent. Each analysis included its original timber price assumptions. The resulting financial estimates are shown in Table 10.3. The staff calculated the cost of the vendor proposal to be $52.0 million. This estimate was not dependent on timber prices since the vendor's proposal does not

TABLE 10.3   Staff Life Cycle Cost Analyses

Timber Prices	District Proposal (million)	Vendor Proposal (million)
District	$52.4	$52.0
Vendor	60.5	52.0

use this disposal method. The cost of the district's proposal varies by about 15 percent depending on the assumptions used for timber prices. In general, the staff felt that the district's timber prices were probably closer to reality than the vendor's, and thus a life cycle cost estimate of $55 million or less seemed most reasonable.

The staff analysis significantly narrowed the range of cost differences between the proposals. In light of the uncertainties about future costs and timber prices, the staff concluded that the two options did not differ significantly in life cycle costs. Thus, the staff recommended that the councilmember not use cost as a major factor in choosing among the options.

The final step in the staff analysis was to identify other factors that should be used by the councilmember to choose between the options. After reviewing the information, the staff presented these factors as advantages and disadvantages for the vendor's alternative:

1. *Advantages.* The staff identified three principal advantages of the vendor's proposal. First, the reduced land area would mean that the treatment plant would have less impact on the park. Furthermore, the facilities required for the vendor's proposal would be less obtrusive than the current system, and thus the plant would appear to be smaller. Second, the number of truck trips through the neighborhood would be reduced, which would please local residents. Third, the end of forest disposal would please residents in the rural area and would eliminate the need to identify more land for sludge application.

2. *Disadvantages.* The staff found three principal disadvantages to the vendor's alternative. First, it had significant technological uncertainty. The vendor's proposed five-year test period would reduce this uncertainty, but problems about what would constitute successful performance would still need to be resolved. Second, the vendor could not guarantee a market for the final product. If a market was not available, the dried sludge would have to be disposed of in a landfill, which would raise costs. Third, a choice to test the vendor's system might prove impossible to reverse at a later date, even if the process were only marginally successful. Public pressure to reduce truck trips, decrease the size of the plant, and avoid forest application would be extremely difficult to overcome once the initial decision for the vendor's process was made.

The staff presented this information to the councilmember without a recommendation of how to vote. The staff indicated that cost factors should not be used to choose between the alternatives, and that the councilmember would need to personally weigh the relative advantages and disadvantages of the vendor's proposal.

10.5   THE OUTCOME

After reviewing the staff report, the councilmember decided to vote for the vendor's alternative. The councilmember felt that the smaller plant size and reduced truck trips were important advantages, and that the risk of failure was sufficiently offset by the vendor's proposed test period. In a close vote, the governing board of the district accepted the councilmember's position.

SUMMARY

This case study points out several important factors. First, it illustrates how differences in technical assumptions, such as discount rates and timber prices, can have major effects on the outcomes of a financial analysis. In this case, it was not immediately obvious which factors accounted for the difference between the two estimates. These key differences were only revealed after work by an independent third party.

Second, the case study shows how some of the assumptions used by different parties can be reconciled, often by developing compromise estimates. In other situations, an independent analysis may agree with one or the other of the competing estimates. Differences in the analyses prepared by two groups are more and more often being reconciled by hiring an independent consultant to review the project and submit a separate analysis.

Third, the case study shows how nonfinancial factors, such as the attitude of the neighborhood, can become the key decision criteria. This is especially true if financial effects of alternatives are similar, or if the nonfinancial factors relate to environmental or quality of life concerns.

QUESTIONS AND PROBLEMS

1. Your councilmember has asked you to prepare a brief written synopsis of your analysis for public distribution. What would you include in such a paper? Would the content or emphasis change depending on who was the intended audience? For example, would you prepare the same summary for review by technical experts or for presentation at a neighborhood meeting?
2. Why do you think the two competing analyses used such different discount rates?
3. How would you have prepared your recommendation if the two analyses had differed in their choice of inflation rates?
4. What other approaches to resolving the differences between the two analyses might have been considered?
5. Why might the city and the district use different real discount rates for their projects?

11

Accounting for the Distribution of Benefits and Costs

11.1. INTRODUCTION

The gains and losses from economic decisions accrue to individuals. The hard fact is that benefit–cost analysis, or any policy analysis for that matter, can only proceed by making some assumption regarding the comparability of individuals' utility. In earlier chapters we derived an equation to express social welfare change in terms of efficiency and equity effects. This is

$$dW = \sum_i \sum_j [P_j \, dX_{ij} + (\alpha_i - 1)P_j \, dX_{ij}] \qquad (11.1)$$

This indicates that a change in welfare depends on an efficiency component and a distributional component. The α_i is the marginal social utility of income (MSUI) for individual i.

Different decision criteria for policy analysis are based on various assumptions concerning the MSUIs. There is a trade-off that must be made between criteria that allow no bad projects but would prevent some good ones (eliminate Type II errors but allow Type I errors) and criteria that would accept some bad projects but would prevent few good ones.[1]

At one extreme we might assume that nothing is known about the MSUI. At the other extreme we could assume we know the MSUI for each individual. In this chapter, we present several criteria that reflect the range of assumptions and show examples of each. We argue that the most practical approach is to simply lay out the distribution of benefits and costs, if the required information

---

[1]Type I errors involve accepting some probability of rejecting a true result or hypothesis. Type II errors involve some probability of accepting a false result or hypothesis.

is reasonably available. If more is required, we then recommend the Harberger Opportunity Cost criterion.

We begin with a policy that allows no bad projects but which rejects good ones and which assumes nothing is known about the MSUI; this is the *full compensation approach*. This is compared with a policy that assumes everyone's MSUI is equal to one, the *potential compensation test* (Kaldor–Hicks). This is the traditional approach of benefit–cost analysis. The simple approach of merely *identifying the winners and losers* (McKean, 1958) and the extent of their losses is aimed at providing decision makers with relevant information and does not presume the choice or foreclose options. Willig and Bailey (1981) develop another approach based on *eliminating undesirable transfers*. Feldstein advocates an approach based on giving *alternative weights to the MSUI* as a function of income.

Finally Harberger (1978) suggests an approach based on *the opportunity cost of transfers*. This approach recognizes that transfers from richer to poorer may be desirable but not at any cost.

11.2.   TECHNIQUES OF ANALYSIS

11.2.1.   The Full Compensation Criterion: Pareto Realized

The central concept of efficiency in economics is that of Pareto efficiency. According to this, a policy is efficient only if there are no losers, and Pareto efficiency is reached when there remain no actions that make someone better off without making someone else worse off.

A decision criterion consistent with the Pareto principle would be *to require that the losers from a decision be fully compensated* from the gains of the winners. Only projects that meet the full Pareto test will be adopted. There would be no losers. Such a criterion assumes that nothing is known about the MSUIs. The advantage of this criterion is precisely that it avoids the difficult question of deciding what values to assign to the MSUIs. Policies adopted under this approach are certain to improve welfare. The weaknesses of the approach are that (1) some policies that would improve welfare are rejected by the criterion, (2) the act of compensation itself may impose costs that decrease social welfare as compared with not carrying out the compensation, and (3) there are costs incurred in carrying out the redistribution.

The full compensation criterion requires not only that the total gains be greater than total losses but that the gains exceed the losses by enough to carry out the distribution. Table 11.1 illustrates the efficiency and distributional

TABLE 11.1

Groups	Marginal Social Utility of Income (α_i)	Net Benefit $(P_j dX_{ij})$	Distributional Effect $[(\alpha_i - 1)P_j dX_{ij}]$	Change in Economic Welfare (ΔW)
Poor	1.2	−$70	−$14	−$84
Rich	0.8	+110	−22	+88
Total		+$40	−$36	+$4

effects of a full compensation policy. The numbers in Table 11.1 and subsequent tables are based on an arbitrary assumption of the MSUIs for the two groups and on arbitrary values for efficiency net benefits.

In Table 11.1, we assume that even though the MSUI is unknown to the policy maker, the values are given so that you can evaluate the policy maker's decisions. The value for the poor is 1.2, that is 20 percent more than the median MSUI, which we assume to be one; the value for the rich is 0.80, 20 percent lower than the median MSUI. We assume that before compensation, net efficiency benefits for the poor are a negative $70. That is, the poor lose. Efficiency benefits for the rich are a positive $110. The distributional effect is obtained by subtracting one from the MSUI and multiplying by the income change. For example, for the poor we have $(1.2 - 1)(-\$70) = -\$14$. The total net benefits for the poor are $-\$70$ plus the distributional effect of $-\$14$ for a total of $-\$84$ as the weighted income change. This could have been obtained also by just multiplying the income change $(-\$70)$ by the MSUI, or $(-\$70)(1.2) = -\$84$. The gains to the rich are $110 before redistributional effects are considered. The rich have a smaller MSUI than the median. Thus the distributional effects of the rich's gain is a negative $22. The total distributional effect for both the rich and the poor is a negative $36. The efficiency effect, however, is large enough so that the poor could be compensated. This policy would be acceptable by the full compensation criterion.

Table 11.2 shows welfare for the situation depicted in Table 11.1 when compensation is actually carried out. The poor have zero net benefits because they are fully compensated for their losses. Carrying out the compensation improves welfare as compared with the uncompensated results shown by Table 11.1 because compensation improves the income distribution.

This need not be the case, as shown by Tables 11.3 and 11.4 for policy two. Table 11.3 shows a project that has both a net efficiency gain and a net distributional gain. The full compensation criterion requires that the rich be fully compensated. This produces results shown in Table 11.4. Table 11.4 shows Table 11.3 with the compensation carried out. Here, carrying out the compensation reduces welfare as compared with not requiring full compensation. The net effect of the policy, however, when compensation is carried out is still positive.

The full compensation requirement may not only reduce the welfare gains, but it may prevent a desirable project from being carried out. Table 11.5 shows such a project.

The project depicted in Table 11.5 could *not* be carried out since full compensation requires the winners to compensate the losers. Although there is a net gain in economic welfare, the winners are unable to compensate the losers. Table 11.5 shows that some projects that improve welfare will be rejected by the full compensation criterion.

The Cost of Transfers.   To this point we have assumed that the transfer of income can be carried out without costs. This is, of course, unrealistic. What are the administrative and other costs of carrying out the compensation? These costs will vary with the project and with the difficulty in identifying winners and losers, and their gains or losses. Let us assume that distribution costs are 20

TABLE 11.2

Groups	Marginal Social Utility of Income (α_i)	Net Benefit $(P_j dX_{ij})$	Distributional Effect $[(\alpha_i - 1)P_j dX_{ij}]$	Change in Economic Welfare (ΔW)
Poor	1.2	0	0	0
Rich	0.8	+$40	-$8	+$32
Total		+$40	-$8	+$32

TABLE 11.3

Groups	Marginal Social Utility of Income (α_i)	Net Benefit $(P_j dX_{ij})$	Distributional Effect $[(\alpha_i - 1)P_j dX_{ij}]$	Change in Economic Welfare (ΔW)
Poor	1.2	+$110	+$22	+$132
Rich	0.8	-100	+20	-80
Total		+$10	-$42	+$52

TABLE 11.4

Groups	Marginal Social Utility of Income (α_i)	Net Benefit $(P_j dX_{ij})$	Distributional Effect $[(\alpha_i - 1)P_j dX_{ij}]$	Change in Economic Welfare (ΔW)
Poor	1.2	+$10	+$2	+$12
Rich	0.8	0	0	0
Total		+$10	+$2	+$12

TABLE 11.5

Groups	Marginal Social Utility of Income (α_i)	Net Benefit $(P_j dX_{ij})$	Distributional Effect $[(\alpha_i - 1)P_j dX_{ij}]$	Change in Economic Welfare (ΔW)
Poor	1.2	+$100	+$20	+$120
Rich	0.8	-110	+22	-88
Total		-$10	+$42	+$32

percent of the amount of money to be transferred. Consider again the problem shown in Table 11.3.

If the costs of carrying out the compensation are $20, which is 20 percent of the $100 that must be transferred, the gains of the winners are insufficient to compensate the losers. This is because the costs of compensation exceed the +$10 net benefit. Full compensation would require $20 in costs plus $100 as compensation for the rich. The poor only gain $110, which is insufficient for compensation. The full compensation criterion may lead to the rejection of a project with both efficiency and distributional gain.

Suppose, however, that the redistributional costs are only 5 percent of the amount redistributed, or $5.00. Then the project shown in Table 11.3 would be carried out under the full compensation principle. Clearly the magnitude of the redistributional costs would influence whether or not a project meets the full compensation procedure.

The full compensation procedure is not attractive because it requires compensation of the rich in some cases. Such compensation may not be desirable. Compensation of the rich would not, for example, be justified if we adopt the assumption that the MSUI is higher for the poor than for the rich either because the marginal utility of income declines with income, or because social justice requires giving a larger weight to income changes for the poor than for the rich. Either (or both) of these assumptions then suggests an *"equitable compensation principle," which we define as requiring compensation only when the poor are the losers*. In our examples, this would improve the criterion because we have assigned a greater weight (marginal social significance) to dollars received or paid by the poor than by the rich.

Are you prepared to accept this assumption? For example, the project shown in Table 11.3 was not carried out because of the cost of compensating the rich. With compensation no longer required, the project is now justified and welfare is improved.

When Compensation Should Be Given.   Compensation for losses that result from public policy can be justified when (1) the costs of compensating the losers are sufficiently small and (2) the winners are sufficiently more wealthy than the losers. In these circumstances justice may make a legitimate claim that losers should be compensated from the gains of the winners. However, when the winners themselves are poor along with the losers, the money for compensation might better come from general revenues.

There are, however, practical limitations to this policy. Costs of compensating the losers or winners include the costs of identifying them and administering the compensation. For many policies, the costs of identifying the losers and winners and the magnitude of their gains or losses are great. The beneficiaries of a policy that lowered the price of some good (for example, butter) will be widely scattered and very expensive to identify. Similarly, a policy that raises butter prices will result in many hard to identify losers, each with small losses. Clearly no compensation should be attempted in cases where compensation costs are high relative to the transfer award.

The full compensation policy has some merit. This is recognized by the fact that the full compensation policy has been adopted in a limited way. For example, the government provides market compensation for taking property. Nevertheless, the full compensation requirement is too restrictive to serve widely and it is costly to carry out. Resources are required just to identify gainers and losers and to effect the transfer. Some policies that increase total wealth would not meet the full compensation criterion. In a larger sense, full compensation may inhibit decisions in a dynamic economy. Perhaps rapid economic growth requires losers. Changes in the legal structure after the American Revolution seemed to have served to promote economic growth by reducing compensation requirements for injuries resulting from growth-producing activities. Was this socially desirable?

By the same token, a full compensation policy may have more acceptance in a mature economy in which growth is less important. There is evidence that developed nations are in fact moving toward providing stricter laws of product liability, environmental protection, and the like. There appears to be more emphasis placed on income and other types of equality as economies become wealthier. There appears to be increasing acceptance of the principle that the marginal social utility of income for a poorer person should be greater than that of a richer individual. This assumption allows us to adopt the less restrictive equitable compensation criterion by which only the poor are compensated rather than everybody.

11.2.2. The Kaldor–Hicks Criterion: Potential Pareto

The most famous of the suggested decision criteria is the potential compensation criterion. Kaldor and Hicks have suggested that a useful benefit–cost measure is one that ignores distributional effects. This is equivalent to assuming the MSUI is the same for all individuals, in which case α would be equal to 1 for all i's. This contrasts with the full compensation approach which assumes nothing is known about the MSUI and that a project can be justified only if there are no distributional effects. Under Kaldor–Hicks, then, the distributional portion of Equation (11.1) becomes zero and we are left only with the efficiency criteria.

$$dW = \sum_i \sum_j P_j dx_{ij} \tag{11.2}$$

As long as the unweighted gains from a policy exceed the losses (benefits exceed costs), the policy would satisfy the benefit–cost test suggested by Kaldor–Hicks. Thus, the Kaldor–Hicks approach simply involves calculating the present value of costs and benefits and determining if the benefits exceed the costs. This is the approach that is often meant when one talks about benefit–cost analysis. But benefit–cost analysis need not be confined to this criterion.

There are, however, two powerful arguments for using Kaldor–Hicks. One argument is that the costs of determining the distributional effects usually outweigh any distributional gains that might be made from attempting to incorporate distributional effects. So as a practical policy, distributional effects should be ignored. This argument is not one for *always* using Kaldor–Hicks but rather a practical argument for using this criterion as a general rule.

A second argument, developed by Musgrave (1969), is that the existing distribution of income is one chosen by the government and therefore project distributional effects can be ignored. That is, one might assume that the government distributional policy is one that concludes that no additional gains can be made because the government is not making them. This argument would be more powerful if the government were able to effect costless redistributions. The logic of the argument is only that the government has exploited distributional gains up to the point where the costs of transfer are greater than the gains. From this perspective, however, Musgrave's argument is not a blanket justification for the use of Kaldor–Hicks. Rather, the Musgrave approach should require that a particular project be examined to see if it can effect a transfer more cheaply than examining the best alternative means available to the government. It follows, then, that if the usual costs of effecting transfers through general tax and redistribution policy are less than transfers realized through individual projects of the sort usually analyzed by benefit–cost analysis, this becomes the first argument above for *usually* ignoring distributional effects of projects.

These and other arguments can be reduced to the essential argument that distributional effects should usually be ignored in project analysis where the gains from considering the distributional effects and of projects will probably be less than the costs of determining the distributional effects and of carrying out the redistribution. This argument is strengthened by the realization that the total size of the pie will be larger under Kaldor–Hicks and by the possibility that all groups will over time gain on the average from the use of Kaldor–Hicks. This result is strengthened by the realization that the process of economic development, that is, of increasing the size of the total pie, often increases income *equality*. In some cases welfare will decrease from using Kaldor–Hicks because of adverse distributional effects that are too costly to identify. However, if on the average the use of Kaldor–Hicks does not impose net costs on the poor, on the average its use will result in welfare gains, so that if over time all groups gain more than they otherwise would, all groups may agree Kaldor–Hicks is acceptable as a general principle to be applied to all decisions.

This argument has considerable merit. It is particularly strong for a developing country that puts a larger premium on economic growth. It is probably appropriate for today's developing countries, and for developed countries in their earlier stages of development.

The argument would lead to less use of Kaldor–Hicks for developed countries today. Concern for income equity is probably a normal or even a luxury good that becomes more important as the society's total wealth grows. Here the likelihood of the distributional gains outweighing the distributional costs are greater. Kaldor–Hicks, then, may not always be a satisfactory guide for policies in which an important concern is income redistribution. Any such policy may be increasingly important in a developed nation.

Kaldor–Hicks is an eminently sensible criterion where the distributional effects are unclear or unimportant or are too expensive to determine. Many projects show these characteristics. The gains and costs are spread among many difficult to distinguish groups; no one bears a large share of the gain or loss or the apparent transfers are among groups not readily or importantly distinguishable by income. In a real world with special interest groups the greater use of Kaldor–Hicks policy decision making will undoubtedly improve policy decision making.

11.2.3. Identify the Gainers and Losers

In this approach, suggested by McKean (1958), the analyst avoids the problems of distributional assumptions. The analyst simply identifies the gainers and losers and how much they will gain or lose. The role of the analyst is to present the distributional information for use by the policy maker. The policy maker could then use this information in choosing among alternatives.

The advantages of this approach are (1) it may be sufficient to call attention to the distributional questions; (2) the information furnished is, arguably, as relevant for policy as that from any other approach and the approach is straightforward and relatively simple; and (3) the approach emphasizes that the

TABLE 11.6   Net Benefits by Income Group

	Poor	Lower Middle	Upper Middle	Upper	Total (Benefits Minus Costs)
Family income	<$6,000	$6,000–15,000	$15,000–30,000	>$30,000	
Number of people	1,000	1,000	1,000	1,000	
Gain or loss	+$100,000	+$10,000	−$75,000	−$25,000	+$10,000

TABLE 11.7   Net Benefits by Income Group

	Poor	Lower Middle	Upper Middle	Upper	Total (Benefits Minus Costs)
Family income	$6,000	$6,000–15,000	$15,000–30,000	$30,000	
Number of people	1,000	1,000	1,000	1,000	
Gain or loss	−$75,000	+$100,000	+$10,000	−$25,000	+$10,000

formal analysis does not make the decision. There is no single number that indicates whether or not the policy is desirable. Table 11.6 shows a simplified version of how data might be presented.

This information is broken down by income group. Other characteristics, such as age, race, sex and location, might be relevant. The information showing gains and losses by income group and other characteristics is presented to the policy maker, who makes the final decisions.

Table 11.6 shows an example which is not likely to cause a problem for the policy maker. Benefits exceed costs and income is taken from the rich and given to the poor. In Table 11.7, however, for the same net gain, the decision may be more difficult. The policy maker might find more information helpful.

Here there is a net benefit overall but the poor lose. On the other hand, the lower middle income group gains. Can the analyst provide more information to the policy maker? The following approaches attempt to do this.

11.2.4.   Willig and Bailey (No Undesirable Transfers)

Willig and Bailey (1981) suggest a practical aggregate procedure based on what they perceive as widely accepted assumptions concerning the marginal social utility of income. These assumptions are that (1) the MSUI decreases as income increases, (2) the MSUI is nonnegative for all individuals, and (3) it is undesirable to transfer money from a poorer to a richer individual.

They then show that policy A dominates policy B if and only if the total net benefits to the poorest h individuals under policy A are greater than under policy B for all values of h. That is, if individuals are ranked from poorest to richest as 1, 2, 3, ..., N, policy A dominates B if

$$\sum_{j=1}^{h} NB_j^A > \sum_{j=1}^{h} NB_j^B \qquad h = 1, 2, \ldots, N \qquad (11.3)$$

for all values of h. Here, NB_j^A is the dollar value of net benefits of policy A to individual j and NB_j^B is the dollar value of policy B to individual j. The condition is that net benefits must be superior at *each* state of the summation

TABLE 11.8

	Poor	Middle	Rich
Net benefits	+$60	−$50	+$20

TABLE 11.9

	Poor	Middle	Rich
Net benefits	+$3	−$3	+$400

process from poorest to richest income group. Policy B might be the policy of doing nothing. Then policy A would be adopted only if the benefits were positive, as richer individuals (or groups) were added to the summation process.

This procedure has the advantage that values of MSUI do not have to be calculated and that there probably would be widespread agreement that a policy which Equation (11.3) satisfied would be preferred. The fact that the Willig–Bailey procedure requires that the poorest person (or group) gain is consistent with a Rawlsian approach. Table 11.8 shows in simplified form the way the Willig–Bailey criterion would work. In this case we are comparing a project with the alternative of doing nothing. First, we array the net gains and losses by income group. Now we sum the net gain or loss from the poorest to richest group as follows:

$$\text{First sum} = +\$60$$
$$\text{Second sum} = +\$60 - \$50 = +\$10$$
$$\text{Third sum} = +\$60 - \$50 + \$20 = \$30$$

The Willig–Bailey test is met if the sum is positive at each stage of the summation; that is, if sum one, sum two, and sum three are all positive. This condition is met in the above example. Note that the procedure requires that total benefits exceed total costs. Thus the Willig–Bailey procedure has the desirable characteristic of accepting only projects with desirable income transfers and with positive overall net benefits.

There are, however, several disadvantages of the Willig–Bailey test. These are (1) some policies with net social welfare benefits (considering both efficiency and equity) would be rejected by the Willig–Bailey test because it disallows regressive transfers regardless of the level of net benefits, (2) the Willig–Bailey procedure gives no guidelines in comparing some projects, and (3) the results might vary depending on how the groups are defined.

Criticism (1) is shown in Table 11.9. This policy would not satisfy the Willig–Bailey test because the loss to the middle income person was equal to the gains for the less wealthy income groups. That is, for $h = 2$, the sum of net benefits is 0, not positive, as is required. Yet, the project results in a desirable income transfer to the poor and creates considerable wealth. (Of course, it would be very easy to modify the policy so that it did meet the Willig–Bailey test; simply transfer a dollar from the rich group to the middle group.) Is the Willig–Bailey assumption that it is undesirable to transfer money from poorer to richer persons a valid assumption regardless of the size of the overall gains? Suppose the middle income group in Table 11.9 has an income

TABLE 11.10   Alternative Projects

	Poor	Middle	Rich
Net benefits for project A	+$2	+$2	+$5
Net benefits for project B	+$3	0	+$6

TABLE 11.11   The Willig–Bailey Test

	Poor	Middle	Rich
Net benefits	+$3	−$2	+$399

about as large as the richer group. Or, suppose the losses to the middle group are scattered among many people and that the losses per person are small. In those circumstances we might not want to eliminate the project.

Second, there are policies that could not be ranked by the procedure. Policy A might be superior to B for certain assumptions but not for others. For example, consider the alternative projects in Table 11.10. Project B is superior for the first sum, with net benefits for the poor of $3 as compared to $2. Project A is superior for the second (net benefits summed over poor and middle) with net benefits of +$4 compared to +$3. They are equal for the third sum (net benefits summed for all three groups). Such indeterminant results could be common.

The final criticism can be considered by examining again the earlier example (Table 11.9). In that example, the middle group suffered a loss of −$3 and the rich a gain of +$400. But suppose a middle income person with a loss of $1 was the richest in the middle group. We move this person to the rich group, decreasing the loss for the middle group by decreasing the gain for the rich group. Now the example meets the Willig–Bailey test as shown in Table 11.11.

The Willig–Bailey test can be used in conjunction with a compensation policy. Compensation could be used with the aim of arranging the costs and benefits to meet the Willig–Bailey test. That is, in Table 11.9, the middle income group could be compensated by the richer group to satisfy the Willig–Bailey test. In sum then the Willig–Bailey approach is intriguing and useful. Certainly there would be considerable agreement that a project that met the Willig–Bailey criterion would be a desirable one. There is, however, apt not always to be agreement that a policy that failed the test would not be a desirable one. The Willig–Bailey test assumes that it is undesirable to transfer money from poorer to richer individuals regardless of the size of the transfer. This means that some policies that increase welfare overall will be rejected.

11.2.5. Distributional Weights

Feldstein (1974) and others suggest a program for using distributional weights.[2] Feldstein suggests that the weights be made a function of income. In particular he suggests that

---

[2]Some authors attempt to infer distributional weights from past government decisions. Such weights don't appear to be very consistent. McGuire and Garn (1969) attempt to build a set of distributional weights based on the preferences of administrators.

TABLE 11.12 ($\delta = 1$)

Income	$\delta = 1$ $y_{50} = 15,000$	Unweighted Net Benefit or Loss	Net Weighted Benefit or Loss
$10,000	1.5	+100	+150
$20,000	0.75	−110	−88.5
Total		−10	+67.5

$$F(y) = \left(\frac{y}{y_{50}}\right)^{-\delta} \qquad (11.4)$$

where y_{50} is the median level of income, and y is the income level in question. The parameter measures the responsiveness of the *marginal social utility of income* (MSUI). If $\delta = 0$, for example, the weights for all y would be equal to that of the median, or 1. For values of $\delta > 0$ the MSUI increases as income decreases, and the more sharply as δ is greater. For example, if $\delta = 1$, the weights are simply the inverse of income of those affected [(10,000/15,000) − 1]. Table 11.12 shows an application of weights when $\delta = 1$. Feldstein's idea is to show the value of δ for which one is indifferent among the alternatives. The policy maker can then, so the argument goes, choose the value of δ he or she prefers.

The value of this approach is simply that it forces an explicit recognition of the MSUI problem. It eliminates the problems of the Willig–Bailey approach in which project choice is indeterminate or in which projects with large net benefits might be rejected. Yet it provides no choice of the MSUI. It is difficult to see that the weighting scheme gives any additional information to the policy maker than the simple indentification of gainers and losers, their incomes, and the extent of their gains and losses. For example, if the policy maker determined that for net values of $\delta = 0.5$ or better, the project was worthwhile, would this have much meaning? Would this have more meaning than simply listing gainers and losers and the amount of their gain or loss? We think not and therefore do not advocate using the Feldstein approach. It complicates unnecessarily the policy process.

There are other reasons for our position. Two important ones are (1) any investment project could be justified by paying a bonus to those affected by the project, for example, workers with a high distributional weight, and (2) projects could be justified on the gains from their distributional effects without sufficient regard for the costs of achieving the improved distribution.

How could any investment project be justified? Table 11.13 shows a project with negative net unadjusted benefits. Suppose also that those bearing the costs and benefits all have income equal to the median income, $15,000, and thus equal weights by the Feldstein criterion. The project would appear to fail. Suppose instead that it is decided to hire workers with an average income of $5000. These workers would have an $F(y)$ of ($5000/$15,000)$^{-1}$ = 3.00, assuming $\delta = -1$ and $y_{50} = $15,000.

The opportunity cost of these workers is, say, $4.00 per hour. They have no net gain if paid $4.00 per hour. Suppose, however, it is decided to pay the workers a bonus and their wage is set at $9.00 per hour. Each worker receives

TABLE 11.13

Project Status	Benefits	Costs	Weighted Benefits Minus Costs
Before hiring new workers (all gainers and losers have a weight of 1)	+$100	−$150	−$50
After hiring	+$200	−$150	+$50
Poorer workers	+300 new workers	−200 cost of new workers	

a benefit of $5.00 per hour, but this is weighted by an $F(y)$ of 3. The total wage package to these workers is, say, $180. Five-ninths of this, or $100, is the net benefit. This receives a weight of $100 \times 3 = $300. Suppose now that the $100 "bonus" given these workers is taken from people with the median income. Suppose further that, because of administrative costs, it is necessary to extract even as much as $200 from the medium income group in order to generate the $100 to transfer to the poorer workers. Our benefit–cost calculus now shows an additional benefit of $300 and an additional cost of $200. The net present value is now positive. These results are shown in Table 11.13.

The problem is that we have justified a poor project by paying a bonus to poorer workers. But isn't this all right? Well, it depends on whether or not the project is an efficient way of transferring money. This one is not. We have extracted $200 from a medium income group to pay a poorer group $100. Earlier we suggested that the costs of transfer should not exceed 20 percent of the amount raised for transfer. That is, the $100 gain of the poorer workers should, at most, be valued at $100 plus 20 percent, or $120. An acceptable approach to the distributional problem should account for the efficiency with which the transfer is made. This defect is remedied by the opportunity cost rule.

11.2.6. The Opportunity Cost Rule (Harberger)

Harberger (1978) suggests an approach that recognizes that the benefit of a transfer cannot be greater than the cost of making the transfer by the most efficient alternative means, an approach we call the opportunity cost approach. This approach is consistent with a kind of distributional Kaldor–Hicks test in the sense that the losers from the redistribution could hypothetically bribe the winners to not proceed with the redistribution if the redistribution could be carried out more cheaply by some other alternative means. The losers would be willing to offer the winners more because they could save themselves more by using the more efficient method of redistribution. The idea is that weights would be given to desirable transfers but that the weight would be limited by the opportunity cost of direct transfers. Harberger correctly notes that it is inefficient to weight the losses or gains of the poor by more than the cost of transferring money by the most efficient alternative. A procedure that we believe conforms to Harberger's suggestions would be as follows: (1) to any net benefits received by the poor add as an additional benefit the costs of transferring these funds by the most efficient direct method; (2) to any net costs born by the poor add an additional cost, the costs of wholly compensating the poor by the most efficient direct transfer. The assumption underlying this

TABLE 11.14   Efficient Transfers

	Poor	Middle	Rich	Benefits and Costs
Net benefits (KH)	+$40	+$29	−$70	−$1

TABLE 11.15   Efficient Transfers

	Poor	Middle	Rich	Transfer Benefits or Costs	Net Benefits
Net benefits (KH)	+$40	+$29	−$70	0	−$1
Net benefits (Harberger)	+$40	+$29	−$70	+$8	+$7

TABLE 11.16   Efficient Transfers

	Poor	Middle	Rich	Transfer Benefits or Costs	Net Benefits
Net benefits (KH)	−$100	+$50	+$58		+$8
Net benefits (Harberger)	−$100	+$50	+$58	−$20	−$12

method is that transfers from rich to poor are desirable but that they should not be valued more than the costs of an efficient transfer method.

Some economists suggest very roughly that the administrative costs and the costs in reduced incentives of transferring money directly from the rich to the poor are 20 percent of the money transferred. Consider the example in Table 11.14 with income groups arranged from poor to rich. The overall net benefits are negative. The project is, however, an efficient means of transferring money from richer to poorer. The net transfer cost is only $1.00. The costs of transferring money directly, however, would be 20 percent of $40 or $8.00. This is an $8.00 saving that is gained by not transferring the money by the alternative means. This adjustment is made in Table 11.15. Thus there is a net social "efficiency" gain of $7.00 reflected in the adjusted net benefit.

Consider another example in Table 11.16. By traditional analysis net benefits would be +$8, so the project would be undertaken. When, however, we reckon the costs of actually compensating the poor at $20.00, the net benefit would thus be negative $12.00 ($8 − $20) and the project should not be undertaken. The project's net gains are insufficient to justify the undesirable wealth transfer.

11.2.7.   Summary

The full compensation test assumes too little about the MSUI; the potential compensation test assumes too much. The Willig–Bailey procedure may give indeterminate results and a project with a large net gain may not be accepted. Feldstein's distributional weights allow a project to be accepted because of the desirable direction of the income transfer, even though the project is an inefficient way to transfer money. The opportunity cost approach (Harberger) avoids these problems while recognizing that transfers from rich to poor are desirable,

TABLE 11.17   Example

			Project A		
Income Group	*<$5,000*	*$5,000–$15,000*	*$15,000–$30,000*	*>$30,000*	*Total*
Number in group	200	900	351	121	1,572
Net benefits	+$5,000	−$6,500	+$6,000	+$7,500	+$12,000
			Project B		
Income Group	*<$5,000*	*$5,000–$15,000*	*$15,000–$30,000*	*>$30,000*	*Total*
Number in group	250	400	60	44	754
Net benefits	+$5500	−$1000	+$5000	+$2500	+$12,000

TABLE 11.18   Compensation Carried Out

Income Group	*<$5,000*	*$5,000–$15,000*	*$15,000–$30,000*	*>$30,000*	*Total*
Net gains					
Project A	+$5,000	0	+$2,533	+$3,167	+$10,700
Project B	+$5,500	0	+$4,200	+$2,100	+$11,800

but not at any cost. *Therefore we advocate combining the informational format of "identify the gainers and losers" with the opportunity costs test to value the transfers.*

11.3.   EXAMPLES

Let us now take an example and analyze it, using the approaches discussed. Table 11.17 shows some data on costs and benefits for two projects. The numbers of people in the different income groups are assumed to be different for the two projects.

11.3.1   Full Compensation Criterion

We continue to assume that the costs of transferring money are 20 percent of the amount transferred. Groups with incomes below, say, $15,000 are considered poor for the purposes of this example. For project A this means $7800 would be required for compensation (20% × $6500 = $1300 + $6500 = $7800). Further, we assume these compensation costs are borne only by the richer groups that are gainers in proportion to their net gains. For example, for project A, the sum of net gains for the two richer gainers is $13,500. For project B, $1200 in compensation would be required (including transfer costs). The two richer groups gain $7500. When compensation is carried out, we have the results shown in Table 11.18. With compensation carried out B is a superior project with net gains of $11,800 compared with net gains of $10,700 for A. Notice that this is a different result from that indicated by a simple sum of the net gains without compensation (the potential Pareto criterion) in which both projects have identical MSUIs.

11.3.2.   The Potential Pareto Criterion

This criterion simply sums the net benefits regardless of the income or other characteristics of the individuals affected. Table 11.19 shows the results. The potential Pareto criterion indicates the two projects are equally meritorious. For

TABLE 11.19   The Potential Pareto Criterion

	Net Benefits
Project A	+$12,000
Project B	+$12,000

project A, $7800 is taken from the richer groups and $6500 is transferred to the next-to-poorest group. Their net gain or loss is then zero. When 58 percent of the income is removed from the two richer groups the net incomes are $2533 and $3167, respectively.

11.3.3.   Identify the Winners and Losers

This technique is the simplest, yet one of the most informative of those discussed. To this point we have only considered presenting gains and losses according to income groups. Table 11.17 already does this, but, of course, these are not the only relevant characteristics. Age, sex, race, geographic location, as well as income level, might well be important to those concerned with equity in decision making.

Table 11.20 shows a sample layout for presenting benefit–cost data. By presenting the data in a less aggregated form, Table 11.20 gives the decision maker additional data. This table shows that projects A and B are equal in terms of aggregate benefits. Project B, however, gives more per capita benefits to residents of both neighborhoods affected by the projects. Project B gives more income to the lowest income category than does project A, and B gives more to residents of neighborhood Q and less to residents of neighborhood P within this category than does project A. For residents of neighborhood Q with incomes below $5000, project B is clearly superior in terms of both total and per capita benefits.

The technique of simply presenting the data in as disaggregated a form as possible recognizes the impossibility of ever presenting all relevant information in terms of a simple statistic. The technique correctly recognizes that the essence of the benefit–cost approach is to present data for a decision maker in a useful manner, not to provide the decision.

11.3.4.   Willig–Bailey Criterion

We compare the projects by summing and comparing benefits over income groups from poorest to richest. This is done in Table 11.21. The results of Table 11.21 show project B is superior, and, in fact, is the only one acceptable under this criterion.

11.3.5.   Distributional Weights

Now assume the median income is $10,000. We now calculate weights according to $(y/y_{50})^{-\delta}$. We arbitrarily let δ be 1 and use the midpoint of the incoming range, which we assume is $40,000, for the upper income. The results are displayed in Table 11.22.

When we use distributional weights, project B is more attractive than project A. This happens because the use of weights increases the gain or loss of income groups below the median, and here project B is superior.

TABLE 11.20 Identify Gainers and Losers

Project A

Income Group	<$5,000		$5,000–$15,000		$15,000–$30,000		>$30,000		Total All Incomes		Combined
Number of families in income group	40		225		117		55		437		12,000
Average number in family	5		4		3		2.2		3.60		437
Neighborhood	P	Q	P	Q	P	Q	P	Q	P	Q	Combined
Net benefits ($)	4,000	1,000	(3,000)	(3,500)	4,000	2,000	6,000	1,500	11,000	1,000	12,000
Number of families in category	30	10	150	75	70	47	40	15	290	147	437
Average persons/category	150	50	600	300	210	141	88	33	1,048	524	1,573
Average net benefits per person ($)	26.67	20.00	(5.00)	(11.67)	19.05	14.18	68.18	45.45	10.68	1.92	7.63

Project B

Income Group	<$5,000		$5,000–$15,000		$15,000–$30,000		>$30,000		Total All Incomes		Combined
Number of families in income group	50		100		20		20		190		12,000
Average number in family	5		4		3		2.2		3.55		190
Neighborhood	P	Q	P	Q	P	Q	P	Q	P	Q	Combined
Net benefits ($)	1,500	4,000	(500)	(500)	4,000	1,000	(1,000)	3,500	4,000	8,000	12,000
Number of families in category	30	40	50	50	5	15	5	15	80	110	190
Average persons/category	100	150	200	200	15	45	11	33	326	428	754
Average net benefits per person ($)	15.00	26.67	(2.50)	(2.50)	266.67	22.22	(90.91)	106.06	12.26	18.69	15.92

TABLE 11.21   Willig–Bailey Summation by Group

	First Sum 0–$5000	Second Sum $5000–$15,000	Third Sum $15,000–$30,000	Final Sum 0–$30,000
Net benefit A	+$5000	−$1500	+$4500	+$8000
Net benefit B	+$5500	+$4500	+$9500	+$19,000

TABLE 11.22   Weighting Costs and Benefits

Income Group	<$5000	$5000–$15,000	$15,000–$30,000	>$30,000	Total
Weights	4	1	0.44	0.25	
Benefit A	$20,000	−$6500(1)	$2640	$1875	+$18,015
Benefit B	$22,000	−$1000	$2200	$625	+$23,825

But, does this provide us with useful information? We think not. First, it is obvious from Table 11.17 that project B benefits the poorer groups relative to project A. The decision to pick B over A could be made on this basis without calculating Table 11.22.

11.3.6.   The Opportunity Cost Criterion

This involves adjusting the net gains or losses of the poor by the cost of transferring money directly to the poor. In this example we classify the bottom two income groups as poor.

The results are shown in Table 11.23. This example indicates project B is superior. It is important to note that the results can be influenced by the poverty definition. For example, if only the lower income group is poor we would have the results presented in Table 11.24. Here additional weight is given only to the poorest group. Project B is now only slightly superior to A.

We advocate combining the identification of gainers and losers with the Harberger opportunity cost evaluation. This was done in Tables 11.20, 11.23, and 11.24. Here, project B is superior to A. Both bottom income groups are counted as poor and only the top group as rich for purposes of the opportunity cost adjustment.

TABLE 11.23   Opportunity Cost Adjustments

Income Group	<$5000	$5000–$15,000	$15,000–$30,000	>$30,000	Transfer Benefits or Costs	Total
Project A						
Adjusted net benefits	+$5000	−$6500	+$6000	+$7500	−$300	+$11,700
Project B						
Adjusted net benefits	+$5500	−$1000	+$5000	+$2500	+$200	+$12,900

TABLE 11.24   Opportunity Cost Adjustments

Income Group	<$5000	$5000–$15,000	$15,000–$30,000	>$30,000	Transfer Benefits or Costs	Total
Project A						
Adjusted net benefits	+$5000	−$6500	+$6000	+$7500	+$1000	+$13,000
Project B						
Adjusted net benefits	+$5500	−$1000	+$5000	+$2500	+$1100	+$13,100

11.4. THE METHOD TO USE FOR DISTRIBUTIONAL WEIGHTS

We feel the best approach is to first identify the relevant characteristics of the winners and losers as in Table 11.20. Next, the income transfers (positive and negative) to the poor should be subjected to the opportunity costs transfer test. Positive transfers to the poor will be valued only to the extent they are efficiently made. Negative transfers from the poor will count as costs to the extent a redistribution to offset them would incur costs. The information provided by these procedures seems about as well as the benefit–cost analyst can do in practice.

In actual use, however, the above procedures are not easily applied as in our examples. First, the analyst must decide what characteristics are important. This will depend on the purposes and circumstances of the analysis. Second, obtaining information disaggregated on the characteristics is often difficult and expensive, and sometimes impossible. For example, we have treated the income level as an important characteristic. But who are the poor? Medical students probably have low incomes, but are they poor? Clearly not when considered from their lifetime income, and surely for most purposes this is the relevant income. We mention these points so the analyst may realize the type of errors that data transfers may easily induce.

Information is never perfect. The emphasis should be on avoiding egregious error, not on avoiding error. Where the distributional effects seem important, in the sense that it seems that substantial transfers would take place involving individuals of lower incomes, consideration might be given to determining the distributional effects. Then, the procedures of identifying the winners and losers by relevant characteristics as far as possible and subjecting transfers to the appropriate cost transfer test gives a flexible and useful way of dealing with the distribution problem.

QUESTIONS AND PROBLEMS

1. Imagine that the President has a new tax proposal that will transfer income from rich to poor as follows:

	Family Incomes		
	<$15,000	$15,000–$30,000	>$30,000
Total (PV)	$350,000,000	($100,000,000)	($340,000,000)

(The numbers in parentheses are losses.)

   a. Evaluate this proposal using the opportunity cost criteria assuming families with incomes over $30,000 are "rich" and those with incomes below $15,000 are "poor," and that the opportunity cost of efficient direct transfer is 20 percent of the amount transferred.
   b. If the above tax is regarded as a project, would it meet the Willig–Bailey test? Why or why not?
2. Develop an argument for ignoring distributional effects in analyzing benefit–cost projects.

3. In Problem 1 above, if you choose a Feldstein distributional weight of $\delta = 0.8$, would you find the project desirable or not? Suppose medium income is $20,000. Explain.

REFERENCES

Bonnen, J. T., "The Distribution of Benefits from Cotton Price Supports," in *Problems in Public Expenditure Analysis,* S. B. Chase, ed., Washington, D.C.: The Brookings Institution, 1968.

Feldstein, Martin, "Distributional Preferences in Public Expenditure Analysis," chaps. 6 and 14, in *Redistribution Through Public Choices,* Harold M. Hochman and George E. Peterson, eds., New York: Columbia University Press, 1974, pp. 136–161.

Harberger, Arnold C., "On the USC of Distributional Weights in Social Cost Benefit Analysis," *Journal of Political Economy* 81, S87–S120, 1978.

Maass, A., "Benefits Cost Analysis: Its Relevance to Public Investment Decisions," *Quarterly Journal of Economics* 80, 1966.

McGuire, M. C., and H. A. Garn, "The Integration of Equity and Efficiency Criteria in Public Project Selection," *The Economic Journal* 79(316), 882–893, December 1969.

McKean, Roland N., *Efficiency in Government Through Systems Analysis,* New York: Wiley, 1958.

Musgrave, R. A., "Cost Benefit Analysis and the Theory of Public Finance," *Journal of Economic Literature* 7, 1969. Reprinted in R. Layard, ed., *Cost Benefit Analysis: Selected Readings*, Harmondsworth, Middlesex, England: Penguin, 1972.

Willig, Robert D., and Elizabeth E. Bailey, "Income Distributional Concerns in Regulatory Policy-Making," in *Studies in Public Regulation,* Gary Fromm, ed., Cambridge, Mass.: MIT Press, 1981.

12

The Ethical Foundations of Benefit–Cost Analysis

12.1. INTRODUCTION

In Chapter 7 we derived an expression for social welfare which consisted of an efficiency and a distribution effect:

$$dW = \sum_j \sum_i P_j dX_{ij} + (\alpha_i - 1) P_j \, dX_{ij} \qquad (12.1)$$

where α_i is the marginal social utility of income. Again, the first term on the right-hand side is efficiency effect and the second term is the distributional effect that depends on the marginal social utility of income. Equation (12.1) is a fundamental welfare equation for the economic analysis of normative issues. Within this chapter we discuss the relationship between ethical theories and the social welfare function as embodied in Equation (12.1).

12.2. ETHICAL THEORIES AND THE SOCIAL WELFARE FUNCTION

To fully implement Equation (12.1) requires the measurement of the willingness to pay or accept and then their conversion into an ordinal utility measure through the calculation of the marginal social utility of income (MSUI). The measurement of the MSU_i is clearly an ethical problem. Various value approaches or theories have been advocated for dealing with this problem. Four of these approaches are presented here: (1) utilitarianism, (2) the Rawlsian function, (3) middle of the road function, and (4) the Kaldor–Hicks criterion.

12.2.1. Utilitarianism

Utilitarianism is a social philosophy that originated in the nineteenth century with Jeremy Bentham and was developed further by others, especially by Henry Sidgwick. It is a leading theory of modern moral philosophy. *The basic assumption of this theory is that everyone's utility should count equally.* The MSU_i equals 1 for all individuals. Note this is not the same as an equal MSUI for all. The economic utilitarian equation is then

$$W = U_1 + U_2 + \cdots + U_N \tag{12.2}$$

Expressed in terms of Equation (12.1), the economic utilitarian change in social welfare would just be the sum of the weighted income changes where the weights are the marginal utilities of income, or

$$dW = \sum_j \sum_i [P_j \, dX_{ij} + (\pi - 1)P_j \, dX_{ij}] \tag{12.3}$$

Notice Equation (12.3) differs from the general welfare Equation (12.1) by the substitution of the marginal utility of income, π, for the more general marginal social utility income term, α. That is, every person's utility counts equally. Income changes receive a different weight that depends only on the individual's marginal utility of income.

The economic utilitarian social indifference curve comparing the utility of two individuals is a straight line. This line has a slope of -1 since the slope of the indifference curve will be given by the ratio of one person's MSU (Park's) to the other person's (McCloskey's). In terms of Parks and McCloskey, the change in welfare is $dW = dU_M + dU_P$. The utilitarian social indifference curve is W_U in Figure 12.1.

Most criticisms of utilitarianism are based on a hedonistic definition of utility. These criticisms generally are not applicable to the approach here in which choice is emphasized. A more trenchant criticism is that utilitarianism is too general a guide to ethical behavior and that a theory with more structure is needed. We will explore these issues later in this chapter.

Figure 12.1

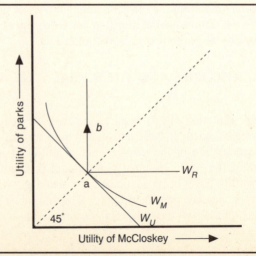

12.2.2.   The Rawlsian Function

John Rawls in his classic book *A Theory of Justice* (1971) suggests that, subject to the establishment of basic rights and liberties (primary goods), justice requires that only the utility of the least advantaged person be given weight. This is called the *difference principle*. The Rawlsian social welfare function would be

$$W = \min (U_1, U_2, \ldots, U_N) \tag{12.4}$$

The Rawlsian change in welfare is

$$d\mathrm{W} = dU_{\min} \tag{12.5}$$

where $dU_{\min}$ is the change in utility of the least advantaged; that is, social welfare is a function only of the group or individual with the minimum utility. A social indifference curve illustrating this welfare function is W_R in Figure 12.1(c). The representative Rawlsian social indifference curve is in the shape of a right angle with its corner on the 45° line. Notice that no distinction is made in the Rawlsian indifference principle between points *a* and *b* both on W_R in Figure 12.1. Thus no weight at all is given to the additional utility of Parks in moving from *a* to *b* even though McCloskey's utility does not fall.

Rawls attempts to justify his social indifference function on the basis of choice. He uses the concept of the original position, which is similar to the initial position developed by Harsanyi, and the concept of the veil of ignorance. The original position and the veil of ignorance constitute circumstances which Rawls saw as required for a representative person to make just or moral choices. The original position constrains the chooser to consider everyone's prospective utility just as in the utilitarian case. The veil of ignorance restricts how much the chooser knows about the characteristics of the individuals whose places she would hypothetically assume. The chooser would not know the proportions of different ethnic or minority groups in the society, would not know the level of technology, and so on.

The difference between utilitarianism as choice presented here and the Rawlsian position is that Rawls introduces constraints on choice that he argues are required by justice. The criticism of the Rawlsian social welfare function by economists is that no matter how thick the veil of ignorance, the chooser would not ignore the utility of the more advantaged unless she had infinite risk aversion, and that empirical evidence is inconsistent with infinite risk aversion. That is, the chooser would not choose as Rawls suggests even when the chooser is in the original position and behind the veil of ignorance. Thus, the Rawls difference principle cannot find its justification in a utilitarian choice framework.[1]

---

[1] There is a great deal more to John Rawls's philosophy than is indicated here. The student is encouraged to read Rawls's *A Theory of Justice,* Harvard Press, 1973. The indifference curves shown in Figures 12.2 and 12.3 as Rawlsian indifference curves are the usual form. They are said to represent the Rawlsian difference principle. For a discussion of this form and the principle and its implications, see Zerbe and Plotnick (1988).

12.2.3.   A Middle of the Road Welfare Function

Curve W_M in Figure 12.1 represents a middle of the road social indifference curve that lies between the utilitarian and Rawlsian curves. Curve W_M is symmetrical around point a and has a slope of -1 at point a. W_M has the usual shape of an indifference curve. It indicates that as one person's utility becomes scarcer, the person's utility becomes relatively more valuable to society. Note that this does not require a declining marginal utility of income. (The student should explain and diagram the differences.)

12.2.4.   Kaldor–Hicks

Kaldor–Hicks (also called potential Pareto) is the standard criterion used in much of benefit–cost analysis. This criterion examines efficiency effects only. Kaldor–Hicks assumes, with utilitarianism, that everyone's utility should be counted equally, but adds the assumption that the marginal utility of income is the same for everyone. The expression for the Kaldor–Hicks measure is the same as the efficiency part of the utilitarian equation; the distributional effects disappear:

$$d\mathrm{W} = \sum_i \sum_j P_j \, dX_{ij} \qquad (12.6)$$

which is just equal to the sum of the income changes. The Kaldor-Hicks (KH) social indifference curve is not shown separately in Figure 12.1 or 12.2. If one assumes constant marginal utility of income, then the utilitarian function is the same as the KH function.

The KH criterion ignores distributional considerations. Yet the welfare evaluation of a policy using Kaldor–Hicks depends on the income distribution in the sense that the value of a new good or service becomes what one is willing to pay for it (or willing to accept to give it up). Other things being equal, a richer person will and can pay more than a poorer one. These types of considerations have led to widespread criticism of Kaldor–Hicks (which in the legal literature is sometimes called wealth maximization instead of Kaldor–Hicks). Yet, a case can be made for using Kaldor–Hicks in defined circumstances.

12.2.5.   Equilibrium

Whatever social welfare function is adopted, the social optimum occurs at the tangency of the social welfare curve with the utility possibility curve GG of Figure 12.2. This tangency gives the highest social welfare that can be reached given the utility possibility curve. The equilibrium condition requires that the social indifference curve slope equals the slope of the utility possibility frontier. Figure 12.2(a), 12.2(b), and 12.2(c) shows the different equilibria that occur with the different social welfare functions when utility transfers are costless. There is equality of utility with the Rawlsian social welfare function, less equality with the middle of the road function W_M, and the least equality with the utilitarian function W_U. The interested student may consider whether or not there are utility possibility curves that would not produce utility equality even with a Rawlsian social indifference curve (the difference principle).

Figure 12.2

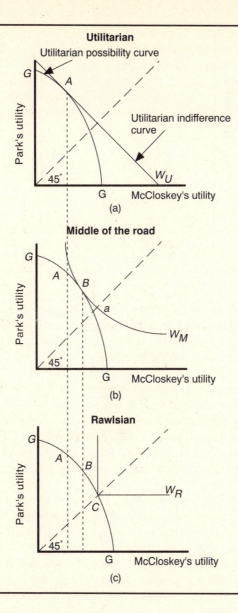

(a)

(b)

(c)

12.2.6. A More Practical Social Welfare Function

Utility cannot be measured. Practically speaking, some substitute or proxy measure must be utilized. Money income is one candidate. Thus, instead of considering the distribution of utility, we can consider the distribution of income or wealth just as we considered the MSUIs rather than the MSU_is.

Figure 12.3 shows the Rawlsian, the utilitarian, the Kaldor–Hicks, and the middle of the road social welfare functions as a function of income rather than of utility. In Figure 12.3, the indifference curve W_U has the characteristic

Figure 12.3

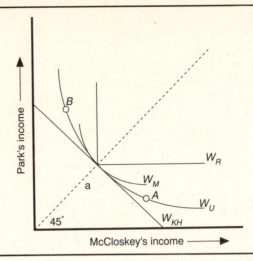

of declining marginal utility of income. As *M* gains additional dollars they become relatively less valuable, so the absolute value of the slope falls as we move from point *B* to point *A* along W_U. Thus, the indifference curve W_U is the utilitarian social indifference curve given that the marginal utility of income declines with income.

A declining marginal utility of income only tells us that the individual obtained more utility from the first or previous dollar than from the last dollar received. A richer person may nevertheless obtain more utility from the last dollar than a poorer person, but the richer person will obtain less utility from the last dollar than from the first dollar. A social indifference curve that expresses the declining marginal utility of income would be bowed inward (convex), as is an ordinary indifference curve.

The Kaldor–Hicks function, W_{KH}, shows a constant and equal marginal utility of income, and is represented by a straight line. Notice that the KH function and the utilitarian function diverge because the KH function assumes a constant marginal utility of income and we have drawn the utilitarian function to reflect a declining marginal utility of income. The indifference curve W_m is the middle of the road social indifference curve shown above. The Rawlsian indifference curve, W_R, is the same as that shown in Figure 12.2. The equilibria of these social indifference curves with a utility possibility curve *GG* are shown in Figure 12.4.

How is benefit–cost analysis to proceed in the face of different ethical approaches? The different ethical theories give different weights to the marginal social utility of income. We could even imagine a theory that distinguished among classes of utility giving more weight to some classes than to others. Benefit–cost analysis used simply as an accounting method for costs and benefits could weigh income and income distributional changes as specified by the ethical theory. Benefit–cost analysis could then use these various weights and thereby correspond to any particular value theory. *Thus, a generalized*

Figure 12.4

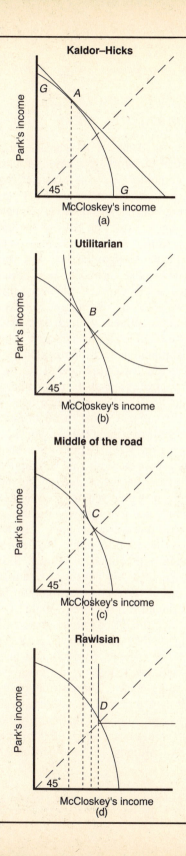

Kaldor–Hicks

Park's income

G

A

McCloskey's income

45°

G

(a)

Utilitarian

Park's income

B

McCloskey's income

45°

(b)

Middle of the road

Park's income

C

McCloskey's income

45°

(c)

Rawlsian

Park's income

D

McCloskey's income

45°

(d)

benefit–cost analysis is, in principle, compatible with virtually any theory of value.

12.3.   THE CASE FOR KALDOR–HICKS

In spite of extensive criticism a substantial ethical case can be made for the use of Kaldor–Hicks in certain circumstances based on utilitarianism and consent in an initial position, combined with the practical requirements of ordinary decisions. Consider again, our chooser in an initial position who seeks a rule to be used by government bureaus in making investment decisions.

The chooser, knowing the relevant laws of the social sciences, is aware that utility cannot be measured and she is familiar with the evidence that as a general rule the marginal utility of income will decline with income. By definition the chooser would like to maximize expected utility summed over the individuals affected by the projects. She does this with a decision rule to maximize incomes weighted by the marginal utility of income in order to adjust for income distribution effects, and adjusted by the risk aversion of the chooser, that is, by representative risk aversion.

Now to convert this utilitarian decision rule into the Kaldor–Hicks criterion it is necessary to suppose only two conditions. First, we must suppose that for some or even most government projects the costs of determining distributional effects, or of appropriately adjusting costs and benefits to reflect them, are large relative to the distributional gains to be made. In this case utility as seen ex ante will be higher if distributional consequences are ignored. Second, we must assume that using the Kaldor–Hicks criterion does not systematically tend to make the already poor poorer. This assumption is necessary because under Kaldor–Hicks we can imagine a situation in which the rich are able to pay more to gain a right, or would require more to give up a right, than the poor would pay or require, and that this would lead to the rich gaining more rights or income over time relative to the poor. This could lead to an income distribution that was less equal than might be chosen in an initial position and thus be incompatible with utilitarian choice. Strictly speaking the first assumption is the only one necessary but the second assumption is desirable so that we remain aware that if the income distribution becomes more unequal, the distributional gains should receive more weight.

One situation in which the distributional gains will be less than the costs incurred in considering distributional effects is when the project involves marginal changes and when income distribution is just in a utilitarian sense. For, if the distribution were just (chosen in the initial position) there would be no distributional gains to be made.[2] The distribution would be more likely to be already just, at least as determined by political decisions, where the costs of affecting transfers are low. Another situation in which there would be little or no distributional gain would occur when the project affects marginally only those of similar incomes, assuming that one cannot, either on the average or

---

[2] A utilitarian chooser would choose an income distribution such that the marginal utilities of money of all were equal if there were no costs to altering income distributions.

in particular cases, distinguish differences in the marginal utilities of income among those of similar incomes.[3]

In many cases the distributional gains to be made will be less than the costs of attaining distributional changes by some other method than through the project in question, reducing the need to consider income distribution effects in project analysis. The existence of an efficient alternative method for affecting distributional changes can ensure that benefit–cost decisions do not systematically cause the poor to become poorer and can reduce the possibility that distributional considerations will reverse the judgment suggested by Kaldor–Hicks. The weight to be given to the distributional effects of a policy will depend on the costs of achieving the same or the reverse effect by alternative methods. Thus we might suppose that explicitly distributional macroeconomic tax and transfer policies would usually be more efficient methods of redistribution than smaller projects, and that the weight given to the distributional transfer effects of benefit–cost analysis would be small because efficient alternatives exist. So, if there is an alternative method of generating distributional changes that is inexpensive, it is less likely that considering distributional effects will change the result of the Kaldor–Hicks benefit–cost analysis, and the need to consider them in a benefit–cost project context is reduced.

12.4.   A CRITIQUE OF BENEFIT–COST ETHICS

12.4.1.   Utilitarianism

In Chapter 3 we introduced the concept of an *initial position*. An initial position (Harsanyi, 1953) is one in which the chooser, having chosen the basic rights and rules, has an equal probability of being any person who might be affected by the rule chosen. Because such choice in an initial position would be more likely to count equally the utility of all, we shall say that in the utilitarian philosophy such choice dominates others. The chooser in such a position maximizes her own and society's utility and thus brings together the economist's concept of utility as a choice problem with the utilitarian requirement that the sum of utilities be maximized. Choice in the initial position is consistent with utilitarianism because (1) it acknowledges the fact that utility cannot be measured, (2) it is realistic in realizing that future risks flow from present choices, and (3) it serves as a device to count everyone's utility equally. In turn, choice in an initial position is consistent with a hierarchy of rights in which rights chosen in an initial position are dominant. Such rights would then be consistent with utilitarian choice (see Zerbe, 1991).

12.4.2.   Benefit–Cost Analysis and Utilitarianism

Utilitarian choice is (1) consistent with rights; (2) considers all individuals; (3) requires a consideration of interpersonal utility effects; (4) requires that all indirect effects be counted; (5) requires the incorporation of distributional effects; (6) recognizes the value of life and of preferences other than human

---

[3]This supposes there are no other utilitarian relevant distinctions.

life; (7) rests on a golden rule principle that treats (the utility of) others as oneself, and as a corollary recognizes the utility of future generations. Finally, (8) utilitarianism also requires that all rights be rejectable, rather than absolute, in the sense that they could be falsified on the basis that they lead to consequences not in the best interests of society.

A benefit–cost analysis can be consistent with utilitarian choice and with a rights structure that is also consistent with utilitarian choice so that benefit–cost analysis can derive justification from utilitarian choice. With no data limitations, a benefit–cost analysis fully satisfying the requirements of economic utilitarianism would (1) present alternative calculations for rights in question by assuming alternative rights, (2) be a general equilibrium analysis, (3) take into account uncertainty and income distribution effects, (4) require that a poorer person's change in utility be given greater weight than a richer person's since evidence suggests that the marginal utility of income declines with income, (5) require a consideration of interpersonal utility effects so that it would recognize that one person's utility is affected by changes in another's, (6) recognize the value of life and of preferences other than human life, (7) rest on a golden rule principle that treats (the utility of) others as oneself, and as a corollary recognizes the utility of future generations. Clearly a benefit–cost analysis that satisfies the utilitarian requirements would be far superior ethically to any likely to be produced.

The ethical issues raised by the use of benefit–cost analysis for public policy making have received considerable attention in recent years. Some analysts have proposed the expanded use of benefit–cost analysis as a way to ensure that all possible consequences of a decision are considered in a fair and equitable fashion. These experts support benefit–cost analysis as a rational alternative to poorly informed and unsystematic decision making. However, other analysts have criticized the ethical foundations of benefit–cost analysis and have cited flaws in its methods. They have proposed alternative approaches that should be used in certain cases. Some of the more important of these arguments are summarized below.

One of the more comprehensive critiques of benefit–cost analysis was published by Steven Kelman in 1981. Since Kelman's article includes most of the standard philosophic criticisms of benefit–cost analysis, its outline will be followed here.

Kelman analyzed the use of benefit–cost analysis for environmental, health, and safety regulation in the United States from an ethical standpoint. He described the case for benefit–cost analysis as being based on three principles:

1. There exists a strong presumption that an act should not be undertaken unless its benefits outweight its costs.
2. In order to determine whether benefits outweigh costs, it is desirable to attempt to express all benefits and costs in a common scale or denominator, so that they can be compared with each other, even when some benefits and costs are not traded on markets and hence have no established dollar values.

3. Getting decision makers to make more use of benefit–cost techniques is important enough to warrant both the expense required to gather the data for improved benefit–cost estimation and the political efforts needed to give the activity higher priority compared to other activities, also valuable in and of themselves.

In reviewing this case for benefit–cost analysis, Kelman concludes that such techniques are overused and sometimes distort important ethical considerations. Kelman bases his conclusion on three major arguments:

1. Benefit–cost analysis is based on utilitarianism, which is not an appropriate moral standard in many cases.
2. Benefit–cost analysis requires the pricing of nonmarketed goods, which distorts the true value of many important rights and duties.
3. The objection of proponents of benefit–cost analysis that people make implicit benefit–cost decisions among nonmarketed goods overlooks a key difference in reasoning.

These three arguments are examined individually in the following paragraphs.

Kelman's first argument begins by examining the utilitarian roots of benefit–cost analysis. He describes utilitarianism as a doctrine supporting the maximization of net benefits. He indicates, as we have also indicated, that most utilitarians include indirect effects in their calculations, such as the likelihood that a lie will reduce society's overall regard for truth and will increase the liar's propensity to lie in the future.

Kelman also notes that some utilitarians broaden the analysis of indirect effects to include the individual's own assessment of her actions. Under this approach, one of the costs of telling a lie is the individual's own dissatisfaction with lying. Kelman rejects this approach as circular. He notes that the utilitarian calculation is trying to determine what is right, but assumes as part of the calculation that the individual knows the action is wrong. Thus, Kelman concludes that utilitarians often assume a set of moral values before they make the calculations needed to determine net benefits.

To support this view, Kelman indicates that utilitarianism often leads to moral dilemmas in which obviously "right" decisions are rejected on utilitarian grounds. He offers Example 12.1 as an illustration of the defects of utilitarianism.

Based on his analysis of its utilitarian roots, Kelman concludes that benefit–cost analysis is an appropriate technique for many simple decisions. However, he believes it is insufficient for decisions involving fundamental rights, such as freedom of speech, or fundamental duties, such as the duties not to lie or kill. He argues that these concepts of rights and duties imply that individuals are to be treated in certain ways, even if the sum of benefits from such treatment does not exceed the sum of costs.

Kelman proposes an alternative to benefit–cost analysis that should be used in situations involving fundamental rights or duties.

In the most convincing versions of non-utilitarian ethics, various duties or rights are not absolute. But each has a prima facie moral validity so that,

EXAMPLE 12.1

Crime and Punishment

A wave of thefts has hit a city and the police are having trouble finding any of the thieves. But they believe, correctly, that punishing someone for theft will have some deterrent effect and will decrease the number of crimes. Unable to arrest any actual perpetrator, the police chief and the prosecutor arrest a person whom they know to be innocent, and, in cahoots with each other, fabricate a convincing case against him. The police chief and the prosecutor are about to retire, so the act has no effect on any future actions of theirs. The fabrication is perfectly executed, so nobody finds out about it. Is the only question involved in judging the act of framing the innocent man that of whether his suffering from conviction and imprisonment will be greater than the suffering avoided among potential crime victims when some crimes are deterred? A utilitarian would need to believe that it is morally right to punish the innocent man as long as it can be demonstrated that the suffering prevented outweighs his suffering.

if duties or rights do not conflict, the morally right act is the act that reflects a duty or respects a right. If duties or rights do conflict, a moral judgment, based on conscious deliberation, must be made. Since one of the duties non-utilitarian philosophers enumerate is the duty of beneficence (the duty to maximize happiness), which in effect incorporates all of utilitarianism by reference, a non-utilitarian who is faced with conflicts between the results of benefit–cost analysis and non-utility-based considerations will need to undertake such deliberations. But in that deliberation, additional elements, which cannot be reduced to a question of whether benefits outweigh costs, have been introduced. Indeed, depending on the moral importance we attach to the right or duty involved, benefit–cost questions may, within wide ranges, become irrelevant to the outcome of the moral judgment.

Kelman goes on to argue that decisions in some areas should not be subject to benefit–cost analysis in order to illustrate their uniqueness and great importance. He describes these as "specially valued things," such as worker safety and environmental protection. He suggests that "when officials are deciding what level of pollution will harm certain vulnerable people—such as asthmatics or the elderly—while not harming others, one issue involved may be the right of those people not to be sacrificed on the altar of somewhat higher living standards for the rest of us." To perform utilitarian benefit–cost analysis in such cases would, in Kelman's view, deprecate the value of the right to clean air and good health, and the value of life itself.

Kelman's second major argument against benefit–cost analysis is that it requires the pricing of nonmarketed goods, such as human lives and environmental quality. He notes that economists try to calculate values for these goods so that a comprehensive benefit–cost analysis can be performed. For example, the value of clean air to homeowners has been estimated by comparing prices for homes in areas with and without heavy smog.

Kelman argues that efforts to price nonmarketed goods suffer from four difficulties. First, he notes that these efforts raise a variety of technical problems. Such technical problems, Kelman believes, undermine the rationale for pricing nonmarketed goods.

Second, Kelman indicates that individuals with an existing right to a nonmarketed good, such as a panoramic view, will value that good more highly than those who would have to pay to acquire the good. He claims that this distinction is rarely made in benefit–cost analysis.

Third, Kelman suggests that prices determined from private transactions are often inappropriate for public decisions. He believes that public decisions give people a chance to value certain things more highly than they do in private transactions. People use their "lower" preferences in private decisions, but want "higher" preferences used in public decisions. Kelman concludes that "the use of private behavior to impute the values that should be entered for public decisions, as is done by using willingness to pay in private transactions, commits grievous offense against a view of the behavior of the citizen that is deeply ingrained in our democratic tradition. It is a view that denudes politics of any independent role in society, reducing it to a mechanistic, mimicking recalculation based on private behavior."

Fourth, Kelman indicates that assigning prices may reduce the perceived value of nonmarketed goods. Nonmarket exchange often involves values not quantified in the marketplace, such as spontaneity or personal affection. In addition, assigning prices removes the concept of something being "priceless" or "not for sale," which implies an unwillingness to trade it for money. Kelman offers the following example: If we proclaim that something is not for sale, we make a once-and-for-all judgment of its special value. When something is priced, the issue of its perceived value is constantly coming up, as a standing invitation to reconsider that original judgment. Were people constantly faced with questions such as "how much money could you get to give up your freedom of speech?" or "how much would you sell your vote for if you could?", the perceived value of the freedom to speak or the right to vote would soon become devastated as, in moments of weakness, people started saying "maybe it's not worth so much after all." Better not to be faced with the constant questioning in the first place. Kelman concludes by noting that assigning a high but finite value to certain things is not the same as saying they are priceless.

Kelman's third principal argument is an attempt to refute a common response by supporters of benefit–cost analysis. These supporters often agree with Kelman that people are reluctant to explicitly value rights and duties, but disagree with Kelman by saying that people implicitly perform such benefit–cost calculations. Kelman offers the example of a regulation that saves 100 lives at a cost of $1 billion, and notes that advocates of benefit–cost analysis would suggest this implies a $10 million value for a human life.

Kelman rejects this statement and says it misses a key difference in reasoning. He argues that benefit–cost analysis assumes equivalencies and values in advance, such as one human life is worth $10 million. In contrast, Kelman argues that the equivalencies should not be assumed in advance. Rather, various consequences should be tabulated and decision makers should be required to confront the questions of equivalencies in reaching their decisions.

Kelman's four arguments lead him to reject the use of benefit–cost analysis in many cases. He accepts the use of benefit–cost analysis for simple decisions that do not involve fundamental rights or duties. He also sees a role for benefit–cost analysis in providing some information for more complex decisions. He rejects efforts to expand the use of benefit–cost analysis in public decision making and especially opposes additional attempts to price nonmarketed goods. He believes that costs are already considered sufficiently in the regulatory process and wants more emphasis to be placed on including ethical deliberations in regulatory decision making.

Kelman's arguments, and those of other opponents of benefit–cost analysis, have been vigorously disputed. The responses fall into two broad categories: (1) those that defend the ethical basis of benefit–cost analysis, and (2) those that defend the importance of pricing nonmarketed goods.

Defenses of the ethical basis of benefit–cost analysis usually revolve around three major points. First, the purpose of benefit–cost analysis is *not* to reduce all factors to a single number (net benefits), but rather to explicitly indicate the major positive and negative factors affecting a decision. Thus, a benefit–cost analysis might show that a new air pollution regulation could prolong 100 lives by an average of three years, at a cost of $10 million and with a loss of 50 jobs. This response suggests that Kelman's view of benefit–cost analysis is too narrow and mechanistic.

Second, many advocates of benefit–cost analysis claim that it is not based on reductionist utilitarianism and that it is not amoral as Kelman implies. James DeLong (1981) notes that benefit–cost analysis is based on the conclusion that "any value system one adopts is more likely to be promoted if one knows something about the consequences of the choices to be made." Robert Solow goes on to indicate that practitioners of benefit–cost analysis have long recognized that "certain ethical or political principles may irreversibly dominate the advantages and disadvantages capturable by benefit–cost analysis." Solow (1981) also notes that a good benefit–cost analysis examines issues of distribution of benefits and costs, not just the absolute magnitude of the net benefits.

Third, the ethical basis of benefit–cost analysis is often defended on the grounds that it provides a consistent set of standards to be used in making decisions. For example, one of the most common uses of benefit–cost analysis is to identify the best way to achieve a particular goal, such as the reduction of water pollution. Policy makers are free to assign weights to different factors affecting the goal and to use benefit–cost analysis as a technique for generating information to support the analysis. Benefit–cost analysis need not be based just on utilitarian values, but even if it is, such analysis will properly recognize rights.

To these defenses we would add a fourth which we consider of fundamental importance. Example 12.1 of crime and punishment violates a rights structure established to protect the innocent, which rights structure is consistent with choice in an initial position and with utilitarianism. Thus, Kelman's example fails as a criticism of the sort of utilitarianism on which we base benefit–cost analysis. Heyne (1988) and Zerbe (1991) point out that benefit–cost analysis has its foundations in the law in the sense that the law defines most rights and duties for the analyst to use. Benefit–cost analysis can, however, in turn help in deciding what are appropriate rights.

Three principal arguments have also been developed that respond to Kelman's criticisms of pricing nonmarketed goods. First, benefit–cost analysis does not need to monetize everything. Instead, benefit–cost analysis is simply a way of comparing what one must give up to achieve something else. This is sometimes done in monetary terms, but it can also be done in terms of lives, leisure hours, or many other factors. For example, a city deciding whether to allocate $10 million to improved fire protection or to an expanded public hospital may well do a benefit–cost analysis in terms of lives saved, rather than in terms of dollars.

Second, Kelman's argument about different values for existing goods or rights and for goods or rights that must be acquired is recognized in standard utilitarian benefit–cost analysis through the economic concepts called the "compensating variation" and the "equivalent variation." Admittedly, many benefit–cost analyses fail to distinguish between these cases, but there is no reason why they cannot be included.

Third, the existence of rights, even nonsalable rights that dominate others, is compatible with utilitarian choice in an initial position and thus with benefit–cost analysis derived from utilitarianism (see Zerbe, 1991). Society chooses to make some rights (moral rights) unsalable because society as a whole may suffer if certain rights are salable, though the individuals making the sale may gain. One cannot sell oneself into slavery or sell away one's right to freedom of speech.

James DeLong (1981) points out the difficulties to which too broad a notion of fundamental entitlements can lead. He notes that such assertions lead to all-encompassing claims, such as "Workers have a right to a safe and healthy workplace." Such claims ignore the obvious fact that any job entails some risk, and that the key question of policy making is to make decisions among different levels of risk. Furthermore, the assertion of absolute rights overlooks the issue that the rights of one imply duties for another; thus, the "right" to clean air implies a duty of others not to pollute the air. If, however, we also assume that individuals have a right to a job, and if some jobs result in air pollution, how are we to determine which entitlement takes precedence? DeLong (1981) concludes that it is better to use benefit–cost analysis as a way to guide painful decisions, than to make decisions in ignorance using an excess of righteous zeal.

Arguments over the ethical basis of benefit–cost analysis are obviously complex and may never be entirely resolved. For the typical user of benefit–cost analysis, it is not necessary to understand all of the subtleties involved in the ethical basis of these techniques. However, there are three important lessons to be learned from this review of the arguments for and against benefit–cost analysis:

1. It is important to understand the philosophical foundations of benefit–cost analysis, since these foundations include certain assumptions that are not universally held. Moreover, the philosophical basis of benefit–cost analysis implies certain standards for the use of these techniques that are not always recognized in practice.

2. It is important to understand the sources of information used in benefit–cost analysis in order to be aware of any hidden assumptions or moral judgments. For example, some data may be based on assumptions about the value of human lives that should be left to the explicit consideration of the policy maker.

3. It is important to present the results of benefit–cost analyses in ways that allow important moral judgments to be made. Issues about rights are usually inherent in benefit–cost analysis. Thus, in many cases no single number can accurately reflect the outcome of the analysis. Instead, separate numbers, such as total costs, lives saved, and pollution avoided, should be provided so decision makers can understand the full implications of different courses of action.

We will return to these lessons in subsequent chapters.

12.5. SOME PRACTICAL IMPLICATIONS OF UTILITARIANISM FOR BENEFIT–COST ANALYSIS

12.5.1. Questions of Rights and Values

Earlier we discussed utilitarianism as a philosophic approach that emphasizes choice in which the utility of all is counted equally. What sort of rights is utilitarianism consistent with?

Our position is that issues of willingness to pay (WTP) are not separable from issues of rights. Whittington and MacRae (1986) consider the question of who has standing to have their preference counted in benefit–cost analysis. This issue can be considered as a question of rights. Consider a benefit–cost analysis of theft, as shown in Example 12.2.

The issue comes up in benefit–cost analyses of programs that affect the existence of robbery. The usual procedure is to count the value of the goods stolen as a transfer (Kemper, Long, and Thorton, 1983). As a policy matter this would lead to less spending on crime prevention than an approach that does not give weight to the thief's valuation of the stolen good.

Yet the language of utilitarianism could be used to argue that a society (or our particular society) would be a better one in which the right to property is defined by saying that the owner has the right for the property to count for zero in the hands of the thief. How can the money in the hands of the thief be counted as zero? Doesn't the thief lose utility when the money is restored to the rightful owner? This question supposes that utility is a hedonistic measure, not a component explaining choice. Is a constitutional-type rule (initial position) that no weight will be given to ill-gotten gains in policy decisions consistent with utilitarianism?

12.5.2. Expert Opinion

A different but related set of issues arises in deciding whether or not to count preferences when they conflict with expert opinion. Suppose that the Seattle AIDS Foundation wants to use a house in a residential area as a hospice for AIDS patients. The homeowners characterize AIDS as a fearful and highly contagious disease and assert that the presence of the hospice will cause terror,

EXAMPLE 12.2

Theft

A simple-minded utilitarian approach requires that the utility of a thief for his stolen goods be counted. But, could there be a benefit–cost justification for a rule that holds that a theft is illegal and that a thief must not be allowed to profit from it? Suppose, for example, that the Federal Trade Commission (FTC) has received complaints about a well-known retailer operating widely throughout the United States. This retailer has a policy of not returning credit balances to consumers who terminate the service.[4] The company bills monthly but the bill is for the future service that is supposed to be provided for the following month. Customers are not aware of this, or have forgotten, so rarely do they ask for their money back. The company sends out no notices of credit balances. As a consequence the company pockets several million dollars per year. As a result of an FTC investigation the company agrees to stop this practice by making provision for automatic refunds. The remaining issue for the FTC is whether or not the company should be required to make restitution to consumers. The FTC conducts a benefit–cost analysis of this issue and discovers that the average refund would be $10 and that the average cost of refund would be $3. The benefit–cost report notes that the net benefit would be negative because the $10 gained by the consumer is $10 lost by the company and is therefore just a transfer. The report goes on to note that there may be some future deterrent value in requiring restitution but the policy makers at the FTC believe this to be small and that other methods of deterrence may be more effective. Should the company be required to make restitution, and if so is there a benefit–cost theory that supports it?

The utilitarian might agree that consumers have a right to the money, but what does this mean? How much should the company be required to spend in order to make restitution? One way to interpret the right to a good is to agree for policy purposes not to count ill-gotten gains. That is, the $10 is counted as zero in the hands of the company. The benefit–cost analyst then counts as a benefit the $10 returned to the customer and compares this with the cost of $3 for making the transfer and concludes that restitution should be made.

---

dread, and trauma. A real estate agent estimates that housing values will fall by 40 percent if the hospice is established. Medical experts, however, are unanimous that AIDS patients cannot transmit the disease and that the physical harm will be zero. In calculating the damages to residents as part of an action for an injunction should the fall in property values be counted? The calculation of damages will differ here depending on whether or not we use a WTP or WTA (willingness to accept) measure of damages. But, this is what the case is about. That is, we use the courts to decide whether or not an injunction should

---

[4]This example is loosely based on an investigation of the FTC in which I was a consultant. The facts as presented make no pretension to accuracy.

EXAMPLE 12.3

Whose Values?: The Nuclear Power Plant

Consider the evaluation of a project to build a nuclear power plant in Seattle, Washington. Suppose that after careful evaluation in a world in which data are complete and accurate, the question whether or not the project is worthwhile turns on the evaluation of the risk to life and limb which building the plant imposes. Let us further suppose that there are no ethical issues as to how to value life that affect the project's assessment. The residents of Seattle incorrectly believe the chances of harm from the plant are much higher than those found by the benefit–cost evaluators who correctly assess the probability of harm and who also know, what in life they can never know, that their own assessment of probability is correct. The nuclear power plant is a very good investment using the project evaluators' assessment of the probability of harm, and it is a very bad project using the residents' evaluation of harm. The benefit–cost question is then which probability of harm should be used?

In a simple-minded utilitarian benefit–cost analysis the assessment of the residents must be used even though the residents' assessment may be based on incorrect information. Even if the actual probability of a nuclear accident is zero, the residents will feel themselves to be worse off if the plant is built and will then suffer a loss of utility from building the plant. What makes this a difficult utilitarian issue is that the residents' own assessment might be endogenous and shaped by the official experts rather than the residents' independent evaluation. For example, once the plant is built and operates without causing harm the residents may come to believe the experts' evaluation. We can imagine a prior utilitarian decision to rely on the experts, consistent with the decision in an initial position. A sophisticated utilitarian approach is consistent with one in which rights can be established by a virtual constitution that lays out who has standing and how preferences will count in a benefit–cost analysis.

---

be granted. If the residents have a right to protection then a WTA measure should be used. How much will the residents accept to allow the hospice to be built in comparison to the WTP of the AIDS foundation? These issues of rights are fundamental to benefit–cost calculation. *Where the rights are unclear, the analyst should present alternative calculations.*

As a political matter agencies must often respond to *perceptions* of risk. Paul Coppinger, Deputy Commissioner for Policy and Planning at the FDA has noted that the death of a few people might force the FDA to act even if the actual risk is negligible and the cost of the action per life saved is high (Souleles, 1987). The analysis here suggests that this practice is not necessarily to be condemned by a benefit–cost standard.

A similar point can be be made with respect to the treatment of voluntary and involuntary risks. Evidence indicates that people are more sensitive to involuntary than to voluntary risks. That is, people will pay more to avoid an involuntary risk than to avoid a voluntary risk of the same magnitude. As long as their preferences count, the benefit–cost analyst should then assign a greater harm to involuntary than to voluntary risks.

Moreover, the value of public participation, that is, participation by the residents, is similarly a value that benefit–cost analysis must recognize. So utilitarian benefit–cost analysis considers the value of process itself, and the importance of process is in fact subject to a benefit–cost test. This point is not always understood. One commentator notes (Byrne, 1987):

> The processes of public decision making depend in such a (cost benefit) model upon the identification of objective values. . . . To involve the citizenry in the process of identifying value could only result in contamination of the process, for citizens can offer merely subjective assessments of their idiosyncratic circumstances. To operate effectively, the world of benefit–cost analysis must be insulated from, and preemptive of, the participation of its citizens.

Clearly, the benefit–cost analysis described is not one rooted in sophisticated utilitarian theory.

These examples show that at this level the distinction between an approach emphasizing the importance of establishing rights and a sophisticated utilitarian approach disappears. Benefit–cost analysis can be applied once the rights are clearly defined so that a benefit–cost analysis could be as well-performed counting the value of the stolen goods to the criminal as zero. But, benefit–cost analysis usually operates in an arena in which at the margin some rights are in dispute. The analyst should then perform alternative analyses making different assumptions about rights.

QUESTIONS AND PROBLEMS

1. (a) Kelman argues that utilitarianism ignores moral values. He gives two examples. In one example your companion on an Arctic trip dies and is buried in the Arctic. You make a deathbed promise to visit his grave and light a candle by it at some point in the future. The second example involves the question of whether or not an old man in Nazi Germany should speak out against the regime if the only observable consequence of his action is that he is killed.

With respect to the argument that utilitarianism ignores moral values, the utilitarian may counterargue that moral values are in fact valued if they produce a better society. Do moral values contribute to a better society?

Kelman maintains that morality requires that you journey to the Arctic to keep the deathbed promise. He condemns utilitarianism because he says it would not allow one to justify the Arctic trip.

(b) Consider a similar example that arises from a letter to Dear Abby: [a letter from "The Truth Hurts," written in response to a letter from "Made A Promise"].

"Dear Abby, 'Made a Promise' asked if she should carry out Granny's request. Granny, on her deathbed, asked that Aunt Mary not be allowed to attend her funeral since they never liked each other. You advised 'Made a Promise' to tell Aunt Mary that Granny didn't want her at her funeral."

Dear Abby, expressing Kelman's morality, said " . . . to make a deathbed promise then conveniently forget it? Never!" However, "The Truth Hurts" expresses the following utilitarian argument:

Funerals are for the living. The living feel the pain and need the comfort. They need to shed tears of loss, grief and even guilt. It's wrong to deprive Aunt Mary of the chance to express her pain. What a terrible guilt trip you have condoned!

Granny wants to carry her grudge to her grave. She's asked for the living to perpetuate her hurtful ways, and she has found a way to haunt Aunt Mary forever. What a power trip she's on!

Aunt Mary deserves a chance to make peace with herself by attending Granny's funeral. I think 'Made a Promise' should use her better judgment and conveniently 'forget' to tell Aunt Mary. What the dead don't know won't hurt them. (*Seattle Times/Post Intelligencer*, Sunday, June 3, 1984.)

Do you agree with Dear Abby and Kelman or with "The Truth Hurts"? Are your arguments utilitarian?

2. Kelman maintains that speaking out against a moral wrong is not supported by utilitarianism if speaking out against a moral wrong would have no impact on the outcome. But, would you rather live in a society in which the existence of self-integrity was widespread, increasing the probability of someone speaking out against moral wrong even if speaking out would have no impact?

Bernard Williams introduces examples similar to Kelman's. The most famous is one in which you are in a Latin American country where the colonel is about to execute a group of ten Indians for no good reason. You ask about it and the colonel gives you the choice of killing one Indian yourself in which case he will let the others go free. Otherwise they all die. Williams does not say you should not kill the Indian. However, he notes that there is a thing of value which he calls *integrity* that among other attributes holds us particularly responsible for our own actions. He notes that integrity may legitimately prevent one from accepting a job to develop weapons of chemical warfare even though one knows one's replacement would develop chemical weapons even faster.

Elaborate on the concept of integrity. Is this a value that utilitarianism will recognize? Williams claims his examples are criticisms of utilitarianism. What do you think? Give a utilitarian counterargument to Williams.

3. Do you see any parallels between Kelman's theft example and the issue of capital punishment and deterrence? Would it ever be morally justifiable to knowingly punish an innocent person? *Suppose the sacrifice of an innocent victim would save the world?*

4. Neither Kelman nor his respondents pay much attention to the limitations of the Kaldor–Hicks criterion. Would this be a better avenue of attack on benefit–cost analysis? Why or why not? (See Chapter 8 for a full discussion of Kaldor–Hicks and its limitations.)

5. Kelman speaks of things that are of "special value." His arguments are rejected by DeLong. Can you develop an argument that some things are undervalued relative to their social value by individuals operating independently? Notice that this is an externality argument and amenable to benefit–cost treatment.

6. Suppose you are in miserable straits and really can improve your welfare by selling yourself into slavery. You strike a bargain that is Pareto superior for both parties. But the law forbids it. Would utilitarianism condemn the law or not? Consider the following from Brodie's *Life of Sir Richard Burton* (1967).

He [Burton] seems to have been the first to point out to Sir Charles [Napier] that though he had signed the death warrants of several rich convicted murderers, the actual man hanged was usually a poverty stricken substitute hired in his stead. Burton interviewed one pauper who had agreed to be executed for a murder he had not committed and asked him why.

"Sain," came the answer. "I have been a pauper all my life. My belly is empty. My wife and children are half starved. This is fate, but it is beyond my patience. I got two hundred fifty rupees. With fifty I will buy rich food and fill myself before going out of the world. The rest I will leave to my family. What better can I do, Sain?"

Would you have stopped the practice as Burton did? Would you stop it if you were a utilitarian? In the utilitarian equation, the disutility of the victims of torture also counts, of course.

Philosophers, but not economists, sometimes distinguish among classes of utility. For example, should torture be included as part of the social welfare function? This question is not innocent and you should give some thought to it before you answer. The distinction among classes of utility on the basis of the type of good or service that gives rise to it can be incorporated in Equation (12.1) by including a term $(\delta W/\delta U_j)$ that reflects the marginal social utility attached to the jth good. It is a weight applied to utility.

7. How would you decide what goods should be excluded from consideration in the social welfare function?

8. Could the problem of whether or not torture should be included among those goods whose utility is part of the social welfare function be approached by differentiating the quantity of utility from various goods? Consider the question of whether or not you would be willing to trade places with someone who was like yourself except that they obtained pleasure from torture. Is it possible or likely that liking torture is associated with less mature emotional development and that one could argue that the loss of utility associated with the lack of emotional development is less than that gained from the pleasure in torture?

9. Should torture be outlawed in all times and places?

10. Should we hold it against utilitarianism that it might allow torture? Suppose the state uses torture, perhaps judiciously and with restraint, but nonetheless uses it. It might even be the case, though this is not necessary to the argument, that in a particular time and place (Elizabethan England?) the limited use of torture was necessary to preserve the state and prevent anarchy. In any event, given that the state uses torture, one might ask the question, for a given amount of torture, is it better to hire a torturer who enjoys his work?

11. Clearly, our utility depends not only on the goods we receive but also on the utility of others. When our utility depends positively on that of others we shall say we *love* them. When our utility depends negatively on that of others we shall say that we hate them, envy them, or are self-proud. The latter relationships we call *envy effects*. The existence of these cross-utility effects represented by the inter-dependence terms of Equation (12.1) give rise to difficult ethical considerations. (a) Should envy effects be counted in the social welfare function? Should envy be discouraged as an unworthy emotion? Does this mean that people should be satisfied with their "place"? (b) How do you do benefit–cost analysis if what people really care about is their relative position?

REFERENCES

Bergson, Abram, "A Reformulation of Certain Aspects of Welfare Economics," *Quarterly Journal of Economics* 52, February 1938.

Brodie, Fawn, *The Devil Drives: A Life of Sir Richard Burton,* New York: W. W. Norton, 1967.

Byrne, John, "Policy Science and the Administrative State," *The Political Economy of Cost–Benefit Analysis* (eds. Frank Fischer and John Forester). 14 Sage Yearbooks in Politics and Public Policy, 1987.

DeLong, James V., Robert Solow, Gerald Butters, John E. Calfree, Pauline Ippoletto and Robert Nesbet, "Defending Cost–Benefit Analysis: Replies to Steven Kelman," *Regulation* 5(2), 39–43, March/April 1981.

Harsanyi, J. C., "Cardinal Welfare, Individualistic Ethics, and Interpersonal Comparisons of Utility," *Journal of Political Economy* 63, 1953.

Heyne, Paul, "The Foundations of Law and Economics," *Research in Law and Economics* 11, 53–71, 1988.

Kelman, Steven, "Cost Benefit Analysis—An Ethical Critique," *Regulation,* January/February 1981.

Kemper, Peter, David A. Long and Craig Thorton, "A Benefit–Cost Analysis of the Supported Work Experiment," *Public Expenditure and Policy Analysis,* edited by Haveman and Margolis, 3rd ed., Boston: Houghton Mifflin, 1983.

Posner, Richard A., *The Economics of Justice,* Cambridge, Mass.: Harvard University Press, 1981, 1983.

Rawls, John, *A Theory of Justice,* Cambridge, Mass.: Harvard University Press, 1971.

Sen, Amartya, "Rational Fools: A Critique of the Behavioral Foundations of Economic Theory," *Philosophy and Public Affairs* 6(4), 317–344, Summer 1977.

Sen, Amartya, and Bernard Williams (eds.), *Utilitarianism and Beyond,* New York: Cambridge University Press, 1982.

Smart, J. J. C., and Bernard Williams, *Utilitarianism: For and Against,* Cambridge, England: Cambridge University Press, 1973.

Souleles, Nicholas, "The Analysis of Social Regulation Under Executive Order 12291," prepared as part of the program 1987 Washington Internships for Students of Engineering (WISE), sponsored by the Society of Automotive Engineering (SAE), 1987.

Whittington, Dale, and Duncan MacRae, Jr., "The Issue of Standing in Benefit–Cost Analysis," *Journal of Policy Analysis and Management* 5(4), 665–682, 1986.

Zerbe, Jr., Richard O., "Comments: Does Benefit Cost Analysis Stand Alone? Rights and Standing," *Journal of Public Policy Analysis and Management* 10(1), 96–105, 1991.

Zerbe, Jr., Richard O., and Robert Plotnick, "Rawlsian Difference Principles in Economic Utilitarianism," *Social Justice Research* 2(3), 207–222, 1988.

13

The Interest Rate for Public Investment Decisions*

13.1. INTRODUCTION

The question of what interest rate to use for government investment decisions has a long controversial history both at the practical and theoretical levels. Table 13.1 shows the history of the level of real rates used by the Corp of Engineers. Clearly there have been enormous changes in the rates used. Early criticisms of the benefit–cost work of the Corp of Engineers, the Bureau of Reclamation, and other government agencies were directed to the use of interest rates that were felt to be too low. It was rather widely believed among economists that low discount rates were used to justify large-scale government projects that would not be justified at higher, more "reasonable" rates (U.S. Congress, Joint Economic Committee Report, 1968; see Fox and Herfindahl, 1968; Haveman, 1969; McKean, 1958).

As a response to these criticisms, the Water Resources Council (WRC) undertook to provide interest rates for use by the Bureau of Reclamation and the Army Corp of Engineers. These rates were coupon rates on government bonds of terms of 15 years or more. After 1978, the WRC rates were changed from coupon rates to yields to maturity. (Coupon rates reflect the rate at the time the bond was issued. Yields to maturity are the current interest for the bond.) Although these rates are market rates and therefore include an expected inflation component, peculiarly the agencies are directed to use these rates as real rates. That is, these rates are used to discount inflation-adjusted (real) benefits and costs. Clearly, however if a 10 percent rate is the correct nominal rate, it is too high a rate to be used with real future benefits or costs.

---

*We would like to thank Jonathan Lesser for useful suggestions.

TABLE 13.1   Discount Rate History of the Army Corp of Engineers (Federal Discount Rate for Project Formulation and Evaluation)

Fiscal Year	B.B.C. A-47	S.D. 97	WRC 1968 Reg.	P & S	WRDA 1974 Sec. 80	WRC 197 Notice
1957	2.500%					
1958	2.500%					
1959	2.500%					
1960	2.500%					
1961	2.625%					
1962	2.625%	2.625%				
1963		2.875%				
1964		3.000%				
1965		3.125%				
1966		3.125%				
1967		3.125%				
1968		3.250%				
1969		3.250%	4.265%			
1970			4.875%			
1971			5.125%			
1972			5.375%			
1973			5.500%			
1974			5.625%	6.875%	5.625%	5.625%
1975					5.875%	5.875%
1976					6.125%	6.125%
1977						6.375%
1978						6.625%
1979						6.875%
1980						7.125%
1981						7.375%
1982						7.625%
1983						7.875%
1984					8.125%	
1985					8.375%	
1986					8.625%	
1987					8.875%	
1988					8.625%	
1989					8.875% [First Half]	

Effective dates of indicated documents:

Budget Bureau Circular (B.B.C.) A-47	December 31, 1952–May 15, 1962
Senate Document (S.D.) 97	May 15, 1962–December 24, 1968
Water Resources Council (WRC)	December 24, 1968–October 25, 1973
Principles and Standards (P & S)	October 25, 1973–March 7, 1974
WRDA of 1974 (Section 80)	March 7, 1974–continuing
Water Resources Council (1974)	August 14, 1974–September 30, 1982 (no staff funds)

Nevertheless the rates used by the Bureau of Reclamation and the Corps of Engineers are roughly consistent with the directive of the Office of Management and Budget (OMB). In 1972, OMB directed most federal agencies to apply a 10 percent real rate of discount when calculating present values of government programs (OMB Circular A-94). Neither the OMB rates nor the Treasury rates provide an adjustment for risk. No developed rationale was given for the choice of the 10 percent rate. Recently, OMB has directed agencies to use a 7 percent real rate.

For many years there have been disagreements among economists on the right conceptual basis for rates, and certainly no agreement on the actual discount rate numbers to use. In addition, there is disagreement on whether or not an adjustment for risk is appropriate for government projects and on the nature and the size of the adjustment assuming one is required. Thus the history of appropriate discount rates to be used has been one of uncertainty and disagreement.

13.2. A SECOND-BEST WORLD

13.2.1. An Economy with Taxes

In Chapter 3 we presented an analysis of the discount rate to use in a first-best world. Here the discount rate to use for public projects equals the market rate, the same rate that will be used by the private sector.

The introduction of a tax on corporate profits and an individual income tax into this first-best world will make our analysis of the discount rate to use more realistic and more complex. Suppose the corporate profits tax is 36 percent and the marginal income tax is 27 percent. For simplicity, suppose further that only corporations undertake investment, that all investment is funded with equity capital, and that all after-tax profits are paid as dividends subject to the personal income tax. Finally, suppose that the after-tax rate of return required by investors is 8 percent. That is, we assume 8 percent is the marginal rate of time preference (MRTP).

In order that shareholders earn 8 percent after taxes they must earn 10.9 percent before taxes, and the corporation must earn about 17 percent before taxes. Shareholders that loan the corporation $1.00 for investment expect to obtain almost $1.11 for a one-year period. A $1.00 investment by the corporation yields $1.17 next year. Of the $.17 earned, 36 percent or about $.06 goes to taxes leaving $.11 to be paid to the shareholder. Of the $.11 the shareholder pays 27 percent or about $.03 in taxes leaving the requisite $.08 to the shareholder.[1]

In equilibrium the required rate of return to private investment of 17 percent must be higher than the marginal rate of time preference of 8 percent. This situation is inconsistent with an optimal allocation of resources. Investments that yield more than 8 percent should be undertaken as long as they yield a return greater than the individual's MRTP. But investments will not in fact be undertaken unless they yield more than 17 percent. The first-best conditions described in Chapter 3 are not met. The level of investment will, *ceteris paribus*, be too low.

13.2.2. Bias Against Longer-Term Investments

This wedge between the rate of return and the MRTP will also create an inefficient bias against longer investments. Consider alternative projects A and B in Table 13.2. Investment A is shorter term than B. Both investments are just worthwhile at 17 percent interest, the market rate of return. (That is, at a discount rate of 17 percent, the $NPV_A = NPV_B = 0$.)

---

[1] We ignore the possible tax deductibility of interest payments.

TABLE 13.2

Time	A	B
+0	−100	−100
+1	63.09	27.85
+2	63.09	27.86
+3		27.86
+4		27.86
+5		27.86
+6		27.86

From the MRTP standpoint, however, B is the better investment since the net present value of A at 8 percent is $12.51, while the net present value of B is $28.75. Thus use of the rate of return to private investment leads both to underinvestment and a bias toward shorter term projects.

13.3.   THE DISCOUNT RATE FOR A SECOND-BEST WORLD

13.3.1.   The Conceptual Problem

Given that we are not operating in an idealized economy and that there are distortions in market interest rates arising from taxes, we are in a second-best rather than a first-best world. The second-best approach seeks to maximize the discounted present value of social welfare taking into account the distortions. This approach is equivalent to determining the optimal level of government spending in a second-best world. The determination of the appropriate discount rate is a by-product of the social welfare maximization process.

In a world in which there are corporate and individual taxes, the choice of interest rate for the evaluation of public projects is no longer obvious. There has been a long-standing debate over the correct rate. Some argue that the MRTP is the correct rate. Others contend that the return to private capital [opportunity cost rate (OCR)] should be used. The simple argument for either of these positions is quite intuitive.

The MRTP represents the rate at which one is willing to trade present consumption for future consumption. If, therefore, an investment is worthwhile when evaluated at the MRTP, it should be undertaken because it will yield enough consumption to make it worthwhile. Yet, no private business would undertake an investment whose yield was only equal to the MRTP. It must consider taxes that it must pay, the cost of funds, and the opportunity cost of other investment. Clearly government must be the one to undertake these investments. Thus advocates of using the MRTP tend to be advocates also of more extensive government investment.

Those advocating use of the OCR rate note that public investment displaces some private investment by diverting investment funds that would otherwise go to private investment. Suppose that a dollar of public investment displaces a dollar of private investment that would otherwise yield 17 percent. If the public investment yields say 8 percent, the public investment causes a net decrease in wealth. Therefore, the argument goes, no public investment should be undertaken that yields less than the rate of return to private investment, that is, less than the OCR. Suppose the government does value investments at the MRTP. An identical investment would be worth more to the government than to private business because the present value of the earnings stream would be calculated at the lower MRTP rate by the government and at the higher OCR by private firms. So, if the MRTP is used, the government could displace investment by private businesses that had greater returns than those undertaken by the government. These arguments, that suggest that the interest rate used by government should be the one used by the private sector, were a motivating factor in the directive of the Office of Management and Budget, issued during the Nixon administration, that the discount rate for evaluating public projects was to be 10 percent in *constant* (inflation adjusted) dollars.

In recent years, it has been realized that there is truth in both the arguments for both the MRTP and the OCR. *The consumption value of investment should be discounted at the MRTP but on the other hand the displacement of private capital should be taken into account.* There is an important caveat, however, to the above rule. *Where a project can be undertaken by either government or private industry, and the evaluation will affect which party undertakes the project, the government evaluation should use the same discount rate as the private sector, that is, the OCR rate.* Otherwise, government will tend to displace private operation even when the private operation is more efficient. The following is the approach when the government is considering whether or not a project should be undertaken.

13.3.2.   A Correct Approach

It has come to be understood, from Bradford (1975), Musgrave (1969), and others, that an approach to determining the public project discount rate involves setting out the consumption that results over time from the investment and then discounting this consumption at the social rate of time preference (SRTP). (See Chapter 3.) The SRTP is by definition the rate at which society is willing to trade off present for future consumption. The SRTP represents the MRTP adjusted for external effects or ethical considerations.

This approach assumes that the value of investments ultimately lies in the consumption they generate and that the willingness of society to forego present consumption for future consumption is measured by the social rate of time preference.

The change of welfare occasioned by a change in consumption is then discounted by the SRTP. Thus,

$$dW = \sum_{t=0}^{T} \frac{\Delta C_t}{(1 + i)^t} \tag{13.1}$$

where ΔC_t is the change in consumption associated with the investment and i is the social rate of time preference (SRTP). Thus far it looks as if we are adopting the MRTP approach because the SRTP is closely related to the MRTP. But the effect of the OCR is taken into account in discovering the change in consumption produced by a private investment.

An investment of $1.00 in public funds displaces some private savings and investment and some consumption. The private investment displaced would itself in turn have generated later consumption. The investment of $1.00 in public funds will itself generate future cash returns. Some of these benefits will return to direct consumption, while the rest will contribute to private investment that will in turn generate additional future consumption and private investment. The trick now is to express the stream of both benefits and costs of an investment in consumption terms.

13.3.3.   The Shadow Price of Capital

To set out the general procedure formally, we define the following variables:

K_0 = original investment at time t
$K(t)$ = the value of the investment at time t
  s = the fraction of the proceeds of an investment that are reinvested in excess of the amount needed to maintain capital
  r = the private investment rate of returns, the OCR
  t = time
  e = the natural log, 2.718 . . .
  i = the social rate of time preference, SRTP

The total capital at time t from an initial investment of K_0 will be

$$K(t) = K_0 e^{srt}$$

The term sr can be thought of as the growth factor. For example, if the investment rate (r) was 8 percent and the fraction reinvested was 100 percent the growth rate would be 8 percent.

The income in any year will be the interest rate r times the stock of capital. The fraction of income consumed will be $1 - s$. The consumption in any year t will therefore be found by multiplying the amount of capital in year t, ($K_0 e^{srt}$), by the returns to capital, r, to give income in year t, and then multiplying this by the marginal propensity to consume ($1 - s$).

This gives consumption per unit of capital in any period t as

$$C(t) = \frac{(1 - s)\, rK_0 e^{srt}}{K_0} = (1 - s)re^{srt} \qquad (13.2)$$

The student may recall from Chapter 3 that the present value of a future sum where discounting is continuous is given by

$$PV = Pe^{-it}$$

where i is the relevant interest rate. Equation (13.2) gives us the consumption flowing from an investment in time t. The present value of consumption in each period is found by discounting it by the social rate of time preference, i. The present value of the consumption for period t only will then be

$$PV_t = (1 - s)re^{srt - it} \qquad (13.3)$$

The present value of the entire consumption stream for all time periods will be

$$PV_c = \sum_{t=0}^{T} (1 - s)re^{srt - it} \qquad (13.4)$$

This will be infinite for the case where $sr > i$. For the usual case, however, where $sr < i$, this reduces to a simple expression:

$$PV_c = \frac{(1-s)r}{i-sr} \tag{13.5}$$

This is a particularly useful expression. *It is the present value of the consumption from $1.00 of private investment,* that is, the shadow price of private capital (SPC). We call this expression V_t (or the SPC) so that

$$V_t = \frac{(1-s)r}{i-sr} \tag{13.6}$$

The amount V_t is the additional amount of consumption that society would expect in place of $1.00 of private capital investment foregone. It is through SPC that the OCR is taken into account. Notice that in a first-best world in which the opportunity cost of capital is equal to the social rate of time preference, SPC is equal to one. That is if $r = i$, then replacing i with r gives

$$V_t = \frac{(1-s)r}{(1-s)r} = 1$$

SPC is the term that can be used to convert those public investments that displace private funds to consumption equivalents. That is, we simply convert all benefits and costs to consumption equivalents using SPC and discount by the social rate of time preference.

We assume that s, i, and r are not functions of time so they can be treated as the same values in different time periods. This allows us to treat V_t as a constant, V, that is time invariant. This is not an unreasonable assumption but it is important because we rely on it in what follows, but we will continue to use the expression V_t rather than V to remind the reader of this assumption.

13.3.4. Present Value Using the SPC

Consider an investment of $1.00 in a public project. Some of the funds will come from consumption foregone. Some will come from private investment foregone. Let θ_c be the fraction of a dollar of public spending that displaces private investment. That is, this is the amount by which private capital formation is reduced as a result of financing an additional dollar of government investment. Then $(1 - \theta_c)$ will be the fraction of public investment funds that comes from consumption. Recognizing that consumption of a dollar in year t has a present value of $1.00 in year t, the present value of a dollar of costs in year t will be

$$PV_c = \theta_c(V_t) + (1 - \theta_c) \tag{13.7}$$

The term θ_c represents the present value of the fraction of the project's costs that come from private capital displaced. The present value of this is found by multiplying it by SPC. The term $(1 - \theta_c)$ is the fraction of the costs that come from foregone consumption. Thus the present value of costs as of year t of costs C_t incurred in year t will be

$$C_t^* = C_t[\theta_c V_t + (1 - \theta_c)] \tag{13.8}$$

where C_t is costs as ordinarily measured and C_t^* is adjusted costs as adjusted by Equation (13.8).

A similar expression can be found for benefits. Let θ_b be the fraction of each dollar of returns from public investment that is returned to private capital. That is, θ_b is the amount by which private capital is increased as result of an increase of $1.00 in the output of the government sector. Thus in any period t the benefits B_t will have a consumption present value in that year of

$$B_t^* = B_t[\theta_b \, V_t + (1 - \theta_b)] \tag{13.9}$$

The change in consumption in each year then can be expressed as

$$\Delta Y_T = B_t^* - C_t^* \tag{13.10}$$

We now have expressions for the present value in each year of the benefits and costs of a project that takes into account the addition to or the displacement of private capital and the consumption gained or foregone. This is done by expressing all effects in terms of the result for consumption and discounting by the social rate of time preference. The change in welfare can then be found by plugging the above values for adjusted benefits and costs into Equation (13.1). The net present value of the consumption value for the project will be then

$$NPV = \sum_{t=0}^{T} \frac{B_t^* - C_t^*}{(1 + i)^t} \tag{13.11a}$$

This equation is the fundamental present value equation for benefit–cost analysis in a second-best world. It incorporates implicitly the correct interest rate for discounting the benefits and costs of public projects. This can be spelled out with all terms to give

$$NPV = \sum_{t=0}^{T} \frac{B_t[\theta_b \, V_t + (1 - \theta_b)] - C_t[\theta_c V_t + (1 - \theta_c)]}{(1 + i)^t} \tag{13.11b}$$

For simplicity we will call the term in brackets on the benefit side F_B [that is, $F_B = \theta_b \, V_t + (1 - \theta_b)$] and the corresponding cost term F_C. When the value of $\theta_b > \theta_c$, then $F_B > F_C$ and discounting by the SRTP will understate the net present value. When $F_C > F_B$, discounting by the SRTP will overstate NPVs. When $F_C = F_B$, however, discounting by the SRTP will give a correct answer. Consider the following cases:

Case 1 $\theta_b = \theta_c$. In this case the fraction of private investment displaced by the project is equal to the fraction of benefits that contribute to private capital, and $F_B = F_C$. When $F_B = F_C$, we shall denote both by F. Equation (13.11a) may then be written as

$$PV = \sum_{t=0}^{t} \frac{F[B_t - C_t]}{(1 + i)^t} \tag{13.12}$$

In this situation F is a multiplier that affects the size but not the sign of discounted benefits and costs. This means that a project that has a positive or negative net present value when discounted by the social rate of time preference will continue to have a positive or negative NPV when adjusted by F. *Therefore in the case where a single project is being compared to the status quo the correct result will follow from using the social rate of time preference applied to ordinary costs and benefits as the discount rate.* That is, if the project is desirable using the SRTP, it is socially desirable when $\theta_b = \theta_c$.

There are several important examples in which the use of the SRTP to discount ordinary benefits and costs is appropriate.[2] First, in an open economy in which there is a high degree of capital mobility, public investment will neither crowd out private investment nor will returns from public projects influence the amount of private investment. The supply of investment will tend to be elastic at the world interest rate. Here discounting ordinary benefits and costs by the SRTP is appropriate. Even if the supply of investment funds is not perfectly elastic, significant elasticity means that θ_c and θ_b will be small and similar. The United States economy is significantly open to world capital; it appears that for most cases, θ_b and θ_c are small and similar.

Second, benefits are sometimes costs avoided whose financing is similar to initial costs. This is likely to be especially important in the case of environmental projects in which future clean-up costs are avoided. Here again the SRTP for benefits and costs should be used.

In *cost-effectiveness analysis* the goal is to compare the costs of alternative methods of reaching the same goal. As long as the financing of the various alternatives is similar, the use of the SRTP should give a correct answer.

Finally, where both benefits and costs are widely dispersed, the effect on private capital for both benefits and costs should be captured in the saving rate. Had the public investment funds remained in the private sector only the portion likely to have been saved would have been invested privately. Thus where benefits and costs are widely dispersed, $\theta_b = \theta_c$ and the SRTP should be used to discount ordinary benefits and costs.

Thus, in five cases the use of the SRTP as the discount rate without further adjustment is warranted.

1. Where analysis indicates that the same portion of benefits as costs affect private capital
2. Where there is little effect of the price on investment funds due to an open economy
3. Where benefits are future costs saved
4. Where a cost-effectiveness analysis is used
5. Where the distribution of benefits and costs are widely dispersed

Case 2 $\theta_b = 1; \theta_c = 0$.   This is the situation in which none of the costs of the project displace private capital but all of the returns to the project go to private capital. In this case the discounting equation is

---

[2]When comparing projects where $\theta_b = \theta_c$ within each project but not across the projects, it may be important to estimate θ_b and θ_c. The size of the NPV will be sensitive to our assumption of the size of θ_b and θ_c. When $\theta_b = \theta_c$, then the NPV will be the same as when the ordinary costs and benefits are discounted by the SRTP. When $\theta_b = \theta_c > 1$, however, the sign of the NPV does not change but the size of the NPV will be larger because the NPV will be multiplied by SPC, which is greater than 1.

$$PV = \sum_{t=0}^{T} \frac{B_t V_t - C_t}{(1 + i)^t} \qquad (13.13)$$

This indicates that discounting both costs and benefits at the SRTP will *understate* the net value of the project, unless an adjustment, multiplication by the SPC, is made to the benefits of the project. Equation (13.13) tells us that in this situation costs are to be discounted by the social rate of time preference. If unadjusted benefits are discounted by the social rate of time preference the present value of benefits will be understated because the SPC is greater than 1. That the SPC is greater than 1 can be seen as follows. V_t may be written as

$$V_t = \frac{r - sr}{i - sr} > \frac{r}{i}$$

Since $r > i$, V_t will be > 1.

Where $\theta_b > \theta_c$, and the SRTP is used to discount benefits and costs, a project with a positive NPV clearly should be accepted.

Case 3 $\theta_b = 0; \theta_c = 1$.   In this case all the costs of the project come from private capital and none of the benefits return to private capital. The discounting equation is

$$PV = \sum_{t=0}^{T} \frac{B_t - C_t V_t}{(1 + i)^t} \qquad (13.14)$$

In this situation it is appropriate to discount the benefits by the social rate of time preference but not the unadjusted costs. Using the SRTP to discount both the unadjusted costs and benefits will overstate the present value.

The SRTP is too low an interest rate in this case. [It can be shown that the return to private capital may be either too low or too high a discount rate in the case where $\theta_c > \theta_b$. (See Zerbe, 1991.)]

Where θ_b and θ_c are unknown, Lesser and Zerbe (1993) show that an adjustment to costs of 10 percent will cover likely cases. *We call this the 10 percent rule for the adjustment of costs.* That is, if the sign of the NPV remains invariant when the costs are adjusted upward or downward by 10 percent, then the sign of the NPV will usually give a correct guide. If one knew that $\theta_b > \theta_c$, costs would only be adjusted downward by 10 percent. A project that was poor even when costs were adjusted downward by 10 percent should then be rejected. When one knows that $\theta_c > \theta_b$, costs should be adjusted upward by 10 percent. A project that passed muster even when costs were adjusted upward by 10 percent will be a good project for any likely values of θ_c and θ_b given that $\theta_c > \theta_b$.

13.3.5.   Ethics and the SRTP

As with any aggregate measure of welfare, the SRTP is ethically determined. The SRTP is the rate society "chooses" according to some ethical theory. For example, in choosing the SRTP the Rawlsian would wish to know whether or not future generations would be less advantaged than current generations. In a utilitarian context, the SRTP will equal the MRTP or the consumption rate of interest in the idealized economy except that external effects may lead to a divergence of the MRTP from the SRTP.

The level of consumption itself may embody an external effect. Suppose, for example, that status in society is a valued good and that status is determined by relative levels of consumption. Then collectively we might wish to reduce current consumption and to increase current savings, lowering the interest rate. Where all reduce consumption, relative status from greater savings remains unchanged. Acting individually, however, we may fail to increase saving because our current status is lowered. One might then argue that in this situation, in the absence of collective action, the SRTP is less than the consumption rate of interest or the MRTP.

An external effect of particular importance is the *intergenerational effect*. A second ethical argument against using the MRTP and in favor of the SRTP is that the preferences of future generations should count in determining the SRTP whereas only the preferences of the current generations determine the MRTP. But, the MRTP shows the rate at which an individual is willing to trade off his own future for his own present consumption. The MRTP will also determine the future wealth of later generations. One could then argue that use of the MRTP is as ethically justified as the SRTP insofar as it derives from a golden rule of treating others as ourselves. This approach gains force also if we postulate that future generations are very like ourselves. It also gains force if the family is viewed as having an indefinite lifetime, unbroken by the births and deaths of individual members. In this situation the household utility function may make considerable allowance for future generations.

13.4.   THE SECOND-BEST DISCOUNT RATE IN PRACTICE

13.4.1.   Empirical Estimates of the SRTP

The SRTP has been identified with the consumption rate of interest and thus with the after-tax rate of return on safe investments. This rate will depend on the growth rate of the economy and on macroeconomic variables. There is no reason to expect that this would be the same in all time periods. Table 13.3 shows inflation-adjusted interest rates for various bonds and for various historical time periods. The range of rates is substantial, the lowest is about 2 percent, the highest about 9.4 percent. If we confine ourselves to those periods in which rates have the lowest outstanding deviation (the SD is shown for just these periods), we have a range from 3.76 to 5.24 percent. Real rates between 4 and 5 percent before taxes seem most appropriate for the period of the 1980s and the early 1990s. On an after-tax basis, they would vary from about 2.7 to about 4.25 percent.

Ideally we would like to use expected real rates. Zerbe (1991) has examined expected real rates, and these suggest a range for projects between 3 and 20 years' duration of about 3.8 to 5.5 percent, consistent with the real rates in periods of economic stability. On an after-tax basis, these range from about 2.6 to about 4.7 percent. All things considered, then, real rates from 2.5 to 5.0 percent seem to cover the range of real rates that should be used to discount public benefits and costs in a second-best world.

TABLE 13.3

Periods	Prime Commercial Paper (CPI Adjusted),[a] Percent	American Railroad Bonds (CPI Adjusted),[b] Percent	Realized Real Yields 1-Year Treasury Notes (CPI Adjusted),[c] Percent	3-Year Treasury Bonds (CPI Adjusted),[c] Percent	20-Year Treasury Bonds (CPI Adjusted),[d] Percent	Inflation Rate CPI,[e] Percent
1857–1860		9.38				
1865–1889		8.86				
1881–1915		4.27 [2.3]				0.16 [2.1]
1885–1893		4.62 [0.13]				0 [0]
1890–1915	5.24 [2.3]	3.76 [2.3]				0.48 [2.1]
1920–1929	5.38	5.16				
1953–1988–1989	1.96		1.9	2.23	2.46	
1977–1989	2.92		3.2	3.56	3.97	
1980–1989	4.27 [0.023]		4.19	4.69	5.17	

NOTE: Figures in brackets are standard deviations.

[a]Historical Statistics of the United States, Bicentennial Edition, U.S. Department of Commerce, Bureau of the Census, Washington, D.C., 1988, pp. 996, 1001, Series X-445.

[b]Historical Statistics of the United States, p. 1002, Series X 456-465.

[c]The Economic Report of the President, Washington, D.C., 1988, 1990, Federal Reserve Bulletin, selected months.

[d]Analytic record of yields and yield spreads from 1945, Salmon Brothers, Inc.

[e]Historical Statistics of the United States, Series E, pp. 210–212, The Economic Report of the President, selected years.

TABLE 13.4

Variables	Expected Values	Bounds (2 std. devs.)
i	3	2.5–4.2
r	8	6.0–10.0
s	7.2	5.5–10

Adjusted from Ruby, 1980.

13.4.2. Estimating the SPC

The best estimates of the size of the shadow price of capital, V_t, are about 2.5 to 3.5. Table 13.4 shows our estimates of the parameters that determine the SPC. These variables give an SPC of about 3.

13.4.3. The Effect of the SPC

Let us consider NPV using different possible discount rates. Consider a simple example in which we wish to find the correct NPV of a project whose present value is about $41 when costs and benefits are unadjusted by the SPC and are discounted with an SRTP of 3 percent.

If θ_b were to equal θ_c, and both were equal to 50 percent, then the NPV would be about $83, using an SPC of 3. Here the adjusted NPV differs considerably from the unadjusted NPV. In an open economy, however, θ_b and θ_c are unlikely to be higher than 2 to 3 percent. If $\theta_b = \theta_c = 5\%$, the NPV will be about $45. Where $\theta_b = 0\%$ and $\theta_c = 3\%$, the NPV will be about $35. Where θ_b and θ_c are less than 5 percent and usually where they are between 5 percent and 10 percent, a 10 percent sensitivity adjustment to costs as suggested by Lesser and Zerbe (1991) will encompass the range of possible values. Where the difference between θ_b and θ_c is larger than this, however, adjustments using the SPC are required.

13.4.4. A Practical Approach

The discount rates suggested here can be regarded as practical rates derived from theoretical underpinnings (Appendix 13B shows another approach, the Harberger weighted average). Lyons argues, correctly we think, that the expected real rate of return on Treasury bonds whose length corresponds to the project in question will give reasonable approximations to the correct discount rate. Dively and Zerbe (1991) show that most municipalities that use a discount rate choose the cost of (private) capital; a majority of municipalities, however, do not use any discount rate at all.

In the context of an air pollution control problem analyzed by Ruby (1980) the uncertainty of the variables θ_b, θ_c, r, i, and s were substantially less than that of certain physical variables such as morbidity and predicted concentrations of the pollution dispersion model. Ruby's results suggest that the rates recommended here should give reasonable estimates.

SUMMARY

We have presented a conceptual framework for determining the discount rate for public projects. This framework involves first tracing the consumption flows generated by the projects' benefits and displaced by the projects' costs. These consumptions flows are then discounted by the SRTP. A general equation was developed to use in discounting public projects. We make the following recommendations (which do not consider risk) for calculating intertemporal benefits and costs:

1. We suggest that the SPC approach be used as the basic approach.
2. The discount rate should be the SRTP.
3. A reasonable approximation to the SRTP appears to be the rate on government bonds of the same term length as the project in question.
4. The SRTP appears to lie within the range of about 2.5 percent to 5.5 percent (adjusted for inflation).
5. Sensitivity analysis with different discount rates should be confined to the range of rates thought to represent the SRTP.
6. In many cases discounting unadjusted benefits and costs by the SRTP will give correct results.
7. Where the contributions or displacements of private capital from benefits or costs is not known, a 10 percent adjustment of costs should be performed to cover likely cases.
8. Where projects are considered in which an issue is whether the government or the private sector should undertake the project, the private sector rate should be used.

QUESTIONS AND PROBLEMS

1. The U.S. government is considering investing in one or two alternative projects. The first will generate additional electricity. The second will produce a solar substitute for electricity. The estimated cash flow for the two projects, A and B, are as follows:

Time	Project A	Project B
	(in $ millions)	
+0	−100	−100
+1	50	16.58
+2	50	16.58
+3	50	16.58
+4		16.58
+5		16.58
+6		16.58
+7		16.58
+8		16.58
+9		16.58
+10		16.58

The government's cost of money is 3 percent and at this cost the two projects seem equally attractive. As a consultant asked to evaluate these projects, you determine that both will return the same (high) percentage of benefits to the private sector and that in their financing both will put the same burden on investment funds that would otherwise go into the private sector. You also determine that the SRTP is 2 percent.

Which of the projects do you recommend on financial grounds, given that you must choose one of them? Why?

2. Calculate the SPC where $r = 10\%$, $i = 3\%$, and $s = 10\%$.
3. The government of Alberta is considering an investment project that provides infrastructure for business development. Their cost of money is a real interest rate of 3 percent. They estimate that 90 percent of the costs will be borne by a reduction in consumption and 10 percent by a reduction in investment. At this discount rate of 3 percent the project just passes muster.

    An analyst is hired who calculates the SPC for Alberta as 3.0. She says that when this is applied to an evaluation of the costs using the 10 percent and 90 percent figures mentioned earlier that costs should be increased by 20 percent. The benefit–cost ratio is now less than one. It seems that the project will not be carried out.
   (a) Members of the government approach you hoping you can provide a technical (discount rate) rationale for the project. Can you?
   (b) Might there be a divergence between the Alberta perspective and a national government perspective?

REFERENCES

Arrow, K., "The Rate of Discount on Public Investments with Imperfect Capital Markets," in *Discounting for Time and Risk in Energy Policy,* R. Lind, ed., Baltimore, Md.: Johns Hopkins University Press, 1982, pp. 115–136.

Arrow, K., and R. Lind, "Uncertainty and Evaluation of Public Investment Decisions," *American Economic Review* 60, 364–378, 1970.

Baumol, W. J., "On the Social Rate of Discount," *American Economic Review* 57, 788–802, 1968.

Boadway, R. W., "Public Investment Decision Rules in a Neoclassical Growing Economy," *International Economic Review* 19, 265–287, 1978.

Bradford, D. F., "Constraints on Government Investment Opportunities and the Choice of Discount Rate," *American Economic Review* 65, 887–899, 1975.

Carlson, J. A., "Short Term Interest Rates as Predictors of Inflation: Comment," *American Economic Review* 67, 469–475, 1977.

Dively, Dwight, and Richard Zerbe, "The Discount Rate Policy for Municipalities," Working Paper, 1991.

Fox, I. J., and O. C. Herfindahl, "Attainment and Efficiency in Satisfying Demands for Water Resources," *American Economic Review* 54(2), 198–206, 1964.

Halvorsen, Robert, and Michael Ruby, *Benefit Cost Analysis of Air Pollution Control,* Lexington, Ky.: Lexington Books, D.C. Heath, 1981.

Harberger, A., "On Measuring the Social Opportunity Cost of Public Funds," in A. Harberger, *Project Evaluation: Collected Papers,* Chicago: University of Chicago Press, 1976.

Haveman, Robert, "The Opportunity Cost of Displaced Private Spending and the Social Discount Rate," *Water Resources Research* 5(5), 947–956, 1969.

Haveman, R., "Policy Analysis and the Congress: An Economist's View," in *Public Expenditure and Policy Analysis,* R. Haveman and J. Margolis, eds., 2nd ed., Chicago: Rand McNally College Publishing Co., 1977.

Lesser, J. A., and R. O. Zerbe, Jr., "Discounting Procedures for Environmental (and Other) Projects," Working Paper, 1993.

Lind, R., ed., *Discounting for Time and Risk in Energy Policy,* Baltimore, Md.: Johns Hopkins Press, 1982.

Lyons, Randolph, "Federal Discount Rate Policy, The Shadow Price of Capital and Challenges for Reforms," *Journal of Environmental Economics and Management* (18), S-29–S-50, 1990.

McKean, N., *Efficiency in Government Through Systems Analysis: with Emphasis on Water Resources Development,* New York: John Wiley, 1958.

Marglin, S. A., "The Social Rate of Discount and the Optimal Rate of Investment," *Quarterly J. of Economics* 77, 95–111, 1963.

Modigliani, F., and M. M. Miller, "The Cost of Capital, Corporation Finance, and the Theory of Investment," *American Economic Review* 48, 261–297, 1958.

Musgrave, R. A., "Cost-Benefit Analysis and the Theory of Public Finance," *Journal of Economic Literature* 7, 759–806, 1969.

Quirk, J., and K. Teresana, "The Choice of Discount Rate Applicable to Government Resource Use: Theory and Limitations," Rand Working Paper, 1986.

Ruby, M. G., "Cost-Benefit Analysis with Uncertain Information," Ph.D. Dissertation, University of Washington, 1980.

Sjaasted, L. A., and D. L. Wisecarver, "The Social Cost of Public Finance," *J. Pol. Econ.* 85, 513–547, 1977.

U.S. Congress, Joint Economic Committee, *Economic Analysis of Public Investment: Interest Rate Policy and Discounting Analysis,* Washington, D.C.: U.S. Government Printing Office, 1968.

U.S. Department of Commerce, Bureau of Economic Analysis, *The National Income and Product Accounts of the United States,* Washington, D.C.: U.S. Government Printing Office, September 1986.

U.S. Department of Commerce, Bureau of Economic Analysis, "U.S. Natural Income and Product Accounts: Revised Estimates," 56(7) and 59(7), *Survey of Current Business,* 1976.

U.S. Office of Management and Budget, *Special Analyses, Budget of the United States Government,* 1978–1980.

U.S. Office of Management and Budget, "Circular No. A-94, Revised," March 27, 1972.

Zerbe, Richard O., Jr., "The Discount Rate for Public Projects," Working Paper, 1991.

APPENDIX 13A

The Harberger Rate

Harberger (1969, *reprinted 1976*) proposed that a discount rate be used that is a weighted average of the return to private investment and foregone consumption. He suggested that the rate of return to public projects should be at least as great as

$$r_H = (\theta_c)r + (1 - \theta_c)i$$

The problem is that the Harberger rate does not give results that correspond to the SPC approach in cases in which there is any reinvestment of proceeds from either private or government investment net of depreciation. The Harberger rate is applicable only to the special case in which there is not reinvestment, as Bradford (1975) has shown. The Harberger rate may give poor results in cases in which there is some reinvestment of proceeds.

Even though the Harberger rate is theoretically incorrect, it is likely to often give reasonable results in practice. In practice, most of the funding for a project will come from consumption so that the Harberger rate will be fairly close to the rate of time preference. For example, if $i = 3\%$ and $r = 8\%$, and 90 percent of the project comes from consumption, the weighted-average rate is just 3.5 percent, not too different from the social rate of time preference of 3 percent. Thus, if the Harberger rates are used for projects in which most of the funding is from consumption and in which the percentage of benefits reinvested is similar to the percentage of displacement of private investment, the Harberger rate will not be unreasonable. Nevertheless, we prefer the use of the SRTP combined with the 10 percent adjustment rule for the adjustment of benefits suggested earlier as the theoretically sound approach.

14

Case Study of the High Ross Dam

14.1. BACKGROUND

Ross Dam is a major hydroelectric power plant on the Skagit River in north-western Washington. The dam is owned by Seattle City Light, which is the City of Seattle's municipally owned electric utility. Ross Dam was originally constructed in 1937 and was subsequently raised to higher levels that would allow more power to be generated. Plans were prepared to increase the height even more under the title of the High Ross Dam, but these were not implemented for several decades due to lack of demand for the power.

One complication for the High Ross Dam relates to the geography of the Skagit River. The Skagit originates in the province of British Columbia, and the High Ross Dam's reservoir would require flooding of about 10 miles of the river gorge in Canada. Under the provisions of the Boundary Water Treaty of 1909, any such flooding would require the permission of the International Joint Commission (IJC), which is a six-member body given the responsibility to "prevent disputes regarding the use of boundary waters . . . and make provisions for the adjustment and settlement of all such questions as may hereafter arise."

In 1942, the IJC gave Seattle permission to raise Ross Dam to its ultimate level, but made the approval conditional on the City of Seattle providing adequate compensation to British Columbia for the flooding of its land. No such agreement was reached for over two decades, largely because there was little pressing need for the power generated by the dam. By 1966, Seattle City Light decided to proceed with planning and construction of High Ross, and reached agreement with British Columbia on compensation for the flooded land in the next year.

However, considerable opposition to High Ross emerged in both Canada and the United States. The opposition focused on the environmental effects of the flooding, including the loss of wildlife habitat and recreational opportunities. This opposition meant that it took City Light until 1980 to obtain final permits from the U.S. federal government for construction of High Ross. While this permitting process was underway, the government of British Columbia repudiated its agreement on compensation for the flooded land and requested that the IJC overturn its 1942 authorization for the construction of the dam.

By the late 1970s, political support for the High Ross Dam began to wane in Seattle. However, the dam represented a very valuable asset for the city because its power could not be provided from any other source at a comparable price. Thus, negotiations were opened between Seattle and British Columbia regarding possible compensation for the city if the High Ross Dam were not constructed. Early in the negotiations, British Columbia indicated its willingness to provide power to the city to make up for the losses that would result from not constructing the dam. Seattle indicated it was still interested in building High Ross but was willing to consider an alternative plan that would provide replacement power from Canada. Seattle's position was based on the premise that any agreement not to build the dam would have to provide sufficient compensation to "make Seattle whole" for the loss of the power from High Ross.

14.2. USES OF BENEFIT–COST ANALYSIS

The complicated issue in the negotiations was exactly what value to assign to Seattle's right to construct the dam and how to evaluate the alternative sources of supply offered by British Columbia. Benefit–cost analysis was used by both parties to support their positions during negotiations, and the differences in assumptions became critical to the outcome of the process. Among the assumptions at issue were the construction costs of High Ross, the costs for supplying alternative power from Canadian sources, inflation rates, and discount rates. For the purposes of this case study, two of these issues will be examined:

1. *Value of energy.* One of the critical differences in the negotiations related to what Seattle would have to pay for replacement power if High Ross were not built. Seattle proposed to pay only the costs that would be equivalent to the price of power from High Ross, while British Columbia wanted to charge prices comparable to those it charged other large customers.
2. *Discount rate.* Seattle and British Columbia disagreed about the appropriate discount rate to be used in evaluating alternatives to High Ross. Seattle sought to use the interest rate actually paid on bonds issued by Seattle City Light, while British Columbia argued for an interest rate based on the prime rate charged by U.S. banks. In the case of High Ross, the value of future benefits and costs would be significantly affected by assumptions made about the appropriate discount rate since the lifespan of the project extended until the year 2066.

The positions taken by the two parties on these issues and the ultimate outcome of the negotiations are discussed in the following sections.

14.3.   VALUE OF ENERGY

In 1979, the two parties agreed to a framework that would allow an alternative to High Ross Dam. Under this framework, British Columbia would provide an amount of power equivalent to that which would be available from High Ross over the lifetime of the project. The parties agreed that the costs for this power would be associated with the escalating operating costs of the British Columbia hydro system. However, it soon became clear that the two parties disagreed on how these escalating costs should be measured.

British Columbia interpreted the price provisions very simply: The province offered power to Seattle in accordance with its Rate Schedule 1821, which was the pricing structure used for large customers. This approach would be the simplest to calculate and would reflect the changing costs of producing power over time.

Seattle interpreted the price provisions in a very different way. The city reiterated its desire to obtain an alternative that would be equivalent to High Ross in capacity and price. Thus, the city proposed that it establish a trust fund equivalent to the present value of the construction and operating costs of High Ross, and that British Columbia draw monies from this trust fund in exchange for providing the power that would replace High Ross.

Both sides quickly moved to denounce the other's proposals. British Columbia noted that the proposed trust fund would not allow payments for the power to keep up with the expected increases in the cost of generation. Over the life of the project, the province's calculations showed that it would have to supply power to Seattle at a cost of less than one-half that charged to other bulk power customers. Seattle, in turn, criticized British Columbia's proposal because the rapid increase in expected energy prices would mean that the city would pay far more for the replacement power than it would pay for High Ross. In addition, Seattle would have no influence on the setting of the rates proposed under Schedule 1821, so its power costs would be entirely in the hands of another country.

With negotiations at an impasse, British Columbia turned to the IJC and asked that body to rescind its earlier authorization to construct High Ross Dam. Before making a decision, the IJC called for an independent benefit–cost analysis by Douglas Gordon and George Berry, two well-known utility financial experts. These experts were asked to assess the value of High Ross to Seattle and to identify a preferred alternative means of providing power that would have a value equivalent to that available through High Ross.

Gordon and Berry's calculations showed that High Ross could be built for an annualized cost of $25,324,000. (The term "annualized cost" refers to the annual amount that would have to be paid over the total life of the project to cover the full construction costs. This concept is discussed in Chapter 9.) Gordon and Berry calculated that the cheapest alternative source of electricity available to Seattle, which would involve a combination of a coal-fired power plant and a combustion turbine, would cost about $58,097,000 per year. However, British Columbia's proposed use of Schedule 1821 would cost $149,018,000 per year, or over six times the cost of High Ross.

After receiving this report, the IJC decided to leave its original 1942 order in effect, which gave Seattle the right to build High Ross. However, the commission also noted that the Gordon and Berry report showed there were alternatives to the dam, and therefore set up a special board with representatives of all parties to continue to explore these alternatives. This board began to meet in July 1982 and immediately applied pressure on both parties to reach a compromise.

By October, the outlines of a compromise were in place. In light of the Gordon and Berry report, British Columbia agreed to drop its demand that power be charged for at the rates included in Schedule 1821. The parties agreed that the province would supply power equivalent to that from High Ross for a period of 80 years. Seattle would pay an annual amount for this power equivalent to the amount that would be generated by the real rate of return (after inflation) from the investment of funds that would otherwise have been spent to build High Ross, plus an amount equivalent to the annual operational costs of the dam. For the first five years of the agreement, the inflation rate would be set at 8 percent and the nominal discount rate set at the rate for the latest City Light bond issue, which was 10.1267 percent. The amounts for each subsequent 5-year period would be adjusted to recognize changes in interest and inflation rates. This breakthrough formed the keystone of the final agreement to avoid the construction of High Ross Dam.

14.4. DISCOUNT RATE

The selection of an appropriate discount rate also proved to be a stumbling block during negotiations. Each party had its own approach for choosing a discount rate and refused to deviate from it. As discussed later in the case study, neither of these approaches was correct in the theoretical sense, and neither party relied on economic theory to derive or justify its choice of a discount rate.

From the outset, Seattle had insisted that its actual cost of funds was the appropriate discount rate to use for the construction of High Ross and that this rate should also be applied to any of the alternatives. In 1977, Seattle City Light had issued bonds at a rate of 5.34 percent, and this rate was what the city proposed to use for evaluating High Ross.

British Columbia had argued that a different rate should apply. At the time City Light sold bonds at 5.34 percent, the U.S. prime rate (the rate charged by banks to their best commercial customers) was 7.00–7.25 percent. British Columbia officials indicated that the true opportunity cost of capital was equal to or greater than the prime rate, and also noted that projects in Canada could not be financed at the same rates available to City Light. British Columbia also contacted several economists at U.S. universities and claimed that their consensus was that the appropriate discount rate should be the prime rate plus 1 percent. Based on this information, British Columbia suggested that a discount rate of 8.75 percent was appropriate.

Seattle responded to British Columbia's analysis by noting that the prime rate is charged to tax-paying entities, and that City Light enjoys a lower interest rate since interest on its bonds is not subject to federal income tax. Seattle also indicated that the only relevant interest rate is the one that would be paid by City Light, because it was the entity that would be foregoing the benefits of constructing High Ross.

The choice of discount rate was critical to the evaluation of alternatives. For example, at one point in the process British Columbia agreed to offer firm energy to replace the output from High Ross, but only for a period of time less than the life of High Ross. At a high discount rate, this proposal seemed attractive because the value of electricity from High Ross in the distant future would be deeply discounted. At a lower discount rate, the alternative proposal would not compare as favorably because the value of future energy would not be as deeply discounted.

The Berry and Gordon report ultimately supported Seattle's position on calculating the appropriate discount rate. However, the effect of this choice was somewhat muted by the rapid rise in all interest rates during the late 1970s and early 1980s. By the time the agreement was signed, City Light's cost of funds had increased to 10.1267 percent, which was about even with the levels originally sought by British Columbia.

14.5. DISCUSSION

The search for an alternative to the High Ross Dam illustrates several basic concepts underlying benefit–cost analysis. These include:

1. *Assignment of property rights.* Discussions regarding alternatives to High Ross began from the basis that Seattle had the right to construct the dam. This right, as embodied in an international agreement, meant that Seattle had a strong basis for seeking compensation if the dam were not to be built. If Seattle had not had this right, British Columbia could simply have refused to permit the flooding of its territory, thereby precluding the construction of High Ross. This illustrates the importance of establishing property rights before beginning a benefit–cost analysis.

2. *Changing values over time.* When Ross Dam was constructed and when the original proposal for High Ross was approved, the citizens and leaders of both Washington and British Columbia put great value on building hydroelectric dams. The power from such facilities was viewed as a critical asset for industrial development in a region trying to escape its dependence on agriculture. Concerns for the environment were almost never brought up in discussions about dams.

   In contrast, when talk of actually building High Ross began in the 1970s, the values of many citizens had changed. The protection of the environment had become much more important, and most residents of British Columbia saw little reason to flood provincial wilderness areas and hurt wildlife in order for Seattle to have cheap electric power. Even many Seattle residents, who were the potential beneficiaries of High Ross, opposed the project on environmental grounds. High Ross illustrates how the values underlying a benefit–cost analysis can change over time, and how decision makers at different times or in different circumstances may make completely different choices from the same benefit–cost data.

3. *Selection of a discount rate.* The assessment of alternatives to High Ross illustrates the sensitivity of many benefit–cost analyses to the

selection of a discount rate. Further, it shows the absence of consensus on the appropriate choice of a discount rate for public projects.

Seattle used a narrow definition of the discount rate that simply reflected its cost of capital. British Columbia proposed a somewhat more general discount rate based on overall commercial interest rates. The two approaches differed in how they defined the scope of the project: Seattle looked only at the costs to City Light, whereas British Columbia looked at the overall economy. The approaches also differed in how taxes were treated: Seattle used tax-exempt rates because City Light did not pay federal tax on its bonds, whereas British Columbia used taxable rates.

It is interesting to note that neither party attempted to develop or use a broader social discount rate. British Columbia's case might well have been buttressed by such an approach, because they might have argued for a high discount rate based on the environmental damage that would occur. The absence of such discussion is partly due to the relatively recent development of information about the appropriate social discount rate, and also stems from the limited exposure of most benefit–cost practitioners to the academic discussions about discount rates.

4. *Selection of a time horizon.* High Ross is somewhat unusual because it represents an extremely long-lived asset. As such, the overall benefits from the project are very sensitive to the selection of the discount rate. In addition, the construction of a major dam presents a unique set of essentially permanent costs and benefits that stem from the long life of the project. On the positive side, most major dams are essentially irreplaceable and will provide low-cost power for decades after they are paid for. For example, it is almost inconceivable to imagine replacing the major power facilities on the Columbia or St. Lawrence rivers given current environmental regulations and economic conditions. On the negative side, dams create permanent changes in the environment that often cannot be mitigated. How these benefits and costs are assessed depends in part on the selection of the lifespan for the analysis.

SUMMARY

The case study of the High Ross Dam illustrates many of the complexities that affect the actual use of benefit–cost analysis. Small variations in assumptions can have major effects on the outcomes of the analysis. These assumptions become even more important in long-term projects because amounts to be received or paid many years in the future can be significantly affected by small changes in calculation techniques or discount rates.

The case study also shows the value of conducting independent benefit–cost analyses in some cases. Negotiations for an alternative to High Ross were stalled until the Gordon and Berry report was prepared, which helped to focus and resolve some of the key differences in assumptions.

Finally, the story of High Ross Dam illustrates the value of benefit–cost analysis as a tool for decision making. Without the techniques of benefit–cost analysis, it is unlikely that decision makers from either side would have been able to reach and justify an agreement. By using benefit–cost analysis, both sides were able to understand the consequences of alternatives and find a compromise acceptable to both parties.

QUESTIONS AND PROBLEMS

1. What would be a more complete approach to developing a social discount rate for the alternatives to High Ross Dam? Would this rate be higher or lower than the rates used by the two parties? How would this have affected the outcome of the negotiations?

2. How could the long-term benefits and costs of a major dam project be considered in a benefit–cost analysis? If the duration of the bonds to pay for such a project is 30 years, how could a longer time frame for analysis be justified?

3. Are there ways in which decision makers could consider the possibility that future generations will have different sets of values than those held at the present? If so, how could they be reflected in benefit–cost analysis?

15

An Introduction to Risk*

15.1. INTRODUCTION

15.1.1. The State of the Art

Neither the practice nor, sadly, even the theory of accounting for risk in public projects is well developed. The norm in practice is not to account for risk at all. One can examine the benefit–cost analyses of the Corps of Engineers or of the Bureau of Reclamation without ever seeing any evaluation of risk. The purpose of this chapter and the following two chapters is to allow readers to be analysts of sufficient sophistication that they will consider risk in evaluating projects. To be sure, the consideration of risk in benefit–cost analysis is as much an art as a science. The sophisticated analyst will not be one who approaches the problem in a cookbook fashion, but will, rather, gain some appreciation of what risk is and how it can be accommodated appropriately in different settings. That is all that can be asked at this stage in the development of the science of risk evaluation.

15.1.2. Risk and Uncertainty

The future is uncertain. Project analysis necessarily involves uncertainty and may or may not involve risk. This chapter and the two following chapters consider risk and uncertainty. This chapter first introduces the concepts of risk, uncertainty, risk aversion, and expected value and expected utility. These concepts are parts of the theory of expected utility which is the dominant theory of choice under uncertainty. This theory has been in the process of development since the early 1940s, and continues to undergo change and scrutiny. Finally, the relationship between risk and variance is explored.

The concept of risk is used in many different ways. Risk commonly refers to a positive probability of a bad outcome. We speak of the risk of driving,

---

*We would like to thank Jonathan Lesser, Dick Parks, and Edward Ricke for useful comments.

swimming, skiing, or of nuclear power plants, where the concern is with injury or death. Similarly we might refer to the risk of a government unit defaulting on a bond (default risk). Anytime there is probability, one possibility is worse than the other so there is risk. Risk of this sort is always present. We are in large part concerned here with *financial risk*, in which the bad outcome refers to a type of variability in benefit or cost streams. Uncertainty is the absence of knowledge about outcomes.[1]

Consider an example (used by Lind, 1982) of an individual who buys fire insurance for his home. The policy pays zero if his home does not burn down, but it pays an amount equal to the value of the house if the house does burn down. The purchase is an investment with an uncertain return. Clearly, however, the insurance reduces financial risk to the individual in the sense that it decreases the variability of a portfolio of assets containing the house. Before the purchase of the insurance, the portfolio was equal to the value of the house if the house did not burn down and equal to zero if it did. The value of the portfolio with insurance becomes equal to the value of the house less the insurance premium.

Suppose that the house is worth $100,000 and that the probability of it burning down is 1 percent. Suppose further that the insurance cost is equal to the value of the house times the probability of the house burning, or $1000, that is, the insurance cost is a fair bet. The insurance has reduced risk because it has reduced the probability of a bad outcome but the same uncertainty exists as to whether or not the house will burn down. The value of the portfolio now with a house, an insurance policy, and −$1000 in the form of an insurance premium, is $99,000 whether or not the house burns down, so that variability has been completely eliminated.

Whether or not the purchase of insurance is a worthwhile purchase for the homeowner depends on her preferences and on the cost of the insurance. Insurance is, of course, not a fair bet. That is, the value of the house times the probability of a fire that requires the insurance company to pay off is less than the insurance cost. This is because there are transaction costs associated with the insurance purchase and because the insurance company makes some return on its investment so that it charges a risk premium. *The purchaser of insurance therefore is making an investment that reduces risk even though it has an uncertain payoff and a negative expected rate of return*. The financial outcome is no longer uncertain for the investor. Yet because the investment reduces risk, it may be worthwhile if it sufficiently reduces risk since reduction of risk has value. The insurance example suggests that (1) reduction in variability per se has value, and (2) there are markets such as insurance which can help reduce variability and risk.

15.2. PROSPECTS AND STATES OF THE WORLD

We shall call a project whose outcome is uncertain a *prospect*. When uncertainty exists we shall say that there exist different *states of the world*. A prospect then

---

[1]Risk is sometimes distinguished from uncertainty by discriminating instances where probabilities are known (risk) from situations in which they are unknown (uncertainty).

involves more than one state of the world. Two states of the world might be rain tomorrow and no rain tomorrow. As the sponsor of an outdoor event, your income may be different according to which state of the world exists, "rain" or "no rain." If it doesn't rain your income will be higher than if it does rain. Similarly, you may consider the purchase of a lottery ticket for which there are only two states of the world; you either win or you lose. In considering whether or not to purchase a lottery ticket therefore one contemplates a prospect. There may be more than two states of the world. In the case of the lottery ticket, for example, you might win either $1,000,000 or $1000, or you might lose. *The question for the analyst is to find how prospects are to be valued.*

15.3. THE EXPECTED VALUE

One approach to valuing prospects, which is very often used in spite of its theoretical deficiencies, is to calculate the *expected value* of prospects. (The expected value is a measure of the value of uncertain outcomes. It is the sum of the values of each alternative outcome times the probability of the outcome.) We will use ExV instead of the usual EV for the expected value to distinguish EV from the EV of Chapters 6 and 7. The formula for expected value is

$$\text{ExV} = P_1X_1 + P_2X_2 + \cdots + P_NX_N \tag{15.1}$$

where P_1 is the probability of receiving the outcome X_1.

This can be expressed more concisely as

$$\text{ExV} = \sum_{i=1}^{N} P_iX_i \tag{15.2}$$

15.3.1. Alternative Projects

The expected value approach is also useful in considering ranking of alternative projects or prospects. Suppose there are alternative projects A and B with the following values if successful and the following probabilities of success:

	A	B
Probability of success (P)	0.20	0.15
Payoff if successful (V)	$1000	$2000
Cost	50	25

The expected value criterion requires us to choose the project with the highest expected value. The expected values are as follows:

$$\text{ExV}_A = 0.20(\$1000) - \$50 = \$150.00$$
$$\text{ExV}_B = 0.15(\$2000) - \$25 = \$275.00$$

The expected value of B is greater than that of A. If A and B are alternative projects should project B be chosen rather than A? Where only one project can be undertaken because of budget limitations, space or other physical constraints, then of course the project with the highest expected value should be chosen if one is using expected values to make the decision.

EXAMPLE 15.1

There is a dam being considered for the Greenbrier River in West Virginia. The life of the dam is 30 years. The value of this dam will depend on the rainfall over the next 10 years. The value of the dam under three different rainfall scenarios and the probability of the different scenarios are as follows:

Scenario	Probability	Present Value of Dam
Low rainfall	0.25	5,000,000
Medium rainfall	0.50	8,000,000
High rainfall	0.25	12,000,000

What is the expected value of the dam? The expected value is the probable value found by using Equation (15.1) to give

$ExV = .25(\$5,000,000) + .5(\$8,000,000) + .25(\$12,000,000) = \$8,250,000$

15.3.2.   Undertaking Both A and B

The example is, however, incomplete because it is possible that undertaking *both* projects is superior to undertaking *either one* of them, even though if both turn out well only one can be used since they are alternatives. That is, the combined project A and B may be superior to either of the individual projects A or B.

   To calculate the expected value of undertaking both A *and* B, however, let us suppose that A will be valuable only if B doesn't succeed. Suppose that P_A and P_B are independent. Then, the expected value of A and B, where ExV_A is the value of A and ExV_B is the value of B, is as follows:

$$ExV_{A+B} = P_A(1 - P_B)X_A + P_B(X_B) \qquad (15.3)$$

where $(1 - P_B)$ is the probability of B not succeeding. This equation makes intuitive sense as follows. The expression $P_A(1 - P_B)X_A$ is the probability A will succeed when B doesn't times the value of $[X_A]$. To this is added the probability that B will succeed times the value of B. Notice that we assume that if both A and B succeed that only B is valuable. The equation can be rearranged to give

$$ExV_{A+B} = P_AX_A + P_BX_B - P_AP_B[X_a] \qquad (15.4)$$

This is the expected value of A plus B minus the expected value of A when both succeed. *Both projects should be undertaken if the value found for their expected values exceeds the expected value of either A or B.* That is, if the value found by using Equation (15.3) exceeds the value found for A or B alone, both projects should be undertaken. The reason why it may pay to undertake both projects even if they are alternatives is that the total probability of success is greater when both projects are undertaken.

EXAMPLE 15.2

Microchip Analysis, Inc., is considering undertaking the development of new computer chips. There are two alternative approaches to developing the chips. Approach A involves a lower probability of success but a higher payoff if successful than approach B. Given the following data should Microchip undertake approach A, approach B, or both together?

	Approach A	Approach B
Probability of success (P)	0.10	0.15
Payoff if successful (V)	$1000	$2000
Cost (C)	50	150

The expected value of approach A is

$$\text{ExV}_A = P_A X_A - C_A = 0.10(1000) - 50 = \$100 - \$50 = \$50.00$$

The expected value of approach B is

$$\text{ExV}_B = 0.15(2000) - 150 = \$300 - \$150 = \$150.00$$

Approach B would seem to be considerably superior to A. However, we must also consider the value of undertaking both A and B. This will be

$$\text{ExV}_{A+B} = P_A X_A + P_B X_B - C_A - C_B - P_A P_B(X_A)$$
$$= 100 + 300 - 50 - 150 - 0.015(1000) = \$185.00$$

Although project A is superior to B, undertaking both projects A and B is superior to either A or B alone. This is true even though A and B are alternatives.

15.3.3. The Expected Value of Projects Given a Budget Constraint

If a project cannot be undertaken because of a budget constraint, the expected value of the project cannot of course be considered in choosing among projects. The project one is unable to undertake is irrelevant. A somewhat more complicated approach must be used when a project *may* be dropped due to a budget constraint.

Suppose that society must choose between two mutually exclusive projects A and B. Suppose further that there are two states of the world with probabilities P_1 and P_2 where $P_1 + P_2 = 1$. Project A has no uncertainty associated with it, and has benefits $B(A)$ of $2000 and costs $C(A)$ of $1000 regardless of the state of the world. Then, the expected net benefit of A, ENB(A), equals $B(A) - C(A)$, and this equals $1000.

The benefits from project B are also invariant to the state of the world and equal $B(B)$. The costs of project B are, however, state-dependent and equal to $C_1(B)$ and $C_2(B)$. Without loss of generality assume that the project budgets are fixed and equal to $C(A)$ and $C_2(B)$, respectively, and that $C_1(B) > C_2(B)$. Assume further that the expected net benefit of B, ENB(B), equals $1000 + e$, where $e > 0$. The decision maker who does not care about the variability of returns (the risk-neutral decision maker) will prefer project B to A, since ENB(B)>ENB(A). The expected net value of project B can be expressed as

$$(P_1 + P_2)(B) - P_1(C_1) - P_2(C_2) = \$1000 + e \qquad (15.5)$$

which is greater than the value of project A by the amount e. But, suppose that project B would be immediately canceled if state 1 occurred because costs would exceed the project budget. Now the decision maker must care about variability. The expected net value of B is the zero value in state 1 in which the project is canceled, plus the value in state 2. The net expected value of B given the possibility of project cancellation is then

$$\text{ENB(B)} = P_2B - P_2(C_2) \qquad (15.6)$$

The difference between Equation (15.6) and Equation (15.5) is $-P_1B + P_1C_1$. The expected net benefits of B when taking into account the fact that B might be canceled will then equal $1000 + e - P_1B + P_1C_1$. The expected value of project B will be higher than A when

$$1000 + e - P_1B + P_1C_1 > 1000$$

This will occur only if

$$e > P_1[(B - C_1)]$$

The point is that the possibility of project cancellation requires that project B must be a better project than if there were no budget constraint.

15.3.4. The Utility of Expected Values

The expected value is a very useful and widely used measure. Expected value, however, may not be the best measure of the economic value of a prospect. Expected value considers the probabilities but does not give full consideration to the variability of outcomes. Consider two alternative projects A and B. Project A has an outcome of 0 with 50 percent probability and an outcome of $1,000,000 with 50 percent probability. Project B has an outcome of $100,000 with 50 percent probability, and an outcome of $600,000 with 50 percent probability. Both projects have equal expected values of $500,000. But one values them differently. Which one do you prefer? Project A shows more variability in its outcome and is more risky than project B. We are interested in the willingness to pay (WTP) or accept (WTA) the projects (see Chapter 7) and expected values may not tell us this.

We can define a *utility of expected values,* which will be the utility associated with the sum that represents expected values. This can be expressed as U(EV). This represents the utility of the amount of expected value. It still does not represent disutility associated with variability. We wish to distinguish the utility of an expected value from a concept we will soon develop, expected utility.

15.4. RISK PREFERENCES

An individual may be (1) risk averse, meaning that he is reluctant to take risks; (2) risk neutral, meaning that he is unconcerned with risks; or (3) risk preferring, meaning that he actively seeks out risks. Research has shown that generally individuals are risk averse. These attitudes toward risk are defined with respect to the relation between the marginal utility of income and the level of income.

Risk Aversity: When an individual's marginal utility of income declines with increasing income, he is said to be risk averse.

Suppose you are offered a prospect of winning $50,000 if a flip of a single coin yields heads. The expected value of this prospect is $[\frac{1}{2}(\$50,000)]$ or $25,000. Would you pay $24,999 for the prospect? On the average you come out ahead by $1.00. Yet, you would probably not pay $24,999 for this prospect. Why not? When you buy the prospect two states of the world will exist: you win or lose. Let your initial wealth before the coin flip be W_0. This gives

	Lose (State 1)	*Win (State 2)*
Net gain	−$24,999	$25,001
Wealth	W_0 − $24,999	W_0 + $25,001

Your wealth is lower in the state of the world in which you lose. If your marginal utility of income declines with income you will value additional dollars more in the state of the world in which you are poorer. Let us suppose, for example, that when your wealth is in the poorer state the utility of each marginal dollar is, in fact, worth $1.00. But, when you are in the wealthier state the utility of each additional dollar is worth 80 percent of what it would be in the poorer state. In this situation you would value the two states as follows:

	Lose	*Win*
Dollar gain	−$24,999	$25,001
Weight	1.00	0.80
Weight value	−$24,999	+$20,001

The expected worth of the prospect to you after the dollar gains or losses are weighted to account for the change in your marginal utility of income would just be $(0.50)(-\$24,999) + (0.50)(\$20,0001) = -\$2499$, a negative amount.

Risk Neutrality: When the marginal utility of income is constant as income changes the individual is said to be risk neutral.

In this situation the individual would pay $24,999 for the prospect of a 50 percent chance of winning $50,000.

Risk Preferring: When the individual's marginal utility of income increases with income, the individual is said to be risk preferring.

Most examples of apparent risk preference by an individual are not examples of risk preference as defined here but instead are examples of utility associated with the undertaking of risk as with an existing bet. Suppose you are willing to bet $1.00 on a one in 10 million chance to win $1,000,000. The expected value of the bet is a negative $0.90. A risk-neutral person would only be willing to bet $0.10, not $1.00 in the absence of utility arising from the gamble itself. Would a person who buys a lottery ticket for $1.00 with this kind of odds be risk preferring?

15.5 EXPECTED UTILITY

We have seen that the expected value of a project may not give the correct valuation of the project for an individual who is risk averse. Let us consider another measure. This is expected utility. The expected utility weights the expected dollar benefits not only by their probability but also by the marginal utility of income.

Consider the situation of a risk-averse individual who wishes to maximize his expected utility in an uncertain world. Suppose there are two mutually exclusive states of the world X and Y. An individual believes that the probability that state X will occur is p and that Y will occur is $(1 - p)$. A project provides a benefit to the individual of B_X if state X exists and B_Y if state Y exists. (State X might be that it rains this week and the individual is a farmer.) The benefits could be negative or positive. The expected monetary gain is the expected value and is $\text{ExV} = pB_X + (1 - p)B_Y$. If we assume the convenience that the utility of the expected value is 1 (Section 15.3.4.), the above expression also expresses the utility of expected value so that $\text{U(ExV)} = pB_X + (1 - p)B_Y$.

The change in expected utility as contrasted with the utility of expected value, however, depends not only on the monetary gain but on how the different parts of this gain are valued in the different states of the world.

The expected utility will be

$$EU = pU(W_X) + (1 - p)U(W_Y) \tag{15.7}$$

A project will cause a *change* in expected utility. This will, approximately, be given by

$$\Delta EU = pB_X MU(W_X) + (1 - p)B_Y MU(W_Y) \tag{15.8}$$

where p is the probability of state X, MU is the marginal utility of income, W_X is wealth in state X, and W_Y is wealth in state Y. This measure takes into account the marginal utility of income in different states of the world. The change in expected utility, ΔEU, will equal the utility of the expected value,[2] U(EV), when $MU(W_X) = MU(W_Y)$. This will occur when $W_X = W_Y$, or when MU is not a function of wealth. W_X will be approximately equal to W_Y when two conditions are met. These are that (1) the changes in wealth caused by undertaking the project are small, and (2) the wealth level is independent of the states of the world given that the project is *not* undertaken (independence).

---

[2]Notice that we compare the utility of expected value with expected utility. We don't attempt to compare expected value alone with expected utility. This is because the standard treatment is to treat a utility function multiplied by a positive constant as equivalent to the original unmultiplied function. Expected values would be invariant to the utility function but expected utility could depend on the arbitrary multiplier as would the utility of expected values so that these latter two can be compared.

Both of these conditions can be summarized by saying that: *wealth cannot significantly differ across the various probable states of the world being evaluated for the change in the utility of ExV to equal the change in EU.*

Consider the first condition. A chance of winning $0.05 if a coin toss is heads or losing $0.05 if a coin toss is tails has an expected value of zero. For most people, the change in expected utility and the expected value will both be zero or close to it, aside from utility arising from the act of gambling.

Suppose, however, the gamble involves $50,000 rather than $0.05. That is, the gambler wins $50,000 on heads but loses $50,000 on tails. For most people, this gamble would have a negative expected utility because they are risk averse: They would require a payment to take the bet. (What payment would you require?)

To understand the independence (second) condition consider an individual, Robert Riley, who is considering building a new apartment building next to an already existing apartment building he owns near the university. If the university expands, state of the world X, Robert will benefit even without the new building. His wealth from the project with the university expansion would be $(W_0 + W_X + B_X)$ where W_0 is initial wealth, and W_X is the addition to wealth from the old building provided by the university expansion even if the *new* building is not built. The term B_X represents Robert's additional wealth from the new apartment building when the university expands. When the project is undertaken, but there is no university expansion, Robert's wealth will be $W_0 + B_Y$, where B_Y is the net benefit from the new apartment building project without the university expansion. The probability of the university expanding is P and the expected utility of the project will then be

$$\Delta EU = pB_X MU_1(W_0 + W_X + B_X) + (1 - p)B_Y MU_2(W_0 + B_Y) \qquad (15.9)$$

Notice the wealth in the two states will differ even if the benefits from the project are small so that B_X and B_Y are small. Notice in fact that wealth will differ even if the magnitude of dollar benefits are unaffected by the two states of the world so that $B_X = B_Y$. The marginal utility weight can differ because of the difference in wealth represented by W_X, the additional wealth caused by the university expansion even without the new apartment project. As long as $W_X + B_X$ is substantially greater than B_Y, the wealth will differ substantially in the two states of the world and the marginal utility weight may also differ. Thus the marginal utility weights for evaluating a project can differ because wealth may differ in two states of the world even though the wealth produced by the project itself does not differ in the states of the world.

Expected values are relatively easy to measure and expected utilities are difficult to measure unless the two conditions just outlined are met that make expected utility equal to expected value. The basic condition is that wealth must be about the same in the states of the world over which the project must be considered. Significant changes in wealth can, however, occur whenever the project itself causes the wealth of individuals to change significantly depending on the state of the world, or when wealth will materially change, even in the absence of the project, depending on the states of the world.

This means that declining marginal utility of income requires that the expected utility will be less than the utility of expected value when wealth changes

Figure 15.1.   The differences between expected utility and the utility of the expected value.

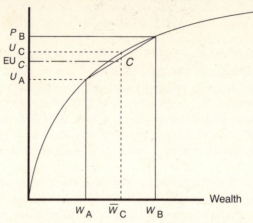

are significant. Declining marginal utility of income implies risk aversion so another way to say this is that risk aversion implies that expected utility will be less than the utility of expected value when wealth changes are significant. To see this consider Figure 15.1. This figure shows a utility function that exhibits declining marginal utility of income. The vertical axis measures the utility of outcomes. The utility of outcome A is U_A and the utility of outcome B is U_B. If A and B are equally probable, the expected utility will be $(U_A + U_B)/2$. The expected utility of A and B will be given by point C that bisects the straight line connecting A and B. The utility of the expected value, however, is given by U_C on the utility curve. Clearly $U_C > (U_A + U_B)/2$. That is, the utility of the expected value will be greater than expected utility.

We can ask the question, what is the smallest certain amount that we would accept in lieu of some gamble? The certain amount you would accept is the *certainty equivalent* of the gamble (see Chapter 16). For example, we could ask, what is the certainty equivalent of a half chance of obtaining $1000? The expected value of the prospect is $500, but with risk aversion the certainty equivalent would be less.

15.6   THE THEORY OF EXPECTED UTILITY

John von Neuman and Oscar Morgenstern in their classic book, *The Theory of Games and Economic Behavior*, set out the conditions under which expected utility will explain choices. The authors develop a set of axioms that underlie the hypothesis that individuals maximize expected utility.[3] Suppose that there are n possible prizes to a lottery and that these are designated by $X_1, X_2, \ldots, X_n$. Furthermore, the value of these prizes is listed in ascending order so that X_1 is the least valuable and X_n is the most valuable. For convenience, we assign arbitrary values to X_1 and to X_n, such that $X_1 = 0$ and $X_n = 1$. Von

---

[3] For a discussion of the axioms and the debates over them see Machina (1987).

Neumann and Morgenstern express the value of some intermediate prize X_i in terms of a gamble involving X_1 and X_n. That is, the gamble is expressed as a certainty equivalent. The most important axioms of the theory require the assumptions of (1) transitivity, (2) continuity, and (3) independence. Transitivity requires that if A is preferred to B and B to C then A will be preferred to C. The axiom of continuity is not important for our purposes (for further information on this and other axioms, see Billingsley, 1968). The independence axiom can be simply stated as requiring that if A > B (read A is preferred to B) then $pA > pB$. [More formally, it states that A > B if and only if $pA + (1 - p)C > pB + (1 - p)C$.]

Von Neumann and Morgenstern ask what is the probability p, of winning X_n that you will regard as equivalent to gaining X_i with certainty? (Note the chances of winning zero, that is, X_1, would be $1 - p$.) *That is, von Neumann and Morgenstern assume that every gamble has a certainty equivalent.* This seems reasonable in that it seems an individual would take a gamble for a larger amount rather than a smaller certain amount as long as the probability of winning the gamble was sufficiently high. Take an extreme case. Suppose that you are given a choice between keeping *all* your wealth on the one hand and doubling your wealth or losing it all on the other. Is there some probability of winning the gamble at which you would undertake it? Would you undertake it at a p of .9999, at a p of .999999, etc.?

Von Neuman and Morgenstern assume that the answer is yes. The von Neumann and Morgenstern technique is then to express the value of X_1 as

$$U(X_i) = p_i U(X_n) + (1 - p_i)X_1 \qquad (15.10)$$

Since we have assumed that $X_n = 1$ and $X_1 = 0$, the above may be conveniently expressed as

$$U(X_i) = p_i \qquad (15.11)$$

Using the von Neumann and Morgenstern formulation, it is possible to show that the individual will prefer the gamble which has the highest expected utility.[4] Thus, in those situations in which it may be assumed that the von Neumann and Morgenstern axioms reasonably hold, we can speak of individuals maximizing expected utility.

15.7.   MEASURING RISK

15.7.1.   A Definition of a Risky Project

A project is said to be risky when its expected utility is less than its expected value. We will show that this occurs when the returns to a prospect vary with the state of the world and when the marginal utility of income declines with income. Table 15.1 shows the distribution of returns for three projects according to three states of the world. (For simplicity, the example assumes that the relevant discount rate is 0 so we do not need to worry about discounted values.) Each state of the world has an identical probability. All three projects

---

[4]For a simple demonstration of this, see W. P. Nicholson, *Microeconomic Theory*, 4th ed. New York: Dryden Press, 1989, pp. 248–250.

TABLE 15.1

Projects	A	B	C
Cost	−$100	−$100	−$100
Returns			
State 1	$250	$120	$108
State 2	60	105	107
State 3	11	96	106

have the same expected value. The expected value of benefits is $107, and the expected value of cost is $100, so that the NPV of each is $7.00.

Which one is better? The expected *utility* of project A is as follows:

$$EU_A = - 100MU(W_0) + \tfrac{1}{3}(250)MU(W_0 + 250)$$
$$+ \tfrac{1}{3}(60)MU(W_0 + 60) + \tfrac{1}{3}(11)(W_0 + 11)$$

This equation shows the expected utility of the cost of the project at the initial level of wealth, plus the utility of the outcome of the project at the resulting levels of wealth. Similar expressions can be written for projects B and C and these can be simplified to give the following for the three projects:

1. $EU_A = -100MU(W_0) + 83.3MU(W_0 + 250) + 20MU(W_0 + 60)$
   $+ 3.7MU(W_0 + 11)$
2. $EU_B = -100MU(W_0) + 40MU(W_0 + 120) + 35MU(W_0 + 105)$
   $+ 32MU(W_0 + 96)$
3. $EU_C = -100MU(W_0) + 36MU(W_0 + 108) + 35.67MU(W_0 + 107)$
   $+ 35.33MU(W_0 + 106)$

We wish to determine which of these projects has the higher expected utility. Consider first the difference between the expected utility for project A and that for project B. We will show that project B has the higher expected utility. The $100 cost is evaluated at the same wealth level in both cases so this is equal for the two projects. The last two states of the world yield a surplus for project B over project A of 15 plus 28.33 or 43.33. This is just equal to its surplus for project A over B in the first state of the world. However, the 43.33 surplus for project A is evaluated at a higher wealth level (W_0 + $250) than is the case for project B. The 43.33 surplus for project B in the latter two states of the world is partly evaluated at the initial wealth level plus $105 and partly at the initial wealth level plus $90. We assume that the marginal utility of income is higher for lower levels of wealth. *The surplus for B in the latter two states of the world is evaluated at a lower wealth level than the equal surplus for project A in the first state of the world. This being the case, the expected utility of project B must be higher than for project A, given diminishing marginal utility of income.* To recapitulate, both projects A and B Have the same expected value. Project A is superior, however, in the first state of the world and project B is superior in the two other states by the same dollar amount. The *value* of the additional earnings of project B in the latter two states of the world is higher than the value of the equal additional earnings of project A in the first state of the world. Why is this? The additional earnings of project B are evaluated when wealth is lower than when the additional earnings of project A are evaluated. Therefore, the marginal utility weights given to project B earnings in states 2 and 3 are greater than the weight given to project A's earnings in state 1. The result is that the expected utility of project A but not the expected value of A is less than for project B.

A similar analysis shows that the expected utility of C is higher than B (the student might work this out). Thus project C is the least risky project because its expected utility is a higher percentage of its expected value than are projects A or B. This suggests the following rule that is extremely important in risk evaluation: *The expected utility as a percent of expected value decreases with the greater variability of the returns.* Consider the following illustrative example:

Projects	A	B	C
Probability			
$\frac{1}{3}$	100	120	150
$\frac{1}{3}$	100	100	100
$\frac{1}{3}$	100	80	50

Project A has no variability. The marginal utility of income weights given to the returns are the same in each state of the world because wealth is the same in each state of the world. Project B has the same expected value as A but must have lower expected utility than A. This is because when the returns of A are surplus over B they are valued at a lower wealth level (with higher marginal utility weights) than when the returns to B are in surplus. Project C has more variable returns than either A or B, and its expected utility will be a smaller percentage of its expected value than in the case of A or B. Thus, project C has the greatest variability and has the lowest expected utility relative to its expected value.

For most people it will be more intuitive to examine the relationship between risk and expected utility diagrammatically. Figure 15.2 shows a utility function that is concave and that therefore exhibits diminishing marginal utility of wealth. This figure can be used to show why a risk-averse individual, faced with the choice between two prospects, will choose the one with less variability. If an individual has diminishing marginal utility of wealth, he will exhibit risk aversion. Suppose that an individual with wealth of W_0, and therefore with utility of $U(W_0)$, is offered a choice between a prospect (gamble 1) in which he has a fifty-fifty chance of winning or losing X, and another prospect (gamble 2) with a fifty-fifty chance of winning or losing $2X$. The expected utility of gamble 1 will be

$$E[U(X)] = \tfrac{1}{2}[U(W_0 + X)] + \tfrac{1}{2}[U(W_0 - X)] \qquad (15.12)$$

The expected utility of gamble 2 will be

$$E[U(2X)] = \tfrac{1}{2}[U(W_0 + 2X)] + \tfrac{1}{2}[U(W_0 - 2X)] \qquad (15.13)$$

Figure 15.2.   Less variability is preferred with risk aversion.

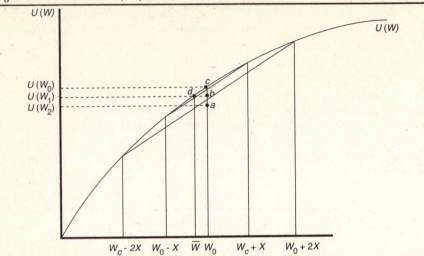

These expressions indicate that the expected utility of each of the gambles is the average utility of the two positions in each of the gambles. Thus the expected utility of gamble 1 will be the average of $U(W_0 + X)$ and $U(W_0 - X)$. From Figure 15.2 it is apparent that the average of these two utilities will be given along a straight line connecting these two utilities at the average wealth, which is just W_0. Similarly the average utility of gamble 2, which has the greater variance, is given by the straight line connecting the two alternative wealth positions associated with gamble 2 at the average wealth which again is W_0. By inspection, the utility of gamble 1 with the smaller variance is greater than the utility of gamble 2. The convexity of the utility function ensures that the average utility of a gamble with greater variance will lie below a gamble with less variance but with the same expected wealth. Clearly, any gambles with an average wealth of W_0 will show an expected utility that is smaller the greater the variance of the gamble. It is clear from Figure 15.2 that the individual will prefer his current wealth with certainty and utility level $U(W_0)$ to either gamble 1 or 2. Figure 15.2 shows that in terms of utility a wealth level $\overline{W}$ with certainty is equivalent to gamble 1 that yields an average of wealth level W_0. The difference between W_0 and $\overline{W}$ represents the amount the individual would pay for insurance that allowed him to avoid gamble 1.

15.7.2.   Measuring Risk Aversion

Often it is useful to have a measure of risk aversion. The most commonly used measure was originally developed by J. W. Pratt in the 1960s. This measure defines risk aversion as

$$\text{Risk}(W) = \frac{-U''(W)}{U'(W)} \tag{15.14}$$

where W is wealth. The term $U'(W)$ is the marginal utility of wealth (the derivative of the utility function with respect to wealth). The term $U''(W)$ represents the rate of change in the marginal utility of wealth. This term will

TECHNICAL NOTE 15A
Difficulties with Expected Utility Theory

The expected utility theory is the dominant theory of choice under conditions of uncertainty. The expected utility model was developed by Ramsey (1931) and by von Neumann and Morgenstern (1944) and by others in the late 1930s and early 1940s. Previously economists have often viewed this model as a sort of logical tautological delineation of choice requirements, that is, as the only form of "rational" behavior under uncertainty, rather than as a refutable scientific hypothesis to be judged against competing theories.

In the last twenty years, however, empirical research, especially by psychologists, has shown consistent choice results that conflict with the predictions of the model. Consider the following example in which you have a choice of C_1 or C_2 and of C_3 or C_4:

Choices		Expected Values
C_1 or	90% chance of $3000	2700
C_2	45% chance of $6000	2700
and		
C_3 or	0.2% chance of $3000	6
C_4	0.1% chance of $6000	6

The expected utility theory suggests that choice C_1 and choice C_3 would be preferred if the marginal utility of money declines with wealth. The expected values of C_1 and C_2 are the same as are the expected values of C_3 and C_4. But, when C_2 and C_4 are successful, wealth is greater than when C_1 and C_3 are successful so that the expected utility of C_1 or C_3 is greater than the expected utility of C_2 or C_4, as long as the marginal utility of money declines. If, however, the marginal utility of income increases with wealth the choice will be C_2 and C_4. In any case the choice would not be C_1 and C_4 or C_2 and C_3, which would violate the independence axiom. That is, these choices would imply that the marginal utility of income is both declining and increasing with income. Kahneman and Tversky in 1979, however, found in a series of empirical experiments, that while 86 percent of the subjects preferred C_1 to C_2, 73 percent preferred C_4 to C_3. The choice of C_4 over C_3 appears to conflict with the assumption that the marginal utility of wealth declines, but the truly unsettling choice to theoreticians[5] is that of C_1 combined with C_4. This type of violation is called the "common ratio" effect (and also the "certainty effect" and the "Berger paradox"). This effect appears to violate the independence axiom of expected utility theory. This is not the only type of systematic violation of the expected utility theory that has been found.

---

[5]Most people, however, intuitively understand the human tendency to ignore differences among small probabilities and to go for the larger pay-off possibility. A better-performing utility theory would incorporate an assumption to this effect.

be negative if the marginal utility of wealth declines with wealth. If the marginal utility of income is positive the denominator will be positive, and this is divided by a negative numerator. Thus, the negative sign in front of the expression makes the Pratt measure of risk aversion positive. Equation (15.14) gives an *absolute* measure of risk aversion. This can also be expressed as a measure of *relative* risk aversion by multiplying the level of absolute risk aversion by wealth:

$$\text{Relative risk aversion} = \frac{-WU''(W)}{U'(W)} \qquad (15.15)$$

An attractive feature of the Pratt measure is that it can be shown to be proportional to the amount an individual will pay for insurance to prevent losing a fair bet. Consider a bet in which you will gain $1000 if a fair coin turns up heads and you will lose $1000 if the coin turns up tails. If for some reason you are committed to this bet, but could pay to avoid the risk of the bet, the amount you would pay is the insurance premium that pays you $1000 if you lose the bet. This premium will be approximately $kU''(W)/U'(W)$ where k is a constant.[6]

15.7.3. Regret Theory

Although it is too early to tell with certainty we suspect that *regret theory* will prove to offer a method of reconciling some of the existing conflicts between experimental results and expected utility theory. Regret theory is a natural generalization of expected utility theory to an intransitive world. Regret theory suggests that your satisfaction will be determined not only by the payoff C_1 but by the payoff D_1 that you would have received if you had chosen D. If D_1 is greater than C_1, you will experience regret. If C_1 is greater than D_1, you will experience extra satisfaction. Consider the following example.

---

[6] k is a term in a Taylor series expansion. Suppose that we are considering a bet that involves a sum h and that the bet is fair so that the expected value of h is zero, $E(h) = 0$. Let p be the insurance premium that would make the individual indifferent between taking the bet and paying the premium. Then:

$$E[U(W + h)] = U[W - p]$$

The Taylor series expansion gives for the left-hand side of the equation:

$$E[U(W + h) = E[U(W) + hU'(W) + h^2 U''(W) + \text{ higher-order terms}]$$

The right-hand side of the equation becomes

$$U(W - p) = U(W) - pU'(W) + \text{ higher-order terms}$$

Setting the terms for the left-hand side equal to those for the right-hand side, recalling that $E(h) = 0$, and letting the term $E(h^2)/2 = k$, for convenience, and dropping the higher terms, gives

$$U(W) - pU'(W) = U(W) + kU''(W)$$

or

$$p = -\frac{kU''(W)}{U'(W)} = \text{Pratt's measure of relative risk aversion}$$

You are considering giving as a birthday gift either $5 cash or a $5 lottery ticket which you already have purchased. If the lottery ticket is the winning ticket, it pays $2,000,000. The two states of the world are that either the lottery ticket is the winning one or it is not. If state 1 of the world occurs so that your ticket is the winning one, and your decision was to keep the ticket and to give cash, your payoff is C_1 and your regret is D_1. If you choose to give the lottery ticket and state 1 occurred, your payoff is D_1 or the $5.00 in cash you saved, and your regret is C_1 or $2,000,000. In making your decision would you consider the possibility of your regret at giving away the winning ticket? Would you feel the same about giving your acquaintance the winning ticket as if he uses your $5 to buy the winning ticket?[7]

This brief excursion into regret theory is meant merely to whet your appetite. Regret theory accounts for the common ratio effect noted earlier as well as most other violations of expected utility theory. One way of interpreting regret theory is not as a violation of the general principle that individuals maximize expected utility, but rather as a statement about the particular form of an individual's utility function. For further elaboration of regret theory see Loomes and Sugden (1982).

15.8.   THE STANDARD DEVIATION AND VARIANCE

In practice risk is measured by expected variability in outcomes. If one prospect is more variable than another it is said to be more risky. We turn now to the question of how to measure variability.

The standard statistical measures of variability or spread are *variance* and *standard deviation.*[8] *The variance of expected returns is the expected squared deviation from the average return.* That is, the *variance S^2* of returns is

$$S^2 = \text{expected value of } \sum_i p_i(r_i - \bar{r})^2 \tag{15.16}$$

where r_i is the ith expected return, $\bar{r}$ is the average return, and p_i is the probability of the ith return. The standard deviation is the square root of the variance, or

$$S = (\text{variance})^{1/2} \tag{15.17}$$

---

[7]Might regret theory be useful in explaining a phenomena that has puzzled one of the authors? Many of us experience a situation where we feel we would be better off with fewer choices. Could it be possible that we might be better off with fewer choices? It seems at first that it could not. Even though one is given an expanded range of choices, one could always choose to limit the number of choices to the original set. Thus, it can be strongly argued that we could not be worse off with fewer choices. Yet, it seems that given an additional choice we often wish to consider it even though the cost of decision making associated with consideration of the choice is greater than the expected value of the choice. There is some probability that the new choice would be very valuable and our regret would be very high if we failed to consider an available option and that option later turned out to be very valuable. Thus, we may actually wish for fewer choices.

[8]The variance is a proper measure of risk when the associated distributions are distributed normally. A little experimentation by the reader will indicate that when distributions are distributed quite unsymmetrically the variance will not be such a good measure.

EXAMPLE 15.3

Calculating Variance and Standard Deviation

Suppose you invest $100 in a gamble that involves two coin flips. For each tail, you get back your starting balance plus 25 percent. For each head you get back your starting balance minus 10 percent. There are four possible equally likely outcomes as follows:

1. Tail and tail gain $50
2. Tail and head gain $15
3. Head and tail gain $15
4. Head and head lose $20

The expected average return is the sum of the returns from each state of the world times the probability of that state. This weighted average outcome is

Expected return = 0.25($50) + 0.5($15) + 0.25(−$20) = $15

The variance and standard deviation can be calculated as follows:

Return Dollars	Deviation from Average	Squared Dollars	Probability	Weighted
+50	+35	1225	0.25	306.25
+15	0	0	0.50	0
−20	−35	1225	0.25	306.25
				612.50

Variance = $612.50

Standard deviation = ($612.50)$^{1/2}$ = $24.75

15.9.   RISK TO A PORTFOLIO: FINANCIAL RISK

Our model is that of an individual who wishes to maximize utility subject to constraints. Utility is a function of goods and services. The individual in considering prospects with future rewards and costs will value equal future goods and services differently depending on different states of the world. We assume that the individual is risk averse so that he will value a given increment to his wealth less when his wealth is greater. (This proposition becomes more problematic when, as in previous chapters, we use the term wealth quite broadly. My utility may be a function of money income but also reports about the fortune of my children. The value of an additional increment to my money income may be greater when I have heard good reports of my children so that my wealth is greater, in which case the marginal utility of money increases with wealth at least when wealth is in the form of good reports about my children.)

In general, the value placed on a risky prospect will depend on its returns in the different states of the world *and by how these returns vary with*

EXAMPLE 15.4

As in the previous example you invest $100 on the outcome of the two coin flips. Now, however, you receive your investment plus a 40 percent return on a tail outcome and your investment minus 25 percent return on a head outcome. The four equally likely outcomes are

Outcomes	Rate of Return
Tail and tail	80%
Tail and head	15%
Head and tail	15%
Head and head	−50%

The expected return is 15 percent as in the previous example. The variance, however, is $2112.5 and the standard deviation is $45.96. The standard deviation is about twice that of the previous example. By the measure of the standard deviation then this second investment is twice as risky as the first bet.

---

wealth. That is, the risk to the investor is not determined by just the variance or standard deviation of a simple investment unless this is the investor's only investment. Rather, the investor is interested in the variability of the *entire* investment portfolio of wealth. A new investment whose returns are variable might nonetheless actually *decrease* the variance of the portfolio because returns from the new investment vary so as to offset the variability in returns to other investments in the portfolio. It is then the variance of portfolio returns that are of interest. *From both the individual and the social standpoint one is interested in how the returns from the project or investment affect the variability of total income. From a national point of view, then, variability of national income is of interest.*

The variability of returns in a portfolio will depend on the variability of returns of the investments in it and on how the investments vary in relationship with each other. A portfolio of investments whose returns are negatively related, so that when returns from one of the investments in the portfolio are up the returns from another investment are down, would clearly have less variable returns to the total portfolio than one whose returns were positively correlated and whose returns therefore moved together.

The extent to which returns from different investments vary with each other is shown by the covariance. The covariance of two investments is the product of the correlation coefficient, r_{12}, and the two standard deviations for the investments:

$$\text{Covariance} = r_{12}S_1S_2 \qquad (15.18)$$

The correlation coefficient is a measure of the extent to which variables move together. It varies from −1 to +1. A correlation coefficient of +1 means the

EXAMPLE 15.5

Suppose 30 percent of an investment is in a project whose expected return is 20 percent. The past standard deviation of returns for this investment was 40. The remaining 70 percent is invested in another project with an expected return of 15 percent and a past standard deviation of 25. The correlation coefficient between returns for these two investments is +0.60. Assume that their past variances are reasonable guides to the future. What is the average expected return and what is the standard deviation for the portfolio of two investments? The average expected return would just be the weighted average of the expected returns of the two investments or 0.3(20%) + 0.7(15%) = 16.5%. The portfolio variance is

$$\text{Portfolio variance (pv)} = W_1^2 S_1^2 + W_2^2 S_2^2 + 2(W_1 W_2 r_{12} S_1 S_2)$$

Filling in the relevant numbers gives

$$pv = (0.3 \times 40)^2 + (0.7 \times 25)^2 + 2(0.3 \times 0.7)(0.6)(40)(25)$$
$$= 144 + 306.25 + 252 = 702.25$$

The standard deviation is then the square root of this, or 26.5. Notice that the portfolio standard deviation is less than the simple average of the standard deviations of the two investments that make up the portfolio.[9]

This interesting fact arises from the relationship between diversification and risk.

variables move exactly together. A correlation coefficient of 0 means there is no relationship between the variables so that the covariance is 0. A correlation coefficient of -1 means the variables move together perfectly but in opposite directions. Since the correlation coefficient can be either positive or negative, so can the covariance. As we have said, for an investor with several investments, what is of interest is the variability of the whole portfolio of investments. This is as true for governments as for corporations or for individuals.

The portfolio variance is influenced both by the variance of the investments and their covariance as follows for a two-item portfolio:

$$\text{Portfolio variance} = W_1^2 S_1^2 + W_2^2 S_2^2 + 2(W_1 W_2 r_{12} S_1 S_2) \qquad (15.19)$$

where W_1 represents the proportion of the first investment to the total portfolio, W_2 the proportion of the second investment to the portfolio, r_{12} the correlation coefficient between investments 1 and 2, and S_1 and S_2 the standard deviations for investments 1 and 2.

15.10. DIVERSIFICATION REDUCES RISK

The standard deviation of a portfolio will always be less than the weighted average of the individual standard deviations, unless the correlation coefficient is $+1$, meaning the returns from the two investments are perfectly correlated and

---

[9]The weighted average standard deviation of a portfolio with two investments will be *greater than* the portfolio standard deviation. This can be shown by comparing the expression for the weighted average variance with the portfolio variance.

therefore move exactly together. The fact that the returns don't move together perfectly reduces the variance of the portfolio. The weighted average of the standard deviation in the previous example is $(0.30 \times 40) + (0.70 \times 25) = 29.5$. Notice this is greater than the portfolio standard deviation of 26.5. Suppose, in our example, that the correlation coefficient were $+1$ instead of $+.060$. We would have

$$\text{Var (portfolio)} = (0.30)^2(40)^2 + (0.70)^2(25)^2 + 2(0.3 \times 0.7)(1)(40)(25)$$
$$= 144 + 306.25 + 420 = 870.25$$

SD (portfolio) = 29.5

This is the same as the weighted average standard deviation.

As the number of investments increases the covariance becomes more important by comparison with the variance. This can be seen by examining the general formula for portfolio variance. This is just an extension of the formula for two investments.[10] This is[11]

$$\text{Portfolio variance} = \sum_i \sum_j W_i W_j S_i r_{ij} S_j \qquad (15.20)$$

If there are N investments there will be N individual variances and therefore N variance terms in the formula. There will be two covariances for each combination of two investments. This can be seen by spelling out Equation (15.20).

As Equation (15.20) indicates, the variance of a portfolio of N stocks will be found by adding up the variance and covariance terms of the N investments. Figure 15.3, borrowed from Brealy and Myers (1984), is useful in seeing this. The diagonal terms show the variance weighted by the square of the proportion invested. The other boxes show the covariance between the pair of securities shown weighted by the product of the proportions invested. Clearly the total number of combinations is N^2. The variance terms are represented by the diagonal and there are N of these. The remaining terms are all covariance terms and there will be N^2 of them minus the number of variance terms or $N^2 - N$. Notice that when N is 1 the number of variance terms is 1 and the number of covariance terms is 0. When N is 2 the number of variance terms is 2 and the number of covariance terms is also 2. When N is 8, however, the number of covariance terms is 56 and the number of variance terms is just 3. *Because the number of covariance terms greatly exceeds the number of variance terms when the number of investments is not small, the covariance dominates the portfolio variance when there are more than a few investments.*

---

[10]For example, with two investments, Equation (15.20) would give the following terms:

$$\text{Portfolio variance} = W_i W_i S_1 S_1 + W_1 W_2 r_{12} S_1 S_2 + W_2 W_1 r_{12} S_2 S_1 + W_2 W_2 S_2 S_2$$

Collecting terms gives

$$\text{Portfolio variance} = W_1^2 S_1^2 + W_2^2 S_2^2 + 2(W_1 W_2 S_1 S_2)$$

[11]When $i = j$, $r = 1$, and $W_i = W_j = 1$, Equation (15.20) just gives the variance of the investment.

Example 15.6

What is the expected return and standard deviation for a portfolio consisting of three investments with the following characteristics?

	A	B	C
Portion invested	0.50	0.30	0.20
Expected return	0.10	0.20	0.30
Standard deviation	20	25	30

where $r_{AB} = .5$, $r_{AC} = 0.3$, and $r_{BC} = 0.2$.
  The expected return will be

$$0.5(10\%) + 0.3(20\%) + 0.2(30\%) = 18\%$$

The portfolio variance will be

$$V = (0.5)^2(20)^2 + (0.3)^2(25)^2 + (0.2)^2(30)^2 + 2(0.5)(0.3)(0.5)(20)(25)$$
$$+ 2(0.5)(0.2)(0.3)(20)(30) + 2(0.3)(0.2)(0.2)(25)(30)$$
$$= 321.25$$
$$SD = (321.25)^{1/2} = 17.9$$

Notice that this is *less than* the standard deviation of any of the three investments.

Figure 15.3.   Variance of a portfolio with N investments.

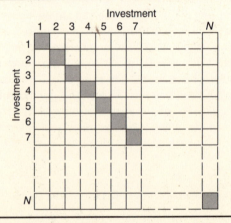

EXAMPLE 15.7

Suppose three investments Have the same variances and covariances as in Example 15.4 but that each investment counts for $\frac{1}{3}$ of the portfolio. What is the relative contribution of the average variance and covariance?

The average variance is $0.33[(20)^2+(25)^2+(30)^2]$ or 641.67. The average covariance will be $0.33[(20)(25) + (0.3)(20)(30) + (0.2)(25)(30)]$ or 193.33. The portfolio variance will be

$$V = \tfrac{1}{3}(641.67) + \tfrac{2}{3}(193.33) = 342.78$$

The portfolio variance is closer to the average covariance than to the average variance even with only three investments in the portfolio. The covariance receives twice the weight of the variance. If a portfolio with the above variances and covariances contained ten investments equal in amount the portfolio variance would be about 238, considerably closer to the average covariance than to the average variance. The covariance receives a weight 9 times greater than the variance.

As more investments are added to the portfolio the covariances become of increasing importance relative to the variances of the individual securities. As N increases the portfolio variance is dominated by the variance. The weight given to the average covariance in determining the portfolio variance will be $(N - 1)$ times the weight given to the average covariance. If, for example, N were 100 the influence of the average covariance would be 99 times that of the average variance. For an N of 11, the average covariance is 10 times as important as the average variance.

15.11. LIMITS TO RISK REDUCTION

Clearly for a well-diversified portfolio the risk can be reduced to that determined by the covariances. Experiments have been performed in which portfolios of different sizes have been formed from samples of stocks and the standard deviation of stock prices has been calculated for each portfolio. Their general results are shown below in Figure 15.4 [see Brealy and Myers (1984, Fig. 7.3)]. Diversification reduces the portfolio variance greatly at first and then quite slowly. Most of the benefit in risk reduction occurs with relatively few stocks (say eight).

If the correlation coefficients between investments were negative it would be possible to eliminate risk. Even if correlation coefficients were 0, increased diversification would reduce risk toward 0 as the covariance terms (which would be 0) receive greater weight with increased diversification. Unfortunately, the returns of most investments are positively related to the general state of the economy so that the correlation coefficients are positive and therefore so are the covariances.

In practice it is not as a general rule possible to eliminate all risk, that is, eliminate all variability in outcomes. The risk that can be eliminated by diversi-

Figure 15.4. Diversification reduces unique risk.

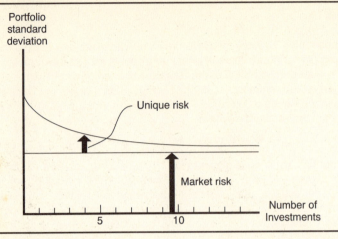

fication is called *unique risk*. Unique risk arises from the uncertainty of returns that are peculiar to a few companies or to a few projects. Sufficient diversification eliminates this risk because in a diversified portfolio the peculiarities of individual companies or projects are no longer important. Diversification, however, still leaves you with risk.

The level of risk remaining after all unique risk is eliminated by diversification is called *market risk*. Market risk exists because there are general economic forces that affect to some extent almost all projects. This is why the values of stock returns for the market of all companies tend to move together.

15.12. THE PORTFOLIO FOR PUBLIC PROJECTS

In considering the risk to a potential public project, one must specify the elements that enter into the utility function and how the returns to the proposed project might then be expected to vary with returns to a portfolio containing these elements, that is, the covariance between the project and the relevant portfolio. One can consider the project from the standpoint of the individuals that are expected to be affected by the project. If these individuals hold portfolios of assets with similar variances then it is possible to consider a single portfolio. One assumption might be that most individuals generally are able to diversify their investments so that they are left with only market risk. That is, their wealth will generally vary directly with swings in the national economy. In fact, given the increased ability to invest internationally, it may be the international economy that is the relevant portfolio. Of course, residents of a particular city will have some assets whose values vary with the national economy, such as a job, and some whose values vary directly with the local or with the state economy, such as a house. The variance in wealth for a local economy may be in large part influenced by the same forces that affect the national economy. *In general, there will be some purely local component of a representative portfolio of assets for inhabitants of one locality.*

Consider a town in Oregon, say Medford, that is contemplating two alternative projects, one involving the tourist industry and the other involving the lumber industry. Suppose that both projects have the same expected value and the same variance, and the same covariance with the national economy. Should Medford be indifferent between the two projects? Medford's economy is closely tied to the timber industry. The asset portfolio of Medford's residents and the portfolio of revenue-generating investments for the city will probably have a local component. In this case, the relevant portfolio of investments to use in determining the risk of the proposed projects also includes a local component. The question is the covariance of the proposed projects with the portfolio that is relevant for Medford. The timber project is likely to have a higher covariance with this portfolio than the tourist project and thus the tourist project is to be preferred, in terms of expected utility.

Another point of view is that of a governmental agency that is primarily interested in the variance in its tax revenues. From this perspective, the portfolio is the tax revenues and indirectly the local economy that gives rise to the tax revenues. Thus, from this point of view also the tourist project is likely to be the better project because it has less covariance with local tax revenues and the same expected value as the timber project.

We return to the Medford project in the next chapter. There we address the issue of practical methods to account for risk in project evaluation. The basis for these methods we have set out in this chapter.

SUMMARY

This chapter addresses questions of the nature of risk and how it affects values under uncertainty. We introduced the concept of expected values and discussed why this concept does not capture values in a world in which the marginal utility of income varies with income. We defined risk aversion, risk neutrality, and risk preference. The von Neumann–Morgenstern theory of expected utility was introduced and we used the theory of expected utility to show the relationship between risk aversion and variance of returns. Finally, we indicated that the variance of interest in project evaluation is portfolio variance. This sets the stage for the introduction for techniques of the incorporation of risk into benefit–cost analysis discussed in the next two chapters.

QUESTIONS AND PROBLEMS

1. As the mayor of Winnipeg, Manitoba, you are considering investing in a public housing project. The value of this project will depend on the future price of housing. The value will be one million when prices are high and will be only half a million if they are low. What is the expected value of the project if the probability of a high price is reckoned at 50 percent?
2. In the Microchip example, Example 15.2, it paid to undertake both alternative projects. Determine what increase in the probability of A succeeding would just result in a choice of A alone rather than A and B.
3. Suppose that Vancouver, British Columbia, is considering the use of a vacant downtown piece of land that it previously purchased as a possible site for a new city hall. The project was abandoned, but Vancouver has retained ownership of the land. This is a quite valuable piece of land and the city is anxious to realize revenue from the

land. The finance director for Vancouver is directed to prepare a report analyzing alternative uses of the land and recommending alternatives. The following report is furnished:

Report of the Finance Director:

Three alternative courses of action have been investigated. These I have labeled options A, B, and C. In order of increasing complexity the three options are as follows:

Option A is the simplest and involves just selling the land. We could sell the land for $8.0 million in year 0.

Options B and C both involve working with a land developer to build a shopping mall. Both of these options require our acquiring abutting land at a cost of $2.0 million. Under option B we would contribute the land but would not contribute to the development costs. Revenues under option B would consist of payments by the developer of $442,500 per year for 50 years, payments to begin upon completion of the mall.

Under option C we would contribute the land and would contribute to development costs with payments of $2.5 million now and $2.5 million upon completion of the project. Revenues from option C would consist of rents from a portion of the shopping mall. Under option C it is my judgment that we could sell our portion of the project upon completion of the project for $12.25 million.

There is substantial uncertainty as to when the mall would be completed. This uncertainty is the main difficulty in assessing the three options. There is no possibility that the mall could be completed during the first year. My assessment is that the chance of completion in year 2 is about 25 percent, in year 3 about 50 percent, and in year 4 about 25 percent. There is no doubt that year 3 is the most likely year for completion. On this basis I have prepared the following tables comparing the net present value of the three options. I have assumed completion of the project during year 3. Our cost of capital, as you know, we reckon at about 6 percent. For a risky venture such as this, however, I believe it would be prudent to assess options B and C at the risk-adjusted interest rate of 8 percent.

Financial Flows (thousands)

Options/Time	0	Year X (Completion of Project)	X + 1 to X + 50
A	+1500		
B	−2000		475.00 per yr
C	−4500	9750	

Present Value at 8% (thousands)

Options	Net Present Value
A	$1500.00
B	2375.19
C	3239.86

Taking into account risk, Table 2 shows clearly that option C is the superior project. Both B and C are superior to immediate sale of the land. Although this is the less risky project, the additional value from adopting option C makes this the most attractive option. It is my recommendation that we adopt option C.

Do you agree with the assessment of the financial officer? Why or why not? Provide your own assessment.

4. Earlier we considered the conditions under which the expected value might be highest if one undertook both projects among two alternatives. Can you derive the conditions under which you would undertake three alternative projects?

REFERENCES

Brealy, R., and S. Myers, *Principles of Corporate Finance,* 2nd ed., New York: McGraw-Hill, 1984.

Graham, D., "Cost Benefit Analysis under Uncertainty," *American Economic Review,* 715–725, 1981.

Lind, R. C., ed., *Discounting for Time and Risk in Energy Policy,* Baltimore, Md.: Johns Hopkins Press, 1982.

Loomes, G., and R. Sugden, "A Rationale for Preference Reversal," *American Economy Review* 73, 428–432, 1982.

Machina, M., "Choice Under Uncertainty: Problems Solved and Unsolved," *The Journal of Economic Perspectives* 1(1), Summer 1987.

Pratt, J. W., "Risk Aversion in the Small and in the Large," *Econometrica,* 122–136, January/April 1964.

Ramsey, F., "Truth and Probability," *Foundations, Mathematics and Other Logical Essays,* London: K. Paul, Trench, Truber and Co., 1931.

von Neumann, J., and O. Morgenstern, *Theory of Games and Economic Behavior,* Princeton, N.J.: Princeton University Press, 1944 (third edition 1953).

16

The Incorporation of Risk into Benefit–Cost Analysis*

16.1. INTRODUCTION

Little if any adjustment for risk is made in the evaluation of public projects. Although in practice the standards for the consideration of risk with respect to private projects are often not particularly high, these standards generally exceed anything that is done for the public sector. We can improve on this state of affairs. Our purpose here is to help the reader to learn to think about risk in a way that allows the incorporation of risk analysis into project evaluation.

We will consider four methods of incorporating risk into benefit–cost analysis. Three of these approaches are based on expected utility and are considered in this chapter. The other approach is the subject of Chapter 17 and consists of a series of techniques for modeling data in a way that is useful for making decisions under uncertainty.

We want to distinguish again between financial risk and uncertainty about outcomes. Uncertainty about outcomes is to be dealt with primarily by calculating expected values. Aside from financial risk, values should be discounted by the standard discount rate (see Chapters 4 and 15). No risk-adjusted discount rates should be used. Where financial risk exists so that differences in the marginal utility of income play a central role, however, we suggest the use of a discount rate that is adjusted to account for the relative riskiness of different projects. This approach is aimed at determining a net present value, NPV, in which the disutility of risk may be said to have been taken into account in some approximate but reasonable way. Most of this chapter is devoted to developing and using risk-adjusted interest rates.

*We would like to thank Jonathan Lesser, Dick Parks, and our reviewers for helpful suggestions.

A second approach considers the ex ante willingness to pay, WTP, for a prospect. The expected value of the EVs or CVs or their proxy, consumer surplus, does not in fact measure the WTP to undertake a risky prospect. This is instead measured by the *option price* or, in a world of complete contingent markets, by the *fair bet price*. These two approaches are based on the theory of expected utility that we have been considering.

A third approach is that of *stochastic dominance*. Here we attempt to say that one project is better than another by considering the results in all states of the world. This approach is also based on the theory of expected utility, but may offer some advantages over the option price approach in certain circumstances.

16.2. A GENERAL MODEL OF RISK ADJUSTMENT: A RISK-ADJUSTED INTEREST RATE

From Chapter 15 we know that the riskiness of a project can be determined by the covariance of the project's return with the relevant portfolio. For public projects, we need to stress that returns mean benefits and costs in the sense of EVs or CVs, and not just financial returns as is the case for private project evaluation.

How is this to be done? Suppose that the Medford Oregon timber and tourist projects, mentioned in Chapter 15, have different expected values, and the projects' returns have different covariances with the relevant portfolio. Suppose that both projects cost $100 today. For now we will say that all the benefits of both projects accrue just one year hence. The timber project has an expected value of $120, the tourist project has an expected value of $115. The covariance of the timber project with the relevant portfolio is 20 and the covariance of the tourist project with the relevant portfolio is 10. Can we combine this information in a way that allows us to say that in a welfare sense, one project is better than another for Medford?

16.2.1. Certainty Equivalents Again

Previously, we introduced the concept of the certainty equivalent of a risky asset. The certainty equivalent is the smallest certain value which you would be willing to trade for the risky asset.

For a one-period case, we know, if we adapt the von Neumann–Morgenstern assumptions, that the PV of a net benefit to be received one period later can be found by discounting the certainty equivalent of the risky benefit by the risk-free rate. That is,

$$PV = \frac{CEQ}{1 + r_f} \tag{16.1}$$

To illustrate this, suppose that you hold the right to a prospect whose expected value is $10,000 to be received one year hence, but the return is risky. You would just be willing to trade this asset for $8000 to be given with certainty one year hence. That is, the $8000 is the certainty equivalent of the $10,000. The present value of the $8000 discounted at the risk-free interest rate must equal the present value of the $10,000 discounted at the risk-adjusted interest rate because the risky $10,000 and the certain $8000 have the same value to you. The present value of $8000 discounted at the risk-free rate of, say, 9 percent, is equal to $8000/1.09 = $7339.45. This can now be used to find the interest rate r that could be used to discount the $10,000 to give the $7339.45 present value as follows:

$$PV = \frac{F}{1 + r} = \frac{CEQ}{1 + r_f} \qquad (16.2)$$

where F is the risky cash flow or benefit, r is the required interest rate, CEQ is the certainty equivalent, and r_f is the risk-free rate of interest.

Solving (16.2) for r gives

$$r = \left[\frac{F}{CEQ}(1 + r_f)\right] - 1 \qquad (16.3)$$

Solving for r in the example given above, using $r = (F/PV) - 1$ gives

$$r = \frac{\$10,000}{\$7339.45} - 1$$

$$= 36\%$$

Clearly in the one-period case, we can solve for r if we can determine F/CEQ.

16.2.2. The Market Price of Risk

The relationship between the F and its CEQ can be expressed in terms of the unit price of risk and the amount of risk. From Chapter 15 we know that the overall risk will depend on the covariance of returns between the specific investment and the portfolio to which it belongs.[1] When the price of risk is multiplied by the amount of risk this gives total risk. For a one-period model, the amount of risk is measured by the covariance between the return to the portfolio and the project's cash flow, $cov(F_1, r_p)$. Let r_m be the returns available in a fully diversified portfolio—the market return. The price of risk per unit of risk is expressed by $[(r_m - r_f)/V_m^2]$ (recall that V_m^2 is the variance of the return). The expression $(r_m - r_f)/V_m^2$ is known as the market price of risk and is usually written as λ (lambda). λ shows the interest rate premium per unit of variance in the market. The covariance between the returns to the prospect and the market's rate of return expresses the amount of risk. The total amount of risk is found by multiplying the project's amount of risk by the price of risk. The certainty equivalent of a value, F_1, received one period in the future will be F_1 minus the total cost of risk. Thus, the certainty equivalent of a cash flow one period later is

$$CEQ = F_1 - \left[\frac{r_m - r_f}{V_m^2}cov(F_1, r_p)\right] \qquad (16.4)$$

---

[1]The assumption made here and in Chapter 15 is that utility depends only on the first two moments of the probability distribution: the mean and the variance. This will be the case when assets are normally distributed, when the expected utility function is quadratic, or when a mean variance model approximates the utility function.

The expression that is subtracted from F_1 is the total risk cost, and this subtraction gives the certainty equivalent of F_1. Equation (16.3) shows an expression for r in terms of the CEQ. Equation (16.4) shows an expression for the CEQ. These can be put together (though it is tricky to do this) to give an expression for r as follows:[2]

$$r = r_f + \left[\frac{r_m - r_f}{V_p^2} \text{cov}(r, r_p) \right] \tag{16.5}$$

16.2.3. Beta

The term $[\text{cov}(r, r_p)]/V_p^2$ is called *beta* (β). Beta is the covariance between the project's rate of return and the portfolio's rate of returns as a percentage of the variance of the market. Thus, the above expression can be written as

$$r = r_f + \beta(r_p - r_f) \tag{16.6}$$

The expression embodied in Equation (16.6) shows the risk-adjusted rate for the one-period case since F_1 is the risky benefit flow for only one period. We shall see, however, that a variant of this equation is a fundamental equation for determining a risk-adjusted discount rate. The beta of any asset i can be calculated by performing the following regression:

$$r_{it} = \alpha_i + \beta_i r_{mt} + e_i$$

where r_{it} is return on asset i in period t and r_{mt} is the market portfolio rate of return. The market portfolio is the ultimate portfolio containing every asset in the economic system in proportion to its value as a percent of the whole. In practice, stock market indexes are usually used.

16.2.4. The Many-Period Case

Equation (16.6) is a fundamental equation for using a risk-adjusted interest rate to discount risky cash flows. *Equation (16.6) can be extended to many periods as long as the assumption can be made that beta is the same during the different periods.* This can be seen as follows. The risk-adjusted interest rate as expressed above is the right interest rate to use in discounting cash flows for the next period, period t_1. Having arrived at the end of the first period, the rate to use for the following period, period t_2, will be the same if beta remains the same, assuming no change in the risk-free rate and no difference between the market rate and the risk-free rate. This is because, having arrived at the end of the first period, it again only requires a one-period model to consider period two. That is, the use of a single risk-adjusted discount rate to discount the cash flows of a many-period project implies that the estimate of beta remains the same throughout the life of the project. The project's returns must tend to vary the same way in each period with respect to the portfolio the investor holds.

---

[2]The trick is to realize that the covariance of $(F_1 r_p)$ can be expressed as the covariance of (r, r_p) because $r = (F_1/\text{PV}) - 1$, and that the only part of the expression that has a variance is F_1 since PV and 1 are single numbers with no variance. See good finance texts such as Brealy and Myers (1988) and Schall and Haley (1991).

A More Systematic Derivation

Let us derive Equation (16.6) for a risk-adjusted interest rate in a more systematic manner. We will assume, as we have been doing, that risk can be characterized by variance so that the value of a prospect can be expressed in terms of mean and variance. This assumption is met if returns tend to be normally distributed, a proposition with some empirical support. We adapt, from the von Neumann–Morgenstern model, the assumption that the present value of a benefit received one period from now can be expressed by discounting the certainty equivalent at the risk-free rate. That is,

$$PV = \frac{CEQ}{1 + r_f} \qquad (16.7)$$

The use of the risk-free rate makes sense because the CEQ already is adjusted for risk. From Equation (16.4), the certainty equivalent of a cash flow of F_1 received one period later can be expressed as

$$CEQ = F_1 - \lambda \, \text{cov}(F_1, r_p) \qquad (16.8)$$

which expresses the certainty equivalent as cash flow in the next period minus the price of risk times the amount of risk. Then, the present value of the project is the certainty equivalent discounted by the risk-free interest rate, or

$$PV = \frac{F_1 - \lambda \, \text{cov}(F_1, r_p)}{1 + r_f} \qquad (16.9)$$

What follows now is straight algebra. Divide both sides by PV to obtain

$$1 = [F_1 - \lambda \, \text{cov}(F_1, r_p,)]/[(1 + r_f)PV] \qquad (16.10)$$

or

$$\frac{F_1}{(1 + r_f)PV} = 1 + \frac{\lambda \, \text{cov}(F_1, r_i)}{(1 + r_f)PV} \qquad (16.11)$$

Writing out the expression for λ and solving for F_1/PV gives

$$\frac{F_1}{PV} = 1 + r_f + \frac{[(r_p - r_f)/V_p^2] \, \text{cov}(F_1, r_p)}{PV} \qquad (16.12)$$

The covariance between F_1 and r_p divided by PV will be the same as between r_1 and r_p. This is because $F_1/PV = r_1 + 1$, and the 1 does not vary or affect the covariance relationship. Thus we can write Equation (16.12) as

$$\frac{F_1}{PV} = 1 + r_f + \frac{r_p - r_f}{V_p^2} \text{cov}(r_1, r_p) \qquad (16.13)$$

Recalling the definition of beta, this can be written as

$$\frac{F_1}{PV} = 1 + r_f + \beta(r_p - r_f) \qquad (16.14)$$

We know that $F_1/(1 + r) = PV$ so that $F_1/PV = 1 + r$. Then

$$1 + r = 1 + r_f + \beta(r_p - r_f) \qquad (16.15)$$

or

$$r = r_f + \beta(r_p - r_f) \qquad (16.16)$$

which is the same equation as (16.6) above.

Projects that consistently yield better or worse returns at times in which the portfolio yields better returns will satisfy this requirement. Projects will also satisfy the requirement for multiperiod analysis that yield either better or worse returns consistently when the portfolio yields worse returns.

The use of a single risk-adjusted discount rate for a many-period project is equivalent to assuming that risk is constant in each period but that cumulative risk grows, so that more distant cash flows are regarded as riskier. Often this will be a reasonable assumption and is equivalent to assuming that beta remains constant over the life of the project.

16.2.5. The Medford Projects

We are now in a position to address the question raised at the beginning of this section, how can we compare the two Medford projects? The timber project is clearly superior to the tourist project if both are discounted at the same rate, as, for example, at the risk-free rate. Suppose that the variance of the relevant market portfolio is 10. Recall that the covariance of the timber project with the relevant market portfolio is 20 and the covariance of the tourist project is 10 (later we will discuss what constitutes the relevant portfolio). We can now calculate the betas for the two projects as

$$\beta \text{ (timber)} = \frac{\text{cov}(r_p, r_i)}{V_p^2} = \frac{20}{10} = 2$$

$$\beta \text{ (tourist)} = \frac{10}{10} = 1$$

Suppose that the risk-free rate is 3 percent and the rate of return to the market portfolio is 9 percent. Then we have

$$r \text{ (timber)} = r_f + \beta(r_p - r_f)$$
$$= 3\% + 2(9\% - 3\%) = 15\%$$

For the tourist industry the risk-adjusted interest rate would be

$$r \text{ (tourist)} = 3\% + 1(9\% - 3\%) = 9\%$$

The present value of benefits for the two projects would then be

$$\text{Timber:} \frac{\$120}{1.15} - \$100 = \$4.34$$

$$\text{Tourist:} \frac{\$115}{1.09} - \$100 = \$5.50$$

The tourist industry project is actually the better project even though its expected value is less. This is because the tourist project is more likely to pay off than the timber project when times are bad in Medford and the value of the payoffs of the tourist project are therefore worth more.

16.2.6. What to Do When Beta Changes During the Life of the Project

Where the assumption of a constant level of risk is not satisfied, we must break the cash flow into segments within which a constant risk-adjusted discount rate can be used. We can imagine a project in which the level of risk is expected to change over the life of the project. For example, suppose that a project involves two phases, an initial test phase and a second phase that will be undertaken only if the test phase is successful. Suppose that the beta for the test phase is estimated to be 2.0, a very large beta. If the test shows the project is not likely to be successful, it will be abandoned and the beta is 0. If the test project is successful, it is estimated that the information gained from the successful test will reduce our estimate of beta for the remaining project to about 0.15. Suppose that the risk-free rate is 4 percent and that the difference between the market rate and the risk-free rate is 8 percentage points. The following costs and benefits are indicated:

Period Cash Flow		
0	−$1,000,000	
1	$500,000 end of test phase	
	If successful (60%)	*If not successful (40%)*
2	−$5,000,000	0
3–12	$1,000,000/year	0

The discount rate for the test period is

$$r_1 = 4\% + 2(8) = 20\%$$

The discount rate for the second phase, if the test is successful, is

$$r_2 = 4\% + 0.15(8) = 5.2\%$$

$$\text{NPV} = \frac{-\$1,000,000 + \$500,000}{1.2} + 0.6\left[\frac{-\$5,000,000}{(1.052)^2}\right.$$
$$\left. + \frac{\$1,000,000[1 - (1.052)^{-10}/(0.052)]}{(1.052)^3}\right] = \$646,958$$

If the entire project was evaluated at the rate of 20 percent, the NPV would be strongly negative.

16.2.7.   The Efficient Form of the General Model

A special case of the general model presented above occurs when we assume that (1) the portfolio of assets in the utility function is fully diversified, (2) the market price of risk is the efficient price, and (3) there are no taxes to drive a wedge between returns provided and required.

The Efficient Portfolio.   The desirable portfolio of investments for an individual, a company, or a government will be one that offers the highest possible expected return for a given portfolio standard deviation. This is known as the efficient portfolio. Sometimes this is expressed the other way around. The set of investments with the minimum variance (the minimum variance set) is the set that has the minimum variance for any given rate of return.

The Efficient Market Price of Risk.   The market price of risk, or if you prefer safety, can be regarded as a price for some commodity. We know that efficiency requires the price to be the same for everyone and that the marginal rate of substitution between safety and money be equal to the marginal rate of transformation between money and safety. This requires that the price of safety equal the marginal cost of production of safety. Efficiency requires that everyone hold a portfolio that is fully diversified and is efficient so that market risk is compensated in the form of a higher return.

When these conditions are met, the market price of risk is efficient and the risk-adjusted interest rate derived from the general model is the efficient interest rate in a first-best world. The market portfolio is the efficient portfolio from this global perspective. In Chapter 13 we discussed the market rate of interest in the first-best world in the absence of risk. This is the market risk-free rate. Then the risk-adjusted interest rate in a first-best world will just be r, where

$$r = r_f + \beta(r_m - r_f)$$

This is the same as Equation (16.6). The only difference is that in this first-best world we assume the market is efficient, and the market rate is determined in a setting in which there are no taxes so it then equals the social rate of time preference, the SRTP (see Chapter 13). Even in a first-best world, this model suggests that risk-adjusted rates should be used. Just as for the general model, this equation can be broken down into the risk-free rate plus a term for the amount of risk represented by the covariance of the prospect with the market and the price of risk. The difference between the efficient model and the general model is that in the efficient model, the market price of risk is the efficient price and the covariance occurs between the returns to the efficient portfolio and the prospect in question.

16.3. CURRENT THEORIES OF RISK-ADJUSTED INTEREST RATES

Leading theories for evaluating risk under uncertainty include the capital asset pricing model, the consumption-based pricing model, and the arbitrage pricing model. These theories are developed mainly in the context of private investments from the perspective of a manager of a stock and bond portfolio. Differences among these theories for evaluating projects under risk concern primarily the nature of what is the relevant portfolio with which the project in question covaries; that is, the different theories argue for different relevant betas.

The capital asset pricing model (CAPM) considers an asset beta. Here the relevant covariance is between returns to fully diversified financial assets and the project in question. The consumption-based asset pricing model assumes that consumption is the argument in the utility function and that therefore the relevant covariance is between consumption and the prospect in question. Chapter 13 assumed that utility comes from consumption in the context of developing adjusted benefits and costs to be discounted at the social rate of time preference. A consumption-based risk model is consistent with this approach. The arbitrage pricing model contains a variety of betas, namely, the betas with various *factors* that are thought to determine the rate of returns to portfolios.[3] Here the question is not the covariance between the asset's returns and the market portfolio, but the sensitivity of the returns to these factors. There is as yet no agreement as to what these factors are or even what they should be.[4] *All these models contemplate estimating a risk-adjusted interest rate (or different rates for different risk periods) and then calculating the NPV based on this interest rate.* All three models agree that riskier projects should be evaluated at higher interest rates than less risky projects. Thus, other things being equal, a more risky project will have a lower net present value than a less risky project. We will consider briefly the most widely used of these models, the capital asset pricing model.

16.3.1. The Capital Asset Pricing Model

The capital asset pricing model, CAPM, is a special case of the general model (GM) derived above and is similar to the efficient model that is discussed as a special case of the GM. CAPM assumes, as does the GM, that the mean return of a portfolio of investments and its variance are by themselves sufficient to characterize the risk of the investment. Similarly, the CAPM model assumes along with the von Neumann–Morgenstern expected utility model and the GM model above that certainty equivalents exist for a prospect. The CAPM model, however, assumes also, along with the efficient model, that the market is efficient, so that the difference between the market return and the risk-free rate measures the efficient price of market risk. Consistent with the efficient market model, the CAPM model assumes that the relevant portfolio is fully diversified so that all risk which it is possible to eliminate is eliminated (called systematic or unique risk), leaving only market risk.

The CAPM model is not, however, used in a first-best world. In practice beta is usually derived from stock market analysis so the covariance that is measured is that of the prospect with the stock market. Also, in practice, certain rather ad hoc adjustments are made to the model so that it yields better predictions. The aim of the CAPM in practice then is to show a portfolio manager what risk-adjusted rate of return can be obtained from the market and thus what risk-adjusted rate of return one needs to obtain from an investment to cover one's opportunity cost.

The CAPM model results in an expression that is identical to Equation (16.6) except that the covariance term is between market returns and the returns to the *i*th prospect, whereas in the Equation (16.6) the covariance is between the

---

[3]The measure of systematic risk is the sensitivity of an asset's returns to the various factors that affect those returns. Factors that have been found significant are (1) industrial production, (2) changes in a default risk premium as measured by the differences in promised yields to maturity between AAA and Baa corporate bonds, (3) differences in promised yields to maturity between long-term and short-term government bonds, and (4) unanticipated inflation.

[4]The arbitrage pricing theory (APT) relies on estimating the covariance between project returns and some portfolio the exact nature of whose contents is not yet clear. We do not discuss this approach here. However, see Haugen (1986).

relevant portfolio and the market return. The fundamental equation of CAPM is then

$$r = r_f + \beta_a(r_m - r_f) \tag{16.17}$$

where r = the required rate of return

r_f = the risk-free rate

r_m = the market rate of return

β_a = asset beta

The Security Market Line.   Equation (16.17) represents the security market line of CAPM. The heart of the CAPM model is the security market line. This shows the relationship between risk and rate of return of investments. The security market line is shown in Figure 16.1.

The vertical axis measures the expected return; the horizontal axis measures the beta of the stock. The security market line indicates the relationship between the level of risk as measured by beta and the expected rate of return. (Note that beta is a regression coefficient in a linear regression between the expected return and the difference between the market return and the risk-free rate of return.) When a project's beta is 0, the project is risk-free and requires the lowest expected return so that the intercept of the security market line with the y axis is the risk-free rate. Projects with higher market sensitivity must have higher expected returns so the line has positive slope. Note that the security market line shows the same relationship as we showed earlier in a more general context except that the beta reflects the covariance between the asset's returns and the market portfolio. The earlier equation did not assume that the relevant portfolio is the market, but rather the actual portfolio being held.

The Asset Beta in the CAPM Model.   If returns are normally distributed and the market portfolio is efficient, the asset beta is an appropriate measure of risk for an individual investment. Beta measures the contribution to risk of an investment relative to the market. The proportion of risk contributed by any one stock to a portfolio consisting of the entire market will be found by dividing

Figure 16.1.   Security market line.

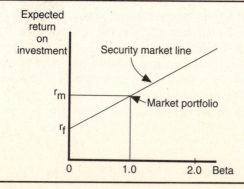

EXAMPLE 16.1

A private firm wishes to use the opportunity cost of capital to discount projects. The asset beta used in conjunction with the security market line equation gives the opportunity cost rate applicable to the firm's existing assets. If new projects have about the same risk as existing ones, then it is appropriate for the firm to use the existing beta to calculate the discount rate for these new projects. (In general, betas refer to the correlation of returns to the market and one may refer to revenue betas, stock or equity betas, debt betas, and so forth.)

Suppose that the risk-free rate is given by the rate on Treasury bills, short-term federal government investments, and that this rate in nominal terms is now about 9.0 percent. On the basis of historical evidence we guess that the difference between the market rate of return and the risk-free rate is about 8.8 percentage points. Suppose now that we are considering two investments A and B with betas of 0.50 and 2.25, respectively. What rate of return should we expect from these investments? Applying Equation (16.17), we obtain

$$A: r_A = 9.0 + 0.50(8.8) = 13.4\%$$

$$B: r_B = 9.0 + 2.25(8.8) = 28.8\%$$

the risk contribution of one stock by the riskiness of the whole portfolio. That is, beta is the expected change in the security's rate of return divided by the associated change in the rate of return of the market portfolio—the national economy. Formally, beta in the CAPM model is

$$\beta = \frac{\text{cov}(r_i, r_m)}{\text{variance } (r_m)}$$

where r_i is the return of the investment in question, and r_m is the return to the market portfolio.

The asset beta used in CAPM in practice has an interpretation as the responsiveness of the investment to changes in the stock market prices. Suppose that portfolio A increased or decreased by 1.5 percent for every 1 percent change in economic activity as represented by changes in stock prices, and that portfolio B increased or decreased by about 0.8 percent for every 1 percent change in economic activity. This tells us the relative responsiveness of the portfolio to the market and therefore indicates the relative market risk of the two portfolios. Portfolio A would have an asset beta of 1.5, and portfolio B an asset beta of 0.8. The percentage increase in value for one investment relative to the market is just the *asset beta* for that investment.[5]

---

[5]The *market portfolio* is defined as consisting of every single risky asset in the world. This portfolio contains each of these assets in the proportion that the asset's market value bears to the total value of all assets. Investments that have more risk have higher rates of return.

16.3.2. Estimating Betas

Betas are usually calculated as a regression coefficient that compares the responsiveness of the investment returns with changes in market returns. Since future returns are unknown, the beta is based on past behavior. Estimates of betas based on the past performances of similar investments can be used.

For private sector investments or for public sector investments that are similar to private ones, published betas can be useful. A number of companies publish beta books that show the betas for stocks of a large number of companies. For example, beta estimates are published by Merrill Lynch, and by Value Line. Most services also publish standard errors of the betas.[6] By examining these betas some idea of the beta for the investment being considered may be gained. These betas are not, however, asset betas but are instead equity or stock betas.

It is asset betas that are of interest for project evaluation, however, since we are interested in market risk which represents the variation of the investment in question with the market. Published betas are generally for the stock of firms. Since these are influenced by the level of debt financing they are not what is required, and betas for stocks need to be adjusted in order to represent the level of variability with the market.

Stock betas can be converted into asset betas by recognizing that the asset value of a firm equals the sum of debt and equity. This allows the derivation of the following relationship:

$$\beta(\text{asset}) = \beta(\text{debt})[\text{debt}/\text{assets}] + \beta(\text{equity})[\text{equity}/\text{assets}]$$

Suppose that the equity beta as determined from a beta book is 1.20 and that the firm uses 40 percent debt financing.[7] This leads to the following estimate of the asset beta:

$$\beta(\text{asset}) = 0 + 1.20(0.60) = 0.72$$

---

[6]For the definition of standard error see any good statistics book.

[7]*Debt financing:* The beta of equity, though not of assets, will be affected by the proportion of financing that is done by debt compared to equity. Suppose you compare your project with betas for companies that undertake similar projects. The standard deviation of the portfolio of betas from all these companies is low, so you have confidence in this estimate of beta. For simplicity suppose that these companies have no debt financing. You, however, plan to finance 50 percent of your project by issuing debt at 10 percent. Now your estimate of beta derived from the beta of these other companies is say 1.50. This implies that the project should return at least 12.0 percent, given a risk-free rate of 4 percent, and a market rate 8 percentage points over the risk-free rate. However, the use of 50 percent debt financing makes your project much more risky for the stockholders. Suppose $10,000 is invested through debt and $10,000 is invested through equity. If the project yields 12.0 percent on the overall investment of $20,000, it will yield 34.4 percent if just the return to equity is considered. The total return will be $2440.00($0.12 \times $20,000$). The return to equity will be $2440.00 minus the payment on the debt of $1000, to give $1440/$10,000 or 14.40 percent. If the market rate of return should increase by 4 percentage points to 16.00 percent from 22.22 percent the return to equity on your investment will increase by 8 percentage points to 22.4 percent. Similarly, if the market return should fall, the return on your investment will fall disproportionately. That is, the effect of the debt is to make the return to equity more responsive to the market return and thereby increase the beta of your return to equity. The increase in beta will be directly proportional to the percent of debt financing. The effect of 50 percent debt financing is, then, to double the equity beta. In this case the equity beta adjusted for debt would be $2 \times 1.50 = 3.00$, a very high beta indeed. An equity beta is found by dividing the unadjusted beta by the extent of equity financing.

EXAMPLE 16.2

Suppose the town of Snohomish, Washington, is considering building an electric plant similar to plants operated by many other electric companies. By checking betas published by Merrill Lynch for other electric companies that operate similar plants, some idea of the beta relevant for the project contemplated may be gained. Very often the betas for such similar companies will be similar and the standard deviation of a sample of these betas may be small. Betas for 23 large electric utilities are shown in Table 16.1.

The estimate for the average beta of 0.45 will be more reliable than the estimate for any one company. Since the variation in the beta is not too great we can judge that the industry average is a reasonable basis on which to proceed. These betas are, however, equity betas, not asset betas. Snohomish PUD has, say, 40 percent of its assets as debt. The asset beta, assuming that the debt beta of Snohomish is 0, will, therefore, be

$$\beta(\text{asset}) = 0(0.40) + 0.45(0.60) = 0.270$$

The estimated cost of capital for Snohomish, using a nominal risk-free rate of 9 percent and a market rate 8.8 percentage points higher than this, gives

$$r = r_f + \beta(\text{asset})(r_m - r_f) = 9\% + 0.27(8.8\%) = 11.38\%$$

TABLE 16.1   Betas for 23 Large Electric Utilities, 1981–1986

Firm	Beta	Standard Error
Baltimore Gas & Electric	0.30	0.15
Boston Edison	0.33	0.15
Carolina Power & Light	0.52	0.15
Central Hudson Gas & Electric	0.44	0.19
Central Maine Power	0.37	0.30
Cincinnati Gas & Electric	0.65	0.24
Cleveland Electric	0.36	0.18
Commonwealth Edison	0.58	0.16
Consolidated Edison	0.33	0.15
Dayton Power & Light	0.40	0.28
Delmarva Power & Light	0.35	0.15
Detroit Edison	0.40	0.15
Florida Progress	0.51	0.13
Houston Industries	0.54	0.15
Idaho Power	0.42	0.13
Indianapolis Power & Light	0.49	0.14
Northeast Utilities	0.50	0.16
Pacific Gas & Electric	0.44	0.16
Pennsylvania Power & Light	0.46	0.19
Philadelphia Electric	0.51	0.19
Public Service Corporation of Colorado	0.45	0.14
Southern California Edison	0.56	0.15
Utah Power & Light	0.38	0.13
Average	0.45	

Source: Merrill Lynch, Pierce, Fenner & Smith, Inc., "Security Risk Evaluation," October 1986. See also Brealey and Myers (1988), 3rd ed., p. 183.

EXAMPLE 16.3

The city of Spokane is considering investing in a water project and financing 40 percent of the project out of bonds. The rest of the project will be financed out of existing money. The city finds that companies that invest in this type of project have betas of 0.8 and that these companies typically have about 10 percent debt with 90 percent equity financing. What beta should the city of Spokane use to evaluate the project? The city can be said to be using 60 percent equity financing. The adjusted beta for Spokane is then $(0.8) \times (0.90/0.60) = 1.2$.

What Factors Affect Betas?   The calculation of betas is hardly an exact science. The analyst must not be mechanical about the calculation of a beta, but must use judgment and must look for information wherever it may be found. The estimation of beta can be informed by an awareness of the factors that affect beta.

You will not be able to make precise evaluations of the riskiness of most projects. Good analysts use a combination of quantitative and qualitative techniques and look at projects from different perspectives to gauge their riskiness. In many cases you may not be able to find published estimates of beta but can analyze the beta of a project from past price data. A city considering a convention center can use data from other centers to determine the correlation between net revenues from such centers and changes in the market. The analyst can in addition consider the various factors that affect risk. These include (1) the cyclical nature of the project revenues, and (2) size of fixed costs as a percent of project costs.[8] Let us consider how these factors will affect risk.

Cyclical Nature of Earnings.   Even if no betas are published that are relevant for your purposes, you will often be able to obtain estimates of cash flow figures for the project in question. These cash flows can be used to calculate the correlation between changes in each flow and the market. That is, you can calculate a beta directly. Projects that tend to have returns that are correlated with other sources of revenue for the government unit will be more risky. Projects that are less correlated, or even negatively correlated, will have less risk, or even negative risk.

The Percentage of Fixed or Sunk Costs.   The PV of an asset is equal to the present value of its expected profits. This can be expressed as

$$PV(assets) = PV(revenue) - PV(fixed\ costs)$$
$$- PV(sunk\ costs) - PV(variable\ costs)$$

[8]For further discussion of factors affecting betas see G. Foster, *Financial Statement Analysis,* 2nd ed., Englewood Cliffs, N.J.: Prentice Hall, Inc., 1986, chapter 10.

It can be shown that the weighted average of a beta for one variable is a weighted average of the beta of its component parts. This gives rise to the following relationship:

$$\beta(\text{asset}) = \frac{\beta(\text{revenue}) \text{ PV (revenue)}}{\text{PV(asset)}} - \frac{\beta(\text{fixed costs})\text{PV(fixed costs)}}{\text{PV(asset)}}$$
$$- \frac{\beta(\text{sunk costs}) \text{ PV(sunk costs)}}{\text{PV(asset)}}$$
$$- \frac{\beta(\text{variable costs})\text{PV(variable costs)}}{\text{PV(asset)}}$$

This can be simplified by realizing that the betas of fixed costs and sunk costs are 0. For convenience we will take advantage of the fact that sunk costs are also fixed costs and use the category fixed costs to represent both of these costs. The betas of revenues and of variable costs are likely to be highly correlated because they are influenced by similar market forces. We will express the beta of variable costs as k times the revenue beta, where k will generally be a number close to 1. The above equation can now be written as

$$\beta(\text{asset}) = \beta(r)\left[\frac{\text{PV(revenue)}}{\text{PV(asset)}}\right] - k\beta(\text{revenue})\left[\frac{\text{PV(variable costs)}}{\text{PV(asset)}}\right]$$

or

$$\beta(\text{asset}) = \frac{\beta[\text{PV}_r - k\text{PV(variable costs)}]}{\text{PV(asset)}}$$

Now we can express the PV_r as follows:

$$\text{PV}_r = \text{PV(fixed costs)} + \text{PV(variable costs)} + \text{PV(asset)}$$

When this is substituted into the previous equation this yields

$$\beta(\text{asset}) = \frac{\text{PV(fixed costs)} + \text{PV(asset)} + \text{PV(variable costs)}(1 - k)}{\text{PV(asset)}}$$

$$\beta(\text{asset}) = \frac{\text{PV(fixed costs)}}{\text{PV(asset)}} + \frac{(1 - k)\text{PV(variable costs)}}{\text{PV(asset)}} + 1$$

This shows that the asset beta is directly related to the ratio of the present value of fixed costs to the (present) value of the asset. The higher the ratio of fixed costs to assets, the higher will be the beta, *ceteris paribus*. Empirical work shows that companies with high ratios of fixed costs to assets have higher betas for their common stock.

Using Betas to Calculate the Risk-Adjusted Present Value of Investments.   The procedure to be used is fairly straightforward. The beta associated with the contemplated investment is used to calculate a risk-adjusted interest rate. This interest rate is used to discount the probability weighted cash flows. Consider Example 16.4.

Example 16.4

The city of Bellevue is evaluating a potential investment in a dam to supply hydroelectric power and water to the city. The returns to this project will depend on what states of the world actually prevail, and particularly on the amount of rainfall and the price of electricity. For simplicity, we will assume that all net benefits are to be realized one period hence. The city determines the following possible net benefits with associated probabilities:

Bellevue Dam Project

	Net Benefits	Probability	Probability Weighted Benefits
1.	$1.5 million	0.3	$0.45
2.	2.2 million	0.5	1.10
3.	1.1 million	0.1	0.11
		Total	1.66

Similar projects have been undertaken throughout the Northwest and elsewhere. Through an analysis of past data, the city's analysts determine that a reasonable estimate of the asset beta for the project would be 0.65. The city estimates the inflation-adjusted (real) risk-free interest rate to be 3.0 percent and the difference between the real market rate and the real risk-free rate to be approximately 8 percentage points. The appropriate risk-adjusted discount rate would then be

$$r = r_f + \beta(r_m - r_f)$$
$$= 3.0\% + 0.65(8\%) = 8.2$$

The present value of the project would then be

$$\frac{\$1.66 \text{ million}}{1.082} = \$1.53$$

The city wishes to compare this project with another one for which the asset beta is 1.4 and which has net benefits one period hence of $1.70 million. The risk-adjusted interest rate for this second project will be

$$r = 3.0\% + 1.4(8) = 14.2$$

The present value of the net benefit flows for this project will be

$$\frac{1.70}{1.14} = \$1.49 \text{ million}$$

All other considerations being equal, the city should undertake the dam project rather than this one.

16.4. RISK-ADJUSTED INTEREST RATES FOR PUBLIC PROJECTS

Let us consider the situation of a public sector decision maker who is involved in the evaluation of alternative risky projects. We will assume that the individual wishes to maximize the expected present value to the public because this will maximize his political support or the support of his superiors whom he wishes to please. The goal of the department then is to achieve the greatest return subject to considerations of risk.

16.4.1. A First-Best World

Case One.   In a first-best world there will be no wedges formed by taxes; in each market the marginal rates of substitution, MRS, will be equal for all consumers, and the marginal rate of technical substitution between any two factors of production will be equal in the production of every good. In addition, the marginal rate of substitution will equal the marginal rate of transformation in production. All markets will be efficient.

In this first-best world there will be, in the absence of risk, one market interest rate that reflects both the rate of time preference and the opportunity cost of capital. Given the existence of risk, the price of risk will be the efficient price and the use of the efficient model will allow the determination of the appropriate risk-adjusted interest rates, subject to knowledge about the probability distribution of returns from a project. Thus, we have

> *Rule for a First-Best World*: Use the efficient model to calculate a risk-adjusted interest rate.

The beta will be determined by the expected correlation between the expected returns to the investment and the expected returns to the efficient market portfolio.

16.4.2. A Second-Best World

Case Two.   In this case we imagine that the first-best conditions are no longer met, but suppose that the political authority has available to it the same array of investment opportunities as the private portfolio manager, and that the only question is whether or not the public sector or the private sector should undertake the investment. Is there any difference in the situation of the public authority and the private portfolio manager? Clearly there is a difference in at least one respect, the treatment of taxes.

The treatment of taxes by public authorities and private investors should be different. The private sector investor is interested in after-tax returns. Tax revenues are, however, a benefit for the public sector authority, at least if they accrue to the public authority that is considering the investment.

Suppose there is a project involving, say, vocational training that the city is considering undertaking. This is also a project in which private investors are interested. The city wishes to determine if it should undertake the project. The city calculates that it will have costs of $2.7 million and that the present value of benefits will be $3.0 million for a net present value of $0.3 million. The private firm estimates that its costs will be $2.5 million plus $0.4 million that

EXAMPLE 16.5

In a first-best world but nevertheless one with drugs, the District of Columbia wishes to undertake an educational program to reduce illegal drug use in the district. The program envisioned involves an initial expenditure of $3,000,000 and yearly expenditures of $200,000. The benefits of the program are estimated to be $600,000 per year. The program is expected to last for 10 years. The risk-free interest rate is 2 percent; beta is estimated to be negative, because the returns to the project are expected to be inversely correlated with the state of the economy, and is estimated to be -0.1; and the market interest rate is 5 percent.

The risk-adjusted interest rate then will be

$$r = r_f + \beta(r_m - r_f)$$
$$= 2\% + (-0.1)(5\% - 2\%) = 1.7\%$$

The risk-adjusted interest rate is just slightly below the risk-free rate because of the negative beta. Recall that in a first-best world the marginal value of a dollar of investment is the same as the marginal value of a dollar of consumption. Thus the adjustments to benefits and costs derived in Chapter 13 for a second-best world, are not required. The present value of the project then will be

$$NPV = -\$3,000,000 + \$400,000 \left[1 - \frac{(1.017)^{-10}}{0.017} \right] = \$650,091$$

it will pay to the city in taxes. Benefits will be $3.1 million for a net present value of $0.2 million. The city concludes that it should undertake the project because the project has a higher net present value if undertaken by the city.

Clearly, however, the City has miscalculated. The taxes that the private sector firm would pay of $0.4 million are a benefit to the city. If the city rather than the private firm undertakes the project the city foregoes $0.4 million. In the city's calculations this $0.4 million should be counted as an opportunity cost. Thus the net present value for the city is a negative $0.2 million. Similarly if a political authority is sponsoring a project that will result in tax revenues these should be counted as benefits to the authority at least if they accrue to the authority.

Failure to consider the value of tax revenues foregone could lead to a justification of a public investment replacing private investment on a large scale. This analysis is pretty straightforward in its logic, but there are stories of political jurisdictions failing to take into account just such foregone taxes. We will not mention the names of such jurisdictions here. In the analysis of taxes we assumed that the public sector should undertake the investment rather than the private sector only if the public sector is more efficient in performing the project in question. This quite reasonable assumption leads to the general provision that except for the treatment of taxes, the public authority that wishes to maximize returns, where the question is whether the public or private sector should undertake the investments, should evaluate potential projects just as would the private portfolio manager. This leads to the following rule:

> *Rule for a Second-Best World in Which the Only Issue Is Whether the Public or the Private Sector Should Undertake the Project:* The public authority should evaluate the project in the same way as the private sector except that for the public sector, tax revenues are a benefit and tax revenues foregone are an opportunity cost.

If the department discounts a risky project at a rate less than shown by the security market line or the empirical market line, it will accept projects that yield less than investments that have the same risk. Certainly, if the issue is whether or not the government or private industry should undertake a particular project, then the government project should be evaluated on the same basis as the private project. *In this case, use of something like the CAPM would seem appropriate for the public sector manager.*

Case Three.   The situation envisioned in case two will not be the usual one. The public sector authority will not have available to it the same array of investment possibilities as will the private sector. Indeed the *raison d'etre* of the public sector is that such public authority has a comparative advantage with respect to certain kinds of investment.

In case three we assume that the clientele of the public sector authority has well-diversified portfolios, and we continue to assume that the public sector authority sees itself as the agent of its voters. This case differs from case two, however, in the fact that the public sector has available to it a different set of investment opportunities than exist for the private sector. There will be potentially valuable public sector projects that the private sector cannot be expected to undertake. This includes potential investments that the private sector could undertake but does not because of low private returns. How should the government evaluate these projects in a second-best world?

The risk preferences and opportunities of the individuals who constitute the clientele of the public authority are expressed in the information about the actual relationship between risk and rate of return as embodied in the CAPM or in some similar model. That is, the public authority should not invest in any project that returns less than their clientele can obtain and this rate of return is shown by something such as the CAPM model. Public projects whose returns accrue to the public should then be subject to the same risk discounting as private projects. Thus, it seems appropriate to use the CAPM as at least a guide to evaluate the risk of a public project as in case two.

However, the measurement of benefits and costs from public investment need to be adjusted as we showed in Chapter 15 to take into account the effect of the project on the availability of consumption over time. In Chapter 15 we obtained an expression for the correct evaluation of net present value in a second-best world. This is

$$\text{NPV} = \sum_{t=0}^{\infty} \frac{(B_t^* - C_t^*)}{(1 + i)^t} \qquad (16.18)$$

where B_t^* and C_t^* are adjustments to ordinary benefits and costs in time t, and i is the social rate of time preference. This expression takes into account the fact that the projects can have different effects on the availability of consumption over time because of their different returns to private capital. *In considering projects not likely to be undertaken by the private sector, the government should take into account the differences between projects in terms of their effects on funds used for private investment.*

In Chapter 13 we argued that the social rate of time preference in the absence of risk, i, can best be identified with the marginal after-tax rate of return of risk-free investments. Equation (16.18) envisions a situation in which an adjustment is made to benefits and costs incurred at time t to convert them to units of consumption at time t. These adjusted benefits and costs are then discounted at the social rate of time preference. The social rate of time preference will, however, be higher for riskier investments. That is, the i of Equation (16.18) becomes the after-tax r_f when there is no risk, and becomes the risk-adjusted after-tax r when there is risk. This discussion leads to the following rule for this case:

Rule for a Second-Best World Where Public Sector Investment Opportunities Are Different from Private Sector Opportunities and Where Portfolios Are Well Diversified: Use the CAPM or the beta from a consumption-based model but adjust benefits and costs to account for returns to private capital.

Case Four.   In this situation, the voters or the clientele of the public authority do not have well-diversified portfolios. Instead, their portfolios consist of local components such as housing to a disproportionate extent. We continue to assume that the public sector authority sees itself as the agent of its voters who will not necessarily have well-diversified portfolios.

The benefits from the public sector investment decisions by the department will vary with time and will covary with the regional economy, that is, with the economy of the locale of those voters that elect officials to govern the department. If the quantity of benefits provided by the department is larger during those periods in which the local economy is booming, these benefits will be of less value to local residents for the sort of reasons already discussed, namely, the declining marginal utility of money. On the other hand, if the quantity of benefits provided by the department to the residents is larger during periods when the local economy is depressed, the benefits will be all the more valuable. That is to say, somewhat the same sort of risk considerations should apply to the investment decisions by the department as to decisions of a private portfolio manager but the relevant beta will be determined with respect to a different portfolio. In this situation the analyst can examine historical data to determine the correlation between the expected returns for the proposed project and the portfolio representative of the clientele.

Government can be regarded as an enterprise whose revenues depend largely on tax revenues which in turn depend on the state of the local or state or national economy, depending on the level of government. Alternatively, government can be regarded as an economy caretaker whose relevant portfolio is the local, state, or national economy. In either case the economy of

EXAMPLE 16.6

Suppose that a government is to choose between two projects, one of which returns benefits to private capital, the other whose benefits are entirely in consumption. Project A will cost $1 million and will return $300,000 in consumption benefits per year for 20 years. For simplicity, we assume that each project is financed in the same way and that 5 percent of the cost will come from private capital. The second project, B, will also cost $1 million and will return benefits of $200,000 per year for 20 years, 25 percent of which will be reinvested privately and 75 percent of which will be consumed. Each project has a beta of 1.5. The rate of return to private capital, r, is 5 percent, the rate of savings is 6 percent, i is 2 percent. What is the risk-adjusted interest rate by which they should be evaluated?

Chapter 13 showed that the shadow price of a dollar of private capital should be considered in evaluating a public project. This price we called V_t. We showed that V_t can be expressed as

$$V_t = \frac{(1-s)r}{i-sr} = \frac{(1-0.06)0.05}{0.02-(0.06)(0.05)} = \frac{0.047}{0.017} = 2.76$$

For both projects A and B the proportion of investment coming from private capital is 5 percent. For project A the proportion of benefits returning to private investment is 0. For project B the proportion of returns going to private capital for reinvestment is 25 percent. From Chapter 13 we recall that B_t^* is

$$B_t^* = B_t[\theta_b V_t + (1-\theta_b)]$$

For project A this gives benefits of $200,000[0(2.76)+1)] = \$200,000$. For project B, however, this gives $200,000[0.25(2.76)+0.75] = \$200,000(1.44)$, or $288,000.

The full expression for C_t^* is

$$C_t^* = C_t[\theta_c V_t + (1-\theta_c)]$$

For both projects A and B this is $3 $million[0.05(2.76) + 0.95] = \$3$ million (1.09), or $3.27 million. The risk-adjusted social rate of time preference for both projects will be

$$r = i + \beta(r_m - r_f) = 2\% + 1.5(5\% - 2\%) = 6.5\%$$

We leave it as an exercise to the reader to complete the example and calculate the NPV of the two projects A and B.

the region over which the government has hegemony, or in which the population served by the government lives, seems an appropriate portfolio. Those projects whose returns vary positively with the economy have positive risk, those whose returns vary inversely with the economy have negative risk, and those whose returns are uncorrelated with the economy are not risky.

Consider the community of Medford, Oregon, whose economic health was largely dependent on the health of the timber industry. The city is again considering two projects: one would support a milling operation for lumber, the other would use wood scrap to make tourist products. Using a riskless discount rate, the two projects have equal NPVs. Which one should be chosen? In this case the answer is easy. The milling project will have returns that are about perfectly correlated with the lumber industry and therefore with the local economy and also with tax revenues. The tourist project, however, has returns that are correlated with the level of tourism. Tourism probably has no correlation, or a weak correlation, with the timber industry. If the returns to tourism are less correlated with the performance of the local economy than the timber industry, the benefits from the tourist project should be discounted at a lower discount rate than the benefits from the milling project. Since the two projects have equal NPVs when discounted by the same riskless rate, the tourist project will probably show a higher net present value when discounted at a lower interest rate than the returns to the milling project. If these two projects both produce benefit streams that cover a similar time period and their benefits are spread out smoothly then it is true that the risk adjustment would favor the tourist project. In any event the milling project will have a higher beta and should therefore be evaluated at a higher interest rate.

Similar reasoning applies to other levels of government. For example, consider federal investment in new energy-saving technology. A reasonable speculation is that the higher energy prices are in the future, the greater the returns to these investments. Furthermore our energy-economic models predict that high energy costs will result in a lower GNP. Therefore, there is a reasonable presumption that the payoffs from energy research and development have a negative correlation with GNP. Thus energy projects have the character of insurance from a national point of view. In this example the appropriate discount rate for federal policy is *below* the riskless rate and might well be negative. Here we suggest the following risk investment rule:

> *Rule for a Second-Best World Where Government Projects Are Different from Private Opportunities and Where Portfolios Are Not Well Diversified:* The beta should be calculated between the investment in question and the relevant portfolio, that is, the general model should be used. Benefits and costs should be adjusted to account for the return to private investments.

16.4.3. Summary

We have seen that risk is not the same as the probability of bad outcomes. We speak of the risk of an accident, the risk that a project will not pay off, etc. These probabilities can be applied to outcomes to give expected values. Risk as defined here occurs when the decision maker is risk averse because the marginal utility of money varies inversely with income. For this kind of risk we have seen that the risk of projects is determined partly by the variance of project returns and primarily by the covariance of the project returns with the portfolio of returns. *This is a general statement that applies to any project whether it is a government project or a private project.*

The particular portfolio against which risk is to be measured will depend on what portfolio is considered by the decision maker. Where the public authorities have available to them the same set of investment opportunities as the private sector, or where the public authorities represent voters that have available to them the same set of investment opportunities, then the use of a similar risk–

EXAMPLE 16.7

The city of Seattle wishes to consider two alternative methods of generating electricity. Both methods will be financed in the same fashion but will yield a different pattern of benefits. The first method involves increasing the height of a dam and the project is known as the High Ross dam project. The returns to this project will depend somewhat on rainfall. When rainfall is insufficient, electricity must be purchased from Canada at considerable expense. This project will cost $5 million and will yield benefits of $600,000 per year for 50 years. About 2 percent of the financing of this project is expected to come from private capital and about 30 percent of the returns from the project will return to private capital.

The second alternative project involves an investment in conservation. This project will cost $3 million and will yield benefits of $350,000 per year for 50 years. About 2 percent of the financing of this project will come from private capital and about 20 percent is expected to return to private capital.

The city determines that the portfolio of its citizens contains a significant local component. Because there is a significant correlation between rainfall and the value of the relevant portfolio, the dam project has a slightly higher beta than the conservation component. Beta for the dam project is 1.3 and for the conservation project is 0.9. The after-tax risk-free rate is 2 percent and the rate of return of the relevant portfolio is 4 percent. Which project will have the higher net present value?

The opportunity cost of private capital (see Chapter 13) will be

$$V_t = \frac{(1-s)r}{i-sr} = \frac{(1-0.06)0.04}{0.02 - (0.06)(0.04)} = \frac{0.0376}{0.0176} = 2.14$$

interest rate relationship (such as is shown by the CAPM) is appropriate. If the public is considering projects outside the possible purview of private firms, then adjustments to costs and benefits should be made to consider the effect of the project on private capital investment. Where the relevant portfolio is quite different from that used in managing private investment, then a different beta should be used by the public decision maker and if the average portfolio return available to the decision maker is also different, then a different market rate of return should be used.

It would appear then that an appropriate and reasonable, though not perfect, adjustment for risk can be made by discounting at a risk-adjusted interest rate such that risky projects are discounted at higher rates. If the project shows different levels of risk at different times over the course of its life, then different risk-adjusted interest rates need to be used for the different time periods. The particular interest rate to use can be found by using the security market line to determine the rate for the class of risk appropriate to the project in question. There are then three steps to this procedure for risk adjustment:

1. Determine the risk class of the project in question or, if the risk class is expected to vary over the life of the project, the risk class for each subperiod in which risk is consistent should be determined.

Project A: High Ross Dam Project:

$$C_t^* = C_t[\theta_c V_t + (1 - \theta_c)] = 9 \text{ million}[0.02(2.14) + 0.98]$$
$$= 9 \text{ million}(1.023) = 9.207 \text{ million}$$
$$B_t^* = B_t[\theta_b V_t + (1 - \theta_b)] = 0.6 \text{ million/year}[0.30(2.14) + 0.70]$$
$$= 600,000(1.34) = 0.8052 \text{ million/year}$$

The risk-adjusted interest rate will be

$$r = i + \beta(r_p - r_f) = 2\% + 1.3(4\% - 2\%) = 4.6\%$$

PV costs = 5.114 million

$$\text{PV benefits} = 0.8052 \text{ million}\left[\frac{1 - (1 + 0.046)^{-50}}{0.046}\right] = 15.65 \text{ million}$$

$$\text{NPV}_A = 15.65 \text{ million} - 5.114 \text{ million} = 10.54 \text{ million}$$

Project B: Conservation Project:

$$C_t^* = C_t[\theta_c V_t + (1 - \theta_c)] = 2.5 \text{ million } (1.023) = 2.251 \text{ million}$$
$$B_t^* = B_t[\theta_b V_t + (1 - \theta_b)] = 0.35 \text{ million } [0.25(2.14) + 0.75]$$
$$= 0.35 \text{ million } (1.29) = 0.45 \text{ million}$$
$$r = i + \beta(r_p - r_f) = 2\% + 0.9(4\% - 2\%) = 3.8\%$$

PV costs = 2.251 million

$$\text{PV benefits} = 0.45\left[\frac{1 + (1 + 0.038)^{-50}}{0.038}\right] = 10.01 \text{ million}$$

$$\text{NPV}_B = 10.01 \text{ million} - 2.251 \text{ million} = 7.76 \text{ million}$$

2. Determine the interest rate associated with each risk class.
3. Discount future benefits and costs by this risk-adjusted interest rate.

16.5. LIMITATIONS OF CAPM

While the CAPM may prove useful in evaluating the value of certain projects, it may be inappropriate in other cases.[9] Defining the relevant market with which to determine covariant risk may be difficult for public projects that produce unpriced commodities. For example, many dams produce electricity, flood control, navigation, and recreation benefits. Unfortunately, no market prices for the latter three benefits generally exist, and the levels of covariance may be difficult to determine.

A further difficulty with the CAPM is the lack of historical data with which to estimate betas for public projects. In general, no data on the relationship between the returns from public investments and changes in national income exist. Indeed, because public projects often produce unpriced commodities, defining a return on investment may be extremely complex.

---

[9] A more complete discussion of the limitations of the CAPM can be found in R. Lind (1982).

The CAPM also does not incorporate nonmarket risks. Suppose, for example, we wanted to investigate the risk associated with pollution from an industrial plant. Suppose the additional pollution from the plant would be expected to increase the death rate from certain cancers within a 100-mile radius of the plant. The CAPM would be inappropriate for considering this project risk because cancer deaths are not a market risk (see, however, Chapter 17).

16.6.   OPTION PRICE AND OTHER VALUES

16.6.1.   Existence Value

The seminal article on option value was written more than 25 years ago by Weisbrod (1964). Weisbrod suggested that important non-use values were not captured as part of *use* value in consumer surplus associated with using the goods. Two concepts of non-use value were introduced in this article that are now recognized as quite distinct. One concept is now called *existence value,* in which the ex ante value of a good consists of the willingness to pay (WTP) of all those willing to pay even though some of those willing to pay may not use or plan to use the good. You might be willing to pay to maintain Denali Park in Alaska in pristine condition even though you (for whatever reasons—perhaps illness) can never see or enjoy the park directly. It is well recognized that such existence value is part of the WTP.

16.6.2.   Option Price

The second issue raised by Weisbrod is quite different. It turns out that the WTP now for a project whose returns are uncertain is, not surprisingly, quite different from the WTP after the future is revealed. Less obviously, the WTP now is also different from the expected value of the various possible willingnesses to pay that would exist after particular futures unfolded.

We have indicated that in a world of certainty, consumer surplus is usually a reasonable approximation of either the WTP or the WTA, the CV or the EV. In a world of uncertainty, which is after all the real world, is expected consumer surplus (or expected utility) the correct measure of ex ante willingness to pay? This is the question raised by the option price concept. It turns out that in general the answer is no.

We are, say, involved in a project whose task is to see whether or not Glacier Park should be preserved. In this connection we are interested in determining the value of Glacier Park. We conduct a travel cost estimation of demand and from this determine the value of Glacier. Many citizens, however, step forward and indicate that the value they give to the park has been overlooked. They are willing to pay sums of money to preserve the park even though they have never visited it and will never visit it. These *existence* values are determined and are added to the previously determined value for the park.

Now, however, another citizen, Mark Elliot, steps forward and says that his value for the park has also been overlooked. He *may* visit the park. Mark will enjoy the park only if his brother Mike can accompany him and will visit the park only if Mike will also go. Mark figures that the chances are about 50 percent that his brother will be able to go. Mark indicates that he is willing to pay $100 to preserve his option to visit the park. *This bid by Mark for the option to use the park is his option price (OP) and should be included in the benefit–cost analysis.* We need to ask, however, if the option price value has already been included as expected consumer surplus and, if not, what is the remaining component that needs to be captured? Consumer surplus may, in fact, capture part—or more than all—of option price. The difference between option price and consumer surplus is option value, which may be a positive or a negative amount. We explore these answers below.

Upon further inquiry we determine that Mark figures that if he does visit the park next year, he will receive a consumer surplus of $300. If he does not visit the park, his consumer surplus from the use of the park is zero. That is, if Mike decides to go, Mark would be willing to pay $300 at that time to be able to visit the Park. Mark's expected consumer surplus is now

$$E(CS) = 0.5(\$300) + 0.5(0) = \$150$$

In this case the expected CS is greater than the option price. Which is the correct measure and why do they differ? Note that if Mark does visit the park his consumer surplus will be $300 which is greater than his expected consumer surplus.

16.6.3. The Relationship Between Option Price and the EV and CV Digression: The Indirect Utility Function[10]

Normally, we think of utility as a function of the goods and services we consume. Depending on the shape of our utility function, we can derive demand functions for these goods and services, which will in turn depend on prices and our income level. Formally, we can write our utility function U as

$$U = U(x_1, \ldots, x_n) \tag{16.19}$$

where the x_i are the amounts of goods and services we consume. Consumption will be constrained by the prices of these goods and services and by our income. So, we write

$$x_1 = x_i(P_i, \ldots, P_n, M) \tag{16.20}$$

where P_i equals the price of good i and M equals our income. If we substitute Equation (16.10) into Equation (16.9), we have

$$U = [x_1(P_1, \ldots, P_n, M), \ldots, x_n(P_1, \ldots, P_n, M), M]$$

Since everything in this equation depends on P_i and M, we can write

$$V(P_1, \ldots, P_n, M) \tag{16.21}$$

The function $V(P_1, \ldots, P_n, M)$ is called the *indirect* utility function.

WTP and the Indirect Utility Function.   The indirect utility function can be used to compare the WTP and the compensating variation, CV. The *compensating variation* can be defined as the amount of money that can be taken away

---

[10]For a complete discussion of the indirect utility function, see Varian (1992).

from the consumer after a price change and leave the consumer as well off as before. That is, the CV is defined implicitly as

$$V(P_{10}, P_2, M) = V(P_{11}, P_2, M - CV) \qquad (16.22)$$

where P_{10} is the original price, P_{11} is the new price, P_2 is the price of other goods, and M is income.

In our park example, there are two states of the world, either Mark wants to visit the park or he does not want to visit the park. We will denote these by the expressions *go* or *nogo*, indicating that Mark wishes to go or does not wish to go. Let us also define a new variable Q which equals 0 if Mark does not have the right to visit the park and 1 if he has this right. Ignoring P_2 for notational simplicity, the value of this right to visit the park in the situation where Mike, and therefore Mark, can go to the park, can be expressed in terms of Mark's CV as

$$V_{go}(M, 0) = V_{go}(M - CV_{go}, 1) \qquad (16.23)$$

where the term V_{go} is the value of going to the park when Mark wishes to go to the park. This equation says that if Mark pays the CV in the state of the world in which he wishes to visit the park, he will be indifferent as between a state of the world in which he wishes to visit the park and one in which he does not wish to visit the park.

If the state of the world exists in which Mark has no interest in visiting the park, because his brother cannot go, his CV would be zero and would be expressed as

$$V_{nogo}(M, 0) = V_{nogo}(M - CV_{nogo}, 1) = V_{nogo}(M, 1) \qquad (16.24)$$

Here Mark's $CV_{nogo} = 0$ because Mark would pay nothing to visit the park when he cannot go anyway.

By visiting the park and paying \$300 Mark's utility will be the same as if he did not visit. Applying the von Neumann–Morgenstern axioms, we determine Mark's expected utility, V_{exp}, from the two states of the world, as

$$V_{exp} = 0.5\, V_{go}(M, 0) + 0.5\, V_{nogo}(M, 0)$$
$$= 0.5\, V_{go}(M - CV_{go}, 1) + 0.5\, V_{nogo}(M - CV_{nogo}, 1) \qquad (16.25)$$

This says that the expected utility in the state of the world in which Mark does *not* have the right to visit the park is the same as paying the CV when he has the right to go. The CV_{go} equals \$300 and the CV_{nogo} equals 0 so the expected value of utility here will be

$$CV = \$150 + 0 = \$150$$

We have determined that Mark is indifferent between visiting the park and paying \$300, and not visiting the park and paying nothing, and that his expected utility, in the von Neumann–Morgenstern sense, in the situation in which he does not know whether he will go but there is no charge for going, will be \$150. Notice that this is different from his option price of \$100.

The option price is the single payment Mark would be willing to make for the option to go before he knows whether or not he will be able to go. As in the case of calculating the expected CV, the answer to the option value question gives a value of going to the park. The difference is that the CV_{go} is not equal to the CV_{nogo} but by definition the OP_{go} equals the OP_{nogo}. That is, the option price will be defined as

$$V_{exp} = 0.5V_{go}(M, \ 0) + V_{nogo}(M, \ 0)$$
$$= 0.5V_{go}(M - OP, \ 1) + 0.5V_{nogo}(M - OP, 1) \tag{16.26}$$

The option price is the payment that Mark would make now that would make him indifferent to which state of the world occurs, going or not going. Both the CV and the option price are payments that will make Mark's welfare in the state of the world in which he has a right to go equal to his welfare when he has no right to go.

To see the relationship between option price and the CV let us recognize that both the CV and the OP are payments that leave Mark indifferent between going and not going. That is both payments give the same expected utility. Equating the expected utility of the equation defining the CV and that defining the OP we have

$$V_{exp} = 0.5V_{go}(M, \ 0) + V_{nogo}(M, \ 0)$$
$$= 0.5V_{go}(M - CV_{go}, \ 1) + 0.5V_{nogo}(M - CV_{nogo}, \ 1)$$
$$= 0.5V_{go}(M - OP, \ 1) + 0.5V_{nogo}(M - OP, \ 1) \tag{16.27}$$

That is for Mark to pay $300 in the state of the world in which he visits the park, and nothing when he doesn't visit the park, is equivalent to Mark's paying $100 to give him the option of going to the park whether or not he is able to go.

The general form of the equation determining the CV or OP is

$$V_{exp} = 0.5V_{go}(M - PAY_{go}, \ 1) + 0.5V_{nogo}(M - PAY_{nogo}, \ 1) \tag{16.28}$$

where PAY_{go} and PAY_{nogo} = payments in the different states of the world. One set of payments that satisfy this is a payment of $300 in the go state of the world and 0 in the nogo state of the world corresponding to Mark's CV in the two states of the world. Another set of payments is a payment of $150 in the go state of the world and $150 in the nogo state of the world that correspond to the relationship for OP which is that $PAY_{go} = PAY_{nogo} = OP$.

In general there will be an infinite number of equivalent payments that satisfy Equation (16.28). For example, perhaps payments of $200 in the go state of the world and $110 in the no go state of the world would also satisfy the equation. Thus, if Mark were offered an arrangement by which he pays $200 if he visits the park and $110 if he doesn't visit the park, he would be indifferent as between an arrangement in which he pays $300 if he visits and $0 if he doesn't, and also be indifferent as between yet another arrangement in which Mark pays $150 whether or not he visits the park. These payments would all give the same expected utility but would not give the same expected values because one values differently the same payments in different states of the world. The locus of all possible pairs that solves Equation (16.28) is called the WTP Locus, and is shown in Figure 16.2.

The vertical axis in Figure 16.2 shows the payments that will be made if the trip is demanded. That is, if Mark is able to go. The horizontal axis shows

Figure 16.2. WTP locus.

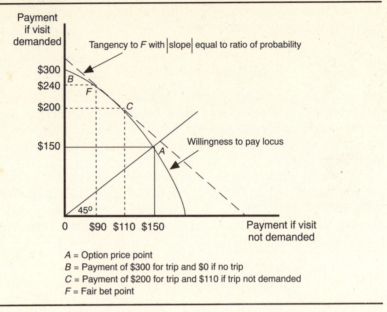

A = Option price point
B = Payment of $300 for trip and $0 if no trip
C = Payment of $200 for trip and $110 if trip not demanded
F = Fair bet point

the payments if the trip is not demanded. Point A is the option price because at point A the same payment is made ($100) whether or not the trip is demanded. Point B shows an ex post payment of $300 and a payment of 0 when the trip is not demanded. Point C shows an ex post payment of $200 and a payment of $110 if the trip is not made. Connecting all such points that are all equally acceptable to Mark (that is, his expected utility is the same) shows Mark's WTP locus.

The slope of the WTP is the MRS between income in the two states of the world. The convex shape of the WTP locus is equivalent to the concave slope of the indifference curve. The convex shape arises because we are not measuring the relative value of two goods but of two payments. The *value* of additional payments in one state of the world, i, relative to those in another state of the world, j, increases as the *amount* of payments in one state, i, increases relative to payments in the other state of the world, j.

The Fair Bet Point.   Point F, the fair bet point, has a special significance that has not yet been discussed. Point F is located by drawing a tangent to the WTP locus with a slope equal to the negative of the ratio of the probabilities in each state of the world. The ratio of the probabilities is analogous to a ratio of prices. In this example, the slope will be equal to -1, since there are equal probabilities of visiting or not visiting the park. The fair bet point represents an efficient equilibrium in the sense discussed in Chapter 2 in the context of equating the MRS with the price ratio. In Figure 16.2 we drew one WTP locus, but imagine a family of such loci. As we move to the southwest, along different WTP loci, Mark is achieving sets of lower and lower payments and his welfare is *increasing*. For any given probability ratio, Mark's equilibrium and his welfare maximum, that is, the lowest WTP locus, will be found by equating MRS with the probability ratio. This occurs at the fair bet point.

The fair bet point will give the largest expected value of all points along the WTP locus. The fair bet point allows Mark to make contingent payments that equalize the marginal utilities of income in both states, go and nogo. Suppose payments at the fair bet point are $240 go and $90 nogo. A risk-neutral entrepreneur that wishes to extract the maximum expected value payment from Mark would offer him the fair bet option. Suppose Mark is offered a choice between an OP of $100 in both states of the world and the fair bet price. He will take the fair bet price even though it involves paying $140 more if he goes and paying only $10 less if he doesn't go. He is willing to do this because the $140 is worth less to him in the state of the world in which he goes than the $10 in the state of the world in which he doesn't go, since the marginal utility of income is greater in the nogo state than in the go state. The fair bet point gives the WTP in a world with the availability of complete contingent contracts, that is, contracts whose payoffs are expressed in terms of contingencies defining possible future conditions.

The difficulty with the fair bet point is that it answers a question that usually does not reflect the realities of choice. In our example, we know that Mark's WTP ex ante is a contingent offer of $240 or $90 depending on whether or not he can go on the trip. In fact no one offers him this sort of contingent contract. The fair bet point gives the right answer in a world of complete contingent contracts, but not the right answer in the real world. Information on the fair bet values gives ex post values where contingent contracts are not available. Knowing Mark's fair bet values doesn't tell us the correct WTP to use in asking whether or not we should preserve Glacier now in a world in which contingent contracts are unavailable. How could we use these values where a decision needs to be made now? The answer is that we could not use the fair bet values.[11] We can, however, use the option price of $100 as the WTP. In this second-best world, the option price is the best measure.

Suppose we are considering whether to preserve the Elwah River from damming. Waiting will lead to a dam. We need a WTP figure for preservation now. The value of the free-flowing Elwah will depend, however, on the success of new, more cost-effective techniques for restoring damaged streams. Some people will only use the Elwah if the new technology is successful and others will use the Elwah to a greater extent if the technology is successful. We cannot wait to see if the new technology develops to decide whether or not to preserve the Elwah for by then the dam will be built. The OP captures a WTP *now* for those people whose value of the Elwah will depend on whether or not the new technology develops.

---

[11]Graham (1981) shows that with perfect contingent claim markets (that is, where insurance markets exist for every possible contingency), and equal assessments of probabilities by all of a large number of people with different state–dependent utility functions, the aggregate value of the WTP of all state-dependent consumers would be the same in different states of the world. Thus, if we knew the aggregate WTP ex ante in such a world this would be the fair bet WTP value to be used. With perfect contingent claim markets, it would be possible to know with certainty the aggregate WTP of all citizens before the state of the world is known. The aggregate WTP would equal or exceed the aggregate consumer surplus or aggregate CVs or aggregate option values.

Option Value.   Option value is the difference between option price and expected consumer surplus. That is,

$$\text{Option value} = \text{option price} - \text{expected consumer surplus}$$

If this value was always small or was of a consistent sign, being positive or negative, we could say more about whether consumer surplus was a lower or upper bound to option price and whether expected consumer surplus was likely to differ much from option price. The sign of option value may be positive or negative, and while its value may often be small, this fact has not been established.

The Use of Option Price in Applied Work.   The first lesson here is that the use of expected consumer surplus will not give the answer to the WTP question. This answer is given by option price. As we have mentioned, expected consumer surplus may be greater or less than option price so that we cannot use expected CS as a bound to the correct value.

The determination of option price will thus be difficult, but not always impossible. Contingent valuation questionnaires are questionnaires that ask people WTP questions about values where these values are contingent upon the state of the world. Such questionnaires hold the possibility of obtaining options values in some, perhaps limited, circumstances. These questionnaires could ask for a hypothetical commitment to be made prior to project completion. For examples of past studies that implement this procedure, see Brookshire, Eubanks, and Randall (1983) and Desousges, Smith, and McGiveny (1981). However, since use value as consumer surplus contains expected consumer surplus, if we add together use value with option price we will be double counting. It is option value, not option price, that should be added to consumer surplus, but option value could be negative.

Much of the discussion in the literature assumes that option value is positive, that is, that option price exceeds expected consumer surplus. Option value is often, and perhaps usually, seen as an additional that needs to be added to estimates of consumer surplus to get total value. Since option value can be negative this is not in general the case. Option value may be viewed as positive because people picture a special setting as the option value context. To clarify this and other value issues let us consider the following setting.

Consider three groups of consumers. One, group A, will consume regardless of the state of the world; the second, group B, will consume depending on the state of the world; the third, group C, will never consume directly but will value the existence of the good. The analyst measures the consumer surplus of group A and finds it to be $100. This is clearly an underestimate. To the amount found for group A, the analyst needs to add the option value, OP, for group B, which is, say, $60. In addition the analyst needs to add the existence value of group C, which is, say, $40. The total WTP is then $200, not just the $100 of group A.

If the world were this neat, option price would be a positive value to be added to consumer surplus.[12] This sort of positive addition to value may

---

[12]Note that option value here is not necessarily positive. We don't know what it is because we have not calculated expected consumer surplus for group B.

be what some analysts have in mind when they treat option value as positive. This is not, however, how values are usually calculated. One envisions a system in which we have calculated the expected consumer surplus of groups A, B, and C. To add option price to this set of values would be to double count since option price and expected consumer surplus are alternative measures of expected utility.

In the real world the situation is unfortunately quite messy. We might calculate expected consumer surplus from existing use of the facility, for example, by use of a travel demand method. Expected consumer surplus consists of the consumer surplus not only of those in group A but also of those in group B. How many of group B are facility users depends on what states of the world exist during the period(s) of data collection. Provided that measurement covers the different states of the world that influence actual use—rain or no rain, for example, perhaps seasonal patterns—one has an ex post estimate of use and thereby of consumer surplus on the part of group B users.

Should an additional amount be added for those group B members who did not use the facility? After all, they have some positive OP. The revealed CS of group B members who actually used the facility, however, will exceed their particular OP. Whether or not the revealed CS for group B users is higher or lower than the entire group's OP we cannot say. Suppose group B consists of Mark Elliot and his sister Mary Alice, each with on OP of $100. If during the period of measurement Mark uses the facility but Mary Alice does not, his measured CS is $300 and hers is zero. The total recorded CS for group B is then $300, which is greater than the $200 sum of their OPs. To add any value to the measured CS in order to represent an option value for group B non-users is to inflate estimates of actual value; by covering reasonable variations in relevant states of the world during data collection, one is allowing all group B members some opportunity to show up and be counted. Ex post values may or may not be reasonable estimates of ex ante consumer surplus. To add OP to these estimates, however, is to double count values.

Option value may not be measurable; the fact that one will often be measuring ex post values has led a number of analysts to despair [for example, see Bishop (1986, p. 149)]. The situation does not seem as pessimistic to us. In practice risks often can be spread so that the information one can collect on the likely ex post willingness to pay is useful in determining an ex ante value. Consider the situation in which only group B exists so that all the estimates we have of the future value of the park are ex post revealed estimates of those who actually use the park but were unsure before that they would be able to use the park, as was the case with Mark. Suppose, on the average over the different states of the world, that 40 percent of those with a prior option demand actually show up. It does not seem unreasonable to decide on whether or not to preserve the park by estimating the ex post WTP of these people and comparing this with the costs of preservation. Private entrepreneurs bear risk and undertake projects on the basis of expected ex post demand. To proceed with public projects on the same basis does not seem unreasonable. The risk of preserving the park today may be undertaken by bond holders who are paid ex post from the fees collected by demanders. In both cases we are asking if users will pay for the values received.

16.7. STOCHASTIC DOMINANCE

There is, however, an empirical technique that we will briefly consider that can be used to rank resources in a way that is consistent with expected utility maximization without having knowledge of the underlying structure of the utility functions themselves. This technique, called *stochastic dominance,* can rank alternative projects and allow us to compute bounds on WTP in certain circumstances. This technique involves determining under what conditions one gamble may be said to dominate another in all probability states.

Suppose we wish to select one project from two alternatives. We have already seen that basing our decision solely on expected net benefits would not account for risk. We have shown how risk can be incorporated into our decision making through the use of financial models like the CAPM to estimate risk-adjusted discount rates. But, as we also discussed, use of these models requires some simplifying assumptions about the structure of risk that may not always hold. And, determining risk-adjusted discount rates may be particularly difficult for public projects (such as hydroelectric dams) where unpriced commodities and nonmarket risks may be the norm.

Stochastic dominance can be used to rank alternative projects based on their expected utilities, without the need to compute risk-adjusted discount rates or limit ourselves to specific types of risk. We introduce stochastic dominance by way of several examples.

Suppose that a decision maker was asked to choose between two gambles, X and Y, with the following outcomes in terms of dollars received:[13]

	Probability					
	$\frac{1}{6}$	$\frac{1}{6}$	$\frac{1}{6}$	$\frac{1}{6}$	$\frac{1}{6}$	$\frac{1}{6}$
X	1	4	1	4	4	4
Y	3	4	3	1	1	4

It is not immediately apparent which is the preferred gamble, since X is better for some outcomes, and Y is better for others. However, we can reorder the gambles, as long as we assume that the outcomes of X are not correlated with those of Y. This is shown as the following:

	Probability					
	$\frac{1}{6}$	$\frac{1}{6}$	$\frac{1}{6}$	$\frac{1}{6}$	$\frac{1}{6}$	$\frac{1}{6}$
X	1	1	4	4	4	4
Y	1	1	3	3	4	4

With this reordering, it is clear that X dominates Y, since X always returns at least as much as Y in every probability state.[14] Formally, we can define the set

---

[13]These examples are taken from Whitmore and Findlay (1978).
[14]Note that, in a mean-variance frontier context, neither gamble can be eliminated since $E(X) > E(Y)$ making X more attractive, but $S_2(X) > S_2(Y)$ making Y more attractive.

U_1 of increasing (in income), continuous, and differentiable utility functions. Any investor with a utility function $u_i \in U_1$ (read u_i and member of the class of utility functions U_1) will therefore prefer X to Y. Equivalently, the expected utility of gamble X, EU(X), is greater than EU(Y), the expected utility of gamble Y, for all $u_i \in U_1$. In other words, X dominates Y in U_1. When one set of outcomes dominates another in regard to the level of risk aversion, it is said that there is a **first-degree stochastic dominance.**

In the preceding example, no mention was made of risk and the marginal utility of income. We only assumed that the decision maker preferred more to less. Since gamble X produces at least as much as gamble Y regardless of the state of the world, the decision maker will always prefer X. We can then say that X shows first-degree stochastic dominance with respect to Y.

In many cases, however, it is not possible to reorder the gambles as in the previous example. To see this, assume the two gambles are as follows:

			Probability			
	$\frac{1}{6}$	$\frac{1}{6}$	$\frac{1}{6}$	$\frac{1}{6}$	$\frac{1}{6}$	$\frac{1}{6}$
X	1	1	4	4	4	4
Y	0	2	3	3	4	4

In this case we cannot reorder the outcomes so that X returns at least as much as Y in all probability states. Thus, even though the expected value of X is greater than Y it does not necessarily follow that the decision maker's expected utility associated with X will be greater than Y. In other words, it is possible to construct utility functions in U_1 such that X will be preferred to Y, and alternative functions such that Y will be preferred to X.[15] We can say, therefore, that neither X nor Y is *dominant* in U_1.

Suppose, however, that we impose the additional constraint of risk aversion, by restricting our attention to the subset U_2 of utility functions in U_1 that are also concave. Thus, $u_i \in U_2$ is concave, if u_i is continuous and differentiable, with $u' > 0$ and $u'' < 0$. The class U_2 restricts the allowable utility functions to those that include risk aversion (diminishing marginal utility of income).

By breaking the gamble in the example into simpler gambles, we can show that, for all $u_i \in U_2$, EU(X) is greater than EU(Y). We can redefine gamble X as a $\frac{1}{3}$ chance of receiving \$1(X_1) and a $\frac{2}{3}$ chance of receiving \$4(X_2). Y is equivalent to a $\frac{1}{3}$ chance of an even gamble between 0 and 2 dollars (Y_1), and an even chance gamble between 3 and 4 dollars (Y_2). Because of diminishing marginal utility of income, utility functions in U_2 will be concave. Therefore, EU(Y_1) = $\frac{1}{2}u(0) + \frac{1}{2}u(2) < u(1) = $ EU(X_1). Similarly EU(Y_2) = $\frac{1}{2}u(3) + \frac{1}{2}u(4) < u(4) = $ EU(X_2). Thus, EU(Y) = $\frac{1}{3}$EU(Y_1) + $\frac{2}{3}$EU(Y_2) < $\frac{1}{3}$EU(X_1) + $\frac{2}{3}$EU(X_2) = EU(X), and X is preferred. That is, the

---

[15]Suppose, for example, that the decision maker's utility function was $u(X) = X$. Then, EU(X) = 3 > EU(Y) = 8/3, and gamble X is preferred. But, if $u(X) = [(X-2)^2 + 0.01]^{-1}$, then EU($X$) = 0.5 < EU($Y$) = 17.08, and gamble Y is preferred.

expected value of Y_1 is the same as X_1, but Y_1 has greater variance than X_1 and is therefore less preferred by risk-averse individuals. The expected value of Y_2 is less than X_2, and Y_2 has greater variance than X_2. Thus, X_2 is preferred to Y_2. Because X_1 and X_2 are preferred to Y_1 and Y_2, X is preferred to Y.

The assumption of risk aversion without specifying its degree may be sufficient to say that one distribution dominates another. It is said that one distribution dominates another in the *second degree* when the assumption of risk aversion alone is necessary for dominance. In general, we read $f >_i g$ as "f dominates g in the ith degree." Let f and g denote two different probability density functions of a (discrete or continuous) random variable x, and let $F(x)$ and $G(x)$ be their respective cumulative density functions, where

$$F(x_i) = \int_{-\infty}^{x_i} f(x)dx$$

Let the set of all possible values of X be denoted X, with $x \in X$. And, let

$$F^1(x) = F(x_i) \quad \text{and} \quad F^2(x) = \int_{-\infty}^{x_i} F^1(x)dx$$

Thus, F^2 set of all (x) equals the area under the cumulative distribution function (cdf) $F(x)$. If one function F^2 dominates another G^2, then there is second-degree stochastic dominance. We could define another function F^3 that equals the area under F^2 and another function G^3 that represents the area under a cumulative density function G^2. Then, if F^3 dominates G^3 we have third-degree stochastic dominance. Each additional degree of stochastic dominance represents more stringent assumptions about risk aversity. First-degree dominance requires no assumption of risk aversion. Second-degree dominance requires just an assumption of some level of risk aversion. Third-degree dominance requires a certain level of risk aversion, and so forth.

Other important properties of stochastic dominance orderings are:

1. Transitivity: If $f >_i g$ and $g >_i h$, then $f >_i h$.
2. Asymmetry: If $f >_i g$, then it is false that $g >_i f$.

Finally, because the class of utility functions U_2 is a subset of U_1, $f >_1 g$ implies $f >_2 g$. The above definition for stochastic dominance leads to two theorems that provide necessary and sufficient conditions for its occurrence.

Theorem 1: $f >_1 g$ iff $G(x) \geq F(x)$ for all $x \in X$.
Theorem 2: $f >_2 g$ iff $G^2(x) \geq F^2(x)$ for all $x \in X$.

[Proofs of these theorems can be found in Hadar and Russell (1969) or Whitmore and Findlay (1978).]

Graphically, Theorems 1 and 2 mean that the dominant distribution is the one whose outcomes lie further toward the right. This is shown in Figure 16.3, where for first-degree stochastic dominance, the cdf $F(X)$ always lies to the right of $G(Y)$. With second-degree stochastic dominance, $F(X)$ could lie to the left of $G(Y)$, but $F^2(X)$ would always lie to the right of $G^2(Y)$.

Figure 16.3.

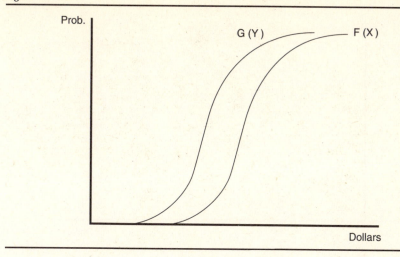

We can use stochastic dominance to rank alternative projects in a manner consistent with expected utility maximization. Suppose, for example, we used a Monte Carlo simulation model (see Chapter 17) to derive distributions of the potential net benefits for two alternative sized dams (A and B), at a site on the Peace River, whose benefits varied depending on the amount of annual rainfall. Using stochastic dominance, we might be able to rank the two dams, such that all risk-averse decision makers would choose (say) dam A. Our ranking would be consistent with expected utility maximization without having any knowledge about the decision maker's specific utility functions, except to assert that decision makers were risk averse (second-degree stochastic dominance). As a result, using stochastic dominance in benefit–cost analysis can allow us to combine theoretical consistency with empirical tractability.

A final advantage of using stochastic dominance techniques to rank resources is that we can avoid calculation of individual risk-adjusted discount rates. In fact, when using these techniques, comparisons of alternative resources must be made using identical discount rates, regardless of the differences in the perceived risks associated with the alternative projects. Identical discount rates must be used because the distributions of the net project benefits will reflect the riskiness of the projects, including any identifiable covariant risk. If different risk-adjusted discounted rates were used to generate distributions of net project benefits, and then stochastic dominance orderings were determined, risk would be "double counted." Thus, the use of stochastic dominance can simplify the debate over the appropriate risk adjusted discount rates.

Stochastic Dominance and Willingness-to-Pay. One useful feature of a stochastic dominance approach is that it can be combined with a willingness-to-pay approach. It may be possible to determine WTP bounds for both of the dams. To see this, consider the case where we have found dam A to dominate dam B in the second degree. We can ask what is the maximum payment that could be attached to A that would not destroy the decision maker's preference for A over B? This amount we call PAY_{max}, but it is actually an approximation

Figure 16.4.

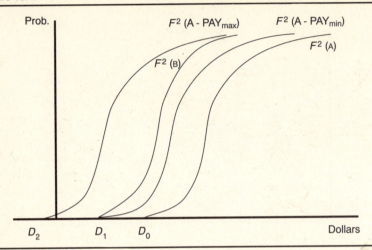

of the lower WTP bound. In the context of the dam example, we could ask what is the most the risk-averse decision maker would pay for the right to build dam A (A would still dominate B). The answer can be found by shifting $F^2(A)$ to the left until, at some point on the curves, $F^2(A - PAY_{max}) > F^2(B)$. We can also ask what is the minimum payment that could be attached to A such that the decision maker would switch his or her preference from A to B. This amount we call PAY_{min}, but it is an approximation of the upper bounds on WTP, which the student can easily see by working out any simple example.

This larger payment, PAY_{min}, can be found by further shifting $F^2(A)$ to the left. In Figure 16.4, $F^2(A - PAY_{min})$ is defined such that $F^2(A - PAY_{max}) - F^2(B) < 0$ always. Thus, at this payment level, all risk-averse decision makers will prefer B to A. To recapitulate, PAY_{max} is the most that the decision maker would pay and still prefer the originally dominant option. PAY_{min} is the larger payment that would just be enough for all decision makers to switch to the other option. We think it is a useful technique to calculate PAY_{max} and PAY_{min} for first- and second-degree stochastic dominance when comparing risky projects.

To illustrate this WTP bounds technique, we use as an example the Columbia River Treaty downstream energy benefits.[16] The Columbia River Treaty was signed by the United States and Canada in 1964. It provided for additional hydroelectric generation in the United States by constructing three hydro storage facilities in Canada. This additional power produced in the United States is called the downstream energy benefits. The treaty stipulated that these benefits would be equally shared between the two countries.

To build the three storage facilities, Canada sold its share of the downstream energy benefits to the United States for 30 years. That sale expires in 2003, at which time the United States will have to transmit Canada's share of the benefits back to the border.

---

[16] A complete description of the Columbia River Treaty can be found in J. Krutilla (1967).

TABLE 16.2   WTP Bounds for the Downstream Energy Benefits—30-Year Purchase (Millions of 1988 Dollars)

ARA Bounds	WTP(1)	WTP(2)
none	$666	$3,010
> 0	$1,100	$1,700
.001-.002	$1,190	$1,210

In a recent study, Lesser (1989) estimated WTP bounds associated with the United States repurchasing the downstream energy benefits.[17] The results of this study are shown in Table 16.2. The first set of estimated WTP bounds place no restrictions on the coefficient of absolute risk aversion. It thus corresponds to the case of first-degree stochastic dominance, where decision makers are not necessarily risk averse. The WTP bounds for this case are relatively large, between $666 million and $3010 million (1988 dollars).

The next set of bounds restricts the coefficient of risk aversion to be positive. In other words, the decision maker is assumed to be risk averse. Adding the constraint of risk aversion, we find that the WTP bounds are tighter, between $1100 and $1700 million (1988 dollars). Finally, the allowable values of the coefficient of absolute risk aversion (ARA) are restricted even further, so that $0.001 < ARA < 0.002$. Using these more restrictive bounds, the WTP bounds are quite close, between $1190 and $1201 million (1988 dollars).

SUMMARY

The concept of willingness-to-pay is extremely important in benefit–cost analysis. It has been the subject of much discussion and argument in the literature as to "correct" measures and empirical applicability. Uncertainty will almost always be present when we evaluate project benefits and costs into the future. We have seen how attitudes toward risk can influence project selection. And, we have seen that uncertainty can change our definition of WTP.

Using an indirect utility framework, we developed the WTP locus and illustrated several alternative payment schemes associated with it. We showed that the fair bet point was the theoretically correct measure of WTP, since it is defined as the maximum WTP along the locus. Because a payment scheme corresponding to the fair bet point would probably not be practical, we discussed option price as a second-best alternative. Option price corresponded to the point on the WTP locus where payments in all states of the world were equal.

Unfortunately, calculation of option price may be difficult or impractical. Thus, a focus of the literature has been to determine whether option price can be bounded by estimates of the compensating variation. Because option price cannot be bounded, however, except under special conditions, a purely

---

[17]Estimating WTP bounds in practice requires the application of Generalized Stochastic Dominance (GSD), first developed by Meyer (1977). First- and second-degree stochastic dominance are special cases of GSD. Testing for GSD is fairly complex. It involves placing specific bounds on the values of the ARA coefficient, and numerically testing for stochastic dominance.

empirical approach to option price will be insufficient. To use option price, utility functions usually must be assumed.

Despite these limitations, policy makers are required to make decisions about resource alternatives. And they must often account for uncertainty. To facilitate decision making, we introduced stochastic dominance. We showed that stochastic dominance could be used to rank alternative resources in a theoretically consistent manner, yet did not require explicit specification of the utility function. Finally, we discussed the use of stochastic dominance to determine WTP bounds for projects, and the use of values for absolute risk aversion, ARA, to narrow those bounds.

QUESTIONS AND PROBLEMS

1. Many municipal governments use their cost of capital to evaluate all their capital projects. What kind of mistakes will they make?
2. A project costs $1 million and offers a single cash flow of $1.5 million in one year. Given a market risk premium, $r_m - r_f$, of 6 percent and a beta of 2 what is the smallest size of the risk-free discount rate under which the project would be accepted?
3. A project with capital costs of $10 million has generated income in year 3 only. The certainty equivalent of this flow is $15 million. If the risk-free interest rate is 4 percent is this a worthwhile investment?
4. ATT is considering two alternative risky investments abroad. The investments will be insured against political risk by the Overseas Investors Protection Corp, OPIC, a quasi-government (U.S.) agency. Each investment has a capital cost of $12 million. For the first investment in Rwanda the cash flow is to be $40 million made in 5 years. The second investment in the country of Ghana involves a return of $20 million after only one year. David Husband, analyst for OPIC, reckons that there is a 20 percent chance that both of these governments will be overthrown before payment is due in which case no payment will be made. OPIC decides to use a discount rate of 30 percent rather than the usual rate of 10 percent to account for political risk. On this basis OPIC indicates they will insure the second project but not the first.
   a. Has OPIC made a mistake? If so, what is its nature?
   b. Which project is better using the 10 percent discount rate?
      Suppose that ATT estimates that the Rwanda project has a beta of 1.5 and the Ghana project a beta of 1.0. ATT has evaluated the projects using these betas in conjunction with its estimate that the market risk premium is 4 percent and the risk-free rate is 4 percent.
   c. What project will they prefer?
   d. Should the ATT evaluation guide OPIC's choice of which investment to insure? Why or why not?
5. a. Problem 15.3 in Chapter 15 considered the net present value under uncertainty of different options for land owned by Vancouver, B.C. Suppose that you know only that the project will not be completed in year 1 and that it could be completed any year after year 1. You do *not* know (unlike Problem 15.3) the probabilities of completion for any year after year 1. That is, the project could be completed any time after year 1. If a choice must be made between options B and C, show how this can be done to produce a clear choice. Assume there is no financial risk. Do the cash flows for one choice dominate the others?

b. Suppose that the city manager for Vancouver wishes to consider yet a fourth option, option D. This would be the same as option C but the city would keep the revenues from the mall rather than sell its share in the project. On the average, revenues are expected to be $630,000 per year for 50 years. Starting in year $X + 1$, revenues will be high in years in which Vancouver is doing well and in which tax receipts are higher and will be low in years in which the local economy is doing poorly. The manager who has now been convinced to use a 6 percent discount rate points out that the net present value of this project will be about $5.430 million using a 6 percent discount rate and suggests that this is the option the city should adopt.

(1) Is his calculation of NPV correct?

(2) Can you present an argument as to why this option may not be the best and why a different discount rate should be used to discount the value of these revenues to present value?

Suppose that by looking at the experience with other malls you find that the simple regression of revenue changes for malls with changes in city tax revenues is

$$\% \text{ change in tax revenues} = 0.04 + 2.10 \ (\% \text{ change in mall revenues})$$

(3) Using this equation and a risk-free rate of 4 percent and a market rate of 6 percent, suggest what discount rate might be used to evaluate the City Manager's suggestion. Do you think that the choice between option C and D is clear cut? Would you choose option B, C, or D? Might the beta for option B be negative?

6. The city of Seattle is considering investing either in a computer system or in a recycling system. They cannot afford to invest in both. The city figures that the payoff for both systems *assuming they are operating successfully* has a beta of only 0.8. The computer system is expected to yield $3 million per year for 10 years in cost savings. The recycling program is expected to yield $2 million per year for 15 years. These cash flows are inflation adjusted. The nominal risk premium is 6 percent, and the nominal risk-free rate is 7 percent. Estimates of inflation are 3 percent. Both projects have a 20 percent chance of going bust with no payoff.

a. What real discount rate should be used for evaluation?

b. The city analyst proposes to add 25 percent to the discount rate calculated in a. Calculate the NPVs using this rate.

c. What do you say the NPVs should be?

REFERENCES

Bishop, Richard C., "Resource Valuation Under Uncertainty," *Advances in Applied Micro-Economics*, 4, 133–152, 1986.

Brealy, R., and S. Myers, *Principles of Corporate Finance*, New York: 3rd Edition, McGraw-Hill, 1988.

Brookshire, David S., Larry S. Eubanks, and Alan Randall, "Estimating Option Prices and Existence Values for Wildlife Resources," *Land Economics* 59, 1–15, February 1983.

Desousges, W., V. Kerry Smith, and M. P. McGiveny, "A Comparison of Alternative Approaches for Estimating Recreation and Related Benefits of Water Quality Improvements," Washington, D.C.: EPA-230-05-83-001, March 1981.

Graham, Daniel, "Cost-Benefit Analysis Under Uncertainty," *American Economic Review* 71, 715–725, September 1981.

Hadar, J., and W. Russell, "Rules for Ordering Uncertain Prospects." *American Economic Review* 59, 25–34, December 1969.

Haugen, Robert A., *Modern Investment Theory*, Englewood Cliffs, N.J.: Prentice Hall, 1986.

Krutilla, J., *The Columbia River Treaty: The Economics of an International River Basin Development,* Baltimore: Johns Hopkins Press, 1967.

Lesser, Jonathan, Renegotiating a Purchase of the Columbia River Treaty Downstream Power Benefits: An Application of Benefit-Cost Analysis Under Uncertainty. Ph.D. Dissertation, Seattle: University of Washington, 1989.

Lind, R. C. (ed), *Discounting for Time and Money in Energy Policy,* Baltimore, Md.: Johns Hopkins Press, 1982..

Meyer, J., "Second Degree Stochastic Dominance with Respect to a Function," *International Economic Review* 18, 477–487, June 1977.

Schall, L. D., and C. W. Haley, *Introduction to Financial Management,* New York: McGraw-Hill, 1991.

Varian, Hal R., *Microeconomic Analysis* (Third Edition), New York: W. W. Norton, 1992.

Weisbrod, Burton, "Collective-Consumption Services of Individual-Consumption Goods," *Quarterly Journal of Economics* 78, 471–477, August 1964.

Whitmore, G., and M. Findlay (eds.), *Stochastic Dominance,* Lexington: D. C. Heath, 1978.

17

Techniques for
Analyzing Uncertainty

M ost benefit–cost analyses of public projects do not include any explicit analysis of risk or uncertainty. These analyses either assume that all future costs and benefits are known or assume that there is no reasonable way to include uncertainty in the calculations. In many cases, such assumptions are reasonable. However, many public sector decisions would benefit from more explicit consideration of the uncertainties affecting future costs and benefits.

Chapter 15 provided an introduction to the basic concepts of risk and uncertainty. Chapter 16 outlined several approaches for incorporating risk into financial analyses. In this chapter, we will focus on three techniques for reflecting uncertainty in basic benefit–cost calculations. These techniques are generally applicable to the types of benefit–cost problems commonly encountered by public sector analysts.

This chapter begins with a review of the nature of uncertainty and a discussion of how and when it is appropriate to employ analytical techniques to deal with uncertainty. The remainder of the chapter is devoted to discussions of three common techniques for including uncertainty in benefit–cost calculations.

17.1. NATURE OF UNCERTAINTY

Many of the examples of benefit–cost calculations presented have assumed that the values of costs and benefits were known exactly and that future events were perfectly predictable. For example, we have assumed that the cash flows resulting from a project were known precisely at the outset; likewise, we have assumed that the lifespan of an asset such as a road, machine, or vehicle is exactly fixed.

Such assumptions are obviously unrealistic. The world is fraught with uncertainty; one need only think of trends in energy prices to see how unpredictable major factors influencing public policy can be. While it is true that in most cases the errors introduced by ignoring uncertainty are not large and can be overlooked, a policy analyst will often confront problems for which a knowledge of uncertainty calculations is essential.

17.1.1. Sources of Uncertainty

There are many causes of uncertainty. For example, agricultural production is influenced by the weather and the presence of pests, neither of which is entirely predictable. The cost of a highway repair project depends upon the condition of the existing roadway, which is often difficult to determine in advance. The revenues generated by a sales tax increase will depend upon the number of purchases that are postponed or are shifted to out-of-state suppliers because of the higher tax. These examples show that no catalog of the sources of uncertainty could ever be complete.

It is useful, however, to distinguish between two types of uncertainty: (1) uncertainty caused by the *unpredictability of future events,* and (2) uncertainty caused by *limitations on the precision of data.*

The first type of uncertainty is a consequence of our inability to foretell the future. An agricultural policy analyst cannot know with certainty what the weather will be in Kansas, Manitoba, or the Ukraine during the fall harvest season and thus cannot be sure how much wheat will be produced. Of course, she will be able to make an estimate based on historical weather patterns, but historical patterns offer no assurance for any single year. The analyst can attempt to cope with this type of uncertainty by using forecasts, but there is no way to completely eliminate the uncertainty caused by our inability to predict future events.

The second type of uncertainty is a consequence of the inability to measure many variables with a high degree of precision at a reasonable cost. It is theoretically possible to precisely measure many variables of interest to policy makers. For example, many types of aid provided by the U.S. federal government are allocated to states and localities based on population. The share of aid given to the city of San Diego is based on the Census Bureau's 1990 estimate of the city's population, which was 1,110,549. The probability that San Diego's population in 1990 was really 1,110,549 is essentially zero; the Bureau undoubtedly missed some individuals and probably counted some people twice. Thus, information on the exact population of San Diego is uncertain, which may affect the federal government's ability to administer policies in the way that was intended. Uncertainty of this type can be reduced by more accurate measurement, but the virtues of this accuracy are often outweighed by the time and expense required to get better information. In some cases it will be appropriate to invest the resources necessary to get more precise data; in other cases, it will be better to utilize the available data and assess the resulting uncertainty using the techniques described in this chapter.

17.1.2. Coping with Uncertainty

Once it is recognized that uncertainty is an important issue for policy analysis, the obvious next question is how to deal with such uncertainty. There are three possible approaches to this problem. First, uncertainty can simply be ignored. This is appropriate in cases where the uncertainty is small, the time span of importance is short, or where the benefit–cost calculations are intended only as rough estimates. Unfortunately, uncertainty is often ignored by policy analysts in cases that do not fall into these categories.

A second approach is to reduce uncertainty to levels at which it can safely be ignored. This usually involves gathering additional data or more accurate information on which to base the benefit–cost analyses.

The final approach is to recognize the uncertainty and factor it into the benefit–cost calculations. Three techniques to do this are described later in this chapter. Besides providing additional quantitative information on the benefit–cost calculation, these methods often yield several other advantages, including:

1. *Recognizing uncertainties.* The explicit recognition of uncertainties helps policy makers understand the quality of information used to support a particular decision and gives them an idea of potential problems in the analysis.
2. *Identifying information needs.* Analyzing the impacts of uncertainty on a benefit–cost calculation often highlights subjects for which better information is needed.
3. *Exploring causes of potential success or failure.* The use of methods to analyze uncertainty usually reveals factors that have the greatest influence on the possible results of a project. Once these factors are recognized, it may be possible to modify or influence them to increase the project's chances for success.
4. *Identifying options once a project is underway.* If uncertainties are analyzed before a project is begun, it is frequently possible to identify strategies to be pursued after the project is underway. In particular, the analysis may suggest conditions that indicate when the project should be terminated.

These other virtues of uncertainty analysis suggest that the analysis be undertaken in some cases when it would otherwise be acceptable to ignore uncertainty.

17.2. ANALYTICAL TECHNIQUES

Many techniques have been developed for dealing with uncertainty. Some of these techniques were developed with public policy analysis in mind, while others have been adapted from uses in other fields. In general, the most important analytical techniques fall into three categories:

1. Sensitivity analysis
2. Simulation
3. Decision trees

The sections below describe these techniques and their advantages and disadvantages.

EXAMPLE 17.1

Variable-by-Variable Sensitivity Analysis

The Seaside City Council is considering a project to improve the community-owned beach for the coming year. The city's engineering department expects to take 45 days to complete the project, but the time could vary between 40 and 55 days depending on construction conditions. Each day of work will cost the city $2000. The city estimates that 20,000 people will use the beach this summer and that the improvements will increase the value of their experiences by an average of $5 each. However, historical data indicate that beach usage could range from 17,000 to 22,000 people. Assume that no benefits of the project will carry forward to future years. Using sensitivity analysis, identify which combinations of variables will produce an attractive benefit–cost ratio.

Step 1: List all important variables. For this analysis, construction days and beach usage are the only important factors.

Step 2: Identify a range of possible values:

	Optimistic	Most Likely	Pessimistic
Days	40	45	55
Usage	22,000	20,000	17,000

Step 3: Calculate the appropriate result. In this case, we will use the benefit–cost ratio, BCR. Note that discounting can essentially be ignored since all costs and benefits are accrued in a short time period.

$$BCR = \frac{\sum_{t=0}^{n} B_t}{\sum_{t=0}^{n} C_t}$$

17.2.1. Sensitivity Analysis

Sensitivity analysis is the simplest and most frequently used method for analyzing uncertainty. In essence, sensitivity analysis measures how sensitive the result of a benefit–cost analysis is to a change in one of the variables.

For example, consider a situation in which a health policy analyst wishes to identify the potential costs and benefits of a government health program that will reimburse patients for the use of a new health care device. In order to compute these figures, the analyst must determine how many people are likely to use the device and what benefits they are likely to obtain. This will be affected by the number of individuals suffering from a problem that the device can correct, the availability of the device, its effectiveness, its side effects, and the availability of alternative treatment methods. None of these factors is likely to be known with certainty.

For the expected values:

$$BCR = \frac{(20,000)(\$5)}{(45)(\$2,000)}$$

$$= 1.11$$

For ranges of construction days:

$$\text{Optimistic: } BCR = \frac{(20,000)(\$5)}{(40)(\$2,000)}$$

$$= 1.25$$

$$\text{Pessimistic: } BCR = \frac{(20,000)(\$5)}{(55)(\$2,000)}$$

$$= 0.91$$

For ranges of beach usage:

$$\text{Optimistic: } BCR = \frac{(22,000)(\$5)}{(45)(\$2,000)}$$

$$= 1.22$$

$$\text{Pessimistic: } BCR = \frac{(17,000)(\$5)}{(45)(\$2,000)}$$

$$= 0.94$$

Thus, the expected values and optimistic values yield desirable BCRs. However, if either variable produces a pessimistic value, the project will have an unattractive BCR. This suggests that steps should be considered to reduce construction time and stimulate beach use.

The analyst would generally calculate the costs and benefits using his best estimate of each of the relevant factors. A more complete analysis would go a step further and test the sensitivity of the result to changes in each of the factors. Thus, the analyst would want to consider the costs and benefits if the device were more effective or less effective than anticipated, had more or fewer users than expected, and so on.

There are two basic approaches to sensitivity analysis:

1. The *variable-by-variable approach,* which treats each variable separately
2. The *scenario approach,* which treats variables in groups

Each approach is described below.

Variable-by-Variable Approach.   One common method of sensitivity analysis is to treat each individual variable separately. This method involves three analytical steps:

1. List all variables that are important for the analysis.
2. For each variable, identify a range of possible values. In the simple problems we have considered so far in this book, we have assumed that each variable has only one possible value. When sensitivity analysis is employed, we consider the different values each variable might have. It is usually appropriate to consider three to five values for each variable, unless the range of possible outcomes for that variable is more restricted. The most common approach is to prepare "optimistic," "pessimistic," and "most likely" estimates for each of the variables. The optimistic and pessimistic values can be defined in terms of a number of standard deviations above or below the mean value, if such information is available. The range of values used in the analysis is often derived from previous experience or from the experiences of other agencies with similar projects.
3. Calculate the appropriate result (such as the net present value or benefit–cost ratio) using each possible value of the variable, holding all other variables at their expected values.

If a calculation of NPV involves three variables labeled A, B, and C, the analysis would begin by listing the variables and developing optimistic, pessimistic, and expected values for each variable. The table would look like this:

Variable	Optimistic	Expected	Pessimistic
A	15	20	30
B	1000	500	200
C	14	13	11

Note that optimistic values can be either higher or lower than expected values. The optimistic value will be higher for benefits, as for items B and C, since we hope that benefits exceed our best estimate. The optimistic value will be lower for costs, as for item A, since we hope that costs are lower than our best estimate. The reverse patterns hold true for pessimistic values. Note also that there need not be a fixed relationship among the optimistic, expected, and pessimistic values; for example, the optimistic value for variable B is 500 more than the expected value, while the pessimistic value is only 300 less than the expected value.

Once the values of the variables are established, the usual calculation of NPV would be made using the expected values of each of the variables. A sensitivity analysis then requires several additional calculations. First, the NPV would be calculated using the optimistic estimate for variable A and the expected values of variables B and C. The calculation would then be repeated using the pessimistic value of A and the expected values of the other variables. These results would show how sensitive the NPV is to changes in variable A. The entire process would then be repeated using the alternative values of variable B and the expected values of

EXAMPLE 17.2

Variable-by-Variable Sensitivity Analysis

A new public hospital is expected to cost $175,000,000 to build. The contractor says the building may cost only $160,000,000 if conditions are ideal, but costs could escalate to $210,000,000 if the weather is bad and materials are delayed. The benefits of the hospital for the first five years are given below in millions of dollars:

Year	1	2	3	4	5
Optimistic	45	55	55	55	55
Expected	40	50	50	50	50
Pessimistic	35	47	47	47	47

Assume the benefits in subsequent years can be ignored at this time. The appropriate discount rate is 8 percent. Using variable-by-variable sensitivity analysis, determine the NPV of this project under different combinations of variables.

Step 1: List all important variables. In this case, these have already been combined into overall costs and benefits.

Step 2: Identify a range of possible values. A range of costs is given, and the present value of the benefits can be found as follows (using the optimistic data as an example):

$$\sum_{t=0}^{n} \frac{B_t}{(1+r)^t} = \frac{45}{1.08} + \frac{55[1-(1.08)^{-4}]}{(0.08)(1.08)}$$

$$= 210.3$$

The other two possibilities are calculated in the same way. This produces the following ranges:

	Optimistic	Expected	Pessimistic
Cost	160	175	210
Benefits	210.3	190.4	176.5

Step 3: Calculate the appropriate result, in this case the NPV. For the expected values:

$$NPV = \$190.4 - \$175$$

$$= \$15.4 \text{ million}$$

Similar calculations are made for the optimistic and pessimistic values for each variable:

Optimistic costs:	$30.4 million
Pessimistic costs:	−$19.6 million
Optimistic benefits:	$35.3 million
Pessimistic benefits:	$1.5 million

Thus, the project is desirable in all cases except when the construction costs are high. The project's managers should carefully monitor these costs and try to find ways to ensure that the original cost estimates are met.

variables A and C, and would be repeated again using the range of estimates for variable C along with the expected values of variables A and B. The final result illustrates the sensitivity of the NPV to changes in each of the variables.

Scenario Approach.   Variable-by-variable sensitivity analysis is useful for many relatively simple analyses. However, this approach assumes that variables operate independently. In our earlier example, we assumed that an optimistic value of variable A could exist with the expected values of variables B and C. In the real world, however, variables are often interdependent, and the optimistic value of variable A may only exist when variable B also assumes an optimistic value or when variable C assumes a pessimistic value.

A good example of this interdependence involves energy demand estimates prepared for the Pacific Northwest region of the United States in the early 1970s. Utility analysts noted that the demand for electricity was rising by about 7 percent per year and calculated that the region's inexpensive hydroelectric power would soon be used up. These analysts suggested that a series of new nuclear and coal-fired power plants were needed. As construction began on these plants, the cost of power began to rise, which in turn reduced demand. The eventual result was that the region had a surplus of power, higher electricity prices, and several abandoned partially completed nuclear reactors. The analysts had generally overlooked the relationship between price and demand and had assumed that rapid growth in demand would continue to exist even with higher prices. In other words, they had combined variables in ways that were not realistic.

Problems such as this can be avoided by using alternative scenarios for sensitivity analysis. Rather than using combinations of variables based upon optimistic, pessimistic, and expected values, several consistent combinations of variables are studied. These combinations are known as scenarios. This type of sensitivity analysis involves two basic steps:

1. Identify several possible consistent combinations of variables.
2. Compute the result (such as the NPV) for each scenario.

The analyst can then see which scenarios are likely to produce favorable or unfavorable results and can make decisions about the project accordingly.

Advantages and Disadvantages.   Sensitivity analysis has several advantages as a technique for analyzing uncertainty. It gives some information about possible outcomes under different circumstances and therefore allows more informed decisions to be made. It forces recognition of key variables and their possible implications, and in scenario analysis it recognizes the interactions among variables. The results may indicate areas in which further research should be conducted to get better data before a project is undertaken.

Sensitivity analysis is subject to important limitations, however. First, there are no definite rules for choosing values for variables or for selecting pessimistic and optimistic estimates for variables, so the meaning of the results is not entirely clear. Second, it is often difficult to get information about alternative estimates for each variable, and it is likewise hard to develop consistent scenarios. Third, the variable-by-variable approach overlooks interaction among the variables and may therefore lead to the analysis of impossible com-

EXAMPLE 17.3

Scenario Approach to Sensitivity Analysis

A state government is considering a new work-incentive program for people receiving public assistance. The program would pay participants $1000 if they received instruction in job search techniques. The total cost per participant is $2000, which includes the cost of the instruction and the payments to individuals. Each individual who obtains a job will save the state $10,000 in public assistance costs. No one is certain, however, how many individuals will participate in the program and what percentage will get jobs. Several scenarios are possible:

Scenario	Participants	Percentage Getting Jobs
1	10,000	22%
2	15,000	15%
3	25,000	12%
4	37,000	10%

Calculate the NPV of this program under each scenario. Assume that all costs and benefits occur simultaneously so no discounting is needed.

Step 1: Identify several scenarios. These are listed above.

Step 2: Calculate the NPV under each scenario. Since no discounting is needed:

$$NPV = \sum_{t=0}^{n} B_t - \sum_{t=0}^{n} C_t$$

For Scenario 1:

$$NPV = (10,000)(0.22)(\$10,000) - (10,000)(\$2000)$$
$$= \$2,000,000$$

This shows 22 percent of 10,000 people getting jobs worth $10,000 each, minus the cost of providing training for 10,000 people at $2000 each. Similarly,

Scenario 2: NPV = −$7,500,000

Scenario 3: NPV = −$20,000,000

Scenario 4: NPV = −$37,000,000

Thus, the program has a positive NPV only if it is relatively small and has a high placement rate. Note, however, that there may be other benefits from the training that are not included in this financial analysis.

---

binations of variables. Finally, the scenario approach is limited in that usually only a small number of scenarios are considered.

These strengths and weaknesses suggest that sensitivity analysis is best suited for relatively simple problems or for problems where rough accuracy is sufficient. Sensitivity analysis is best used to illustrate the range of possible outcomes and to identify variables for which better information or more precise controls are needed.

EXAMPLE 17.4

Monte Carlo Simulation

A state highway department is considering a plan to improve lighting on a dangerous section of a rural highway. The improvements would cost $5,000,000 and would last for eight years. The lighting would help to reduce accidents, but the department's planners do not know exactly how many accidents would be prevented. Based upon experience at similar sites, they have prepared probability estimates for the number of accidents that would be prevented each year.

Accidents Prevented	Probability
9	30%
10	40%
11	20%
12	10%

Each accident that is prevented will yield $100,000 in benefits. If the discount rate is 10 percent, is this project a worthwhile investment?

This problem can be solved using Monte Carlo simulation. It is a relatively simple problem and could be solved using other techniques, but it will help to illustrate the approaches used to solve more complex simulation problems.

Step 1: Develop a computer model. There are only three variables involved in this problem: costs (C), benefits (B), and the number of accidents prevented (N). The costs are fixed:

$$C = \$5,000,000$$

The benefits are a function of the number of accidents prevented:

$$B = \$100,000 \times N$$

This equation is the only one necessary for the computer model.

Step 2: Specify the probabilities. The probabilities for N are shown in the table above. The same probabilities apply to each of the eight years of the project's lifespan, so only one set of calculations needs to be made.

Step 3: Sample the distribution and calculate cash flows. The computer now uses the equation relating B to N and the probability distribution for N to calculate values for B. It chooses values for N in proportion to their probability; that is, the computer is four times more likely to choose an N of 10 than an N of 12 since the probability of N being 10 is four times greater than the probability of

17.2.2. Simulation

The second important technique for dealing with uncertainty is simulation. Simulation is an outgrowth of sensitivity analysis that considers many possible combinations of variables, rather than a few estimates or a few scenarios. It

N being 12. For each choice of N, the computer calculates B and stores the result. After several hundred calculations, the computer produces a probability distribution for B such as is shown in Figure 17.1.

Based upon these results, the expected value of B, $E(B)$, is $1,010,000.

The NPV of this project can be calculated using the expected value of the benefits:

$$\text{NPV} = \sum_{t=1}^{8} \frac{1,010,000}{(1.10)^t} - 5,000,000$$

Simplifying the calculation gives

$$\text{NPV} = \$1,010,000 \left[\frac{1 - (1.10)^{-8}}{0.10} \right] - \$5,000,000$$

$$= \$5,388,275 - \$5,000,000$$

$$= \$388,275$$

The project has a positive net present value and should be pursued.

Figure 17.1. Probability Distribution of Benefits.

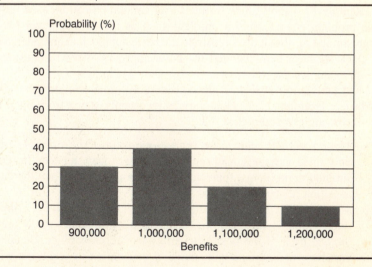

can thus be a very powerful analytical tool. Unfortunately, this power comes at the expense of requiring a great deal of information about the project under consideration.

A wide variety of simulation techniques have been developed for use in business, economics, engineering, and other fields. Some simulation techniques are relatively simple, while others are extremely complex and time consuming. In this book, we will present only one simulation technique, known as *Monte Carlo simulation*. This technique gets its name because it relies on choosing values for variables based upon the laws of probability, somewhat like a roulette wheel at the casino in Monte Carlo establishes winning numbers. Monte Carlo simulation is probably the most widely used simulation technique for financial analysis.

Monte Carlo simulation relies on a computer to perform a large number of calculations that reflect many possible combinations of variables. This technique requires three major analytical steps:

1. Develop a computerized model of the project's cash flows (or other factors of interest). The model should include equations showing the relationships among the different variables.
2. Specify the probabilities for different results for each of the variables.
3. Sample the probability distributions and calculate the resulting cash flows.

The analyst must conduct the first two steps, while the computer performs the calculations required in the third step. Hundreds or thousands of combinations of variables are tested by the computer in a typical simulation.

The result of the simulation is a probability distribution of the project's cash flows. This distribution reveals the range of possible cash flows resulting from the project and shows which results are more likely than others. The expected value of the cash flow, which is found from the mean of the probability distribution, can be used to calculate the NPV, the BCR, or other results of interest. The variance of the simulated distribution can also be determined.

Example 17.4 shows how Monte Carlo simulation can be used for a very simple problem. In practice, a problem such as this would never be solved through simulation, but it does illustrate the basic approach in an understandable way. Once we have demonstrated the basic approach, we will consider more complex examples.

Most simulation problems are considerably more complex than the one described in Example 17.4. This complexity usually stems from one or more of the following characteristics:

1. *More variables with more interrelationships.* The example included only three variables, and only two of them were related. In most real simulation problems, there are several more variables and the variables are often related in complex ways.
2. *More complex probability distributions.* The probability distribution in the example is very simple. Only four discrete values for N are possible and each of the possibilities has a fixed probability. Usually, each variable can assume a wide range of values, which yields a continuous rather than a discrete probability distribution.
3. *Variability over time.* In Example 17.4, the relationships among variables and the probability distribution for N do not change over time. This allows us to use the same result for B for each of the eight years of the project's lifespan. In many simulation problems, however, the relationships among variables and the probability distributions do change

in successive years. In fact, it is common to have problems where the results in a particular year are dependent upon the results of previous years.

These complications make simulation much more difficult, but also make it more valuable. Simulation is expensive and unnecessary for simple problems but it is often the only way to approach more complex situations.

Advantages and Disadvantages. Simulation is an extremely powerful technique that allows many combinations of variables to be explored. A simulation analysis produces information about the range of likely results, along with an estimate of the expected value. Simulations often reveal combinations of variables that produce unexpected outcomes, which allows the project to be redesigned to accommodate these outcomes. For all these reasons, simulation can be very valuable in analyzing complex projects.

However, simulation suffers from three disadvantages. First, it is often difficult to prepare good probability estimates for each of the variables. Second, it is also often difficult to develop equations that reflect all the possible interactions among variables. Third, preparing a computer model can be expensive and time consuming, although the availability of powerful computers and standardized statistical software have made this problem less significant.

A review of these advantages and disadvantages suggests that simulation is best suited for relatively complex projects and for projects that need to be very carefully analyzed. In these cases, the time and expense involved in preparing a simulation are usually justified. For simpler projects or projects that do not require detailed uncertainty analysis, simulation is usually unnecessary.

17.2.3. Decision Trees

The third common approach for analyzing uncertainty is the *decision tree*. This approach begins with a graphic representation of the different possible outcomes of a decision, and then uses probability analysis to calculate the overall expected value of the project.

Decision trees are generally used for projects that have costs or benefits in several time periods. The decision tree shows these possible outcomes in a consistent and easily understood format. However, decision trees can become very complicated for projects with long durations or large numbers of possible outcomes.

Analytical Approach. In the decision tree technique, different options for a project are analyzed on a sequential basis. The possible outcomes in each period are identified and assigned probabilities. These outcomes and probabilities are shown on a flowchart that resembles tree branches, hence the name of the technique. The results are then aggregated over time to calculate the expected value of each option for the project. The option with the highest expected value is the preferred choice. There are five steps involved in the development and use of decision trees:

1. Identify decision points in the project. These are points at which the project's operators can choose among various options, such as which of

EXAMPLE 17.5

Simple Decision Tree

Seaview City has a 20-year-old public aquarium that presently loses $1,000,000 per year. The City Council is considering a plan to upgrade the aquarium by spending $1,000,000 on new exhibits. If the exhibits are purchased, attendance may improve, which in turn will generate more revenue. A consultant's report indicates that three outcomes are possible if the exhibit is built:

Outcome	Probability	Profit in Year 1	Profit in Year 2
1	0.3	$1,000,000	$1,000,000
2	0.5	0	0
3	0.2	−$1,000,000	−$1,000,000

If the exhibit is not built, there is a 90 percent probability that the aquarium will continue to lose $1,000,000 per year and a 10 percent probability that it will break even in each of the next two years due to added publicity from the City Council debates. The new exhibits will have no effect on revenues after the second year. The appropriate discount rate is 10 percent. Using a decision tree, determine if Seaview City should undertake the project.

Step 1: Identify decision points. The only decision point is whether to add the new exhibits.

Step 2: Identify possible outcomes. These are listed above.

Step 3: Estimate probabilities of outcomes. These are listed above.

Step 4: Prepare the tree diagram. Using the information given above, the following tree diagram can be prepared for this project:

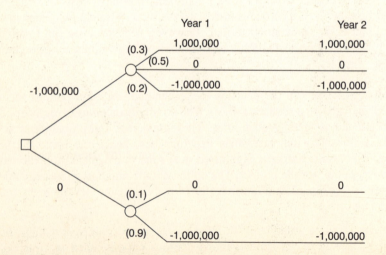

Step 5: Calculate the expected value of each option:

$$Ex(NPV) = \sum_{i=1}^{n} P_i(NPV_i)$$

For the option of the new exhibits:

$$Ex(NPV) = -1,000,000 + 0.3\left[\frac{1,000,000}{1.10} + \frac{1,000,000}{(1.10)^2}\right]$$

$$+ 0.5(0 + 0) + 0.2\left[\frac{-1,000,000}{1.10} + \frac{(-1,000,000)}{(1.10)^2}\right]$$

This shows the three possible outcomes and their probabilities. The cash flows for each outcome are discounted to represent their present values. Completing the calculations gives

$$Ex(NPV) = -1,000,000 + (0.3)(1,735,537)$$

$$+ (0.5)(0) + (0.2)(-1,735,537)$$

$$= -\$826,446$$

For the option without the new exhibits:

$$Ex(NPV) = (0.1)(0 + 0) + 0.9\left[\frac{-1,000,000}{1.10} + \frac{-1,000,000}{(1.10)^2}\right]$$

$$= (0.9)(-1,735,537)$$

$$= -\$1,561,983$$

These figures indicate that the first option is preferred. Although adding the new exhibits results in a negative NPV for the aquarium, this NPV is larger than if the exhibits are not added. Therefore, the project is preferable to the present operation.

---

three pieces of equipment to purchase. In many situations, decision points only occur at the beginning of the project. However, more complex projects often involve several decisions at different times.

2. Identify the possible outcomes of each option for each decision point. Some options have only one outcome, while others may yield several possible outcomes depending on the circumstances. For most financial analyses, outcomes are expressed in terms of cash flows.

3. Estimate the probability of each outcome for each option. These probabilities are usually estimated from previous experience or from information about the results obtained for similar projects. The probabilities for the outcomes of each option must sum to 1.

4. Prepare the tree diagram. This diagram illustrates the decision points and the possible outcomes of each decision. It is organized chronologically, with the starting point on the left. Decisions are represented by squares and alternative outcomes are represented by circles. For each branch of the tree, the outcome (such as a cash flow) and its probability are listed. The probabilities are usually represented as decimals, and are shown in parentheses or in the form "$p = 0.7$." Some branches of the tree may

extend for more time periods than other branches. A typical tree diagram might look like this:

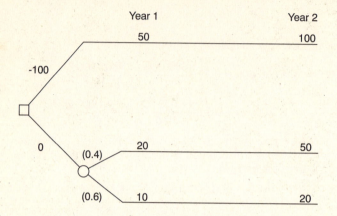

This diagram shows a decision between two options, as denoted by the square on the far left. The first option involves an immediate cost of $100, with a return of $50 in the first year and $100 in the second year. Note that no probabilities are shown for these figures since each is known with certainty. The second option has no initial cost and has two possible outcomes, as indicated by the circle before year 1. One outcome pays $20 in the first year and $50 in the second, and has a probability of 0.4, or 40 percent. The other outcome pays $10 in the first year and $20 in the second, and has a probability of 0.6, or 60 percent. The total of the probabilities sums to 1.0, as required.

5. Calculate the expected value of each option from the information in the tree diagram, using the equation developed in Chapter 15:

$$\mathrm{ExV} = \sum_{i=1}^{n} P_i V_i \qquad (15.2)$$

where ExV is the expected value for that option, N is the number of possible outcomes, P_i is the probability of the ith outcome, and V_i is the value of outcome i. Thus, for net present value,

$$\mathrm{Ex(NPV)} = \sum_{i=1}^{n} P_i(\mathrm{NPV}_i) \qquad (17.1)$$

Similar equations apply if other measures of the results of a project are used. Each separate path through the tree from right to left is a separate outcome. All outcomes must be included in the calculation in order to obtain accurate results.

For the example shown above, the NPV of the first option would be calculated in the usual fashion since all values are known with certainty. Using a discount rate of 8 percent, the NPV of this option is $32.03. Determining the NPV of the second option requires analyzing cash flows on two separate paths. The upper path has a present value of $61.39 and the lower path has a present value of $26.41. Applying Equation (17.1) gives

$$Ex(NPV) = (0.4)(\$61.39) + (0.6)(\$26.41)$$
$$= \$40.40$$

Since the expected value of the second option is higher than that of the first option, the second option is the preferred choice.

The tree diagram produces an estimate of the most likely value of each option for a project. These estimates can be used to decide if the project should be pursued and to determine which option has the largest expected value.

The problem shown in Example 17.5 is relatively simple, involving only one decision and two time periods. Most projects are not this simple. Two types of complications often arise in decision tree calculations:

1. *Different probabilities in different periods.* In this situation, branches may occur at several different times, as shown below:

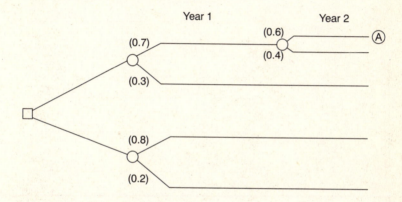

It is important to recognize that probabilities in later years are dependent on probabilities in earlier years. Thus, on path A in the diagram, the actual probability in year 2 is $0.7 \times 0.6 = 0.42$, not just the 0.6 shown for year 2.

2. *More than one decision point.* Many projects involve decisions that occur at different times. For example, a contractor building a highway may choose materials in the second year based on the types of soils encountered in the first year. Graphically, these situations appear as follows:

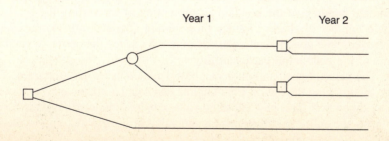

EXAMPLE 17.6

Decision Trees with Dependent Probabilities

Seaview City is also considering a more elaborate aquarium-remodeling project. The consultant has prepared estimates for the benefits of this project for two years. As before, there are no additional benefits beyond the second year. These estimates are shown on the following decision tree, along with the two options analyzed in Example 17.5:

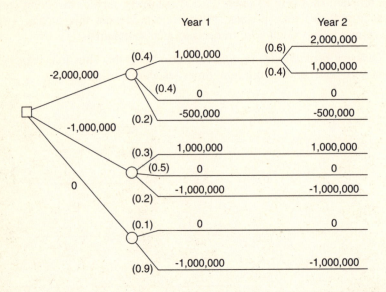

Such situations must be analyzed from right to left on the diagram. The later decisions are analyzed to identify the best option. The expected value for this preferred option is then used in calculations made for earlier decisions.

These two situations are explored in the following examples.

Value of an Option.   Decision trees can also be used to calculate the value of an option in a project. Many projects include options that can be exercised at the discretion of the individual or group controlling the project. For example, many corporate bonds give the bondholder the option of converting the bond into a certain number of shares of stock on a certain date at a predetermined price. Likewise, some government contracts give the agency the option to change the terms of the contract at particular times.

The value of such an option can be calculated using decision trees. This is done by dropping the option from the tree and calculating the expected value of the modified tree. This new expected value can be subtracted from the expected value for the entire tree to determine the value of a particular option. It should

Note that the outcomes in year 2 are dependent on the outcomes in year 1. Using this decision tree, determine if Seaview City should undertake this project.

Steps 1 to 4 for analyzing a decision tree have already been completed. Step 5, the calculation of the NPV, is done as follows:

For the option with the $2,000,000 remodeling:

$$Ex(NPV) = -2,000,000 + 0.4\left[\frac{1,000,000}{1.10} + \frac{(0.6)(2,000,000)}{(1.10)^2}\right.$$

$$\left. + \frac{(0.4)(1,000,000)}{(1.10)^2}\right] + 0.4(0 + 0)$$

$$+ 0.2\left[\frac{-500,000}{1.10} + \frac{-500,000}{(1.10)^2}\right]$$

Note how the 0.4 probability for the upper path in the first year also applies to the 0.6 and 0.4 probabilities in the second year. Solving this equation gives

$$Ex(NPV) = -2,000,000 + (0.4)[909,091 + (0.6)(1,652,893)$$

$$+ (0.4)(826,446)] + (0.4)(0) + (0.2)(-867,769)$$

$$= -\$1,280,992$$

The expected NPVs of the other two options were calculated in the last example:

For the $1,000,000 investment: Ex(NPV) = -$826,446

For no additional investment: Ex(NPV) = -$1,561,983

A comparison of the three options indicates that the new $2,000,000 proposal is better than doing nothing, but it is not as good as the $1,000,000 proposal described in Example 17.5.

---

be noted than an option can never actually have a negative cash value, since such an option would never be exercised.

One special application of the concept of the value of an option occurs in the field of environmental economics. In this field, attention is often paid to the additional information that can be gathered if a decision is postponed. For example, consider a situation in which a policy maker must choose today whether to open a wilderness area to mineral exploration. At present, there is incomplete information about the consequences of this development. If the decision could be delayed for a year, additional information might be gathered. The value of this future information is referred to as the *quasi-option value*. This concept is discussed in more detail in Appendix 17A at the end of this chapter.

Option to Bail Out.   Decision trees can also be used to determine the value of an option to "bail out"; in other words, the value of an option to quit a project before its conclusion. Such situations most often arise in projects that require investments over several years. If a project is not progressing satisfactorily, or if funds run out, a bail-out option may be valuable.

EXAMPLE 17.7

Multiple Decisions

One of the Seaview City council members has proposed that the city defer a decision about part of the expansion until the second year of the project. Under her proposal, several of the new exhibits will not be installed unless the first set of exhibits has boosted attendance. If attendance has increased, the City Council will reexamine the issue and may authorize other exhibits. This proposal would involve a $750,000 investment for the first year, followed by an optional $250,000 investment before the second year. The resulting decision tree looks like this:

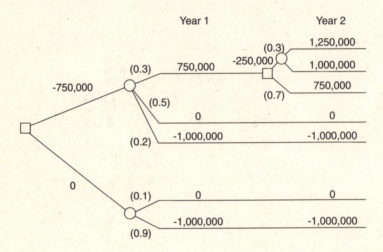

In comparison with the option to do nothing, is this proposal a good one?

Steps 1 to 4 for analyzing a decision tree have already been completed. Step 5, the calculation of NPV, is done as follows.

For the new option, the decision after year 1 must be analyzed first. In this case, the upper branch following the decision in year 1 has an expected value in year 1 of

$$Ex(NPV) = -250,000 + (0.3)\left(\frac{1,250,000}{1.10}\right) + (0.7)\left(\frac{1,000,000}{1.10}\right)$$

The bail-out option is evaluated by adding another branch to the tree. This branch is based on a decision to terminate the project and sell off any assets. The expected value of the project is then calculated with this new branch. The value of the option to bail out is found by subtracting the original expected value of the project from the expected value with the bail-out option included.

Advantages and Disadvantages. Decision trees have the advantage of making all alternatives explicit and easily understood. Different outcomes are easily rec-

Note that these values are only discounted for one year at this stage of the analysis.

$$Ex(NPV) = \$727,273$$

The lower branch following the decision in year 1 has an expected value in year 1 of

$$Ex(NPV) = \frac{750,000}{1.10} = \$681,818$$

Thus, after year 1, the City Council should choose to invest the extra $250,000 in new exhibits since this investment yields a higher expected NPV than the option of no additional investment. This means that the lower branch for this decision can be dropped from further analysis. So, the expected value of the new option can be found from

$$Ex(NPV) = -750,000 + 0.3\left[\frac{750,000}{1.10} - \frac{250,000}{1.10}\right.$$

$$\left. + \frac{(0.3)(1,250,000)}{(1.10)^2} + \frac{(0.7)(1,000,000)}{(1.10)^2}\right]$$

$$+ 0.5(0 + 0) + (0.2)\left[\frac{-1,000,000}{1.10} + \frac{-1,000,000}{(1.10)^2}\right]$$

There are three important points to note in this equation. First, the 0.3 probability for the upper outcome in year 1 applies to the additional investment and returns in year 2. Second, the $250,000 investment after year 1 must be discounted to the present. Third, the result of our earlier calculation for the present value in year 1 could have been used as part of this equation. Substitute this result into the equation and see if the answer is the same. Completing the analysis gives

$$Ex(NPV) = -750,000 + (0.3)(681,818 - 227,273 + 309,917 + 578,512)$$

$$+ (0.5)(0) + (0.2)(-909,091 - 826,446)$$

$$= -\$694,215$$

The expected NPV of the other option was calculated in Example 17.5:

$$Ex(NPV) = -\$1,561,983$$

Therefore, the new option is better than the option of making no additional investment in the aquarium. In fact, this new option is the best of all that have been analyzed.

ognized, and steps can be taken to reduce the likelihood of adverse outcomes. Decision trees are also useful in identifying the values of options and the value of bailing out.

However, the information needed to build decision trees is sometimes difficult to obtain. Figures on the probabilities of various outcomes are especially difficult to get for many projects. In addition, the trees can become very complex if a project has many decision points and possible outcomes, or if the project has a long duration. Thus, decision trees are most often used in situations of moderate complexity where simulation is unnecessary.

EXAMPLE 17.8

Value of an Option

Using the information contained in Example 17.7, calculate the value of the option proposed by the city council member in comparison with the options for the $1,000,000 and $2,000,000 investments. If the contractor wants to charge an additional $100,000 in order to give the city this option, is it worthwhile?

From earlier examples, the expected NPVs of these options are as follows:

City council member plan: Ex(NPV) = −$694,215

$1,000,000 investment: Ex(NPV) = −$826,446

$2,000,000 investment: Ex(NPV) = −$1,280,992

The value of the option proposed by the city council member is simply the difference between this option and the others. Therefore, for the $1,000,000 investment:

Option value = −$694,215 − (−$826,446) = $132,231

For the $2,000,000 investment:

Option value = −$694,215 − (−$1,280,992) = $586,777

Thus, the option proposed by the city council member is quite valuable. The option is even worthwhile if the contractor wants the additional $100,000.

SUMMARY

In many situations, the information needed for benefit–cost analysis is not known with certainty. As a result, several techniques have been developed to include uncertainty in benefit–cost calculations.

Sensitivity analysis is the simplest type of uncertainty calculation. Individual variables or groups of variables are analyzed at optimistic, expected, and pessimistic levels to develop a range of estimates for the outcome of a project. Sensitivity analysis is useful for simple situations, but is somewhat arbitrary and incomplete for more complex problems.

Simulation extends sensitivity analysis to cover wide ranges of possible values for each variable. The technique produces extensive information on the range of possible outcomes and the project's expected value. However, the extensive information and analysis requirements of simulation mean that it is best suited for complicated problems that require very thorough analysis.

Decision trees are used to analyze problems with a range of options and outcomes. This approach allows options to be compared and is particularly suited for projects that cover several time periods. For very complex projects, the decision trees become complicated and hard to analyze, so simulation is often better in such cases.

EXAMPLE 17.9

Value of an Option to Bail Out

Seaview City has decided to undertake the two-stage aquarium-remodeling project proposed by the city council member. As noted in the original description, the city insists on an option to bail out after one year and not spend the additional $250,000 before year 2. What is the value of this option to bail out?

The expected NPV of the two-stage aquarium project was found to be −$694,215 in Example 17.7. If there were no bail-out option, the $250,000 investment in year 2 would be mandatory. This would change the calculation of the expected NPV to

$$Ex(NPV) = -750,000 - \frac{250,000}{1.10}$$

$$+ 0.3\left[\frac{750,000}{1.10} + \frac{(0.3)(1,250,000)}{(1.10)^2} + \frac{(0.7)(1,000,000)}{(1.10)^2}\right]$$

$$+ (0.5)(0 + 0) + 0.2\left[\frac{-1,000,000}{1.10}\right] + \frac{(-1,000,000)}{(1.10)^2}$$

This equation differs from the earlier version in that the $250,000 is required for all three outcomes, not just the outcome with a positive $750,000 cash flow in the first year. The revised NPV is, therefore,

$$Ex(NPV) = -750,000 - 227,273 + (0.3)(681,818 + 309,917 + 578,512)$$

$$+ (0.5)(0) + (0.2)(-909,091 - 826,446)$$

$$= -\$853,306$$

Therefore, the option to bail out is worth

$$\text{Option value} = -\$694,215 - (-\$853,306) = \$159,091$$

This answer can be easily confirmed by observing that it represents the added probability of the $250,000 investment before year 2. This investment originally had a probability of 0.3, but if the bail-out option is eliminated the probability increases to 1.0. Therefore, the option value should be

$$\text{Option value} = \frac{(0.7)(250,000)}{1.10} = \$159,091$$

which matches our earlier result.

QUESTIONS AND PROBLEMS

1. A project's discounted costs and benefits have the following expected, optimistic, and pessimistic values:

	Optimistic	Expected	Pessimistic
Costs	130	175	200
Benefits	185	180	175

Perform a sensitivity analysis using the discounted benefit–cost ratio. What do the results suggest about ways to manage the project?

2. A proposed state computer system is designed to facilitate motor vehicle licensing by speeding the processing of licenses and eliminating duplicative functions. The system is expected to cost $5,000,000 to implement. In another state, the same vendor proposed a similar system at an identical cost, but actual implementation was more complex than anticipated and thus final costs turned out to be $6,500,000. The vendor now claims that this previous experience should allow costs to be reduced, so they optimistically estimate costs at $4,250,000. All costs can be considered as initial costs and need not be discounted. The system's benefits result from reduced staff time. In the most optimistic case, 90,000 hours would be saved each year for the five-year expected life of the system. The expected value for annual savings is 70,000 hours, and a pessimistic estimate is 50,000 hours. For each hour saved, the state's total cost is $20. However, this is an optimistic estimate of the potential dollar savings, since some staff positions may not be eliminated even though the time demands are reduced. Thus, a savings of only $14 is expected for each hour. Critics of the system have claimed that few workers will actually be replaced, so that actual savings are $7 per hour. Perform a variable-by-variable sensitivity analysis of this project, using the net present value at a discount rate of 6 percent.

3. The project described in Problem 2 has been redefined by the state in order to lessen the chance of costs exceeding benefits. The governor has told the department director that staff levels will, in part, be tied to the costs of the computer system. The governor has laid out three scenarios:
   a. Initial costs are $5,000,000, with annual savings of 70,000 hours at $14 per hour for five years.
   b. Initial costs are $6,500,000, with annual savings of 70,000 hours at $20 per hour for five years.
   c. Initial costs are $4,250,000, with annual savings of 70,000 hours at $14 per hour for five years.

   Using net present value at a 6 percent discount rate, which of these scenarios produces a desirable project?

4. A proposed project has a decision tree as follows:

	Year 1	Year 2	Year 3
(0.4)	2,000	3,000	5,000
(0.6)	5,000	4,000	3,000
(0.7)	3,000	2,000	2,000
(0.2)	3,000	3,000	2,000
(0.1)	3,000	3,000	3,000
(0.5)	1,000	1,000	
(0.5)	0	1,000	

-10,000

-7,500

0

Using net present value and a discount rate of 8 percent, determine if either choice for this project is desirable.

5. A proposed project has a decision tree as follows:

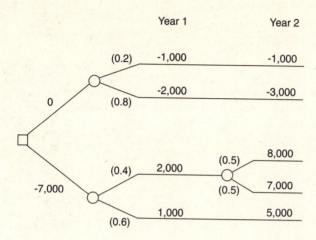

Using net present value and a discount rate of 8 percent, determine if this project is desirable.

6. A port district must decide how much to invest in refurbishing a container terminal. It must spend at least $200,000 for routine maintenance. As an alternative, it can invest $1,700,000 in a full-scale remodeling, which would increase traffic and revenue. The effects of the project would last for two years. Port staff have prepared a decision tree reflecting the potential costs and benefits of the options:

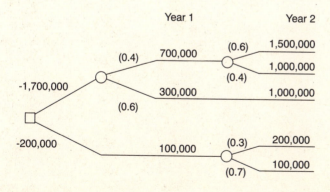

Using net present value at a discount rate of 7 percent, determine which option the port should pursue.

7. A variation of the remodeling option in Problem 6 would allow the port to pursue a two-phase project. In this case, the upper branch of the decision tree would appear as follows:

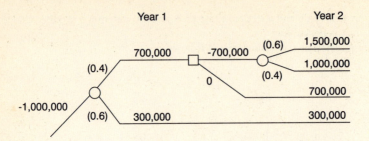

Using a discount rate of 7 percent, what is the value of this option, if any?

8. What is the value of the option to bail out that is shown in Problem 7?

APPENDIX 17A

Quasi-Option Value

This more formal treatment of quasi-option value is stylized and restricted for ease of exposition. Consider a decision that would allow development of oil fields in Glacier Park. Assume two periods, $t = 1, 2$. Assume that oil development will take place now or in the second period, or not at all. Let d_1 be the amount of development in the first period and d_2 the amount of development in the second period. For simplicity we will assume that d_1 may equal either 0 or 1, and that d_2 can equal either 0 or 1 given that $d_1 = 0$, and $d_2 = 0$ if $d_1 = 1$. That is, partial development is not possible and full development takes place only in either period 1 or in period 2 or not at all.

Associated with each period are net benefits B_1 and B_2, and total net benefits will be

$$B = B_1 + B_2$$

where B_1 and B_2 represent the net benefits in the first period and in the second period, respectively. By net benefits we mean benefits net of investment and operating costs. Net benefits in the first period will be

$$B_1 = B_{1d}(d_1) + B_{1p}(d_1)$$

where B_{1d} are net benefits from development and B_{1p} are net benefits from preservation. If $d_1 = 1$ there will be no benefits from preservation and only developmental benefits. If $d_1 = 0$, there are only benefits from preservation for period 1. These benefits we assume are known with certainty. Benefits in the second period are expressed as

$$B_2 = B_{2d}(d_1 + d_2, d_2, A) + B_{2p}(d_1 + d_2, d_2, A)$$

where A represents the amount of oil. For simplicity we assume that A can only take two values; oil will be found to be either abundant or scarce. This equation expresses the fact the benefits of development during period 2 are a function of the total level of development $(d_1 + d_2)$, the development during period 2, and the abundance of oil. Given that the optimal level of development can be determined with certainty once period 2 arrives, the correct decision maker includes this forthcoming information in his decision. The correct decision maker wishes to maximize

$$V^*(d_1) = B_1(d_1) + E\{\max[B_2(d_1 + d_2, d_2, A)]\}$$

where E represents the expected value, A represents the amount of oil determined at the beginning of period 2, and d_1 and d_2 are previously defined.

The mistaken decision maker will maximize

$$V^{**}(d_1) = B_1(d_1) + \max\{E[B_2(d_1 + d_2, d_2, A]\}$$

Both decision makers will treat the benefits in period 1 the same. The difference is in the evaluation of period 2.

The question is should development proceed now? When there is no development in period 1, the value as seen by the correct decision maker will be

$$V^*(0) = B_1(0) + \{E \max[B_2(0, 0, A), B_2(1, 1, A)]\}$$

That is, the value of no development in period 1 will be given by the benefits in period 1 with no development, plus the benefits in period 2 which may or may not involve development in period 2. The second expression is the expected value of the maximum benefit in period 2 taking into account the value of information at the beginning of period 2. With development in period 1 the value will be

$$V^*(1) = B_1(1) + \{E[B_2(1, 0, A)]\}$$

The value with development in period 1 will be the benefits in period 1 with development plus the benefits in period 2 given that development has occurred in period 1. Development should occur in period 1 only if $V^*(1) > V^*(0)$.

The value of no development in period 1 for the incorrect decision maker will be

$$V^{**}(0) = B_1(0) + \max\{E[B_2(0, 0, A)], E[B_2(1, 1, A]\}$$

The second expression on the right-hand side maximizes the expected value of development in period 2 from the point of view of information now and takes no account of the additional information that will be forthcoming at the end of period 1. The value of development in period 1 to the incorrect decision maker will be

$$V^{**}(1) = B_1(1) + E[B_2(1, 0, A)]$$

The incorrect decision maker would choose to develop in period 1 if $V^{**}(1) > V^{**}(0)$. Note that if development occurs in period 1 the values of both periods are the same for both the correct and the incorrect decision maker. If development does not occur in period 1, however, the values are different. The benefits in period 1 from nondevelopment are known to both decision makers and these are the same, that is, equal to $B_1(0)$. The ex ante value of nondevelopment in

---

EXAMPLE 17.A.1

In this example we assume that some development can occur in both phases.

The value of oil development during the first phase is $100. When there is a large amount of oil the value of development during the second phase will be, say, $300. When there is little oil the value of development during the second phase will be zero. The value of preservation during the first phase will be $50. The value of preservation during the second phase will be $200.

Both the correct and the incorrect decision maker look at the net benefits from development during the first phase in the same way. The value of development will be the benefit of $100 during the first phase plus the expected value of $P(\$300)$ plus $(1 - P)0$.

The correct decision maker will look at the value of preservation during the first phase differently than the incorrect decision maker. Since information will be available with certainty at the start of the second phase, the correct decision maker will see the value of preservation as the $50 gained during the first phase, plus the maximum amount that can be gained during the second phase, which is $300. The value of preservation during the first phase is then $350 for the correct decision maker. For the incorrect decision maker the value of nondevelopment is $50 plus $P(\$300)$ plus $(1 - P)\$200$. This can be simplified to $100P + 250$. The value of nondevelopment for the first phase for the incorrect decision maker will only be as great as for the correct decision maker when $P = 1$. Of course, if $P = 1$, both decision makers would opt for immediate development.

The correct decision maker will develop as long as $\$100 + P(\$300) > \$350$, or as long as $P > \frac{5}{6}$. The incorrect decision maker will choose to develop as long as $\$100 + P(\$300) > \$250 + 100P$, or as long as $P > \frac{3}{4}$. Thus the correct decision maker requires a higher probability than the incorrect decision maker of there being a large amount of oil in Glacier before proceeding with development during the first phase.

---

period 1, however, is viewed quite differently in terms of the benefits to be had in period 2. These will be higher for the correct decision maker since

$$E\{\max[B_2(0, 0, A), B_2(1, 1, A)]\} > \max\{E[B_2(0, 0, A)], E[B_2(1, 1, A)]\}$$

That is, the expected value of the maximum benefits in period 2 which is the perspective of the correct decision maker is greater than the expected value of the benefits in period 2. The value of nondevelopment in period 1 will be greater for the correct decision maker since $V^*(0) > V^{**}(0)$. The correct decision maker has a stronger incentive to preserve, while the incorrect decision maker has a bias in favor of development in period 1.

The decision tree is often the most illuminating way of analyzing the value of an option. The problem in the above example can be expressed in a decision tree as the following:

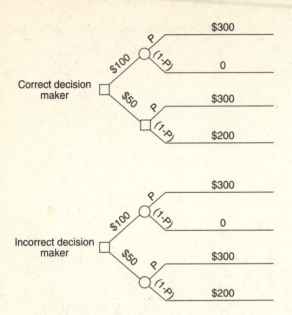

Note that steps 1 to 4 for analyzing a decision tree have already been completed. Step 5, the calculation of NPV, is as follows:

Correct decision maker NPV (upper branch)	$100 + P(300)$
NPV (lower branch)	$50 + 300 = 350$
Incorrect decision maker NPV (upper branch)	$100 + P(300)$
NPV (lower branch)	$50 + P(300) + (1 - P)200$

The correct decision maker will set up the decision tree recognizing the future decision node. The incorrect decision maker treats the decision node as a probability branch, and is led then to put too low a value on the option. To account for quasi-option value is to recognize that flexibility in decision making has a value.

The lesson of quasi-option value is straightforward. The value of future information should be considered when making a benefit–cost decision. This is true as long as there are sunk costs associated with a decision now and there is a potential for additional information that will make a future decision one of fuller information than a present decision. Even if a decision to develop now is reversible there would normally be sunk costs incurred and costs associated with reversing development. What is gained by delaying development, in the form of new information, must be weighed against what is lost.

In the Glacier Park example the value of earlier development must be weighed against the loss of the park. In the Pacific Northwest during the late 1970s and early 1980s huge sums were committed to the development of nuclear power before it was clear that these plants would be needed. Although large sums were spent, these plants were never completed. In retrospect it seems clear that policies that increased flexibility and allowed a delay of development would have been more cost-effective. This is the sort of lesson that the concept of quasi-option value provides. The general rule then may be expressed by comparing the expected advantages of earlier development against the expected value of future information. Unlike our earlier example this information may not be perfect, and may be probabilistic, and the value of earlier rather than later development may also be probabilistic. The decision tree approach is generally the most illuminating way to model these situations.

18

Introduction
to Nonmarketed Goods

18.1. INTRODUCTION

Most approaches to valuation fall into one of three categories. These are (1) market approaches, (2) contingent valuation (interviews, experiments, or questionnaires), and (3) travel cost methods. Market approaches consist of direct estimates and indirect estimates usually known as hedonic price approaches.

Market prices are useful in benefit–cost analysis because they convey information. In a competitive market, the price contains information about both the cost of production and about marginal valuation to the consumer. Even noncompetitive prices may convey information about costs and the marginal consumer evaluation.

Many of our most important goods do not trade in directly observable markets. One does not go to the store to buy clean air, quiet, or less crime. Alternative travel costs are an important component in any location decision. A transportation analyst, for example, will want to consider travel costs including waiting time in making any policy decisions about location of transport facilities.

18.2. MARKET APPROACHES

18.2.1. Direct Estimates

In the case of such nonpriced goods, the analyst will have to consider *shadow prices* for the nonmarketed good or service.

Shadow Price: The shadow price is an accounting price that reflects an estimate of the opportunity cost of providing or eliminating an additional unit of the good.

In a market without distortions, the market price represents the opportunity cost. The market price represents both the marginal valuation to consumers and the marginal cost of production. A market may, however, be distorted by government regulations or other interference, or by external effects. The price may be adjusted to account for taxes or subsidies the good receives. In the example of the Mid-State project considered in Chapter 1, the issue arose as to whether the market price of farm products should be considered or the price should be reduced to take out the effect of government price supports. Such an adjusted price represents an attempt to use a shadow price.

The market may fail to exist because of high costs of running a market, such as costs of excluding nonpayers (see the discussion of public and collective goods in Chapter 2). In this case, the shadow price may refer to an estimated price for nonmarketed goods.

Market data on price can be combined with elasticity estimates to generate estimates of shadow price. Consider the following examples.

Housing: Rent Control.   Figure 18.1 shows the demand and supply for apartments in Trenton, New Jersey. The market price would be P_1, but rents are controlled at a price of P_2. The government is considering building new housing and wishes to perform a benefit–cost analysis of the proposed project. If the government values new housing at the rent-controlled price of P_2, it will understate the benefits of the new housing. Suppose that, in fact, the project is not financially justified at this low valuation. The marginal willingness to pay for new housing is given by P_3, assuming that the new housing is rationed among new users by their willingness to pay. In this situation, the price P_3 is the shadow price of housing, and should be used as the basis for evaluation of the building of new housing. If housing is not to be rationed on the basis of WTP, then the use of P_3 no longer has a special significance, and the appropriate marginal valuation must be determined by other considerations. If housing is rationed randomly among all users willing to pay more than the controlled price P_2, for example, one might then use the average willingness

Figure 18.1.

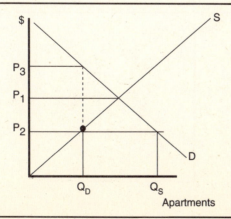

to pay of all persons in the relevant section of the demand curve as a proxy for the willingness to pay of those who will obtain the housing.

Housing: The Shadow Price Where There Is a Tax.   Consider now a government proposal to build additional housing in a market that has an excise tax. In Figure 18.2, the price with the tax is P_1 and the price net of tax to suppliers is P_2. The additional government demand will increase the market price slightly (Why do we call this additional government demand rather than a change in supply?). The loss of consumer surplus will be area A. The resource cost of the additional housing will be area B. The opportunity cost of the government housing is then area $A + B$. The cost *per unit* of additional housing will then be a weighted average of these two areas A and B. The size of areas A and B will depend on their width and height. If the size of government demand is small so that the change in demand and supply prices is small, we can ignore triangles *abc* and *def,* which would then be small. The social opportunity cost per unit of government housing will then be a weighted average of P_1 and P_2 where the weights are the widths of boxes A and B, that is, the weights are the change in quantity demanded and the change in quantity supplied. Suppose that α is the decrease in consumption of the taxed good for *each extra unit* of the good used by the project, and $(1 - \alpha)$ is the increase in production of the good. Then for each extra unit used by the project, the shadow price is the gross of tax price times the change in quantity consumed plus the net of tax price times the change in quantity produced. The shadow price will then be

$$P_s = \alpha P_2 + (1 - \alpha)P_1 \tag{18.1}$$

Harberger (1969, in Harberger 1972) provides the following formula expressed in terms of elasticities:

$$P_s = \frac{E_2 P_2 + E_1 P_1 (Q_d/Q_s)}{E_2 + E_1 (Q_d/Q_s)} \tag{18.2}$$

Figure 18.2.   Shadow price of housing.

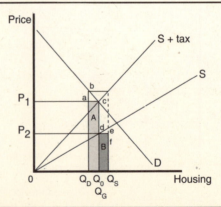

where P_s = shadow price

P_1 = price gross of tax

P_2 = after-tax price

E_2 = supply elasticity

E_1 = demand elasticity (expressed as > 0)

Q_d = quantity available to the private sector after the government intervention

Q_s = quantity supplied by the private sector

Q_g = the quantity demanded by government, is the difference between Q_s and Q_d

Suppose that the demand elasticity is 2, the supply elasticity is 0.5, price including tax, P_1, is $100, and the after-tax price to suppliers is $75. Let Q_d be 1000 and Q_s be 1010. The shadow price of an additional unit of housing is then

$$P_s = \frac{0.5(\$75) + 2(\$100)\frac{1000}{1010}}{0.5 + 2\frac{1000}{1010}} = \$94.96$$

Notice that the shadow price lies between the demand price of $100 and the supply price of $75. The price is closer to the demand price because the demand elasticity is greater. Notice also that the difference in Q_s and Q_d is small and that the shadow price of capital ignoring this difference is just $95. Q_d and Q_s are not very different in the case where government intervention is small or where the elasticities are small. Then the shadow price formula is just

$$P_s = \frac{E_2 P_2 + E_1 P_1}{E_2 + E_1} \tag{18.3}$$

(The reader might consider what the shadow prices should be when the elasticity of supply is infinite or zero.)

Foreign Currency Control: Exchange Controls.   The currencies of many countries are subject to exchange controls. The supply and demand for dollars in terms of rubles is illustrated by Figure 18.3. The demand for dollars is derived from a demand for goods produced in the United States. Russia, for example, wishes to buy grain from the United States. The supply of dollars represents the willingness to trade dollars for rubles, or more fundamentally, to trade U.S. goods for those produced in Russia.

Governments often fix the price of foreign currency below the level that it would reach in a competitive market. This was the case in Russia. With a price of dollars fixed at P_2 below the market price there was an excess demand for dollars. Russia could for a time meet this demand by running down its reserves of dollars, but in the long run it could maintain the artificially low price only if it rationed by exchange controls. Russia's problem was that it naturally wanted

Figure 18.3.

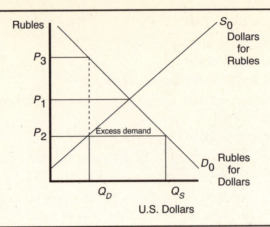

the available supply of dollars to be allocated to their socially most valuable use. This would be the case only if the users of foreign currency behaved as if the price were P_3. To ensure that the shadow price of P_3 is used for the exchange rate, a government might impose a tax on the use of foreign currency such that the price to users is, in fact, P_3. Imports thus might be taxed, and in this sort of situation often are taxed.

A government project that considers the use of imports should count the cost of dollar imports at the opportunity cost, or shadow price, of P_3 as long as dollars can be allocated efficiently. As with the rent control example, however, if dollars are allocated on a random basis, it can no longer be concluded that the marginal value is P_3.

RUBLE IS DEVALUED IN SOME CASES; STEP TO SPUR SOVIET ECONOMY SEEN

Moscow, Oct. 25—With the relaxation of travel restrictions, the number of Soviet citizens traveling to Western countries as tourists, on business, and in exchange programs has increased dramatically. And their demand for foreign currency has strained the Soviet Union's hard-currency resources.

The Soviet Union today announced a drastic cut in the ruble exchange rate that applies mainly to foreigners in the country and to Soviet citizens traveling abroad. The move, which puts a more realistic value on its currency, is apparently a step along a difficult path toward making it possible for anyone to exchange rubles for other world currencies.

The biggest news is not what has happened, but what is likely to happen next. Sweeping changes in currency regulations are expected over the next few months that should reduce the control of Moscow planners over foreign transactions.

Effective Nov. 1, the rate of exchange will plummet in certain dealings, not all of which were defined by Gosbank, the state bank, in an announcement carried by Tass, the official press agency. The ruble, now officially worth about $1.60, will then be worth just 16 cents. Officials of Gosbank, the Finance Ministry and the Foreign Ministry refused to comment on the announcement.

UNREALISTIC OFFICIAL RATES

The new "special rate" would apply to foreigners in the Soviet Union, who have long been outraged by the unrealistic official rates, particularly when compared with rates 20 times as high that are offered by black marketeers.

According to a report in the Government newspaper *Izvestia*, the new rate would apply only to the tiny fraction of transactions that do not involve imports and exports. The official rate would continue to be used, presumably for all transactions aside from direct buying and selling of currencies.

In recent weeks, the black market rate in Moscow was reported to be about 10 rubles to the dollar, and as high as 20 to the dollar in Leningrad and the Baltic republics.

At the New York offices of Deak Pereira, the foreign currency exchange concern, the rate this week was 7.7 rubles to the dollar.

EFFORT TO CURB SPECULATION

A Tass commentator, Andre Orlov, wrote in an article distributed by the press agency tonight that "The purpose of the decrease in the value of the ruble is to put currency payments in order, attract more foreign currency to the U.S.S.R., help normalize the consumer market and cut short currency speculation."

Exporters who now earn foreign currency must negotiate with the planning bureaucracy to determine how many rubles they will collect. The planners' decisions have more to do with politics and power than with economics.

Under the new system, Moscow's discretion to favor some exporters at the expense of others would be sharply curtailed. And exports would be determined by the more efficient and objective criteria of supply and demand.

"This act is aimed primarily at the black market, so dollars will flow to official exchange points and not to profiteers," said Mikhail L. Berger, an economics specialist at Izvestia, who wrote today's article. "When you have a choice of the bank offering 60 rubles for $100 or some guy on the street giving you 1500 rubles, that's no alternative. It's clear most people would prefer the second."

SOURCE: *The New York Times,* October 26, 1989.

The Shadow Price of Foreign Exchange with a Tariff. Equations (18.1) and (18.2) apply also to any situation in which there is a tax. A tariff is a tax, so we can calculate the shadow price of foreign exchange if we have data on elasticities. Suppose that in equilibrium the tariff is 10 percent and the import price is then 200 rubles; then the export price is 180 rubles. The elasticity of private sector exports is 1 and the elasticity of private sector demand for imports is 0.4. Using Equation (18.2) on the grounds that the difference between imports and exports is not great, we would have

$$P_e = \frac{1(180) + 0.4(200)}{1 + 0.4} = 185.71$$

A Note on the Social Opportunity Cost of Public Funds.   Earlier we considered and rejected the opportunity cost of funds approach suggested by Harberger. Yet the Harberger formula comes from the same considerations that led to Equations (18.1) and (18.2). Why do we recommend these formulas for the kinds of cases considered here and not for deriving the discount rate, the social opportunity cost of funds, to be used for public projects? The answer is that there are important general equilibrium effects that affect the social opportunity cost of funds. The shadow price approach used here takes no consideration of the reinvestment of project benefits into the private sector. The models here are essentially one-period models in that they do not consider feedback effects in future time periods. In the case of the social cost of capital the feedback effects can be large because the displacement of private capital in one period can have effects over time on future investment and the available benefits from the project can also provide private capital in the future. The assumption of no feedback is an appropriate assumption in cases where these feedback effects are small.

Labor Market Examples in a Development Context.   A worker leaves a job in the mines paying $14.00 per hour to take a job teaching welding at $7.00 per hour. National income goes down. Has economic welfare decreased? We must, in the words of Arnold Harberger, "presume because he acted voluntarily that he conceives his welfare to have improved (or at worst stayed the same) . . . ." (1971, in Harberger, 1972, p. 165). Mine workers, for example, have a great probability of getting silicosis and the accident rate is rather high, so that there are these and other good reasons why the worker may have improved his position by taking the lower-paying job.

Harberger (1971, in Harberger 1972) considers situations in less-developed countries in which rural workers leave low-paying jobs to migrate to much higher-paying jobs in the city. A worker who leaves a job in the country paying 1000 rupees to accept a job in the city paying 2500 rupees will increase national product by 1500 rupees. Even though national product has risen, Harberger argues that welfare may not have improved much because the worker requires a much higher wage to even consider working in the city. If the worker were, for example, willing to work in the country for 1000 rupees and only willing to work in the city for 2000 rupees, the gain from moving from the job paying 1000 rupees in the country to a *government-subsidized job* in the city paying 2500 rupees is 500 rupees, not 2500 rupees. Now since we cannot usually ask each worker his opportunity cost wage we cannot calculate exactly in each case the welfare change. We can, however, examine the wages for the city in the *unprotected* sector. The wages in this sector will show the market equilibrium wage at which the marginal worker will voluntarily offer his labor. Suppose that the wage in the unprotected sector is 1950 rupees. We would then say that the opportunity cost wage for the new worker in the city is 1950 rupees and that the gain to the worker is 550 rupees rather than the 1500 rupee increase in national product represented by the difference in wages between the rural wage and the subsidized city wage of the worker.

18.2.2.   Indirect Estimates

The above examples of calculating the shadow price of housing and of foreign exchange use direct estimates. Market data can also be used indirectly to make valuation estimates. For example, market wage rates across different labor markets in which there are differences in the degree of workers' risk have been used to estimate the price of risk and the value of life. Similarly, estimates of differences in property values with different exposures to environmental amenities such as water or clean air have been used to estimate the value of these amenities. Where differences between markets are used to estimate the value of some characteristic that varies across markets, this is called *the hedonic price approach*.

Land Value Approaches.   The value of a piece of land is the present value of the benefits associated with the land. Such environmental values as access to water, view, and clean air are reflected in market price differences in land value. Similarly, differences in level of crime, the quality of schools and neighbors, and access to shopping and to the workplace are also captured in differences in land values.

The usual approach is in two stages. First, a multiple regression equation is used to estimate property values as a function of property characteristics, neighborhood and location variables, and environmental amenity variables. An equation estimator of property values might take the following general form:

$$\ln \text{PP} = a \ln \text{PCHAR} + b \ln \text{NEIGH-LOC} + c \ln \text{ENV} \qquad (18.4)$$

where   PP = property value

PCHAR = property characteristics

NEIGH-LOC = neighborhood and location characteristics

ENV = environmental characteristics

ln refers to natural logarithm, and a, b, and c are vectors of coefficients for the various variables. In a study attempting to find a hedonic price for certain environmental variables, this sort of equation can give the relationship between property values and these variables. From such an equation we might, for example, be able to determine the value of living closer to Lake Washington in Seattle or to the ocean in Vancouver, B.C., or the value of having a residential view. A number of studies have focused on the relationship between air pollution and property values. Figure 18.4 shows the type of relationship that can be discovered from an equation such as (18.4). [For a summary of studies that calculate PP for clean air and property values, see Pearce and Turner (1990)].

Figure 18.4.   Property price and environmental quality (from Pearce and Turner, 1990).

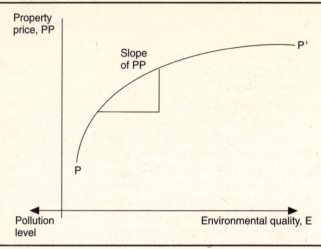

The relationship depicted in Figure 18.4 expresses Equation (18.4) in which PP is a function of environmental quality. From Equation (18.4) the slope of PP can be determined as a function of environmental quality. This is shown by curve AA in Figure 18.5. If all households were identical, the slope of the curve shown in Figure 18.5 would be a demand curve and the WTAs could be calculated from it. Because households will differ in income, tastes, or other characteristics, however, the slope cannot be interpreted as a demand curve. Suppose that there are two individuals that define two points on PP. One of the individuals is very sensitive to air pollution, the other is not. They are identical in other respects. The individual that is less sensitive to pollution lives

Figure 18.5.

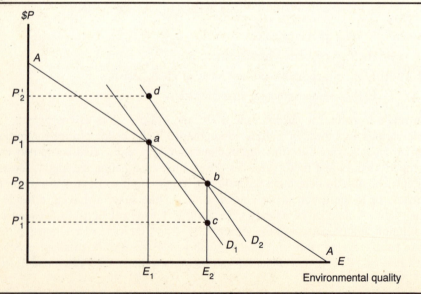

in an environment with an average level of air pollution, as shown by level P_0 in Figure 18.5. The second lives in a much cleaner environment as shown by point P_1. In moving from one pollution level P_0 to another higher level P_1 we are moving from the equilibrium position of one individual to the equilibrium position of another. The individual with greater sensitivity to pollution would pay a good deal not to be exposed to greater pollution. His demand curve goes through point P_0 and is shown by DD_1. The less sensitive individual has demand curve DD_2. Using the curve AA to calculate consumer surplus may lead to an incorrect estimate. Ideally the analyst would next calculate the various demand curves of different types of households. If we can do this we can then calculate the WTPs of the various types of households and find the aggregate WTP.

18.3. NONMARKET APPROACHES

18.3.1. Contingent Valuation Methodology

A third approach is called the *contingent valuation method* (CVM); it is a direct but nonmarket technique. Contingent valuation refers to interview or questionnaire techniques in which people are asked how much they are willing to pay for a good, or how much they are willing to accept to bear a loss. In a contingent valuation study, interviews or questionnaires and sometimes experimental techniques which elicit subjects' responses to the setting can be used to determine answers to valuation questions. The idea is to elicit bids that reveal what people would be willing to pay for a benefit or to accept to bear a loss.

The use of surveys to value public goods became commonplace during the 1980s as a result of the need for damage assessments under the Comprehensive Environmental Response, Comprehensive Liability Act of 1990 (CERCLA). CVM has now undergone federal court review. The court has supported the use of CVM as a legitimate alternative to property value, travel cost, or other approaches.

The CVM methodology has been accepted in large part because a number of CVM studies yield WTP estimates similar to indirect approaches such as hedonic or travel cost methods. Other studies have compared actual purchase decisions with responses to questions about hypothetical purchases. Hypothetical behavior has been predictive of actual behavior.

CVM has also been used because it has the potential to generate value estimates that may not be obtainable in other ways. In valuing environmental goods, both *use* and *non-use* values have been considered important. Non-use values include the WTP for the mere *existence* of a resource aside from use and *behest* value, the WTP to leave a resource to posterity. It is difficult to determine these values without CVM.

Associated with the use of the CVM is some interesting recent methodological research that suggests that, at the least, a good deal of care must go into developing the CVM in each study to obtain reliable results. There are a number of important potential sources of bias in using CVM. These are (1) large positive bid outliers, (2) refusals to bid or zero bids, (3) viewing public goods as joint products (embedding), and (4) survey context.

Particularly where survey respondents are unfamiliar with buying the goods in a market (for example, clean air) the variance in hypothetical bids can be large. Empirical work indicates that there will be a few bids that are very large relative to other bids, and that often these bids may reflect market inexperience with respect to the good in question. (The variance of bids decreases as questionnaire respondents gain market-type experience with respect to the good.) The few large bids result in the mean bid of the sample being greater, sometimes much greater, than the medium bid. For this reason very often the medium bid is preferred to the mean in CVM studies.

Another source of bias in CVM studies arises when respondents refuse to bid or bid zero values, even though they really do not have zero values for the good in question. Instead some respondents give a zero or no value for the good because they identify a positive bid with their personal responsibility for the problem, such as air pollution, and these respondents do not believe they are personally responsible.

Other respondents view bids for a specific public good as if they were giving bids for a more general public good. This problem is sometimes called *embedding*. For example, the expressed WTP through increased taxes of Toronto residents to prevent a drop in fish stock in a small part of Ontario called Muskow was almost as large as the WTP to prevent the same reduction throughout all of Ontario. This phenomenon, in which a part of a good is valued as if it were a more inclusive category in which the original good is embedded, is found in a number of studies [see especially Kahneman & Knetsch (1991)]. Similarly, the WTP responses can be much larger when the payment is expressed as a long-term commitment than as a one-time outlay. Kahneman and Knetsch (1991) appear to suggest that the embedding effect may render unusable the CVM methodology.

Finally, the way in which a setting is described for respondents may influence their bid. For example, asking respondents if they would be willing to be "taxed" to gain cleaner air may result in refusals to give a value not because clean air has no value but because they are upset by the level of current taxes.

These difficulties are formidable. They can be significantly reduced by careful use of the CVM methods. An example of a quite good CVM study, which attempts to overcome the sort of difficulties mentioned here, may be found in a report done for the EPA. Some reassurance about the use of the CVM is obtained from the fact that the range of estimates between CVM and other techniques is not outside the usual range of errors in estimates for demand functions in economics [Pearce & Turner (1990)]. The best CVM studies are those that do not ask open-ended questions about what something is worth but instead develop data from interrelated questions from which WTP or WTA measures can be extracted.

18.3.2.   Use and Non-Use Values

Suppose you will never visit Kruger National Park in South Africa. Knowing this, would you nevertheless pay something to prevent the destruction of this park? In recent years non-use values for goods, particularly for environmental goods, have become very important. Non-use values have been part of the discussion of a wide variety of resources from beaches along Lake Michigan in

Chicago, to non-use river values, to lake values, to wilderness areas. Usually two types of non-use values are considered, existence value and option value. (These concepts are also discussed more technically in Chapter 16.)

Existence Value.   *Existence value* is the WTP for the existence of a good over and above the WTP for the use of the good. Thus existence value is the amount one would pay for the existence of a good that one knew one would never use. That is, there is a WTP for just the existence of a grand canyon or for old growth forest. These values are known as *existence values*. CVM suggest that often these existence values are quite large. Note that this suggests that environmental goods can be regarded as very valuable even when discounting reduces the present value of use value to a small amount. Existence value is a legitimate part of consumer surplus value. Since existence value will not usually be captured by use value, it will not be reflected in the demand curve for use of a good. For this reason the CVM has become the primary tool for the calculation of existence value.

Although it is recognized that existence value is a legitimate value, there is disagreement about whether the incorporation of existence value into valuation measures considered in benefit–cost analyses is desirable or possible. (Many market goods, e.g., also have existence values.) Discussions of the issues may be found in articles by Rosenthal & Nelson (1992) and by Kopp (1992).

Option Price, Option Value, and Quasi-option Value.   Since Weisbrod introduced the concept of option value in 1964, a good deal of confusion has arisen over the definitions of these concepts and their applications, at least partly because the labels attached to them are not particularly apt.

An option that keeps open one's choices until, for example, more information is available of course has value. The amount one would pay for this option to defer a decision, given realities now, is called by economists the *quasi-option value*. This was considered in Chapter 17 as the value of an option. (For a clear discussion, see Bishop, 1980.)

Option value (a largely technical term without an obvious intuitive analogue), and option price, however, refer to values under uncertainty about what state of world will prevail in the future. As long as the marginal utility of income varies with the level of income, the consumer will value the good differently in different states of the world because her income will differ in these states. Thus the consumer surplus of the good will differ in different states of the world, and expected consumer surplus will in general give an incorrect value unless the marginal utility of income is assumed not to vary according to the level of wealth.

The correct measure of the ex ante (before the fact) value of a prospect is called the option price. The option price is the single payment that one is willing to make to preserve the option now of obtaining the good in the future before one knows the other circumstances of the future. Expected consumer surplus, however, takes the consumer surplus in the different states of the world and sums these according to their probabilistic realization. It then measures the value of the good accordingly. Expected consumer surplus may be greater or lesser than the option price.

The technical term option value is defined as the difference between expected consumer surplus and option price. That is:

$$OP = OV + E(CS) \tag{18.5}$$

where OP = option price,

OV = option value, and

$E(CS)$ = expected consumer surplus.

Option value may be positive, negative, or zero. In practice, option value is often conceived as a positive value that should be added to expected consumer surplus to obtain the option price. Since option value may be negative, this is incorrect.

Suppose, for example, that the marginal utility of income does not vary with income. In this case, option price and expected consumer surplus are equal, and the option value is zero. Determining an option value that is to be added to expected consumer surplus in this situation would give an overestimate of the option price.

Consider the issue of preserving Glacier Park. Suppose that the marginal utility of income is constant so that we can use the expected value as a decision criterion. The values of using Glacier for Mark and Mike Elliott are $150 and $100, respectively, *if they use the park*. These values are constant over time. Mark figures he has a 60 percent probability of going to Glacier in the future and Mike thinks he has a 50 percent chance of seeing Glacier. Assuming the discount rate is zero, the expected present value of the park for Mark and Mike is $140 (60 percent of $150, plus 50 percent of $100). This is the correct expected value for the park.

Suppose, however, that Mark would pay $90 and Mike $50 to preserve the option of their future use of the park. We examine the history of Glacier Park use by Mark and Mike and find that on the basis of actual visits their use value of the park is $140. This would be the empirical derivation of the value of expected consumer surplus as shown above. If now we add the value that Mark and Mike would pay for an option on future park use to the expected value of the park as determined by actual use, we are double counting. This addition would give a value of $280, $140 greater than the correct figure of $140. The option value was in a sense already included in the calculation of expected consumer surplus.

Clearly, where option value is conceptually confused with either option price or quasi-option value, and is treated as necessarily a positive value to be added to use value, there is a potential for double-counting values. The confusing fact is that usually we don't know even the correct sign of option value let alone its magnitude. Studies in which option value is an important component should be examined carefully. They are, in fact, suspect (see Bishop, 1986).

The Persistence of Option Value Misuse.   The concept of option value as an automatically positive value that needs to be added to consumer surplus to capture total value is an idea that is incorrect but persistent. Why? The insistence and persistence of the misuse of option values in a discussion of environmental goods may reflect a confusion with existence values in some instances, but seems more likely to reflect a feeling that there are important values just not otherwise being captured by a benefit–cost analysis. For most environmental goods, the difference between the WTP and the WTA will be very large. The WTP of the Sierra Club, for example, to preserve old growth forest in the Northwest may be large but it is likely to be very much smaller than the willingness to sell (WTA) of the Sierra Club if they owned the rights to the old growth forest. Our guess is that the insistence in misusing option value is just a reflection of a more fundamental notion that there should be public entitlements to important environmental goods. This is a notion to which we are sympathetic but would like to see this addressed directly in the analyses rather than through a sort of subterfuge, the misuse of option value.

18.4. TRAVEL DEMAND METHOD

18.4.1. Case Study: The Value of a Recreation Area[1]

The valuation of benefits from a recreation facility poses many theoretical and practical problems. One of the best ways to illustrate these problems is to examine a fairly small recreation facility with only one major use. The results of this simplified analysis can then be extrapolated to larger and more complex facilities.

This case study will focus on Grafham Water, a popular trout fishing location in England. Anglers drive considerable distances to visit Grafham and some stay for more than one day. The recreation benefits of Grafham Water were originally studied in the late 1960s, at which time the entrance fee for fishing was 20 shillings per day.[2]

Basic data for the analysis were gathered using a survey of people visiting Grafham Water. A total of 1000 questionnaires were distributed, of which 685 completed forms were returned. Each questionnaire solicited information on the mileage traveled, the number of people in the vehicle, and an estimate of the traveling costs incurred in visiting Grafham Water.

The benefits of Grafham Water were estimated using the travel cost method, originally developed by Clawson (1959). As discussed earlier, this method requires the development of a total demand curve for use of the site. This demand curve indicates the number of visits that can be expected at different total costs of access. The total cost of access includes both the travel cost and the admission fee, if any. The total area under the demand curve defines the economic benefits of the recreation site. The application of the Clawson method to Grafham Water required seven principal steps:

1. *Definition of origination areas*. The calculation of travel costs requires the identification of the origin of trips to the recreation site. Since it is impractical to consider each trip individually, origins are usually

---

[1]From R. J. Smith (1971).
[2]The currency in use at the time was the old system of the British pound sterling (£), where £1 equaled 20 shillings equaled 240 pence. This system was subsequently replaced with a decimal system. The values of the currency units are not important for this case study. The 1971 *Statistical Abstract of the United States,* published by the Census Bureau, however, reports a 1969 exchange rate of £1 = $0.4166 (U.S.).

divided into several concentric rings surrounding the recreation site. In this case, eight zones were defined.

Zone A, for example, included all trips originating within a 20-mile circle from Grafham Water. At the other extreme, Zone H included all trips originating outside of a 200-mile circle around the site. The specifications for the other zones are shown in Table 18.1.

In some analyses, an average distance traveled for each zone is calculated using the midpoint of that ring. For example, the average distance traveled from Zone A would be defined as 10 miles. However, the true mean distance traveled for each zone will obviously depend on the population distribution within that zone, as is shown in Table 18.1.

2. *Estimation of costs per mile.* The Clawson method requires some average measure of costs per mile traveled in order to estimate the benefits of the site. Obviously, visitors to a site will provide different individual estimates of these costs. For Grafham Water, these estimates ranged from 1 penny to 2 shillings per mile. The wide dispersion of the estimates made it impractical to use a standard arithmetic average, especially since the few high estimates would skew the average substantially. Instead, three other measures of central tendency were calculated: the mode was 3.0 pence per mile, the median was 2.94 pence per mile, and the geometric mean was 3.09 pence per mile. Since all three measures were very close to 3.0 pence per mile, this figure was chosen for subsequent calculations.

The cost per mile figure was then used to calculate costs per person per day for each visit. The cost per person includes both the travel cost and the admission fee. In addition, the cost is affected by the average number of persons traveling in each car, which the survey revealed to be 1.7 for Zone A and 2.1 for all other zones. As shown in Table 18.1, the costs per person ranged from a low of about 25 shillings to a high of over 80 shillings.

3. *Resolution of boundary problems.* In order to calculate the area under the demand curve, it is necessary to know at what cost the demand for the recreation facility falls to zero. The data for Grafham Water did

TABLE 18.1   Basic Data for Grafham Water Zone

	Zone Boundaries (miles)	Mean Distance Traveled (miles)	Cost per Person per Visit (shillings)	Visits per 100,000 Population
A	0–20	34.5	25.074	516
B	21–40	71.3	28.488	339
C	41–60	115.0	33.690	74
D	61–80	158.7	38.893	29
E	81–120	241.5	48.750	7
F	121–160	326.6	58.881	2.5
G	161–200	414.0	69.286	1
H	201+	506.0	80.188	13

not initially reveal such a figure; some visits were occurring even at a cost in excess of 80 shillings per day. However, a follow-up questionnaire to visitors traveling long distances revealed that almost all these individuals were in the area for other reasons or stayed for several days. The results of this second questionnaire allowed Zone H to be eliminated from further analysis since no occupants of this area were making single-day trips to Grafham Water. Furthermore, the cost at which no visitors would come to Grafham Water appeared to be about 90 shillings.

4. *Specification of the demand curve.*

a. An estimate of the benefits of a recreation area may be very sensitive to the form specified for the demand equation. The Grafham Water case illustrates this situation. Two forms of equation were used for preliminary analysis:

$$\log V = \log a_0 + a_1 \log C + \log e \qquad (18.6)$$
$$\log V = b_0 + b_1 c + e \qquad (18.7)$$

where V is the total number of visits per 100,000 population, C is the total cost per visit, a and b are calculated parameters, and e is a random error term.

A least squares analysis was used to fit the existing data to each of these forms. The results showed that the form of the equation has a major impact on calculated results. For example, a proposal to increase the fishing charge by 4 shillings would reduce the total number of visits to 15,109 under Equation (18.6), while under Equation (18.7) the number would drop only to 18,903. Similar discrepancies were noted for many other potential uses of the equation. Thus, it was necessary to reanalyze the data in order to minimize the problems associated with the form of the equation.

b. The demand curve must now be respecified. The information gathered in the survey was restudied to specify the origin areas more precisely. Instead of using eight zones, the origins were divided into 27 categories. The least squares analysis was then repeated to give the following two equations:

$$\log(V + 1) = 10.663 - 5.7041 \log C \qquad (18.8)$$
$$\log(V + 1) = 4.3920 - 0.06996 \, C \qquad (18.9)$$

Both of these equations provided statistically valid representations of the revised data. Equation (18.8) has the form of Equation (18.6), while Equation (18.9) has the form of Equation (18.7). The term $(V + 1)$ was used instead of V in order to allow V to fall to zero at some finite cost.

These new equations showed far less variability in results than the earlier equations based on eight zones. Thus, they served as the foundation for further analysis.

5. *Calculation of the final demand curve.* The initial demand curves listed above show the number of visits that are expected at different costs. These equations can be used to derive final demand curves for the

site by calculating the number of visits that would result for different admission charges. The area under the final demand curve can then be measured to identify total benefits and consumer surplus. For Grafham Water, the analysis began with the existing entrance fee of 20 shillings and increased in 4 shilling increments. The number of visits reached zero at a charge of about 90 shillings. The total benefits of trout fishing were calculated to be approximately £27,500, and the consumer surplus was nearly £7000.

6. *Analysis of the value of time*. The recreation benefits of Grafham Water were initially calculated by assuming that anglers assigned no value to their time other than the cost of traveling. In practice, individuals do assign values to their leisure time, although these values are usually difficult to measure or predict. Several approaches to calculating the value of time for the users of Grafham Water produced widely divergent results.

   Since no precise measure of the value of time was available, the benefits of Grafham Water were recalculated using a range of possible values for leisure time. Total benefits increased to over £30,000 if a time value of 3 shillings per hour was assigned. A further increase in total benefits to nearly £34,000 was noted if a time value of 6 shillings per hour was used.

18.4.2. Lessons

This case study of Grafham Water illustrates how the travel cost approach can be used to calculate the benefits from a recreation area. It also reveals five key lessons that need to be remembered when applying this technique:

1. *Data collection is very important*. Most efforts to calculate the value of a recreation area are based on information gathered from surveys of users. If such a survey is to be employed, it is essential that all the necessary information be identified in advance. For example, in the Grafham Water case it was important not only to collect information on the number of vehicles visiting the site, but also the average number of people in each vehicle.

   In addition to completeness, it is important to try to ensure that the survey reflects a representative sample of all users of a recreation area. This is fairly easy for small areas with single uses, but can be much more complicated for larger multi-use areas. Surveys should be designed to include all important categories of users (tourists, local residents, and so on) and all principal uses, which may require the survey to be conducted on several occasions during a year. In addition, the survey should include individuals who have traveled from a variety of distances.

2. *Origins must be carefully specified*. The Grafham Water study shows the importance of carefully defining the origins of trips to the recreation site. The method of concentric circles works well, but the average distance traveled from each ring should reflect actual highway miles and population distribution rather than simply the midpoint of the ring.

Furthermore, it is desirable to have a fairly large number of origins in order to reduce the impact that the form of the equation has on the results.

3. *Average costs must be carefully estimated.* It is essential to include all factors that significantly affect average cost, including travel costs, tolls, admission fees, and other expenses. If data are collected for vehicles rather than individuals, it is also important to know the average number of users in each vehicle.

4. *Equations must be specified using appropriate forms.* The form of the equation can often have a substantial impact on the results of a travel cost analysis. It is always useful to compare the results of several different forms to see how much variability is introduced in this way. Using large numbers of origins can help to reduce the effects introduced by different forms of equations.

5. *The value of time should be included, if possible.* In many cases, the value of leisure time can be a critical factor in calculating the value of a recreation area. Considerable research is currently underway on this subject. It appears that the value of leisure time is increasing, and that many individuals now assign values to leisure that equal or exceed their wage rates. If good figures are available, a single value of time can be included in the analysis. If figures are not available for the types of users being studied, the Grafham Water approach of calculating results for a range of values of time can be employed.

SUMMARY

Benefit–cost analysis is most often used where there are nonmarketed goods to value, such as environmental goods. To measure such values, a number of concepts and measurement techniques have been developed. A central concept is that of the *shadow price*. The shadow price is an estimate of the opportunity cost of providing or eliminating an additional unit of the good.

Both market and nonmarket approaches are used to evaluate nonmarketed goods. The hedonic price approach is a market approach that uses price differences among markets to value some attribute that varies across markets. For example, differences in land values are used to measure the value of clean air and quiet. In recent years there has been extensive use of questionnaire studies called contingent valuation measures (CVM) to measure environmental values. There is significant controversy about the accuracy of values gained from using the CVM approach. An older and widely used approach is the travel demand method in which willingness to bear expenses to travel to the good are used to derive a WTP for it.

Especially in the environmental area, the concepts of *existence value, option price,* and *option value* have been introduced and have assumed importance. Existence value is the value one would pay for the existence of some good over and above the use value of the good. There is concern that using existence value for, say, environmental goods gives too much weight to environmental values because most goods may have existence value that is not counted. Option value is the difference between option price and expected consumer surplus. This value may be positive or negative though it is often incorrectly treated as if it were only a positive value. Studies that add option value to use value to gain a measure of value are suspect.

QUESTIONS AND PROBLEMS

1. Describe several goods for which shadow prices might be calculated. Describe how you would calculate these shadow prices.
2. An African country imports trucks, and taxes them. The price of trucks is given by the world market and this world price is not influenced by actions of the African country. The government is considering a project that will require the import of five ore trucks. There are no exchange controls. The world price of trucks is $12,000, and the price with the country's tax is $15,000. Should the shadow price of trucks be calculated at the price with the tax, the price without the tax, or something in between? What number represents the shadow price of trucks.
3. In the above problem involving the importation of trucks, suppose instead that there were exchange controls such that the government was committed to maintaining a fixed exchange rate. Now what would be the shadow price of trucks? Why?
4. A famous example of the use of non-use values is the report of the Environmental Defense Fund (EDF) on the Clavey-Wards Ferry project on the Toulumne River. This was a part of the Hetch Hetchy Valley, over whose preservation John Muir had fought so hard and which led to a strong Sierra Club. EDF measured the total U.S. option value of retaining the Toulumne without the two proposed dams as $33.5 million. The EDF estimated the value of the project at about $188 million, and the total social costs including the option value at about $184 million for a surplus in favor of not proceeding with the project of about $26 million. The major other cost of the project was about $134 million in construction costs. The EDF apparently meant by option value the non-use value of the river.

   User value for fishing and rafting was constructed from a travel cost calculation that gave a yearly benefit of about $3 million. EDF estimated that per capita user value for California residents was about $184 per user. Per capita user value for other regions in the United States was about $393 per user.

   EDF surveyed nine studies showing use and non-use values and determined that the ratio of non-use to use value averaged 60 percent. The ratio ranged from 0.47 to 1.39. The non-use value for California was then determined by multiplying the use value by 60 percent to give a value of $110 and multiplying this figure by the California membership of the Sierra Club. The argument is that this represents a conservative number for interested non-users.

   Non-use value for the United States was determined by multiplying the use value of $393 by 45 percent rather than by 60 percent to help account for the greater remoteness. This figure is then multiplied by one-half the Sierra Club membership for the United States outside of California.

   The work of the EDF played a substantial role in preventing the Clavey-Ward project. In large part it allowed politicians in favor of preservation to cite benefit–cost figures to those in favor of the project. The EDF study furnished an acceptable rationale for a no vote.

   a. Is what EDF calculated as option value, in fact, option value? Why or why not?

   The EDF study is famous as a Harvard case study called "Saving the Toulumne." The Harvard study notes that EDF estimated " 'option value': the amount interested non-users would be willing to pay to ensure access to rafting on the river at some future time."

b. If this is, in fact, the definition EDF was using, is their procedure for adding use value and non-use value correct? Why or why not? (You may need to refer to Chapter 16 to give a complete answer but a reasonable answer can be given on the basis of this chapter.)

c. Is the Harvard case study definition consistent with the definition of option value given here?

d. If the Harvard case study definition of option value is used, then should existence values also have been calculated?

e. Do the size of the non-use values seem reasonable to you? Why or why not?

f. Do per capita non-use values higher than per capita use seem reasonable? Why or why not?

g. What would have been the result if the EDF had used the lower bound figure of 47 percent for the ratio of non-use to use value? Incidentally, this figure came from a study by Mitchell and Carlson in 1981 (Fisher and Raucher, 1984), two of the best-regarded figures now working in the field of contingent valuation.

REFERENCES

Bishop, Richard, "Resource Evaluation Under Uncertainty: Theoretical Principles for Empirical Research," in *Advances in Applied Microeconomics*, Vol. 4. V. Kerry Smith, ed., Greenwich, CT: JAI Press, 1986, 133–152.

Clawson, Marion, *Methods of Measuring the Demand for and the Value of Outdoor Recreation*, Washington: Resources for the Future, 1959.

Doyle, J., S. Elliott, G. McClelland, and W. Schulze, "Valuing the Benefits of Groundwater Cleanup: Interim Report," USEPA, Office of Policy, Planning and Evaluation, January 1991.

Fisher, Ann, and Robert Raucher, "Intrinsic Benefits of Improved Water Quality: Conceptual and Empirical Perspectives," in *Advances in Applied Microeconomics, Vol. 2*, V. Kerry Smith, ed., Greenwich, CT: JAI Press, 1984, 184–201.

Harberger, A., *Project Evaluation: Collected Papers,* Chicago: The University of Chicago Press, 1972, Chapter 5.

Kahneman, D., and J. Knetsch, "Valuing Public Goods: The Purchase of Moral Satisfaction," *Journal of Environmental Economics and Management* 22(1), 57–70, 1992.

Kopp, Raymond J., "Why Existence Value Should Be Used in Cost-Benefit Analysis," *Journal of Policy Analysis and Management* 11 (1), 123–130, Winter 1992.

Pearce, David W., and R. Kerry Turner, *Economics of Natural Resources and the Environment,* Baltimore: Johns Hopkins University Press, 1990.

Rosenthal, Donald H., and Robert H. Nelson, "Why Existence Value Should Not Be Used in Cost-Benefit Analysis," *Journal of Policy Analysis and Management* 11 (1), 116–122, Winter 1992.

Smith, R. J., "The Evaluation of Recreation Benefits: The Clawson Method in Practice," *Urban Studies* 8 (2), 89–102, 1971.

19

The Cost of Risk
(The Value of Life)*

19.1. INTRODUCTION

Imagine that you live with 99 other residents in a high-rise condominium in Toronto, Canada. The residents appear, at first glance, to be a rather homogeneous lot, apparently similar in age and income. Some residents express a concern over the risk of fire in the building. The major concern is over the threat to life posed by fire; the condominium residents have an insurance policy that is considered adequate for damages to property from fire. A meeting is called to discuss whether or not more should be spent to decrease the risk of fire.

There is no question the building can be made safer with respect to fire. There is in fact a considerable range of options, from increasing the number of fire extinguishers, which is relatively cheap, to replacing the existing system of overhead sprinklers with a more expensive and sophisticated system, which is expensive, to making major structural changes in the building, which is very expensive indeed.

The residents ask the fire marshal to speak about the effectiveness of the alternatives. She indicates that the more expensive options will be more effective. In North America over the last five years there have been 300 apartment fires. There were 15 fires in apartments that had the type of sprinkler system that the condominium now has. A total of five lives were lost from these 15 fires. There were 14 fires in buildings that had the more expensive sprinkler system, and in these fires two lives were lost. She believes it likely that the more expensive system explains the difference in lives lost. She thinks that adding more fire extinguishers and keeping the existing sprinkler system would

*We thank Pauline H. Ippolito for useful comments on early drafts of this chapter.

be less effective than putting in the new sprinkler system but would give about half of the *additional* protection of the new sprinkler system. She says that, if the major structural changes are made, the risk to life from fire would decrease dramatically and that if the new sprinkler system is combined with the structural changes, the risk would be about as low as it is possible to make it. One resident, however, does point out that the risk could be reduced even further were they to tear down the existing building and erect a new fireproof building.

The residents express different views about what should be done. One says that saving lives justifies any expenditure and that both the structural changes and the new sprinkler system should be purchased. Others say that the risk from fire is low to begin with and that no additional expenditures are necessary. One resident wants to know what level of expenditures will maximize the value of the building.

As one knowledgeable about benefit–cost analysis you point out that the issue being discussed is in fact the value of life. And, you further note, the solution to the problem posed would depend on you and your fellow residents' willingness to pay (WTP). You comment that those who say that saving lives justifies any expenditure must not really mean this since even this group did not propose tearing down the building and erecting a safer structure. A resident responds that she is not willing to sell her life for any amount so how can you talk about the value of life. You reply that we are talking about the value of increased safety, not the willingness to sell one's life.

As one who is able to use economic thinking you use the data the group has collected to present Table 19.1 in order to clarify the choices of the group. This table shows the cost of each option and the probable lives saved over a 50-year period. The cost is divided by the probable lives saved to obtain a value per life. A number of the residents object to putting a value on life. You maintain that the group is considering purchasing additional safety. Members of the group are demonstratively willing to pay to increase safety. Calculating the implicit value of life is just a way of expressing the cost of additional safety. With this understanding you present to the residents the figures illustrated by Table 19.1.

Option 5, erecting a new building, is eliminated immediately as too expensive. The cost would be $50,000 per resident. After some discussion option 4, which involves major structural change, is also eliminated as too expensive, although the woman who earlier said that no price is too high to pay to save

TABLE 19.1.

Options	Lives	Total Cost	Additional Cost per Life Saved
1. Fire extinguisher	0.010	$10,000	$1,000,000
2. New sprinkler system	0.040	200,000	5,000,000
3. Extinguishers + sprinklers	0.045	208,000	4,622,222
4. Structural changes	0.050	750,000	15,000,000
5. New building	0.20	5,000,000	25,000,000

lives would prefer option 4. (This woman is also reputed to be the wealthiest among the tenants.)

This exercise suggests that people do in fact put a value on life all the time, in the sense of determining what should be spent on safety. The value of life is then consistent with the WTP approach we have used elsewhere for other goods. It also suggests that people's tastes for safety differ and further suggests that as with other goods one's willingness to pay for more safety is likely to be greater the greater one's income.

The federal government spends over $100 billion on health, safety, and pollution control programs aimed at prolonging the lives of Americans.[1] The private sector spends an unknown additional amount. *Decisions concerning these expenditures implicitly put a price on life*. Product design decisions, quality control standards, labor training, and by-product disposal require management decisions that make a trade-off between higher costs and greater safety. Increasingly, private firms' decisions involving issues of health and safety are scrutinized by governments. Questions of appropriate safety standards for business products are now important matters of policy. Data on the value of life are fundamental to these decisions.

The purpose of considering the value of life is to determine (1) whether or not more lives would be saved if these sums were allocated differently among life-saving programs, and (2) whether they represent money well spent. Bailey notes that "Preliminary evidence indicates that the public health and government-stimulated private resources allocated to safety and health would save more lives if there were more effective government management and policy." The measurement of benefits and costs of life-saving programs is required if our goal is to more effectively use resources.

Bailey (1980, p. 26) offers the data in Table 19.2 as showing the potential for better management. The substantial discrepancies in the table indicate dramatic opportunities to save more lives by using resources more effectively.

We consider first briefly some philosophical and ethical issues in attaching a value to life. The economists' approach is then spelled out followed by a description of procedures for evaluating the value of life and limb or, more properly, of risk. We then present the results of empirical studies. Finally, we conclude with using value of risk.

19.2. PHILOSOPHICAL UNDERPINNINGS

Assigning values to lives has been the subject of intense controversy for many years. Although dozens of different views have been advanced, there are two basic philosophical positions in this controversy. The *moralists' view* is that it is unethical and immoral to place a value on life.[2] In this view, it is inappropriate to discuss lives using the language of material values. Instead, lives should be discussed in the language of rights and justice. In contrast, the *economists' view*

---

[1] M. J. Bailey (1980) calculated expenditures at over $70 billion in 1979.
[2] Many adherents of this position also believe it is inappropriate to assign values to other things, such as the existence of animal species. In this view, any action that risked the destruction of an entire species would be unacceptable, regardless of benefits that would result.

TABLE 19.2. Sample Estimates of the Cost per Life Saved in Programs Supported, Operated, or Mandated by Government

Program	Cost per Life Saved (1979 dollars)
Medical expenditure[a]	
Kidney transplant	72,000
Dialysis in hospital	270,000
Dialysis at home	99,000
Traffic safety	
Recommended for benefit–cost analysis by the National Safety Council	37,500[a]
Estimate for elimination of all railroad grade crossings	100,000[b]
Military policies[a]	
Instructions to pilots on when to crash-land airplanes	270,000
Decision to produce a special ejector seat in a jet plane	4,500,000
Mandated by regulation	
Coke oven emissions standard, OSHA	4,500,000–158,000,000[c]
Proposed lawn mower safety standards, CPSC	240,000–1,920,000[d]
Proposed standard for occupational exposure to acrylonitrile, OSHA	1,963,000–624,976,000[e]

[a] Dan Usher, "An Imputation to the Measure of Economic Growth for Changes in Life Expectancy," in M. Moss, ed., *The Measurement of Economic and Social Performance,* New York: National Bureau of Economic Research, 1973.

[b] Robert F. Baker, *The Highway Risk Problem,* New York: Wiley, 1971, p. 127.

[c] Statement on behalf of the Council on Wage and Price Stability by Dr. John F. Morrall III before the Occupational Safety and Health Administration, Washington, D.C., May 11, 1976.

[d] Comments of the Council on Wage and Price Stability before Consumer Product Safety Commission (CPSC), August 15, 1977.

[e] Statement on behalf of the Vistron Corporation by James C. Miller III before the Occupational Safety and Health Administration, Washington, D.C., April 4, 1978.

SOURCE: "Reducing Risks to Life" by M. J. Bailey, 1980. Reprinted with permission of the American Enterprise Institute for Public Policy Research, Washington, D.C.

is that determining the value of life is no different than determining the value of any other good. Proponents of this view note that individuals, companies, and governments must make implicit or explicit determinations of the value of life all the time, especially when the value of life must be compared with the value of other goods such as economic growth or environmental protection.

For the purposes of this book, it suffices to note that policy analysts often must assign values to lives under existing laws and regulations, and to consider the following four issues.

Purpose. First, it is important to note that the value placed on a human life depends on the purpose of the evaluation. In war the value placed on the lives of enemy soldiers is usually negative. The value generals place on the lives of their own men seems to be the opportunity cost of other uses of their lives to win the war. In some cases, lives may be valued *ex post* (after the fact) for the purpose of compensation. In other cases, lives may be valued *ex ante* (before the fact) for the purpose of preventing death and injury. Lives may be seen in the abstract where the names of the individuals are not known, such as when investments are made in highway guard rails as a way to save lives. Alternatively, lives may be seen in the particular where the names of the individuals are known, such as when prodigious efforts were made to free Brigitte Gerney after a construction crane fell on her as she walked along Manhattan's Third Avenue in May 1985. These contrasts illustrate that valuing lives does not lend itself to a simple and direct approach that applies in all circumstances.

Compensation.   The second philosophical issue is that refusing to place a value on life cannot reasonably be thought to apply to the provision of compensation for lives wrongfully lost. Such compensation is widespread today and has been provided in many past societies. The Aztecs created an elaborate system of compensation for injuries and death, and similar provisions were included in the Babylonian Code of Hammurabi. In ancient and medieval English law a sum of money (*Wergild* in Old English) was paid by a guilty party to the family of the person injured or killed. Currently, state laws in the United States differ in their provisions for compensation. For example, in suits for damages under wrongful death theory, in Georgia people are worth what they would have earned, while in New York or Washington State they are worth what they would have contributed to their family (that is, their earnings less their own personal consumption). Thus, the wrongful death of a young unmarried doctor is a small case in New York or Washington but a major case in Georgia in terms of monetary values.

Indemnification for a life wrongfully lost should not be regarded as a payment for a life.[3] The practical question is whether or not it is better (more just and more efficient) to have compensation when a life is wrongfully lost, or not to have compensation. Most societies have determined that compensation is desirable. Efficient compensation promotes greater care and reduces accidents. Thus, compensation for wrongful death is not unethical but rather is desirable.

The third philosophical issue involves how the value of life should be applied to saving future lives. If no consideration at all is given to the value of life, lives will be lost since there would be no way to choose between two otherwise equal projects, one of which saved more lives. However, the issue of actually valuing lives can be side-stepped by attaching equal and infinite weights to all lives, in which case the object of decision making would be to maximize the total number of lives saved. This approach has the advantage of allowing some efficiency considerations in policy while avoiding any moral qualms about putting a value on life. Similarly, a cost-effectiveness approach based on maximizing the number of lives saved makes sense when there is already a fixed budget allocated for this purpose. Efficiency in allocating this budget can be achieved without putting a value on life. An objection to putting an infinite value on life is that this eliminates all other values; thus, there can be no trade-offs. Under the infinite value of life approach, all resources should be devoted to saving lives. No resources at all should be devoted to other purposes, including enhancing the quality of lives. This approach is not generally adopted and is unacceptable when the issue is how much to spend

---

[3]This is consistent with the fact that damage to the deceased is not ordinarily a part of the court's considerations. See W. S. Malone (1965).

on saving statistical lives. However, some value of life must be used if lives are to be considered in policy analysis.

Discounting Future Lives.   If some value is to be given to lives, as we think it should, this leads to questions of the relative value of present and future lives. In short, should future lives be discounted? Many have held that it is immoral to discount future lives. Consider, however, the following example. Suppose there are two individuals, one who will be born twenty years after the other, but who are otherwise identical. Policy A will save the first-born individual, individual 1; policy B will save individual 2. It would seem that one cannot choose between policy A and B. If individual 1 is saved, however, his earnings or some portion of his earnings can be taxed to generate a sufficient amount to save the life of 2. Even if the tax on the earnings would be insufficient, it may be that if the tax revenues are invested they will grow enough to save 2. The point is that if individual 1 has a WTP that exceeds the value of the risk, the net benefit could be invested to generate funds that in the future could be devoted to saving lives. *The essential point is that failure to discount statistical lives will lead to a situation in which fewer total lives will be saved.*

Under extremely plausible assumptions, Cropper and Portney (1990) show that the lives of future generations as well as the future life of an existing generation should be discounted. These assumptions are (1) individuals are willing to trade off increases in mortality risk for money, (2) there are alternative uses for life-saving resources, and (3) capital investments yield a positive rate of return. Horowitz and Carson (1990) have shown that people do in fact discount future lives in their decisions. (See also Horowitz, 1991.) The authors are able to reject the hypothesis that discount rates for saving lives are zero or nonexistent and generally are not able to reject the hypothesis that these rates are the same as market rates. Applying five different approaches, Moore and Viscusi (1990) find that workers discount future health risks and that the estimated discount rates "do not deviate substantially from financial market rates" (p. 394).

For reasons that are unclear, people seem to use a higher discount rate in decisions more likely to affect their own lives than the lives of others (Horowitz and Carson, 1990).

Quality of Life.   The final issue involves the quality of life. If an analysis focuses only on the number of lives saved, not the quality of those lives, serious philosophical issues can be raised. For example, this approach would not differentiate between saving for a short time a life in pain, such as saving a hospitalized person for one week, and a longer-term saving of an apparently higher quality of life. This approach would be somewhat more acceptable if it focused on the days of life saved, thereby making the distinction between saving a life for a short time and a longer time. Other quality considerations would, however, still be ignored. Suppose there were a single kidney machine that could be used to save either a physically ill psychopath or a young Mozart. Should a distinction on the merits be made? There is no doubt that such distinctions raise difficult ethical questions. However, these distinctions are increasingly a part of policy analysis.

Assigning values to lives obviously is a complex and sometimes morally upsetting problem. The moral issues involved can never be resolved to the satisfaction of everyone. Economists and policy analysts have chosen to address these issues by comparing the *value of risk* to other values in a way that reflects the willingness of society to pay or accept. This approach is discussed in detail in the following section.

19.3.   THE ECONOMISTS' APPROACH

Economists' approach to value of life questions is the same as for other valuation questions. For them, the unavoidable comparison is how much we should value improved physical well-being as opposed to more scenic views, better looks, greater economic growth, or some other outcome. Dollar values are the convenient basis of comparison.

Economists' estimates of the value of life are estimates of the WTP for additional safety or the WTA payment for bearing additional risk to life. Assuming a right to life, the value of accepting an increased risk is the amount one is willing to accept to undertake it. The question asked by this methodology is what will one accept as monetary compensation to undertake an additional risk or what will one pay to avoid an additional risk. The usual custom is to calculate the WTP for benefits and the WTA for costs.

Suppose you are willing, for \$5, to undertake an additional risk of one in a million chance (1×10^{-6}) of fatal injury. For simplicity, suppose all injuries in this activity are fatal. In this case the value of your life would be \$5 × 1,000,000, or \$5,000,000. It is these sort of figures that are used to generate "value of life" calculations. But this \$5,000,000 figure is misleading if used as a single value of life. The premium is specific for the initial level of risk and for the added risk assumed. For a larger risk we would expect you to require a larger premium per unit of risk. As one takes on greater risks one's valuation per unit of risk increases. This reflects the fact that for safety, as for most goods, the value of additional units of safety falls as one gains more safety.

For example, suppose you are asked to assume a risk of one in ten thousand (1×10^{-4}), a hundred times more risk than in the previous example. We would expect that your premium would be more than 100 × \$5. It would be, say, \$1000. This would give a value of life of \$10,000,000, twice that for the previous risk. Thus assuming the person has a right to life, there is no unique value of life for even a single person. The value of life depends on the initial risk and the additional risk as well as the risk aversion of the particular person.

The willingness to pay for or to accept risks can be depicted by the indifference map for income and safety in Figure 19.1. Initial equilibrium is at point A on budget line $Y_A S$. A decrease in the price of safety moves equilibrium to $Y_A S_2''$ at B. The compensating variation for this decrease is $Y_B - Y_A$. The equivalent variation is $Y_C - Y_A$. The CV for a price decrease is the willingness to pay to obtain the decrease. The EV for a price decrease is the amount one would accept to forego the price decrease. For a normal good, the equivalent variation is greater than the compensating variation for a price decrease because of a positive income effect. In a legal sense the difference between the CV and the EV for a price decrease is that the CV assumes one has to buy into the

Figure 19.1. Compensating and equivalent variations for safety.

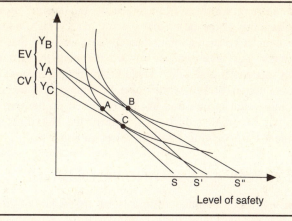

benefit. The EV assumes one has the benefit initially. That is, one can regard this as a difference in the initial assignment of rights. For a price decrease, the EV shows a positive income effect as compared with the CV because the initial income is assumed higher for the EV than the CV as reflected in the assignment of the right.

In consideration of the value of life, the right to life or to safety and health is at issue, so the difference between the CV and EV will tend to be very large where the risk is large. The distinction reflects the difference between the questions posed by two killers. The honest killer asks (1) how much will you accept to allow me to shoot you? The dishonest killer asks (2) how much will you pay me not to shoot you? The second question assumes you have the right to life; the first does not. Clearly the compensation required (the CV) to accept an increased risk amounting to certain, or even almost certain, death, is very high if not infinite.

This may be reflected in society's willingness to spend very large sums to save a life when the person's name is known. When Brigitte Gerney was trapped for six hours by a construction crane, no questions were raised about the costs of freeing her.[4] Hundreds of police officers rerouted traffic. Two cranes were brought from other boroughs to lift the fallen one. Doctors set up a mobile hospital. Emergency service workers risked their lives to save her. Police halted traffic for 30 blocks to speed her trip to the emergency room. Lieutenant Thomas Fahey of the NYPD said, "There's no point where you say that's too expensive." This attitude, similar to the philosophic view that you

---

[4]Update on Gerney, Kirk Johnson, *The New York Times,* "New Yorker Pinned by Crane Testifies in Trial," Apr. 15, 1986.

> Nearly 11 months after a 35-ton crane fell and crushed her legs, Brigitte Gerney entered a Manhattan courtroom yesterday—on crutches but on her own—to tell her story to a State Supreme Court jury. . . .
> Mrs. Gerney, who is 50 years old, has also filed a $35 million civil suit against the defendants and a long list of co-defendants, including the City of New York. . . .

cannot place a value on life is, however, consistent with an economic approach that recognizes a person's right to life and accepts the person's own evaluation.

An understanding of the point that placing a very high value on the life of a *known* person is consistent with benefit–cost analysis that recognizes a right to life would go some distance toward reducing the distance between the economists' approach and other value-oriented approaches. Criticism of the economic valuation of life would also be muted if it were understood that the economic value in question should be based on the individual's own willingness to pay for small reductions in risk or the individual's willingness to accept payment for accepting small increases in risk.

19.4.   METHODS OF CALCULATING VALUE OF LIFE

Four methods are used to make estimates of the value of life and limb: (1) estimates of wage premiums for accepting risk, (2) estimates of premiums paid in consumption choices (hedonic prices), (3) contingent valuation on interview studies, and (4) foregone earnings.

19.4.1.   Estimates of Wage Premiums

The use of premiums as measures to accept additional risk is straightforward and follows the logic of the previous examples. If you accept a job with a greater than usual risk, say an additional risk of 1×10^{-4} of death, and require a wage premium of $40 to accept this additional risk, the value is 4×10^4, or $400,000. We must now ask how representative is your risk evaluation, and how representative your value of life at the specified level of risk is to your implicit value at other levels of risk.

To illustrate these points, let us assume for simplicity that individuals in the labor force can be divided into three groups and all employers likewise can be divided into three groups. This is shown in Figure 19.2. As Figure 19.2 indicates, the risk premium per unit of risk will be greater the greater the risk and the greater the initial level of risk. Thus an additional risk of 2×10^{-4} will involve a premium more than twice as great as a 1×10^{-4} level of risk.

Figure 19.2.   Marketplace observed and underlying relations between risk and wage premiums.

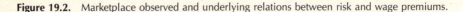

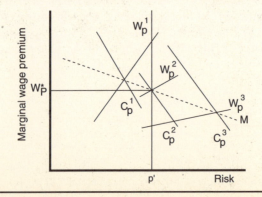

That is, the implicit value of life, ceteris paribus, for a risk level of 2×10^{-4} will be greater than for a risk level of 1×10^{-4}. The first group of individuals is relatively risk averse, with the curve W_p^1 indicating the wage premium that would be required by workers if they are asked to accept a given level of risk. Curves W_p^2 and W_p^3 indicate the same for the less risk-averse groups. The payments that employers are willing to offer if workers will forego greater safety (assume more risk) in their jobs are indicated by curves C_p. Employers with a lower cost of safety have C_p^1. Firms with the greatest cost of safety have C_p^3. The curves slope downward indicating that as the marginal cost of providing more safety increases, the firm will pay more. The three curves represent employers with differing costs of providing safety. The actual wage premium paid to the workers in each group will be determined by the level of risk, such as $p*$, where it becomes less expensive for the employer to provide increased job safety than to increase the wage premium by W_p^*. It is W_p^* and $p*$ that will be observed, not the W_p and C_p curves. Thus, a regression analysis relating marketplace wages and risks will yield the dashed line M in Figure 19.2.

Figure 19.2 shows the observed market relationship decreasing as risk increases. There is no theoretical requirement that M increase or decline with increasing risk, but Olson (1981) and Viscusi (1983) have been able to confirm that M does in fact decline for wage premiums in U.S. industry. This implies that studies with data taken from occupations with high risk levels will report a lower average value of life than studies that focus on occupations at lower risk.

The correct price of increased risk to life for a benefit–cost analysis would be the arithmetic average of the values of all the W_p curves at the appropriate risk level. For example, if the initial risk of the project to be analyzed were p^* in Figure 19.2, the price would be the average of W_p^1, W_p^2, and W_p^3 where they cross the vertical line through p^* (assuming there are equal numbers in each group and all the individuals in each group have identical preferences). Without knowledge of the slopes of the W_p^1 and W_p^3 curves it is not possible to say if W_p^* will be an overstatement or an understatement of the average. If we relax our assumptions our uncertainty increases. Since the individuals in each group do not have identical preferences their individual curves will not fall on a single line, such as W_p^2. The observed market position (W_p^*, p^*) will represent the values of the marginal worker, the last worker attracted into that labor group by the wage premium. That position will represent a surplus for some workers.

19.4.2. Estimate of Premiums Paid in Consumption Choices

Just as risk premiums can be determined from choice among jobs of differing risk, so also can risk premiums be derived from consumer choices among alternatives and different risk levels. Given an increase in income one might choose a safer car, use a seat belt more often, or smoke less. A change in the convenience of using seat belts will change usage. New information about the danger of smoking will reduce smoking. It is from these kinds of changes that risk premiums can be determined. The issues of interpretations of those premiums are similar to those for risk from job choices.

19.4.3. Contingent Valuation Studies

Recently, questionnaire studies have been used in interesting ways to yield exciting results concerning behavior under risk. In a number of cases these studies have involved actual monetary payoffs to individuals and in this sense have been realistic, though the results tend to confirm those in which no actual payoffs are given. A few of these studies have generated value of life estimates but small sample sizes for these studies reduce confidence in some of them. A recent contingent valuation study by Gerking et al. (1988) gives an estimated 2.6 million in 1984 dollars. This is within the range of most other estimates.

Potential data problems exist for any approach. Wage premium estimates, for example, have very substantial data deficiencies. Whether or not, and to what extent, interview data are reasonably reliable is an empirical question whose answer will depend in part on the procedures used to collect the data. A great advantage of interview studies is that the interviewer can often generate data not otherwise available.

19.4.4. Foregone Earnings

The foregone earnings approach bears little theoretical relationship to the concepts of WTP or WTA for risk which underlie the economists' approach. The foregone earnings approach nevertheless is the major approach used by the courts in calculating damages for cases involving wrongful death. The foregone earnings approach sees the value of life as flowing from one's lifetime consumption. That is, the value of life is approximately what one will add to the national product discounted to present value. Using foregone earnings as a criterion would mean choosing among health and safety activities in order to produce the largest measured real national product.[5] This approach gives a rough approximation of willingness to pay to save a life or to avoid a very high risk in the sense that one's willingness to pay is one's income. It is deficient as a value measure because one's income may differ substantially from the figure one would accept or pay to undertake an increase in risk. A person with lifetime earnings of $10,000 per year for twenty years has a present value of life of $200,000 using a zero discount rate. This person might, however, be willing to pay $10,000 for a reduction in risk of 1×10^{-3} with an implicit value of life of $10,000,000.[6]

The foregone earnings approach, of course, may bear no relation to the WTA a loss of life. Mr. Smith, who earns $20,000 per year, may require $50 per year to accept a yearly risk of 1 in 100,000. This gives a value of life of $5,000,000 per year. This result is not surprising when we consider the relationship of earnings to life value. Mr. Smith makes $10 per hour and works 8 hours a day, 260 days per year producing an income of $20,800 per year. Mr. Smith's life expectancy is, say, 40 years, for a present value of earnings of $832,000 at a zero discount rate. The value of life as measured by Smith's

---

[5]E. J. Mishan (1971).

[6]There is an abundance of evidence showing that most investors are risk averters (that is, they would not accept a fair bet where the amount to be invested was sizable). Bailey (1980, p. 29) points out that this implies that safety and health benefits are greater than discounted future amounts of lost earnings. This would be the case at least if a risk-free interest rate is used to do the discounting.

WTA to bear the specified risk level is over six times his lifetime earnings. If one is going to use the foregone earnings approach and assume a right to life, then the value of leisure must also be valued. The value of Mr. Smith's additional after-work leisure is worth at least as much per hour and probably more than his wage. Mr. Smith would then certainly require at least $10 per hour for 24 hours per day for every day of the year, or $3.5 million for 40 years using a zero discount rate. This is, of course, far greater than the $832,000 found by the simple earnings approach.

19.4.5. Net Earnings

A variant of the net income approach occurs where one calculates only the monetary value of the person to others, that is, the estate value. This approach is the basis for most wrongful death claims. The net income method subtracts from the decedent's expected earnings that portion of the earnings the deceased is expected to have consumed. That is, the loss to others from the death is the expected value of the savings that the deceased might have had available to leave to others. This approach suggests the value of an older, retired person who may have no labor earnings but who will continue to consume is negative. Yet the person's friends and relatives (as well as the person herself) would usually be willing to pay to increase the probability of longer life for the person.

We see then that foregone earnings are not a good theoretical approximation of either the WTP or WTA for the loss or gain of risk (life). The foregone earnings approach is theoretically discredited as a benefit–cost approach. Empirically, however, the fact is that the value of life calculated by the foregone earnings approach seems to be a rather consistent percentage of the value of life calculated by a theoretically correct economic approach. Cave (1986a) has found that lifetime earnings are consistently about 6 percent of the value of life calculated in a theoretically correct manner.

The foregone earnings approach is used now mainly, and importantly, to establish awards in wrongful death and injury cases. The approach has the advantage of being subject to fairly objective calculation. Here the approach makes sense as a measure of the economic loss to survivors. Compensation for death must necessarily be arbitrary. Though in some states gross earnings are used, in most states estimates of the person's own consumption is subtracted to yield an estate value. In the case of injury, the present value of gross earnings foregone (plus medical expenses) is calculated. The calculation of lawful damages for wrongful death or injury has reached a considerable degree of refinement and detailed handbooks are available to assist in these calculations.[7]

19.4.6. Conclusion

The economists' approach to the value of life is useful and consistent with the general economic approach to valuation. Questions may nevertheless be raised. Note that (1) the value of one's life will still depend on one's wealth, ceteris paribus; and (2) anomalies arise because the value of life is greater for a named than an unnamed person. One's WTP to reduce risk is clearly constrained by one's wealth, but even one's willingness to accept payment for

---

[7]E.g., S. M. Speiser (1979).

the assumption of risk will be affected by one's wealth. Other things being equal a poorer person will be more likely to accept a given wage premium for assuming greater risk than a rich person. Some may object to this aspect of the value of life calculation. One could, of course, calculate the value of life for some standard level of wealth and use this figure for all wealth levels. One then can use the same figure for a richer and poorer person. With respect to the second point, consider a rather fanciful hypothetical case.

Suppose there are two alternative projects A and B. Project A subjects 100,000 people to a risk of 1×10^{-4}; we expect ten lives to be lost. Project B subjects only John Jones to certain death. Otherwise, the two projects are identical. On a value of life approach we might prefer project A because unnamed lives are worth less than named lives. That is, the 100,000 people affected by project A each require a wage premium of, say, $6. This adds $600,000 to the project cost. The value of the life that will be lost is $600,000. John Jones quite naturally is not, however, going to accept $600,000 or even $6,000,000 in exchange for his life. He will require considerably more, if indeed any amount is sufficient. So, on a benefit–cost basis, project A may be preferred over B even though A costs ten lives and B one life.

19.5. EMPIRICAL ESTIMATES OF THE VALUE OF LIFE AND LIMB

19.5.1. Wage Premium Approaches

Most estimates of the premiums required to accept risk are based on studies of wage differentials for jobs of varying degrees of riskiness. As noted earlier, the idea is that if one accepts a more risky job in exchange for a higher wage then the higher wage is a risk premium representing the amount one is willing to accept for the additional risk. There are problems with this approach. We have discussed some of the conceptual problems in connection with Figure 19.2. These problems involve applying estimates once they are made.

There are also difficulties in making the initial estimates. Workers receive wage premiums for other aspects of the job than risk. For example, miners may receive more because of working in the dark or because the job is dirty. Workers are not randomly chosen for jobs of different levels of risk, but can choose jobs based on attitudes toward risk. Construction workers and race car drivers may accept much higher levels of risk than the typical consumer or worker. There is also a question of whether or not workers' perceptions of risk accord with actual risk. Finally the data themselves are often not of high quality. Different researchers obtain different estimates from the same set of data under different specifications of the risk acceptance equation.[8]

Dillingham (1985) shows that much of the variation in the wage premium studies is due to different risk variables and equation specifications.

---

[8]For example, Dillingham (1985) used a cross section of workers similar to those used in the Smith and Viscusi studies. Dillingham utilized detailed risk data by industry and occupation and was able to assign workers to more detailed risk categories than those used in other studies. His estimates of the value of life are considerably below those of Smith (1976), Viscusi (1978), and Olson (1981).

By accounting for the effects of different risk variables, Dillingham is able to produce much more uniformity in the estimates. His work indicates that the appropriate range for value of life estimates is in the $1–$2 million range (1979 dollars). *This gives a range in 1990 dollars of $1.75 million to $3.50 million.*

19.5.2. A Different Approach

A different approach to the cost of risk was made by Ippolito and Ippolito (1984) and by Blomquist (1981). Ippolito and Ippolito provide an interesting measure of value of life by looking at the cigarette market. Changes in information and beliefs about the life expectancy effects of smoking were compared with changes in individuals' demand for cigarettes. Estimates were made of what the demand for cigarettes would have looked like in 1980 had no disclosures appeared about the hazards of smoking. These estimates were compared with the actual demand for cigarettes in 1980. The reduction of demand was then compared to the change in perceived risks to give a value of life figure. Sensible adjustments were made for the deterioration in cigarette quality and this contribution to the reduced demand was separated from those due to health disclosures. The assumption is made that lower health levels, such as shortness of breath, coughing, etc., attributable to smoking were known equally well before and after disclosures about risks of death for smoking. If this assumption is incorrect the Ippolito result is too low. On the other hand, no account is taken of the psychic cost of cigarette withdrawal. Ignoring this cost may also give an underestimate to Ippolito and Ippolito's calculation of the value of life.

Ippolito and Ippolito found an average value of life of about $460,000 in 1985 dollars, or approximately $580,000 in 1989 dollars. That is, on average, individuals are willing to pay up to $580 to reduce the risk of death by 1/1000 or up to $52 to reduce the risk of death by 1/10,000.

This estimate is lower than most of those in the literature. It is based on a situation in which information about health risks are rather well known. In addition, there is a direct connection between the observed behavior and the risks to life. Finally, the study corrects for possible errors in consumer beliefs about the risks and for differences in their educations or safety.

Blomquist compared estimates of seat belt usage with estimates of the risk reduction achieved by seat belt usage and with the cost of seat belt usage to calculate a value of life. The idea is that using the seat belt takes more time (and causes discomfort) to which the individual attaches a value but also accomplishes a reduction in risk. Blomquist used evidence that the value of a driver's time is approximately one-half his wage and found that seat belt usage varied directly with the wage, holding lifetime income constant. After correcting for the value of avoided injuries, Blomquist estimates a value of about $40 (1978 dollars) for a risk reduction of 1×10^{-4}. Since he estimates the discomfort and inconvenience cost of seat belts is at least seven times the fastening cost, a more accurate premium may be $280. These premiums translate into a value of life between $400,000 and $2,800,000 in 1978 dollars. Blomquist also finds that the elasticity of his estimate with respect to foregone earnings is only about 0.3, which is consistent with the contention that the foregone earnings approach substantially understates the value of life.

TABLE 19.3.   Labor Market Value of Life Estimates

"Low" Estimates			"High" Estimates		
Study	Estimate	Data Source	Study	Estimate	Data Source
Thaler and Rosen (1975)	$730,000	Actuarial— Thaler/Rosen	Smith (1976)	$4,045,000	BLS (1970)[a]
Brown (1980)	$1,000,000	Actuarial— Thaler/Rosen	Viscusi (1978)	$4,213,000	BLS (1969)[a]
Amould and Nichols (1983)	$340,000– $967,000	Actuarial— Thaler/Rosen	Olson (1981)	$4,957,000– $9,106,000	BLS (1973)[a]
			Marin and Psacharopoulos	$3,291,000	OPCS[b] (1970–1972)
			Dillingham	$1,858,000– $2,365,000	Census and Workers' Compensation Data (1970)

[a] Bureau of Labor Statistics
[b] Office of Product and Consumer Safety
SOURCES: Dillingham (1985) Estimated Updated CPF

19.5.3.   Summary

Table 19.3 summarizes the results of the major risk premium studies. Dillingham shows that differences in definitions of risks and other statistical problems explain much of the variation in estimates. Dillingham also finds that the low end estimates of Table 19.3 are derived from actuarial data that give estimates that are biased downward. *For these and other reasons, Dillingham argues that the estimates below about 1.7 million and above 3.4 million (1990 dollars) should be ignored.* Thus the range of value of life estimates derived from wage or occupational studies is considerably narrower than indicated by Table 19.3. Although one can feel rather confident using a range of say $1.7 million to $3.4 million in 1990 dollars, this is still a wide range.

The Environmental Protection Agency has ordered that virtually all remaining asbestos production in the United States be phased out, capping a 17-year struggle to end the manufacture of a substance that has been causing cancer for decades.

While previous orders have cut annual production from 561,000 metric tons in 1979 to less than 85,000 metric tons today, EPA Administrator William Reilly said the mineral still is used in a variety of products from brake pads to roofing. The order will cut production to less than 6000 tons by 1996, he said.

Reilly said the order would save about 300 lives over 13 years, at a cost to the economy of $459 million, or more than $2 million per life. He said that was a small price to pay to end production of a substance that "has left a terrible legacy of dead, dying, and crippled."

Between 3000 and 12,000 people die each year from asbestos-caused disease. The mineral, which is used because it is heat- and fire-resistant, odorless, and very durable, breaks down into tiny fibers that are easily inhaled. It can take 20 to 40 years for the inhaled fibers to cause cancer; cases are now being diagnosed in people exposed during World War II.

The EPA order will ban the manufacture, import, and processing of most asbestos products in three stages, starting August 17, 1990, and ending in 1996.

Auto makers will have to stop using asbestos in car and truck brakes, starting with the 1994 models. Shingles and other new roofing materials will have to be free of asbestos by 1996.

The White Lung Association, representing victims of asbestos illness, said it welcomed the ban but said it wants the EPA to go further and recall asbestos products already in use.

Source: Seattle Times, May 5, 1991.

19.6. APPLYING VALUE OF LIFE FIGURES

There are four considerations that should be kept in mind in applying valuation of risk. These are (1) the level of risk and the applicable risk class, (2) the value of life to others, (3) whether or not the risk is voluntary or involuntary, and (4) the distribution of risks.

19.6.1. The Level of Risk and the Risk Class

The most reasonable value of life to use will depend on the level of risk and on the risk class of the individuals involved. Since in most cases the risk class will not be known, a range of estimates can be used and sensitivity analysis performed (see Chapter 17).

The appropriate risk premium will differ at different levels of risk for a single individual as we have indicated. For the same individual a greater risk will suggest a larger value of life. In addition, at the same level of risk, different risk premiums will apply to different individuals. Available evidence suggests that the value of life will be less for those who voluntarily expose themselves to large risks.

Also, the value of life for people of one risk category may be inappropriate for those not in the category. The estimates of Thaler and Rosen (1975) for a high–risk–bearing group are, for example, inappropriate for a typical worker. Olson (1981) indicates that the slope of M in Figure 19.2 is negative. The Ippolito and Ippolito study indicates consumers vary considerably in their risk preferences and that the distribution of these preferences is decidedly skewed. More than 40 percent of the population had a value of life of less than $350,000 ($350 of 1×10^{-2} risks) though the average value was $460,000. Yet, 20 percent of the population shows a value of life of more than $670,000 ($670 to reduce risks by 1×10^{-3}). These results indicate that a minority of consumers are willing to pay a sizable premium for safety while others are willing to pay considerably less. In fact, in the Ippolito and Ippolito study 70 percent are unwilling to pay the estimated mean of \$460 to eliminate risks of death by 1×10^{-3}. This same skewed distribution was found in a questionnaire study by Jones-Lee (1980) in which individuals were asked directly about their willingness to pay.

Viscusi's 1983 study, as Olson's 1981 study, helps to throw light on how the risk premium varies with the level of risk. As Viscusi points out, value of life studies should not be directed at estimating an elusive value of life number (Viscusi, 1983, p. 103). There is instead a schedule of values representing the WTA of those with different attitudes toward risk.

Those who price their life the cheapest are drawn into the market first. Higher wages must be paid as additional workers with increasing levels of risk aversion are hired. Viscusi (1981) divides workers into categories of on-the-job risk; his findings indicate that value of life estimates among workers in the first, second, and third quartile scarcely differ, which indicates that three-fourths of all workers have very similar values of life (in the range of \$6 to \$10 million in 1980 dollars, depending on the form of equation used). There is a dramatic decline in the value of life as one considers workers in the most hazardous (fourth) quartile.[9] Thus this quartile is not representative of most workers.

These estimates suggest that of all the various disparate wage study estimates, value of life estimates may not be contradictory at all. The value of life to workers in the lowest risk level was 2.7 times the value for those in the higher risk group. This is well within the upper-range estimates for the value of life estimates. Clearly more work needs to be done to explain the existing range of estimates.

19.6.2.   Value of One's Life to Others

Needleman (1976) used data on the behavior of kidney donors in the United States to estimate the willingness to pay on the part of family and friends to save a life. The value of one life to those not family or friends is assumed to be zero. The figures Needleman finds are modest and sensible. For example, the value a child places on the life of a parent is only 3 percent of the value the parent places on his own life. Ruby (1981) applies Needleman's calculations to the 1980 population characteristics of the United States. He finds that the cost to others is about 44 percent of the value the individual puts on his own life. The consideration of the value of one's life to others requires some upward adjustment to the range of figures in Table 19.3.

19.6.3.   Involuntary Risks

Work by Slovic, Lichtenstein, and Fischaff (1979) and others indicates that the risk premium is greater when the risk is involuntary. In this study a panel of adults was asked to assign relative social value to deaths from a number of causes. The higher the value the greater the social cost of the death. Deaths due to one's own personal choice or negligence (for example, mountain climbing) were assigned values near 1. Deaths due to common, voluntarily accepted risks

---

[9]Since the value of life falls off very steeply as the risk level is increased, low estimates such as those obtained by Thaler and Rosen (1975) for high-risk populations are not implausible.

EXAMPLE 19.1

Choose between alternatives:

Alternative A: Person 1 dies, person 2 lives.

Alternative B: 50 percent chance that person 1 dies and that person 2 lives, and 50 percent chance that person 2 dies and that person 1 lives.

In these two alternatives the expected number of fatalities is the same. Under both alternatives one person will die. An analysis that ignored the distribution of risks (such as the von Neumann–Morgenstern utility function) would predict indifference between the alternatives. In fact, however, alternative B will be chosen by a majority of people. In alternative B each person has an equal chance of dying.

(for example, automobiles) were rated about 1.25. Deaths from involuntary and insidious risks (for example, pesticides) received a rating of from approximately 1.5 to 2. Thus it could be argued that the wage premium estimates, which of course represent voluntary risk, should be increased by the ratio of the value of involuntary risks to that of voluntary risks when accounting for involuntary risks, such as air pollution or pesticide exposure. This would require the value of a voluntary risk to be multiplied by about 1.2 to 1.6 to properly represent a willingness to pay for additional risks relative to involuntary risks. For our purposes here we will use a value of 1.4 to represent the adjustment from voluntary to involuntary risks. Whether the value of risk to others is also affected by whether the risk is voluntary is not known.

The Total Social Value of Risk.   We let V stand for the value of voluntary risk not counting the value of life to others. Assuming that the value of life to others is not affected by whether or not the risk is voluntary, the total value of life taking into account both the value of life to family and friends and the involuntary nature of risks would be $V + 0.44V + 1.4V =$ total value or $1.84V$ where V is a value of life determined prior to the two adjustments. *Thus the total value for an involuntary risk, taking into account the value of one life for others, and using a range for the value of V from 1.7 to 3.4 million dollars, would be about 3 million to 6 million dollars in 1990 dollars.*

19.6.4.   The Distribution of Risks*

People care not only about the level of fatalities or injuries but also about the *distribution of risks*. One should consider not only the number of expected fatalities or injuries but also how the risks are distributed over the members or groups of society.

---

*This section relies on Keller and Sarin (1988).

EXAMPLE 19.2

On an island within your jurisdiction 100 miners are trapped in one location in a mine. There is a way to rescue these miners by sending a rescue team through an unused tunnel. You have dispatched a rescue team of 10 rescuers to this tunnel. The team has come upon a portion of the tunnel which is dangerous. They need to station a rescuer at this point in the tunnel for the next 10 hours to listen and watch for any signs that the trapped miners send to the team. However, there is a chance that sometime in the next 10 hours, a cave-in will occur which will be fatal to the rescuer stationed there. The rest of the tunnel is safe, so the rescuers are not at risk in other parts of the tunnel. The team is able to communicate with you at a command post via a portable radio. The team has contacted you for your orders about what to do next. They want to know if they should station one rescuer at the key point in the tunnel for 10 hours, or have each rescuer take a 1-hour shift. There is a 10 percent chance that a cave-in will occur, and only one cave-in would occur, if any.

The rescuers will definitely be able to save the 100 miners, no matter which option is taken.

Option A.   One rescuer does the entire 10 hour shift. This rescuer has a 10 percent chance of death. The other nine rescuers have a 0 percent chance of death.

Preference group: 17% ($N = 53$)
Fairness group: 4% ($N = 53$)

Option B.   Each of the 10 rescuers takes a 1 hour shift. Thus each rescuer has a 1 percent chance of death, because each would be in the tunnel one-tenth of the time, and one-tenth times 10 percent is 1 percent.

Preference group: 83% ($N = 53$)
Fairness group: 96% ($N = 53$)

Option B was ranked above Option A in terms of preference and fairness by a majority of subjects. In both options A and B, the probability distribution over number of fatalities is identical (10 percent chance one person dies and 90 percent chance no person dies).

Two concepts of equity have emerged as important in considering risk. The first is ex ante equity:

Ex Ante Equity: A distribution of risks is more equitable the more equal are the probabilities of risk for relevant individuals or groups, ceteris paribus.

The second equity concept is that of ex post equity:

Ex Post Equity: A distribution of risk is more equitable the more equal the distribution of final consequences, ceteris paribus.

EXAMPLE 19.3

On an island within your jurisdiction, 100 miners are trapped in two locations in a mine. There are 50 miners trapped in location A and 50 miners trapped in location B. You can attempt to rescue all the miners in both locations or direct your efforts to only one of the locations. You would choose which location to direct your attention to by the flip of a coin. If all of your efforts go to one location all the miners at that location will be rescued. All the others at the other location will die. These options have the following probabilities:

1. Attempt to rescue all miners: 50 percent chance all will be rescued and 50 percent chance that all will die.
2. a. 50 percent chance that A will be chosen so that all 50 at A will be rescued and 50 at B will die.
   b. 50 percent chance that site B will be chosen so that all 50 at B will be rescued and all 50 at A will die.

Note that ex ante each miner has a 50 percent chance of being rescued. The outcomes, however, will be different. If the first option is chosen either 100 miners will be rescued or all will be dead. If the second option is chosen 50 miners will be alive and 50 will be dead. In an experiment by Keller and Sarin (1988), 91 percent of subjects preferred option 1.

Risks Should Match Rewards.   The preference for greater ex ante and ex post equity is not at the expense of an equitable distribution of risks and benefits. People apparently believe that the distribution of risks should parallel the distribution of benefits.

Case I.   On an island in your jurisdiction, there are two communities. Each community has an equal population size. Community 1 has an industrial plant that brings in many jobs and much income to the residents of this community. The residents of community 2 do not receive any of the benefits of this plant. However, the plant also is producing toxic waste. The problem is to determine where the waste should be stored. There are two waste storage facilities on the island. One is in community 1 and one is in the other community, community 2.

Where should the waste be stored? There are two proposals for storing this waste.

Proposal A.   Store all the waste in community 1. In this case, it is expected that ten additional people from community 1 will die within one year due to exposure to this toxic waste. No people from community 2 will die due to this waste, since they will not be exposed to it.

Preference group: 89% ($N = 53$)
Fairness group: 87% ($N = 53$)

Proposal B. Store half the waste in community 1 and half the waste in community 2. In this case, it is expected that five additional people from community 1 will die within one year due to exposure to this toxic waste. Likewise, it is expected that five additional people from community 2 will die within one year due to exposure to this toxic waste.

Preference group: 11% ($N = 53$)

Fairness group: 13% ($N = 53$)

Case II. In this case, the situation and options are the same as in Case I above, except that the industrial plant is located halfway between both communities, so the plant brings in an equal number of jobs and equal income to the residents of each community. The waste from the plant must still be stored in one or both of the waste storage facilities on the island.

Where should the waste be stored? There are two proposals for storing this waste.

Proposal A′. Store all the waste in community 1. In this case, it is expected that ten additional people from community 1 will die within one year due to exposure to this toxic waste. No people from community 2 will die due to this waste, since they will not be exposed to it.

Preference group: 6% ($N = 53$)

Fairness group: 6% ($N = 53$)

Proposal B′. Store half the waste in community 1 and half the waste in community 2. In this case, it is expected that five additional people from community 1 will die within one year due to exposure to this toxic waste. Likewise, it is expected that five additional people from community 2 will die within one year due to exposure to this toxic waste.

Preference group: 94% ($N = 53$)

Fairness group: 94% ($N = 53$)

In Case I, the majority of the subjects preferred to allocate the risks to community 1, presumably since they received all the benefits of the plant. In Case II, the majority of the subjects split the risks equally between the two communities, just as the benefits were split. The fairness judgments followed the same pattern as the preference judgments.

This scenario illustrates that an even distribution of risk is considered fair if the distribution of benefits is also even. However, if the benefits accrue to one group, then it is considered fair that the group should also bear a higher risk. *A fairness concept of "proportional equity" which may be implicit in these judgments is that the fraction of benefits should equal the fraction of risk.*

19.7.   POLICY CONSIDERATIONS: SUMMARY

Estimates of the value of life and limb as reflected in willingness to accept risk have a sufficiently solid basis both in theory and in data to be useful in benefit–cost studies. Such estimates are now being increasingly used in policy work.

TABLE 19.4.   Breakdown of Policy Options by Agency and by Net Cost per Life Saved (1989 Dollars)

Agency	Total	Under $599,000	Between $600,000–$1,499,000	Between $1,500,000–$2,999,999	Between $3,000,000–$5,999,999	Above $6,000,000
		Number of Cases Where Net Cost per Life Saved Was				
NHTSA[a]	24	3	2	0	0	29
HHS[b]	5	0	0	0	0	5
CPSC[c]	4	1	1	0	0	6
EPA[d]	4	0	1	0	5	10
OSHA[e]	0	0	0	1	6	7
Total	37	4	4	1	11	57

[a]NHTSA = National Highway Traffic Safety Administration
[b]HHS = Department of Health and Human Services
[c]CPSC = Consumer Product Safety Commission
[d]EPA = Environmental Protection Agency
[e]OSHA = Occupational Safety and Health Administration
SOURCE: Calculated from John D. Graham and James W. Vaupel, "Value of Life: What Difference Does It Make?" *Risk Analysis* 1, 1 March 1989.

Still, there is a strong reluctance to make explicit trade offs between dollars and lives and this is a mistake. Quite possibly it costs lives. Transferring resources from programs with a high marginal cost per life saved to those with a lower marginal cost per life saved will increase the number of lives saved. Table 19.4 shows the implicit value of life as used by different agencies.

An alternative approach is a cost-effectiveness analysis. Instead of using figures of the value of risk one estimates the *number* of lives saved through different programs and allocates funds to produce the greatest number of lives saved. This will work reasonably well, however, when only lives and not other values represent the objectives sought. This is not usually the case. Considerations other than just lives saved should clearly be used in budget allocations. It is more appropriate from a policy perspective, for agencies such as OSHA, Medicare, the NRC, etc., to use the same explicit value of life in their project analysis. Clearly, it is inefficient to allocate funds to these agencies on the basis of their different spendings per life saved.

QUESTIONS AND PROBLEMS

1. Is the method the courts use to determine the value of life in wrongful death cases acceptable? Why or why not?
2. Discuss the Toronto apartment building example. How has reading this chapter changed your discussion of this example?
3. At a lower level of risk and for some activities, it is argued that risk can have positive utility. If this is the case, what shape would this imply for an indifference curve drawn with wealth on the horizontal axis and probability of survival on the vertical axis? (*Hint:* Consider extending the indifference curve beyond the vertical axis.)

4. People are less concerned about risk when it is voluntary than when it is involuntary. Consider the differences in values that people place on voluntary versus involuntary risk. Is this a measure of the value of the freedom to choose? What explains this difference?

5. The EPA is considering a more stringent regulation to control benzene in the work place. The cost schedule for various levels of control is as follows:

ppb (parts per billion)	Total cost (millions)	Total Benefits (wtp) (millions)
20	100	300
10	150	400
5	170	430
2	190	450
1	300	460

The benefit estimates are derived from a contingent valuation survey of a random sample of citizens.

a. If the above figures are accepted, at what level should the EPA set the benzene level?

b. An analyst hired by the EPA questions the use of the benefit figures on the grounds that the population sampled is more risk averse than are workers exposed to benzene. If this analyst's judgment is accepted on this point, would the optimal level of regulation tend to be higher or lower than it is now? Why?

c. At a citizens' hearing before the EPA, a plant official, Smith, maintains that benefits should not vary with the risk aversity of the exposed population. Rather, benefits should be constant and related to health. Smith maintains that benefits should be based on estimates of medical costs avoided at different levels of benzene so that there is a uniform value of life for lives lost. What are the merits and defects of Smith's proposal? Should the lost wages of workers made ill by benzene be added if Smith's approach is taken?

d. Which approach do you think the courts are most likely to accept?

6. Do you find reasonable and acceptable the assumptions that Portney and Cropper demonstrate as sufficient to justify discounting life values? If so, why? If not, why not?

7. To reduce pollution of the Ohio River, the EPA requires the states of West Virginia and Ohio to reduce chemical river pollution. They plan to require a reduction of 1,000,000 tons per year for each state. The cost schedule for the reduction of pollution is $TC_1 = \$2(E_1)^2$ for West Virginia, and $TC_2 = \$4(E_2)^2$ for Ohio, where E_1 and E_2 are the amounts of emissions reduced in West Virginia and Ohio, respectively, in millions of tons, and TC is in millions of dollars. This will increase the value of the river and will save human life. The risk of death in downstream states is 1×10^{-3} per 100 tons of emission regardless of which state reduces the emissions or the amount of emissions produced.

a. What value of life would yield a total benefit equal to the total cost of reduction?

b. What would be the efficient distribution of reducing 2 million tons between West Virginia and Ohio? At the efficient distribution, what value of life is required to justify the reduction?

c. If the value of life is $2,000,000 per life, what is the optimal level of pollution, and how should the reduction be distributed among the states?

REFERENCES

Bailey, M. J., *Reducing Risks to Life,* Washington, DC: American Enterprise Institute for Public Policy Research, 1980.

Blomquist, G., "Value of Life Saving: Implications of Consumption Activity," *Journal of Political Economy* 87, 540–558, 1979.

Blomquist, G., "The Value of Human Life: An Empirical Perspective," *Economic Inquiry* 29, 156–164, January 1981.

Broome, J., "Trying to Value a Life," *Journal of Public Economics* 9, 91–100, 1978.

Brown, C., "Equalizing Differences in the Labor Market," *Quarterly Journal of Economics* 94, 113–134, 1980.

Cave, Jonathon A. K, "Adjusting Benefits Measures for Type of Risk," Working draft, Rand, 1986a.

Cave, Jonathon A. K, "Age, Time, and the Measurement of Mortality Benefits," Working draft, Rand, 1986b.

Cooper, B. S., and D. P. Rice, "The Economic Cost of Illness Revisited," *Social Security Bulletin* 39, 21–36, February 1976.

Cropper, Maureen, and Paul Portney, "Discounting and the Evolution of Life Saving Programs," *Journal of Risk and Uncertainty* 3, 369–379, 1990.

Dillingham, Alan E., "The Influence of Risk-Variable Definition on Value-of-Life Estimates," *Economic Inquiry* 24(2), 277–294, April 1985.

Gerking, S., et al., "The Marginal Value of Job Safety: A Contingent Valuation Study," *Journal of Risk and Uncertainty* 1, 57–74, 1988.

Horowitz, John K., "Discounting Money Payoffs: An Experimental Analysis," in *Harvard Book of Behavioral Economics 2b,* S. Kaish and B. Gaild, eds., Greenwich, CT: JAI Press, 309–324, 1991.

Horowitz, John K., and Richard T. Carson, "Discounting Statistical Lives," *Journal of Risk and Uncertainty* 3, 403–413, 1990.

Ippolito, Pauline M., and Richard A. Ippolito, "Measuring the Value of Life Savings from Consumer Reactions to New Information," *Journal of Public Economics* 25, 53–81, 1984.

Johnson, Kirk, "New Yorker Pinned by Crane Testifies in Trial," *The New York Times,* April 15, 1986.

Jones-Lee, N. W., "Maximum Acceptable Physical Risk and a New Measure of Financial Risk Aversion," *Economic Journal* 90, 157–164, 1980.

Kaplan, R. M., J. W. Bush, and C. C. Berry, "Health Status: Types of Validity and the Index of Well-Being," *Health Services Research* 11, 478–507, 1976.

Keller, R., and K. Sarin, "Equity in Social Risks: Some Empirical Evidence," *Risk Analysis* 8(1), 135–146, 1988.

Linnerooth, J., "The Value of Human Life: A Review of the Models," *Economic Inquiry* 17, 52–74, 1979.

Malone, W. S., "The Genesis of Wrongful Death," *Stanford Law Review* 17, 1043–1076, 1965.

Mishan, E. J., "Evaluation of Life and Limb: A Theoretical Approach," *Journal of Political Economy* 79, 687–705, 1971.

Moore, Michael, and W. K. Viscusi, "Environmental Health Risks: New Evidence and Policy Implications," *Journal of Environmental Economics and Policy Management* 18(2), 551–562, 1990.

Needleman, L., "Valuing Other People's Lives," *Manchester School of Economic and Social Studies* 44, 309–342, 1976.

Olson, C. A., "An Analysis of Wage Differentials Received by Workers on Dangerous Jobs," *Journal of Human Resources* 16, 165–185, 1981.

Ruby, Michael Gordon, "Benefit–Cost Analysis with Uncertain Information: An Application in Air Pollution Control," Doctoral dissertation, University of Washington, 1981.

Slovic, P., S. Lichenstein, and B. Fischhoff, "Images of Disaster: Perception and Acceptance of Risks from Nuclear Power," in *Energy Risk Management,* G. T. Goodman and W. D. Rose, eds., 219–245, London: Academic Press, 1979.

Smith, R. S., *The Occupational Safety and Health Act: Its Goals and Implications,* Washington, DC: American Enterprise Institute for Public Policy Research, 1976.

Speiser, S. M., *Recovery for Wrongful Death: Economic Handbook,* 2nd ed., San Francisco: Bancroft-Whitney, 1979.

Thaler, R., and S. Rosen, "The Value of Saving a Life: Evidence from the Labor Market," in *Household Production and Consumption,* N. E. Terleckyj, ed., 265–298, *Studies in Income and Wealth,* vol. 40, New York: Columbia University Press (for National Bureau of Economic Research), 1975.

Viscusi, W. K., "Labor Market Valuations of Life and Limb: Empirical Evidence and Policy Implications," *Public Policy* 26, 359–386, 1978.

Viscusi, W. K., *Employment Hazards: An Investigation of Market Performance,* Cambridge, MA: Harvard University Press, 1979.

Viscusi, W. K., *Risk by Choice: Regulation Health and Safety in the Workplace,* Cambridge, MA: Harvard University Press, 1983.

APPENDIX 19A

Empirical Estimates of the Value of Life

The first widely cited estimate of the compensating wage differential for risk was published by Thaler and Rosen (1975). Using multiple regression procedures the wages of a sample of workers in hazardous occupations were analyzed for dependence on personal characteristics (for example, age, race, education, etc.), job characteristics (for example, hours worked, unionization, occupation, etc.), and relation with the incidence of fatalities by occupation. No variable was included for injuries, so the fatality measure would include whatever wage premiums are paid for other safety hazards to the extent they are correlated with fatalities. Thaler and Rosen found an incremental premium of approximately $40 in 1978 U.S. dollars for a change in risk of 1×10^{-4}. This translates into a value of life in 1989 dollars of approximately $719,000. However, their average worker faced an annual fatality risk of 10×10^{-4}, more than ten times the risk faced by the average worker. Since the Thaler and Rosen sample was for workers in high-risk occupations, it is unclear how applicable their results are for more typical workers.

As indicated previously, the premium per unit of risk will be larger for a larger risk. This would mean the Thaler and Rosen results overstate the wage premium for a typical worker. As Figure 19.2 shows, however, riskier jobs are held by workers with a greater acceptance of risk (less risk averse), which tends to lower the wage premium. If the wage gradient slopes downward as in Figure 19.2, as the work of Olson and others indicates, the Thaler and Rosen estimates understate the value of life for a typical worker.

Also, the occupational fatality data used by Thaler and Rosen report a mortality rate for all fatalities, not just for those directly related to occupation. (Thaler and Rosen attempted to correct for this but it is unclear that this correction was successful.) Certainly the fatality pattern is interesting and suspect. For example, cooks face three times the death risk of firemen, elevator operators face twice the death risk of truck drivers or electricians, waiters face sixty-seven times the death risk of linemen or servicemen, and actors face a higher death risk than fishermen, foresters, power plant operatives and individuals in many other more physically demanding operations.

Brown (1980) utilized a richer data source in order to reduce the potential for omitted variable bias by including more variables on personal and job characteristics. The workers in his sample were young men who were followed for seven years. He used the same data on occupational fatalities as Thaler and Rosen and like them did not include an injury variable. In his sample the average annual fatality risk was 2.25×10^{-4}, about one-fourth that for the sample used by Thaler and Rosen. Brown found an incremental wage premium approximately three times larger than Thaler and Rosen, that is, about $120 in 1978 dollars for a change in risk of 1×10^{-4}, or a value of life in 1989 dollars of about $2,277,000. He specifically tested for the inclusion of the less risky occupations as the source of the difference, but concluded it was due to the improved specification in his model.

Smith (1976), Viscusi (1979), Olson (1981), and Viscusi (1983) have been able to build a still larger data base by using industrial rather than occupational statistics. These statistics also contain information on industrial injuries. However, they reflect the average risk within each industry, rather than the specific risk of the individual's occupation. (Because differences among jobs within the industry are ignored, measurement error is introduced which will lead to an underestimation of wage premiums if the error is random.)

Viscusi in the 1979 study used a sample of blue-collar workers that included specific details on their job characteristics and hazards. This sample also was more broadly representative of workers in all industries, with an average risk exposure very close to the all-industry average. His regressions included variables for job characteristics that might tend to affect wages, such as overtime, fast work, a necessity not to make mistakes, or occupational group. He also included a variable for all occupational injuries. His measured wage premium for a change in the risk of 1×10^{-4} was greater than $200 (in 1978 U.S. dollars). He attributes the difference between his value and those reported earlier primarily to his inclusion of more risk-averse workers employed in less risky industries. Viscusi attempted in a separate regression to evaluate the risk premium contingent on the perception of job hazards by the employees. His injury variable suggests a separate wage premium for the risk of injury of $1 (1978 U.S. dollars) for a change in the annual risk of 1×10^{-4}. It is not clear what type of injury this corresponds to since approximately 60 percent of all injuries are not sufficiently serious to result in an average two weeks to six months away from work in different industries.

The employee data base used by Olson was not as rich in job characteristics as Viscusi's but did include a greater number of workers, which permitted him to improve the specification of his model.[1] Previous models implicitly assumed

---

[1] All previous models had utilized a linear or semi-log model, which effectively assumed the observed market-clearing relationship M in Figure 19.2 to be an understatement of the wage premium. Olson used a semi-log model with both a linear and a squared item in fatal accident frequency, which then allows M to be negatively sloped. His results confirm a decline of the marginal risk premium at higher levels of risk and a regression of his data without the square term lowers his estimate of the wage premium by a factor of two.

that the slope of M in Figure 19.2 was horizontal or positive. Olson used a squared term to test for the slope of M and found a value that varied inversely with risk indicating that M in Figure 19.2 is negatively sloped. Olson obtains expressions for the marginal wage premium of a form that varies with the level of risk, $WP = a - bx$, where x is the probability of a fatality multiplied by 10^4. His estimates range from $\$548 - 75x$ to $\$500 - 71x$. At the same average risk level, Olson's estimate is approximately twice the wage premium obtained by Viscusi. By determining the slope of M, Olson was able to reproduce Viscusi's results. Olson also was able to improve the specification of his variables for the premium associated with the risk of injury.[2] The severity of accidents was measured by the number of workdays lost. Olson's results indicate a separate wage premium associated with risk of injury. The additional wage premium would vary with the average number of days that are expected to be lost from an accident. The premium would be about $\$0.50$ (1978 U.S. dollars) for each day lost where the risk was about 1×10^{-4}. Thus for an average accident that resulted in ten days (two workweeks) absence, the total premium would be about $\$5$ for a change in annual risk of 1×10^{-4}. An accident that would result in a full year away from work would require a premium of approximately one-fourth that associated with a fatality.[3]

---

[2]The severity of accidents was measured by the number of workdays lost following an injury in each industry. Olson found the most satisfactory results with additive, linear terms in risk and severity, although he also attempted regressions with squared and product terms. Like the results for fatal injury risk, the improved specification increased the total estimated premiums.
[3]This ratio is consistent with the subjective evaluation of disease states reported by Kaplan, Bush, and Berry (1976).

20

The Evaluation of Health Risks in Bonneville Power's Weatherization Program*

20.1. INTRODUCTION

This is a story about a public agency, the Bonneville Power Administration (BPA), which needed to make a decision in which consideration of the value of life played a role and in which substantial uncertainty existed. The story arose because the Pacific Northwest Electric Power Planning and Conservation Act of 1980 (PL 96-501) altered substantially the degree to which environmental factors affect the resource acquisition policies of BPA. It did this through the establishment of the Northwest Power Planning Council and the mandating of certain priorities and considerations.

The Planning Council was to prepare, adopt, and transmit to the BPA administrator a regional conservation and electric power plan. This plan was to "...give priority to resources which the Council determines to be cost effective. Priority shall be given: first to conservation...."[1]

The definition of certain terms in the Act also tended to impose significant constraints on BPA. For example, the term *cost effective* was defined as a resource available "...at an estimated incremental system cost no greater than that of the least cost similarly reliable and available alternative measure or resource...."[2] The term *system cost* included those "quantifiable environmental costs and benefits...(that) are directly attributable to such measure or

---

*This case study was prepared with the substantial help of Robert Jones.
[1]U.S. Congress, "The Pacific Northwest Electric Power Planning and Conservation Act of 1980" (PL 96-501), Sec. 4(e)(1).
[2]Ibid, Sec. 3(4)(A)(ii).

resource."[3] Finally, the Act provided that "the estimated incremental system cost of any conservation measure or resource shall not be treated as greater than that of any non-conservation measure or resource unless the incremental system cost of such conservation measure or resource is in excess of 110% of the incremental system cost of the non-conservation measure or resource."[4]

Thus, in December 1980 the Bonneville Power Administration found itself subject to the provisions of a new federal statute which mandated that (1) quantifiable environmental costs and benefits be included in system cost calculations, (2) new resource acquisitions be cost effective, and (3) conservation measures be treated not just as an equally viable option but instead be given priority in the form of a 10 percent advantage in evaluating cost effectiveness.

Bonneville Power responded by accelerating work on conservation plans, especially a plan to weatherize residences in the Pacific Northwest. However, an Environmental Assessment (EA) prepared in April 1981 revealed the fact that the weatherization program, as envisioned at that time, could have a significant impact on the quality of the human environment.

The environmental review showed that the proposed weatherization measures would reduce the air exchange rate in the homes and thereby increase the air pollutant concentrations and increase the risk of adverse health effects to the occupants. The National Environmental Policy Act (NEPA) requires that a full Environmental Impact Statement (EIS) be prepared before a final decision is made unless the EA makes a Finding of No Significant Impact (FONSI). Bonneville Power felt a full EIS would take an additional one to two years with a significant loss of potential energy savings. Therefore, the Home Weatherization Program was revised to make the tightening measures available only to those homes where certain characteristics made the health risk from indoor air pollutants minimal. Eight such characteristics were identified that served as criteria for excluding riskier homes. They were[5]

1. Homes built slab on grade
2. Homes with basements
3. Homes without fully ventilated crawl spaces
4. Homes supplied with private well water
5. Homes containing wood stoves
6. Homes having unvented combustion appliances
7. Homes with urea-formaldehyde foam insulation (UFFI)
8. Mobile homes

Excluding homes with one or more of these characteristics allowed a Finding of No Significant Impact in the revised EA issued in September 1981 and the initial weatherization program was then promptly implemented. However, excluding homes with one or more of these characteristics also meant that only 30 percent of the homes in the Northwest were eligible for tightening

---

[3]Ibid, Sec. 3(4)(B).
[4]Ibid, Sec. 3(4)(D).
[5]BPA, *Issue Backgrounder: The Health Impact of Home Weatherization* (DOE/BP-180, Bonneville Power Administration, Portland, Oregon, 1983), p. 2.

measures.[6] A full 70 percent were excluded. Clearly much potential energy savings was being excluded and Bonneville Power began additional research into the health risks of weatherizing those homes excluded under the initial program.

That research resulted in the Expanded Residential Weatherization Program and a decision by the BPA administrator that house-tightening measures should be made available to all electrically heated homes in the BPA service area if otherwise eligible for the program.[7]

20.2.   THE FIRST DILEMMA

The dilemma for BPA then is that to exclude homes that allowed a finding of no significant impact is to exclude most homes in the Northwest. If BPA wishes to have a major impact on energy savings through conservation these homes must be included. If these homes are included, however, BPA must, perforce, perform an Environmental Impact Statement that would have the disadvantages of (1) requiring one to two years with loss of energy savings in the meantime, and (2) deal in this assessment with the difficult issue of the value of life.

The question posed at this point is what course of action should BPA take? (A class discussion is useful here.)

As a first step what BPA did was to survey the literature on the value of life and on the damage functions for the various pollutants.

20.2.1.   The Pollutants

Bonneville Power traced the concern over indoor pollutants to the early 1970s when researchers began examining homes near highways to see if auto exhaust pollutants were tending to concentrate in them. What they found was not exhaust pollutants but other pollutants attributed to sources inside the home. Ongoing research has focused attention on the following ones:

Radon.   Radon is an odorless, colorless, gaseous radioactive product of radium, which is part of the decay chain from uranium to lead. Radium is a naturally occurring trace element in the soil and rock found virtually everywhere, although concentrations vary widely from place to place. Radon enters buildings through cracks and openings in the structure, through porous material such as concrete, through the use of certain minerals in construction materials, and through the use of well water. Uranium miners exposed to very high concentrations of radon have been shown to have increased incidence of lung cancer. The concentration in homes is, of course, much lower, and the incidence of radon-induced cancer more uncertain, but nonetheless radon is believed to account for between 5 and 20 percent of all lung cancers.[8]

---

[6]Ibid.
[7]BPA, "Record of Decision, the Expanded Residential Weatherization Program," *Federal Register* 49 (203), 40959, October 18, 1984.
[8]BPA, *Indoor Air Quality and Building Energy Efficient Homes* (DOE/BP-351, Bonneville Power Administration, Portland, Oregon, December, 1984), pp. 13–15.

Formaldehyde (HCHO).   A colorless water-soluble gas with excellent bonding properties, it is used extensively in the glues which are used to manufacture plywood, particle board, and textiles, It is also used to manufacture urea-formaldehyde foam insulation (UFFI). The formaldehyde gas tends to be released over time from those products in which it is a component; a process known as off-gassing. This process varies with temperature, humidity, and time with about one-half of the amount in a material released in about five years. It enters the home through plywood and particle board used in construction, furniture, carpentry, drapes, and UFFI. Mobile homes tend to have higher concentrations because they are constructed with more particle board and plywood. Thus, the homes with a significant formaldehyde problem are usually mobile homes or homes with UFFI. The most common health effect is irritation such as burning eyes or irritated upper respiratory tract, but about 10 to 20 percent of the population is highly sensitive and can have more severe reactions such as coughing, constrictions in the chest, rapid heartbeat, or changes in the structure and performance of the respiratory system. Of particular concern is the fact that animal studies have shown formaldehyde can cause nasal cancer. [9]

Benzo-α-pyrene.   This is a tarry by-product of wood combustion and tobacco smoke. It is a known carcinogen and enters the home through the use of wood-burning stoves and the use of tobacco.[10]

These three, radon, formaldehyde and benzo-α-pyrene, are the ones of greatest concern because of the carcinogenic effect. Other indoor pollutants considered in the FEIS include respirable suspended particulates (RSP), oxides of nitrogen (NO_x and NO_2), carbon monoxide, and carbon dioxide, but the effects of these were not considered significant in doing the cost calculations, at least not compared to the mortality effects of the known carcinogens.

20.2.2.   Determining the Impact

Bonneville Power compiled regional data concerning housing types, sizes, air infiltration rates, climatic factors, etc.; conducted a radon-monitoring study to ascertain the high-, low-, and mid-range radon emission areas; and then took this and other pollutant emission data and computed estimated average daily indoor pollutant concentrations in this area.

Then, using various models, BPA calculated the annual risk of cancer resulting from the no-action alternative and the incremental increase in risk above the no-action level for each of the other four alternatives. This was done by pollutant for each of the three carcinogenic pollutants and then summed up for the total. (Detailed information about the modeling techniques is contained in the appendices to the FEIS.)

Pollutant concentration estimates generated a minimum, mid-, and maximum figure. For instance, minimum concentrations would be estimated for residences with the largest volume, lowest pollution emission rate, and highest

---

[9]Ibid, pp. 16, 17.
[10]Ibid, p. 23.

air exchange rate while the maximum figure would be for a residence with the smallest volume, highest emission rate, and lowest air exchange rate. These and other factors resulted in a range of uncertainty for the estimated annual cancer risk.

The Baseline.[11]   The baseline effect per 100,000 population per year, independent of any weatherization program is

Expected cancers per year by pollutant:
  Benzo-α-pyrene: 2.6
  Radon: 2.5
  Formaldehyde: 0.2
Total expected cancers: 5.3 per year
Range of uncertainty: 1.78 to 35.05 per year

The No-Action Alternative.[12]   The incremental increase in cancer risk per 100,000 per year *above the baseline figure* is

By pollutant:
  Benzo-α-pyrene: 0.04
  Radon: 0.004
  Formaldehyde: 0.003
Total incremental increase: 0.047
Range of uncertainty: 0.0074 to 0.39

The BPA Preferred Alternative.[13]   The incremental increase in cancer risk per 100,000 per year *above the no-action alternative* is

By pollutant:
  Benzo-α-pyrene: 0.43 (approx.)
  Radon: 0.31
  Formaldehyde: 0.04 (approx.)
Total incremental increase: 0.78
Range of uncertainty: 0.092 to 7.95

The no-action alternative demonstrates some increased risk above the baseline because no action means no change from the existing program. Approximately 30 percent of the homes had already received tightening measures under the initial program. These were the homes without any of the exclusion criteria, and some minimal health risk above the baseline data was associated even with that program.

---

[11] BPA, "Record of Decision, the Expanded Residential Weatherization Program," p. 40961.
[12] Ibid.
[13] Ibid, p. 40962.

The BPA preferred alternative is the one alternative that will be used to illustrate the benefit–cost analysis of incremental increase in cancer risk under this program.

20.2.3. Calculating the Cost

After having ascertained the number of cancer deaths expected to result from the preferred option and the range of uncertainty, BPA set out to calculate a cost value for this incremental health risk, a necessary step if such risk was later to be evaluated as an external cost. The basic approach taken was that of compensating variation. That is, the appropriate welfare measure for health risks imposed on "victims" by the agency is deemed to be the level of compensation necessary to induce them to accept the health risks voluntarily. A victim is defined as one who bears costs for which there are no compensating benefits.

Numerous assumptions were made prior to performing the calculations. The most significant were[14]

1. 1,209,000 homes are eligible and will participate.
2. There are 2.71 persons per household.
3. An average of 105.4 megawatts of energy will be saved annually.
4. The increased probability of contracting cancer for an individual is 0.0000078 or 0.78 per 100,000 people per year.
5. The incidence of cancer will occur within 20 to 25 years.
6. An incidence of cancer is assumed to equate to death. (This is a worst-case assumption as some cancers will not lead to death.)
7. All values are compared to the no-action alternative.
8. All homes receive equal savings and all people are exposed and respond equally to health risks.
9. There are no other health risks. That is, low-level health effects such as increased incidence of colds, allergic reactions, minor discomfiture, etc., are possible but cannot be quantified and therefore are excluded from this calculation.
10. A 3 percent real discount rate is the proper rate.
11. Program participants are fully informed.

Following these assumptions the levelized cost of health risks associated with the expanded weatherization program were calculated in the following manner:[15]

1. For each year in the future, calculate the number of deaths associated with the energy savings under the program.
2. Multiply those deaths by the value of a lost statistical life.
3. Discount each year's value back to the present.
4. Divide the present value of all costs associated with the yearly energy savings by that annual energy savings to get a levelized cost expressed in mills per kilowatt-hour.

---

[14]"Health Risk Cost of Expanded Residential Weatherization Program," Unpublished working paper of BPA staff, p. 2, and telephone conversation with Shep Buchanan, BPA economist.
[15]Ibid., p. 3. Levelized cost is the periodic, usually annual, cost found by converting the present value of total cost to an annuity.

The mathematical notation is

$$\text{Levelized cost of health risks (LEC)} = \left[\sum_{i=T_0}^{T_t} \frac{(V^*)(P_i)(N)}{(1+r)^i} \right] \frac{1}{E}$$

where i = year of incidence of death

T_0 = first year of incidence

T_t = last year of incidence

V^* = value of life

P_i = probability of incidence in year i

N = total incidences arising from annual savings

r = discount rate

E = annual energy savings

BPA then made a simplifying assumption for calculation purposes. To wit, assume the incidence of cancer is uniformly distributed over years 20 to 25. With a discount rate of 3 percent, the equation can be reduced to

$$\text{LEC} = \frac{(V^*)(N)/(1.03)^{22}}{E} = \frac{(0.522)(V^*)(N)}{E}$$

N = 25.55 and is calculated in the following way:

1,209,000 homes $\times$ 2.71 persons per home = 3,276,390 persons

$(32.76 \times 100,000$ persons$) \times (0.78$ death$/100,000$ persons$)$ = 25.55 deaths

E = 915,420,000 kWh/yr from the following:

(104.5 MW) $\times$ (8760 hr/yr) $\times$ (1000 kW/MW) = 915,420,000 kWh/yr

The problem then arose of selecting the value of a statistical life lost. Bonneville Power surveyed the literature (see Appendix 20A for references and see Chapter 19) and found estimates ranging from a low of $113,000 (Acton) to a high of $874,000 (Low and McPheters). (What do you think of this range of estimates?) For calculation purposes BPA selected a low value of $113,000 and a high of $1,000,000 which was deemed to bracket a plausible range of valuations of a statistical life lost or saved.

The levelized cost of the health risks can now be calculated by substituting these values in the equation.

For the low valuation of a statistical life:

$$\text{LEC} = \frac{(0.522)(\$113,000)(25.55)}{915,420,000} = 1.65 \text{ mills/kWh}$$

For the high valuation of a statistical life:

$$\text{LEC} = \frac{(0.522)(\$100,000,000)(25.55)}{915,420,000} = 14.60 \text{ mills/kWh}$$

Since the impact assessment studies showed not just a single probability of cancer risk but a range, BPA calculated the levelized costs for the extremes of the range as well as the expected value of 0.78 cancer per 100,000 population. The high probability case was 7.94 cancers per 100,000 and the low probability case was 0.092 cancer per 100,000. The results for all three probability cases and the high and low statistical life valuations are summarized below.

| | Levelized Cost of Increased Cancer Risk | |
| | Valuation of a Statistical Life | |
Risk	High ($113,000)	Low ($1,000,000)
High probability (7.94)	148.63 mills/kWh	16.80 mills/kWh
Expected value (0.78)	14.60 mills/kWh	1.65 mills/kWh
Low probability (.092)	1.72 mills/kWh	0.19 mill/k/Wh

SOURCE: "Health Risk Cost of Expanded Residential Weatherization Program," Unpublished working paper of BPA staff, p. 6.

The extraordinarily wide range of the cost estimate from 0.19 to 148.63 mills/kWh reflects the high level of uncertainty involved in the cancer risk and the wide range of estimates for the value of a statistical life.

20.3. THE SECOND DILEMMA

The high estimate of the cost of cancer risk is 782 times the lowest estimate. The estimated savings from the weatherization program lie well within these estimates. BPA is interested in proceeding with their preferred alternative program. Yet their excursion into attempts to generate hard numbers has proved to be a quagmire of uncertainty. They appear to be able to obtain little help there.

The question for the student is whether or not this means no decision by BPA can be made?

Is there a more subtle way in which BPA can finesse the issue and yet keep within the policy context of benefit–cost analysis?

The Implied Health Risk Valuation

The data above can also be used to do an implied value analysis (IVA) to estimate the maximum compensation residents will require to subject themselves to the incremental increase in cancer risk. The analysis is based on the assumption that if residents elect to receive the home-tightening measures, and are acting rationally when they do so, they are willing to trade the increased risk of cancer for the economic gain of lower utility bills. Therefore, the cost of the increased health risk can be no greater than the savings the resident expects to receive by his or her participation in the program.

For the purposes of this analysis the expected value of the probability of contracting cancer (0.78 annual case per 100,000 population) is used as the true value since this is what the residents will be advised is the best estimate when they make the decision to participate or not. The procedure is as follows:[16]

---

[16]"Implied Health Risk Valuation," Unpublished working paper of BPA staff, p. 1, and telephone conversation with Shep Buchanan, BPA economist.

1. Calculate an average energy savings in kilowatt-hours per year per person by dividing the average annual energy savings E by the number of people affected or exposed to the health risks.
2. Divide that figure by the change in probability of contracting cancer per person per year to get the number of kilowatt-hours necessary to compensate a lost statistical life.
3. Multiply that value by the dollar savings per kilowatt-hour to get an implied discounted dollar value per lost statistical life.

The mathematical expression of this procedure is

$$V^\circ = \frac{(E/R)(\$/kWh)/P}{A_{rt}}$$

where V° = implied value of a statistical life lost

$\quad\quad E$ = average annual energy savings in the region

$\quad\quad R$ = number of residents in the region associated with E

$\quad\quad P$ = incremental increase in the probability of contracting cancer

$\quad \$/kWh$ = saving per kilowatt-hour not purchased

$\quad\quad A_{rt}$ = present value of future cost occurring in year t at discount rate r, that is, $1/(1+r)^t$

From the previous analysis,

$$E = 915,420,000 \text{ kWh/yr}$$
$$R = 3,276,390 \text{ persons per year}$$

BPA's best estimate of P is 0.0000078 cancer per person per year.

The value of energy savings per kilowatt-hour not purchased depends on the utility rate the resident must pay. For calculation purposes the BPA analyst used the rates of Pacific Power and Light Company applicable to Portland residents. PP&L has a two-tier pricing system with a different changeover threshold for each of the two seasons. The costs are 2.376 cents per kilowatt-hour up to 600 kWh and 4.814 cents beyond that during the summer months. In winter the rates are 2.376 cents up to 1300 kWh and 4.814 cents beyond that. Although the higher rate is probably more appropriate since energy saved comes off the final kilowatt-hour used, both rates were used by the analyst.[17]

Once again the cancer cases were assumed to occur uniformly between years 20 and 25 and condensed into year 22 for calculation purposes. However, the choice of appropriate discount rate involved some judgment. The prior analysis used a value of 3 percent which is apparently the standard used in BPA cost effectiveness studies and is defined as the "social rate of time preference." That is, it is a general value not necessarily applicable to every situation.

Here we have a situation in which one's health and well being are at risk.

---

[17] Ibid, p. 2.

20.4. A TECHNICAL DILEMMA

The second and final analyst responsible for the third implied health value analysis was concerned that to use the 3 percent discount rate as the first analyst had done would be to hold that the residential consumer's personal rate of time preference for incurring health risks is the same as the rate at which consumers as a group value money. The analyst thought that a reasonable inference would be that people tend to value time with respect to health issues more valuably than they do in general. Note that this assumption is at variance with the evidence noted in the previous chapter.

The analyst considered a rate of 0 percent but that would imply that the home owner viewed the risk as immediate when the evidence indicates it is most likely to manifest itself 20 to 25 years later. The analyst's conclusion was that the proper rate is more than 0 percent (since a rational resident will prefer the incidence of cancer occur later rather than earlier) but less than 3 percent (the rate at which consumers generally value time). A value of 1 percent was selected as most appropriate.[18]

The question we ask here is whether or not the use of the lower discount rate is appropriate for the reasons asserted. Is this discount rate a value–of–health problem?

The value of A_{rt} [that is, $1/(1 + r)^{22}$] was calculated for each of the three discount rates. For 0 percent it is 1.00, for 1 percent is it 0.803, and for 3 percent it is 0.522. The data were then substituted in the equation as in the following example done for the high kilowatt-hour price and the 1 percent discount rate.

$$VI = \frac{(915{,}420{,}000 \text{ kWh/yr})(\$0.04814/\text{kWh})/(3{,}276{,}390 \text{ persons/yr})}{0.0000078 \text{ death/person}/0.803}$$

$$= \$2{,}145{,}000$$

The complete results for all three discount rates are tabulated below:

| | Implied Compensation Value for Life Lost | |
Discount Rate	Low Energy Rate ($0.02376/kWh)	High Energy Rate ($0.04814/kWh)
0%	$ 850,000	$1,722,000
1%	1,059,000	2,145,000
3%	1,628,000	3,299,000

SOURCE: "Implied Health Risk Valuation," Unpublished working paper of BPA staff, p. 6.

The BPA analyst is quick to point out that these figures are not a value of life itself but, assuming rational behavior, they are the maximum value residents would require as compensation in order to accept the incremental increase in

---

[18]Ibid, p. 3.

risk of contracting cancer as a result of the expanded residential weatherization plan.

20.5.   THE DECISION

At this point you have all the data available to explain how, in fact, BPA was able to finesse the difficult value of life issue, to come to a decision and, in fact, to proceed with the decision they wanted.

Your question is, "Can you predict what BPA did?"

After engaging in substantial research as to the risk of adverse health effects and calculating the costs of such effects, BPA held in its final decision that *no* environmental costs would result from the expansion of the residential weatherization program.

It reached this conclusion after making several preliminary findings. First BPA held that the incremental increase in the risk of ill health was the only quantifiable effect directly attributable to program expansion. In particular,[19]

1. The employment effects of expansion cannot be counted as benefits because they are already included as expenses for the labor to install the conservation devices.
2. Land and water effects are indirect effects of this program and would become direct effects only if additional generating plants are acquired. If that happens they would be evaluated in that decision-making process.
3. Other effects of weatherization such as increased home comfort cannot be quantified or priced.

The administrator then explained that a principal element of the selected alternative is an information program in which potential participants are made aware of the increased health risks associated with house tightening. If, after being informed of the risks, they volunteer to participate, there are risk mitigation options offered. BPA's position is that the residents will have the opportunity to weigh the estimated health risks against the potential economic gain from reduced energy bills and make a voluntary decision as to whether to participate in the program or not.

BPA holds that when an individual elects to participate in the program with knowledge of the health risks he or she must also accept the health costs. In this way the costs are internalized to the individual's decision-making process and they are not an environmental externality to enter in BPA's cost calculations. Remember, a "victim" is defined as one who bears a cost for which there is no compensating benefit. In this case BPA is saying there are no victims, only informed volunteers, and no victims means no externalities. Reasoning this way permits them to logically conclude the environmental cost of the selected alternative is zero.

It should be pointed out that Bonneville Power does not arbitrarily dismiss the health risk issue. Instead, in its Record of Decision, it proclaims "it is

---

[19]BPA, "Record of Decision, the Expanded Residential Weatherization Program," p. 40963.

clear that the wide uncertainty range of the health risk estimates would, if converted to dollars, produce cost values which are much less meaningful than a straightforward social policy consideration based on the number of lives at risk from house tightening."[20]

This straightforward social policy consideration is the subjective comparison of the health risk under the ERWP with other risks which people are normally willing to accept. For example, the incremental risk of cancer from one person participating in the expanded program is similar to the risk of one person contracting cancer out of 100,000 who smoke 10 to 30 cigarettes over a lifetime, or the risk of one person having a fatal accident out of 100,000 who travel in a motor vehicle for 600 miles.[21]

The decision states that the administrator has "fully considered these risks in the context of BPA's responsibility for public health and energy efficiency." The administrator presumably concluded the incremental increase in risk to health is relatively low when compared to other risks which people are normally willing to accept.

SUMMARY

The expanded residential weatherization program seems to illustrate well two elements of practical cost–benefit analysis. First, it demonstrates how multiple uncertainty can rapidly deflate the confidence of your estimates until those estimates are almost meaningless. In its Record of Decision BPA cites that "the high end of the risk range for the no-action alternative overlaps with the low end of the risk range for the preferred alternative."

The second thing the project illustrates is one way an agency can "dodge a bullet." The agency avoided confronting the difficult questions of the value of life and environmental costs. This paper did not determine if the environmental costs as quantified would have been so great as to render the project no longer cost effective, but such a scenario is possible. By designing the program in a way that internalized the environmental costs to the home owners, BPA was able to meet the statutory requirements of PL 96-501 without really having to be concerned about the true cost of the environmental impact. But the fact remains, there *will* be an environmental impact.

QUESTIONS

1. In Chapter 19, question 7, we referred to an EPA decision to reduce chemical pollution in West Virginia and Ohio. Can you suggest an approach that the EPA could take that might reduce its political risks in considering value-of-life issues?
2. What do you think of the value of life estimates used by BPA? What range of estimates would you choose?

---

[20] Ibid.
[21] Ibid.

REFERENCES

BPA, *Issue Backgrounder: How BPA Performs Environmental Cost Analysis,* DOE/BP-405, Bonneville Power Administration, Portland, Oregon, June 1983.

BPA, *Issue Backgrounder: The Health Impact of Home Weatherization,* DOE/BP-180, Bonneville Power Administration, Portland, Oregon, September 1983.

BPA, *Expanded Residential Weatherization Program: Final Environmental Impact Statement,* DOE/EIS-0095F, Bonneville Power Administration, Portland, Oregon, August 1984.

BPA, "Record of Decision, the Expanded Residential Weatherization Program," *Federal Register* 49 (203), October 18, 1984.

BPA, *Indoor Air Quality and Building Energy Efficient Homes,* DOE/BP-351, Bonneville Power Administration, Portland, Oregon, December 1984.

Buchanan, Shep, Bonneville Power staff economist. Telephone interview. November 25, 1984.

Eco Northwest Ltd., *Review of Methodologies for Assessing the Environmental Costs and Benefits of Acquisitions,* Bonneville Power Administration, Portland, Oregon, 1981.

"Health Risk Cost of Expanded Residential Weatherization Program," Unpublished working paper of BPA staff.

"Implied Health Risk Valuation," Unpublished working paper of BPA staff.

Northwest Power Planning Council, *Northwest Conservation and Electric Power Plan,* Vol. 1, Portland, Oregon, April 27, 1983.

United States Congress, *The Pacific Northwest Electric Power Planning and Conservation Act of 1980* (Public Law 96-501), December 5, 1980.

APPENDIX 20A

This is the selected bibliography used by the Bonneville Power Administration staff analysts to arrive at a dollar value for a statistical life lost or saved.

Acton, J. P., "Evaluating Public Programs to Save Lives: The Case of Heart Attacks," R-950-RC, Rand Corp., January 1973.

Blomquist, Glenn, "Value of Life Saving: Implications of Consumption Activity," *Journal of Political Economy* 87 (3), 1979.

Dardis, Rachel, "The Value of Life: New Evidence from the Marketplace," *The American Economic Review,* December 1980.

Low, Stuart A., and Lee R. McPheters, "Wage Differentials and Risk of Death: An Empirical Analysis," *Economic Inquiry* XXI, April 1983.

Portney, Paul R., "Housing Prices, Health Effects, and Valuing Reductions in Risk of Death," *Journal of Environmental Economics and Management,* 72–78, 1981.

Thaler, R., and R. Rosen, "The Value of Saving a Life: Evidence from the Labor Market," in *Household Production and Consumption,* Nestor Terleckyj, ed., New York: Columbia University Press (for National Bureau of Economic Research), 1975.

21

Benefit–Cost Analysis
in General Equilibrium*

21.1. INTRODUCTION

In previous chapters we have analyzed how a shift in supply or demand in a single market affects the amount of a good traded and its equilibrium price. In conducting such an exercise one usually treats the prices of other goods and services, consumers' incomes, tastes, and so forth as given. Such economic analysis focusing on the individual market, or restricting consideration of effects to few markets, is known as "partial equilibrium" analysis.

In contrast, an exercise in which one explicitly models the interactions among markets is known as "general equilibrium" analysis. General equilibrium analysis accounts for the simultaneous determination of prices and incomes throughout an economy. General equilibrium thus accounts for the effects that a change in one market makes in all other markets.

The tools of partial equilibrium analysis are the supply and demand curves of the *individual* market and the standard set of assumptions used in constructing those curves. The fundamental tool of general equilibrium analysis is the *general equilibrium model,* by which the economist formally describes the interrelationships between markets. One general equilibrium model involves the computation of supply and demand curves for all markets.

In previous chapters we focused our attention on the problem of measuring welfare gains and losses in a partial equilibrium setting. For example, we demonstrated how one might compute the consumer's willingness to pay (in terms of the EV and CV) to avoid a tax, under the assumption that the prices of other goods and services and the consumer's income remain fixed (that is, unaffected by the tax). In reality no policy change affects only one market.

---

*Nicholas Pealy wrote most of this chapter.

Partial equilibrium analysis is none the less appropriate where the effects on other markets and on income are small.

However, there are a variety of circumstances in which a change in government policy, aimed soley at changing the behavior of consumers and/or firms in a single market, will end up producing significant cross-market effects. These cross-market effects will appear as price changes in markets beyond that at which the government policy change is directed, and as changes in consumers' incomes and firms' profits. In the language of economists, a government policy change will often have ***general equilibrium*** effects.

Consider an example. Suppose the federal government imposes a $0.50 per gallon excise tax on gasoline. Clearly such a policy will have an economic impact beyond the gasoline market. First, having raised the price of gasoline, the tax will induce shifts in the demand curves for other goods and services such as the market for automobile trips. Second, the prices of other goods and services whose supply curves are upward sloping will change, inducing second-round or "feedback" effects on the demand for gasoline. Third, productive resources will be reallocated across industries as the production of different goods and services changes, thereby changing the incomes to different factors of production (including *labor*). Finally, in spending the proceeds of the tax, the government will redistribute income across private agents in the economy; since private agents may differ in their propensities to spend transfer income, the transfer of income from consumer group X to consumer group Y may change the pattern of relative demands for different goods and services. These general equilibrium changes, because they result in a new vector of consumption and production prices, directly affect the rate of productive capital accumulation, technological innovation, labor supply, and thus the economy's dynamic growth path. By affecting this growth path, the long-run effects of a general equilibrium analysis can differ substantially from the short-run effects.

These "other effects" of a government policy change alter the whole nature of the problem of measuring welfare gains and losses. The yardstick in nearly every partial equilibrium exercise in welfare measurement is a single Marshallian demand and its associated compensated demand. As a consequence of the indirect effects of a governmental policy change—which shift the position of supply and demand curves throughout an economy—we cannot be sure that a single set of Marshallian demands is the appropriate yardstick for a welfare analysis. In fact, it is not even clear that the EV and CV are reasonable measures of welfare gains and losses when a governmental policy change has general equilibrium effects.

To find a sensible solution to the problem of measuring welfare change in general equilibrium, we need to consider two questions. First, what are the channels by which a change in government policy directed at one market affects behavior in other markets? We can answer this question by examining the structure of a few examples of general equilibrium models. Second, what is a reasonable measure of welfare change in general equilibrium? We will turn to this question later in the chapter. There we will introduce a technique to calculate general equilibrium welfare changes that is much more simple than determining supply and demand equations in all markets.

21.2. GENERAL EQUILIBRIUM MODELS: AN INTRODUCTION

In this section, we present two examples of general equilibrium (GE) models. Although hardly useful for real-world policy analysis, the examples serve three functions: first, they give you a sense of what a general equilibrium model is; second, they provide a basis upon which to compare general and partial equilibrium analysis; and third, they illustrate the ways in which government policy changes work their way through an economy.

21.2.1. What Is a General Equilibrium Model?

A general equilibrium (GE) model is a complete mathematical description of the relationship between each market in an economy.

While there are many different examples of GE models, *every* well thought-out GE model is rigorously built around five basic elements. These elements are (1) the utility functions and budget constraints of each household in the economy; (2) the production functions of each firm in the economy; (3) the government's budget constraint; (4) the resource constraints of the economy; and (5) assumptions about the nature of consumer and producer behavior (that is, are consumers and producers price-takers?).

Pay careful attention to the role of these five elements in the construction of each of the examples discussed below.

21.2.2. A Robinson Crusoe Economy

Many of you will be familiar with this example from introductory and intermediate price theory. Consider an economy composed of a single individual who derives utility from two goods, food (F) and entertainment (E). Call this individual Crusoe.

Crusoe's indifference map appears in Figure 21.1. Note that his indifference curve has the usual shape, reflecting the principle of diminishing marginal rate of substitution between goods. Of course, Crusoe's utility increases as one moves northeast on the indifference map.

At his disposal, Crusoe has constant-returns-to-scale (CRS) technologies for producing both food and entertainment. These technologies require Crusoe's

Figure 21.1.   Crusoe's indifference map.

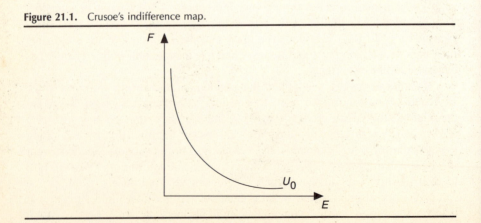

labor time, but nothing else. (You will recall that a CRS production function is one in which a doubling of inputs results in a doubling of outputs.) Formally, Crusoe uses the production functions

$$F = a_f L_f \tag{21.1}$$

and

$$E = a_e L_e \tag{21.2}$$

to produce food and entertainment, respectively. The coefficients a_f and a_e are the marginal products of Crusoe's labor time in the production of food and entertainment. It is straightforward to show that an $X\%$ increase in L_f (respectively, L_e) increases F (respectively, E) by $X\%$. This is just the property of CRS. (The student should show this.)

  Crusoe's production possibilities are constrained by the availability of his labor time as well as by the production technologies for F and E. We assume that he has L^* units of labor (hours) with which to produce goods.

  We use a four-quadrant diagram (Figure 21.2) to illustrate Crusoe's production possibilities. In the southwest quadrant we graph the constraint on Crusoe's labor time, $L_f + L_e = L^*$. The slope of this constraint (-1) reflects the fact that a unit of labor reallocated to the production of $F(E)$ must be taken from the production of $E(F)$. Notice that the intercepts of this constraint, $L_f^* = L^*$

Figure 21.2. Crusoe's production possibilities.

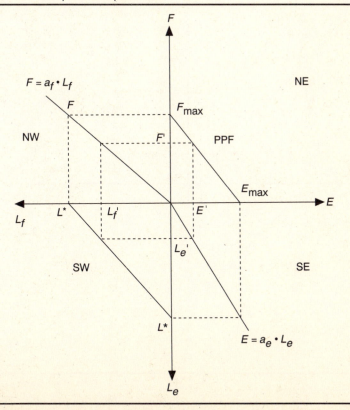

and $L_e^* = L^*$, depend solely on the amount of time Crusoe has available for production.

In the northwest and southeast quadrants we graph the production functions for food and entertainment—equations (21.1) and (21.2). Since these equations are both linear functions of labor, their slopes are precisely the marginal products of labor. In principle, these functions extend indefinitely into their respective quadrants; that is, if Crusoe had enough labor he could produce any amount of F or E.

Using the labor time constraint and the production functions for F and E, we can draw the production possibilities frontier (PPF) for food and entertainment.

Suppose $L_f = L^*$. With all his available labor allocated to food production, Crusoe can produce F_{max} units of food, but, of course, no entertainment. Conversely, if he allocates all his labor time to entertainment production, Crusoe can produce E_{max} units of entertainment, but no food. He can produce positive amounts of F and E by allocating positive amounts of labor time to the production of both goods. For example, by allocating L_f' units of labor to food production and L_e' to entertainment production, Crusoe can have F' units of food and E' units of entertainment.

Notice that Crusoe's PPF is linear. This is a result of the fact that the production functions for F and E are both linear.[1] In Figure 21.3 we draw

Figure 21.3.   Slightly concave production possibilities.

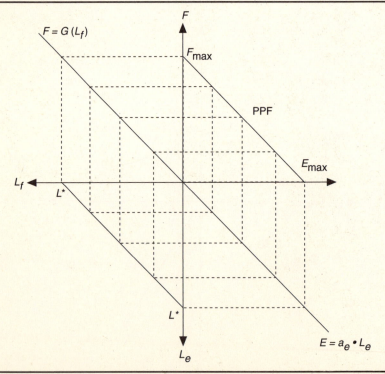

---

[1]Prove this to yourself. Try to develop an algebraic expression describing the PPF corresponding to Equations (21.1) and (21.2) and the labor time constraint.

Crusoe's PPF under the assumption that the production function for food is slightly concave, that is, the production of food exhibits diminishing marginal productivity of labor.

This simple model of a Robinson Crusoe economy exhibits an important feature—a feature characteristic of other, considerably more complex, models. Like many other (model) economies, Crusoe's world is one in which only technological change (increases or decreases in a_f or a_e) or changes in resource constraints can improve (or worsen) the consumer's consumption possibilities.

So how, you ask, should Crusoe divide up his labor time between the production of F and E? The answer is simple if you have recognized the fact that PPF plays the role of a budget constraint as in the standard theory of consumer behavior. That is, we can find Crusoe's "optimal" consumption of F and E simply by superimposing his indifference map in the same quadrant where we have drawn the PPF. Crusoe's utility is maximized at the point where he has reached the highest attainable indifference curve consistent with his budget constraint, that is, the PPF. At this point, Crusoe's marginal rate of substitution of F for E is just equal to the rate at which technology permits him to transform F into E. (See Figure 21.4.).

Figure 21.4.   Optimum allocation by Crusoe.

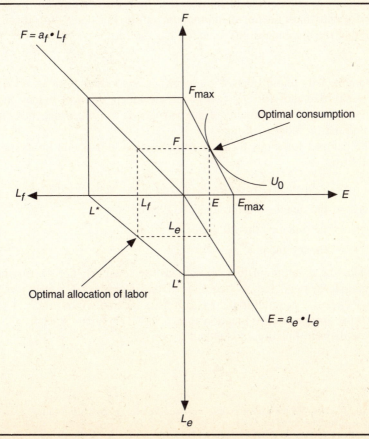

Having found the combination of F and E that maximizes his utility, Crusoe can simply "work backwards" through the northwest and southeast quadrants to determine how he should allocate his labor between L_f and L_e.

Suppose now that there is a shift in the production function so that Crusoe can now produce more food per unit of labor. This increase in productivity will show as a larger value for a_f. This will shift outward the PPF and will result in a new equilibrium at a higher indifference curve. The value of this change can now be measured as the shift to a higher indifference curve with the CV or the EV.

An Alternative Interpretation.   We can provide a reinterpretation of the discussion above which imparts a greater sense of realism to the Robinson Crusoe model, and which sheds some light on some of the more subtle but complicated problems of building general equilibrium models.

Suppose the Crusoe economy is actually an economy populated by many consumers and many firms. Specifically, let there be L^* households, n_f food producers, and n_e entertainment producers.

Each household has 1 unit of labor, which it supplies to the labor market inelastically. Moreover, each household has demand functions for both food F and entertainment E. In calculating the aggregate demand for $F(E)$ we wish to avoid the problem of adding up L^* *different* demand functions for $F(E)$, one corresponding to each of the L^* households. To avoid this problem we assume that households have identical **homothetic** utility functions. Specifically, we assume that the common utility function has the form:[2]

$$U = F^r E^{1-r} \qquad 0 < r < 1 \tag{21.3}$$

Homotheicity implies that, for a given set of goods and prices, an individual's *relative* demands for any two goods are independent of money income. That is, the ratio of the amounts of any two goods consumed depends only on prices and not on money income.

The demand functions for a consumer with a homothetic utility function take the form:

$$X_i = f_i(p_1, \ldots p_i, \ldots p_n) \cdot I \qquad i = 1, \ldots, n \tag{21.4}$$

where X_i = the quantity of the ith good consumed

p_i = the price of the ith good

I = money income[3]

Under the assumption that households are identical, (21.4) implies that the aggregate demand for X_i (the sum of the individual demands for X_i) is simply $f_i(p_1, \ldots, p_n)$ multiplied by aggregate income. (Why?)

For the specific utility function shown in (21.3) it can be shown that the aggregate demand functions for F and E are

$$\overline{F} = \frac{r\overline{I}}{p_f} \tag{21.5}$$

---

[2]This utility function has the well-known Cobb-Douglas form. It can be shown that $r/(1-r)$ is the fraction of income spent on $F(E)$.
[3]Demonstrate to yourself that the ratio X_i/X_j is independent of I.

and

$$\overline{E} = \frac{(1-r)\overline{I}}{p_e} \tag{21.6}$$

where p_f and p_e are the prices of F and E which, of course, the consumer takes as given. Bars over variables denote aggregate quantities.[4] To obtain (21.5) and (21.6) we first maximize (21.3), subject to the consumer's budget constraint, $p_f F + p_e E = I$ We then sum the L^* consumer's demand functions to obtain F and E. (Later in the chapter we actually "grind" through the mathematics required to derive these demand functions.)

Now if we assume that food (entertainment) producers are identical, we can sum across the $n_f(n_e)$ food (entertainment) producers to obtain an aggregate production function for food (entertainment). (We continue to assume that there is no government so that government does not affect either the demand or the production functions for food or entertainment.)

Because the economy in this example is populated by many consumers and producers, we cannot say much about the general equilibrium of the economy unless we make some assumptions about the way consumers and producers behave. We adopt the usual convention that consumers and producers are price-takers, that is, competitors.

The assumption of competition implies three things: (1) consumers individually equate the marginal rate of substitution of food for entertainment to the ratio of p_f to p_e; (2) the producer equates the value of the marginal product of labor to the wage he pays; and (3) supply is equated to demand in each market (F, E and labor).[5]

A description of the general equilibrium of this economy is complete once we impose a condition that labor be efficiently allocated across industries. This condition amounts to requiring that the value of the marginal product of labor be equal in food and entertainment production. Put differently, free mobility of labor requires that the wage rate be equal in food and entertainment production. If this condition did not hold, labor would flow to the most profitable alternative until wage rates were equal.

The model is summarized in the following four relationships:

$$\frac{rI}{p_f} = a_f L_f \tag{21.7}$$

$$\frac{(l-r)I}{p_e} = a_e L_e \tag{21.8}$$

$$L_f + L_e = L^* \tag{21.9}$$

and

$$p_f p_{af} = w_f = w = w_e = p_e a_e \tag{21.10}$$

---

[4]See Silberberg (1978, chap. 8) for a discussion of the derivation of Equations (21.5) and (21.6).
[5]Of course, no consumer can exceed his budget constraint.

Equations (21.7), (21.8), and (2.9) are self-explanatory. Equation (2.10) is the condition that the value of the marginal product of labor in each industry be equated to the wage in that industry, and to wages in all other industries as well.

Equations (21.7) to (21.10) *define* an equilibrium for this simple economy. In words, these equations state that a general equilibrium of the Crusoe economy consists of a set of prices (p_f, p_e, and w) that equate supply and demand in every market (including that for labor), ensure that each consumer's utility is maximized, and ensure that the profit of each producer is maximized.

The system of equations describing the Crusoe economy shares a feature with equation systems describing most other general equilibrium models. This feature is the property that only relative prices can be determined from the equations describing the economy (model). This property reflects an idea you should already be familiar with: In an economy in which resources are allocated through a price system, it is **relative** prices, not absolute prices, that allocate resources.[6]

To clarify how one uses Equations (21.7) to (21.10) to describe the equilibrium of the economy, consider a numerical example. Suppose $r = \frac{3}{4}$, $a_f = \frac{1}{2}$, $a_e = \frac{2}{3}$, and $L^* = 100$. Aggregate household income is just $100w$, using Equations (21.7), (21.8), and (21.9) and the fact that $w_f = w = w_e$. Using these parameter values, it is easy to show that $L_f = 75$, $L_e = 21$, $F = \frac{75}{2}$, and $E = \frac{50}{3}$. You should check to see that you can compute these numbers yourself.

Before you read the next example examine the structure of the Crusoe economy carefully. Note the fundamental role of preferences, technology, and resource constraints (specifically the labor time constraint) in determining the equilibrium production levels of food and entertainment. Only changes in these three "fundamentals" can alter the equilibrium configuration of output in the economy.

21.2.3. A Profits Tax in General Equilibrium

Government policy changes often produce "secondary" effects on the economy, many of which cannot be captured by a partial equilibrium analysis. Our gasoline tax example is a case in point.

At the level of the individual consumer, we can analyze the effect of a tax on gasoline in terms of well-known substitution and income effects. These are illustrated in Figure 21.5. You will all recognize that the substitution effect is the movement $A - D$ on indifference curve U_0 and the income effect is the movement from D to B.

But is it appropriate to analyze the tax simply in terms of its effect on the individual consumer? As our discussion in the Introduction indicated, the answer is "No."

To see how a government policy change produces effects beyond just the standard income and substitution effects (see Figure 21.5) let us examine a

---

[6]To see that only relative (the ratio of) prices matter in the Crusoe economy, multiply each price—including wages and money income—by the same content. The equilibrium of the economy will not change; that is, the quantities of food and entertainment demanded and supplied will not be affected.

Figure 21.5.

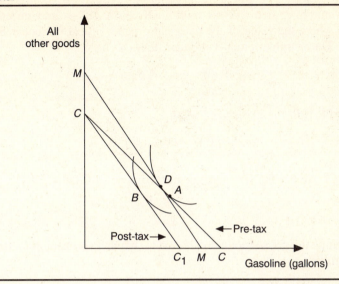

model of an economy where the government taxes the profits of firms. This profits tax alters the income of firm owners, which, of course, are households. But the way in which the tax affects household income is somewhat peculiar; let us see why.

Suppose there is only one good produced in the economy, call it "X." Because we wish to examine how a tax on the profits of producers of X affects the general equilibrium of the economy, we must ensure that X-producers actually make profits in equilibrium. To that end, we assume that the aggregate production function for X is

$$X = L^{1/2} \tag{21.11}$$

where X = the aggregate quantity of X produced, and L = the aggregate amount of labor used in the production of X.

Equation (21.11) has the property of decreasing-returns-to-scale (DRS). As you know from intermediate price theory, only in the case where a competitive industry is characterized by a DRS technology is it possible for the industry to make economic profits.[7]

After-tax profits of X-producers are given by

$$PR^* = (1 - t)(pL^{1/2} - wL) \tag{21.12}$$

where PR^* = after-tax-profits

p = the price of X (competitively determined)

w = the wage rate

t = the tax rate on profits

---

[7]We assume that the number of X-producers is fixed. This model can best be thought of as a model of a short-run general equilibrium. In a strict sense, then, the model is partial equilibrium because we have not permitted the possibility for profits in the X-industry to be competed away by entry.

Since $PR^* = PR(1 - t)$, where PR is before-tax profits, PR^* is maximized at the same value of L as before-tax profits. Of course, PR is maximized at the value of L where the value of the marginal product of labor is equated to the wage rate. The marginal product of labor, dX/dL, is

$$\frac{dX}{dL} = \frac{1}{2}L^{-1/2} \tag{21.13}$$

Therefore, PR (PR^*) is maximized when

$$\left(\frac{p}{2}\right)L^{-1/2} = w \tag{21.14}$$

Solving for L we get the (industry) demand function for labor:

$$L = \left(\frac{p}{2w}\right)^2 \tag{21.15}$$

If we substitute this expression into (21.12) we get an expression for *maximized* after-tax profits

$$PR^*_{max} = \frac{(1 - t)p^2}{4w} \tag{21.16}$$

The consumer side of the economy is modeled in the same way as we modeled the consumer side of the Crusoe economy. Now, however, instead of deriving utility from two produced goods, consumers derive utility from the single produced good X, and from leisure $(1 - L)$. The utility function of the representative consumer is

$$U = X^a(1 - L)^{1-a} \qquad 0 < a < 1 \tag{21.17}$$

where X = the individual household's consumption of X.

By introducing leisure into the utility function, we have introduced the possibility that the consumer's labor supply will vary with the wage rate, the price of X, and other variables. In contrast to the Crusoe example, the one productive resource in the model will now be used in variable amounts depending on the relative return to the use of labor in market production versus "leisure production."

Since the total demand for labor in X production is L and there are L^* consumers in the economy, in equilibrium each consumer will supply L/L^* units of labor to the market and will receive PR^*_{max}/L^* in profit income.

The consumers' budget constraint is

$$\frac{pX}{L^*} = \frac{wL}{L^*} + \frac{PR^*_{max}}{L^*} \tag{21.18}$$

In (21.18) we have made explicit the fact that each consumer buys an equal share of the X production, receives an equal share of profit income, and supplies an equal share of the labor required to produce X. *Most important*, we have assumed the proceeds of the tax are *not* redistributed from the government back to households; that is, the government simply throws the proceeds of the tax away. It is easy to see that if the profits of tax revenues were returned to households in equal shares, household after-tax income would equal household before-tax income; the transfer of tax revenue back to households would exactly offset the reduction of profit income resulting from the imposition of the tax.

Using lowercase letters to denote per capita consumption and profits, we can rewrite the household's budget constraint as

$$px + w(1 - L) = w + pr \qquad (21.19)$$

Equation (21.19) states that the consumer's expenditures on goods (x) and leisure $(1 - L)$ must be equal to his/her "full income," that is, the market value of his/her endowment of available time (w *times* 1), plus his/her profit income. Equation (21.19) is written in a way that envisions the consumer as selling all of his available time to the market (for which he receives w) and then buying some of it back $(1 - L)$ at the price w.

Since Equation (21.17) is identical to the utility function used in the Crusoe example (apart from notational differences), we can write the demand functions for x and $(1 - L)$ immediately. They are

$$x = \frac{a(w + pr)}{p} \qquad (21.20)$$

and

$$(1 - L) = \frac{(1 - a)(w + pr)}{w} \qquad (21.21)$$

where $w + pr$ is the consumer's income.

An equilibrium for this economy is a set of prices (w and p) that equate supply to demand in the goods (x) and labor (L) market, and ensure that each consumer's utility and each firm's profit is maximized.

Now (21.20) and (21.21) were obtained from the consumer's maximization problem, so utility maximization is already "built into" these demand functions. The profit-maximizing demand for labor is given by Equation (21.15) and the profit-maximizing supply X is obtained by substituting (21.15) into the production function (21.11). The result is

$$X_{\max} = \frac{p}{2w} \qquad (21.22)$$

Equating (21.22) to the *aggregate* version of (21.21), we get the equilibrium condition for the goods market

$$\frac{p}{2w} = \frac{aL^*(w + pr)}{P_1} \qquad (21.23)$$

$$\frac{w}{p} = \frac{2 - (a + at)^{1/2}}{4aL^*} \qquad (21.24)$$

Equation (21.24) is the expression for the equilibrium real wage rate, w/p. Note that t raises the real wage above what it would be in the absence of the tax (that is, when $t = 0$).

To see the implications of (21.24) for the behavior of the economy, use (21.22) along with (21.24) and (21.15) to solve for the equilibrium levels of X and L as functions of the tax rate, t. We get

$$X = \frac{1}{2}\left[\frac{4aL^*}{2 - (a + at)^{1/2}}\right] \tag{21.25}$$

and

$$L = \frac{1}{4}\left[\frac{4aL^*}{2 - (a + at)^{1/2}}\right]^2 \tag{21.26}$$

As you can see, a positive tax lowers both X and L, that is, raises the quantity of leisure demanded. The reduction in X (per capita X) tends to reduce utility, while the increase in leisure demands tends to raise utility.

Can households be made better off with an increase in t? While it is somewhat complicated to show formally, the answer is clearly "No." (You might try proving this to yourself.)

To see exactly what the tax does in general (as opposed to partial) equilibrium, let us draw the budget line and indifference map of a representative consumer.

In Figure 21.6, the consumer is initially at an optimum at point A, enjoying utility level U_0. The budget line is (initially) the segment $CAB1$. If the representative consumer were to stop working altogether—that is, choose $1 - L = 1$—he could consume x_1 of X, *as long as his withdrawal of labor supply from the production of X had a negligible effect on total profits*. If each consumer were to simultaneously choose $1 = 0$, economywide profits would drop to 0 and every consumer would be at point 1 on the horizontal axis.

With the slope of the budget constraint as it is $(-w/p)$ the consumer maximizes utility at point A. Suppose the profits tax rises from its initial level, say 0, to some positive level. From (21.24) we know that the real wage rises. This causes the budget constraint to pivot upward around point B (see Figure 21.7). Utility actually appears to increase, as the consumer moves to point D!

Figure 21.6. Optminum consumer equilibrium.

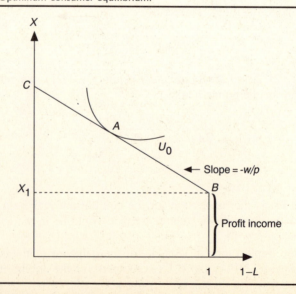

Figure 21.7. Change in the profits tax.

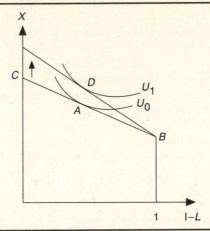

Figure 21.8. Final equilibrium or consumer with profits tax.

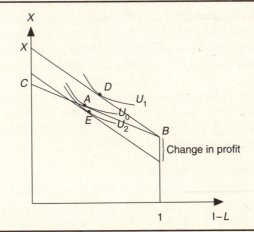

However, the increase in w/p reduces economywide profits. Hence segment B_1 becomes shorter. The reduction in profit per capita has a pure income effect. The final optimum of the consumer is actually at a point like E in Figure 21.8. The consumer is worse off than before.

A partial equilibrium analysis of the profits tax would have highlighted the pure income effect of the tax—that is, the reduction in profit income of the consumer resulting from the imposition of the tax. However, only a general equilibrium analysis indicates that the profits tax actually has one substitution effect and *two* income effects.

To summarize, government tax and spending changes often have secondary effects on the economy. Intuition often fails to suggest the channels by which these secondary effects arise. Careful modeling of the interactions between sectors of an economy is often a cure for failing intuition.

21.2.4. Conclusion

Useful general equilibrium models are rigorously built around the five basic elements discussed at the beginning of this section. Unless one specifies household preferences, budget and resource constraints, production technologies, the nature of the government taxing and spending policies, and assumptions about the degree of competition in the economy one can arrive at faulty conclusions about the economywide impact of a government policy change. Armed with an adequate general equilibrium model one can (at least) say something about the way a change in the government's tax and/or spending policies affects the prices of goods and services and the amounts of those goods and services traded. We have yet to consider the question of how one should evaluate the welfare effects of policy changes in general equilibrium. This question is considered in Section 21.4.

21.3. GENERAL EQUILIBRIUM MODELS: A GENERIC VIEW

General equilibrium (GE) models of economies in which consumers are assumed to purchase more than, say, three goods can be extraordinarily difficult to manipulate. This is true even if we assume that households have identical homothetic preferences and firms (in the same industry) have identical production technologies. Drastic efforts to reduce preference and technology aggregation problems do not eliminate all the technical difficulties associated with modeling "large" economies.

The discussion in this section is aimed at giving you a heuristic feel for how large GE models are put together. As was the case with the two simple examples discussed above, "more general" GE models are rigorously built around the five basic elements listed in section 21.2.1.

21.3.1. The Generic GE Model

Households. The economy consists of H households. Households consume K different goods, one of those goods being leisure. In general, preferences for the K goods will be different across households, so household utility functions must be subscripted accordingly. These utility functions are written in the general form

$$U_h(x_{1h}, \ldots, x_{kh}) \qquad h = 1, \ldots, H$$

The household's budget constraint is

$$p_1 x_{1h} + \ldots + p_{k-kh} = I_h$$

where I_h is unearned income. I_h includes profit income, government transfer payments, and the value of the household's endowment of goods.

If households are price-taking utility maximizers, we can generate a set of (Marshallian) demand functions for each household ($h = 1, \ldots, H$). These demand functions will be written as

$$x_1 h(p_1, \ldots, p_k, I_h) \qquad k = 1, \ldots, K, h = 1, \ldots, H$$

The demand function for the ith good for the hth household is a function of the K goods' prices and the household's unearned income, I_h.

The x_{ih} functions are called *gross* demand functions. In principle, households can be suppliers as well as demanders of goods; that is, it is possible for x_{ih} to be negative, zero, or positive. Therefore, we adopt the convention that a positive value of x_{ih} means that household h is a "gross demander" of good i, and a negative value for x_{ih} means that household h is a gross supplier of good i. The household's *net* demand for good i is

$$y_{ih} = x_{ih} - z_{ih} - x_{ih}^E$$

where z_{ih} = the government's transfer (receipt) of good i to (from) household h, and x_{ih}^E = the hth household's endowment of good i. y_{ih} can be positive or negative depending on whether household h is a net demander or a net supplier of good i.

Firms. There are F firms in the economy. Firms are permitted to supply and demand any number of the K different goods in the economy. We use the notation y_{if} to denote the supply (demand) of the ith good by the fth firm. If y_{if} is negative, the fth firm is a demander of good i. We assume that these supply (demand) functions are a product of profit maximization on the part of firms. Firms are assumed to be price-takers, but we do not assume that firms producing the same goods (necessarily) use the same technologies.

21.3.2. Market Equilibrium

As we saw in the profits tax example (Section 21.2.3.), a household's unearned income is a function of its endowment of resources (that is, labor), the prices of goods and services (which affect the market value of endowments as well as profit income), and tax rates (which affect the relative prices of goods and services and profit income). Suppose, for convenience, that government revenues are raised by a system of per-unit taxes on goods and services. Then we can write an explicit function for I_h which reflects its dependence on the aforementioned quantities:

$$I_h = I(x_{ih}^E, \ldots, x_{kh}^E, p_1, \ldots, p_k, t_1, \ldots, t_k, \ldots)$$

It is instructive to review the profits tax example to see where this function comes from. In the profits tax example, unearned income consisted of the market value of the household's endowment of time (w times 1 unit), and the household's profit income ($\mathrm{PR}_{\max}^*/L^*$) which was a function of the tax rate t and parameters from the household utility function and industry production function. Thus, by analogy with the profits tax example, we can see that the function for I_h written above reflects the general equilibrium dependence of unearned income on prices, tax rates, and so forth.

To solve for an equilibrium set of relative prices for the model described above, we need to compute the I_h function for each of the H households. Having done this (which might be a hideous mess), we can substitute these "income functions" back into the appropriate set of demand functions (that is, we substitute the income function for consumer h into each of his K demand functions). From here we *sum* the demand functions for the ith good ($i = 1, \ldots, K$) *across the H consumers to obtain aggregate* gross demand functions for each of the K goods. Finally, we form a set of K equilibrium conditions by equating the aggregate gross demand for the ith good ($i = 1, \ldots, K$) to the aggregate supply of the ith good.

What we obtain is a set of K equations that take the form

$$x_i(p_1, \ldots, p_k, t_1, \ldots, t_k) = Y_1(p_1, \ldots, p_k)i = 1, \ldots, K$$

It will always be the case in a model with the structure of the one above, that only relative prices can be computed from the K equilibrium conditions.

21.3.3. Conclusion

With a bit of scrutiny you can see that the general model described above has exactly the same form as the profits tax example discussed in Section 21.2.3. While the structure is the same, we repeat: When the model gets "large" it becomes very difficult to evaluate how a change in government policy affects equilibrium prices and so forth.

All the difficulties aside, it is important that you develop a feel for how typical GE model is put together. The discussion above should be enough to get you started. We will use the generic GE setup as a background for our discussion of welfare measurement in general equilibrium.

21.4. THE MEASUREMENT OF WELFARE CHANGE IN GENERAL EQUILIBRIUM

21.4.1 The Setting

We will use the generic GE model described above as the foundation for our discussion of how one might measure welfare change in a general equilibrium setting.

Assume, for simplicity, that there are three goods in the economy and that the first good, x_1, is subject to a per-unit tax, t_1. In addition, assume that households have identical homothetic preferences; as we explained earlier this assumption makes it possible to treat the representative household's utility function as the "aggregate" utility function for households as a group. In essence, we have reduced the problem of measuring the aggregate welfare change associated with a change in t, to a problem of calculating how a change in t affects the representative household's utility.

21.4.2 Writing Utility as Function of the Tax

In order to be able to write utility as a function of the tax, we need to backtrack through the discussion of Section 21.2.3. Using the utility function of the representative household and the *aggregate* household budget constraint, we can solve for the aggregate demands for x_1, x_2, and x_3. These demands will be functions of the three goods prices (p_1, p_2, p_3) and unearned income (that is, profit income), I.

By solving for the industry supply curve for each of the goods, equating supply to demand in each market, and by noting the fact that the price received by producers of x —call it q—is equal to $p_1 - t_1$, we can solve for what we have previously labeled the reduced form income function, $I^R(t_{1j}P_1O_2P_3)$. This function describes the way in which household income varies with t_1 and goods prices; these functional dependencies arise from the fact that *households own firms*.

Substituting this income function back into the demand functions, and again equating supply to demand in each market, we obtain a set of three equilibrium conditions which permit us to solve for *reduced form price* functions, $P_1^R(t_i)$ and $P_2^R(t_i)$, which only depend upon t_1 and parameters of the model.[8]

Finally if we substitute these price functions into the demand function we obtain three reduced form demands that depend solely on t_1 and parameters. We write these functions as

$$X_1^R(t_1 \alpha) \qquad X_2^R(t_1 \alpha) \qquad \text{and} \qquad X_3^R(t_1 \alpha)$$

where α is a set of parameters (that is, coefficients from the utility function and industry supply functions).

21.4.3. Computing the Utility Change Resulting from a Change in t_1

Now that we have reduced form demand functions, we can substitute the reduced form demand functions into the utility function to obtain

$$U = U[X_1^R(t_1), X_2^R(t_1), X_3^R(t_1)] \tag{21.27}$$

Before we consider how a change in t_1 affects utility, let us think carefully about the information contained in Equation (21.27). At first glance, it would appear that (21.27) only contains information about household utility. Such a conclusion would be wrong. Since the reduced form functions, $X_i^R(t_1)$, were obtained only after using the condition for market equilibrium [that is, supply as well as demand] (21.27) contains information about producer as well as consumer welfare. In fact (21.27) tells us everything we need to know to compute the aggregate welfare change associated with a change in t_1.

Computing the change in utility resulting from a change in the tax is straightforward. It is

$$U = U[X_1^R(t_1^1), X_2^R(t_1^1), X_3^R(t_1^1)] - U[X_1^R(t_1^0), X_2^R, (t_1^0), X_3^R(t_1^0)] \tag{21.28}$$

In words, the change in utility accompanying a change in the tax from t_1^0 to t_1^1 is just Equation (21.27) evaluated at t_1^1 minus Equation (21.27) evaluated at t_1^0. In order to use (21.28) as a device for computing welfare change it is necessary to have an explicitly functional form for the utility function, and for each of the reduced form quantity functions, $X_1^R(t_1)$, $i = 1, \ldots, n$.

21.5. A PRACTICAL GUIDE: COMPUTING WELFARE CHANGE WITH LIMITED INFORMATION

At this point, the student may despair of considering general equilibrium benefit–cost problems outside of large models built with major investments of time and money. The above discussion suggests that a complete model of the economy must be built and that some explicit, but perhaps incorrect, utility function must be assumed.

---

[8] Again only relative prices can be determined. We have chosen P_3 as the "numeraire," so that $P_1^R(t_{ij})$ and $P_2(t_{ij})$ are really reduced form *relative* price functions.

Edlefsen (1983) has, however, demonstrated how one can conveniently approximate a change in welfare for a change in either additive or ad valorem taxes when all goods $X_1, \ldots, X_n$ are subject to either additive or ad valorem taxes. We think it is highly likely that a similar simplification to that derived by Edlefsen will give the expression for the welfare effects of a policy change when goods are subject to distortions of various forms. Edlefsen's approximation requires substantially less information than is required to use Equation (21.28) and relies on information that is often available from estimated demand and supply functions found in statistical demand studies. In general, one needs information on the changes of quantity in the initially affected market and the changes in quantities only for those markets with distortions, and on the size of the distortions evaluated over the change in quantities.

Edlefsen begins by demonstrating that a change in aggregate welfare may be expressed as

$$\Delta U = \Delta W \equiv \lambda \int_{t_1^0}^{t_1^1} \sum D_i^R(t, w) \partial \frac{X_i^R}{\partial t_1} dt_1 \tag{21.29}$$

where ΔU = the aggregate change in welfare (utility)

ΔW = the aggregate monetary change in welfare

t_1^0, t_1^1 = the initial and final values of t

$D_1^R(t, 1)$ = reduced form distortion functions

$X_i^R(t, w)$ = quantity of the ith good

t = the complete vector of tax rates

w = the complete vector of supply and demand parameters describing the economy

$\partial X_i^R / \partial t_1$ = the marginal change in X_i^R due to a change in t_1

λ = the average marginal utility of income over the range of $t = t_1^0$ to $t = t_1^1$

Edelfsen calls ΔW the *Hotelling-Harberger* measure of welfare change in general equilibrium. What Equation (21.29) tells us is that we can calculate the Hotelling-Harberger measure if we can calculate the quantity changes produced by the tax under consideration, and the size of the distortions over which the quantity changes are felt. This approach was discussed in Chapter 7.

Figure 21.9 shows the welfare change from a tax on butter where the margarine market is also taxed and where no other markets are affected. The difference between the measures here and partial equilibrium measures is that changes in quantities reflect full general equilibrium effects.

In the case in which we wish to evaluate an additive tax and the only form of distortions on other goods are also additions taxes, Equation (21.29) reduces to a particularly simple expression:

$$\Delta W \equiv \lambda \int_{t_1^0}^{t_1} t_1 \frac{\partial X_1^R}{\partial_1^t} dt_1 + \sum_{i \neq 1} t_1(x_1^1 - X_1^0) \tag{21.30}$$

Figure 21.9.   Welfare change of a tax on butter given that margarine is taxed.

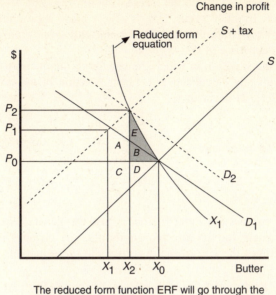

The reduced form function ERF will go through the initial and final equilibrium

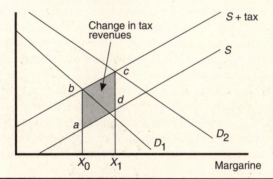

where $X_i^1 - X_i^0$ denote the pre- and posttax on the quantities of the ith good; and the other expressions are previously defined.

The first expression on the right-hand side of Equation (21.30) is just the amount of the tax, times the change in quantity of the taxed good in response to the tax, evaluated over the change in the tax. This is similar to just the traditional deadweight loss area along a compensated demand curve for the taxed good except that market interactions affecting the changes in the quantity of the taxed good have been taken into account. To this is added the second expression which is just the sum of the tax revenue changes in all the other goods.

ΔW can often be computed with very little information. In the case of an additive tax one need only know the initial and final taxes, t_1^0, t_1^1, the *total* change in tax revenues from all other goods $[t_i(X_1^1 - X_0^1)]$, and the reduced form quantity function whose tax rate has changed, $\partial X_1^R / \partial t_i$.

The truly important (and comforting) feature of the estimate of ΔW, is that it will rarely deviate from the true ΔW by more than a few hundredths of a decimal point. In other words, ΔW is a very close approximation to ΔU, a measure of *exact* welfare change. *This is the case even though we have not specified the exact form of the utility function.*

Consider the situation in which the change in the quantity of taxed goods can be approximately calculated as a linear function of the tax rate. That is, note that if $X_1^R(t_1)$ is linear in t_1,

$$X_1^R(t_1) = a + bt \qquad a,\ b > 0$$

then $\partial X_1^r(t_1)/\partial X = b$, and

$$\Delta W = \frac{1}{2}b(t_1^1 - t_1^0)^2 + \sum_{i \neq 1} t_i(X_1^1 - X_1^0) \qquad (21.31)$$

a very simple expression, indeed. This is just the general equilibrium dead-weight loss triangle for the affected goods plus the changes in quantities in other markets times the size of the distortions in those markets.

21.5.1.   The Reduced Form Functions $X_i^R(t)$—A Special Case

You may still be wondering about the question "Where, in practice, does one obtain estimates of the reduced form quantity functions?" Instead of attempting to answer this question for a general system of demand equations (which is difficult), we restrict our discussion to a three-good world in which the demand function for the taxed good is linear.[9] Linear demand functions are often estimated in applied demand studies.

Suppose X_1 is gasoline and X_2 is "food." The third good, X_3, is "all other goods," but we treat this good as the numeraire, (that is, as money with a price of \$1.00). Since we know that a three-good general model only generates enough information to make it possible to compute two relative prices, we choose to normalize P_3 such that $P_3 = 1$. Note, also, that when the markets for X_1 and X_2 clear, the market for X_3 will clear as well.[10] Hence, we can essentially confine our attention to the demand and supply curves for X_1 and X_2; any changes in the equilibrium of the market for X_3 will be summarized by changes in the equilibria for X_1 and X_2.

Suppose the demand and supply functions for X_1 and X_2 are

Demand: $X_1 = -16.34 - 14.22p_1 + 21.29p_2 + 0.082I$

$X_2 = 379.6 + 48.08p_1 - 72p_2 - 0.2773I$

Supply: $Y_1 = 42.685 + 14.22q_1$

$Y_2 = 72.0 + 72q_1$

where q_1 and q_2 are the prices of X_1 and X_2 received by producers and $Y_i(i = 1, 2)$ is the supply of good i.

---

[9]We assume that the second and third goods are not taxed, that is, t_1 and t_3 are zero. This means that the second term of (21.31) will disappear.

[10]This is just Walras' law.

Since X_1 is subject to an additive tax (t_1), $p_1 = q_1 + t_1$. To make the analysis easy, we assume that I is fixed at $I = \$720$.[11]

Our first step is to find the reduced form price functions $P_1^R(t_1)$ and $P_2^R(t_1)$. By equating supply to demand in each market, setting I to \$720, and using $p_1 = q_1 + t_1$, $p_2 = q_2$, and $p_3 = q_3$, we can show that

$$P_1^R(t_1) = 0.75 + 0.66t_1 \qquad \text{and} \qquad P_2^R(t_1) = 1.00 + 0.22t_1$$

To get the reduced form quantity function for X_1 simply substitute $P_1^R(t_1)$, $P_2^R(t_1)$, and $I = 720$ into the demand function for X_1. You should get

$$X_1^R(t_1) = 53.321 - 4.701t_1$$

At this point, one can apply $\partial X_1^R(t_1)/\partial t I = b = -4.701$.

We leave it as an exercise for the student to calculate ΔW where $t_1^1 = \$0.05$, and $t_1^0 = 0$.

21.5.2. Relationship of the Hotelling-Harberger to Other Measures of Welfare Change

Some advocate the use of the partial equilibrium well-known deadweight-loss triangle as a measure of the welfare loss attributable to an increase in, say, an additive tax. The deadweight loss is depicted in Figure 21.10.

This is just the deadweight loss of partial equilibrium that we discussed in Chapter 7. Some argue that feedback effects (of the type discussed in the introduction to this chapter) would not significantly affect the position of the supply and/or demand curve of the good upon which the tax is levied and therefore the cross-hatched area is the appropriate measure of the welfare loss associated with the tax. This amounts to arguing that the prices of other goods

Figure 21.10.

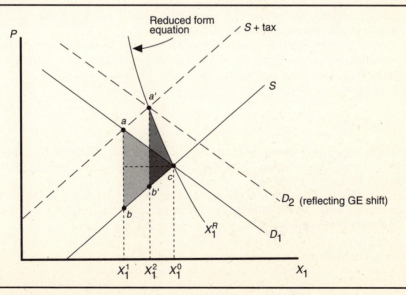

---

[11]That is, we are assuming that changes in P_1 and P_2 do not affect I.

and services are *not* functions of the tax itself and therefore will not change in response to a change in the tax in such a way as to affect the position of the demand curve for the good whose tax has changed.

This argument is clearly wrong. This can be seen by inspecting the expression for $P_2^R(t_1)$ and $X_1^R(t_1)$ in the previous section. The price of X_2 is clearly a function of t_1, the tax on good 1 (in fact, p_2 is an increasing function of t_1). Therefore, an increase in t_1 will raise p_2 and (if X_1 is a gross substitute for X_2) cause the demand function for X_1 to shift outward. Edlefsen shows that the welfare loss associated with the tax is really the shaded area under the $X_1^R(t)$ curve shown in Figure 21.10.

Generally, Edlefsen's "Hotelling-Harberger" measure produces a much smaller measure of the welfare change resulting from a tax change than that produced by the conventional deadweight-loss triangle. This is to be expected. When all markets are considered, the ability of the economy to cushion the effects of a change in one market is considerable. On the other hand, general equilibrium analysis can take into account the effect of policies on the dynamic growth path of the economy over time. For example, when a policy reduces investment and produces slower growth, the adverse effect on welfare can be much greater than that suggested by a partial equilibrium analysis (see Hazilla and Kopp 1986). Yet, as Edlefsen shows, ΔW is a much more accurate measure of welfare change than that given by the traditional, partial equilibrium deadweight loss.[12] It seems likely that the long-run future of benefit–cost analysis will be in the area of general equilibrium analysis.[13]

QUESTIONS AND PROBLEMS

1. Show graphically the welfare change from a tax on bolts that affects the markets for nails and screws. Assume no markets are subject to previous distortions.
2. Show graphically the welfare changes as in Problem 1 but now assume that both nails and screws are subject to ad valorem taxes.
3. Assume that the Hotelling-Harber welfare measure can be used for any distortions in markets. Show graphically the welfare change in Problem 1 where there is no tax on nails or screws, but now assume that screws are monopolized.
4. Find the welfare change for the problem given in Section 21.5.1.

REFERENCES

Edlefsen, Lee, "The Deadweight Loss Triangle as a Measure of General Equilibrium Loss: Harberger Reconsidered," Working paper, Department of Economics, University of Washington, 1984.

Edlefsen, Lee, R. Zerbe, and N. Pealy, "Measurement of General Equilibrium Welfare Loss Using Limited Information," Working paper, Department of Economics, University of Washington, 1983.

---

[12]That is, W deviates much less from U than does the deadweight-loss measure of welfare change.
[13]It seems to us likely that Edlefsen taxes can be treated as any additive distortion that exists in markets, and that nonadditive distortions (for example, an ad valorem tax) will yield similar simplifications to that found here in Equation (21.29). The existence of large-scale computing techniques on microcomputers, such as made available by the Gauss program, promises to thus allow general equilibrium calculations on a much more widespread basis.

Hazilla, Michael, and Raymond Kopp, "The Social Cost of Environmental Quality Regulations: A General Equilibrium Analysis," Discussion paper QE86-02, *Resources for the Future,* August 1986.

Hazilla, Michael, and Raymond Kopp, "The Social Cost of Alternative Ambient Air Quality Standards for Total Suspended Particulates: A General Equilibrium Analysis," Discussion paper QE86-06, *Resources for the Future,* 1986.

Silberberg, Eugene, *The Structure of Economics: A Mathematical Analysis,* New York: McGraw Hill, 1990.

22

Government Uses
of Benefit–Cost Analysis

T he most common use of benefit–cost analysis today is for the analysis of projects to be undertaken by governments. Many of the techniques implicit in benefit–cost analysis are derived from approaches used in the private sector, but the use of comprehensive benefit–cost analyses is most often encountered in public agencies. Until the mid-1960s, benefit–cost analysis was extensively used only at the national level, but in the last 25 years these techniques have been used quite frequently by state, provincial, and local governments.

There are several reasons for these trends of increasing use of benefit–cost analysis at all levels of government. First, benefit–cost analysis *can be* an objective method to assist governments in making decisions. Second, benefit–cost analysis can be used to clarify factual information about a politically controversial project and thereby make the range of choices more apparent. Third, benefit–cost analysis is sometimes used by one or more groups concerned about a project to support a particular position, with different information being used in order to allow the analysis to reach different conclusions. Fourth, the need to conduct a benefit–cost analysis is sometimes used as a reason to delay a decision and thereby postpone a controversial action.

This chapter will cover four major topics about how governments use benefit–cost analysis. The first section discussed basic approaches to the use of benefit–cost analysis by governments, ranging from approaches that merely recognize costs and benefits to those that require a decision to be based solely on a strict comparison of costs and benefits. The second section summarizes several major issues related to the use of benefit–cost analysis by governments, most of which were discussed in more detail in previous sections of this book. The third section provides recommendations on the appropriate ways to present information from benefit–cost analyses to decision makers. The final section is a brief forecast about future governmental use of benefit–cost analysis.

22.1.   APPROACHES TO BENEFIT–COST ANALYSIS

Benefit–cost analysis now has an extensive history of uses by government agencies. Beginning in the 1940s and 1950s, the techniques of benefit–cost analysis began to receive extensive use by some agencies of the U.S. government, particularly the Bureau of Reclamation and the Army Corps of Engineers. At the outset, benefit–cost analyses were restricted to capital projects, particularly those with large construction costs and long-term streams of benefits, such as dams and flood control projects. Gradually, the uses of benefit–cost analysis were broadened to include many regulatory and noncapital projects, culminating in a policy that all major federal project proposals had to undergo a benefit–cost analysis during the administration of President Jimmy Carter in the late 1970s. The use of benefit–cost analysis eventually spread to state and local agencies, too.

There have been several attempts to classify the uses of benefit–cost analysis by governments into different categories of application. One of the most successful was prepared by William Rodgers in 1980.[1] In Rodgers's classification, four models can be used to describe uses of benefit–cost analysis: (1) cost-oblivious, (2) cost-effective, (3) cost-sensitive, and (4) strict benefit–cost analysis. Each of these is discussed briefly below.

Cost-Oblivious Model.   This is a model in which decision makers reach a decision without regard for the costs involved. The most obvious examples of such situations involve environmental regulations. Many pollution control or health protection standards mandate achievement of specified control levels regardless of the costs. In some cases, these decisions may reflect implicit benefit–cost analyses conducted by the decision makers. More often, a moral or political judgment is involved, in which the policy makers determine that a particular standard is necessary even though careful benefit–cost analyses would suggest that different standards or exceptions in some cases would be appropriate. Debates about cost-oblivious standards are often couched in terms of "no one can put a value on a human life" or "the benefits of this policy cannot be compared to mere financial costs."

Cost-Effective Model.   This model involves identifying the best approach to meet a particular goal. Often, the goal itself has been set through a separate process that may or may not have recognized the costs and benefits. Once the goal is set, policy makers may specify that efforts to achieve the goal be assessed and implemented based on their cost effectiveness. In such cases, administrators are required to review alternative approaches and choose those that will allow the goal to be achieved at the lowest cost. Once again, such situations are often encountered in environmental regulation, where various options to achieve specified air and water pollution standards will be compared to find those that impose the least economic cost in progressing toward a fixed goal.

---

[1]William H. Rodgers, Jr., "Benefits, Costs, and Risks: Oversight of Health and Environmental Decision Making." *Harvard Environmental Law Review* 4 (19), 191–226, 1980.

Cost-Sensitive Model.   This model requires that the costs of a policy be considered, but stops short of requiring a strict benefit–cost analysis. In such cases, economic costs are often only one of the factors that an agency is required to consider in establishing policies or regulations. The agency may also be required to analyze effects on specified groups, impacts on other policies or programs, and costs or benefits that cannot easily be expressed in economic terms. The cost-sensitive approach is probably the most common model used in federal and state policy making in the United States since it allows elected officials to set major policy goals while also allowing the development of detailed policies and regulations to be left to specialized agencies. One consequence of this approach is that it often results in court challenges to agency decisions since the legislative directive to be sensitive to costs can be interpreted in a wide variety of ways.

Strict Benefit–Cost Analysis Model.   This model requires a formal benefit–cost calculation to be used in reaching a policy decision. The early uses of benefit–cost analysis for water projects were ostensibly examples of this approach, since the costs and benefits of various projects were calculated and compared to identify the best investments of federal funds. In practice, political pressures and systematic underestimation of costs tended to undermine the validity of the approach. Some recent federal policies still rely on strict benefit–cost analysis, including some aspects of the National Environmental Protection Act. Strict benefit–cost analysis is also commonly encountered in public works decision making at all levels of government. It is also used frequently in making investment and purchasing decisions, such as determining whether to replace a fleet of vehicles or deciding what type of computer systems to acquire.

22.2.   MAJOR ISSUES RELATED TO THE USE OF BENEFIT–COST ANALYSIS

While the use of benefit–cost analysis by government has been growing, there has been a parallel growth in criticism of benefit–cost techniques. This criticism first flowered in the 1960s as a result of the emerging environmental movement. For example, environmentalists began to review the benefit–cost analyses used to justify water projects and quickly identified problems such as unrealistically low discount rates and the failure to include many of the indirect costs of the projects. This criticism played a major role in stopping several projects and in supporting legislation to govern the appropriate use of benefit–cost analysis.

Within a few years, criticisms of the data used in benefit–cost analyses and the comprehensiveness of the studies began to evolve into opposition to the basic techniques underlying the analysis. Some critics claimed that benefit–cost analysis was inherently biased in favor of quantifiable values, especially financial outcomes, at the expense of more qualitative considerations, such as environmental protection. These critics often favored cost-oblivious regulatory approaches. The high cost of some of these regulations eventually produced a backlash against such inflexible decision making, which in turn regenerated interest in benefit–cost analysis. This tension between the advocates and critics of benefit–cost analysis continues to exist today.

There are at least six major issues currently confronting the use of benefit–cost analysis in the public sector. This issues have already been described in different sections of this book, but are summarized here for convenience. The six issues are (1) the appropriateness of using benefit–cost analysis, especially in valuing nonmarketed goods; (2) the accuracy of benefit and cost estimates; (3) accounting for the distribution of benefits and costs; (4) the appropriate time horizon; (5) the appropriate discount rate; and (6) dealing with risk and uncertainty. It is important to recognize that the issues are interrelated and often cannot be dealt with in isolation.

22.2.1.   Appropriateness of Using Benefit–Cost Analysis

There is considerable debate about the value of benefit–cost analysis for certain types of public projects. Many critics contend that benefit–cost analysis is misused and often applied in inappropriate situations.

Such concerns are most often encountered when nonmarketed goods are involved. Attempts to put values on human life, the preservation of wildlife, clean air, or other environmental issues are frequently criticized. For example, attempts by government agencies to assign values to the birds and animals killed by the Prudhoe Bay, Alaska oil spill in 1989 met with widespread opposition and ridicule from environmental groups and considerable adverse comment in the press. Similarly, attempts to quantify the value of lives lost due to construction of facilities that cause air pollution often receive significant opposition from the public.

Questions about the appropriateness of using benefit–cost analysis in these types of situations generally are of two types: (1) questions about the moral justification of benefit–cost analysis; and (2) questions about the accuracy of the techniques that are employed. The first type of criticism suggests that it is immoral or inappropriate to attempt to put values on certain items, such as human life or the preservation of a species. While such criticism has appeal, it ignores the reality that choices sometimes *must* be made that involve trade-offs among nonmarketed goods. However, in such cases the criticisms can often be avoided if information on the trade-offs between financial and nonfinancial costs and benefits is presented without attempting to assign a precise value to the nonmarketed goods.

The second criticism, which focuses on the accuracy of the techniques that are used to evaluate nonmarketed goods, has considerable basis in fact. As discussed in Chapter 21, there are a variety of methods available to assign values to nonmarketed goods, each of which has shortcomings in some situations. Thus, it is usually best to try a variety of methods and present the results of each, rather than settle on a single approach and assert that it is flawless.

22.2.2.   Accuracy of Benefit and Cost Estimates

In many cases, challenges are made to the accuracy of figures used in benefit–cost analyses. These challenges fall into two general categories: (1) claims that certain costs or benefits are omitted, and (2) concerns that specific costs or benefits are overstated or understated.

The first challenge usually arises when certain impacts or costs are not included in an analysis. This most often occurs in situations involving environmental impacts, such as pollution or loss of wildlife habitat. As noted previously, it is often appropriate to omit such factors from the financial portion of a complete benefit–cost analysis, but they should be listed as part of an overall decision-making package.

The second challenge usually involves concerns about systematic over-statement of benefits. This is the type of problem that has occurred with many analyses of water projects, for which the benefits of increased agricultural production or flood control are exaggerated. This type of problem can be avoided by considering the true overall benefits of a project, not just those that might accrue to a small group, and by using well-documented values in calculating benefits.

22.2.3. Accounting for the Distribution of Benefits and Costs

Many benefit–cost analyses completely omit a discussion of the distribution of benefits and costs. In some cases, this omission is appropriate, especially if the benefits and costs are widely dispersed, are fairly small, or are restricted to the same group. However, if the costs and benefits are significant and accrue to different groups, it is often important to recognize distributional issues.

Several options for accounting for the distribution of costs and benefits were identified in Chapter 13. As noted therein, the most common method is the Kaldor–Hicks or potential Pareto approach, which assumes that the income of all individuals is valued equally and thus distributional effects can be ignored. While this approach has considerable theoretical support, it rarely satisfies critics. Thus, it is probably better to employ the McKean approach of identifying winners and losers, or the Harberger opportunity cost criterion in performing distributional analyses.

22.2.4. Appropriate Time Horizon

In performing benefit–cost analyses of long-term projects, the question of the appropriate time horizon often arises. Government agencies rarely conduct analyses for longer than 20 to 30 years, and some critics believe this tends to ignore costs or benefits in the more distant future. While this is true, there are at least three reasons to use time horizons of this scale.

First, benefits and costs beyond 20 to 30 years have very little present value as long as a positive discount rate is being employed. Second, it is rarely possible to make accurate estimates of costs and benefits for time periods beyond 20 years. Third, most government financing is restricted to time periods of these durations, so financial analyses for longer periods may have little practical meaning.

Thus, unless there are significant costs or benefits that are expected to occur in the more distant future, it is generally appropriate to use time horizons of 20 to 30 years. One exception to this rule may be for very long-lived assets whose future replacement cost would be very large, such as hydroelectric facilities. It is probably still appropriate to evaluate such proposals over the time period used for their financing, but it is also appropriate to recognize the very long-term costs and benefits that are associated with such facilities.

22.2.5. Appropriate Discount Rate

As discussed in Chapter 15, the choice of a discount rate is often critical to the outcome of a benefit–cost calculation. A variety of approaches for selecting a discount rate are discussed in that chapter, along with guidance in selecting a preferred method. In addition to using these approaches, it is often desirable to perform sensitivity analyses using different discount rates. This will reveal how critical the choice of discount rate is to the final outcome of the analysis.

The selection of a discount rate is often related to the choice of an inflation rate. As discussed in Chapter 9, there are a wide variety of inflation measures available, each of which has particular value for some applications. In some cases, it may be useful to consider inflation measures that apply to government purchases only, as are shown in Figure 22.1.

22.2.6. Dealing with Risk and Uncertainty

Many public sector benefit–cost analyses involve considerable uncertainty due to the complexity of projects, the long time horizons involved in assessing costs and benefits, and the difficulty in assessing certain types of impacts. Analyses are often criticized for failing to recognize these uncertainties.

Approaches for dealing with risk and uncertainty were discussed in Chapters 15 through 17. The most useful approach for public sector projects is usually to do sensitivity analyses for key variables or for different scenarios. In more complex cases, these sensitivity analyses can be broadened to full-scale simulations. In cases where a variety of outcomes are possible, decision trees may be a useful technique. Decision trees are especially valuable when several decision points exist at different phases of a project.

Figure 22.1. Governmental implicit price deflators: 1980–1990.

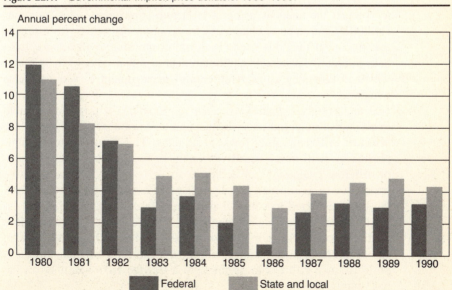

22.3. PRESENTING INFORMATION

Public sector policy makers are increasingly presented with the results of benefit–cost analyses as a means of providing support for making decisions. However, the presentation of benefit–cost information is often not in a form that is readily accessible to these policy makers, especially in light of the wide range of issues they must deal with and the limited time available. Thus, the effective use of benefit–cost analysis in the public sector requires an understanding of how the results of such analyses can best be communicated to decision makers and the public. The following six rules may be of use in planning presentations of benefit–cost data:

1. *Identify key factors used in the analysis.* Most decision makers are familiar with the basic approach for performing a benefit–cost analysis. Thus, it is usually valuable to identify important factors used in the analysis, including (a) the types of costs and benefits included in the calculations; (b) the sources of information used to assess the costs and benefits; (c) the discount and inflation rates, as appropriate; (d) the time horizon; and (e) any contingencies or uncertainties that were included. This listing of key factors should be done briefly, without excessive attention to theoretical issues involved in the selection of the values.

2. *Focus on outcomes, not calculations.* Once the basic assumptions are presented, decision makers and the public usually are interested in the outcomes of the analysis, not detailed explanations of how the calculations were done or which special models were employed. Succinct presentation of the results is usually the most important part of explaining a benefit–cost analysis.

3. *Use a variety of analytical techniques if available.* In situations where several options exist for calculating costs and benefits, it is usually best to conduct the analysis using at least two approaches. This increases credibility and reduces challenges from opponents who try to discredit the analytical methods used. Performing multiple analyses may also help to identify needs for additional data or major risks of the project, which in turn may allow more careful management to avoid adverse outcomes.

4. *Use uncertainty calculations when appropriate.* It is often valuable to recognize potential uncertainties and perform analyses showing the effect of different values for key variables. This is most often accomplished by performing sensitivity analyses for different discount rates or different evaluations of certain costs or benefits. If there is active opposition to a proposed project, it is often useful to request data from the opponents and to consider performing a comparative analysis using this data. Presenting such information to decision makers enhances credibility and allows a more informed choice to be made. It also can be valuable information to assist with careful implementation of a project, since efforts can be made to avoid the risks identified in the uncertainty analysis.

5. *Be brief and avoid jargon.* Many presentations of benefit–cost results get bogged down in excessive explanation and project-specific jargon. This quickly reduces credibility and tends to bore policy makers and members of the public. It is usually best to allow time for questions about technical details rather than try to anticipate all such questions in the presentation itself.

6. *Use visual aids as much as possible.* Many benefit–cost analyses are presented using seemingly endless tables of data. This approach tends to make it difficult to understand the results and leads to confusion about what the information means. It is usually much better to provide results using graphs or charts, with the tabular data available as a backup if needed.

Using these six rules should result in clear, concise, and easily understood presentations of benefit–cost information.

22.4. THE FUTURE OF PUBLIC SECTOR BENEFIT–COST ANALYSIS

Benefit–cost analysis has become an indispensable tool for governmental decision making. Policy makers and the public are gradually becoming more interested in ways to balance the advantages and disadvantages of proposed projects and programs, so the use of benefit–cost techniques is likely to spread. However, these same groups are also becoming more informed about the strengths and weaknesses of a typical benefit–cost analysis, so practitioners will need to become more skilled in addressing concerns raised by critics.

Several specific topics related to benefit–cost analysis are likely to receive more attention in the next few years. Foremost among these is the continuing effort to recognize the value of nonmarketed goods. This issue will be especially important in fields of environmental protection and species preservation as these goals increasingly conflict with economic and employment considerations.

A second area of interest will be in broadening the scope of application of benefit–cost analysis. Most analyses now focus on capital projects or investment decisions. In the next few years, efforts to apply similar techniques to social and educational programs will receive more emphasis.

A third area of emphasis will probably be in analyzing the distribution of costs and benefits. As resources for governmental initiatives grow scarcer, more attention will be paid to the allocation of benefits of programs. In particular, it seems likely that the impact of many programs on low-income individuals will become an important criteria for assessing proposals.

Overall, the use of benefit–cost analysis by governments is almost certain to grow. However, analysts will need to be increasingly sophisticated in applying techniques, recognizing uncertainties, and presenting results if benefit–cost analysis is to attain its ultimate usefulness as a tool for policy making.

QUESTIONS AND PROBLEMS

1. Should government use different models for the application of benefit–cost analysis in different cases? Specifically, should some policies be adopted on a cost-oblivious

basis while others must comply with a strict benefit–cost analysis? Would a policy of applying the same model in all cases be realistic?

2. Are there governmental projects or programs for which a benefit–cost analysis should never be performed? If benefit–cost analysis should not be used in some cases, what other tools to assist decision making should be applied?
3. Should the use of benefit–cost analysis by government be subject to review by an independent group in order to minimize inappropriate uses such as artificially low discount rates? If so, what type of group should be given this review authority?
4. What aspects of a typical benefit–cost analysis are likely to be most confusing for decision makers and the public? How could these aspects be better explained?

REFERENCES

Rodgers, William H. "Benefits, Costs, and Risks: Oversight of Health and Environmental Decision Making." *Harvard Environmental Law Review* 4 (19), 191–226, 1980.

Thompson, Mark. *Benefit–Cost Analysis for Program Evaluation,* Beverly Hills, CA: Sage Publications, 1980.

23

The Case of the Snail
Darter and the Tellico Dam

Chapter 1 presented a case study of the Mid-State Project. There we raised
a number of questions about the conduct of benefit–cost analysis. These
questions were as follows:

1. What criteria can be used to compare projects with different life spans,
   or different initial outlays?
2. Are costs to be subtracted from benefits, or divided into them, or is
   some other index to be preferred?
3. Should the WTP of different individuals be compared directly? How
   should the distributional effects of policies that apportion gains and
   losses among different individuals be evaluated?
4. When should general equilibrium analysis be used and how may it be
   reasonably applied?
5. When should market prices be used as measures of value and what
   should be used instead if market prices cannot or should not be used?
6. What discount rate should be used and why?

We have attempted to answer these questions in the course of this book.
There is no reason to think that all these questions have absolute answers.
The questions do, however, have some answers that are more useful, more
supportable, and in a real sense better than other answers. Experience indicates
that the quality of answers can improve over time. The following case study
shows in fact how improvements in the quality of answers were used by the
Department of the Interior and the Endangered Species Committee to vitiate
an earlier benefit–cost study performed using outdated methodology.

The case study, however, raises another set of policy questions concerning
political processes. Economists, policy makers, and others, who want their
work to have an impact and who subscribe to the progressive school of policy

methodology, must first learn the technical lessons of benefit–cost analysis, but must also learn the broader policy lessons that the following case illustrates so well. We think the lesson here concerns the desirability of integrating political and technical processes.

For a substantial period of time, the snail darter stopped the completion of a great dam, the Tellico Dam. The following is Robert Davis' story of the role of analysis in the completion of the Tellico Dam. This story is taken (with substantial editing) mainly from *Environmental Resources and Applied Welfare Economics: Essays in Honor of John Krutilla* (ed. V. Kerry Smith), *Resources for the Future,* 1988 (Washington, D.C.). Some small parts are also taken from an unpublished manuscript by Davis [with the same title as the published article (1986)].

23.1. LESSONS IN POLITICS AND ECONOMICS FROM THE SNAIL DARTER*

23.1.1. Prologue

To some the snail darter is the symbol of the ridiculous lengths to which protection of endangered wildlife can be driven. Prohibiting beneficial activities to favor a 3-inch fish which is never caught, much less eaten, seems irrational. To others the case is a symbol of the economic wastefulness of water resource projects which place local and sectional interests above national resource efficiency and of the intransigence of a public agency pursuing its historical mission at all costs. This story is based on my experiences as staff person to the Endangered Species Committee when it took up the case of the snail darter and as an observer of the ensuing legislative battle over the dam.[1]

A direct descendant of the pioneering studies of Krutilla and Eckstein (1958) and Eckstein (1958), the benefit–cost analysis presented in this paper was one of many factors in an extended and sometimes heated decision-making effort that involved not only a Supreme Court decision but, ultimately, various players from all three branches of the federal government, and led to a nine-month legislative battle. The cause of the conflict was the expected incompatibility of a newly discovered, endangered species of fish, *Percina tanasi* —the snail darter—with the completion of a federal public works project, the Tellico Dam and Reservoir, being constructed by the Tennessee Valley Authority (TVA) on the Little Tennessee River.

Tellico brought attention to the Endangered Species Act of 1973 as prohibitive policy—a strong, comprehensive, symbolic statement—and how government can deal with such a policy. [For an illuminating discussion of the act as prohibitive policy, see Yaffee (1982).] Before the 1978 amendments were

---

*By Robert K. Davis (edited by Zerbe and K. Reed).
[1] The story related in this chapter is based on Davis' experiences in the late 1970s, first as the principal staff member assigned by the U.S. Department of the Interior to assist the Endangered Species Committee in the case of the snail darter and then as a close observer of the ensuing legislative battle. The serious time constraints imposed on the committee by law resulted in a schedule that allowed less than a month for the staff work that would be the basis for the decision in the snail darter case. The report produced for the committee (U.S. Department of the Interior, 1979) provides much of the substance of this chapter.

passed, the Endangered Species Act called for no discretion or balancing. If a species or its critical habitat were to be jeopardized by an action of a federal agency, that action was forbidden. The snail darter, however, shattered the prohibitive purity of the act. Tellico and a sister case, Grayrocks, which involved the whooping crane and a water project, were the first two cases to be considered by the newly established Endangered Species Committee—the committee having been created by the 1978 amendments which were specifically designed for making a choice between each water project and wildlife species involved.

23.1.2. Introduction to the Issues

The celebrated endangered fish which is featured in this paper is no longer considered endangered and the much contested public works project is now Tellico Dam and Reservoir on the Little Tennessee River. The case raises many good questions about the economics and politics of water projects but it demands to be treated as a good story about how Washington works; that what is done and what is said often represent two different games. The story also bears out the statement that our representative government operates on principles but our first principle is flexibility.

The case raises questions about the usefulness of benefit–cost analysis. Is it useful to compare the benefits and costs of alternatives where the emotional content is high and the politics of an issue should be obvious? Congress was not pleased with the re-analysis of the economics of its decision to authorize the Tellico project and showed its displeasure by legislating the completion of the project, thereby reversing the findings of a cabinet-level committee created by Congress to choose between the dam and the fish.

The case illuminates the drive of the water resource agencies to see their plans realized. The experience leaves no doubt about the singlemindedness of TVA and its supporters with regard to the particular kind of multipurpose water resource development found in Tellico and raises questions about the costs to TVA of winning a bitter struggle.

The Tellico Project. Completed in 1979, the Tellico project—the dam and reservoir on the Little Tennessee River a short distance from where it joins the Big Tennessee south of Knoxville in a reach known as Watts Bar Lake—had been conceived in 1936 as part of the grand design for the Tennessee Valley.[2] A canal cut between Fort Loudon Lake (upstream from Tellico) and the new Tellico reservoir was planned to extend navigation into the new lake and create enough head to generate additional electricity from the hydroelectric plant at Fort Loudon Dam. Wartime shortages, however, had caused postponement of the Tellico project in 1942. It was reproposed with modifications in 1963, and Congress reauthorized it and approved its initial appropriation in 1966. Construction began in 1967.

The conflict over the Tellico project and the snail darter began to take shape in about 1976 when much of the Little Tennessee about the dam site

---

[2]The history of Tellico is reviewed in the staff report to the Endangered Species Committee (U.S. Department of the Interior, 1979) and in a report of the Tennessee Valley Authority (1978).

was designated as the critical habitat of that endangered species. But Tellico had first come under fire some ten years earlier when Congress was in the process of reauthorizing the project: Opponents of the structure, in Congressional hearings at that time, emphasized the unique natural characteristics of the river and the cultural and historic values of the valley as arguments against the dam. These values included the archaeological record left by the Cherokee and their precursors and the presence of the sites of early European occupation of Tennessee. Congress approved the appropriation for the project in spite of arguments to the contrary.

In 1971, with project construction under way for about four years, opponents of the project filed a suit in federal court successfully contending that the Tennessee Valley Authority had not filed an adequate environmental impact statement (EIS), as required by the National Environmental Policy Act (NEPA) of 1969. A 21-month delay in construction ensued while TVA prepared the EIS, which was approved in 1973, by which time half of the project's funds had been spent.

In preparing the EIS, TVA emphasized the benefits of multipurpose water projects in the Tennessee Valley and asserted that the analysis of alternative means for supplying comparable benefits is basic to the analysis of a particular project (Tennessee Valley Authority, 1972). Nevertheless, TVA never seriously considered nonreservoir alternatives, according to a U.S. General Accounting Office (1977) report. The EIS considered, instead, four scaled-down versions of the dam and development of 33 miles of river, and rejected all the versions because of their "failure to realize the benefits that will be provided by the Tellico project" (Tennessee Valley Authority, 1972, p. I-1-46).

The Snail Darter.   The snail darter—*Percina tanasi,* a member of the perch family and a 3-inch-long riffle fish with the unique habit of feeding on snails— assumed its role in the Tellico controversy in the mid-1970s, at which time it was believed to exist only in the Little Tennessee River. ("Tanasi," the name of an Indian village on the Little Tennessee in the 1700s, is Cherokee for "Tennessee.")

The seemingly tardy entry of the snail darter into the chronology of this story is explained in part by the fact that it was only discovered on August 12, 1973, by David Etnier, a biologist at the University of Tennessee. Two years before actually discovering the fish, Etnier had mentioned that four endangered species—the blotchside logperch, the smoky madtom, the spotfin chub, and the then-undescribed darter—might be in the Little Tennessee River and, if so, would be threatened by the Tellico Dam (Tennessee Valley Authority, 1972, p. I-1-20) because the shallows where the fish spawned would be inundated by the reservoir. At the time of its discovery, the darter was spawning in the shallows of the river above the dam. The fingerlings then moved downstream, matured in one year, and came back upstream to spawn. The full reservoir would inundate the spawning areas, making them uninhabitable by the fish. (As of 1978, the project was not impeding the migration of the mature fish.)

Following Etnier's discovery in 1973, the U.S. Fish and Wildlife Service listed it as an endangered species in 1975. In 1976, publication of the description of the *Percina tanasi* (Etnier, 1976) established the species status of the fish.[3] In the spring of the same year, the U.S. Fish and Wildlife Service listed the Little Tennessee as critical habitat for the snail darter, and in October 1976 the agency delivered its biological opinion: "The continued existence of the snail darter will be jeopardized and its critical habitat will be destroyed" if Tellico Dam is completed and the sluice gates are closed on January 1, 1977, as planned.[4] Since the Endangered Species Act of 1973 precluded any federal action that could jeopardize an endangered species or its habitat and since the TVA was intent upon completing its project, the stage was set for conflict.

23.1.3. The Issue Moves to Court

TVA had every intention of completing its project. Who would speak for the darter? On February 18, 1976, Hiram G. Hill, Jr., a native of the Tellico area who had become interested in this issue as a student of Professor Zygmunt Plater at the University of Tennessee School of Law in Knoxville, filed *Hill vs. TVA* in the district court in Tennessee to enjoin the Tellico project as a violation of the Endangered Species Act of 1973.[5] Although the district court refused to grant an injunction because "it would be an absurd result," it agreed that closure of the dam would jeopardize the snail darter. The Sixth Court of Appeals in Cincinnati then enjoined closure of the dam but permitted construction to continue as long as it did not endanger or jeopardize the snail darter.

The case next moved to the U.S. Supreme Court where it was heard in the spring of 1978. Attorney General Griffin Bell had been asked by President Carter to plead the case of the snail darter, but he had refused (Bell, 1982, p. 44). Instead, Bell appeared in court on behalf of TVA and ridiculed the situation in which a 3-inch fish was holding up a TVA project. The government's case on behalf of TVA was weakened because its brief contained material from the U.S. Department of the Interior taking the side of the snail darter. The respondents in the case were represented by Zygmunt Plater.

In the decision handed down on June 15, 1978, the Supreme Court upheld the Endangered Species Act, stating the "Congress had spoken in the plainest of words making it abundantly clear that the balance has been struck in favor of affording endangered species the highest of priorities, thereby adopting a policy which it described as "institutionalized caution" (*Tennessee Valley Authority v. Hill,* 11 ERC 1721). The majority opinion made it clear that if Congress was unhappy with the outcome of the case, its solution was to change the law. Mr. Justice Lewis F. Powell, Jr., wrote the dissenting opinion. Powell leaned over the bench during the trial to ask Zygmunt Plater what good this fish was. Could it be caught? Could it be eaten? Powell was bothered by the "absurd result" of the majority opinion and concluded that "Congress will amend the Endangered Species Act to prevent the grave consequences made possible by today's decision. Few if any members of that body will wish to defend an

---

[3]Eugene Kinkead chronicles the discovery and further studies of the snail darter in *The New Yorker* (January 8, 1979, pp. 52–55).

[4]The opinion was contained in a letter of October 12, 1976, from Lynn A. Greenwalt, director of the U.S. Fish and Wildlife Service, to Lynn Seeber, general manager of the Tennessee Valley Authority.

[5]Most of the information in this section is taken from *Tennessee Valley Authority v. Hill,* U.S. Supreme Court decision no. 76-1701 of June 15, 1978.

interpretation of the Act that requires the waste of at least $53 billion . . . and denies the people of the Tennessee Valley area the benefits of the reservoir that Congress intended to confer" (11 ERC 1728).

Shortly after the Supreme Court decision, there was evidence of shifting attitudes in the Tennessee Valley Authority toward the Tellico project and in Congress toward the Endangered Species Act. Developments reflecting these changes included the collaboration of TVA and the U.S. Department of the Interior on a study of alternatives to Tellico, and the passage of amendments to the Endangered Species Act.

23.1.4. Collaborative Study by TVA and the Interior

In 1977 President Carter had appointed S. David Freeman to the TVA board, replacing Aubrey J. Wagner, who as board chairman since 1962 had strongly defended Tellico. As chairman, Freeman began to question publicly the soundness of the Tellico project and to suggest that perhaps there were superior alternatives. In testimony before the House Committee on Fisheries, Wildlife, Conservation and the Environment shortly after the Supreme Court decision, Freeman suggested that it might be just as well for taxpayers that legal constraints on completing the dam would necessitate a harder look at how to best make use of the government's investment in the land, and he went on to suggest that the real waste of the taxpayers' money might be in flooding the land (Freeman, 1978).

Another indication of changing perspectives was the collaboration in the summer of 1978—after many previous failures to consult on the issue of the endangered snail darter—between TVA and the Department of the Interior on a report on the alternatives to the Tellico project (Rechichar and Fitzgerald, 1983). Economists, including this author, from the Office of Policy Analysis of the Department of the Interior participated in the benefit–cost review and, as it turned out, delivered the first substantive criticisms to TVA's benefit–cost analysis, which until then had been impregnable: TVA's claimed navigation benefits were found to be unsupportable, its recreation benefits analysis primitive, and its claim to regional benefits unacceptable in a national accounting framework. The recreation analysis was reworked with help from Interior economists and made credible. Under pressure from non-TVA economists and possibly from its own chairman, TVA began to reduce the benefits claimed for the project (Tennessee Valley Authority, 1978).

A joint report was to have been issued by TVA and the Department of the Interior on the alternatives to the Tellico project. A draft of this report was issued on August 10, 1978, but by the time of the final report in December 1978 it was apparent that an endangered species committee would be established to settle the Tellico project and the Department of Interior could not remain a co-author on the final report.

The TVA report presented two distinct pieces of evidence that there was movement within that agency on the questions surrounding Tellico:[6] (1) for the

---

[6]Rechichar and Fitzgerald (1983, pp. 52–57) note that Freeman's entrance disrupted the TVA board's unanimity on the project.

first time, TVA had found an alternative—protection and use of the free-flowing river—with net benefits of comparable magnitude to those of the reservoir; and (2) benefits claimed for the dam were revised downward in response to criticism from non-TVA economists.

23.1.5. Endangered Species Act Amendments of 1978

After the June 1978 Supreme Court decision, Congress began to consider changes to the Endangered Species Act, and on July 19, 1978, the Senate passed amendments to the act. Congress could not legislate an exemption for the Tellico project merely by continuing to appropriate funds for construction. It would have to pass legislation exempting the project from the Endangered Species Act. But John C. Culver, the Democratic senator from Iowa who headed the Resource Protection Subcommittee of the Senate Committee on Environment and Public Works and whose committee was in charge of reauthorizing the Endangered Species Act, successfully argued against all attempts under the 1973 act to have Congress declare the Tellico Project exempt. He had argued that if Congress legislated an exemption for Tellico, it would have "one exemption case per week" in which it would be forced to weigh the merits of an action against the protection of endangered species, something for which Congress was ill-equipped.

Instead his committee proposed the creation of a committee of cabinet officers, to be called the Endangered Species Committee, that would be empowered to decide all such cases. (The amendments that created the committee came to be known as the Culver-Baker amendments—Culver eventually having been joined in this effort by Tennessee Senator Howard H. Baker, Jr.)

The Culver-Baker amendments were debated on July 18 and 19, 1978 [see Drew (1979)]. Culver opened the debate with a fervent plea for the preservation of species[7] and went on to point out that, without the flexibility afforded by the committee process, the act would be under pressure for elimination or emasculation. Culver had come to the floor with a unanimous position from his Environment and Public Works Committee, but during the debate he faced amendments from both sides that would undo the compromise. Senator John C. Stennis of Mississippi offered an amendment that vented the frustrations of those senators who saw Tellico as a symbol of development stymied. The Stennis amendment called for "grandfathering" all the projects begun before the 1973 enactment of the Endangered Species Act and would have allowed the head of the agency to determine which projects to finish in the case of a conflict with an endangered species. The debate on the Stennis amendment laundered in public the concerns over the apparent inflexibility of the act, but it also gave Culver the opportunity to expand on the advantages of a committee "better equipped by background, training and expertise to make informed scientific, knowledgeable judgments, not to be buffeted by the political winds of the moment."[8] The Stennis amendment lost, 76 to 22.

Senator Gaylord A. Nelson of Wisconsin, on the other hand, represented the forces that wanted the act to remain unchanged. His position was that all

---

[7] 124 *Cong. Rec.* S10973, July 18, 1978.
[8] 124 *Cong. Rec.* S11022, July 19, 1978.

the conflicts except Tellico had been resolvable and that Tellico should not have been started—nor should it be completed.[9] Nelson saw the joint authorship of the amendment as suspicious and thought that the amendment "punches a big hole in a very good law . . . [O]ur wisdom is insufficient for me to trust a handful of people to make that decision [on survival of a species] for us."[10]

At this point Senator Baker entered the debate to defend the committee process for exemption, saying that he "did not believe exemption for particular projects is a legitimate function of Congress." But he also made clear his position on Tellico: It might have been a mistake to build the dam, but "you cannot go back and undo that decision and you cannot carry off that $116 million worth of concrete. My point is you ought to go ahead, finish it and make the law conform to it."[11] The debate continued for another day, but on the afternoon of July 19, 1978, the Culver-Baker amendments came to a vote and were passed, 94 to 3.

On November 10, 1978, President Carter signed the Endangered Species Act Amendments of 1978. The law directed the Endangered Species Committee to begin proceedings within 30 days, and to consider Tellico and make a decision within 90 days of the law's enactment. Failing action by the committee, Tellico would become exempt. The charge to the committee was as follows: In considering the case, it could grant an exemption "if it finds there are no reasonable and prudent alternatives to the agency action, the benefits of such action clearly outweigh the benefits of alternative courses of action consistent with conserving the species or its critical habitat, and such alternative action is in the public interest."[12]

23.1.6. Economic Analysis Prepared for Committee

It was December before the Endangered Species Committee process was set up, and mid-December before the Office of Policy Analysis in the Department of the Interior was assigned to staff the committee. Staff work began on December 22. A first draft report was prepared in two weeks. A second draft, done the next week, assimilated the record of hearings held in Knoxville and Washington, D.C. (on January 8) and other submissions and was circulated to committee members for comment on January 12, 1979. The final report was prepared on January 19, four days before the committee meeting.

The Office of Policy Analysis staff members assigned to work for the committee used the legislative history (U.S. House of Representatives, 1978) to understand crucial terms and concepts. Although the legislative history allowed some leeway in the choice of procedures for establishing the benefits of various alternatives, the legislative language was influenced by the instructions pertaining to impact analysis contained in Executive Order 11949. The staff, however, chose *Principles and Standards for Planning Water and Related Land*

---

[9]Nelson had privately told Culver that he did not think Senator Baker would get his dam from these amendments (Drew, 1979, p. 49).

[10]124 *Cong. Rec.* S11028, July 18, 1978.

[11]124 *Cong. Rec.* S11029-30, July 18, 1978.

[12]Endangered Species Act Amendments of 1978, P.L. 95-632, 92 Stat. 3758, amending 16 U.S.C. 1536, Sec. 10(i)(1) and Sec. 7(h)(1)(A)(i),(ii) as amended.

Resources of the U.S. Water Resources Council (1979) as its standard for the economic analysis.

By law the committee had the following options: It could (1) deny an exemption, (2) grant an unqualified exemption, or (3) grant an exemption while requiring one or more mitigation measures (U.S. Department of the Interior, 1979, p. 5.2), such as delaying the closure of the Tellico Dam long enough to be sure that the populations of snail darters in other rivers were going to survive—by this time the fish had been transplanted in two other rivers; finding other rivers for transplantation; or requiring studies of propagation in captivity.

Benefits of the Project.   Table 23.1 summarized the benefits and costs of the project and of the river alternative. The committee staff estimated the total annual project benefits to be $6.50 million. Originally, TVA had estimated that total benefits would be $16.53 million, distributed among land enhancement, flood control, navigation, power, recreation, water supply, and employment purposes as shown in column (1) of Table 23.1. With costs at $5.02 million

TABLE 23.1.   Estimated Annual Benefits and Costs of the Tellico Dam and Reservoir and the River Development Alternative, Ignoring Environmental Factors (millions of 1978 dollars)

Benefits and Costs	Original TVA Estimate[a] (1)	1978 Revised TVA Estimate[b] (2)	Committee Staff Estimate[b] (3)	River Development Alternative: Committee Staff Estimate[b] (4)
Total benefits (*B*)	16.53	6.85	6.50	5.10
Land enhancement[c]	1.62	0.34	—	—
Flood control	1.13	1.04	1.04	—
Navigation	0.89	0.31	0.10	—
Power	0.89	2.70	2.70	—
Recreation	3.70	2.30	2.50	3.10
Water supply	0.16	0.05	0.05	—
Agriculture[d]	—	0.11	0.11	2.00
Employment	8.14	—	—	—
Total costs, $(r + d)K$	5.02	3.19	7.22	6.29
Dam	5.02	3.19	3.19	2.26
Land[e]	—	—	4.03	4.03
Net benefits, $B - (r + d)K$	11.51	3.66	−0.72	−1.19
Benefit–cost ratio, $B/(r + d)K$	3.29	2.15	0.90	0.81

NOTE: Dash = not applicable.

[a] Taken from the U.S. General Accounting Office, *The Tennessee Valley Authority's Tellico Dam Project: Costs, Alternatives, and Benefits*, (Washington, D.C., October 1977), table 1. All numbers are converted to 1978 dollars by multiplying by 2.23, the ratio of the gross national product (GNP) price deflator in 1978 to that in 1968 (the base year).

[b] Taken from U.S. Department of the Interior, *Tellico Dam and Reservoir*, Staff Report to the Endangered Species Committee, (Washington, D.C., 1979, exhibit 3). Midpoints are used whenever ranges are shown in the original source.

[c] For land surrounding the reservoir.

[d] On land included in and surrounding the reservoir.

[e] Of land included in the reservoir.

SOURCE: Edward M. Gramlich, *Benefit–Cost Analysis of Government Programs*, © 1981, p. 150. Adapted by permission of Prentice-Hall, Inc., Englewood Cliffs, N.J.

and a benefit–cost ratio of 3.29, the project appeared to provide a comfortable margin of net benefits. But after the criticism of its results mentioned earlier, TVA revised its benefit estimates downward by a considerable margin, as shown in column (2). For one thing, TVA could not count land enhancement benefits and also navigation and recreation benefits, both of which are free services that are likely to be capitalized in land values (Knetsch, 1964). The change in the flood control estimate [see column (2)] took place because TVA began using an altered concept of the maximum probable flood. In addition, TVA's navigation benefits fell by almost two-thirds under criticism from a variety of sources; the final figure still represented what some felt was a highly dubious claim.

On the other hand, power benefits, as shown in the table, reflected an increase in the cost savings that resulted from substituting additional hydro-generation for the nuclear and coal-fired plants that would have been operated instead. The methodology for estimating the recreation benefits was also improved in that the new estimate was based on the travel-cost/demand method and incorporated the concept of substitution between sites: recreational visits to the Tellico reservoir that would otherwise have occurred on another reservoir were not counted.[13] Employment benefits were a victim of the classic arguments over secondary benefits; water supply benefits applied only to one small town, Vonore, Tennessee, which later would refuse to accept them.

In TVA's 1978 estimate, costs also diminished because funds had already been sunk in the project. TVA had estimated the remaining costs for the dam project to be $35.1 million, which included $14.5 million to enable spillways to handle a larger maximum flood. The total benefits of $6.85 million less the incremental costs of $3.19 million left net benefits of $3.66 million, or a benefit–cost ratio of 2.15, in 1978.

The committee staff estimates, in column (3) of Table 23.1, show a change of major importance on the cost side: The staff assigned an opportunity cost to the project lands, reasoning that although the land might have been purchased, it was not irretrievably committed until the reservoir was created.[14] The staff used current market values of $2500, $1400, and $650 per acre, respectively, for "prime," "statewide-important," and "other" classes of land for a composite value of $1196 per acre and a total value of $43.2 million.[15]

The cost of the land was annualized at the private opportunity cost of capital: the 10 percent discount rate. Had the staff used the 6.63 percent discount rate on the land value, its estimate of net benefits for completing the project would have been a positive $0.55 million instead of a negative $0.72 million. The difference in net benefits on this item made the percentage a crucial issue. The staff believed, however, that using the private discount rate to annualize the cost of land acquired at prices set in private markets was the correct procedure [see Eckstein (1958, p. 146)].

---

[13]This argument assumes that the new and the displaced sites provide comparable services so there is no improvement in quality at the new site or avoidance of congestion at the site experiencing the displacement.

[14]Letter dated January 8, 1979, from Leonard Shabman to Secretary of the Interior Cecil D. Andrus.

[15]A crucial line was omitted from the staff report, however, creating the erroneous impression that a market price of $2500 per acre had been used as the value of all the land in the reservoir site.

Benefits of Alternative Courses of Action.   Column (4) in Table 23.1 shows the benefits and costs of the river development alternative. The principal benefits of the alternative came from recreation and agriculture; the opportunity costs of land were the same as in the dam-reservoir alternative. Additional costs were involved in river development, however, in the removal of the dam, restoration of historic sites, and construction of highways. Thus, the estimated costs of river development exceeded the benefits by a margin of $1.19 million, and the river development alternative was inferior (by about $0.5 million per annum) to completing the project.

TVA's attempt to find agricultural benefits in the river development alternative led it to envision 1000 acres of high-value fruit and vegetables growing on 73 farms and, additionally, 60 dairy farms. TVA was prepared to go into partnership with farmers using intensive agricultural practices to take advantage of the markets for seasonal fresh fruits and vegetables in Chattanooga, Knoxville, and Atlanta. The 1979 edition of the U.S. Water Resources Council's *Principles and Standards* did not allow specialty crops nor livestock benefits to be used to account for agricultural benefits; however, to be consistent, the staff cut TVA's agricultural benefits to $1.5 million but allowed $0.5 million in resource cost savings for the employment of underemployed resources. Agricultural benefits under the river development alternative thus totaled $2.0 million (U.S. Department of the Interior, 1979, pp. 2–3).

The Special Case of River Recreation.   In its 1978 report, TVA used unit day values to estimate recreation days. Moreover, its model for estimating recreation use on a new site did not correct for use transferred in from existing sites. By December 1978, TVA's recreation estimates were based on a travel-cost model, its estimates of use took account of alternative sites, and its comparisons of alternatives were sensitive to the comparative uniqueness of reservoir and river recreation. Table 23.2 shows the basis for the recreation benefit calculations. The cross-elasticity of demand, which is used to account for substitution, is assumed to be between 0.5 and 5.0 for the river alternative; the cross-elasticity of the reservoir is assumed to be in the range of 2.0 and 20.0. Using 0.5 for the river cross-elasticity and 10.0 for the reservoir cross-elasticity, allowing for slightly higher growth rates in the demand for recreation on the river, and assuming (for lack of data) equal capacity constraints, recreation benefits are $3.10 million for river development and $2.50 million for reservoir development.[16]

23.1.7.   The Committee Decides

When the Endangered Species Committee convened on January 23, 1979, the Tellico case opened with a 10-minute briefing on the staff report. A question from the Secretary of the Army established the fact that TVA had not made a recommendation to the committee. The representative of the state of Tennessee, William R. Willis, Jr., of Nashville, confirmed that TVA's river development alternative was a reasonable alternative to the completion of the dam. Then,

---

[16]Note the parallels with the Cicchetti-Krutilla analysis of High Mountain Sheep dam in Hells Canyon (Krutilla and Fisher, 1985, chap. 6).

TABLE 23.2.   Annualized Recreation Benefits for the Reservoir and River Development Alternatives (millions of dollars)

Cross-Elasticity[a]	Capacity Assumption[b]	Reservoir			River		
		2.5%	3.5%	5.0%	3.5%	5.0%	7.0%
0.5	L				2.409	2.829	3.390
	M				2.558	3.040	3.732
	H				2.673	3.300	4.241
1.0	L				2.305	2.673	3.163
	M				2.495	2.924	3.538
	H				2.651	3.244	4.109
2.0	L	1.998	2.201	2.554	2.232	2.546	2.955
	M	2.169	2.447	2.867	2.451	2.826	3.356
	H	2.264	2.658	3.278	2.639	3.193	3.977
5.0	L	1.966	2.139	2.436	2.176	2.441	2.766
	M	2.154	2.408	2.773	2.416	2.742	2.186
	H	2.262	2.646	3.226	2.629	3.146	2.847
10.0	L	1.954	2.115	2.389	2.155	2.399	2.686
	M	2.148	2.393	2.735	2.402	2.708	3.112
	H	2.262	2.642	3.204	2.625	3.126	3.788
20.0	L	1.948	2.102	2.363			
	M	2.145	2.384	2.713			
	H	2.262	2.639	3.191			
30.0	L	1.946	2.098	2.354			
	M	2.144	2.382	2.707			
	H	2.262	2.638	3.187			

[a] Cross-elasticity is the ratio of the percentage change in visitation to the percentage change in the price of alternative recreation opportunities. This coefficient is a measure of the availability of close substitutes for recreation at the site.

[b] L = design capacity; M = 1.30 × design capacity; H = 2.00 × design capacity. Design capacity is defined as boating and camping activities only.

SOURCE: Adapted, by permission of Butterworth Scientific Limited, from F. Reed Johnson, "Federal Project Evaluation and Intangible Resources," *Resources Policy,* September 1981, p. 205.

with almost no further preliminaries, Charles Schultze, chairman of the President's Council of Economic Advisors, asked to be recognized.[17] Upon being given the floor by Chairman Cecil Andrus, Schultze said

> Well, somebody has to start....I have not prepared a resolution; however, I think the sense of it would be clear. It seems to me the examination of the staff report (which I thought was excellently done) would indicate that it is very difficult...to say there are no reasonable and prudent alternatives to the project. The interesting phenomenon is that [this] project...is 95 percent complete, and if one takes just the cost of finishing it against the benefits

---

[17] The unexpected presence of Schultze on an Endangered Species Committee finds explanation in the legislative history of the committee. The chairman of the Council on Environmental Quality was first designated as a member of this committee, together with the Secretary of the Interior, of Agriculture, and of the Army, and the heads of the National Oceanic and Atmospheric Administration (NOAA) and of the Environmental Protection Agency (EPA). The balance of the committee looked as though it might favor preservation, however, and so the president's economic advisor was substituted for his environmental advisor. Interestingly, the economist proceeded to strike a blow for the darter rather than for the dam.

and does it properly it doesn't pay, which says something about the original design.

The proceedings were interrupted by applause at this point. Events would show Schultze's remark to be at the crest of a popular reaction against pork barrel spending.

Mr. Schultze goes on to say:

It's also true that the particular river development plan posed by TVA as an alternative also has negative net benefits, slightly larger, negative benefits. I note that the staff report points out the market value of the raw land involved, which is still available for liquidation as an alternative, is something in the neighborhood of $40 million which appropriately discounted gives you $4 million a year. The staff notes that in further developing any specific river development plan, the TVA would have to look very carefully at what mix of private and public ownership, lease and purchase . . . would maximize the total value. On the basis of this, it seems to be that a completion of the project returning negative net benefits to the development alternative, which at the moment also has negative benefits, but only slightly larger, an alternative which does preserve some archaeological sites, some scenic value, I don't see how it's possible to find that there is no reasonable and prudent alternative, nor do I see how it is possible to find that the benefits of alternatives consistent with conserving a species. Therefore Mr. Chairman, . . . I would move that we deny an exemption (U.S. Department of the Interior, Endangered Species Committee, 1979).

The motion was seconded, there was a chorus of ayes, and there was applause in the audience. The snail darter had prevailed unanimously over the dam. Chairman Andrus went on to make some statements about how well the committee process had worked on this occasion and how that boded well for the future, anticipating many more such cases.

23.1.8.   The Road to Exemption

The day after the Endangered Species Committee made its decision, Senator Baker was quoted in the January 24, 1979, edition of the *Washington Post* as saying: "If that's all the good the committee process can do, to put us right back where we started from, we might as well save the time and expense. I will introduce legislation to abolish the committee and exempt the Tellico Dam from the provisions of the act." Baker's statement was the beginning of a nine-month fight by the Tennessee Congressional delegation to overrule the committee. At a hearing of the Culver committee (that is, the Resource Protection Subcommittee of the Senate Committee on Environment and Public Works) in May 1979, Baker repeated his earlier support for the amendment creating the committee.[18] He also introduced an amendment to exempt the

---

[18] As recorded in personal notes taken by this author at the May 10, 1979, hearing, Senator Pete V. Domenici of New Mexico expressed interest in Baker's statement that the species was not endangered. With the help of staff, Culver explained that the snail darter recovery team believed that up to 15 more years were needed to determine the viability of the population of darters in the Hiwassee River. When Domenici declared a lack of interest in this level of detail, Culver jumped at the opportunity to make his often-repeated point that this was just the kind of detail the Senate *must* review if it is to make exemptions to the Endangered Species Act in each case of irreconcilable conflict.

Tellico project in order to "close the gates on a dam we bought and paid for." The committee voted against the Baker amendment, 10 to 3.

Yet Baker continued to pursue the exemption. The Culver committee had been working on an extension of the Endangered Species Act which came to the floor of the Senate on June 13, 1979, and Baker offered his amendment for exemption. The amendment failed by a vote of 52 to 43, and this step exhausted the normal legislative remedies available to the Tennessee delegation.

By June 18, the action had moved to the House. When the House public works bill containing energy and water appropriations was being considered late in the afternoon, Tennessee Congressman John J. Duncan proposed an amendment to exempt Tellico from any federal law impeding its completion. Duncan asked that the amendment not be read and instead began to explain it. Before he could finish, John T. Myers of Indiana jumped to his feet and said that he had read the amendment and would accept. Tom Bevill of Alabama, the chairman of the Appropriations Subcommittee that wrote the bill and in whose district the Tennessee-Tombigbee waterway was under construction, announced that he also accepted the Duncan amendment. Thus, with no further explanation of its contents, the amendment was passed by what a UPI wire service story of June 18 called a "mumbled voice vote apparently with few on the House floor aware of what was happening."

The amendment authorized and directed TVA to complete the dam. It was the Tennessee delegation's first victory over the snail darter in many months. The Senate Appropriations Committee then approved the House version of the bill, but on July 18 Culver again prevailed on the floor of the Senate (by a 53-to-45 vote) and the Tellico language was removed from the Senate appropriations bill. The language was reinserted by the conference committee, however, and on September 10, 1979, after a lengthy debate the Senate voted 48 to 44 to grant an exemption. Howard Baker thus had finally won a victory over the fish he had been calling "the bane of my existence, the nemesis of my golden years, the bold perverter of the Endangered Species Act." Although professing to have nothing personal against the snail darter—"he seems to be quite a nice little fish as fish go"—Baker said the snail darter had become the unfortunate symbol of a type of environmental extremism that could spell the doom of the environmental protection movement and that advocated the perversion of the Endangered Species Act as a device "to challenge any and all federal projects."[19]

The Rhetoric of Exemption.   The rhetoric used to argue for the exemption of the Tellico project drew a great deal of strength from the U.S. energy situation.[20] In 1979 the nation was feeling the inflationary bite of the price hikes of the Organization of Petroleum Exporting Countries (OPEC), and President Carter was promoting energy independence. When completed, Tellico would light 20,000 homes with hydroelectric power. Senator Baker thus urged his colleagues "to seize this opportunity to redeem our commitment to energy production." The Tellico supporters had also found openings for disputing the

---

[19]125 *Cong. Rec.* S12234, September 10, 1979.
[20]All quotations in this subsection, The Rhetoric of Exemption, are taken from the September 10, 1979, edition of the *Congressional Record* (pp. S12234–S12239).

analysis of benefits and costs presented to the Endangered Species Committee. Senator James R. Sasser of Tennessee switched from Baker's earlier tactic of declaring the matter to be an environmental question; rather, Sasser said, "It is an economic question," and he proceeded to argue against letting the $111 million already sunk in the project go down the drain. (The $111 million claimed as the sunk cost of the dam was repeated refuted by the Culver forces, who reiterated that only $22 million had actually been spent on the dam itself.) Sasser also cited the earlier benefit–cost ratio of 2.3 found in TVA's alternatives report (Tennessee Valley Authority, 1978) and accused the committee of making its decision based on some "creative accounting." Senator J. Bennett Johnston, Jr., of Louisiana continued the attack on the committee's economics, in particular objecting to the inclusion of the opportunity costs of the land among the costs of completing the project.

Although the exemption forces were about to win, Senator Culver summarized the list of arguments against the motion. They included:

The difficult responsibility that Congress would now face in having to make highly complex decisions on more cases of endangered species

The Tellico project's lack of economic viability and the Endangered Species Committee's findings that the completed project would not pay

The waste of most of the prime farmland in the project area (it would be flooded by the reservoir, according to the U.S. Department of Agriculture)

Opposition to completion of the project by the Office of Management and Budget

The minute (one-thousandth) portion of TVA's total energy capacity that Tellico would provide, in addition to which TVA was deferring further construction of nuclear power units

The expenditure of only $22.5 million (rather than $111 million, as claimed by project supporters) on the dam by that time and the fact that all the rest of the federal expenditures could be put to beneficial use

The endangered status of the snail darter and the question of the viability of transplanted populations

The violation of the jurisdictional prerogatives of the Environment and Public Works Committee that exemption would constitute

The unprecedented exemption of a project from all other laws

Why the Committee Was Snubbed.   The 48-to-44 vote on September 10, 1979, in favor of exempting the Tellico project was a reversal of the 53-to-45 margin of July 17 because three northern senators (Mathias, Ribicoff, and Danforth) and three western senators (Cannon, Dole, and Gravel) switched to the exemption side on the final vote. The reversal also occurred because eight senators who had previously supported Culver's position were not present to vote.[21] In addition, there were four senators (Cohen, Magnuson, Chiles, and Stone) who switched from favoring exemption to opposing it.

---

[21]The eight "no-shows" were Bayh, Durenberger, Muskie, Pell, Bumpers, Armstrong, Inouye, and Pressler.

TABLE 23.3.   Regional Breakdown of Senate Vote on Tellico Exemption

| | July 17, 1979 | | September 10, 1979 | |
Region	No. for Exemption	No. Against Exemption	No. for Exemption	No. Against Exemption
North	7	30	9	25
South	23	5	21	6
West	15	18	18	13
Total	45	53	48	44

SOURCE: *Congressional Quarterly Almanac 1979*, Washington D.C.: Congressional Quarterly, pp. 31-S, 45-S.

In all three of the previous votes the division of the Senate on Tellico had followed regional lines. The South had supported the water project, and the rest of the country had opposed it. In the final vote, the West swung to the other side and favored exemption. Table 23.3 shows the breakdown of the voting by region.

A number of lessons in the current realities of the political process can be drawn from this campaign. One is found in the words of Howard Baker: "This project has been bought and paid for." In other words, a deal that has been made must be kept; a project that has been authorized must not be deauthorized. Once such a deal is made and a project is authorized and begun, its beneficiaries have established claims—property rights to the promised benefits.

A second and corollary proposition was that sunk costs could not be ignored because they were the down payment on the "contract." To ignore sunk costs would have been to disavow the bargain that had been struck. To the members of Congress defending Tellico, there was no consideration of the proposition that they might be "throwing good money after bad." Costs that are economically sunk may not be sunk psychologically or politically. To admit that taxpayer's money was wasted was a greater crime than the wasting of more money.

A third lesson was that incremental benefit–cost analysis of a project which was underway was considered an affront to the Congress when it was at odds with the decision to authorize the project. Once Congress had determined that a project was economic—on whatever grounds—it did not want to be second-guessed on economic grounds.

A fourth lesson was that when regional projects reach the final vote, they must be presented as national projects. Although the trade-off in this case involved gains for the regional beneficiaries of the project balanced against net costs to the nation at large, little was heard of regional arguments in the final debates.

Carter's Dilemma.   The fiscal year 1980 energy and water appropriations bill that emerged from the Congress contained the Tellico exemption, funds for completing the dam, and funds for the Hart Senate Office Building. To make a threatened veto all but impossible, Congressman Bevill of Alabama tacked the $10.8 billion appropriations bill onto the continuing resolution to keep the government operating after October 1. There were some signs that the president might veto this exemption as he was being urged to do by Secretary of the

Interior Andrus. The press began to take sides after it became apparent that Congress was going to uphold the exemption: Numerous editorials called the project a waste, urged an end to the pork barrel, and generally echoed Charles Schultze's sentiments about a project that was 95 percent complete and still did not pay its way.

President Carter had established a record as an environmentalist and also as an enemy of pork barrel projects. He had vetoed the public works bill in October 1978 and recalled later that "the battle left deep scars" (Carter, 1982). In 1979, as he faced a decision on the Tellico project, he was already deeply embroiled in the issues of Panama Canal legislation, Salt II, the creation of a department of education, and initiatives in energy policy, and he was anticipating his reelection campaign of 1980. It was not a good time to pick a fight, especially one that involved letting a 3-inch fish stop the federal government in its tracks. The snail darter had already borne widespread ridicule for stopping a $100 million reservoir project. On September 25, 1979, the president made this statement: "It is with mixed emotions that I sign H. R. 4388, the Energy and Water Development Appropriations Bill,"[22] explaining his reason for not vetoing the bill:

> While I believe firmly in the principles of the Endangered Species Act and will enforce it vigorously, I do not consider that the action by Congress on the Tellico matter implies congressional intent to overturn the general decision process for resolving conflicts under that Act. Furthermore, I am convinced that this resolution of the Tellico matter will help assure the passage of the Endangered Species Act reauthorization, without weakening amendments or further exemptions (Office of the White House Press Secretary, "Statement by the President," September 25, 1979).

Carter also expressed the hope that by being reasonable on this bill he would get support from Congress for a water project review function to be lodged with the Water Resources Council, which itself was having difficulty getting funded. Environmentalists, however, were not pacified. Brent Blackwelder of the Environmental Policy Center said Carter "had a chance to show leadership and he blew it" (*Congressional Quarterly,* 1979).

23.1.9. TVA Wins—and Loses

By the day after the president had signed the appropriations bill, TVA's bulldozers were rolling. By November 13 the last two farmers had been evicted, and at 11:23 A.M. on November 29, 1979, the gates of the dam were dropped into place. Former TVA chairman Aubrey Wagner attended the event. Wagner, according to whom the "only appropriate course of action had been closure of the gates of Tellico" (Rechichar and Fitzgerald, 1983, p. 52), told reporters, "I'm glad to see it filled, finally" (AP news wire story, November 30, 1979). On that November day, persistence was rewarded. TVA had begun with a mission to improve navigation in the Tennessee and Mississippi River basins. It

---

[22]According to a conversation of the author with Zygmunt Plater, the law professor who had taken the snail darter to the Supreme Court, President Carter telephoned Plater the night before he signed the bill and spoke of his mixed feelings about the act and the conflict between his sympathies for the cause of the fish and the realities of his situation.

had been charged by President Franklin D. Roosevelt with the broader duty of "planning for proper use, conservation and development of natural resources of the Tennessee River drainage basin and its adjoining territory" (Hodge, 1938, p. 36). As a result of its interpretation of that charge, TVA had become irrevocably committed to completing a system of dams conceived in the 1930s to regulated the flow of the Tennessee and its tributaries.

Although local opposition and unprecedented regulation of its activities by the National Environmental Policy Act and the Endangered Species Act severely tested TVA's resolve, the old coalition of businessmen, newspaper editors, and local officials never wavered in its support of Tellico. Although Tennessee Congressman John J. Duncan found that, in his district of 190,000 households, 82 percent of 13,046 persons responding to a mail survey favored completion of Tellico (U.S. Department of the Interior, 1979, p. 31), we will never know whether the majority of local residents perceived a need for the dam.

23.1.10.   Where Is the Snail Darter Now?

At the time the Endangered Species Committee met, the snail darter was known to exist in two places in Tennessee and to be established in only one of them. It now appears that the entire controversy may have revolved around a dam that was not worth building in the first place and a fish that did not really need to be saved. On August 6, 1984, the Fish and Wildlife Service downgraded the status of the snail darter from "endangered" to "threatened."

Within six years after the dam was completed, the snail darter was found in Chickamauga Creek in Chattanooga and in Watts Bar Lake on the Big Tennessee below Tellico, a puzzling development because at the time of the committee deliberation, one would have thought that if there were any other snail darter populations in Tennessee, TVA would have found them.[23] In Watts Bar Lake, adult snail darters have been found in depths of 20 feet or more, where, according to biologists, visibility is poor, seining is costly, and only one snail darter may be the reward for a day's work. In 1981 and 1982, biologists again found darters in Watts Bar Lake but could make no positive identification of young for either of those years. It was known that if the darters could reproduce it would indicate that they could survive in deeper water as long as there were clean riffle conditions, which apparently existed in this location.

There are several other locations in the Tennessee River system—Sewee Creek, Sequatchie River, and Point Rock River—in which populations of snail darters are being found under similar circumstances, and there are also other sites in Alabama and Tennessee that are considered promising.

SUMMARY

The snail darter case closely resembles that of Hells Canyon (Krutilla and Fisher, 1985). Like the Low Mountain Sheep–Pleasant Valley Dam project in Hells Canyon, the Tellico Dam was found to have a negative net benefit without

---

[23] Chickamauga Creek was a polluted, urban waterway crisscrossed with freeways; it was difficult to get to and unpleasant to work in. Biological surveys bypassed it for many years. When it was finally sampled, it yielded both snail darters and another endangered species, the logperch.

even counting any environmental effects, which for Tellico included flooding one of the few remaining natural river reaches in the Tennessee Valley.

But as in the Hells Canyon case, there was another aspect of the problem that required an analysis of the environmental amenity benefits that would have to be foregone. In the Tellico case, the law of exemption required a comparison of the project with alternatives that were consistent with the preservation of an endangered species; this meant the dam had to be compared with preserving the free-flowing Little Tennessee River.

In Hells Canyon, the pathbreaking analysis of the loss of amenities that would occur if High Mountain Sheep Dam were constructed led to the reasonable conclusion that the small gain in the net value of hydroelectricity was not worth the loss of the amenity benefits the area provided in its preserved state. In the Tellico case, the amenities preserved with the free-flowing river were sufficiently valuable that the Endangered Species Committee could say, without direct analysis of the economic values of the snail darter, that preservation was a reasonable alternative to the dam.

In their impact on policy, the cases diverged sharply. Consistent with the economic analysis, Hells Canyon was added to the National Wilderness Preservation System in 1975, and thermal power-generating capacity appears to be providing an economic substitute for the hydroelectric potential of the site (Krutilla and Fisher, 1985, p. 143). Contrary to the economic analysis, Tellico Dam was completed in 1979, adding yet another body of flat water to the Tennessee Valley and ostensibly jeopardizing the existence of the snail darter.

One of the risks in pursuing applied welfare analysis is that occasionally events turn out contrary to the results of the analysis. When this happens, we must ask whether the events as they turned out have nothing to do with the analysis or whether there is a flaw in the model—the progressive model—that most analysts follow when they engage in such work. The progressive model emphasizes good science, systematic and rigorous analysis, and rational decision making based on that analysis. Progressivism is so closely identified with good behavior in government that, given a sound, systemic staff analysis according to progressive rules, Congress might not have been able to vote against the snail darter without the help of sleight-of-hand legislative strategies driven by long-established claims for the project.

Analysts do not expect as many of the actors to fail to match assumptions as they did in the snail darter case. A president who lived the progressive faith was oddly immobilized amidst a crescendo of opposition to the economic inefficiencies of the pork barrel and "blew it," according to one environmentalist. TVA, a blend of engineering, economic boosterism, and conservationist zeal founded on New Deal progressivism, felt sunk costs were not sunk. Finally, the scientists and technicians who were responsible for upholding the tradition of thorough biological investigation failed to find other populations of snail darters when such information might have rendered the question of preservation moot and kept the economics of Tellico from becoming a nationwide issue.

Although most analysts practice economics as though the progressive model were alive and well, the principal lesson of the snail darter may be that we should look for a more realistic premise for our craft. This is a tall order but we should remember that practice may always be about 20 years behind the frontiers. At the frontier today our progressive models are being challenged and rethought.[24] Meanwhile, we need to apply economic analysis to problem solving with a sense of the nature of the problem and the kind of information that would be most useful in solving it.

It is an encouraging sign that a number of scholars are beginning to pursue these questions. There is more analysis by economists of the behavior of economists in the policy process (Leman and Nelson, 1981; Nelson, 1987; Shabman, 1983). Attention is also being paid to the art of persuasion in economics (McCloskey, 1985). More to the point, Mann and Plummer (1992) provide the beginnings of a policy analysis of the Endangered Species Act itself. Those of us who continue to labor on the policy issues would do well to maintain an ongoing inquiry into the reasons for our successes and failures.

CASE QUESTIONS

1. Discuss changes that the Department of Interior and the Endangered Species Committee made to the previous analysis by TVA. Were these improvements?
2. What additional work could you suggest that would improve the benefit–cost analysis? Consider this question in light of the questions asked at the beginning of the chapter.
3. Is such formal analysis of benefit–cost analysis useful?
4. How could the impact of progressive analysis be greater?

REFERENCES

Bell, Griffin B., *Taking Care of the Law,* New York: William Morrow, 1982.

Carter, Jimmy, *Keeping the Faith—Memoirs of a President,* New York: Benham Books, 1982.

Congressional Quarterly, September 29, 1979, p. 2140.

Davis, Robert K., "Lessons in Politics and Economics from the Snail Darter," *Environmental Resources and Applied Economics: Essays in Honor of John V. Krutilla,* V. Kerry Smith, ed., Washington, D.C.: Resources for the Future, 1988.

Drew, Elizabeth, *Senator,* New York: Simon and Schuster, 1979.

Eckstein, Otto, *Water Resources Development: The Economics of Project Evaluation,* Cambridge, MA: Harvard University Press, 1958.

Etnier, D. A., "*Percina (Inostoma) tanasi,* a New Percid Fish from the Little Tennessee River, Tennessee," *Proceedings of the Biological Society of Washington* 88, 469–488, 1976.

Freeman, S. David, "Testimony Before the House Committee on Fisheries, Wildlife, Conservation and the Environment," 95th Cong., 2d sess., June 23, 1978.

Hodge, Clarence Lewis, *The Tennessee Valley Authority: A National Experiment in Regionalism,* New York: Russell and Russell, 1938.

Knetsch, Jack L., "Economics of Including Recreation as a Purpose of Water Resources Projects," *Journal of Farm Economics,* pp. 1148–1157, December 1964.

---

[24]Robert Nelson, 1984. "Ideology and Public Land Policy—The Current Crisis," in *Rethinking Federal Lands,* Sterling Brubaker, ed., Baltimore: Johns Hopkins University Press/Resources for the Future, 1984, pp. 235–298, and Leonard Shabman, "Nonmarket Valuation and Public Policy: Historical Lessons and New Direction," in *Nonmarket Valuation: Current Status and Future Directions,* John R. Stoll, Robert N. Shulstad, and Webb M. Smathers, Jr., eds., *Proceedings of a Regional Workshop,* published by the Southern Rural Development Center and the Farm Foundation, May 1983, pp. 62–99.

Krutilla, John V., 1967, "Conservation Reconsidered," *American Economic Review* 57, 777–786, September 1967 (Resources for the Future Reprint 67).

Krutilla, John V., and Otto Eckstein, *Multiple Purpose River Development: Studies in Applied Economic Analysis,* Baltimore, MD: Johns Hopkins Press for Resources for the Future, 1958.

Krutilla, John V., and Anthony C. Fisher, *The Economics of Natural Environments: Studies in the Valuation of Commodity and Amenity Resources,* rev. ed., Washington, D.C.: Resources for the Future, 1985.

Leman, Christopher K., and Robert H. Nelson, "Ten Commandments for Policy Economists," *Journal of Policy Analysis and Management* 1(1), 97–119, 1981 (Resources for the Future Reprint no. 198).

Mann, Charles, C., and Mark L. Plummer, "The Butterfly Problem," *The Atlantic*, vol. 269(1), pp. 47–70, Jan. 1992.

McCloskey, Donald N., *The Rhetoric of Economics,* Madison: University of Wisconsin Press, 1985.

Nelson, Robert H., "The Economics Profession and the Making of Public Policy," *Journal of Economics Literature* 25(1), 49–91, 1987.

Plater, Zygmunt J. B., "Reflected in a River: Agency Accountability and the TVA Tellico Dam Case," *Tennessee Law Review* 49, 747–787, 1982.

Rechichar, Steven J., and Michael R. Fitzgerald, 1983, *The Consequences of Administrative Decision: TVA's Economic Development Mission and Intergovernmental Regulation,* Knoxville, Bureau of Public Administration, University of Tennessee, 1983.

Shabman, Leonard, "Nonmarket Valuation and Public Policy: Historical Lessons and New Direction," pp. 62–99 in *Nonmarket Valuation: Current Status and Future Directions,* John R. Stoll, Robert N. Shulstad, and Webb M. Smathers, Jr., eds., Proceedings of a Regional Workshop, May 1983 (Southern Rural Development Center and Farm Foundation).

Tennessee Valley Authority, *Environmental Statement, Tellico Project,* Chattanooga, Tenn., TVA, Office of Health and Environmental Science, February 10, 1972.

Tennessee Valley Authority, *Alternatives for Completing the Tellico Project,* Knoxville, Tenn., 1978.

U.S. Department of the Interior, 1979, *Tellico Dam and Reservoir,* Staff Report to the Endangered Species Committee, Washington, D.C., 1979.

U.S. Department of the Interior, Endangered Species Committee, "Transcript of the Meeting of January 23," Washington, D.C., 1979.

U.S. General Accounting Office, *The Tennessee Valley Authority's Tellico Dam Project— Costs, Alternatives, and Benefits,* Report to Congress, Washington, D.C., October 14, 1977.

U.S. House of Representatives, *Conference Report on the Endangered Species Act Amendments of 1978,* H.R. Rep. No. 95-1804, 95th Cong., 2d sess., 1978.

U.S. Water Resources Council, "Principles and Standards for Planning Water and Related Land Resources," *Federal Register* 44(242), 72,892–72,990, Dec. 14, 1979.

Yaffee, Steven L., *Prohibitive Policy: Implementing the Federal Endangered Species Act,* Cambridge, MA: MIT Press, 1982.

Glossary

annuity   A stream of uniform payments at constant intervals for a specified time.

benefit–cost analysis   To organize data so as to compare benefits of an action with its costs. To be used correctly, both benefits and costs should be discounted.

benefit–cost ratio   The ratio of benefits to costs. Properly, the ratio of NPV benefits to NPV costs. Sometimes, benefits minus costs divided by costs.

best available alternative rate (BAAR)   The highest return that can be earned by an investor. The opportunity cost rate.

beta   A measure of market risk. The covariance between a project's return and the market return as a percentage of the variance of the market.

CAPM   Capital asset pricing model. A model for valuing risky prospects.

certainty equivalent   The smallest certain amount that would be accepted in lieu of some gamble.

common pool problem   The situation that exists when no one owns a valuable resource.

compound interest   Interest that applies to principal and to accumulated interest.

contingent valuation   Valuation based on a questionnaire, usually applied to environmental goods.

CS: consumer surplus   Approximately the maximum amount one is willing to pay minus the amount actually paid.

CV: compensating variation   The difference between indifference curves measured at final prices. The amount of money transfer that will leave one as well off as before the economic change.

decision tree   A graphic representation of the outcomes of decisions under uncertainty.

depreciation   The allowance made for the loss in value of an asset over time for tax purposes.

difference principle   A principle of justice developed by John Rawls in which only the utility of the least-advantaged person would be given weight, but subject to basic rights and liberties.

discount rate   The interest rate used to discount future cash flows to present value.

dissipation of rents   When potential net gains in consumer or producer surplus are eliminated by well-specified property rights.

e   The natural logarithm. Part of the expression for present or future values when compounding of interest is continuous.

economic efficiency   Either Pareto or potential Pareto efficiency, or some form of utilitarian-based efficiency.

effective rate (of interest)   The actual rate paid when allowance is made for compounding.

equivalent annuities   The net present value of projects converted to annuities for the period of the project. Used to compare projects with different lives.

EV: equivalent variation   The difference between indifference curves measured at original prices. The amount of money transfer that will leave one as well off as after an economic change in the absence of the change.

existence value   The willingness to pay for the existence of a good over and above the willingness to pay for use of the good.

expected utility, EU   The sum of utilities in different states of the world.

expected value, EV   The sum of the values of each outcome times its individual probability.

financial risk   Variability in benefit or cost streams.

future value   The value of cash amounts or flows assessed at a specified time in the future.

general equilibrium model   A model that explicitly portrays interactions among markets and accounts for income effects.

good   Anything of value.

Harberger redistribution test   A test to take into account distributional effects of benefit–cost analysis.

initial position   Hypothetical decisions in which the one making the decision has an equal chance of being any person affected by the decision.

interest rate   A percentage rate charged for the cost of credit. Usually expressed on an annual basis.

inflation   A general increase in the price level over time.

internal rate of return   The discount rate at which benefits just equal costs for a project.

Kaldor–Hicks criteria   The potential Pareto criterion.

market risk   Risk that cannot be eliminated by diversification.

Monte Carlo simulation   A technique that simulates outcomes after probabilities have been assigned.

MRS   Marginal rate of substitution.

MSU_i, the marginal social utility of i   The weight given by society to a unit of i's utility.

MSUI, marginal social utility of income   The value that society places on the marginal dollar for the ith person.

MUI_i, marginal utility of income   The utility of a change in one dollar for the ith person.

nominal rate (of interest)   Either the yearly interest before compounding is considered or the interest rate including the inflation component.

NPV, net present value   The present value of benefits minus the present value of costs.

opportunity cost   The value of what is given up by a decision.

option price   The willingness to pay for a prospect under uncertainty.

option value   The value of an option. In environmental economics, however, option value is the difference between option price and expected consumer surplus. This may be positive or negative.

original position   A hypothetical decision-position concept developed by Rawls to satisfy the requirements of justice; similar to the initial position with additional requirements of various sorts of ignorance on the part of the decision maker.

Pareto efficiency   When no reallocation of goods or resources can fail to harm some-one.

Pareto superiority   One position is said to be Pareto superior to another when a move from the second to the first position harms no one while helping someone.

payback period   The time required to recover the initial investment.

perpetuity   An annuity with an infinite life.

potential Pareto test   A Kaldor or a Hicks test. A test that determines if a Pareto superior move is possible, ignoring the transaction cost of redistribution.

present value   The value today of a prospect or project.

principal   The amount of money invested at the outset.

producer surplus   Approximately the maximum amount a producer would pay for a factor of production minus the amount actually paid. (A change in producer surplus is equal to a change in profits in most cases.)

prospect   A project with uncertain flow of benefits or costs.

public goods   Goods with high exclusion cost and nonrivalry in use.

quasi-option value   The value of expected future information associated with valuing a project.

real rate (of interest)   The rate of interest after removing inflation. $[(1+i)/(1+I)]-1$ where i is the nominal interest rate and I is the inflation rate.

risk   A positive probability of a bad outcome.

risk aversity   When marginal utility of income declines with income.

risk neutrality   When the marginal utility of income is constant with changes in income.

risk preferring   When the marginal utility of income increases with income.

salvage value   The value of an asset at some future time. Similar to terminal value.

security market line   A line that shows the relationship between expected return and market risk.

sensitivity analysis   A technique for evaluating risky decisions based on changing assumptions.

shadow price   A social accounting price that reflects an estimate of the opportunity cost of providing or eliminating an additional unit of the good.

shadow price of capital (SPC)   The present value of the consumption flowing from $1.00 of private investment. The opportunity cost of private investment.

simple interest   Interest that applies only to the original principal.

simulation   A complex sensitivity analysis.

social welfare function   A decision rule to apply to decisions affecting more than one person.

SOCR   Social opportunity cost rate.

SRTP   Social rate of time preference.

terminal value   The value of a project at some future date.

travel demand model   A technique to calculate consumer surplus usually for an environmental asset by examining the willingness to pay for travel.

uniform growth series   The same as an annuity except that the periodic amounts are increasing at a constant growth rate.

unique risk   Risk that can be eliminated by diversification.

utilitarianism   A philosophy associated with Jeremy Bentham based on treating everyone equally in some sense and "maximizing the greatest good for the greatest number." In economics, a normative model based on utility maximization.

utility   A concept used to aid in modelling choice. What individuals seek to maximize.

utility of expected value, U(EV)   The amount of expected value times the MUI.

wealth-maximizing rate   The rate of return that predicts the future amount that a project will actually yield. This rate is superior to the internal rate of return in that it is easier to calculate, gives the right ranking of projects (if adjusted for scale of projects), and provides only one rate for one project.

Willig–Bailey criterion   A method of considering distributional effects based on allowing no undesirable transfers.

willingness to accept (WTA)   The amount a person is willing to accept to give up a good or to bear a harm.

willingness to pay (WTP)   The amount a person is willing to pay to secure a good or to avoid a loss.

Answers to Selected Problems

CHAPTER ONE

1. a. This problem raises two issues. First, should the comparisons be made between the two 10-acre sites or should 20 acres be used since the school board will not buy the 10-acre site at B? Second, what value should be given to the land now owned at site A?

 The analyst can finesse the first issue by accepting the school board's judgment that the 20-acre site is preferred to the 10-acre site at face value. Then, if a comparison of the 10-acre site shows B to be superior, then the 20-acre site at B must a fortiori be superior to the 10-acre site at A. If the 10-acre site at B is superior, then the school board's preference for the 20-acre site suggests that the 20-acre site B should be chosen. The second issue is one of the role of opportunity cost. The cost of site A should include the market value of the land they now hold. This is the **opportunity cost** of using the land. That is, the market value of A represents a value the board could realize by selling this land. The fact that the board now owns site A is irrelevant in determining the cost of site A. On this basis we could set out the following figures.

Cost Category	Site A	Site B
Capital cost of site	$1,500,000	$1,250,000
Capital costs of building on site	$2,000,000	$1,000,000
Busing costs		$1,000,000
Total costs	$3,500,000	$3,250,000

 On this basis, the 10-acre site at B is superior, and therefore the 20-acre site at B is rated superior to that at A.

b. One factor to mention to the parents is the cost of the children spending more time on the bus. How would you conceptually put a value on this? (See Chapter 18 generally, and consider a contingent value survey.)

CHAPTER 2

1. In the figure below, Q_c is the output under a competitive regime and P_c is the competitive price. P_m is the monopoly price and Q_m the monoply output. (The student is referred to Chapter 6 for a discussion of consumer and producer surplus.) Consumer surplus under competition will be $A + B + C$. There is no producer surplus. Under monopoly consumer surplus will be area A. Producer surplus is not the gain in profits or area B. The loss in welfare due to monopoly is area C, which is also known as the dead-weight loss.

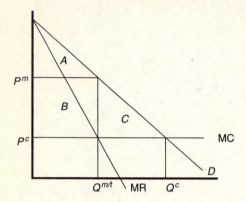

Under competition the price will equal MC of P^c and output will be Q^c. Total of consumer surplus will be $A + B + C$. Because the supply curve is flat, under competition there will be no producer surplus.

Under monopoly price and output are $P^m Q^m$. Consumer surplus is A and producer surplus is B. Area C is lost to both consumers and producers and is called a dead weight loss.

3. Clean water, clean air, fisheries, wild game, etc.

5. The existence of externalities or public goods is *not* a sufficient reason for public intervention. A relevant economic question is under what alternative arrangements will the net social product be higher. To answer this question is the role of benefit-cost analysis.

7. **a.** Since the lighthouse is a public good, demand must be summed vertically. Solve for P:

$$P = 40 - 2L$$

Multiply by 50 for aggregate demand for 50 ships:

$$P = 2000 - 100L$$

b. Set MC = demand. Then, $P = 100 = 2000 - 100L$

$$L = 19 \text{ days per year}$$

c. The total demand will not change.

d. If two companies are excluded from using the lighthouse, then the demand for the remaining three companies with a total of 40 ships is found by multiplying the demand of a single ship by 40 so that

$$P = 1600 - 80L$$

The output level will then be 18.75 days per year. Too few days will be provided.

CHAPTER 3

1. **a.** The net present value criterion seems the best.
   b. Use the SRTP to calculate the NPV.

$$\text{NPV} = -100 + \frac{50}{1.04} + \frac{50}{(1.04)^2} + \frac{50}{(1.04)^3}$$

$$= -100 + 48.08 + 46.23 + 44.45$$

$$= \$38.76$$

The project is worthwhile.

   c. No, because in a first-best world the market rate is the SRTP.

3. The present value of \$50,000 per year for 10 years at 6 percent is \$368,004.35. This should be added to the cost of site B. (For a simpler method of calculating the present value see Chapter 9.)

CHAPTER 4

1. $P = \$500$
   a.

$$F_t = P(1 + r)^t \qquad r = 0.0575$$

$$= \$500(1 + 0.0575)^3$$

$$F_3 = \$591.30$$

   b.

$$F_t = P\left(1 + \frac{i}{h}\right)^{ht}$$

$$i = 0.0575 \qquad h = 12 \qquad t = 3$$

$$F_t = \$500\left(1 + \frac{0.0575}{12}\right)^{12(3)}$$

$$F_3 = \$593.89$$

   c. Same formula as (*b*) with $h = 52$; $F_3 = \$594.08$

3. Simple:

$$F_t = P(1 + rt)$$

$$r = 0.03 \qquad P = \$100 \qquad t = 111$$

$$F_{111} = \$100[1 + (0.03)(111)]$$

$$= \$433.00$$

Compound:

$$F_t = p(1 + r)^t$$

$$F_{111} = \$100(1 + 0.03)^{111}$$

$$= \$2660.31$$

5.

$$(1 + \bar{r}) = \left(\frac{F_t}{P}\right)^{1/t}$$

$$F_t = P(1.05)(1.02)(1.13)(1.20) \qquad \text{Applies interest rates each year}$$

$$= 1.452P$$

$$(1 + \bar{r}) = \left(\frac{1.452P}{P}\right)^{1/4}$$

$$\bar{r} = 0.0978 = 9.78\%.$$

Note: A straight average would have given 10 percent.

7.
$$F_6 = \$10,000$$

$r = 0.01$ per month   Work entire problem in months

$$F_6 = P(1 + r)^6$$
$$\$10,000 = P(1 + 0.01)^6$$
$$P = \$9,420.45$$

After 9 months:

$$F_9 = P(1 + r)^9$$
$$= \$9,420.45(1.01)^9$$
$$= \$10,303.01$$

The difference between 6 months and 9 months is, therefore,

$$\$10,303.01 - \$10,000.00 = \$303.01$$

The firm should ask for \$303.01 for the delay.
Note that this result could be calculated directly from

$$F_6(1 + r)^3 = F_9$$
$$\$10,000(1 + 0.01)^3 =$$
$$F_9 = \$10,303.01$$

9.
$$A = F\left[\frac{r}{(1 + r)^n - 1}\right]$$

$F = \$17,000,000 \qquad n = 14 \qquad r = 0.08$

$$A = \$17,000,000\left[\frac{0.08}{(1.08)^{14} - 1}\right]$$

$$= \$17,000,000(0.0413)$$
$$= \$702,046$$

11.
$$P = \frac{G}{r}\left[\frac{1 - (1 + r)^{-n}}{r} - \frac{n}{(1 + r)^n}\right]$$

$G = \$500 \qquad r = 0.07 \qquad n = 10$

$$P = \frac{\$500}{0.07}\left[\frac{1 - (1.07)^{-10}}{0.07} - \frac{10}{(1.07)^{10}}\right]$$

$$= \frac{\$500}{0.07}(7.024 - 5.083)$$

$$= \frac{\$500}{0.07}(1.94)$$

$$= \$13,858$$

13.
$$F = X\left[\frac{1 - (1 + k)^{-n}}{k}\right](1 + r)^n$$

$X = \$500$ $g = 0.05$ $r = 0.065$ $n = 10$

$$1 + k = \frac{1 + r}{1 + g}$$

$$= \frac{1.065}{1.05}$$

$$k = 0.01429$$

$$F = \$500\left[\frac{1 - (1.01429)^{-10}}{0.01429}\right](1.065)^{10}$$

$$= \$500(9.257)(1.877)$$

$$= \$8688$$

15. This problem can be treated as an annuity. Assume payments are made on an annual basis throughout.

$$F = A\left[\frac{(1 + r)^n - 1}{r}\right]$$

$$A = (0.15)(\$20,000) = \$3000$$

$$n = 35 \qquad r = 0.06$$

$$F_{35} = \$3000\left[\frac{(1.06)^{35} - 1}{0.06}\right]$$

$$= \$334,304.34$$

a. If drawn out at \$24,000 per year,

$$P = A\left[\frac{1 - (1 + r)^{-n}}{r}\right]$$

$$\$334,304.34 = \$24,000\left[\frac{1 - (1.06)^{-n}}{0.06}\right]$$

$$0.83576 = 1 - (1.06)^{-n}$$

$$(1.06)^{-n} = 0.1642$$

Iterate (guess values of n) until result is approximately correct:

$n = 10$ $(1.06)^{-n} = 0.5584$

$n = 20$ $(1.06)^{-n} = 0.3118$

$n = 30$ $(1.06)^{-n} = 0.1741$

$n = 31$ $(1.06)^{-n} = 0.1643$

It would take about 31 years to use up the money.

b. At \$12,000 per year:

$$\$334,304.34 = \$12,000\left[\frac{1 - (1 + r)^{-n}}{0.06}\right]$$

$$1.6715 = 1 - (1 + r)^{-n}$$

$$(1 + r)^{-n} = 0.6715 \leftarrow \text{Cannot be true for any value of } n$$

This money can never be used up since the annual interest exceeds the amount being withdrawn.

CHAPTER 5

1. The reason why Mr. James may be better off shopping at Safeway is because relative prices differ as between Safeway and Tradewell so that Mr. James will purchase different market baskets at the two stores. Calculate the amounts bought for shopping at the two stores.

	Meat	Fruit	Canned Goods	Total $
Tradewell first				
Prices	10	8	10	
Quantities	1	3	1	
Total spent	10	24	10	$44
Safeway cost for same basket				
Price	8	10	8	
Quantity	1	3	1	
Total spent	8	30	8	$46

If, however, Mr. James shopped at Safeway for the optimal market basket his purchases would be different.

	Meat	Fruit	Canned Goods	Total $
Safeway first				
Prices	8	10	8	
Quantities	3	1	3	
Total spent	24	10	24	$58
Tradewell cost for same basket				
Prices	10	8	10	
Quantities	3	1	3	
Total spent	30	8	30	$68

Notice that it cost more to buy the optimal Safeway market basket at Tradewell just as it cost more to buy the optimal Tradewell basket at Safeway.
     Now compare consumer surpluses for the optimal baskets:

	Units	WTP	Amount Paid	Surplus
Tradewell				
Meat	1	$10	$10	$0
Fruit	3	27	24	3
Canned goods	1	10	10	0
Total				$3
Safeway				
Meat	3	$27	$24	$3
Fruit	1	10	10	0
Canned goods	3	27	24	3
Total				$6

Shopping at Safeway provides Mr. James with twice the consumer surplus as shopping at Tradewell.

3. a. The change in Don's utility from his increase in records would be

$$2 \text{ records} \times \$4 \text{ per record} \times 2(\text{MUY}) = 16 \text{ utils}$$

The increase in Don's utility from the increase in Dick's income would be

$$5 \text{ books} \times \$8 \text{ per book} \times (0.2)(\text{Don's weight for Dick's income}) \times 2(\text{MUY}) = 16$$

This gives a total of $16 - 16$, or 0 utils. Don's envy of Dick leads to no utility change for Don from a policy that increases the quantity of records for Don and books for Dick.

b. The weight Don gives to Dick's utility is -0.5 which gives a utility change to Don from the change in Dick's income of $\$40 \times (-0.5)(\text{weight}) \times 2(\text{MUY}) = -40$. When this is combined with the gain of 16 that Don has from the increase in the records he receives, the total change to Don's welfare is -24. Don's envy is so strong that he loses when both he and Dick gain income because Dick gains more income than Don.

c. Don would be better off if both he and Dick had no income.

d. The interdependence multiplier would be less than one. Don's utility could decrease even though his money income increased. The negative weight Don gives to Dick's utility times the interdependence multiplier is less than negative one.

CHAPTER 6

1. a. Dick's income increases by $100 which is weighted first by 2 (the MUY), and then by 0.8 (the MSU of Dick) to give a value of 160. Don's income increases by $50 which is weighted by 1 and then 1 (the MUY and the MSU) to give a value of 50. Don's income of $50 is, however, valued negatively by Dick and receives a weight of -0.2 to give an additional income to Dick of $10.00. Notice that since the income increase to Don is a harm to Dick, that the willingness to accept measure may be used for the CV measure. This is then weighted by 2 and by 0.8 to give an effect on social welfare of -16. The sum of these gains and losses is $160 + 50 - 16$ or 194.

b. Under the Kaldor–Hicks measure, the marginal utilities of income are treated equally, weights of one, and the MSUs are all 1. This gives a welfare gain of $\$100 + \$50 - \$10 = \$140$. Notice that Dick's negative investment in Don's income increase is still counted under Kaldor–Hicks because this is part of the CVs.

c. Without using the Kaldor–Hicks measure we cannot say whether or not the policy is a good one. This is because the cost is given in dollars and is not expressed in terms of utility units so that it cannot be compared with the gain of 194 in Problem a above. Using the Kaldor–Hicks measure we can say that the arts policy measure should not be undertaken since the gain of $140 is less than the cost of $150.

3. a. The benefits for garbage disposal as opposed to none are shown by the total WTP of all groups and this amounts to $3550. The benefits of developing the north-end site are shown by the WTP for the site by members of group N_1 of $100, and the WTP for garbage disposal of $3550. Similarly, for the south-end site the benefits of this site are shown by the WTP of S_1 of $50 and the WTP for disposal of $3550. The costs of the north-end site are the $1650 for construction and development and the $300 WTA of group N_2. The costs of the south-end site are similarly $850 plus the WTA of $95 by the members of S_2 who would be harmed by building the site. The net benefits of using the county would be the $3550 WTP for disposal minus the $3000 fee. Thus we have

	North-End Site	South-End Site	County
Benefits			
WTP disposal $(N_1 + N_2 + S_1 + S_2)$	$3550	$3550	$3550
WTP site $(N_1 \ or \ S_1)$	100	50	0
Costs			
WTA (construction)	−1650	−850	−3000
WTA (site) $(N_2 \ or \ S_2)$	−300	−95	—
NPV	1700	2655	550

The site in the south end has the greatest net benefits.

There is a tendency to include in the WTP for the north-end site the WTP of those south enders that are willing to pay $75 not to have the site in the south end. And, to include as one of the benefits of the south-end site the WTP of $100 by north-end residents to not have the site in the north end. This tendency presumably arises because clearly the desires of the north- and south-end losers to not have the site located in their area should be considered. Yet, these desires not to have the site in their area are considered in their WTA to bear the burden of the site in their area. That is, the desires of residents of, say the north end, to not have the site in their area is part of the calculation only if the north end is being considered and in this case the use of the CV requires these residents' WTA be included as a cost if the status quo point is no plant in the north end.

Suppose that you are willing to pay $10,000 not to have a nuclear power plant located in a vacant lot located nearby. Should this WTP be included among the benefits in considering locating a nuclear power plant in another state, say, New Jersey? Clearly not unless the vacant lot is being considered as a location. If it is to be considered as a location then the WTP to not have the site locally will be considered in calculating the EV of the site. See c below.

b. Notice that this approach will not be different from an approach that assumes that the garbage must be disposed of and ignores the WTP for disposal. The WTP for disposal is common to all sites. The south-end site still has the lowest net costs.

c. We can calculate the EV also. The benefits will be the WTA for not having the site at the specified location plus the WTA for not having garbage disposal. We are not given this later figure but on the assumption that garbage disposal is a normal good, the figure for all alternatives must be greater than the $3500 WTP for garbage disposal. We will say that the amount by which the WTA exceeds the WTA is e so that the EV benefit of garbage disposal is $3500 + e$. The costs of building on a site will consist of the $1650 in actual construction costs plus the WTP to have the site elsewhere. The results are shown in the table below:

	North-End Site	South-End Site
Benefits:		
WTA $(N_1 + N_2 + S_1 + S_2)$	$3500 + e$	$3500 + e$
WTA $(N_1 \ or \ S_1)$	150	80
Costs:		
WTP	−1650	−850
WTP $(N_2 \ or \ S_2)$	−100	−75
NPV	$1900 + e$	$2655 + e$

Both the EV and the CV show that the south-end site is superior. By coincidence they also show that the EV and the CV are the same for the south-end site. Is this logically possible? Why or why not?

CHAPTER 7

1. The extent of cross-market and income effects should be considered in deciding whether or not to use market equilibrium in general equilibrium analysis.
   a. Partial equilibrium analysis
   b. A difficult call, probably general equilibrium analysis
   c. General equilibrium analysis
   d. General equilibrium analysis
   e. Partial equilibrium analysis
3. A key issue is whether or not changes in production are the only pollution mechanism. If this is the case we have the following diagram.

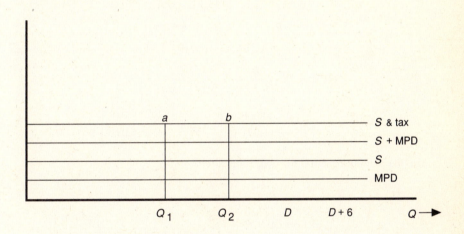

The social cost is the production cost plus the additional pollution damage.
5. This optimum is not an economic optimum that balances marginal cost and marginal value.
7. **a.** TSC $= 100 + .0025X^2 = 100 + 0.0025(1800)^2 = \$8200$ per lane per hour.
   b. MSC $= 0.005X = 0.005(1800) = 9.00$ per car per lane per hour
   c. MPC $= $ ASC $= \frac{\text{TSC}}{X} = \frac{100 + 0.0025(1200)^2}{1200} = 3.08$ per car per lane per hour.
   d. The optimum Pigovian(?) tax will equal the difference between MSC and MPC $= 9.00 - 3.08 = \$5.92$ per car/per hour.
   e. The margin of (?) will equal MSC in equilibrium or $\$9.00$ per car.

CHAPTER 8

First Case

1. The second case in this chapter shows the answer. The student should, however, *attempt* to answer this question before looking at the next case.
3. This would increase the welfare under regulation because price would be lowest closer to marginal cost.

Second Case

1. This could be consistent with a public interest theory of regulation. Such a theory might argue that where social gains are larger it will pay to exert more effort to secure them ceteris paribus.

3. This could occur where the value of information conveyed to the customer is high relative to the welfare loss from higher prices. Suppose that the value of the service, is much greater with quality regulation. The gain in quality may offset the higher price. Can you draw a graph to illustrate this?

Third Case

1. The analyst must look to the law, the client, and to social custom to resolve such issues of standing. (See Chapter 12.)

CHAPTER 9

1.

$$C_0 = \$50,000$$

$$C_1 = \cdots = C_{10} = \$500$$

$$B_1 = \cdots = B_{10} = \$8000$$

$$n = 10, \qquad r = 0.07$$

$$\text{NPV} = \sum_{t=0}^{n} \frac{B_t}{(1 + r)^t} - \sum_{t=0}^{n} \frac{C_t}{(1 + r)^t}$$

$$= \sum_{t=1}^{10} \frac{\$8000}{(1.07)^t} - \left[\$50,000 + \sum_{t=1}^{10} \frac{\$500}{(1.07)^t} \right]$$

Use the annuity equation for both summation:

$$P = A \left[\frac{1 - (1 + r)^{-n}}{r} \right]$$

$$\text{NPV} = \$8000 \left[\frac{1 - (1.07)^{-10}}{0.07} \right] - \left\{ \$50,000 + \$500 \left[\frac{1 - (1.07)^{-10}}{0.07} \right] \right\}$$

$$= \$8000 \, [7.0236] - [\$50,000 + \$500(7.0236)]$$

$$= \$56,188.65 - [\$50,000 + \$3511.79]$$

$$= \$2676.86$$

Since NPV > 0, the subway system should buy the equipment.

3. NOTE: Periods are *months*.

					Month				
	0	1	2	3	4	5	6	7	8
Costs		$200	$200	$200	$200	$200	$200		
	$5000			$300	$300	$300	$300	$300	$300
Benefits		$1500	$1500	$1500	$1500	$1500	$1500		

$$r = 0.10$$

First, find an equivalent monthly discount rate:

$$1 + r = \left(1 + \frac{i}{h} \right)^h, \qquad h = 12$$

$$1 + 10 = \left(1 + \frac{i}{12}\right)^{12}$$

$$\frac{i}{12} = 0.00797 = 0.797\% \text{ per month}$$

$$\text{NPV} = \sum_{t=0}^{n} \frac{B_t}{(1 + r)^t} - \sum_{t=0}^{n} \frac{C_t}{(1 + r)^t}$$

$$\text{NPV} = \sum_{t=1}^{6} \frac{\$1,500}{(1.00797)^t} - \left[\$5,000 + \sum_{t=1}^{6} \frac{\$200}{(1.00797)^t} + \sum_{t=3}^{8} \frac{\$300}{(1.00797)^t}\right]$$

Use the annuity equation for the three summations. Note that the pollution fines start in month 3, and thus must be discounted by two additional months.

$$\text{NPV} = \$1,500 \left[\frac{1 - (1.00797)^{-6}}{0.00797}\right]$$

$$- \left\{\$5,000 + \$200\left(\frac{1 - (1.00797)^{-6}}{0.00797}\right) + \frac{\$300\left[\frac{1 - (1.00797)^{-6}}{0.00797}\right]}{(1.00797)^2}\right\}$$

$$= \$1,500\,[5.836] - \left[\$5,000 + \$200(5.836) + \frac{\$300(5.836)}{(1.00797)^2}\right]$$

$$= \$8754.19 - [\$5,000 + \$1167.22 + \$1723.26]$$

$$= \$863.71$$

NPV > 0; therefore this is a good investment.

5. a.

Option #1	Option #2	
$C_0 = \$200$	$C_0 = \$550$	$C_4 = \$25$
$n = 2$ months	$r = 0.083$	$n = 6$ months

First, find the equivalent monthly discount rate:

$$1 + r = \left(1 + \frac{i}{h}\right)^h$$

$$1.083 = \left(1 + \frac{i}{12}\right)^{12}$$

$$\frac{i}{12} = 0.00667 = 0.667\% \text{ per month}$$

Assuming the benefits are equal, three repetitions of Option 1 are required to match Option 2. Thus, for Option 1:

$$C_o = \$200, \qquad C_2 = 200, \qquad C_4 = \$200$$

$$\text{NPV} = \sum_{t=0}^{n} \frac{B_t}{(1 + r)^t} - \sum_{t=0}^{n} \frac{C_t}{(1 + r)^t}$$

$$= 0 - \left[\$200 + \frac{\$200}{(1.00667)^2} + \frac{\$200}{(1.00667)^4}\right]$$

$$= -\$200 - \$197.36 - \$194.75$$

$$= -\$592.11$$

Similarly, for Option 2:

$$NPV = 0 - \left[\$550 + \frac{\$25}{(1.00667)^4}\right]$$

$$= -\$550 - \$24.34$$

$$= -\$574.34$$

Option 2 costs less and is thus preferred.

b.

Option #1	Option #2	
$C_0 = \$200$	$C_0 = \$550$	$C_4 = \$25$
$n = 2$ months	$r = 0.083$	$n = 6$ months

$$r = 0.083$$

First, find the equivalent monthly discount rate:

$$1 + r = \left(1 + i/h\right)^h$$

$$1.083 = \left(1 + i/12\right)^{12}$$

$$i/12 = 0.00667 = 0.667\% \text{ per month}$$

Assume benefits are equal and set them equal to zero for convenience:

$$NPV = \sum_{t=0}^{n} \frac{B_t}{(1 + r)^t} - \sum_{t=0}^{n} \frac{C_t}{(1 + r)^t}$$

OPTION # 1:   NPV $= 0 - \$200 = -\$200$

The equivalent annuity is:

$$P = A\left[\frac{1 - (1 + r)^{-n}}{r}\right]$$

$$-\$200 = A\left[\frac{1 - (1.00667)^{-2}}{0.00667}\right]$$

$$A = -\$101.00$$

OPTION # 2:   NPV $= 0 - \left[\$550 + \frac{\$25}{(1.00667)^4}\right] = -\$574.34$

The equivalent annuity is:

$$P = A\left[\frac{1 - (1 + r)^{-n}}{r}\right]$$

$$-\$574.34 = A\left[\frac{1 - (1.00667)^{-6}}{0.00667}\right]$$

$$A = -\$97.97$$

Option # 2 costs the least on an equivalent lifecycle and is thus the better choice.

7.

	Year				
	0	*1*	*2*	*3*	*4*
Costs	$10,000		$1000		
Benefits		$3000	$3000	$3000	$3000

$$r = 0.05$$

$$BCR_d = \frac{\sum\limits_{t=o}^{n} \dfrac{B_t}{(1+r)^t}}{\sum\limits_{t=o}^{n} \dfrac{C_t}{(1+r)^t}}$$

$$BCR_d = \frac{\sum\limits_{t=1}^{4} \dfrac{\$3,000}{(1.05)^t}}{\$10,000 + \dfrac{\$1,000}{(1.05)^2}}$$

The payment series of benefits can be calculated using the annuity equation:

$$P = A\left[\frac{1 - (1+r)^{-n}}{r}\right]$$

$$BCR_d = \frac{\$3,000\left[\dfrac{1 - (1.05)^{-4}}{0.05}\right]}{\$10,000 + \dfrac{\$1,000}{(1.05)^2}}$$

$$BCR_d = \frac{\$10,638}{\$10,000 + \$907} = 0.975$$

$$BCR_n = [BCR_d - 1] \times 100\%$$

$$BCR_n = (0.975 - 1) \times 100\% = -2.5\%$$

Since the $BCR_d < 1$ and the $BCR_n < 0$, this project is *not* a good investment. Both the BCR_d and the BCR_n would decrease if $r = 0.10$ since the benefits are more heavily discounted than the costs.

9.
$$C_0 = \$325,000$$

$$B_1 = \cdots = B_7 = \$100,000, \quad r = 0.10$$

For payback:

$$\sum \frac{x_t}{(1+r)^t} \geq 0$$

At four years:

$$\sum \frac{X_t}{(1+r)^t} = -\$325,000 + \sum\limits_{t=1}^{4} \frac{\$100,000}{(1.10)^t}$$

Applying the annuity equation for the benefits:

$$\sum \frac{X_t}{(1+r)^t} = -\$325,000 + \$100,000\left[\frac{1 - (1.10)^{-4}}{0.10}\right]$$

$$= -\$325,000 + \$100,000\,[3.170]$$

$$\sum \frac{X_t}{(1+r)^t} = -\$8,013$$

Since $\sum[x_t/(1+r)^t] < 0$ after four years, the firm would *not* purchase the invention using a four-year payback period.

For NPV:

$$NPV = \sum_{t=0}^{n} \frac{B_t}{(1+r)^t} - \sum_{t=0}^{n} \frac{C_t}{(1+r)^t}$$

$$= \sum_{t=1}^{7} \frac{\$100,000}{(1.10)^t} - \$325,000$$

$$= \$100,000\left[\frac{1-(1.10)^{-7}}{0.10}\right] - \$325,000$$

$$= \$100,000[4.868] - \$325,000$$

$$= \$161,842$$

Under the NPV approach, the firm *would* purchase the invention.

Alternative payment stream:

$$C_0 = \$50,000$$

$$C_1 = \cdots = C_5 = \$90,000$$

$$B_1^2 = \cdots = B_7 = \$100,000$$

For payback:

$$\sum \frac{X_t}{(1+r)^t} = -\$50,000 + \sum_{t=1}^{4} \frac{\$10,000}{(1.10)^t}$$

$$= -\$50,000 + \$10,000\left[\frac{1-(1.10)^{-4}}{0.10}\right]$$

$$= -\$50,000 + \$10,000[3.170]$$

$$= -\$18,301$$

The firm would still not purchase the invention.

For NPV:

$$NPV = \sum_{t=1}^{7} \frac{\$100,000}{(1.10)^t} - \$50,000 - \sum_{t=1}^{5} \frac{\$90,000}{(1.10)^t}$$

$$= \$100,000\left[\frac{1-(1.10)^{-7}}{0.10}\right] - \$50,000 - \$90,000\left[\frac{1-(1.10)^{-5}}{0.10}\right]$$

$$= \$100,000[4.868] - \$50,000 - \$90,000[3.791]$$

$$= \$95,671$$

Although the NPV is lower, the firm would still purchase the invention.

11.

	Year			
	0	*·1*	*2*	*3*
Costs	\$10,000			
Benefits		\$4000	\$4000	\$4000

$$r = 0.08$$

NPV:

$$NPV = \sum_{t=0}^{n} \frac{B_t}{(1+r)^t} - \sum_{t=0}^{n} \frac{C_t}{(1+r)^t}$$

$$= \sum_{t=1}^{3} \frac{\$4,000}{(1.08)^t} - \$10,000$$

Using the annuity equation:

$$NPV = \$4,000 \left[\frac{1 - (1.08)^{-3}}{0.08} \right] - \$10,000$$

$$= \$4,000 \, [2.577] - \$10,000$$

$$= \$308$$

This is a good investment since NPV > 0.

BCR_d:

$$BCR_d = \frac{\displaystyle\sum_{t=0}^{n} \frac{B_t}{(1+r)^t}}{\displaystyle\sum_{t=0}^{n} \frac{C_t}{(1+r)^t}}$$

The same benefit and cost calculations apply as for NPV:

$$BCR_d = \frac{\$4,000[2.577]}{\$10,000}$$

$$BCR_d = 1.03$$

This is a good investment since $BCR_d > 1$.

BCR_n:

$$BCR_n = \frac{\displaystyle\sum_{t=0}^{n} \frac{B_t}{(1+r)^t} - \sum_{t=0}^{n} \frac{C_t}{(1+r)^t}}{\displaystyle\sum_{t=0}^{n} \frac{C_t}{(1+r)^t}} \times 100\%$$

$$BCR_n = \frac{\$4,000(2.577) - \$10,000}{\$10,000} \times 100\%$$

$$BCR_n = 3.08\%$$

This is a good investment since $BCR_n > 0$.

IRR:

$$\sum_{t=0}^{n} \frac{B_t}{(1+IRR)^t} = \sum_{t=0}^{n} \frac{C_t}{(1+IRR)^t}$$

$$\sum_{t=1}^{3} \frac{\$4,000}{(1 + IRR)^t} = \$10,000$$

Guess $IRR = 9\%$
$$\sum_{t=1}^{3} \frac{\$4,000}{(1.09)^t} = \$4,000 \left[\frac{1 - (1.09)^{-3}}{0.09} \right]$$
$$= \$10,125$$

Guess is slightly too low; choose $IRR = 9.5\%$:

$$\sum_{t=1}^{3} \frac{\$4,000}{(1.095)^t} = \$4,000 \left[\frac{1 - (1.095)^{-3}}{0.095} \right]$$
$$= \$10,036$$

Guess is still to low; choose $IRR = 9.77\%$:

$$\sum_{t=1}^{3} \frac{\$4,000}{(1.097)^t} = \$4,000 \left[\frac{1 - (1.097)^{-3}}{0.097} \right]$$
$$= \$10,000$$

Since the IRR is greater than the opportunity cost of capital, this is a good investment.

13.

	Year			
	0	*1*	*2*	*3*
Costs	$10,000		$10,000	
Benefits		$8000	$8000	$8000

$$r = 0.08$$

Formulas and mathematics are similar to Problem 12.

$$NPV = \sum_{t=1}^{3} \frac{\$8,000}{(1.08)^t} - \$10,000 - \frac{\$10,000}{(1.08)^2}$$

$$= \$8,000 \left[\frac{1 - (1.08)^{-3}}{0.08} \right] - \$10,000 - \frac{\$10,000}{(1.08)^2}$$

$$= \$8,000[2.577] - \$10,000 - \$8,573$$

$$= \$2,043$$

Since NPV > 0, this is a good investment.

$$BCR_d = \frac{\$8,000 [2.577]}{\$10,000 + \$8,573}$$

$$= 1.11$$

Since $BCR_d > 1$, this is a good investment.

$$BCR_n = \frac{\$8,000 [2.577] - \$10,000 - \$8,573}{\$10,000 + \$8,573} \times 100\%$$

$$= 11.0\%$$

Since $BCR_N > 0$, this is a good investment.

For *IRR*:

$$\sum_{t=1}^{3} \frac{\$8,000}{(1 + IRR)^t} = \$10,000 + \frac{\$10,000}{(1 + IRR)^2}$$

Guess *IRR* = 10%:

$$\sum_{t=1}^{3} \frac{\$8,000}{(1.10)^t} = \$10,000 + \frac{\$10,000}{(1.10)^2}$$

$$\$8,000 \left[\frac{1 - (1.10)^{-3}}{0.10} \right] = \$10,000 + \frac{\$10,000}{(1.10)^2}$$

$$\$19,895 = \$18,264$$

Guess is too low; choose *IRR* = 20%:

$$\$8,000 \left[\frac{1 - (1.20)^{-3}}{0.20} \right] = \$10,000 + \frac{\$10,000}{(1.20)^2}$$

$$\$16,852 = \$16,944$$

Guess is to high; choose *IRR* = 19.4%

$$\$8,000 \left[\frac{1 - (1.94)^{-3}}{0.194} \right] = \$10,000 + \left[\frac{\$10,000}{(1.194)^2} \right]$$

$$\$17,011 = \$17,014$$

Since the *IRR* is greater than the opportunity cost of capital, this is a good investment.

15.   Alternative A : $C_o = \$250,000; n = 2; 7\%$ annual interest

Alternative B : $C_o = \$850,000; B_4 = \$1,250,000$

Alternative C : $C_o = \$1,000,000; B_1 = B_2 = B_3 = \$375,000$

BAAR = loan rate = 0.08;   initial capital = $1,000,000

To use WMR, outlays and lifespans must be equal. Thus, set the initial outlay at $1,000,000 and the lifespan at 4 years.
For A: Replicate 4 times at outset:

$$C_o = \$1,000,000$$
$$B_2 = \$1,000,000(1.07)^2 = \$1,144,900$$

At start of year 3 (end of year 2), reinvest $1,000,000 in project for 2 more years. Invest balance ($144,900) at BAAR.

$$B_4 = \$1,000,000(1.07)^2 + \$144,900(1.08)^2$$
$$= \$1,144,900 + \$169,011 = \$1,313,911$$

For B: Invest remaining $150,000 at BAAR:

$$B_4 = \$1,250,000 + \$150,000(1.08)^4$$
$$= \$1,454,073$$

For C:

$$C_0 = \$1,000,000, \qquad B_1 = B_2 = B_2 = \$375,000$$

This must be treated as a four-year investment for comparability. The WMR calculation will reinvest the proceeds at the BAAR.

Summary of cash flows:

Year	A	B	C
0	−1,000,000	−850,000 − 150,000	−1,000,000
1			375,000
2			375,000
3			375,000
4	1,313,911	1,454,073	

$$C_0(1 + WMR)^n = \sum_{t=0}^{n} B_t(1 + BAAR)^{n-t}$$

In all cases, $C_0 = \$1,000,000$, $n = 4$, BAAR $= 0.08$.

For A:

$$\$1,000,000(1 + WMR)^4 = \$1,313,911(1.08)^{4-4}$$
$$(1 + WMR)^4 = 1.3139$$
$$WMR = 0.0706$$

For B:

$$\$1,000,000(1 + WMR)^4 = \$1,454,073(1.08)^{4-4}$$
$$(1 + WMR)^4 = 1,454$$
$$WMR = 0.0981$$

For C:

$$\$1,000,000(1 + WMR)^4 = \$375,000(1.08)^{4-1} + \$375,000(1.08)^{4-2}$$
$$+ \$375,000(1.08)$$
$$\$1,000,000(1 + WMR)^4 = \$472,392 + \$437,400 + \$405,000$$
$$(1 + WMR)^4 = 1.3148$$
$$WMR = 0.0708$$

Project B is the only one with WMR > BAAR; therefore, it should be pursued.

17. $K = \$19,000$; $N = 5$

a. Straight-line

$$d_t = \frac{K - 5}{N}$$
$$= \frac{\$19,000}{5}$$
$$= \cdots = d_5 = \$3,800$$

b. Double-declining balance: $d_t = 2B_t/N$; $B_{t+1} = B_t - d_t$

$$B_1 = K = \$19,000$$

$$d_1 = \frac{2(\$19,000)}{5} = \$7,600$$

$$B_2 = \$19,000 - \$7,600 = \$11,400$$

$$d_2 = \frac{2(\$11,400)}{5} = \$4,560$$

$$B_3 = \$11,400 - \$4,560 = \$6,840$$

$$d_3 = \frac{2(\$6,840)}{5} = \$2,736$$

$$B_4 = \$6,840 - \$2,736 = \$4,104$$

$$d_4 = \frac{2(\$4,104)}{5} = \$1,642$$

$$B_5 = \$4,104 - \$1,642 = \$2,462$$

$$d_5 = \frac{2(\$2,462)}{5} = \$985$$

c. Double-declining balance switching to straight-line in year 4. From (b):

$$d_1 = \$7,600$$
$$d_2 = \$4,560$$
$$d_3 = \$2,736$$

To switch in year 4, set $K = B_4$. From (b), $B_4 = \$4,104$. For straight-line:

$$d_t = \frac{K - 5}{N}$$

$$d_4 = d_5 = \frac{\$4,104}{2} = \$2,052$$

d. Sum-of-the-years'-digits: $d_t = \left[\dfrac{N - (t - 1)}{N\left(\dfrac{N + 1}{2}\right)} \right] K$

$$d_1 = \left[\frac{5 - (1 - 1)}{5\left(\dfrac{5 + 1}{2}\right)} \right] (\$19,000)$$

Similarly:

$$d_1 = \$6,333$$
$$d_2 = \$5,067$$
$$d_3 = \$3,800$$
$$d_4 = \$2,533$$
$$d_5 = \$1,267$$

e. ACRS: $d_t = P_t K$

Similarly:
$$d_1 = (0.20)(\$19,000)$$
$$d_1 = \$3,800$$
$$D_2 = \$6,080$$
$$d_3 = \$4,560$$
$$d_4 = \$3,040$$
$$d_5 = \$1,520$$

CHAPTER 10

1. A good answer might include the following points: The content of any paper should be geared to the specific audience involved. A paper presented to a neighborhood meeting should be brief and should emphasize conclusions and the reasons for them. A paper intended for review by technical experts should be longer and should focus much more on the methods used to reach a decision. In both cases, tables or charts should be included since these are often an effective way of summarizing information for presentation to the public.

3. A good answer might emphasize the folllowing: One option would be to evaluate the two inflation rates and decide which is most reasonable. Alternatively, such an evaluation might conclude that a third option is more reasonable, as was concluded in the review of discount rates. Once an inflation rate was chosen, the competing analyses could be recalculated using this inflation rate.

   A second option would be to remove the effect of inflation from both analyses and compare the two calculations on a real (as opposed to nominal) basis. In this approach, inflation would be treated as a separate variable that differs between the two analyses, with no attempt made to decide which analysis was correct.

5. A good answer might emphasize the following: The city and the district might assign different values to the time value of money because of their relative emphases on current versus future costs and benefits. The two might also differ because the types of capital projects they build differ; for example, the appropriate time value of money for sewer projects might be different than that for streets.

CHAPTER 11

1. **a.** On a straight KH criterion the project shows a welfare gain of zero (350 million − 10 million − 340 million).

   The cost of making this transfer to the poor by the most efficient alternative means is, however, 20% × 340 million, or 68 million. The opportunity cost approach counts this as a gain so the project shows a gain of 68 million. Thus, the financial criterion suggests the project is undertaken.

   b. This project would not meet the Willig–Bailey test because it does not meet the KH test.

3. The project would be financially desirable where the Feldstein weight is 0.8. The income to the poorer group would increase by 26% $\left(\frac{15}{20}\right)^{-0.8}$, and the income to the richer group would receive a weight less than 1. For example, families with income of 30,000 would receive a weight of 0.67.

CHAPTER 12

1. **a.** This depends on the quality of morals. The support of morals that do contribute to a better society is consistent with a sophisticated utilitarian position.

   b. This is a tough problem. We think a view that lets the dead bury the dead, for example and ignores sunk cost, leads us to agreement with "The Truth Hurts."

3. We don't think abstract moral principles justify ignoring outcomes.

5. The presence of existence values found in environmental benefit–cost work suggests values beyond personal use value. On market values we ask, would you sell your child's favorite toy for twice its market value?

7. The answer here must be subjective.

9. Another tough question. Consider another question that may be related. Would vegetarianism as a moral philosophy be more appropriate in a richer or poorer country, or in a more technologically advanced or less technologically advanced country? (See Arthur Clarke, *The Deep Range*, New York: Harcourt, Brace, 1957.)

11. a. A simpleminded utilitarian approach must count envy as a value. We can, however, imagine that a prior constitutional decision has been made by society to not count envy as a value—this is consistent with sophisticated utilitarianism.

   b. You then count the value of relative position.

CHAPTER 13

1. The discount rate of 2% (the SRTP) should be used, which favors the solar project. The SPC, θ_c and θ_b, will be the same for both projects so these will not be a determinative.

3. a. The existence of benefits that return to private capital will produce a multiplier for benefits using the SPC approach. As long as more than 10% of the benefits return to private capital the project will pass the financial test.

   b. Yes. The returns for business may just be a relocation to Alberta at the expense of other provinces.

CHAPTER 14

1. Insofar as the discount rate legitimately differs for the two parties, the issue is a property rights question. If Seattle has the right, they should be compensated at the appropriate discount rate for them.

3. Certainly the possibility of a change in values could be considered. This may, however, unduly complicate an already complex analysis.

CHAPTER 15

1. EXV = 0.50(1 million) + 0.50(1.5 million) = 1.25 million

3. Risk due to probable values should *not* be treated by adjusting the discount rate. (See Chapter 16 to determine the conditions when the discount rate should be adjusted.) Instead, expected values should be calculated and discounted at a rate unadjusted for risk. Thus,

$$PV_A = 1500$$

$$PV_B = -2000 + 0.25\left[475\left[\frac{\left(1-(1.06)^{-50}\right)}{.06}\right]\right](1.06)^2$$

$$+ 0.50\left[475\left[\frac{\left(1-(1.06)^{-50}\right)}{.06}\right]\right](1.06)^3$$

$$+ 0.25\left[475\left[\frac{\left(1-(1.06)^{-50}\right)}{.06}\right]\right](1.06)$$

$$= -2000 + 1665.83 + 3143.06 + 1482.58$$

$$= \$3861.00$$

$$PV_C = -4500 + \frac{0.25(9750)}{(1.06)^2}$$

$$+ \frac{0.50(9750)}{(1.06)^3} + \frac{0.25(9750)}{(1.06)^4}$$

$$= -4500 + 2169.37 + 4093.14 + 1930.72$$

$$= \$3693.23$$

Option B is the better project. Using the higher discount rate of 8%, as did the financial director, results in a bias against B which is the longer-term project.

CHAPTER 16

1. They will tend to undertake projects that have undue financial risk.
3. Yes. Use the risk-free rate to discount the certainty equivalent. The NPV is $15/(1.04)^3 - 10 = 3.33$ million.
5. a. One can see that at an interest rate of 6% option B shows first-degree stochastic dominance over project C. At 6% the present value of benefits from project B at time X is $7063.10. This is $2686.90 less than the value of benefits of project C at this time. When this difference is discounted for 2 years or more at 6% it is less than the difference in the costs of the projects so that B is the better project. Also, the longer the period for completion the better B looks compared with C.

The following table shows the NPVs for several completion dates:

Completion Date	A	B	C
2	1500	4286.13	4177.47
3	1500	3930.31	3686.29
4	1500	3594.64	3222.91
5	1500	3277.96	2785.77

b. (1) The managers calculation of NPV is incorrect because this is a project with financial risk.
(2) This equation yields a very high beta of 2.10 and a risk-adjusted discount rate of about 8.2%. Benefits for option D have a present value in year X of $6962.65. This is less than for option B so option D is not the superior option.

CHAPTER 17

1.

	Optimistic	Expected	Pessimistic
Discounted costs	130	175	200
Discounted benefits	185	180	175

$$BCR_d = \frac{\sum\limits_{t=0}^{n} [B_t/(1+r)^t]}{\sum\limits_{t=0}^{n} [C_t/(1+r)^t]}$$

For expected values:

$$BCR_d = \frac{180}{175} = 1.03$$

Holding costs at expected value:

Optimistic benefits: $BCR_d = \dfrac{185}{175} = 1.06$

Pessimistic benefits: $BCR_d = \dfrac{175}{175} = 1.00$

Holding benefits at expected value:

Optimistic costs: $BCR_d = \dfrac{180}{130} = 1.38$

Pessimistic costs: $BCR_d = \dfrac{180}{200} = 0.90$

Thus, the project is attractive unless costs exceed expected values. Efforts should focus on cost containment.

	Scenario a	Scenario b	Scenario c
C_o	$5,000,000	$6,500,000	$4,250,000
Annual hours saved	70,000	70,000	70,000
Value of hours saved	$14	$20	$14

$$NPV = \sum_{t=0}^{n} \frac{B_t}{(1+r)^t} - \sum_{t=0}^{n} \frac{C_t}{(1+r)^t}$$

$$n = 5 \text{ years} \qquad r = 0.06$$

Scenario a:

$$NPV = \sum_{t=1}^{5} \frac{70,000(\$14)}{(1.06)^t} - \$5,000,000$$

Using the annuity formula:

$$NPV = 70,000(\$14) \left[\frac{1 - (1.06)^{-5}}{0.06} \right] - \$5,000,000$$

$$= 70,000(\$14)(4.212) - \$5,000,000$$

$$= \$4,128,117 - \$5,000,000$$

$$= -\$871,883$$

Similar calculations yield

Scenario b: $NPV = -\$602,691$

Scenario c: $NPV = -\$121,883$

No scenario produces a positive NPV. If an option must be chosen, scenario c would be preferred since it does the least to decrease real wealth.

5.

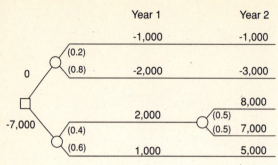

	Year 1	Year 2
(0.2)	-1,000	-1,000
(0.8)	-2,000	-3,000
(0.4) 2,000	(0.5)	8,000
	(0.5)	7,000
(0.6) 1,000		5,000

$$\text{NPV} = \sum_{t=0}^{n} \frac{B_t}{(1+r)^t} - \sum_{t=0}^{n} \frac{C_t}{(1+r)^t} \qquad r = 0.08$$

For the upper branch (no project):

$$\text{Ex(NPV)} = 0.2\left[\frac{-1000}{1.08} + \frac{-1000}{(1.08)^2}\right] + 0.8\left[\frac{-2000}{1.08} + \frac{-3000}{(1.08)^2}\right]$$

$$= 0.2(-926 - 857) + 0.8(-1851 - 2572)$$

$$= -\$3,895$$

For the lower branch (with the project):

$$\text{Ex(NPV)} = -7000 + 0.4\left[\frac{-2000}{1.08} + \frac{(0.5)(8000)}{(1.08)^2} + \frac{(0.5)(7000)}{(1.08)^2}\right]$$

$$+ 0.6\left[\frac{1000}{1.08} + \frac{5000}{(1.08)^2}\right]$$

$$= -7000 + 0.4(1851 + 3429 + 3001) + 0.6(926 + 4287)$$

$$= -7000 + 3312 + 3128$$

$$= -\$560$$

Although the project has a negative NPV, it is less costly than the no-action alternative. Thus, the project is desirable.

7.

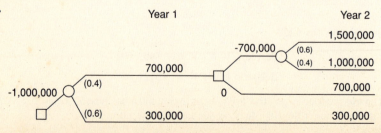

	Year 1		Year 2
		-700,000 (0.6)	1,500,000
(0.4) 700,000		(0.4)	1,000,000
-1,000,000		0	700,000
(0.6) 300,000			300,000

$$\text{NPV} = \sum_{t=0}^{n} \frac{B_t}{(1+r)^t} - \sum_{t=0}^{n} \frac{C_t}{(1+r)^t} \qquad r = 0.07$$

Consider first the decision after year 1:

Upper branch (additional investment):

$$\text{Ex(NPV)} = -700,000 + 0.6\left(\frac{1,500,000}{1.07}\right) + 0.4\left(\frac{1,000,000}{1.07}\right)$$

$$= -700,000 + 841,122 + 373,832$$

$$= \$514,954$$

Lower branch (no additional investment):

$$\text{Ex(NPV)} = 0 + \frac{700,000}{1.07}$$

$$= \$654,206$$

Thus, the port should choose *not* to invest the additional $700,000 after year 1. So, the Ex(NPV) for this new option is

$$\text{Ex(NPV)} = -1,000,000 + 0.4\left[\frac{700,000}{1.07} + \frac{700,000}{(1.07)^2}\right] + 0.6\left[\frac{300,000}{1.07} + \frac{300,000}{(1.07)^2}\right]$$

$$= -1,000,000 + 0.4(1,265,613) + 0.6(542,405)$$

$$= -\$168,312$$

Compared to the previous full-scale remodel plan, this option is worth

$$\$291,842 - \$168,312 = \$123,530$$

However, it is still undesirable compared to the routine maintenance option; thus, the new option has no net value.

CHAPTER 18

1. The supply of trucks is elastic to the country. The increase in demand does not therefore affect the price consumers pay. The price should be net of tax. In Equation (18.1), $\alpha = 0$

3. The number of unpriced or socially mispriced goods are legion, including air pollution, space at your university, collegiality, and highway congestion. Available methods of determining the shadow price are contingent valuation, travel demand models, and calculation from supply and demand data generated through noncontingent valuation surveys.

   c. Among possible benefits of Smith's proposal are the fact that establishing a constant figure for all may be more ethically acceptable, that medical costs may be more accurately determined than WTP costs, and that medical costs should in any event be a component in a WTP measure. A major deficit is that such costs take no account of pain and suffering, and are likely to give an answer for benefits that are too low. Another deficit is that medical costs are not the right theoretical answer, though they may be included in the correct answer.

   d. We believe the courts would be more likely to accept the medical costs approach as more understandable.

7. a. With both West Virginia and Ohio reducing pollution by $1 million, the total cost would be $6 million.

    b. Marginal costs will be $4E_1$ for West Virginia and $8E_2$ for Ohio. The reduction should be divided so that these are equal at the margin. Thus $E_1 = 2E_2$. Thus 67% of the reduction or 1.33 tons should be reduced by West Virginia and 0.67 million tons by Ohio. The total costs would then be about $5.35 million.

    c. This is a rather more difficult problem. The two marginal costs curves must be combined. The equation of the new curve will be approximately: MC(millions) = $2.67[E_1 + E_2]$. This can be derived graphically or mathematically by adding together the two equations horizontally. [This is found by noting that $MC_1/4 + MC_2/8 = E_1 + E_2$. Setting $MC_1 = MC_2$ gives MC (millions) = $8/3[E_1 + E_2]$.] Now setting MC = MB. MB will be $2 million for each million tons. Solving for $E_1 + E_2 = .75$ million tons, much smaller than the requested reduction. Of course this assumes that the reduction in emissions is divided efficiently between Ohio and West Virginia.

CHAPTER 19

1. It is easy to find court practices that will be philosophically objectionable. For example, some may object that the value of a more educated person is greater than for a less educated person, or that the value of a younger person just entering the work force is greater than that of an older worker, or that a woman or person of color may be worth less in a wrongful death case than a white male. To eliminate these distinctions means a weakening or eliminating of compensation based on earnings. It is considerably more difficult to suggest a replacement methodology. Recently, hedonic measures have been introduced to give a somewhat different basis for calculating the value of life lost.

3. The indifference curve would cut the vertical axis below the point of unity probability. A point on the indifference curve to the left of the vertical axis indicates a person would pay a sum in order to enjoy a risk. Pick a point on the indifference curve shown below and characterize the risk and the positive value of the risk.

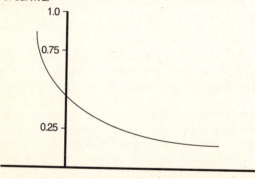

5. a. Set MC = MB. The optimal level is 2 ppb.

    b. The WTP reflected in benefits would be lower so that the point at which MC = MB would be at a lower level of control and a higher level of benzene.

CHAPTER 20

The EPA, as pointed out in Chapter 19, could of course increase the efficiency of its regulations by having West Virginia reduce twice as much pollution as Ohio. Thus, a first step of the EPA toward efficiency is the efficient reduction of waste. It could be argued that this saves lives, even though the reduction in chemical waste in Ohio is the same, if the EPA could realistically claim that the cost savings would be used in some other fashion that would also save lives. For example, perhaps the EPA could negotiate a change in the distribution of pollution reduction in exchange for some greater efforts by the Ohio plants to reduce pollution in some other areas.

In deciding on the right level of pollution control for chemical pollution going into the Ohio River, the EPA could refer to studies on the value or cost of risk and avoid terminology such as "the value of life." To refer to the cost of risk is both technically correct and probably politically expedient.

The EPA could also adopt as figures for the cost-of-risk figures used by other federal agencies. This may also help it to get off the hook.

Finally, the EPA could request that the Office of Management and Budget suggest figures to be used by Federal agencies.

CHAPTER 21

1. Draw a reduced form demand curve that incorporates the cross effects with the other markets and the income effects. The shaded area is now the welfare cost of the tax.

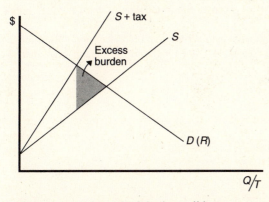

3. Clean water, clean air, fisheries, wild game, etc.
5. The existence of externalities or public goods is *not* a sufficient reason for public intervention. A relevant economic question is under what alternative arrangements will the net social product be higher. To answer this question is the role of benefit–cost analysis.
7. **a.** Since the lighthouse is a public good, demand must be summed vertically. Solve for P:

$$P = 40 - 2L$$

Multiply by 50 for aggregate demand for 50 ships:

$$P = 2000 - 100L$$

b. Set MC = demand. Then, $P = 100 = 2000 - 100L$

$$L = 19 \text{ days per year}$$

c. The total demand will not change.

CHAPTER 22

1. A good answer might include the following points: The answer to this question depends on your personal value system and sense of priorities. For most people, it is reasonable to apply different models in different cases. Some people, particularly

economists, might argue for a strict cost–benefit model in all cases. Only in very rare cases does anyone truly believe in a cost-oblivious model; eventually, the cost of achieving some benefit becomes too great for virtually anyone.

3. A good answer might include the following: There have been several recommendations in the last 30 years that an independent technical review group be established to review government uses of cost–benefit analysis. A typical proposal calls for a group of economists, engineers, or other experts in a specialized field to be empowered to review analyses and either propose or require changes in methodologies. However, there is not universal consensus on the correct approach to cost–benefit analysis, or on key issues such as how to select a discount rate. Thus, the outcome of an independent review would depend on who the reviewers were, and such review would not eliminate controversy about particular assumptions or approaches.

CHAPTER 23

1. Clearly, the changes suggested by Interior and the Committee were improvements. They might have been able to improve on their suggestion of the discount rate and we would suggest more weight be given to the inundation of the Cherokee burial grounds.

3. Only by subjecting benefit–cost analysis to scrutiny and to discussion will improvements result both for the particular project and for the use of benefit–cost analysis in general.

Name Index

Subject Index

Page numbers in italics refer to examples, figures, and tables.